The Student Writer
Editor and Critic

FIFTH
EDITION

The Student Writer
Editor and Critic

BARBARA FINE CLOUSE

Boston   Burr Ridge, IL   Dubuque, IA   Madison, WI   New York   San Francisco   St. Louis
Bangkok   Bogotá   Caracas   Lisbon   London   Madrid
Mexico City   Milan   New Delhi   Seoul   Singapore   Sydney   Taipei   Toronto

McGraw-Hill Higher Education

*A Division of The **McGraw-Hill** Companies*

THE STUDENT WRITER: EDITOR AND CRITIC

This book is printed on acid-free paper.

1 2 3 4 5 6 7 8 9 0 QPF/QPF 9 0 4 3 2 1 0 9

ISBN 0-07-043486-7

Editorial director: *Phillip A. Butcher*
Sponsoring editor: *Sarah Touborg Moyers*
Developmental editor: *Alexis Walker*
Marketing manager: *Lesley Denton*
Project manager: *Kimberly D. Hooker*
Production supervisor: *Debra Benson*
Freelance design coordinator: *Mary Christianson*
Freelance cover designer: *The VISUAL*
Cover photograph: © *L. Lefkowitz/Masterfile*
Photo researcher: *Judy Kausal*
Compositor: *Shepherd Incorporated*
Typeface: *10/12 Plantin Light*
Printer: *Quebecor Printing Book Group/Fairfield*

Library of Congress Cataloging-in-Publication Data

Clouse, Barbara Fine.
    The student writer : editor and critic / Barbara Fine Clouse.—
5th ed.
        p.   cm.
    Includes index.
    ISBN 0-07-043486-7 (softcover)
    1. English language—Rhetoric.   2. Report writing.   3. Criticism.
4. Editing.   I. Title.
PE1408.C537 1999
808'.042—dc21   99-11790

http://www.mhhe.com

In loving memory of
Rose Lewin

About the Author

BARBARA FINE CLOUSE is a seasoned writing instructor who has taught all levels of college composition, first at Youngstown State University in northeastern Ohio and then at Slippery Rock University in western Pennsylvania. She has written a number of composition texts for McGraw-Hill including *Writing: From Inner World to Outer World; Working It Out: A Trouble-Shooting Guide for Writers; Transitions: From Reading to Writing; Patterns for a Purpose: A Rhetorical Reader;* and *Jumpstart! A Workbook for Writers.* In addition, she has developed *Cornerstones: Readings for Writers,* a short prose reader for developmental students, which is the newest addition to Primis, McGraw-Hill's electronic database. Barbara's publications also include *Process and Structure in Composition* and the fourth edition of *Progressions* for Allyn and Bacon.

Barbara appreciates getting comments and suggestions from instructors and students who use her texts, so feel free to write to her:

Barbara Clouse
c/o College English Editor
McGraw-Hill, Inc.
2 Penn Plaza
New York, NY 10121

Contents

14   *Writing the Research Paper*   393

Student and Professional Essays

Preface

The Student Writer: Editor and Critic aims to help students develop their own successful writing processes. To this end, the text describes a wide range of procedures for handling idea generation, drafting, organizing, revising, editing, and proofreading, and it helps students sample these procedures to discover techniques that work well for them. Throughout the text, students consider what they do when they write, evaluate the effectiveness of their procedures, and try alternative techniques as necessary, in an ongoing effort to improve their processes.

A second focus of *The Student Writer* is to help students learn to revise by accurately judging the strengths and weaknesses of a draft and successfully effecting the necessary changes. To help students judge writing reliably so they can make accurate revision decisions, the text includes a large number of student essays with both strengths and weaknesses. Students study these essays and assess those strengths and weaknesses to hone their critical abilities and thereby become better judges of their own drafts. To help students learn how to effect necessary changes, many revision strategies are described for students to sample until they discover their own effective revision procedures.

The focus on revision gives the text its subtitle: *editor* is used in its broad sense in reference to one who makes changes to improve writing; *critic* refers to one who *evaluates* writing to determine what changes need to be made.

In addition to focusing on process, *The Student Writer* also treats essay structure and the qualities of an effective essay with discussions of essay characteristics, sentence effectiveness, and rhetorical patterns. In fact, throughout the text, the dual concern for process and structure is apparent.

FEATURES OF THE TEXT

Part 1, The Basics of Process and Structure, has the following features:

- Procedures for helping students identify their own processes and ways to improve those processes.

- Descriptions of a wide range of techniques for shaping topics, generating ideas, determining purpose, establishing audience, drafting, revising, editing, and proofreading.
- Charts headed "Process Guidelines" that highlight important aspects of the writing process and essay structure.
- A detailed treatment of essay structure.
- Explanations and illustrations of the qualities of effective writing, including logical organization; adequate, relevant detail; and sentence effectiveness.
- An annotated essay to illustrate essay structure.
- Exercises that help students write their first essay of the term and experiment with procedures.
- Collaborative and individual exercises.
- Sections headed "Computer Tips" that offer suggestions for those who compose at the computer.
- Sections headed "Pitfalls to Avoid" that call common trouble spots to students' attention.

Part 2, Patterns of Development, has a chapter each on description, narration, illustration, comparison-contrast, process analysis, cause-and-effect analysis, definition, classification, and argumentation-persuasion. Each of these chapters has the following features:

- A discussion of detail, structure, audience, and purpose.
- A discussion of combining the pattern with other patterns.
- A discussion of using the pattern across the curriculum and in nonacademic settings.
- A section headed "Pitfalls to Avoid" that calls common problems to students' attention.
- Charts headed "Process Guidelines" that highlight important aspects of writing in the pattern.
- Professional essays, which are followed by study questions, and student essays, including an annotated student essay.
- A generous number of writing topics, including topics based on individual readings, multiple readings, the rhetorical pattern, and thematic issues.
- Revision checklists.
- Prompts for securing reader response to drafts.
- Exercises that give students an opportunity to practice skills and techniques associated with the pattern under discussion.
- Collaborative activities for evaluating the student essays.
- Topics for group discussion or journal writing after each professional essay.

Part 2 also includes a chapter on research writing; it contains the new MLA guidelines, information on evaluating sources, instruction in locating and documenting electronic sources, and exercises for skill reinforcement. In addition,

Part 2 includes a chapter on writing in response to reading that explains how to handle some of the more frequently occurring writing tasks students will encounter across the curriculum. The chapter addresses the process of reading analytically as well.

Part 3, An Editing Guide to Frequently Occurring Errors, treats word choice, sentence fragments, run-on sentences and comma splices, subject–verb agreement, tense shifts, pronoun problems, problems with modifiers, punctuation, and mechanics. Each chapter also includes exercises for reinforcement.

CHANGES FOR THE FIFTH EDITION

The fifth edition has been thoroughly revised to incorporate the following features:

- "Computer Tips" that give new strategies for composing at the computer.
- An expanded discussion of collaboration and more collaborative activities.
- "Process Guidelines" charts with composing strategies.
- Expanded discussion of the thesis with added exercises.
- Expanded discussions of introductions, supporting details, diction, and peer response.
- "Pitfalls to Avoid" sections to alert students to common troublespots.
- Additional revision exercises.
- Information on using the patterns of development across the curriculum and beyond the classroom.
- Information on combining patterns of development, including essays that illustrate various combinations.
- New student and professional essays, including the addition of annotated student essays in every pattern.
- The addition of both content and critical thinking questions after each reading.
- Additional essay topics calling for analytic thinking and response to one or more readings.
- Expanded discussion of argumentation-persuasion, with the addition of advertisements to analyze for persuasive technique.
- New emphasis on reading analytically and expanded discussion of writing a summary.
- Expanded treatment of the research paper, including information on evaluating sources, using and documenting electronic sources, and deciding what to document.
- New MLA guidelines.
- New exercises, including additional paragraphs to edit.

ACKNOWLEDGMENTS

I am deeply indebted to the following reviewers, whose sound counsel informs this book: Richard Betting, Valley City State University; Mary Alice Palm Diehr, Schoolcraft College; Robert McIlvaine, Slippery Rock University; John Reid, Rowan Cabarrus Community College; Linda Rollins, Motlow State Community College; Paulette Vrett, McHenry Community College; Nancy B. Culberson, Georgia College and State University; Anita G. Gorman, Slippery Rock University; Gail K. L. Levy, Leeward Community College; M. Elaine Brown, New York Institute of Technology; Ellie Bunting, Edison Community College; Michael Hricik, Westmoreland County Community College; John S. Terhes, Chemeketa Community College; and Dawn L. Leonard, Charleston Southern University.

As always, I owe profound gratitude to my husband, Dennis, and to my sons Gregory and Jeffrey for their patience, understanding, and indulgence. For her contribution to the first edition, I thank Joy Johnson DeSalvo. She is a respected colleague, a superior teacher and administrator, and a cherished friend. At McGraw-Hill, I thank Sarah Moyers, sponsoring editor; Alexis Walker, developmental editor; Stephanie McCusker, copyeditor; and Kimberly Hooker, project manager for their support and sound advice.

Barbara Fine Clouse

PART 1

The Basics of Process and Structure

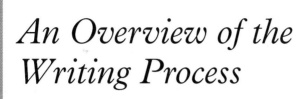

An Overview of the Writing Process

Ask 20 successful writers what they do when they write, and you could get 20 different answers because different people approach their writing in different ways. Ask one successful writer what happened when he or she wrote 20 different pieces, and once again you could get 20 different answers. This is because the same person does not always do the same things. Thus, we can make two important points about the writing process. First, there is no *one* process, and each varying approach can work well. Second, the same person does not always use the same procedures—an individual may adjust the process for a number of valid reasons.

Now what if I told you it is possible to identify steps in the writing process? "Ah," you might say, "this is not as tricky as I was starting to think. I just learn the steps and perform them in order, right?" Actually not. You see, the nature of the writing process is such that writers often find themselves stepping back before going forward. Say, for example, you have shaped a topic and generated ideas that please you, so you begin to consider ways to arrange your ideas. However, while you are arranging, you discover a relationship between your ideas that had not occurred to you before. This discovery prompts you to go back and shape your topic a bit differently. You have stepped back before going forward, which illustrates that the writing process is not linear (advancing in a straight line through the steps) but **recursive** (advancing with some doubling back and more advancing—perhaps in a new direction).

What, then, can we say for sure about the writing process? Three things, actually, and they appear in the following chart.

 PROCESS GUIDELINES: SAFE GENERALIZATIONS

1. The procedures writers follow vary from person to person.
2. The same person might use different procedures for different writing tasks.
3. The writing process is recursive rather than linear.

IMPROVING YOUR WRITING PROCESS

One goal of this text is to help you discover writing procedures that work for you. If you can learn what to do and when to do it, then your writing is bound to improve. A second goal of this text is to help you write efficiently, in ways that bring good results with a minimum of wheel spinning. To learn to write effectively *and* efficiently, you will be working toward discovering your own particular productive writing process.

You may be wondering how to discover which procedures work best for you, when the writing process varies from writer to writer. The answer lies in experimentation. This text describes a variety of ways to handle each aspect of writing. To discover your own effective, efficient writing process, you should sample several of the different techniques. Afterwards, evaluate the success of what you sampled and make a decision about whether to retain a procedure because it worked well or try something else. If you experiment and evaluate this way throughout the term, you will improve your writing process—and hence your writing.

Before discussing the writing process any further, you should identify what you currently do when you write by answering the following questionnaire.

A Writing Process Questionnaire

Answer the following questions as completely as possible.

1. How do you get ideas to include in your writing?
2. How do you establish your audience and purpose?
3. How do you decide how to order your ideas? When do you decide this? Do you outline?
4. Do you typically write more than one draft? If so, how many?
5. How do you decide what changes to make in your drafts? At what point do you decide this?
6. Do you ask other people to read your work before you submit it? If so, whom?
7. What do you do when you get stuck?
8. Under what circumstances do you produce your best work (in a quiet room, at night, a week before deadline, with a special pen, etc.)?
9. Do you write a piece in one sitting or leave your work and come back to it? If you do the latter, when do you leave and when do you return?

Your answers will tell you what you currently do when you write. However, you should also identify how successful your current process is by answering the next questions.

1. Which features of your process produce satisfactory results in a reasonable amount of time?
2. Which features take too long or fail to produce satisfactory results?

Your response to question 2 indicates aspects of your process to improve. Make note of these aspects, and the next time you write, try techniques described throughout this text to handle these aspects (consult the index to find the techniques under the following headings: Topic selection, Idea generation, Audience, Purpose, Outlining, First draft, Revising, Editing, Proofreading). After trying a new technique, evaluate its effectiveness, determine whether you need to experiment further, and choose the next technique you will try.

SIX AREAS OF THE WRITING PROCESS

Even though writers do different things when they write, most successful writers turn their attention to these six areas.

1. Generating ideas, establishing purpose, and identifying audience.
2. Ordering ideas.
3. Writing the first draft.
4. Revising (improving content, organization, and the expression of ideas).
5. Editing (correcting errors in grammar, usage, capitalization, and punctuation).
6. Proofreading (making corrections in the final copy).

Since we know that successful writers deal with these six areas, you may be wondering why there is so much variety among the writing processes of different writers. The explanation is that although successful writers attend to these six areas, they vary in the way they handle each area. Furthermore, they attend to these areas in different orders, and sometimes they attend to two areas at once. This variety explains the different approaches to writing.

Your efforts to discover the process that works best for you will involve you in understanding each of the six areas, becoming aware of the various approaches to handling each of the areas, and experimenting to learn which approaches work for you.

Now look again at the list of six areas, but this time let's group the areas to shed more light on the writing process.

WRITER-BASED	*Prewriting*	*1. Generating ideas, establishing purpose, and identifying audience*
		2. Ordering ideas
	Writing	*3. Composing the first draft*
READER-BASED	*Rewriting*	*4. Revising*
		5. Editing
		6. Proofreading

The diagram above illustrates that the six areas in the process can be divided into two groups: *writer-based activities* and *reader-based activities*. In other words, as writers move from idea to finished piece, they first concentrate on what *they want* for their writing and then move to what their *readers need* from their writing. Of course, during writer-based activities the reader is still considered, just as the writer's orientation is a concern during reader-based activities. The division really represents the *primary* focus of each of the six areas of the process.

The chart also shows that the six areas can be grouped into three categories: **prewriting** (activities performed prior to writing the first draft), **writing** (composing the first draft), and **rewriting** (making changes in the first draft to get the piece ready for a reader). Prewriting and writing are primarily writer-based activities, while rewriting is primarily reader-based.

As you study the chart, remember the recursive nature of the writing process: You may not always move sequentially through the areas; instead your work in one area may prompt you to step back and make changes in an area handled earlier, and these changes will affect what you do when you go forward again.

WRITING REALITIES

As you experiment to discover your own effective, efficient writing process, keep in mind the following "writing realities."

1. WRITING IS USUALLY HARD WORK

You may think that while you are straining over the page, the rest of the world is out there merrily writing away with no trouble. On the contrary, writing is seldom easy for anyone. Sure, there are a few who write easily and well, but they are the exception. For everyone else, writing is hard work.

2. WRITING TAKES TIME

Think for a minute about the writing process. If you are to attend to all the stages, you must have time on your side. If you wait until the last minute, you will build in frustration and failure.

3. EVERYONE GETS STUCK SOMETIMES

When this happens to you, leave your writing for a time and refresh yourself by doing other things. When you return to your work, you may have the solution to your problem. If not, try to discover why the problem exists by asking the following questions.

Is my topic too broad?

Am I trying to write about something I do not know enough about?

Am I worried about getting everything "right" too soon?

Do I need a different organization?

If these questions do not help you solve the problem, ask a reliable reader to review your work and identify a way around the problem.

4. MORE THAN ANYTHING ELSE, WRITING MEANS REVISION

Do not expect your first efforts to be top quality. Professional writers are always making changes, so why should you expect to get it right the first time? If you look at an early effort and discover everything is not what it should be, do not despair or conclude that you cannot write. Instead, get in there and revise.

5. WRITING CAN START OUT AS ONE THING AND END UP AS ANOTHER

When you revise, you make changes and sometimes the changes are sweeping. Thus, you may end up with something very different from what you initially had in mind.

6. SOMETIMES YOU MUST START OVER

Even though you planned carefully and executed your plan well, you may discover that what you have is not working. This unpleasant discovery can be made at any point in the writing process. When you realize you have major problems and no attempts at revision help enough, you may have to begin again. This can be frustrating, but take comfort in knowing that writers often must discover what they do *not* want to do before they learn what they *do* want to do.

7. KEEP YOUR WRITING IN MIND WHILE YOU ARE DOING OTHER THINGS

People do not write only at a desk. You can think about your work while you are cleaning the bedroom, walking the dog, or stuck in a traffic jam. Any time your mind is not fully occupied, you can think of ideas, toy with approaches to your introduction, consider different organizations, and so on. If you do this, you are mentally planning ahead, so when you do sit down to your paper, the writing will move along more smoothly. Thinking about your writing in this way can be especially helpful when you have hit a snag. As you pursue other activities, let a portion of your brain consider solutions to your problem.

8. YOU HAVE INSTINCTS THAT CAN BE SHARPENED AND RELIED ON

You have heard, read, spoken, and written the language so much that a great deal of what you know about it has been internalized. As a result, you sometimes function more by instinct than by conscious awareness. When it comes to writing and reading your own writing, you often have an intuitive sense of what is and is not working. Sometimes you sense a trouble spot even though you cannot identify what the problem is. Trust your instincts and assume there is a problem when you sense one. If your intuitive sense could stand some sharpening, read a little bit every day. Subscribe to a weekly newsmagazine or read books about subjects that interest you. Regular exposure to effective writing will help you internalize awarenesses about language and sharpen your instincts.

WRITERS ON WRITING

In the following selections, two professional writers comment on writing and their writing processes. These selections make a number of important points you should keep in mind as you consider your own process and how to improve it.

About "The Watcher at the Gates"

In "The Watcher at the Gates" Gail Godwin writes of the "inner critic," the restraining voice in writers that can interfere with inspiration and creativity if not held in check in the early stages of writing. Yet Godwin makes it clear that the inner critic should be set free to exercise vigilance during revision and editing. Finally, Godwin confesses to the reason she, like many student writers, errs by turning the inner critic loose too soon.

The Watcher at the Gates

Gail Godwin

I first realized I was not the only writer who had a restraining critic who lived inside me and sapped the juice from green inspirations when I was leafing through Freud's "Interpretation of Dreams" a few years ago. Ironically, it was my "inner critic" who had sent me to Freud. I was writing a novel, and my heroine was in the middle of a dream, and then I lost faith in my own invention and rushed to "an authority" to check whether she could have such a dream. In the chapter on dream interpretation, I came upon the following passage that has helped me free myself, in some measure, from my critic and has led to many pleasant and interesting exchanges with other writers.   *1*

Freud quotes Schiller, who is writing a letter to a friend. The friend complains of his lack of creative power. Schiller replies with an allegory. He says it is not good if the intellect examines too closely the ideas pouring in at the gates. "In isolation, an idea may be quite insignificant, and venturesome in the extreme, but it may acquire importance from an idea which follows it. . . . In the case of a creative mind, it seems to me, the intellect has withdrawn its watchers from the gates, and the ideas rush in pell-mell, and only then does it review and inspect the multitude. You are ashamed or afraid of the momentary and passing madness which is found in all real creators, the longer or shorter duration of which distinguishes the thinking artist from the dreamer . . . you reject too soon and discriminate too severely."   *2*

So that's what I had: a Watcher at the Gates. I decided to get to know him better. I discussed him with other writers, who told me some of the quirks and habits of their Watchers, each of whom was as individual as his host, and all of whom seemed passionately dedicated to one goal: rejecting too soon and discriminating too severely.   *3*

It is amazing the lengths a Watcher will go to keep you from pursuing the flow of your imagination. Watchers are notorious pencil sharpeners, ribbon changers, plant waterers, home repairers and abhorrers of messy rooms or messy pages. They are compulsive looker-uppers. They are superstitious scaredy-cats. They cultivate self-important eccentricities they think are suitable for "writers."   *4*

And they'd rather die (and kill your inspiration with them) than risk making a fool of themselves.

My Watcher has a wasteful penchant for 20-pound bond paper above and *5* below the carbon of the first draft. "What's the good of writing out a whole page," he whispers begrudgingly, "if you just have to write it over again later? Get it perfect the first time!" My Watcher adores stopping in the middle of a morning's work to drive down to the library to check on the name of a flower or a World War II battle or a line of metaphysical poetry. "You can't possibly go on till you've got this right!" he admonishes. I go and get the car keys.

Other Watchers have informed their writers that: *6*

"Whenever you get a really good sentence you should stop in the middle of *7* it and go on tomorrow. Otherwise you might run dry."

"Don't try and continue with your book till your dental appointment is *8* over. When you're worried about your teeth, you can't think about art."

Another Watcher makes his owner pin his finished pages to a clothesline *9* and read them through binoculars "to see how they look from a distance." Countless other Watchers demand "bribes" for taking the day off: lethal doses of caffeine, alcoholic doses of Scotch or vodka or wine.

There are various ways to outsmart, pacify, or coexist with your Watcher. *10* Here are some I have tried, or my writer-friends have tried, with success:

Look for situations when he's likely to be off-guard. Write too fast for him *11* in an unexpected place, at an unexpected time. (Virginia Woolf captured the "diamonds in the dustheap" by writing at a "rapid haphazard gallop" in her diary.) Write when very tired. Write in purple ink on the back of a Master Charge statement. Write whatever comes into your mind while the kettle is boiling and make the steam whistle your deadline. (Deadlines are a great way to outdistance the Watcher.)

Disguise what you are writing. If your Watcher refuses to let you get on *12* with your story or novel, write a "letter" instead, telling your "correspondent" what you are going to write in your story or next chapter. Dash off a "review" of your own unfinished opus. It will stand up like a bully to your Watcher the next time he throws obstacles in your path. If you write yourself a good one.

Get to know your Watcher. He's yours. Do a drawing of him (or her). Pin *13* it to the wall of your study and turn it gently to the wall when necessary. Let your Watcher feel needed. Watchers are excellent critics after inspiration has been captured; they are dependable, sharp-eyed readers of things already set down. Keep your Watcher in shape and he'll have less time to keep you from shaping. If he's really ruining your whole working day, sit down, as Jung did with his personal demons, and write him a letter. On a very bad day I once wrote my Watcher a letter. "Dear Watcher," I wrote, "What is it you're so afraid I'll do?" Then I held his pen for him, and he replied instantly with a candor that has kept me from truly despising him.

"Fail," he wrote back. *14*

About "How I Wrote 'Fat Chance' "

In the following selection, Barbara Wright makes important points about the writing process. She notes the occasional necessity to begin again, the reality of writer's block, the fact that writing is hard, the usefulness of writing ends before middles, the purpose and nature of revision, the fact that writing takes time, the need to get some distance, the unreliability of inspiration, the fact that writing is a form of discovery, the fact that final versions can vary greatly from first drafts, and the role of instinct and how to sharpen it.

How I Wrote "Fat Chance"

Barbara Wright

Writing a short story, I find myself changing things from the moment the first 1 word is committed to paper until the last word of the final draft is typed. Even as I proofread, I see changes I want to make. The only thing that saves me is that I am too lazy to retype the story. Someone once said that a work of art is never finished, only abandoned. I agree.

Although the process of some writers seems to fit in neat categories with the 2 first, second, and third drafts on pink, blue, and yellow paper, the process I go through is haphazard, totally chaotic. I usually start with an image of the main character and an ill-defined intent. I never know what is going to happen in my stories until I have finished one draft, which takes an average of a month, writing three hours every day except Sunday.

In "Fat Chance" I started out to write a story with an unreliable narrator 3 named Jenny, a nineteen-year-old, 250-pound woman who goes to a weight reduction clinic and meets one of the waiters in the dining hall, who she deludes herself into thinking is attracted to her. I wanted to make the reader know more than the first-person narrator, to play with the tension between Jenny's fantasy and the reality.

Before beginning I read several books on obesity to find out how fat men 4 and women perceive the world, the prejudices they encounter, how they view their fatness, and the problems they have in trying to reduce. Then I sat down and in two three-hour sessions wrote fifteen pages on Jenny's childhood, how she was taken advantage of by people in her high school, how they would use her to tell all their problems to, but wouldn't invite her to go on beach weekends because, as they told her, they didn't think she could swim. I wrote of the time she passed an anti-abortion activist on the street who didn't hand her a pamphlet, assuming that no one would sleep with her, so she wouldn't need any information.

Rereading what I had written, I realized that all of this was background in- 5 formation. There was no story. Nothing had happened. Those pages were necessary for me to write in order to get to know the character better, but they had nothing to do with the story I was about to tell, although I didn't know what that story was. However, I did discard the idea of the unreliable narrator. The Jenny who emerged on the page was different from the character I originally intended to create. This character was vulnerable, and tried to cover her vulnerability with tough language and humor, but she was basically honest and would never delude herself into thinking someone liked her if he didn't.

What had happened thus far was this: I had started with an intent, but in writing, was forced to discard the intent, although I hadn't replaced it with another. So there I was with 15 pages that had to be thrown out. *6*

I was able to salvage about three pages from different parts of the original and started from there. Now came the difficult part. For the next month, I worked on the first draft. *7*

To explain why it takes me so long to write, I must divulge one of my dirty little secrets: I have writer's block, a mild form that makes it difficult for me to sit down and commit myself to paper. *8*

In *Writing with Power* (New York: Oxford University Press, 1981) Peter Elbow identifies two kinds of difficulties in writing. The first he compares to carrying an unwieldy load across a stream on slippery rocks. This is the most noble, productive difficulty because it involves working through language, figuring out thoughts, developing ideas. One is struggling with the writing itself, and the task of mastering words and ideas can be overwhelming, thus causing the block (p. 199). This kind of writer's block derives from the fear of the unknown. When I know that a good idea is being formed, however inchoate and messy, as new ideas always are, there is a sense of real engagement, but also a pulling back, a terror of the unknown that causes me to panic, afraid I am going to blow the idea. *9*

The second kind of difficulty is more neurotic, and, sadly, I suffer from it more than anything else. Peter Elbow describes it this way: "You are trying to fight your way out from under a huge deflated silk balloon—layers and layers of light gauzy material which you can bat away, but they always just flop back again and no movement or exertion gets you any closer to the open air" (p. 199). In this type of block, the writer has no sense of direction and keeps going around in circles. Elbow attributes this behavior to fear of the generalized audience some writers carry in their heads. *10*

The dangerous audience in my head is composed of two factions. To stage left are all my critics, past, present, and future: the junior-high-school English teacher who read one of my essays in a voice like Bullwinkle's; all the people who have looked at my work and said something noncommittal, unable to disguise the screaming subtext; my eighty-year-old Quaker grandmother, whose heart may not be able to withstand the shock of sex scenes and vile language; people who may think they recognize themselves among my characters. *11*

To stage right are my supporters, equally dangerous. These are people who think I have talent, who think I am going to make it. I am afraid I am going to disappoint them, make them reassess their view of me, expose the *real me*. Both these groups form a Gestapo, and I can't shake what one writer called "the feeling that the Gestapo is going to come to my door and arrest me for impersonating an intellectual." *12*

So this is the audience for the drama that happens every morning as I sit *13* down to write. The principal actors are the angel, the demon, and me. The props: a desk and a typewriter.

Angel: It's nine o'clock. Time to sit down and write.

   Me: But I can't think of anything to say. I have no idea what my character is going to do. I've got to get Jenny out of the fat farm and downtown so she can meet Marvin.

Demon: The plants need watering.

Angel: Don't do it. You know you'll waste ten minutes.

Demon: Well the least you can do is clean up this mess. I mean, it's disgusting—coffee stains, flakes from the white-out, eraser dust, paper on the floor. We can't write in this filth.

Angel: Don't listen to him. Why don't you just get started?

   Me: I don't know. I sit down to write and nothing quite . . . you know . . . jells. Maybe if I clean up . . .

Angel: Try freewriting. You can throw it away. No one is going to see it but me and . . . (whispers) . . . him.

   Me: It only depresses me. I sit down and write ten minutes worth of crap, and nothing can be salvaged. It only makes me feel worse.

Demon: You'd better check the mail. There's probably another rejection slip.

Angel: (Ignoring him) Okay, then just write one sentence and see if that leads you to another.

   Me: I can't seem to do it. When I write letters, they are full of life, everyone loves to get them—and I'm not counting my mother. But when I write a story, it never quite . . .

Angel: So write some background information on Marvin. You don't know what kind of a guy he is yet.

   Me: Okay. (Sigh. Write a sentence, rip it out of the typewriter carriage, crumple it up, aim at the wastebasket, and miss.)

Demon: (Taunting) You're going to have to say something difficult, aren't you? You don't know if you have the talent to do it, do you? I saw that pitiful, decaffeinated sentence you just wrote. And you call yourself a WRITER? I've got news for you, Toots. That's never going to pass muster.

Angel: (To demon) Will you cut the clichés? (To me) If you absolutely have nothing to say, then just sit down and stare at the blank paper. It's not going to hurt. What is it that you're afraid you're going to do?

Demon: Fail.

Considering this daily drama, the brouhaha of the audience in my head, *14* and my own expectations, which are always higher than I can ever meet, the wonder is not that I write so little, but that I write at all.

For a long time I thought my difficulty with writing was nature's way of handing me a rejection slip, but I have since learned that others share this. When asked if he enjoyed writing, William Styron said, "I certainly don't. I get a fine warm feeling when I'm doing well, but that pleasure is pretty much negated by the pain of getting started each day. Let's face it, writing is hell."[1]

Yet the fine warm feeling is worth the pain, especially when one has the heady experience of the writing taking over and writing itself. These rare moments, gifts from the unconscious, are to be cherished. In "Fat Chance" this happened to me on the last three pages. I had been working on the first part of the story, describing what goes on at Dr. Bonner's rice clinic where Jenny goes to reduce. I had also been tinkering with a later section in which Jenny meets a black waiter named Marvin in a railroad-car diner when she goes in to order black tea. Marvin was still vaguely defined and I didn't know exactly what was going to happen between him and Jenny, but I knew it would be something horrible to make her abandon her diet and go on a super-binge. For some reason, I felt I had to write the last scene before I could go on with the middle part. Every morning for two weeks I wrote and rewrote the ending. The results were abysmal, depressing. The garbage can was overflowing with discarded pages. I couldn't get it right. Not even one sentence was redeemable. For me it was not a problem of what to say, but how to say it; the two are indistinguishable in fiction. Some days I would sit for three hours and produce nothing. At this point in my life, nothing was going right. The freshman English classes I was teaching were uninspired, I was not doing good work in my graduate-school classes, and my personal life was dormant. All these problems were aggravated by my inability to produce even one good sentence after two weeks of solid work. I knew that I had to get the ending right before I could go on.

Then, one night after teaching, I came back from school and decided that instead of studying or reading I would take a walk to relax. I could feel the pressure building up from all points in my life. When I came back, I felt an urgency to sit down at the typewriter, even though I had already done my three-hour stint and rarely write twice a day. Typing as quickly as I could, I wrote the entire last scene in ten or fifteen minutes. It appears in the final draft almost exactly as I wrote it. I was typing full speed when suddenly, out of nowhere, the image of a phoenix tattooed on Jenny's stomach appeared. As she gorges herself on junk food, she imagines the red and green wings blurring as her stomach expands until the tattoo is no longer recognizable as a bird. Clacking along, I typed: "But no one would see it but me. No one would ever see it but me." I came to an abrupt stop. I knew that I had the last line. And I knew I had the ending to the story. There was an immediate feeling of ecstasy. One of those rare moments in writing that make up in intensity what they lack in frequency.

Popular misconception has it that writers' inspiration falls from the sky and thwacks them over the head. Actually, the moments of clarity are born of hard

[1]*Writers at Work: The Paris Review Interviews* (First Series), ed. Malcolm Cowley (New York: Penguin Books, 1977), p. 271.

work, false starts, discarded efforts. It is only through the struggle that what was brewing in the unconscious is able to shoulder its way through to consciousness.

Often the conscious mind needs a rest, needs to regroup. When the final *19* breakthrough occurs, it seems so simple, and we wonder how we could have been so stupid as to miss it. The reason is that we were not psychologically ready to see it.

This is why I write every day. Inspiration is infrequent, and the periods of *20* drought are frustrating and debilitating, but necessary to make creative break-throughs possible.

After the ending to "Fat Chance" was written, I had to create a catalyst for *21* Jenny's binging. This time, the unconscious deserted me. The first draft ended up like this: Jenny and Marvin go to the movies. She invites him back to her room. On the way there, two thugs from the Ku Klux Klan stop them, insult Marvin, tell him he's hard up to be going out with a fat woman, then beat him up. Jenny runs to call the police. By the time the police get there, Marvin has disappeared. He quits his job and won't talk to her. Jenny goes to his house but his sister slams the door in her face. Then she goes on the binge.

By this time I had been working on the story so long I had lost all critical *22* faculties, so I asked the help of a friend, an excellent critic whom I trust. She made the following observations: The voice was inconsistent, the first three pages, which were from the initial fifteen I had written, were irrelevant, and the whole bit about the thugs was fake and depended too much on plot. Also the symbolism of the tattoo didn't work.

Armed with this information, I went back to work. Usually, after the painful *23* first draft, I work more quickly. I started the story in the middle of page four. I rewrote sections to make the voice consistent and tried to make the tattoo work. In the first draft, I had written one paragraph about the one time Jenny had been rebellious and got a phoenix tattoo on her stomach. This didn't do the trick, my friend told me, because her motivation for doing so wasn't clear. Now I added a scene in which Jenny's mother takes her to the department store on her sixteenth birthday to buy her a dress. Jenny tries on the largest size, but it is too small. Her mother humiliates her in front of the clerk, saying that they would take the dress anyway, since it would give Jenny incentive to reduce. Jenny changes in the cubicle, leaves the dress in a heap on the floor, then leaves without her mother, taking the subway home. On the way, she passes a tattoo shop and decides to get a phoenix tattooed on her stomach.

In this version, her motivation was still not clear. So finally I added a sec- *24* tion in which she looks in the window of the shop and sees a life-sized photo of an obese oriental man stripped to the waist with a two-headed dragon tattoo winding up his stomach. Jenny remembers her mother's looking at the photo several weeks before and saying, "Can you imagine anyone showing off their blubber like that?" Now, juxtaposed against the department-store scene and the fact that her mother is always taking potshots at fatsos, the motivation is—I hope—clear. It is an act of self-hatred to get back at her mother.

To find the details of the tattooing, I called a friend who had had a tattoo *25* put on her chest. She told me about the reclining dentist-type chair and how the needles sounded and felt.

Next I completely rewrote the catalyst for Jenny's binge. Now she goes to *26* the restaurant where Marvin works. They overhear his friends in a booth, saying he must be hard up to be going out with an obese woman—and white at that. Marvin jerks his hand away from hers and goes to the front of the store. Jenny leaves and calls him from Pizza Hut, but he doesn't say anything and she can't think of anything to say either, so she hangs up. Trapped in Pizza Hut, thick with the smell of oregano, tomatoes, and dough, she thinks a fast-food fix will make it easier for her to think clearly. This is the start of the binge.

Most of what appears in the final draft was not in the first draft. Yet I was *27* able to write it in two weeks. The first draft was so difficult because I didn't know what was going to happen, who the characters were, or even what my intent was. I started out with an intent, a preconception of what the work would be. But through writing I was constantly reassessing the intent, adapting and changing it to fit what the writing produced. At other times the preconception forced a revision of the writing. Each time I reworked a scene, a paragraph, or even a sentence, it caused a restructuring of the whole. Everything was in flux. Fiction writers, more than any other kind of writers, are familiar with Keats' negative capability and are used to swimming in uncertainty and doubt, without the ability to grasp onto something firm.

After the first draft, when one aspect of the writing had stabilized—in this *28* case, the intent—it was much easier for me to work. Thus, I was able to complete the second draft in half the time.

In revision, the only help I have to make changes is an internal Geiger *29* counter that registers when something is not quite right. This Geiger counter is partly intuitive, partly educable. When it starts registering dissonance, I have to stop, diagnose the problem, and decide what to do about it: whether to modify the intent or the writing.

For example, toward the end of the first draft, I was having trouble revising *30* the scenes at Dr. Bonner's clinic. I tried to put them in past tense, but they seemed awkward and unnatural. So I asked myself to whom and how soon after the incident was Jenny relating the story. I realized that she had to be relating it soon after the binge because the sense of self-hatred that comes out in the scene would have to be relatively fresh. I decided that she was telling the story while she was still at the clinic, having had to stay longer after the setback of her superbinge. She would be telling the story to someone who hadn't been to the clinic, but who knew she was still there. Thus the reader would have to put himself in the position of being a confidant. Walter Ong talks of writers who "fictionalize their audiences, casting them in a made-up role and calling on them to play the role assigned."[2] In my case, this tactic is often intuitive. Only when problems arise do I consciously analyze these relationships.

[2]"The Writer's Audience Is Always a Fiction," *PMLA* 90 (1975), p. 17.

The more I read literature and the more I work on my own fiction, the *31* more sensitive my Geiger counter becomes, and the more often it registers dissatisfaction. I feel worse about my writing after two years of graduate school than I did when I first started because the development of my Geiger counter has outdistanced the development of my writing. I can see the possibilities of what can be done with the short story form and have become increasingly frustrated with my inability to reach the goal.

In her study of children's rewriting strategies, Lucy Calkins found that one *32* group of third graders, whom she called transitional children, would start and abandon piece after piece of writing. Nothing seemed to satisfy them. Calkins writes: "As children develop high standards for themselves and become more self-critical, they become more and more frustrated with what they have done, and more and more unwilling to reread, recopy, and refine what they view as 'lousy' to begin with."[3]

I find that when my freshman writing students do their best work at the end *33* of the semester, they are invariably the most uncertain, the most self-critical. This is because over the course of the semester, they have learned what good writing is and how to identify the problems, but are not yet confident of their ability to solve the problems. Their Geiger counters have developed more rapidly than the skills to quiet them.

Even though it seems the longer I write the more dissatisfied I become, I *34* know that my only chance is to write regularly to develop the craft.

---

[3]Lucy McCormick Calkins, "Children's Rewriting Strategies," unpublished manuscript, University of New Hampshire, p. 18.

Shaping Topics, Discovering Ideas, and Developing a Thesis

Many people believe that a writer's ideas come in a blinding flash of inspiration, in some magic moment of discovery that propels the writer forward and causes word upon wonderful word to spill onto the page. Yes, such moments occur from time to time, but they are the exception rather than the rule. More typically, writers cannot depend on inspiration, because it does not make scheduled appearances. Often it does not arrive at all.

So what is a writer to do in the absence of inspiration? Fortunately, when ideas do not come to the writer, there are ways the writer can go after ideas. That is what this chapter is about—ways you can discover ideas when inspiration does not strike at the moment you need it.

THE WRITING SUBJECT AND THE WRITING TOPIC

Sometimes your writing topic is determined for you by an instructor, boss, or situation (such as when you write a letter to a company protesting an incorrect bill). When your topic is not predetermined, however, your first step is topic selection.

If you need a writing topic and you are not inspired, you can take steps to discover one. However, before discussing those steps, let's consider the difference between a writing subject and a writing topic.

A **subject** is a broad area you want to write about. A **topic** is the narrow territory within that subject area that you stake out as the specific focus for your writing. For example, say you want to write about presidential elections. That is a subject area because "presidential elections" takes in a great deal. If you settle on arguing that electing the president by popular vote is better than by electoral vote, then you have a topic—a narrow focus for your essay. In the most general sense, **topic selection** involves choosing a broad subject area and paring it down until you have a narrow topic.

Finding Your Subject

Anything can serve as the subject for an essay. However, when you are seeking your own subjects, there may be little comfort in knowing that you can write about anything. You need to discover which of the many "anythings" you want to write about. Fortunately, writers can do several things to find subjects, and some of these techniques are described here.

1. TRY FREEWRITING

Freewriting shakes loose ideas by freeing writers of worry about correctness, organization, and even logic. To freewrite for a writing subject, write nonstop for 5 or 10 minutes. Record *everything* that comes to mind, even if it seems silly or irrelevant. DO NOT STOP WRITING FOR ANY REASON. If you run out of ideas, then write names of your family members; or write, "I don't know what to say," or write the alphabet—anything. You will not be sharing your freewriting with a reader, so you can say what you want and you can forget spelling, grammar, neatness, and form. Just get your ideas down any way you can. After 5 or 10 minutes, read over your freewriting and you will likely find at least one idea for a writing subject. Here is an example that yields several possible subjects.

> I have to find a writing subject. Let's see, there's politics and school, but politics is boring and school is done to death (and it's going to kill me, hah). What else? Television, there ought to be a lot there. The shows, the commercials, the sex and violence. I could do something with arguing about the violence. Pop culture is possible too, especially MTV. I haven't watched it for awhile but it used to be really racy. What about soaps? Let's see, what else? A B C D E F G H What else? My friends, my family. I could write about Dad—he'd be a book, not an essay. Especially if I write about his drinking—no, better not. I could write about Janet's accident and the courage she showed or I could write about courage in general. That could be hard. I don't know, what else? Teachers roommates studying grades? Stress? I should have enough now.

2. BROWSE THROUGH A DICTIONARY

You may not want to write about aardvarks or Zyrian, but there are many entries in between that you may wish to discuss. Perhaps an entry will trigger your thinking because it is associated with something. Who knows? The entry for *balloon* might remind you of that summer day at the fair when you were six and your first helium balloon escaped your grasp, an episode that could make a fine narrative essay.

3. READ YOUR LOCAL AND CAMPUS NEWSPAPERS

The events, issues, controversies, and concerns reported in newspapers can be essay subjects. Tax hikes, building projects, curriculum changes, pending legislation, demonstrations, actions of officials or citizens or students—all of these and more are reported in the papers and can suggest interesting, worthwhile subjects.

4. KEEP AN ESSAY-SUBJECT NOTEBOOK

Get a small spiral notebook to keep in your backpack, pocket, or purse. During the day you will have thoughts and experiences that could serve as future essay subjects. If you write these down, you can refer to them later when you are searching for things to write about.

5. FILL IN THE BLANKS

You can discover a subject by filling in the blanks in key sentences like these:

```
I'll never forget the time I _____.
_____ is the most _____ I know.
After _____ I was never the same again.
College can best be described as _____.
Is there anything more frustrating (interesting/exciting) than
_____?
This world can certainly do without _____.
What this world needs is _____.
_____ made a lasting impression on me.
After _____ I changed my mind about _____.
My biggest success (failure) was _____.
Life with _____ is _____.
Life would be easier if only _____.
I get so angry (annoyed/frightened) when _____.
_____ is better (or worse) than _____.
The main cause of _____ is _____.
The main effect of _____ is _____.
Most people do not understand the real meaning of _____.
The best way to do _____ is _____.
```

6. GIVE YOURSELF ENOUGH TIME

Deciding on a writing subject can take time, so allow yourself a day or two for ideas to surface. Go about your business with a portion of your brain considering what you experience and observe. You may be inspired. For example, a routine walk across campus may not ordinarily prompt an essay subject. However, if you take that walk aware that you need a subject, you might see the library you pass every day as the subject for an essay, perhaps one about the different ways people study in the library.

Shaping Your Topic

When you shape a topic from a subject, keep the following points in mind.

1. SHAPE A TOPIC THAT WILL HAVE AN IMPACT ON YOUR READER

A topic should interest you as the writer, but it should also have significance for the reader. After all, you are writing something that will be read by someone else, and you do not want to bore your reader. To determine whether your topic can have an impact on a reader, ask yourself these questions:

    a. In what ways can the topic inform a reader?
    b. In what ways can the topic entertain a reader?
    c. In what ways can the topic influence a reader to think or act differently?
    d. In what ways can the topic arouse a reader's emotions?
    e. Why would the topic interest a reader?
    f. How can I make my topic interesting to a reader?

2. SHAPE A TOPIC YOU KNOW ENOUGH ABOUT

Shape a topic you have some firsthand experience with or one you know through observation, reading, or classwork. It makes little sense, for example, to write about saving the whales if you did not know they were in trouble until you saw that bumper sticker yesterday.

3. SHAPE A TOPIC THAT CAN BE HANDLED IN AN APPROPRIATE LENGTH

It is better to treat a narrow topic in depth than a broad topic superficially. A superficial treatment will never satisfy a reader because the essay will be vague and general. If your topic takes in too much territory, then to develop it appropriately you would be forced to write a very long piece. For example, how would you like to be stuck writing 500 words on stress? You would not be able to treat every aspect of stress adequately. If you did, your essay would be so long that three friends would have to help you deliver it to your instructor. However, if you narrowed your topic to effects of stress on college freshmen, you could treat a topic in depth in a comfortable length.

How to Narrow

Shaping a topic can involve a series of narrowings. Say, for example, that you have decided to write about unemployment. Now you must narrow this subject to something that can be managed in a reasonable length. You could narrow first by deciding to write about the causes and effects of the unemployment rate in our country. Yet it is unlikely one essay could say everything about the causes and effects of unemployment, so another restriction is necessary. You may settle on a discussion of the causes *or* of the effects. These are narrower, but they still take in quite a bit, so another narrowing is in order. Perhaps you could narrow to discuss the effects of your father's unemployment on your family. If you feel there is too much to say about that topic, you could narrow once more to discuss the effects of your father's unemployment on you. Such a topic would be narrow enough for treatment in a single essay.

Here is a graphic representation of the process of shaping a topic from a subject.

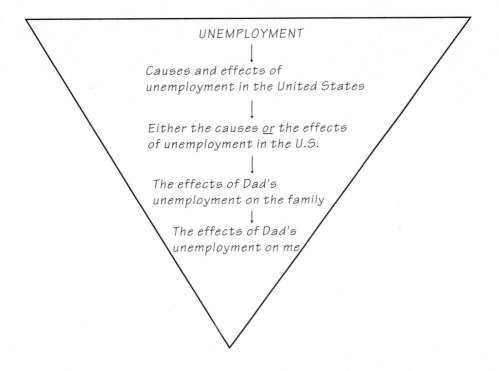

UNEMPLOYMENT

↓

Causes and effects of
unemployment in the United States

↓

Either the causes _or_ the effects
of unemployment in the U.S.

↓

The effects of Dad's
unemployment on the family

↓

The effects of Dad's
unemployment on me

For help narrowing a subject to a topic, try the following procedures.

1. FREEWRITE

To find a topic, try 10 to 15 minutes of freewriting on your general subject. (See page 18 on how to freewrite.) Here is a sample freewriting on soap operas, one of the subjects that surfaced as a result of the freewriting on page 18.

> Soap operas have been around a long time. They are hugely popular. They're on day and night. Lots of different kinds of people watch them. Even very bright, professional people who you would think have better things to do. What now? ABCDE. Let's see. Soaps are interesting to some people and entertaining to others, but why I don't know because I think they are pretty stupid. Have you ever really listened to these things? Must be a reason people like them. Maybe several reasons. Entertainment? People are bored? Lots of famous actors started on soaps. I can't think of who, though. At 1:00 half my residence hall meets to watch All My Children. Some people even schedule their classes around their favorite soaps. Good grief. My mother used to call them her "stories."

This freewriting suggests several possible topics, including: who watches soaps, why they watch soaps, what soaps are like, and how the author's mother felt about her soaps.

2. MAKE A LIST

Write your subject at the top of a page and below it list every aspect of the subject you can think of. Do not evaluate the worth of the items; just list everything that occurs to you. A list for the subject "stress" might look like this:

Stress

effects on health

stress management

fear of failure

exam anxiety

school stress

job stress

stress in children

stress in athletes

peer pressure

Sometimes this list is enough to prompt a suitable topic. For example, you might look at it and decide to write about "exam anxiety," perhaps focusing on ways students can cope with this anxiety. Other times, you may need a second list to narrow a subject in the first list. For example, you could look at the first list and narrow to "school stress." That is a step in the right direction, but "school stress" is still broad and without a specific focus. You could try a second list, which might look something like this:

School Stress

exam anxiety

coping with a roommate

picking a major

dealing with stress

effects on studies

fear of flunking out

trying to fit in

Your second list could lead you to one of several topics. For example, studying this list could lead you to write about ways a college student can deal with stress.

3. EXAMINE YOUR SUBJECT FROM DIFFERENT ANGLES

Another way to move from subject to topic is to ask these key questions about your subject, so that you can view it from different angles.

Can I describe my subject?

Can I compare my subject with something?

Can I contrast my subject with something?

What is my subject related to? What does it remind me of?

Can my subject be broken down into parts?

Can I explain how my subject works?

Is my subject good for something? Would anyone find my subject useful?

What arguments or controversies surround my subject?

Answers to these questions can reveal aspects of your subject to help you discover ways to narrow to a topic.

4. TRY CLUSTERING

To cluster, write your general subject in the center of a page and circle it, like this:

Next, let your thoughts flow freely and record all the associations that occur to you; circle and connect these associations to the core circle, like this.

As ideas continue to strike you, write them and connect them to the appropriate circles.

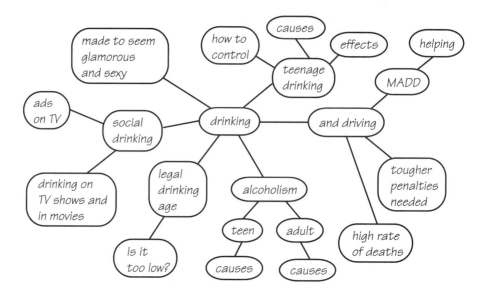

This clustering reveals several areas to explore for topics based on the subject "drinking":

1. *The causes of teenage drinking*
2. *The effects of teenage drinking*
3. *How to control teenage drinking*
4. *How MADD (Mothers Against Drunk Driving) is working to end drunk driving*
5. *The need for tougher penalties for drunk driving*
6. *The causes of teenage alcoholism*
7. *The causes of adult alcoholism*
8. *What the legal drinking age should be*
9. *How drinking is made to seem glamorous and sexy on television and in the movies*

Do not censor yourself; instead, allow a free flow of ideas without evaluating their worth. If you get stuck, doodle or trace over what you have already written until new ideas surface.

PROCESS GUIDELINES: SHAPING TOPICS

1. Sometimes writers identify a broad subject they are interested in and then carve a narrow topic from that broad area.
2. Techniques to help the writer find subjects and topics include
   a. Freewriting.
   b. Browsing through a dictionary.
   c. Reading newspapers.

      d. Filling in the blanks in sentences.
      e. Keeping an essay-subject notebook.
      f. Thinking and observing.
      g. Making lists.
      h. Examining the subject from different angles.
      i. Clustering.
3. Remember, suitable essay topics should
      a. Have an impact on the reader.
      b. Be narrow enough to be treated with penetration in a reasonable length.
      c. Be something the writer knows enough about.

Student Essay: Discovering a Subject and Topic

To discover a writing subject, student author Peg filled in blanks in a number of sentences, including this one: Life with _____ is _____. Her result was "Life with my family has been interesting." To narrow to a suitable writing topic, Peg wrote this list:

always a crisis

never enough money

learned the value of sharing

always someone to play with or talk to or help out

many difficulties

learned what is important in life

went without things others had

lots of love and laughter

After reviewing her list, Peg decided to write about the difficulties she experienced as a member of her family. Later in this chapter and in the next ones, you will watch Peg as she discovers ideas to develop her essay and as she outlines, drafts, revises, and edits.

EXERCISE | **Shaping Topics**

1. Identify five subjects you could write an essay about. If you cannot arrive at five after some thought, try one or more of the techniques for finding subjects described in this chapter.
2. For each topic below, write a *B* if the topic is too broad to be handled with penetration in a 500- to 700-word essay. Write an *N* if the topic is narrow enough to be handled in a 500- to 700-word essay.
      a. The day I learned a lie can be less harmful than the truth
      b. My favorite people
      c. Being the oldest of six children has dozens of disadvantages
      d. Being the oldest of six children has two chief disadvantages

    e. It's a mistake to teach children to read in kindergarten
    f. Cigarette smokers have their rights too
    g. Our public schools are deteriorating in every way
    h. How to teach a six-year-old to ride a bike
    i. There are more similarities than differences among modern religions
    j. Computer science should be taught in elementary school
    k. Television soap operas present an unrealistic and potentially dangerous view of the ways people relate to each other
    l. For pure fun, nothing is better than watching an old monster movie

3. Using three of the five subjects you gave as your response to number 1 above, shape three suitable essay topics. If necessary, use one or more of the techniques described in this chapter.
4. Below are five broad writing subjects. Select two of them and write one narrow topic for each. Use any of the techniques described in this chapter.
    a. Studying for exams
    b. Team sports
    c. The changing role of women (or men)
    d. Difficult decisions
    e. Interesting (or unusual) people

ESTABLISHING YOUR PURPOSE

Early on you should ask yourself why you are writing a particular piece. The answer to this question will form your **purpose.** In the most general sense, writers can establish one or a combination of these four purposes for their writing:

1. To express feelings or ideas to the reader and/or relate experiences.
2. To inform the reader of something.
3. To persuade the reader to think or act a certain way.
4. To entertain the reader.

Writers must be clear about their purpose because the reason for writing influences the nature of the piece. Say, for example, that your writing topic is the difficulties you encountered during your first term of college. If your purpose is to relate your experiences, you might include accounts of what went wrong for you, along with descriptions of your emotional reactions to these happenings. If your purpose is to inform your reader that college life is not as easy as it seems, you might provide explanations of the problems you encountered, without a discussion of your reactions. If your purpose is to persuade your reader that a better orientation program is needed, you might offer only those unpleasant experiences that could have been avoided if a better orientation program existed. If your purpose is to entertain your reader, you could tell amusing stories of the difficulties you encountered.

Even this does not fully indicate how clearly your purpose should be established. You should be even more precise by asking yourself *why* you want to express yourself or inform or persuade or entertain. Return to the purposes for writing about the difficulties encountered during the first term of college to see how asking "why" can sharpen your purpose. If you ask why you want to relate your experiences of the first term, you might answer, "To vent frustration and earn some sympathy." If you ask why you want to inform your reader that college is not as easy as it seems, you might answer, "So my reader understands better what college life entails," or "So my reader knows what to expect when he or she begins college." If you ask yourself why you want to persuade your reader that a better orientation program is needed, you might respond, "So pressure is applied on the administration to institute the program." If you ask yourself why you want to entertain your reader, you might answer, "To help my reader appreciate the humor or absurdity of a situation."

To establish your purpose, you can answer the following questions:

1. What ideas, feelings, or experiences can I express to my reader?
2. What can I inform my reader about?
3. In what way can I entertain my reader?
4. In what way can I persuade my reader to think or act a particular way?

IDENTIFYING YOUR AUDIENCE

Like your purpose, your audience shapes your writing. An essay about freshman life may need a great deal of explanatory information if it is written for someone who knows little about college. However, such information would not be necessary for the reader who recently attended the same school you do. Similarly, if you wish to convince the administration to improve the orientation program and it claims there is no money to do so, then you must show that the program's cost is affordable. Such cost information might not be necessary if you were writing to persuade the student council to run the program and the council had the money. To convince the council, though, you might discuss how such a program could increase student support for council-sponsored activities. This latter fact, however, would not appear in writing aimed at the administration.

Audience and purpose must be compatible. For example, if your purpose for writing about your first-term difficulties is to vent frustration and earn sympathy, your audience could be your parents or your advisor. If your purpose is to inform readers about the nature of college life, your audience might be college-bound high school seniors. If your purpose is to convince the reader that a better orientation program is needed, your audience could be the dean of student services.

You might be thinking that because you are in a writing class, your audience is your instructor. Of course, you are right. Yet writing teachers can assume the identities of different readers, so you are free to write for different audiences. You can also identify your audience as "the average, general reader"—someone who knows something about your subject but less than you do. You might think of the average, general reader as the typical reader of a large daily newspaper.

To decide on a suitable audience for your writing, you can answer the following questions:

1. Who could learn something from my writing?
2. Who would enjoy reading about my topic?
3. Who could be influenced to think or act a certain way?
4. Who shares an interest in my topic?
5. Who would find my topic important?
6. Who needs to hear what I have to say?

Once identified, your audience must be assessed to ensure that you provide the detail that will meet your reader's needs and help you achieve your purpose. These questions can help:

1. What does my reader already know about my topic?
2. What information will my reader need to appreciate my view?
3. Does my reader have any strong feelings about my topic?
4. Is my reader interested in my topic or will I have to arouse interest?
5. How receptive will my reader be to my view? Why?
6. Will my reader's age, gender, level of education, income, job, politics, or religion affect reaction to my topic?

DISCOVERING IDEAS TO DEVELOP YOUR TOPIC

After shaping a topic and considering audience and purpose, you are ready to begin writing your essay, so you pour yourself a cold drink, empty the last of the potato chips into a bowl, and push the clutter on your desk to one side. You get comfortable, reach for some fresh paper, and begin—and idea after idea tumbles forth as you write through your first draft, right? Yes, if you are lucky enough to be inspired. No, if inspiration is too busy helping the redhead in the third row to bother with you. So once again, if ideas do not come to you, you must go after the ideas.

All writers (not just students) experience writer's block. Sometimes we draw a blank—not a single idea comes to mind. Sometimes we have a hazy idea but it is too vague to get us anywhere, so we find ourselves saying something like, "I know what I want to say, but I can't explain it."

Fortunately, writer's block can be overcome with techniques that start the flow of ideas. These techniques come under the broad heading of prewriting. Although the term **prewriting** suggests that the techniques occur *before* writing, they are really writing procedures that stimulate thought. Actually, you already know something about prewriting because the techniques you learned for discovering subjects and shaping topics are forms of prewriting. The next pages, however, will offer ways to use prewriting to overcome writer's block.

Freewriting

You learned that freewriting helps a writer find subjects and topics. (For a review of freewriting, see page 18.) However, it can also help the first-draft writer who needs ideas to develop a topic. To freewrite for ideas to develop a topic, write down everything that occurs to you about your topic without evaluating the worth of the ideas. You can shift direction to pursue a new idea that suddenly strikes you, or you can pursue a single idea as far as you can take it. You can make random, wild associations, be flip, serious, or angry. Just be relaxed, and go with your flow of thoughts.

After 10 minutes or so, read what you have (most likely about two pages). It will be rough, but you will notice at least one or two ideas that can be polished and developed in an essay. Underline these ideas. Sometimes they will be enough to start you off on an outline or draft. Other times you may need a boost from a second freewriting. If so, write for 5 to 10 more minutes, this time focusing on the ideas you underlined in the first freewriting. When you are done, read your material and again underline the good ideas. Between the two freewritings, you may generate what you need to get started.

A Sample Freewriting

Here is a sample freewriting written to discover ideas for an essay on why people watch soap operas. (This topic was discovered as a result of the freewriting on page 21.) Potentially usable ideas have been underlined.

> *Why do people watch soap operas? I guess <u>some people find them</u> <u>entertaining</u>, but they must like pretty mindless stuff. Probably <u>the</u> <u>sick and elderly get hooked on them</u>. <u>After awhile the people on soaps</u> <u>probably seem like family</u>. I don't know what to say now. cow how sow plow Let me think. Well, <u>sometimes people want entertainment that</u> <u>doesn't require them to think too much</u>. Also, <u>today's soaps can be</u> <u>very steamy</u>. <u>And people love to watch sex</u>. Anything else? <u>They deal</u> <u>with important social issues</u>, <u>like Aids</u>. Are people who watch lonely? Not always. Lots of people I know watch them and I'm sure they're not all lonely. <u>Soaps are campy and fun</u>. That may be why college students like them. ABCDEFGHIJKL I can't think of anything else right now. Maybe <u>the storylines are good</u>. I'll have to watch some more and see.*

List Writing

You have read about list writing as a technique for shaping topics from subjects (see page 22). This prewriting activity is also helpful for generating ideas to develop these topics: In a column, list every idea that occurs to you about your topic. Do not stop to decide whether you like these ideas or whether they will "work" in your essay. When you run out of ideas, review your list. Now you can evaluate whether or not each idea is suitable for your essay. If you find ideas that do not seem relevant to your topic or do not seem worthy of inclusion for some other reason, simply cross them out. Next, study the first idea remaining on your list. Think about it a few moments. As you do, you may discover one or two related ideas that can be added. Proceed this way down your list, studying each idea and adding thoughts.

Many writers find that this list writing meets their needs. Others like to go one step further by turning their list into a **scratch outline.** To turn a prewriting list into a scratch outline, group together related ideas. For example, say you have a list of ideas for an essay about the day you baby-sat for two-year-old twin boys. You want the essay to explain that the experience was one of the most nerve-wracking of your life. When you look over your list, you discover that three of your ideas pertain to feeding the children lunch, four of them pertain to trying to bed them down for a nap, and five of them pertain to keeping them out of mischief. If this is the case, you make three lists—one of ideas about lunch, one of ideas about the nap, and one of ideas about mischief. When you group ideas in this way, you are doing more than listing your ideas; you are also organizing them.

A Sample List and Scratch Outline

Below is a list one student developed before writing an essay about the trauma he experienced when his family moved to a new town and he had to change schools.

> *loved old school*
>
> *comfortable with friends—knew them 12 years*
>
> *at new school I was outsider*
>
> *everyone belonged to a clique*
>
> *sleepless nights for weeks before the move*
>
> *asked if I could live with my aunt so I wouldn't have to move*
>
> ~~*my parents tried to reassure me*~~
>
> *I knew I would never see my old friends again*
>
> *scared to leave familiar for unknown*
>
> *new school was ugly*
>
> ~~*I resented my parents for transplanting me*~~
>
> ~~*I became argumentative with my parents*~~
>
> *I was behind in my school work at new school*
>
> *I didn't get on basketball team at new school*

Some of the ideas in the list are crossed out because after reviewing the list the writer decided he did not wish to treat these ideas after all, probably because they focused on his relationship with adults, and he wanted to center on his adjustment to the school and his relationship with his classmates.

After the writer eliminated ideas unsuited to his purpose, he reviewed his list and added ideas he thought of. After this step, the list looked like this:

> *loved old school*
>
> *comfortable with friends—knew them 12 years*
>
> *at new school I was an outsider*
>
> *everyone belonged to a clique*

sleepless nights for weeks before the move

asked if I could live with my aunt so I wouldn't have to move

~~*my parents tried to reassure me*~~

I knew I would never see my old friends again

scared to leave familiar for unknown

new school was ugly

~~*I resented my parents for transplanting me*~~

~~*I became argumentative with my parents*~~

I was behind in my school work at new school

I didn't get on basketball team at new school

~~*new math teacher tried to help me adjust*~~

at new school I was stared at like a freak

I would skip lunch because I didn't know anyone to sit with

I was popular & respected at old school—at new I was a nobody

new school was old, needed repair—describe ugly classrooms

math & science classes were way ahead of my old ones & my grades suffered

I was center on basketball team before—at new school I didn't make team

I couldn't go to games & cheer for a team I wasn't playing on & felt no loyalty toward

After adding new ideas to the list, the writer decided to form a scratch outline by grouping together related ideas. Here is the result:

Before Move

loved old school

comfortable with friends—knew them 12 years

sleepless nights for weeks before the move

I knew I would never see my old friends again

asked if I could live with my aunt

scared to leave familiar for unknown

After Move

Classmates

I was outsider

everyone belonged to clique

stared at like a freak

skipped lunch cause had no one to sit with

I was a nobody instead of popular & respected

Basketball

didn't make team—was center before

couldn't go to games & cheer for a team I wasn't playing on & felt no loyalty toward

Surroundings

new school was ugly

new school was old & needed repairs

describe classrooms

School work

I was behind

math & science classes way ahead of me & my grades suffered

The ideas in your list will not necessarily cover every point, example, and piece of detail in your essay. Instead, your list can provide a starting point.

Answering Questions

Answering questions about your topic is a good way to generate ideas for developing that topic. Some of the most useful questions are the standard journalistic ones: Who? What? When? Where? Why? How? These questions can be shaped in a variety of ways, according to the nature of your topic. Here are some examples; you will develop your own to suit your particular topic.

Who is involved?	When is it important?
Who is affected?	Why does it happen?
Who is for (or against) it?	Why is it important?
Who is interested in it?	Why is it interesting?
What happened?	Why is it true?
What does it mean?	Where does it happen?
What causes it?	How does it happen?
What are its effects?	How does it make people feel?
What is it like (or different from)?	How does it change things?
What are its strengths (weaknesses)?	How often does it happen?
What are its parts?	How is it made?
When does it happen?	How should people react to it?
When will it end (or begin)?	

Sample Questions and Answers

Below are the questions a student asked herself for an essay about what happened when her friend died of leukemia.

1. *What happened?*
   Judy died of leukemia.
2. *What was the effect?*
   I became depressed.
3. *What was the effect of the depression?*
   I wouldn't associate with people.
4. *Why wouldn't you associate with people?*
   I was afraid of getting close and then losing them.
5. *How long did that last?*
   a year
6. *What ended it?*
   my pastor
7. *How did your pastor end it?*
   He gave me a copy of the book When Bad Things Happen to Good People.
8. *How did the book help?*
   It made me realize I couldn't stop living.

9. *How is your experience significant to others?*
   We all lose loved ones and must find a way to keep going.
10. *How has Judy's death changed you?*
   I don't take anything or anyone for granted anymore.
11. *Why is this important?*
   My life is richer now because I appreciate the people around me more.

When the student wrote her essay, she did not use all the points that resulted from her questioning. Also, her essay included ideas she developed along the way, *after* her questioning. That is fine.

Clustering

On pages 23–24 you read that clustering can help a writer move from general subject to restricted topic. However, clustering can also help a writer discover ideas to develop a topic. Just write your topic in the center of a page and circle it. Below is one of the restricted topics discovered in the clustering illustrated on page 24.

(how to control teenage drinking)

Next, let your thoughts flow freely and record all the ideas that occur to you, circling and connecting the ideas as appropriate. Do not pause to evaluate ideas; just go with the flow of your thoughts. If you run out of ideas, study the branches of your clusters to see relationships among ideas. These relationships may suggest new ideas. Or try retracing what you have written until ideas strike you. Here is a clustering to generate ideas for an essay about how to control teenage drinking.

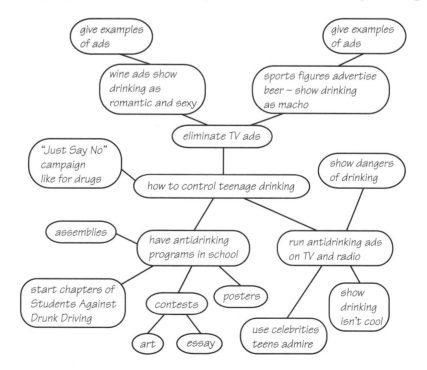

NOTE: Your clustering can include ideas that never make it into your first draft, and your draft can include ideas not in the clustering.

Letter Writing

Sometimes writers have trouble generating ideas because they do not relax enough to allow a free flow of thought. If this happens to you, try letter writing, a prewriting technique that relaxes the writer. Simply write a "letter" to someone you feel comfortable with and can open up to easily. The subject of your letter is your essay topic. Use this letter as an opportunity to explore ideas about your topic. Since you are writing to someone you are comfortable with, you will not hold anything back. Of course, this is all just a way to stimulate thought, so you need not actually mail your letter.

To discover ideas for developing her topic—the changing roles of women—a student wrote the letter that appears below. The letter explores some difficulties the writer faces meeting the demands of her various roles.

Dear Liz,

I guess I'm what you'd call a modern woman, but I'm not sure I like it very much. I know this is what I asked for, but it's a lot rougher than I expected and frankly less exciting.

The kids are 10 and 13 now, so they are fairly independent, but they still make a lot of demands on my time. Katie's adolescence has her turned inside out, and half the time she's crying and the other half she's mad at me for something. She's really on my mind a lot. Jenny is pretty together, but her gymnastics, Camp Fire activities, and swim meets really keep me on the fly. She makes a big demand on my time.

Then there's the job. I know it's only part-time, but those 20 hours really eat up my week. I can't keep up with the cleaning or the kids. And poor Jim really gets shortchanged. Actually, I feel pretty guilty that he works all day and then has to come home and help with laundry, dinner, and things. He doesn't mind, but I do. I feel like he's always picking up my slack and I'm not pulling my weight.

To top it off, now I'm in school. I must be crazy to make my work load even heavier than it already is. Still, I want my degree badly. I don't know, maybe I'm just in a slump, but I feel like I'm not doing anything well. Being liberated is not all I thought it would be. It's really very hard. I think I'm paying a big price for being a modern woman.

Love,

Marge

Keeping a Journal

Journal writing is more than a prewriting activity; it is a way to record thoughts, feelings, and responses to the events in your life. Because keeping a journal allows you to explore and examine what you think and feel, it can be a very satisfying experience. In fact, many people make journal writing a routine part of their lives because it can be so rewarding.

Sometimes instructors collect and respond to journals, but even so, they are considered private, rather than public writing, so you need not worry about grammar, spelling, and such. Also, some instructors give specific assignments for journal entries. At other times, students can write on whatever they want. (Keep in mind, though, that a journal is not a diary that merely records the events of your day.) If you need ideas for journal entries, try some of these.

1. Freewrite by beginning with the first thought that comes to mind.
2. Write about someone you admire.
3. Write about how your writing class is going.
4. Write about your feelings about college.
5. Explore your goals for the coming year.
6. Explain where you see yourself five years from now.
7. React to a book you recently read or to a movie you recently saw.
8. Write about a problem you have and explore possible solutions.
9. Write about your best attribute.
10. Record a vivid childhood memory.
11. Write about an event of the day that caused you to feel a strong emotion (anger, fear, frustration, happiness, relief, etc.).
12. Write about your family relationships.
13. Describe your writing process.
14. Tell about a change you would like to make.
15. Tell about a valued possession.

Journals can be handwritten in a special notebook reserved for the journal, or they can be a separate file on your computer. Either way, date and begin each entry on a new page. Write each day or two religiously, and soon journal writing will become a habit. Then, when you need ideas for topics or details to develop a topic, scan your journal for ideas.

Working Collaboratively: Generating Ideas

To stimulate their thinking, writers often collaborate. In fact, many of the idea-generation techniques explained in this chapter can be adapted for use with two or more people. For example, to list collaboratively, one person acts as the recorder. Group members speak whatever ideas occur to them, and the recorder writes the ideas down in list form. Collaborative listing is productive because the comments of one person often stimulate other people to come up with ideas.

To answer questions collaboratively, one person asks another person questions about the topic. The person answering records his or her responses for later consideration for the draft. Answering questions collaboratively is a powerful idea-generation strategy because an objective party can often think of many more questions than the writer can think of. Clustering, too, can be done collaboratively. In this case, one person is assigned to write while everyone else speaks ideas and suggests where to connect them. Like list writing, clustering is a productive collaborative technique because one person's thoughts will inspire another person's.

Perhaps the simplest way to collaborate on idea generation is to approach other people and ask them what they think about your topic. Their ideas may be both useful in their own right and helpful as prompts to other ideas.

Computer Tips

Most of the prewriting techniques can be very effective when done on a computer. However, you may find the following strategies particularly helpful:

Try freewriting. Simply sit at the keyboard with a blank screen in front of you and write whatever comes to mind without deleting anything, moving the cursor, or pausing. Fill the screen with what occurs to you, print what you have, and underline useable ideas. If necessary, do a second freewriting that focuses on one or more ideas in the first.

A powerful variation of this technique is to turn down the brightness dial on your monitor until you can no longer see what you type in and *type "blindfolded."* When you are finished, you are likely to have many typographical errors, but ignore them. You are also likely to have a number of useable ideas because your inability to see (and hence censor) what you are writing allows for a very free flow of thought.

Many people like to list and *develop a scratch outline* at the computer. To do so, type in the first idea that occurs to you and press the enter key. Then type the second idea and hit the enter key again. Continue in this fashion until you run out of ideas. Then you will have your list. Study this list and use your delete function to eliminate ideas you do not care to use and your insert key to add ideas that occur to you. Finally, use your copy-move functions to arrange the ideas in the order you want. Of course, with the computer, you can rearrange your ideas as many times as you need to in order to come up with a suitable sequence. Once you have that sequence, you have your scratch outline.

PROCESS GUIDELINES: PREWRITING

1. Regardless of the prewriting techniques you favor, some generalizations can be made.
   • Writing seldom progresses in a straight line from step 1 to step 2 and so on. Often writers move forward and then step back to alter something done earlier. For example, while drafting, you may think of additional

ideas—even though formal idea generation came earlier. While revising, you may decide to reshape your topic a bit. Always be receptive to good ideas, no matter where in the process they occur to you.
- Idea generation takes time, so procrastination undermines the process.
- You may find that combining idea-generation techniques yields more ideas than using one technique by itself.
- Try many of the prewriting techniques to discover what works best for you. If a previously successful technique lets you down, try another strategy and return to the favored technique another time.

2. If you have trouble coming up with ideas
- Try a prewriting technique you have never used before.
- Leave your writing and think about your topic while you are doing other things.
- Consider what people who disagree with you might say and use their views as a departure point.
- Make sure you are writing about what you know.
- Do not reject rough ideas. Nothing is polished in the early stages of writing, so look at the possibilities your rough ideas offer up.
- Force yourself to write because the act of writing stimulates thinking. Just sit down and fill a page or a computer screen. Then look for possibilities.

3. If you have trouble establishing a purpose for your writing
- Ask yourself, "What *can* I accomplish with this writing?"
- Ask yourself, "What would I *like* to accomplish with this writing?"

4. If you have trouble identifying a suitable audience for your writing
- Ask yourself who would benefit from reading your writing.
- Let your reader be someone who would disagree with you.
- Let your reader be someone in authority with the power to act in response to the ideas in your essay.
- Write to the "average, general reader"—someone who knows something about your topic, but less than you do.

Student Essay: Establishing Purpose, Identifying Audience, and Generating Ideas

Refer to page 25 to see the list that led student writer Peg to decide to write about the difficulties she experienced as a member of her family. Peg decided that her writing purposes were to relate her experiences, express her feelings, and inform. Because Peg was an adult learner in a class of younger students, she decided to make her classmates her audience because she wanted them to understand what it was like for her growing up during a difficult and different time.

To discover ideas to develop her topic, Peg wrote the following idea-generation list. The circles and checkmarks are her personal notation for grouping related ideas. Notice that Peg crossed out an idea she decided not to include and that she bracketed some ideas and wrote a note to remind herself of what she wanted to emphasize.

Effects of growing up in a large family

√ *food—Milk dry & canned,*   *Beans*

• *trips—none*   *Soups*

√ *money—little*   *Oats & Mush*

√ *eating out*

•√ *Christmas*

• *Birthdays*   *Points to bring out*

√ *Clothing—hand me downs*

√ *Shoes—1 pr—worn a longtime*

√ *Haircuts*

√ *teeth*

√ *Nothing new*

~~*treats once every 2 wks payday*~~

• *Car—old—wouldn't go real far*

   Helen's Hungry Brood—Title

   Commercial—50's—intro?

   Mom—pregnancy—easy deliv.

   Dad—Bakery Checker

   Dad—Budgeted finances

• *farthest went was to town 3 mi away*

   Ending

      8th Grade—Father died

EXERCISE | **Establishing Purpose, Identifying Audience, and Discovering Ideas**

1. Assume you must write an essay about campus life.
   a. First, develop a topic about campus life, using one or more of the techniques described in this chapter. Then establish a purpose for an essay on this topic by answering the questions on page 27.
   b. Establish the audience for this essay by answering the questions on page 28.
   c. Determine the nature of the audience by answering the questions on page 28.
   d. Use any two techniques described in this chapter and generate at least five ideas that could be included in an essay with the topic from *a*. After generating the ideas, determine whether they are compatible with the audience and purpose you have established.
   e. If some of your ideas will not work with your audience and/or purpose, what options do you have?

2. When you responded to number 3 and number 4 of the exercise on page 26, you shaped a total of five essay topics. (If you did not complete this exercise, do so now.) For each of these topics, discover at least four ideas worthy of inclusion in an essay. To generate these ideas, try each of the techniques described in this chapter (freewriting, listing, answering questions, letter writing, and clustering) at least once.
3. For each idea you generated for number 2 above, note the technique that yielded the idea. Which technique(s) do you think worked best for you? Which are you likely to use in the future?
4. *Collaborative Activity.* Assume you are writing an essay about your proudest or most embarrassing moment.
   a. What moment will you write about?
   b. Team up with a classmate and work collaboratively to discover ideas by taking turns asking each other questions about your topics.
   c. Next, work together to develop clusterings for each of your topics.
   d. Do you find collaborative idea generation to be productive?

DEVELOPING A PRELIMINARY THESIS

A *thesis* is the statement of what an essay is about. Usually appearing early on in an essay, the thesis lets the reader know what the writer's topic is, and it lets the reader know what opinion the writer has about the topic. For example, an essay can have this thesis:

```
The current television rating system does little to help
parents make wise programming choices for their children.
```

This thesis presents both the writing topic and the writer's opinion:

```
        topic: the current television rating system
writer's opinion: It does little to help parents decide what
                  their children should watch.
```

The thesis is an exceptionally important part of an essay, important both to the writer and to the reader. The thesis is important to the writer because it provides the focus for the essay and hence guides the writer. A writer decides what points to make and how to develop those points based upon how well the details develop or support the thesis. A point unrelated to the thesis must be struck from the essay, no matter how much the writer would like to include it. Similarly, the thesis is important to the reader, who develops expectations for an essay according to what the thesis promises the essay will be about. Because the thesis is so important, you must shape it carefully, and that means approaching your first draft with a preliminary thesis in mind.

A *preliminary thesis* is an early version of your thesis; it is the version you use to guide your first draft, to focus and help organize it. The preliminary thesis states your topic and your opinion on the topic, but it does so in an early, rough form. Like everything else in a first draft, the preliminary thesis is subject to change—that is why it is called "preliminary." In fact, so preliminary is this thesis that it may bear little or no resemblance to the thesis in the final version of your essay because, in the course of drafting and revising, you may decide to shift your focus or change your topic dramatically. Because writing is an ongoing act of discovery and revision, such changes are common and not a source of concern.

Once you have decided on your writing topic, established your purpose, identified your audience, and discovered some ideas for developing your topic, you are ready to shape your preliminary thesis. When you do so, keep in mind the following qualities of an effective thesis.

The Qualities of an Effective Thesis

1. **State your topic and your opinion on that topic.** Consider this thesis:

> More and more high school students are working while they attend school, but this trend is not a healthy one.

Both the topic and the writer's opinion are clear.

> *Topic:* high school students who work
>
> *Writer's opinion:* It is not healthy for high school students to work.

Be sure your opinion is clearly and directly stated, so your reader knows exactly what your view is.

> *Unclear opinion:* Although there are pros and cons on both sides of the issue, I have decided how I feel about affirmative action.
>
> *Unclear opinion:* A number of states are reevaluating their affirmative action laws, creating a great deal of public debate.
>
> *Better:* Although there are pros and cons on both sides of the issue, I am convinced that affirmative action laws do more harm than good.
>
> *Better:* States that have eliminated their affirmative action laws undermine the goals of equal rights initiatives.

2. **In addition to stating the topic and your opinion of that topic, your thesis can state the main points to be covered in your essay.** Here is an example:

> *Thesis:* Working mothers have changed the character of the American family by contributing a second paycheck, by popularizing day care, and by creating a new division of labor in the home.

> *Main points to be* the contribution of a second paycheck; the
> *discussed:* popularizing of day care; a new division of
> labor in the home

3. **Limit your thesis to one topic.** If your thesis mentions two topics, you will be forced to write about two topics, which will split your focus and confuse your reader. Consider this thesis, for example:

> The violence on television has an adverse effect on children,
> as does most of MTV's programming.

An essay with this thesis requires a discussion of two topics: the adverse effects of television violence on children and the adverse effects of most of MTV's programming on children. That is one topic too many.

> *Better:* The violence on television has an adverse effect on
> children.

> *Better:* Most of MTV's programming has an adverse effect on
> children.

4. **Express your opinion in specific words.** Because the reader relies on the thesis for a clear indication of what the essay is about, the narrowing should be expressed in specific words. Consider this thesis, for example:

> It is interesting to consider the various meanings of <u>love</u>.

The word *interesting* is vague, so the reader cannot be sure what the writer's opinion is. In the following revision, the opinion is stated in specific words, so the reader has a clear sense of the focus of the essay.

> *Better:* We apply the word <u>love</u> to a broad spectrum of
> emotions.

Pitfalls to Avoid

1. **Avoid broad statements.** A thesis that is too broad will force the writer into a vague, superficial discussion that will never satisfy a reader because it will never get beyond statements of the obvious. The following thesis statement is too broad:

> The role of women has changed drastically in the last 50 years.

This broad thesis presents a problem for the writer. Fifty years is a long time; to discuss in depth all the changes in that time span would require more pages than the typical college essay runs. If the essay were to run a more manageable length, the writer could do little more than skim the surface and state the obvious. Below is a more suitable thesis, one that is sufficiently narrow.

> The leadership role of women in state politics has changed
> drastically in the last 10 years.

This thesis is better because it is narrowed to include only one role of women in one political arena and because the time span is more reasonable.

2. **Avoid stating two opinions.** A thesis with two opinions will force you to write about too much and likely lead to a superficial treatment of both opinions, which your reader will find unsatisfying. Instead, aim for an in-depth treatment of one opinion.

Two opinions: Divorce would be less traumatic if custody laws were revised and if attorneys counseled their clients more carefully.

Better: Divorce would be less traumatic if attorneys counseled their clients more carefully.

Better: Divorce would be less traumatic if custody laws were revised.

3. **Avoid factual statements.** Factual statements do not make suitable thesis statements because they leave the writer with nothing to say.

Factual statement: The water department is considering a rate increase.

Better: The water department's proposed rate increase is unnecessary.

4. **Avoid an announcement.** A thesis such as "This paper will show why I have always hated team sports" is an announcement. In some disciplines, particularly some of the sciences and social sciences, the announcement is acceptable, but in English classes and many of the humanities, it is considered poor style.

Announcement: I will explain why our board of education should consider magnet schools.

Better: Our board of education should consider magnet schools.

Announcement: The next paragraphs will present the reasons Americans value youth.

Better: Americans value youth for surprising reasons.

5. **Avoid expressions such as "in my opinion," "I believe," "I think," and "it seems to me."** You are writing the paper, so it is obvious that you are expressing what you think. Including such expressions weakens the impact of your thesis by making you seem unassertive.

Unassertive: In my opinion, the Women's Center performs a valuable service on campus and deserves a budget renewal.

Better: The Women's Center performs a valuable service on campus and deserves a budget renewal.

PROCESS GUIDELINES: DEVELOPING A PRELIMINARY THESIS

1. Be sure to develop your preliminary thesis with your audience, purpose, and idea-generation material in mind so all these aspects of your writing are compatible with each other.
2. Feel free to alter your audience and purpose to make them more compatible with your preliminary thesis.
3. Once you have developed your preliminary thesis, you may decide not to use some of your idea-generation material, or you may decide to do some additional prewriting to discover more ideas.
4. Remember that your preliminary thesis is subject to change, particularly during drafting and revising.

E X E R C I S E

The Thesis

1. In the following thesis statements, identify the topic and the opinion.
    a. No experience is more exasperating than taking preschool children to the grocery store on a Saturday to do a week's worth of shopping.
    b. My brother, Jerry, taught me the meaning of courage.
    c. Television news does not adequately inform the U.S. public.
    d. It has been said that Benjamin Franklin was a great diplomat; however, no one is more skilled at diplomacy than people who make their living selling clothes.
    e. Many people believe a little white lie can be better than the truth, but even these seemingly harmless fibs can cause trouble.
2. In the following thesis statements, identify the topic, the opinion, and the main points to be developed in the essay.
    a. Socrates Pappas would make an excellent mayor because he is an experienced manager, because he is fiscally conservative, and because he is well-connected in the state capital.
    b. Different communication styles and different agendas make it difficult for men and women to communicate effectively.
    c. Her eccentricity, her courage, and her unusual lifestyle would make Juliette Low, the founder of the Girl Scouts, the subject of an entertaining movie.
    d. The speed limits on our highways should be 55 mph to save lives and reduce the cost of automobile insurance.
    e. The student production of *Macbeth* is a big hit because of its excellent production values and daring direction.
3. Decide whether each of the following thesis statements is acceptable or unacceptable. If the thesis is unacceptable, explain what the problem is.
    a. There are many game shows on television.
    b. Schools should not be funded by property taxes.
    c. I would like to explain why I am an avid reader.
    d. Higher education is in need of reform.

e. College students can learn to handle stress if they follow my advice.

f. My Christmas cruise to the Bahamas was nice.

g. The Nontraditional Student Center and the International Student Union are two university organizations that serve students well.

h. My parents own a beach house.

i. This essay will explain the best way to choose a major.

j. I do not think that soap operas deserve their bad reputation.

k. For today's young people, the shopping mall offers a variety of entertainment options.

l. The wise woman learns how to manage her own finances, and she learns how to take care of her car.

4. Rewrite the unacceptable thesis statements from number 3 to make them acceptable.

5. When you completed number 1 in the exercise on page 38, you shaped a topic about campus life, established a purpose, identified an audience, and generated some ideas. Now review that material and develop a preliminary thesis that is compatible with it. Do you need to revise your topic, audience, or purpose? Do you need to eliminate some of the ideas you generated or generate additional ideas? Explain.

6. *Collaborative Activity.* Below are four broad subjects. With a classmate, select two of them and write a thesis for an essay about each. Narrow so that you are treating a topic manageable in 500 to 700 words.

> *Example:* Saturday morning cartoons: `If parents took the time to watch Saturday morning cartoons with their children, they would be surprised by how violent these programs really are.`

a. sports

b. large parties

c. a childhood memory

d. grades

WRITING ASSIGNMENT

When you completed the chapter exercises, you shaped an essay topic about campus life. In addition, you determined a purpose for this essay, established and assessed audience, discovered at least five ideas, and wrote a preliminary thesis. Now you can develop this material into an essay. As you do so, keep the following points in mind:

1. Nothing is sacred about the material you have already developed. Any or all of it can be changed. You can even start over with a new topic.

2. You may have to discover additional ideas to include in your essay.

3. To plan your draft, list your ideas in the order you think they should appear.

4. Write a rough draft from this list of ideas. Do not be concerned about the quality of this draft; just get your ideas down the best way you can without worrying about anything, particularly grammar, spelling, and such.
5. Leave your rough draft for at least a day. Then go over it and make necessary changes. To decide what changes to make, you can ask yourself the following questions:
   a. Is each idea clearly explained?
   b. Is each idea backed up with examples and/or explanation?
   c. Are all ideas related to the topic?
   d. Do ideas appear in a logical order?
6. After making changes in your draft, recopy it and ask two classmates to read it and make suggestions.
7. Check your work for correct grammar, spelling, and punctuation.

CHAPTER 2

Ordering Ideas and Writing the First Draft

Prewriting is often disorganized. We make random associations, travel round-about, double back over the same path, and test offbeat relationships. Illogical though it may seem on the surface, this process can be very productive—when we are discovering ideas. However, a reader cannot be expected to follow such twists, turns, repetitions, and leaps. Thus, once you have some ideas formed and have settled on which of them to include, you are obligated to help your reader by presenting those ideas in an orderly way.

FROM PREWRITING TO ORGANIZING

Before ordering your material, evaluate your ideas and make preliminary decisions about which to use and which to reject. Make those decisions on the basis of which ideas best develop your preliminary thesis, suit your purpose, and accommodate your audience. After your evaluation, you may discover you have rejected quite a few ideas. Or you may decide to alter your thesis, purpose, or audience. If this happens, more ideas may be needed and you can find yourself prewriting and evaluating again. Actually, this prewriting and evaluating process can occur any number of times until you are satisfied that your thesis, purpose, audience, and ideas are established well enough to form a departure point. Then you can think about ways to organize your ideas.

Ordering Ideas (Writer-Based/Prewriting)

Ordering ideas is a writer-based activity because writers decide in what order *they* want to present their ideas. At the same time, deciding on order is partly reader-based because writers must find an arrangement that will help the reader appreciate the sequence of ideas and how they relate to each other.

Some writers organize mentally by reviewing their ideas from prewriting and arranging them logically in their heads. This usually works when there are only a few ideas to deal with. Some writers organize as they write their first draft.

They decide which idea to treat first, write through it, and then decide what comes next when they get there. Other writers are more successful if they plot their organization in a separate outlining step between prewriting and the first draft. Regardless of whether you go from prewriting to draft or from prewriting to outlining, at some point you will have to concern yourself with the logical organization of ideas.

Outlining

Many student writers resist outlining because they see it as time-consuming, difficult, and somehow unnecessary. Yet outlining does not deserve this reputation. Because it helps writers organize their ideas before drafting, outlining can help ensure the success of an essay. Furthermore, any time and effort put into the outline is worthwhile because outlining makes drafting easier. You see, if you do not order and group your ideas prior to drafting with some kind of outline, you will have to order and group your ideas as you draft, which complicates the drafting process, causing writers to start over frequently and become frustrated.

Outlines can be detailed or sketchy, formal or scratch. The kind of outline you use will often be determined by your writing task. Long, complex pieces often call for formal, detailed outlines, while briefer pieces can be planned with less-detailed, scratch outlines.

The detail you include in your outline—whether everything that will appear in your first draft or just the main points—will come from your prewriting ideas. However, since outlining stimulates thought, new ideas may occur to you. If so, include these ideas in your outline. Similarly, outlining may lead you to reject some of your prewriting ideas, and that is fine too. In other words, outlining does not mark the end of idea generation.

THE FORMAL OUTLINE

The formal outline, which is the most detailed, structured outline, allows you to plot all your main points and major supporting details. This is the outline that uses roman numerals, letters, and arabic numbers. Main ideas are designated with roman numerals; supporting details to develop a main idea are designated with capital letters; points to further develop supporting details are designated with arabic numbers. The format looks like some variation of this:

Thesis
    I. Main idea
       A. Supporting detail
       B. Supporting detail
       C. Supporting detail
   II. Main idea
       A. Supporting detail
          1. Further development
          2. Further development
       B. Supporting detail

Here is an example of a formal outline written for an essay about the attitudes of children toward food.

Thesis: Children can be taught to have healthy attitudes about food.

    I. Parents should stress health and fitness.
       A. Teach nutrition.
       B. Serve healthy foods.
       C. Exercise with children.
       D. Set an example.
   II. Parents should make mealtimes pleasant.
       A. Keep conversation enjoyable.
          1. Avoid discussing problems.
          2. Avoid arguments about food.
       B. Serve balanced meals and let children choose
          quantities.
       C. Avoid eating in front of the television.
  III. Parents should not forbid children to eat certain foods.
       A. Children will want what they cannot have.
       B. Reasonable amounts of sugar and fat are not harmful.
   IV. Parents should praise children for their behavior, not
       their appearance.
       A. Children should take pride in what they do, not how
          thin they are.
       B. Those with a tendency toward carrying more weight need
          to like themselves.

Sometimes a topic outline, rather than a sentence outline, works well. An outline for an essay on the causes of eating disorders could have a topic outline that looks like this in part:

    I. Poor self-image
       A. Caused by media emphasis on thinness
       B. Caused by self-hatred

If you have trouble completing your outline, you may need to go back to prewriting to generate additional ideas.

OUTLINE CARDS—METHOD I

Outline cards have many of the advantages of the formal outline, but they often simplify matters because the writer does not have to be concerned about roman numerals, letters, and numbers. To outline using cards, you need several large index cards (or you can use sheets of paper). Use one card to plan each paragraph. On each of your cards you can list your details in the order they will appear in the paragraph the card represents.

One advantage of cards is flexibility. A writer can easily shuffle paragraph cards into different sequences to examine alternative arrangements. Also, it is easier to rework parts of the outline when cards are used. A writer can throw out one or two cards and redo just those without having to rewrite the entire outline.

OUTLINE CARDS—METHOD II

An interesting form of outlining was shown to me by a student. She would take every idea she generated, whether a main point or a subpoint, and place it by itself on an index card. If she had 12 ideas, then she had 12 cards. Next she would examine each card and place it in a pile. A card with an idea related to something on another card would go in the same pile as that card. If she encountered a card that could go in more than one pile, she made the appropriate number of duplicate cards and placed them in the appropriate piles. After all her cards were sorted, she decided which pile to handle first, second, and so on. Then she studied the cards in the first pile to be handled and arranged them in the order she wanted the ideas to appear. This she did for each pile of cards. When an idea appeared in more than one pile, she decided which card to eliminate from which pile. Finally, she stacked her cards and wrote her draft from them. If she discovered her organization was not working, she would rearrange the order of her cards and try again.

OUTLINE WORKSHEET

The outline worksheet, like outline cards, allows writers to plot organization in as great or as little detail as they require. Also like outline cards, the worksheet does not make use of roman numerals, letters, and numbers. While it is not as easy to rework parts of the outline when the worksheet is used (this is the advantage of cards), it is easy to get a clear overview of your organization (this is one advantage of the formal outline).

Below is a sample outline worksheet. To use it, fill in the blanks with the amount of detail that works for you.

Sample Outline Worksheet

Introduction

Detail to generate reader interest _____

_____

_____

Preliminary thesis _____

_____

Paragraph

Main idea _____

Support_____

_____

_____

Paragraph

Main idea_____

_____

Support_____

_____

_____

(NOTE: The number of paragraph sections will correspond to the number of paragraphs planned for the first draft.)

Conclusion

Detail to provide closure_____

_____

_____

THE OUTLINE TREE

An outline tree helps writers see the relationships among ideas. It also helps writers determine where more ideas are needed. The following example uses ideas discovered in the clustering on page 33.

To develop an outline tree, first write the central idea (this will be shaped into a thesis in the draft). Then place the first branches of the tree, using the ideas that can be main points.

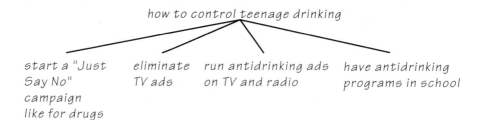

Each of the first branches will be the focus of one or more paragraphs.

Next, build the tree by adding additional branches.

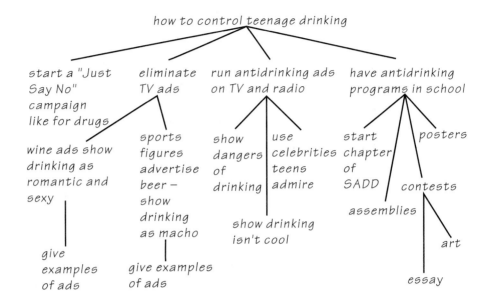

The branches after the first level represent supporting detail to develop main points. You can study your outline tree to determine where detail is needed. For example, studying the above outline tree reveals that supporting details are needed to develop the main point that a "Just Say No" campaign could be started. If detail cannot be developed for this point, it should be eliminated or combined with "antidrinking programs in school." Further study shows that examples of wine ads and sports figures must be generated.

THE SCRATCH OUTLINE

You learned about the scratch outline when you read about idea generation (p. 30). This outline is for writers who prefer to come to the first draft knowing only the main points that will be made and maybe the order they will be made in. The outline does not usually include much of the detail that will develop main points, so writers who use it must have in mind how their ideas will be supported, or they must be capable of developing the ideas as they draft. For some writers, such an outline is not very helpful because too little is brought to the draft. For others, this is the preferred approach because they find a more-detailed, structured outline constraining. They do better when less is determined prior to the first draft and they can "create" as they go along. For an example of a scratch outline, see page 30.

Computer Tips

If you listed ideas for developing your topic, you can turn that list into a scratch outline. See Computer Tips on page 36 for an explanation of how to do this.

If your computer has an outline program, you can use it to outline by filling in the various levels designated. If your computer uses Windows, click on "Format" on the toolbar to get the drop-down menu. Then click on "Bullets and Numbering" to find "Outline Numbered," which will give you an outline format to use, if you like.

Some writers like to write an outline *after* they draft in order to check their organization. To do this, create a second copy of your draft by renaming the file with an "out" extension (for "outline"). For example, a file named "essay" would be renamed "essay.out." Now go through that second file and identify the sentence in each paragraph that states the main idea and the sentences that give the major supporting details. Then delete everything else in the paragraph. Next, identify your thesis and move it to the top of the page. Now, using roman and arabic numbers and capital and lowercase letters, form the thesis and sentences into a formal outline. Study this outline to determine if any adjustments should be made in your draft.

PROCESS GUIDELINES: OUTLINING

1. Writers vary in the amount of organizing they do before the first draft. Some writers require detailed outlines that amount to a blueprint of the essay, while others do better with only a rough sketch. Other writers prefer not to outline at all, feeling it stifles their creativity. These writers order their ideas the best way they can when they draft and then adjust their organization afterward as necessary.
2. Some writers like to write a formal outline after they have written their first draft to be sure everything has a logical placement. They do this when they have not written an outline earlier, when they have deviated from their original outline, or when their original outline was sketchy.
3. In general, the more detailed the outline, the more quickly the first draft goes and the less revision the draft requires.
4. During outlining, writers often think of new ideas or make discoveries that cause them to step back and alter their thesis, audience, purpose, ideas for support, or plan for organization.
5. You may have to revise your outline several times before you are ready to draft.

Student Essay: Writing an Outline

After determining her purpose, identifying her audience, and generating and grouping some ideas (see p. 38), student author Peg numbered the ideas in her idea-generation list to develop a scratch outline.

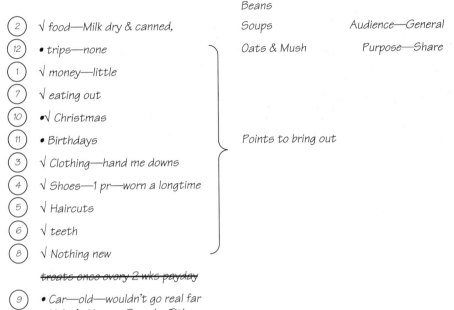

Idea-Generation List

Effects of growing up in a large family

		Beans	
②	√ food—Milk dry & canned,	Soups	Audience—General
⑫	• trips—none	Oats & Mush	Purpose—Share
①	√ money—little		
⑦	√ eating out		
⑩	•√ Christmas		
⑪	• Birthdays	Points to bring out	
③	√ Clothing—hand me downs		
④	√ Shoes—1 pr—worn a longtime		
⑤	√ Haircuts		
⑥	√ teeth		
⑧	√ Nothing new		

~~treats once every 2 wks payday~~

⑨ • Car—old—wouldn't go real far
    Helen's Hungry Brood—Title
    Commercial—50's—intro?
    Mom—pregnancy—easy deliv.

EXERCISE | **Essay in Progress**

Directions: After completing this exercise, save your responses. They will be used later in this chapter and the next ones as you work toward a completed essay.

1. Assume you have won a writer's contest. As first-prize winner, you may write a four-page, typed article that will be published in the magazine of your choice. You may write on any topic. What topic will you write about? (Use the idea-generation techniques described in Chapter 1 if you have trouble shaping a topic.)
2. For what purpose will you write this article? (If necessary, determine your purpose by answering the questions on page 27.)
3. What magazine will you publish your article in?
4. What are the typical readers of this magazine like? (If necessary, answer the audience-assessment questions on page 28.)
5. Generate as many ideas as you can to include in this article. Try using at least two of the idea-generation techniques described in Chapter 1.
6. Study the ideas you have generated. Do they suggest you should alter your audience (magazine choice) or purpose in any way? If so, do that now.

7. Select the outlining technique that most appeals to you and outline your ideas.
8. Now select a different outlining technique and outline your ideas a second time.
9. Do you like one of the outlining techniques better than another? If so, which one and why? Do you think still another technique might work even better?

WRITING THE FIRST DRAFT (WRITER-BASED/WRITING)

When your prewriting is complete, you are ready to write a first draft. Although drafting moves you out of prewriting and into writing, this activity is still writer-based because your focus is less on getting your writing ready for a reader than on expressing your ideas the best way you can at the time.

A first draft, commonly known as a **rough draft,** is an early effort to transform the prewriting ideas and outline into an essay, without worrying about grammar, usage, spelling, and such. This early effort is tentative, subject to changes of every kind. It can be loaded with errors and rough spots, but still it forms a base—material to shape and alter until the desired product is reached. By the time the final product *is* reached, so many changes may have occurred that it might bear little resemblance to the original draft.

Writers who work from detailed, formal outlines may have to do little idea generation and organizing while drafting. However, the less detailed and structured the outline, the more ideas writers will have to develop while drafting and the more organizing they will become involved in.

When you write your draft, you may get stuck. That is common. Simply skip the troublesome section and go on, leaving space for the omitted part to be added later. Many writers use this strategy for their introductions. If you cannot get started, begin in the middle and return to the introduction later. If you have an idea about how to approach a difficult part but you cannot get the words down, make a note in the margin to remind yourself of what you had in mind. Also, if you cannot find the right word, leave a blank or use an alternative and underline it for later revision. Skipping troublesome sections prevents you from becoming bogged down at any one point. Also, if you skip a troublesome part, you may find when you return to it that the words you needed surfaced while you were working on other parts of the essay.

Computer Tips

Place your outline in a window or print it out to serve as a guide for your work. If you have trouble expressing an idea, use the copy-move sequence to insert the appropriate section of your outline into the draft to hold the place. You can work the troublesome part through later, when you revise.

You have, no doubt, heard it before, but be sure to back up your draft on a diskette in case of a power or hard-drive failure. In addition, if you are keeping a writing portfolio, print out each version of your draft for inclusion in that portfolio.

PROCESS GUIDELINES: DRAFTING

1. Some writers do not handle a first draft as a rough draft; they prefer to revise as they go. Such writers really combine the first-draft and revision steps. They are uncomfortable with rough copy, and so they write a paragraph or perhaps just a sentence or two and then go back over what they have to shape and refine it. These writers push on better when they know that what they have left behind is in pretty good shape.

2. Some writers have strong feelings about their introductions. They have to get the opening paragraph close to perfect before they can go on comfortably. These writers will revise or start over repeatedly until they are satisfied with their introduction, and then they go on to produce the rest of the first draft in rougher form.

3. Idea generation occurs during first-draft writing, so be receptive to new ideas and discoveries, and be prepared to go back and alter decisions made before the first draft if necessary.

4. In general, the more planning done prior to the draft, the less revision the draft will need.

5. Remember that first drafts are *supposed* to be rough. If you expect perfection at this point, you will become frustrated unnecessarily.

6. If you have trouble drafting

   a. Skip your introduction and begin with the next paragraph. You can write your introduction later.

   b. Select one idea—one you know the most about or feel most comfortable with—and write up that point in its own paragraph.

   c. Write your draft as you would speak your ideas to a close friend, or write the draft as a letter to a friend.

   d. Stop and generate more ideas; you may not have enough material yet to begin a draft.

   e. Write your draft from start to finish without stopping and without evaluating your work. Feel free to ramble and write silly notions when you are stuck—you can refine later; for now just get something down with which you can work.

   f. Reshape your topic to something easier to write about.

   g. Leave your work for a while. Your ideas may need an incubation period before you come to your draft. However, think about your draft while you are doing other things.

STRUCTURING YOUR ESSAY

In order to write an essay—indeed, in order to draft an essay—you need to understand essay structure. Fortunately, essay structure is something you already know something about: An essay has a beginning, a middle, and an end. The beginning is the introduction; the middle is the body; and the end is the conclusion. Let's take an overview of these three parts and then deal with each in more detail.

1. The first paragraph (or paragraphs) of the essay forms the **introduction,** which serves two purposes: It lets your reader know what your essay is about, and it arouses your reader's interest in your topic. That is your beginning.
2. Next comes the middle. This is two or more **body paragraphs.** The body paragraphs present detail to develop your topic. They form the real meat of the essay.
3. The end of your essay is the **conclusion.** This final paragraph (or paragraphs) brings your essay to a satisfying finish.

Before looking more closely at the function and structure of the three parts of an essay, read the essay that follows. The notes in the margin call your attention to the structural features, features that will be referred to throughout the rest of this chapter.

The Iowa State Fair

Paul Engle

paragraph 1
This is the introduction. It functions to engage interest and present the thesis. The thesis is the first sentence. It gives the topic: the Iowa State Fair. It also gives the author's opinion: the fair is the best of all worlds.

If all you saw of life was the Iowa State Fair on a brilliant August day, when you hear those incredible crops ripening out of the black dirt between the Missouri and Mississippi rivers, you would believe that this is surely the best of all possible worlds. You would have no sense of the destruction of life, only of its rich creativeness: no political disasters, no assassinations, no ideological competition, no wars, no corruption, no atom waiting in its dark secrecy to destroy us all with its exploding energy.   1

paragraph 2
This is a body paragraph. The first sentence is the topic sentence, which tells what the paragraph is about (the peaceful energy of the fair). The rest of the paragraph is the supporting detail, which comprises descriptive examples to develop the topic sentence. In all, the paragraph helps support the thesis idea.

There is a lot of energy at the Fair in Des Moines, but it is all peaceful. The double giant Ferris wheel circles, its swaying seats more frightening than a jet plane flying through a monsoon. Eighty thousand men, women, and children walk all day and much of the night across the fairgrounds. Ponies pick up their feet in a slashing trot as if the ground burned them. Hard-rock music backgrounds the soft lowing of a Jersey cow in the cattle barn over her newborn calf, the color of a wild deer. Screaming speeches are made all around the world urging violence; here there are plenty of voices, but they are calling for you to throw baseballs at Kewpie dolls, to pitch nickels at a dish which won't hold them, to buy cotton candy, corn dogs, a paring knife that performs every useful act save mixing a martini.   2

paragraph 3
This is a body paragraph. The topic sentence (the first) tells

Above all, you would believe there was no hunger in the world, for what the Iowa State Fair celebrates is not only peace but food. It walks by you on the hoof, the Hereford, Angus, Charolais, Shorthorn   3

that the paragraph will focus on food. The rest of the paragraph (the supporting details) develops the topic sentence idea. The paragraph helps develop the thesis.

paragraph 4
This is also a body paragraph, and it focuses on the carcass competition; this focus is given in the topic sentence (the first). The supporting details to develop the topic sentence are an example.

paragraphs 5–8
The focus is on the 4-H kids; the topic sentence ideas (which give the focus of each paragraph) are in the first sentence of each paragraph. The supporting details of each paragraph develop the topic sentence, and each paragraph helps develop the thesis.

steer, the meat under its hide produced by a beautifully balanced diet more complicated than a baby's formula. These thousand-pound beef animals look at you with their oval, liquid eyes, not knowing that in human terms they are round steak, rib roast, tenderloin, chuck, and hamburger.

The Fair has always specialized in show-ring competition for 4 swine and cattle, but in recent years this has been extended to the slaughtered and dressed carcass. Often the animal which won on the hoof will not actually be as good a meat specimen as one graded lower on its "figure." Probably the most important single event at the Fair is also the quietest and most hidden: the judging of the carcass by experts in white coats in a refrigerated room. The months of elaborate feeding, of care to prevent injuries, all have their meaning when the loin eye is measured and the balance between fat and lean is revealed. At the 1974 Fair, Roy B. Keppy's crossbred hog placed second in the live competition, but first in the pork carcass show. It yielded a chop which measured 6.36 square inches, one of the largest in the history of the Fair. A little more than an inch of fat covered the rib (loin-eye) area.

If you saw close up the boys and girls of 4-H, you would also 5 believe that this world was lived in by the best of all possible people. These are not the drugged youth of the newspapers. They are intelligent and sturdy and have carried into the present the old-fashioned and sturdy ideas: The four-H concept means thinking HEAD, feeling HEART, skilled HAND, and strong HEALTH. They walk with the ease of the physically active and the confidence of people who have done serious and useful projects. They understand animals, machines, fibers.

Nor are they the "hicks" of rural legend. Newspapers, radio, 6 television have brought the world into their home; before their eyes they see what is happening not only in the nearest city but in a country five thousand miles away. Nor are they dull. Often a 4-H boy and girl will work together washing down their steers, shampooing the tails and polishing the hooves, and then go off to spend the evening dancing or at a rock concert.

One of the great sights in 4-H at the Fair is the weeping face of 7 a bright, attractive farm girl whose steer has just won a championship. She has raised the animal herself. She has kept a daily record of how much she fed it each day, of how many pounds of feed it took to make pounds of grain (a cornfed beef steer's daily growth is frightening and fattening). She has washed and brushed and combed it, taught it to lead with a halter, to stand still on order.

The final moment of truth comes when she leads it into the 8 show ring and the judge examines it with a hard and expert eye. If a Blue Ribbon is awarded, tears of joy on the cheeks of the 4-H girl, after her months of loving care and the tension of competing. Then the auction, for which she receives much more per pound than the average because she has the champion, with tears of sadness because the creature who had become a pet at home is led off to be slaughtered. Head, Heart, Hand and Health of that devoted girl went into the profitable health of that sexless steer.

paragraph 9
This body paragraph has a topic sentence (the first), that presents the paragraph's focus as the "pulls." The rest of the paragraph develops the topic sentence and contributes to the development of the thesis.

9   One of the dramatic examples of energy at the Fair is in the tractor, draft team, and pony "pulls," in which the machine and the animals rear up as they try to pull a weighted sledge. The tractor is the usual case of a souped-up engine performing a task it would never do on a farm, with a great snorting and straining. The fun is in the horse and pony pulls, where the animals dig into the turf and drive themselves beyond their real strength, as if they understood the nature of competition.

paragraph 10
This paragraph presents its focus in the topic sentence (the first).

10   Above all, the Fair gives a workout to the body's five senses they could get nowhere else in the U.S.A. Apart from the fact that most people walk far more than they realize in their four-wheeled daily life, one reason for the healthy tiredness at the end of a morning-afternoon-evening at the Fair is that eye, hand, ear, tongue, and nose are exercised more than in all the rest of the year.

paragraphs 11–15
These paragraphs develop the focus on sensory experiences with descriptive detail that pertains to each of the five senses. Notice how specific the word choice is.

11   *Eye* sees the great, full udders of Holstein cows swaying between those heavy legs, the rounded bellies of hogs unaware that the symmetry will lead to an early death, the sheep struggling under the shearer's hand as he draws red blood on their pink skin in his haste, the giant pumpkin glowing orange as an autumn moon, the Ladies' Rolling Pin Throw contest (you wouldn't argue with one of them), the blue-purple-white stalks of gladioli from home gardens, the harness horses pulling goggled drivers as they trot and pace frail sulkies in front of the grandstand.

12   *Hand* touches surfaces it never meets at home unless it belongs to a farmer: softness of Guernsey hide or of the five-gaited saddle horse sleek from the currycomb, the golden feel of new oat straw, the fleece of Oxford Down or Shropshire lambs, the green surface of a John Deere eight-row corn picker, smooth as skin and tough as steel, the sweet stickiness of cotton candy.

13   *Ear* has almost too much to take in: the hog-calling contest with its shrill shrieks, the husband-calling contest combining seduction with threats, the whinnying of Tennessee walking horses, the lowing of cattle bored with standing in the showring, the male chauvinist crowing of roosters at the poultry barn, loudest at daybreak (the champion crowed 104 times in half an hour), the merry-go-round playing its old sentimental tunes, the roar of racing cars, the barkers praising the promised beauty to be revealed at the girlie show, the old fiddler's contest quivering the air with "Buffalo Gal," "Texas Star" and "Tennessee Waltz," the clang of horseshoes against each other and against the stake.

Tongue learns the taste of hickory-smoked ham, the richness of *14*
butter on popcorn with beer, the tang of rhubarb pie, sour elegance of
buttermilk served ice cold, the total smack of hamburger with onion,
pickle, mustard, and horseradish, many-flavored ice cream, chicken
fried in sight of their live cousins in the poultry barn, barbecued pork
ribs spitting their fat into the fire as fattened hogs waddle by on their
way to be judged.

Nose has an exhausting time at the Fair. It smells the many odors *15*
rising from the grills of men competing in the Iowa Cookout King
contest, grilling turkey, lamb, beef, pork, chicken, ham with backyard
recipes which excite the appetite, the delicate scents of flowers in the
horticulture competition, the smell of homemade foods, the crisp smell
of hay. People drive hundreds of miles in air-conditioned cars which
filter out smells in order to walk through heavy and hot late summer
air across the manure-reeking atmosphere of the hog, cattle, horse, and
sheep barns, to sniff again the animal odors of their childhood.

paragraphs 16 and 17
These paragraphs support the
thesis with a catalog of
activities that show the richness
and variety of the "sane" fair
activities.

You can watch the judging of home-baked bread or listen to the *16*
latest rock group. You can watch free every day the teenage talent
search or pay money to hear the same nationally known acts you can
watch free on television. The 4-H sewing contest, in which con-
tenders wear the clothes they made, was startled in 1974 to have a boy
enter himself and his navy blue knit slacks and jacket with white trim
(he grew up on a hog farm, but wants to design clothes). A girl won.

The Iowa State Fair is a great annual ceremony of the sane. *17*
Young girls still stand all night behind dairy cows with pitch forks to
keep the freshly washed animals from getting dirty before being
shown in the morning. Boys milk cows at 10 P.M., 2 A.M., and 3 A.M.
to be sure their udders are "balanced" when judges look at them. This
is hardly the view of teenagers we often hear. A six-year-old boy wins
the rooster-crowing contest. There is Indian Wrestling (arm-hand
wrestling) with a white and black sweating in immobile silence; the
judge was John Buffalo, a real Indian from the Tama reservation.

paragraph 18
The topic sentence of this
paragraph is the first sentence.
It presents the focus as the
continuity of the fair. The rest
of the paragraph develops the
topic sentence idea.

Year after year this rich and practical ritual of life is repeated. *18*
Animals whose ancestors competed many Fairs ago come back. So do
people, returning by plane and automobile to the grounds their
grandparents visited by train and buggy. Three-hundred-and-fifty
horsepower internal-combustion engines have replaced the one-horse
hitch or the two-horse team, but the essential objects of life are the
same: the dented ear of corn, the rounded rib of steer and pig, that
nourishment of the human race which is the prime purpose of the
plowing and harvesting State of Iowa.

paragraph 19
This is the conclusion. It
provides closure by repeating
the thesis idea that the fair is
the best of all worlds, and
therefore it represents how
things ought to be.

To some, the Fair seems corny. To others, the world still needs *19*
to catch up to the human and animal decency which each year digni-
fies a corner of this corrupt world. A few hundred acres of human
skill and animal beauty in Des Moines, Iowa, prove to the space cap-
sule of Earth how to live.

THE INTRODUCTION

First impressions are important because they often dictate our responses. Think about it a moment. Have you ever dropped a course after attending only one class session? Have you ever made an excuse to walk away from a person you have just met? Have you ever selected a restaurant on the basis of its name? We all do such things, and we do them in response to first impressions. Because first impressions are so important, the introduction of your essay must be carefully handled so that your reader's initial reaction is favorable. In addition to creating a first impression that will engage your reader's interest, the introduction can serve another purpose. It can tell your reader what your essay is about by including your **thesis.** If you need to review the purpose and qualities of a thesis, return to page 40.

Creating Interest in Your Topic

In addition to presenting your thesis, the introduction should engage your reader's interest in your essay. Below are 13 approaches you can take to stimulate that interest. Each approach is illustrated with an introduction taken from a student essay. (The thesis is underlined as a study aid.)

APPROACH 1: PROVIDE BACKGROUND INFORMATION

Rick was always taking crazy chances. Even in elementary school, he was the one to lock himself in the teacher's supply closet or lick a metal pole in the dead of a subzero winter. By high school, Rick had moved on to wilder things, but his drinking was the biggest concern. <u>I guess that is why no one was really surprised when he drove off the road and killed himself the day after his 18th birthday</u>.

APPROACH 2: TELL A PERTINENT STORY

Last winter while home alone, I tripped on the garden hose and fell in my garage while the door was down. The pain was excruciating, and I could not move. I lay there for two hours, sobbing, until my son came home. Now, I am not an old woman; I am just 45. <u>However, that experience made me feel fearful of growing old and living alone</u>.

APPROACH 3: EXPLAIN WHY YOUR TOPIC IS IMPORTANT

The recent tuition hike proposed by the Board of Trustees has serious implications for everyone on this campus, students, faculty, and staff alike. If tuition goes up 45 percent as expected, fewer students will be able to attend school, which will mean fewer faculty and staff will be employed. Once the cost of school becomes prohibitive for all but the wealthy, then this university will begin a downward spiral that will eventually mean its demise. There is only one way to solve our economic woes. <u>We must embark on an austerity program that makes the tuition hike unnecessary</u>.

APPROACH 4: PRESENT SOME INTERESTING IMAGES OR USE DESCRIPTION

It was a cool, crisp October morning. Sunrise was complete, the countryside awake and responding to another day. As I turned and slowly made my way into the woods, <u>I had no idea what lay ahead on the path I was to follow that day</u>.

APPROACH 5: PRESENT AN INTRIGUING PROBLEM OR RAISE A PROVOCATIVE QUESTION

Are you a Dr. Jekyll who transforms into Mr. Hyde the minute you get behind the wheel of a car? Are you a kind little old lady who becomes Mario Andretti's pace car driver the instant you hit the freeway? Are you an Eagle Scout by day and a marauding motorist by night? The chances are you are because <u>people's personalities change the moment they strap on that seat belt and head out on the highway</u>.

APPROACH 6: PRESENT AN OPPOSING VIEWPOINT

People opposed to putting warning labels on CDs with sexually explicit or otherwise offensive lyrics have their reasons. They cite free speech and they say teens will be encouraged to buy the CDs with the advisory labels. Even so, <u>I favor warning labels on certain kinds of CDs</u>.

APPROACH 7: ESTABLISH YOURSELF AS SOMEONE KNOWLEDGEABLE ABOUT THE TOPIC

<u>Believe me, racial prejudice is still a fact of American life, no matter what you hear to the contrary</u>. You see, I am what is known as an "army brat." My dad is a career army man who gets moved from post to post. Since he takes his family along with him, I have lived in eight cities over the course of my 19 years. I have known small towns and large, northern cities and southern, rural environments and urban centers. And no matter where I have lived, as an African-American, I have encountered prejudice.

APPROACH 8: OPEN WITH AN ATTENTION-GRABBING STATEMENT

What your family doctor does not know may surprise you—or it may kill you. We assume our doctors are smart and caring, that they will do whatever it takes to keep us well. We put our trust in them and never question their advice or decisions. Unfortunately, such trust is often misplaced. <u>For the best health care, we need to learn to question our doctors carefully</u>.

APPROACH 9: EXPLAIN YOUR PURPOSE

<u>All students should contact the Dean of Academic Affairs to protest the cancellation of the artist-in-residence program</u>. If enough students express their unhappiness, the dean will be forced to reinstate the program.

APPROACH 10: FIND SOME COMMON GROUND TO ESTABLISH A BOND WITH YOUR READER

None of us goes through life without doing something that we later regret. In fact, we often have many regrets. Fortunately, we are often given second chances and we redeem ourselves. It should not be any different for people released from prison after serving their sentences. These people should not be denied their second chances. <u>Convicted felons who have served their sentences should be allowed to vote</u>.

APPROACH 11: PROVIDE AN INTERESTING QUOTATION

Mark Twain said, "Man is the only animal who blushes—or needs to." <u>I take comfort in that statement when I recall the most embarrassing night of my life</u>.

APPROACH 12: DEFINE SOMETHING

A good teacher is someone who sees what students <u>can</u> do, rather than what they cannot do. A good teacher shares knowledge, helps students achieve their potential, and fosters self-esteem. <u>Without a doubt</u>, <u>Dr. Sorenson is a good teacher</u>.

APPROACH 13: GIVE RELEVANT EXAMPLES

<u>Sometimes telling a lie is better than telling the truth</u>. When a friend asks you what you think of the glasses he just paid $100 for, when your grandmother asks you what you think of the rubber chicken she lovingly prepared for your birthday, when your girlfriend asks if her dress makes her look fat, it is best to lie.

Pitfalls to Avoid

1. **Avoid referring to your title as if it were an integral part of your introduction.** For example, if your title is "The Impact of the Internet," avoid beginning with "It has changed the way we work and live." Instead, write "The Internet has changed the way we work and live."

2. **Avoid an introduction that is not suited to your audience, purpose, or thesis.** For example, a humorous story would not be a suitable way to open an essay arguing against capital punishment.

3. **Avoid an introduction that is out of proportion to the rest of your essay.** A very long introduction is out of balance with a short essay. Similarly, a long essay can have an introduction that runs more than one paragraph.

4. **Avoid opening with dictionary definitions.** This approach is overused and, therefore, likely to be boring.

5. **Avoid opening with tired expressions.** Expressions like "It's always darkest before the dawn" and "Fools rush in where angels fear to tread" are overused and should be avoided. For an explanation of overused expressions (clichés), see page 98.

6. **Avoid apologizing.** Statements like "I really don't know much about this topic" or "I doubt that anyone can understand this issue" will cause your reader to lose confidence in what you have to say.

Computer Tips

If you cannot decide which approach to your introduction is the best, execute the keystrokes that allow you to divide the screen in half. Try a different approach to your introduction on each half of the screen and compare the two to decide which you like better. You can then compare the preferable approach with *another* that you write after erasing the half you did not like as well.

Sometimes your conclusion can be turned into an excellent introduction with some reworking. Try moving your conclusion to the beginning of your essay to determine if it holds more promise as an introduction than as a conclusion.

PROCESS GUIDELINES: WRITING INTRODUCTIONS

If you have trouble writing your introduction

1. Skip it and come back to it after drafting the rest of your essay, but jot down your preliminary thesis to guide and focus the remainder of your draft.

2. Keep your introduction short and simple, perhaps writing just one or two sentences to create interest and then a thesis.

3. Supply background information or explain why your topic is important.

| **The Introduction**

1. Find three essays in books, newsmagazines, or newspapers. Then read the introductions and decide whether or not they engage your interest and why.
2. Below are three introductions written by students, each in need of revision. Revise each introduction so that it stimulates interest and has a suitable thesis.

> ```
> It was snowing when I boarded the plane. But I was terrified. I
> have always been afraid of air travel, and hopefully I will
> someday overcome this fear.
> ```

Some suggestions for revision: Create some images. Describe the weather in more detail. Specify the kind of airplane and explain more carefully the feeling of terror. Also, does the thesis present one or two narrowings? It should only present one.

> ```
> I set the alarm two hours earlier than usual and spent the
> morning cleaning like crazy. At 11:00 I went to the grocery
> store and bought all the necessary food. All afternoon I
> cooked; by 5:00 I was dressed and ready; but still the first
> meal I cooked for my in-laws was terrible.
> ```

Some suggestions for revision: Be more specific. What time did the alarm go off? Give an example or two of the cleaning you did. What food did you buy? Was it expensive? What did you cook? How bad was it? Can you find a word or words more specific than *terrible?*

> ```
> Does crime pay? Does justice win out? Do the police always get
> their man? The day I shoplifted a box of candy I learned the
> answers to these questions.
> ```

Some suggestions for revision: Substitute more interesting questions for these trite, rather boring ones—perhaps some questions that focus on the writer's feelings, such as "Have you ever wondered what a criminal feels when he or she gets caught?" Create some interest by naming the brand or type of candy and giving its price and by giving the name of the store.

3. Below is a list of four subjects. Select one and shape a topic from it. (If necessary, prewrite to find a suitable topic.) Then establish an audience and purpose. Next, write an introduction for an essay that discusses that topic.
   a. A first experience
   b. A disagreement with a friend
   c. A pleasant (or unpleasant) surprise
   d. The best (or worst) feature of your university
4. Write a second introduction using the thesis, audience, and purpose you shaped for number 3 above, only this time use a different approach. That is, if you told a story the first time, try something else—say, creating images—this time. If you wish, you may state your thesis differently in this second introduction. (As an alternative, select a subject different from what you used for

number 3. Just be sure to narrow, establish audience and purpose, and use a different approach than you did for the first introduction.)

5. *Collaborative Activity.* Pair up with a classmate and select one of the thesis statements you shaped when you responded to number 6 on page 44. Establish an audience and purpose and write an introduction for an essay that might use that thesis. Feel free to alter the original thesis somewhat.

THE BODY PARAGRAPHS

The paragraphs after your introduction form the **body** of your essay. The purpose of the body paragraphs is to present the detail that supports, explains, defends, describes, illustrates, or otherwise develops the idea given in your thesis. Obviously the body is the real core of an essay, for here you present the material to convince your reader of the validity of your thesis.

Each body paragraph has two parts: the topic sentence and the supporting detail. The **topic sentence** provides focus by presenting the point the body paragraph will deal with. This point will be something to support the thesis. While the topic sentence can appear anywhere in the body paragraph, many student writers find it easiest to place the topic sentence first. After the topic sentence comes the **supporting detail.** This is all the information that explains, illustrates, defends, describes, supports, or otherwise develops the idea presented in the topic sentence. Look again at the body paragraphs of "The Iowa State Fair" on page 56, and notice each topic sentence and the supporting details.

Adequate Detail

You cannot expect a reader to understand and appreciate the view in your thesis if you do not provide enough convincing support for that view. Let's say someone walked up to you and said, "This town stinks." You respond by asking why. The first person replies, "It's awful here; I hate it. I'm going to leave, and you should too." Would you agree that the place is awful? I doubt it, because you were not given convincing evidence to support the claim that the place stinks. That is the way it is with supporting detail: If it is not adequate, no reader will believe the thesis.

To ensure that you supply adequate detail, remember that you cannot just *tell;* you must also *show.* Thus, the person who *told* by saying that the town stinks should also *show* with specific evidence, such as there is no symphony or museum, there is only one theater, the government is corrupt, the public schools are poorly funded, the roads are in disrepair, and the people are snobs.

When writers show rather than tell, they are supporting generalizations. A **generalization** is a statement offered as truth. The support is what is offered as proof. Say, for example, that you believe buying books at your school is too much of a hassle. That would be your generalization—your statement of truth. To convince me, you would have to do more than just make the statement. After all, why should I accept your statement as fact just because you make it? If I am to believe that buying books is a hassle, you will have to prove it to me. Here is a list of some evidence you could provide to support your generalization.

> *long lines*
>
> *crowded facilities*
>
> *too few copies of books*
>
> *confusing procedures*

If you were writing an essay about the hassles of buying books, you could write one body paragraph on each of the points in the above list. However, you would have to support every generalization in every body paragraph by showing in addition to telling. Thus, the paragraph about crowded facilities must describe the nature and extent of the crowding in enough detail to convince the reader that crowding really exists. This need to support generalizations holds for every generalization you make everywhere in the body of your essay.

To appreciate the structure of a body paragraph and the need for adequate detail, let's return to "The Iowa State Fair" (p. 56). Remember, the thesis idea of that essay (expressed in the first sentence) is that the fair is the best of all possible worlds. To begin supporting that thesis, the author writes this body paragraph:

Topic Sentence

```
[There is a lot of energy at the Fair in Des Moines, but it is
all peaceful.] The double giant Ferris wheel circles, its swaying
seats more frightening than a jet plane flying through a
monsoon. Eighty thousand men, women, and children walk all day
and much of the night across the fairgrounds. Ponies pick up
their feet in a slashing trot as if the ground burned them.
Hard-rock music backgrounds the soft lowing of a Jersey cow in
the cattle barn over her newborn calf, the color of a wild deer.
Screaming speeches are made all around the world urging
violence; here there are plenty of voices, but they are calling
for you to throw baseballs at Kewpie dolls, to pitch nickels at
a dish which won't hold them, to buy cotton candy, corn dogs, a
paring knife that performs every useful act save mixing a
martini.
```

Supporting details

Notice first that the topic sentence of this body paragraph (the first sentence) serves two purposes:

1. It mentions a point that helps support the thesis.
2. It states the focus of the body paragraph.

Next, notice that the supporting details (the remainder of the paragraph) have two characteristics:

1. They develop the topic sentence by showing and not just telling.
2. They help support the thesis by adequately developing the topic sentence.

In order for your essay to have adequate detail, you must do two things:

1. You must provide enough topic sentence ideas in enough body paragraphs.
2. You must develop each of your topic sentence ideas in enough detail.

Ways to Develop and Arrange Supporting Detail

To provide the adequate detail a reader requires, you have a number of strategies at your disposal, including using the patterns of development that are the focus of Part 2 of this book. For now, to give you an idea of how they can help you provide adequate detail, here are examples of ways you could use the patterns to support this thesis: "This country does not do enough to solve the problem of homelessness."

Description *(the writer describes something):*	You could describe the living conditions of the homeless.
Narration *(the writer tells a story):*	You could tell the story of how you became interested in the plight of the homeless.
Illustration *(the writer provides examples):*	You could give examples of how the homeless are treated.
Process analysis *(the writer explains how* *something is made or done):*	You could explain how to pass a law to help the homeless.
Comparison and contrast *(the writer points out* *similarities and differences):*	You could compare the treatment of the homeless to the treatment of stray animals.
Cause-and-effect analysis *(the writer explains the causes* *and effects of something):*	You could predict the effects of passing a law to aid the homeless.
Definition (the writer explains *what something means):*	You could define *compassion*.
Classification (the writer *explains how items are grouped):*	You could classify the reasons people become homeless.

Regardless of the kinds of details you provide, those details must be presented in a logical order so your reader can easily follow the sequence of ideas. Several arrangements are possible, and these are discussed in detail in Part 2. For now, this information will give you an idea of some of the possibilities.

Chronological order: This is a time order. You begin with what happens first, move to the second event, on to the third, and so on. This is a useful order for storytelling.

Spatial order: With this arrangement, you move across space in some logical way, say top to bottom, outside to inside, left to right, and so on. Writers who describe frequently use a spatial arrangement.

Progressive order: With this order, you move from the *least* compelling (important, surprising, convincing, or representative) idea to the most compelling. Writers who aim to persuade often use a progressive order to save the most compelling argument for last.

Deductive order: In this order, you begin with a generalization and then give specific details to support that generalization. With this arrangement, the thesis is at the beginning of the essay.

Inductive order: In this order, you begin with specific details and end with the generalization to be drawn from those details. With this order, the thesis would come at the end of the essay.

Relevant Detail

In addition to being adequate, your supporting detail must be *relevant,* which means that every detail in a body paragraph must be clearly and directly related to the topic sentence idea of that paragraph. Thus, in "The Iowa State Fair," the first body paragraph (which has a topic sentence that presents the focus as the peaceful energy of the fair) cannot include a description of an elderly man asleep on a bench. Since a sleeping man does not show energy, that detail is not relevant.

Sometimes writers include detail that is not relevant because they become so concerned about supplying *enough* detail that they overlook the need to include the *right* detail. You know the feeling, that sense that if you only write enough, in there somewhere you will say something terrific. This common impulse can lead you to write ideas that do not belong because they are not related to the topic sentence.

In addition to being sure that the detail in a paragraph is relevant to its topic sentence, you must be sure that each topic sentence is relevant to the thesis. If you have a topic sentence—and hence a paragraph—that does not pertain to the thesis, a portion of your essay will stray from the stated topic. Thus, "The Iowa State Fair," whose thesis states that the fair is "the best of all possible worlds," cannot include a topic sentence that says the prices at the fair are very high. That statement would not be relevant to the thesis idea.

To ensure relevance, think of your thesis and topic sentences as contracts between you and your reader. They guarantee that your essay and body paragraphs will be about what your thesis and topic sentences say they will be about.

Run a careful check on both your topic sentences and supporting details to be sure you have not violated the terms of the "contracts."

When to Begin a Paragraph

You can begin a new paragraph each time you begin discussion of a new point to develop the thesis, with the following exceptions:

1. If the discussion of a point requires a very long paragraph, you can break up the discussion into two or more paragraphs as a courtesy to your reader, who may find one very long paragraph taxing.
2. You can begin a paragraph to emphasize a point. If a point can appear in a paragraph along with other ideas but you want that point to receive special emphasis, you can place it in a paragraph of its own.
3. You may use one body paragraph to make a point and then illustrate that point with a long example or a series of short examples. If including the example or examples in the paragraph that makes the point would create an overly long paragraph, the example(s) can appear in a separate paragraph.

Pitfalls to Avoid

1. **Avoid one- or two-sentence paragraphs.** You often see these in magazines and newspapers, but journalistic style differs from essay style. In an essay, a one- or two-sentence paragraph gives you a topic sentence with little or no supporting detail.

2. **Avoid ending a paragraph with a new idea.** Let the new idea begin the next paragraph.

3. **Avoid repeating the same idea in different ways.** Such repetition makes a paragraph look longer, but it does not contribute to adequate detail. Here is an example of the kind of repetition to avoid. (The underlined sentences are repetitious.)

> Weightlifting is an excellent physical activity for women. It increases bone density and thus wards off osteoporosis. <u>It really does women a great deal of good</u>. However, weightlifting helps more than women's bones, for it also builds muscle, which increases metabolic rate. The increase in metabolic rate is good because it means that more calories are burned. <u>The protection afforded bones, though, is the big benefit</u>. Still another advantage to weightlifting is the fact that muscles are strengthened and thus better able to protect various body parts. <u>A woman's stronger muscles are far better able to protect various parts of the anatomy</u>.

4. **Avoid including more than one idea in a body paragraph.** One of those ideas is likely to be insufficiently related to the topic sentence.

PROCESS GUIDELINES: EVALUATING YOUR SUPPORTING DETAIL

1. TO EVALUATE THE ADEQUACY OF YOUR DETAIL
   a. Underline every generalization and bracket off the details that support each generalization. Look at the bracketed material and ask yourself whether you are *showing* the truth of the generalization in enough detail.
   b. Ask someone who can be objective to read your draft and note in the margin any additional information he or she needs in order to appreciate your thesis.
   c. Count the number of sentences in each of your body paragraphs. If you have a paragraph with fewer than five sentences, ask yourself if you have developed your topic sentence adequately.
   d. For each body paragraph, answer the following questions:
      1.) Why would my reader find the information in this paragraph helpful?
      2.) How does the information advance my purpose?
          If you cannot justify the inclusion of certain details, then these details are probably not appropriate.
2. TO EVALUATE THE RELEVANCE OF YOUR DETAIL
   a. Examine each topic sentence against your thesis and ask yourself whether each is clearly related to the thesis.
   b. Examine each sentence of every body paragraph and ask yourself whether each is clearly related to its topic sentence.
   c. Ask someone who will be objective about your work to read your draft and underline any detail that does not seem relevant.

EXERCISE | **Body Paragraphs**

1. The following essay, written by a freshman, has definite strengths as well as some problems. Read the essay and answer the questions after it.

Exhaustion

All of my friends told me it would be hard for me to attend college *1* at my age because I was 18 years removed from any study habits that I may have once had. However, I'm finding that the hardest part of attending college is not lack of study habits but coping with the exhaustion from trying to keep up with attending classes, working 40 hours a week, raising a family of three exuberant boys, and taking care of household chores.

A typical day starts for me at 6:00 in the morning when I crawl *2* out of my toast-warm bed and stumble over the dog. Flicking on the lights in each of the boys' rooms, I grope my way carefully down the stairs, with eyes half open. My first encounter is with three hungry, mewling cats and a dog who lets me know he has to be let out. Next I grab a cup of coffee and gulp half of it down so I can pry my eyes open enough to take care of all the urgent matters of the morning. Gulping coffee and grabbing quick puffs of my cigarette, I stumble around packing school lunches. Now it's time for the real work, pushing the boys to get ready for school. "Greg, don't forget to brush your teeth." "Bob, take that shirt off. I don't care if it is your favorite; you wore it yesterday." "Mike, you can't comb your hair like that; it makes you look like Alfalfa." By the time I get them out the door, I'm ready to go back to bed, but work is waiting and I have no time to lose. Eight-thirty finds me on the job, brushed, curled, and ready to begin.

The hands on the clock finally reach twelve and it's time for   *3* my lunch hour. Lunch? What is that? I have one hour to do my grocery shopping for the day and pay any bills that need paying. I rush home, put my milk and bread away, take care of the pets again, and hurry back to work by one o'clock.

Work is filing, typing, taking payments, balancing my money   *4* drawer, and putting my data on the computer as fast and efficiently as possible so I can exit quickly at 4:30 P.M.

My first class in the evenings at college starts at 5:40, and I   *5* live 40 miles from campus, so my trip usually takes 45 to 50 minutes. By the time I find a parking place, I barely make it to class on time. Algebra class is over at 9:30. I then have a 45-minute drive home.

Packing lunches for the next day, bathing and washing my hair,   *6* finding something to eat, and relaxing enough to go to sleep usually puts me in bed as late as 1:00 A.M. Most of the time I fall asleep immediately because I am so worn out.

I knew attending college and working would be hard, but I did   *7* not realize it would be this exhausting. However, I feel that when I graduate it will have been worth the exhaustion to achieve at last a degree which I have always wanted.

---

a. What is the thesis of "Exhaustion"?
b. When you finished the essay, did you feel there was enough detail to demonstrate the validity of the thesis? That is, is the thesis adequately developed in the body paragraphs? Explain.

    c. What is the topic sentence for each body paragraph? Are all these topic sentences relevant to the thesis?

    d. Which topic sentence receives the most development?

    e. Which topic sentence receives the least development? How do you react to the paragraph with that topic sentence?

    f. Do any paragraphs need additional supporting detail because the author is telling without showing?

    g. Are any details not relevant to the appropriate topic sentence?

2. Assume you are writing an essay using one of the following thesis statements.

The best thing about _____ is _____.
(You fill in the blanks.)
The worst thing about _____ is _____.
(You fill in the blanks.)

    Decide which thesis you will use, and prewrite until you discover two main ideas for developing that thesis. For example, if your thesis is "The best thing about college life is meeting interesting people," you might describe the people you meet in class and the people you meet in your dorm. Or develop one paragraph about Chris, the guy you met from Zimbabwe, and another about Dr. Schwartz, the prof who got you interested in cellular biology. Develop each main point in a body paragraph. (You may want to prewrite a second time to discover supporting detail.)

3. *Collaborative Activity.* Bring your completed body paragraphs and thesis to class and exchange them with a classmate. After reading each other's work, write a note to the person whose paragraphs you read, and in the note, answer the following questions:

    a. Are the topic sentences relevant? If not, what specifically is the problem?

    b. Are all the supporting details relevant? If not, what detail is not relevant? Why?

    c. Is the supporting detail adequate in each paragraph? If not, where is the detail needed? What kind of detail should it be?

    d. Is the order of details logical? If not, what is wrong?

When you get back your paragraphs, study your classmate's responses. Decide whether you agree with the evaluation. If not, discuss your disagreement with your instructor.

THE CONCLUSION

The conclusion of an essay is important because it influences your reader's final impression. Have you seen a movie that starts out strong and then fizzles at the end? As you walked out of the theater, you probably talked about the disappointing ending, not the strong beginning or middle. Writing works the same way. Even if it has a strong introduction and body, an essay with a weak conclusion will leave your reader feeling let down. For this reason, the same care that goes into your introduction and body should go into your conclusion.

Consider for a moment the conclusion a student wrote for an essay with the thesis "The way Mr. Wang communicated with students, challenged them, and spent his own time with them made him the teacher I respected most." The essay with this thesis had three body paragraphs, one on communicating with students, one on challenging students, and one on spending his own time with students. The conclusion read like this:

> Therefore, Mr. Wang is the teacher I most respected because of the way he communicated with students, the way he challenged them, and the way he spent his own free time helping them.

How do you react to this conclusion? Do you find it boring? Are you annoyed by the repetition of the thesis? Boredom and annoyance are valid reactions to this conclusion. Actually, the student's essay had interesting detail, but the writer did not craft his conclusion carefully, so the reader comes away disappointed.

Now react to a conclusion handled with more care. This conclusion was for an essay describing a night spent at the beach.

> As the sun rose to signal the start of a new day, I walked away, not feeling at all tired but instead fulfilled. The beach had offered me all of her beauty, and the night we spent together would remain a pleasant memory always.

This second conclusion is more interesting than the first, so a reader will leave the second essay with a better reaction. The point to be drawn from all this is that, like first impressions, final reactions are significant.

Now look again at "The Iowa State Fair" on page 56. Is the conclusion effective? Why?

Ways to Handle the Conclusion

1. LEAVE THE READER WITH AN OVERALL REACTION

With this approach, you extract from the major points of the essay some overriding impression, observation, or reaction to leave the reader with a final sense of how you feel about things. Here is an example for an essay with the thesis "Ability grouping is harmful to many students":

> Clearly, ability grouping causes many students to feel unsuccessful, and it damages their self-esteem. That fact, alone, should be enough to prompt educators to discontinue such a harmful practice.

2. SUMMARIZE THE MAIN POINTS OF THE ESSAY

Save a summary conclusion for those times when a brief review would help the reader. If you have written a relatively short essay with easily understood and easily remembered ideas, your reader does not need a summary and may grow annoyed by the repetition. On the other hand, if your essay has many ideas, some of which are complex, your reader may appreciate a final summary.

3. INTRODUCE A RELATED IDEA

An effective conclusion can include an idea not appearing elsewhere in the essay, but the idea must be clearly and closely related to the ideas that appear in the body, so the reader is not caught off guard by an idea that seems to spring out of nowhere. Here is an example for an essay with the thesis "With so much discussion of the advantages of computers, we tend to overlook the fact that these machines have serious disadvantages as well":

> If we overlook the drawbacks of computers, we risk becoming enslaved by these machines. Certainly this happened with the automobile. We routinely drive even short distances, never even considering walking instead. As a result, our physical fitness suffers and we have fewer opportunities to enjoy the splendor of a beautiful day.

4. MAKE A DETERMINATION

Frequently, the ideas in the body lead to some significant point or determination. When this is the case, the final paragraph(s) can be used to state and explain that point. Here is an example for an essay with the thesis "Co-workers should never attempt to become friends outside of the workplace":

> Co-workers who socialize outside of the workplace do not remain friends for long. I regret the strain my socializing created on the relationship I had with my colleagues at work, and I regret having to quit my job. Next time, I will know better.

5. RESTATE THE THESIS OR ANOTHER PORTION OF THE INTRODUCTION

You can conclude an essay by repeating the thesis or another part of the introduction. However, use this approach at the wrong times and the effect is unsatisfactory. For example, the conclusion you read on page 73 (about Mr. Wang) seems lazy; it is certainly dull. Yet this approach *can* succeed if you keep two things in mind. First, if you repeat the thesis or another part of the introduction, restate the idea using different language. That is, restate the idea in a new way. Second, the restatement is best used to achieve the dramatic effect that comes from repetition. For an example of restatement in a new way, read "Horse Sense" on page 228.

6. EXPLAIN THE SIGNIFICANCE OF YOUR TOPIC

This approach is particularly effective when your essay tells a story and you want to note why that story is important. Here is an example from an essay that tells the story of the time the author's house burned down.

> Although young people generally think they are immortal, as a result of that fire, I no longer take my safety for granted. Wherever I live, I plan an escape route in the event of fire, I

have two smoke detectors, and I keep a chain ladder by my
second-story bedroom window.

7. MAKE A RECOMMENDATION OR CALL YOUR READER TO ACTION

This approach is often appropriate for persuasive essays. Here is an example for
an essay with this thesis: "Because there are too few organs for all the patients
needing transplants, federal laws should govern how the limited number of organs are allocated."

It is time that we began a letter-writing campaign to urge our
representatives and senators to support organ allocation
legislation. If enough people write, we can have equitable
distribution of organs.

8. EXPLAIN THE CONSEQUENCES OF IGNORING YOUR VIEW

This approach also works well for persuasive essays. Here is an example for the
thesis used in number 7:

If we do not legislate the allocation of transplant organs,
then we cannot be sure that the sickest patients will be first
on the list. Instead, the wealthy and the famous will use their
influence to get organs that more appropriately belong to
others.

9. COMBINE APPROACHES

Your conclusion can combine two or more strategies. You can restate the thesis
and then summarize. You can make a determination and then give an overall reaction. A related idea can appear with a restatement. Any combination of approaches is possible.

The length of the conclusion varies. Sometimes a single sentence serves
very well. Other times you may need a paragraph of several sentences. For a long
essay, a conclusion of more than one paragraph may be in order. Regardless, the
function of a conclusion is to bring your writing to a satisfying finish. Effective
writing does not screech to a halt but closes off neatly.

Pitfalls to Avoid

1. **Avoid a conclusion that is out of proportion to the rest of your essay.**
Short essays should have short conclusions, and longer essays can have longer
conclusions.

2. **Avoid a conclusion that is not suited to your audience, purpose, or thesis.** Say that you are writing about the ways to combat discrimination against overweight people, and your audience is overweight people themselves. There is no
need to close by explaining what would happen if your view were ignored; your audience already knows this because they know about the effects of discrimination.

3. **Avoid expressions like "in conclusion," "in summary," "to conclude," "to summarize," and "in closing."** These expressions are overused.

PROCESS GUIDELINES: CONCLUSIONS

If you have trouble with your conclusion:

a. Try an approach other than the one in your draft.
b. Summarize your main points if this will be helpful to the reader.
c. Give your thesis or main points a larger application by showing their significance beyond the scope of your essay.
d. Keep your conclusion brief—perhaps even a single sentence.

EXERCISE | **The Conclusion**

1. Locate three essays with formal conclusions. You might check the library for books of essays, weekly newsmagazines, and newspaper editorial pages. Read the essays and answer the following questions.
   a. Does the conclusion bring the essay to a satisfying close? Explain.
   b. What approach is used for the conclusion? Is this approach effective? If not, explain why.
   c. Is the length of the conclusion appropriate? If not, explain why.
   d. Does the conclusion leave you with a positive final impression? If not, explain why.
2. *Collaborative Activity.* Below is a clever essay written by a student. The conclusion has been omitted, so with two classmates write your own. In class take turns reading your conclusions and note the variety of approaches. You will find it interesting to see how many different ways the conclusion can be handled.

Beware the Body Brigade

I honestly believe that if all the health fanatics were piled in   *1*
one big heap, the mound would make Mount Everest look like an
anthill. These joggers and protein-poppers seem to be banding
together armed with sweatsuits and wheat germ to descend upon the
junk food junkies and those chumps whose only exercise is climbing
in and out of bed morning and night. The poor slovenly souls in the
latter group struggle to defend themselves against the psychological tactics of what I call the "Body Brigade." Disguised as
run-of-the-mill let's-get-a-pizza people, they are actually
brainwashers. Take your Big Mac and run the other way if you come
face to face with a Body Brigader. The breed works in potent ways.

Take for instance the health food nut. The health food nut will   *2*
weaken your resistance and convert you to a Body Brigade Believer
by threatening you with immediate, self-inflicted death if you
continue eating "whatever that awful stuff is you're feeding
yourself. As you open your lunchbox, empty stomach growling, and
begin to gobble your bologna sandwich, he or she will grab your
arm, yank the sandwich from between your teeth, and proclaim,
"You're *killing* yourself eating that junk. Don't you know they put *rat
meat* in bologna?" Because you now believe that you will not rise
from the lunch table upon consuming your rat bologna, the carrot
sticks and plain, natural yogurt your patron Brigader offers you
begin to look appetizing. Watch out, Burger Barn addict—you are
beginning to weaken.

If you ever hear a pair of sneaker-clad feet running up behind   *4*
you—don't turn around. You are being chased by the jogger. The
jogger will snare you by pounding into your head the "I used to
look *like you* before . . . " line. A common conversation goes
something like this: "You take the bus to work? And it's only five
miles to your office? You have to be kidding." Mr. Addidas here
believes that you should run the "short five-mile jaunt" each
morning, despite the fact that walking just the two blocks from
your doorstep to the bus stop leaves you gasping for air. The next
line is "I used to look *like you*" (and the Brigader puckers up his
face on the "like you") "before I started running each morning. I
used to have a pot belly just like you do, and look at me now." You
do look at the jogger—no gut. You look at yourself—big gut. Never
worried before about your pot belly, now you feel as if you have an
overblown beachball beneath your shirt. The self-disgust maneuver
is working on you, and you begin to feel inferior to the Brigader.

Student Essay: Writing the First Draft

Using her outline on page 53 as a guide, student author Peg wrote the following
first draft:

In the '50s or '60s there was a commercial on T.V. that
made reference to a big family. It showed the husband and wife
looking out their window at a car pulling up to their house
with kids in it packed like sardines in a can. The wife
screams, "Here come Helen and her hungry brood, what are we
gonna do for food?" I really thought at the time that they were

referring to my family. Someone in the neighborhood had to have told them about us. My mother's name was Helen. She had seven children. To get us all in the car to go anywhere was a real fiasco. The doctor told her she was built to have kids.

I guess the most devastating fact about being in this large family was not enough money. My dad had a steady job at the bakery as a checker, but the pay was pretty crummy. My dad never took a vacation. We needed the money too badly. He had to do some pretty tight budgeting to pay the bills. This lack of money led to many other hardships.

Food was a problem. We never went hungry but the foods we ate were those you could make a large amount of at one time, that stretched a long way and weren't too expensive, like beans, soup, and mush. Since only nine quarts of mild were delivered to our house, we had to substitute canned milk and water or powdered milk on our cereal quite a few times. We rarely got store bought candy or sweets. We never experienced the privilege of going to a restaurant. Again the culprit is lack of money.

We were never choosy about the clothes we wore. We couldn't afford to be choosy. Since we girls had two older brothers, we ended up wearing old faded jeans. I can never remember getting any new clothing. It was always my brothers' or sisters' or someone elses'. The one thing I do remember getting new are shoes. We had one pair each. We wore them a long time till they couldn't be patched and on payday we got a new pair. That was a great feeling.

Professional haircuts were not to be had. We didn't have the money for such frivilous things. My uncle cut everyone's hair. Regular dental work was also out of the question. We only went to the dentist when we had a toothache or when we might loose a tooth through decay.

We never owned a real nice car. My dad would keep the thing running but you couldn't depend on it to go too far. The grocery store was about the extent of our travel.

As a member of a large family you took a few things for granted: you never took long trips, Christmas was never thought of for its material gain, and birthday parties were unheard of. These are a few of the disadvantages experienced.

When I was in 8th grade, I was sitting in English class and the teacher was lecturing. Our principle appeared in the doorway and calmly said to the teacher that I was supposed to go with him. I wondered what all the mystery was about. I knew I hadn't done anything wrong. What could he want with me? When we reached the corridor I saw my older brother standing there waiting for me. I knew something was wrong. "Dad died," he managed to get out. I couldn't believe it. We hugged and cried.

Living within a large family structure had meant many hardships, but the hardship of living without a dad was one that would never be overcome.

NOTE: See pages 123 and 126 for the revised drafts and final version of this essay.

EXERCISE | **Essay in Progress**

Directions: After completing this exercise, save your draft. You will use it later as you work toward your completed essay.

1. Using one of the outlines you wrote when you completed the exercise on page 53, write a first (rough) draft in one sitting. Do not worry about getting anything down in perfect form; just write your ideas the best you can. Skip any troublesome sections.
2. Study your draft. Does it suggest that you should return to an earlier stage in the process? If so, which one(s) and why? Return to those stages now and do what is necessary.
3. Were you comfortable writing your first draft? If not, what will you do differently the next time you draft? Why?

WRITING ASSIGNMENT

The broad subject for this essay is how you feel about writing and/or taking a writing course and why you feel as you do. Your audience is your writing instructor, a person who is interested in your thoughts and feelings about this subject. The purpose of your writing is to communicate honestly and accurately the attitude you are bringing to your writing course in order to help your instructor better understand your feelings about your work.

Before you begin, review the following suggestions. You may want to try some of them, although you are not obligated to do so.

1. To generate ideas, consider your past experiences: whether you have enjoyed writing in the past, how successful your past writing has been, the kinds of writing you do and do not enjoy, what you hope to learn this term, what you see as your strengths and weaknesses, whether you are glad to be in a writing course, what you perceive as the purpose of your writing class, how good your previous writing instruction has been, what you think your chances of doing well are, and so on.

2. If you have trouble generating ideas for support, use some of the prewriting techniques.

3. Once you feel you have enough ideas to bring to a draft (and different writers will vary in their needs here), number your ideas in the order you wish to handle them.

4. Write your first draft, but let it be a rough one. Just get your ideas down the best way you can without worrying over anything. Try to go from start to finish in one sitting. If you have trouble getting started, skip your introduction and return to it after everything else is drafted.

5. Make any changes in your draft that you deem necessary.

6. Type your reworked draft and ask two of your classmates to read it. Have your readers respond in writing to the following questions:
   a. Does the introduction hold your interest? If not, why?
   b. Is there a stated or strongly implied thesis? What is it?
   c. Are all generalizations adequately supported? If not, where is more detail needed?
   d. Are there any relevance problems? If so, what are they?
   e. Is there any detail not appropriate to the audience or purpose?
   f. Are there enough points to develop the thesis adequately?
   g. Is there anything you do not understand? If so, what?
   h. Does the conclusion leave you with a positive final impression? If not, what problems exist?
   i. What are the chief strengths of the draft?

7. Rework your draft, taking into consideration the reactions of your readers. If you question the validity of a reader response, ask for your instructor's opinion.

8. Check your essay slowly and carefully for spelling, punctuation, and grammar errors.

9. Type your essay into its final form and check it for typing errors.

CHAPTER 3

Revising and Editing the Draft

No matter how rough the first draft is, it gives the writer raw material to work with. There it is on the page—the first expression of the writer's ideas, ready to be shaped into polished form. There are rough spots, gaps, errors, and lots of things that are not working, but it can be transformed into something that satisfies the writer and engages the reader. This process of reworking is **revision.**

REVISING (READER-BASED/REWRITING)

The first draft completes the work that is primarily writer-based, so the writer can begin getting the piece ready for a reader. The job of rewriting (revising) begins.

Revision is the essence of the writing process, so much so that there is simply no way to overemphasize its crucial role. Despite the importance of revision, not every writer understands its nature and function. For example, many students say they feel frustrated after completing a first draft, reading their work over, and discovering that it is nowhere near ready for a reader. They seem surprised that they have written so many pages but none of them is "right" yet, and they conclude that they cannot write. These students are expecting too much of themselves by looking for a finished product too soon. Only the rare writer gets it right the first time. The rest of us produce drafts that need a major overhaul.

Some writers recognize the need to revise but fail to appreciate how much time and effort must go into the process. They think that revising means going through the draft to fix spellings, insert some punctuation, and change a few words. Sure, a blessed few write quickly and produce near-perfect first drafts, but most people must make significant changes before turning a piece over to the reader.

The word *revision* (re-vision) means "seeing again." The revision process calls upon writers to look again at their work. However, because revision marks the point when writers cross the line from writer-based to reader-based activity, revision involves us in seeing our work from the reader's point of view.

How, you may be wondering, can writers view their work as their readers will? How do writers know what to change in their drafts? These questions go to the heart of the revision process, and the following process guidelines will help you answer them.

PROCESS GUIDELINES: THINKING LIKE A READER

1. Before revising, leave your work for several hours at least, a day or more if possible. The longer you can stay away, the better. Getting away is important because after generating ideas, outlining, and drafting, you know what you mean so well that you may not recognize when you have failed to clarify an idea for a reader who does not have the same awareness. Getting away is also important for helping you make the very important shift from writer to reader.

2. If you drafted with a pen or pencil, type your draft after it is written. Your essay will resemble printed matter, which makes it easier for you to view it as "someone else's work," an orientation that lends objectivity. Also, when you view your work in type, you can spot problems more easily, as when you see that a paragraph is running only two typed lines, an indication that your detail may not be adequate.

3. Another way to achieve a fresh perspective is to read your draft out loud and approach it from the sense of sound rather than sight. Writers often hear problems that they overlook visually.

4. Trust your instincts. If you sense a problem, the odds are high that a problem exists—even if you cannot give it a name.

5. Use a revision checklist, like the one on page 117, so you are reminded of everything you need to check for.

As you approach the revision of your draft, keep in mind that revising is a time-consuming, multifaceted process. You will need to evaluate and make changes in your *content, organization,* and *expression of ideas.*

REVISING FOR CONTENT

In Chapter 1, you learned about the qualities of an effective thesis, and in Chapter 2 you learned about the qualities of effective introductions, body paragraphs, and conclusions. When you revise, you must carefully evaluate these features of your draft and make necessary changes. Answering the following questions can help you.

Questions for Evaluating Content

1. Does your thesis express your topic and your opinion of that topic? Does it express just one topic and opinion? Is your opinion expressed in specific language?

2. Have you avoided writing a thesis that includes a broad statement, a factual statement, an announcement, and expressions like "in my opinion"?

3. Is your thesis compatible with your audience and purpose?

4. Is your introduction calculated to engage your reader's interest? Is it well-suited to your audience, purpose, and thesis?

5. Have you avoided a dictionary definition, tired expressions, apologies, and reference to the title in your introduction?

6. Is the length of your introduction in proportion to the rest of your essay?

7. Have you proven the truth of all of your generalizations, including your thesis and topic sentence generalizations, with sufficient detail? That is, did you *show* rather than just *tell?*

8. Are the details in each body paragraph clearly related to their topic sentence? Is each topic sentence clearly related to the thesis?

9. Did you write your details with your audience and purpose in mind? Have you included everything your reader needs in order to understand your topic and opinion?

10. Have you avoided one- and two-sentence paragraphs and repeating the same idea in different ways?

11. Does your conclusion bring your essay to a satisfying close? Is it in proportion to the rest of the essay? Is it well-suited to your audience, purpose, and thesis? Have you avoided expressions like, "in conclusion"?

PROCESS GUIDELINES: REVISING FOR CONTENT

1. If you discover you have a relevance problem
   a. Try to reshape the detail or slant it so that it becomes relevant.
   b. Alter your thesis or topic sentence to accommodate the detail, but be careful that the change does not create a relevance problem elsewhere.
   c. Eliminate the irrelevant detail.

2. If your detail is not adequate
   a. Place a check mark next to each generalization in your draft, and then look at how much support each generalization gets. For each sketchily supported or unsupported generalization, add several sentences of explanation.
   b. Use examples to show rather than just tell.
   c. Ask a reliable reader what additional information he or she needs.
   d. Write each underdeveloped generalization on a separate sheet of paper and list every point that could be made about it. Review your list of points for ones you can add to your essay.
   e. If you are unable to generate adequate detail, consider the possibility that your thesis is too narrow and should be broadened to be less restrictive.

3. If you decide you don't like your draft
   a. Do not make any final decisions on the worth of your draft until after leaving your work to restore your objectivity.
   b. Have realistic expectations for your draft. Remember, it is supposed to be rough.
   c. Do not reject your draft without trying to identify portions that can be salvaged and improved with revision.
   d. Do not reject your draft without asking a reliable reader to react to it; this reader may see merit where you do not, or the reader may be able to suggest changes that make the draft salvageable.
   e. If you must begin again, take a hard look at your topic to determine if it is the source of your difficulty, and consider reshaping it. Starting over is not a tragedy; sometimes writers must discover what does not work before they discover what does work.
   f. If necessary because of time constraints, do the best you can with what you have.
4. If you have trouble deciding what revisions to make
   a. Ask yourself if you are considering too many aspects of your draft at the same time. Consider evaluating your draft in stages.
   b. Ask a reliable reader to review your draft and make suggestions.
5. If you are having trouble making your revisions
   a. Leave your draft for a day to clear your head and allow time for ideas to form.
   b. Revise in stages, taking a break after each stage or two. Avoid attempting too much at one time.
   c. If you cannot solve a problem, try to get around it by expressing an idea in another way, using a different example, generating another idea to replace the one you are having trouble writing, and so forth.
   d. Work your easiest revisions first to build your momentum and confidence.
   e. Settle for less than ideal. Once you have done your best, no more can be expected, even if your best is not as good as you want it to be this time.

REVISING FOR ORGANIZATION

In Chapter 2 you learned how to structure an essay. In addition to that information, you need to understand how to demonstrate the relationships among your ideas. That means you need to understand how to use transitions effectively.

Use Transitions

Transitions are connective words and phrases that show the relationship between ideas. Because they show how ideas relate to each other, transitions aid organization and prevent abrupt, annoying shifts. Consider, for example, the following sentences taken from an essay a student wrote about what she experienced when her boyfriend, Dave, broke their engagement:

> For weeks I wondered what I had done wrong until friends helped me realize that I was not necessarily responsible. Dave's explanation that "people change" became more acceptable to me.

The movement from the first to the second sentence is abrupt and confusing. Look what happens, however, when a transitional phrase is used to bridge the gap between the two sentences by clarifying the relationship between ideas.

> For weeks I wondered what I had done wrong, until friends helped me realize that I was not necessarily responsible. As a result, Dave's explanation that "people change" became more acceptable to me.

The transitional phrase *as a result* is added at the beginning of the second sentence to signal that the ideas in the first sentence function as a cause, and the ideas in the second sentence function as the effect of that cause. By demonstrating this cause-and-effect relationship, the transition smooths the flow of ideas and helps the reader understand how the writer is connecting thoughts.

In addition to connecting ideas in different sentences, transitions can clarify the relationship between ideas in the same sentence as the following sentence shows:

> In her campaign speech, the senator claimed she favored economic aid to the unemployed and the elderly; however, her voting record demonstrates otherwise.

However functions as a transition that indicates contrast. That is, it signals to the reader that what comes after it is in contrast to what comes before it.

Transitional words and phrases can signal a variety of relationships. Be sure to check the Transition Chart on pages 86-87, which presents these relationships and some common transitions used to signal them.

Use Repetition to Achieve Transition

Another way to achieve transition is by repeating key words. At some point, you may have been told that repetition is annoying to the reader and a waste of words. Often this is true. However, at times deliberate repetition is appreciated by the reader because it clarifies the relationship between ideas, bridges gaps, and hence aids comprehension. Consider these sentences:

> Exam anxiety is more prevalent among students than many instructors realize. Many students who understand the material are prevented from demonstrating their knowledge.

These sentences have a relationship to each other (cause and effect), but that relationship is not revealed as clearly as it could be. Also, an awkward gap exists between the sentences. To alleviate these problems, strategic repetition can serve as a transition.

(*continued on page 88*)

Transition Chart

Relationship Signaled	Transitions That Signal the Relationship	Example
addition	also, and, and then, too, in addition, furthermore, moreover, equally important, another, first, second, third . . .	The mayor fully expects the city council to approve her salary recommendations for city employees. <u>In addition</u>, she is certain she will gain support for her road-repair program.
time sequence	now, then, before, after, afterward, earlier, later, immediately, soon, next, meanwhile, gradually, suddenly, finally, previously, before, next, often, eventually	<u>Before</u> an agreement can be reached between the striking hospital workers and management, both sides must soften their stands on the economic issues.
spatial arrangement	near, near to, nearly, far, far from, beside, in front of, next to, beyond, above, below, to the right, to the left, around, surrounding, on one side, inside, outside, across, opposite to, far off, behind, alongside, there	As you leave the fair grounds, turn right on Route 76. <u>Just beyond</u> the junction sign is the turnoff you need.
comparison	in the same way, similarly, just like, just as, in like manner, likewise	The current administration must not abandon its commitment to the poor. <u>Similarly</u>, it must not forget its promise to the elderly.
contrast	but, still, however, on the other hand, yet, on the contrary, nevertheless, despite, in spite of	<u>In spite of</u> the currently depressed housing market, money can still be made in real estate.

Relationship Signaled	Transitions That Signal the Relationship	Example
cause and effect	because, since, so, consequently, hence, as a result, therefore, thus, because of this	Because of this year's frost, almost 30 percent of the state's fruit crop was lost.
purpose	for this purpose, so that this may occur, in order to	In order to pass the school levy, the school board must make clear just how desperately additional money is needed.
emphasis	indeed, in fact, surely, undoubtedly, without a doubt, certainly, truly, to be sure, I am certain	Adolescence is not the carefree time some adults view it to be. In fact, it can be the most unsettled period in a person's life.
illustration	for example, for instance, as an illustration, specifically, to be specific, in particular	Most of the parents complained that the schools were not tough enough. They said, for example, that their children were rarely assigned homework.
summary or clarification	in summary, in conclusion, as I have shown, in brief, in short, in other words, all in all, that is	The used car Joshua bought required brake pads, shocks, and a fuel pump. In other words, it was in terrible shape.
admitting a point	although, while this may be true, granted, even though, while it is true that	While it is true that too many Americans cannot read and write, this country's literacy rate is among the best in the world.

```
Exam anxiety is more prevalent among students than many
instructors realize. Such anxiety prevents many students who
understand the material from demonstrating their knowledge.
```

The relationship between ideas is clarified by the repetition of *anxiety* at the beginning of the second sentence. In addition, this repetition smooths the flow from the first sentence to the second.

You can also create transitions by repeating a key idea rather than a key word. To understand this, first look at the following sentences:

```
Mr. Ferguson, driving at close to 60 miles per hour, took his
eyes off the road for only a second to light a cigarette. A
three-car pileup put two people in the hospital.
```

The relationship between these two sentences is not as clear as it should be. Further, the gap creates an abrupt shift. The repetition of a key idea can serve as a transition and solve these problems:

```
Mr. Ferguson, driving at close to 60 miles per hour, took his
eyes off the road for only a second to light a cigarette. This
momentary lapse caused a three-car pileup that put two people
in the hospital.
```

At the beginning of the second sentence, the phrase *this momentary lapse* refers to Mr. Ferguson's eyes taken off the road for only a second. It repeats that idea to achieve transition.

One other way to achieve transition is to use synonyms to repeat an idea. Consider these sentences:

```
Jenny has been in bed with strep throat for a week. Her illness
may force her to drop her courses this term.
```

Notice that the second sentence begins with *her illness*. The word *illness* is a synonym for *strep throat*, which appears in the first sentence. This synonym repeats a key idea to achieve transition.

Use Transitions to Connect Paragraphs

Transitions can link ideas between the end of one paragraph and the beginning of the next. When used in this way, transitions tighten organization by demonstrating how the ideas of one paragraph relate to those of another, and they improve the flow of paragraphs by eliminating abrupt shifts.

The transitional devices you have learned so far—using transitional words and phrases, repetition of key words, repetition of key ideas, and using synonyms—can all be used to bridge paragraphs as the following examples show:

1.   *End of one*
      paragraph: The students believe that the proposed
                   library will not meet their needs.

      Beginning of
      next paragraph: In addition, students oppose construction of
                   the library for economic reasons.

Transitional
device: The transitional phrase *in addition* signals that the idea in the second paragraph functions as a supplement to the idea in the first paragraph.

2.   *End of one*
paragraph: Clearly, teacher burnout is a serious problem.

Beginning of
next paragraph: Unfortunately, teacher burnout is not the only serious problem facing our schools.

Transitional
device: ·Repetition of the key words *teacher burnout* and *serious problem* signals the connection between the two paragraphs.

3.   *End of one*
paragraph: For the first time in years, the American divorce rate is beginning to drop.

Beginning of
next paragraph: The reasons for this new trend deserve our attention.

Transitional
device: In the second paragraph, *this new trend* is a repetition of the key idea in paragraph 1, *the American divorce rate is beginning to drop.*

4.   *End of one*
paragraph: All signs indicate that the safety forces strike will continue for at least another week.

Beginning of
next paragraph: If the work stoppage does last seven more days, the effects will be devastating.

Transitional
device: In the second paragraph, *work stoppage* is a synonym for *strike,* which appears in the first paragraph. Also, in the second paragraph, *seven more days* is a synonym for *another week,* which appears in the first paragraph.

EXERCISE | **Transitions**

1. Write sentences and supply transitions according to the directions given. The first one is done as an example.
   a. Write two sentences about the way women are portrayed in television commercials. Link the sentences with a transitional word or phrase signaling contrast.

example: Television ads do not depict women realistically. However, today's commercials are an improvement over those of five years ago.

b. Write one sentence about exams that has a transitional word or phrase of addition to link two ideas.

c. Write two sentences about a television show. Link the sentences with a transitional word or phrase signaling emphasis.

d. Write one sentence about Thanksgiving (or another holiday) that has a transitional word or phrase of contrast.

e. Write two sentences that describe the location of things in your bedroom. Link the sentences with a transitional word or phrase to signal spatial arrangement.

f. Write one sentence about a campus issue with a transitional word or phrase for admitting a point.

g. Write two sentences about someone you enjoy being with. Link the sentences with a transitional word or phrase of illustration.

h. Write two sentences, each about a different relative. Link the sentences with a transitional word or phrase of either comparison or contrast.

i. Write two sentences about what you do upon waking in the morning. Link the sentences with a transitional word or phrase to show time sequence.

j. Write two sentences about your toughest instructor ever. Link the sentences with a transitional word or phrase of clarification.

2. In the following sentences, fill in the blanks with one or more words according to the directions given. The first one is done as an example.

a. *Repeat key word:* I am uncomfortable with the principle behind life insurance. Basically _such insurance_ means I am betting some giant corporation that I will die before my time.

b. *Repeat key word:* Over the years the registration process has become increasingly complex, causing students to become confused and frustrated. This _____ is now being studied by campus administrators in an effort to streamline procedures.

c. *Use a synonym* for *additional week:* Because so many students found it impossible to complete their term papers by Friday, Dr. Rodriguez was willing to give an additional week to work on them. _____ helped everyone feel more comfortable with the assignment.

d. *Repeat key idea:* The Altmans returned from their weekend trip to discover that their house had been broken into and ransacked. _____ was so extensive, it took them two full days to get everything back in order.

e. *Repeat key idea:* According to the current charter, the club's president can serve for only one term. _____ was meant to ensure that there would be frequent change in leadership.

Questions for Evaluating Organization

1. Does every body paragraph have a clearly stated or strongly implied topic sentence that is directly related to the thesis?

2. Have you begun a new body paragraph with each new main point or for some other appropriate reason? Have you avoided ending with a new idea or including more than one main idea in a paragraph?
3. Are all your body paragraphs and supporting details arranged in a logical order?
4. Have you demonstrated the relationships among your ideas and smoothed awkward gaps with transitions?

PROCESS GUIDELINES: REVISING FOR ORGANIZATION

If you have trouble organizing your ideas

a. Try an outlining technique you have not used yet.
b. Ask yourself whether your ideas seem to follow a chronological, spatial, or progressive order.
c. Write your draft without an outline and see what happens. When the draft is complete, check for logical ordering, and if there is a problem, number your ideas in the way you think they should appear.
d. Check to see if instead of having an organization problem, you really lack transitional devices that signal how your ideas relate to one another and flow one to the next.

REVISING FOR EFFECTIVE EXPRESSION

An important part of revising involves evaluating your draft and making changes to be sure you are expressing your ideas as effectively as possible. After all, even the best ideas—if poorly written—will fail to capture and hold a reader's attention. Revising for effective expression is a process that focuses on your words and sentences. The next sections discuss much of what you need to consider. Additional sentence-level concerns are taken up during editing, and these are discussed in Part 3.

Use the Appropriate Level of Diction

Diction means "word choice." Levels of diction can be formal, popular, or informal. A *formal level of diction* is appropriate when you are writing for specialists. If you were writing a government report, an article for a scholarly academic journal, a master's degree thesis, or an annual report for a corporation, you would use a formal level of diction. Typically, formal diction requires strict adherence to all the rules of grammar. Technical language is common, sentences are long, *I* and *you* are not used, and contractions are avoided. The tone is impersonal, humorless, and unemotional.

A *popular level of diction* is used in many magazines, newspapers, and books. Popular diction requires you to adhere to grammar rules, but contractions, *I,* and *you* are usually permissible, as is the expression of emotion and humor. Overall, the tone is more relaxed and the writer's personality can show through. The popular level of diction is suitable for most college essays written in your English class.

An *informal level of diction* is very much like the way you speak to your friends. There are no specialized terms, sentences are short, and slang expressions may appear. Strict adherence to the grammar rules is not expected. Informal diction is not acceptable for college papers (unless you are reproducing someone's exact words), but it is often used for friendly letters, e-mail, and personal journals.

When you revise your papers, be sure that you do not lapse into informal diction.

Use Words with the Appropriate Connotation

Words have both denotation and connotation. *Denotation* is a word's literal dictionary definition; *connotation* refers to the emotions and ideas associated with a word. For example, the denotations of *excited* and *agitated* are similar, but their connotations are different. A negative nervousness is associated with *agitated,* and a positive enthusiasm is associated with *excited.* If you use words with the wrong connotations, you risk alienating your reader and confusing your meaning. For example, notice the different meanings conveyed in these sentences with verbs that have similar denotations but different connotations.

```
Lee chewed the steak.

Lee gnawed the steak.
```

When you revise, pay attention to the connotations of your words.

Avoid Slang and Colloquial Language

Slang is language that originates with one group of people—musicians, teenagers, truck drivers, nurses, athletes, and so forth. Sometimes slang makes its way into wider usage, but regardless, it should be avoided in college essays. Below are some examples of slang that originated with office workers. (Because slang is ever-changing, by the time you read them, they may no longer be current.)

```
I-way (the information superhighway)

ohnosecond (the fraction of a second when you realize you have
made a mistake)

keypal (e-mail pen pal)

Dilberted (exploited by the boss)
```

Colloquial language is informal. It includes abbreviated forms ("b-school" for "business school"), ungrammatical usages ("It's me"), and informal words ("tough break"). Colloquial language is used among friends, with family, and in speech. Generally, colloquial language is not suitable for college essays. The following examples of colloquial language will give you an idea of the kinds of expressions to avoid.

| cool | awesome | feeling lousy | sweet (very good) |
| off the wall | bummed out | having a cow | chill out |

When you revise, eliminate slang and colloquial language.

Use Specific Diction

General words present a broad (and often vague) sense of your ideas, while *specific words* present a more precise sense. Here are some examples to help you appreciate the difference between general and specific words.

General Words	Specific Words
shoe	combat boot
hat	baseball cap
woman	Mrs. Hernandez
went	stormed out
nice	colorful

Most often, you should use specific words because they give the reader a more precise understanding. Consider, for a moment, the following sentence:

I walked across campus, feeling good about the test I just took.

The word *walked* is general and vague. Some of the more specific alternatives to *walked*, ones that would be accurate when combined with *feeling good*, include

| strolled | strutted | bounced |
| sauntered | trotted | lilted |

If we pick a more specific word for *walked*, one sentence we could get is

I strutted across campus, feeling good about the test I just took.

Now we have a more-accurate sense of how the writer moved across campus, because of more-specific word choice. However, there is still room for improvement because *good* is vague and general. Here are some more specific alternatives:

| positive | elated | at ease | delighted | jubilant |
| pleased | satisfied | exhilarated | cheerful | optimistic |

Next let's select a word that works with *strutted*. We need something that conveys lots of good feeling because we strut when we are really feeling up. For example, if we select *exhilarated*, we get

I strutted across campus, exhilarated by the test I just took.

Now that is a more-effective sentence than what we started out with because it is more specific.

When you revise, work to make your sentences more specific by focusing
on nouns and verbs. Instead of general nouns like *magazine, hat,* and *dog,* use the
more-specific *Newsweek, stocking cap,* and *collie.* Instead of general verbs like *said,
moved,* and *drank,* use the more specific *blurted out, bolted,* and *sipped.*

Adding specific modifiers can also make a sentence more precise. For example, instead of "Cans and candy wrappers are on the floor," you can revise to
get "Smashed Coke cans and crumpled Milky Way wrappers are scattered across
the floor."

Of course, you must be careful not to overdo because too much specific
word choice, especially description, can create a bulky, overwhelming sentence,
like this:

> Dozens of smashed, twisted, red-and-white Coke cans, lying bent
> on their distorted sides, and at least forty crumpled, brown,
> wadded-up, misshapen Milky Way wrappers representing two weeks
> of my traditional midnight sugar intake are scattered messily
> in heaps everywhere across the green, plush-carpeted floor of
> my small, third-floor bedroom with its green walls and white
> ceiling.

Use Simple Diction

Some writers believe that effective, sophisticated sentences require big, $20-
words. These people use *pusillanimous* when *cowardly* would do as well—even
better, actually. If these writers do not have words like *egregious* or *inveigle* in their
vocabularies, they pull them out of a dictionary or thesaurus and plunk them into
their writing. When this happens, the writer is guilty of using *inflated language,*
which is overblown usage that makes the writer seem self-important. Such language is wordy and full of important-sounding substitutes for common expressions, like this:

> *Inflated:* It would appear that the functionality of the new
> generation of personal computers can be demonstrated
> most readily by a cursory exhibition.
>
> *Better:* The function of the new generation of computers can
> be shown with a quick demonstration.

Writers who believe "the bigger the words, the better the sentence" forget
that a sentence cannot be effective if the reader cannot understand it. Also, they
do not appreciate that they can be specific and accurate by using the wealth of
simple, clear words they have at their disposal. Consider for a moment the following sentences taken from student essays.

> The impetuous drive of youth mellows into the steady pull of
> maturity.

```
The car vibrated to a halt.
Unnoticed, light filters in beneath the blinds.
```

These sentences are interesting and clear because of the specific word choice. Although specific, the words are simple ones that are part of our natural, everyday vocabularies. Words like *filters, mellows, impetuous, drive, pull, vibrated,* and *halt*—words as simple as these make effective sentences. You need not hunt for high-flown words because specific yet simple words create an appealing style. On the other hand, when writers use unnecessarily big words, the reader is put off by a style that seems unnatural.

In addition to avoiding inflated language, you can keep things simple by avoiding jargon. *Jargon* is the technical language of a particular profession. It is the language of insiders and should only be used when you are addressing the in-group. Thus, you can use terms like *mitochondria* and *endoplasmic reticulum* when you are addressing cellular biologists, but for other audiences, you need more easily understood substitutes.

Use Gender-Neutral Language

We are past the time when it is acceptable to use language that excludes women or that ascribes particular roles to particular genders. Your word choice will reflect that fact if you follow these guidelines:

1. Avoid masculine pronouns that inappropriately exclude females.

    No: Each student should bring his catalog to orientation.

    Yes: Each student should bring his or her catalog to orientation.

    Yes: Each student should bring a catalog to orientation.

    Yes: All students should bring their catalogs to orientation.

2. Use gender-neutral titles.

Yes	No
police officer	policeman
firefighter	fireman
table server	waitress
mail carrier	mailman
chair/chairperson	chairman

    No: The committee will elect its own chairman.

    Yes: The committee will elect its own chairperson.

3. Avoid assigning roles to a single gender.

    No: It is understandable for mothers to worry when their children leave home.

Yes: `It is understandable for parents to worry when their children leave home.`

4. Avoid using terms that demean a gender.

   No: `The company promoted three girls to district manager.`

   Yes: `The company promoted three women to district manager.`

5. Avoid referring to women with the *-ess* suffix.

   No: `Emily is a promising young poetess.`

   Yes: `Emily is a promising young poet.`

Eliminate Wordiness

When you draft, you work to get your ideas down any way you can. Naturally, conciseness is not one of your concerns. However, when you revise for effective expression, you should eliminate unnecessary words. The following tips can help:

1. *Reduce empty phrases to a single word.*

Phrase	Revision
at this point in time	now
in this day and age	now
due to the fact that	because
in many cases	often/frequently
on a frequent basis	often/frequently
has the ability to	can
being that	since
at that time	then
in the event that	if
for the purpose of	so
in society today	today
we as people	we

wordy: `The mayor has the ability to alter that policy.`

revision: `The mayor can alter that policy.`

2. *Eliminate redundancy.* A **redundancy** is a phrase that says the same thing more than once.

Redundancy	Revision
the color yellow	yellow
circle around	circle
mix together	mix

reverted back	reverted
the reason why	the reason
very unique	unique
the final conclusion	the conclusion
true fact	true

wordy: The Joint Chiefs of Staff felt an increased military budget was <u>very necessary</u>.

revision: The Joint Chiefs of Staff felt an increased military budget was <u>necessary</u>.

3. *Eliminate deadwood.* Words that add no meaning are *deadwood,* and they should be stricken.

wordy: Joyce is a clever <u>type of</u> person.

revision: Joyce is a clever person. [Joyce is clever.]

wordy: A multiple choice <u>kind of</u> question is difficult to answer.

revision: A multiple choice question is difficult to answer.

4. *Eliminate unnecessary repetition.*

wordy: The first car in the accident was <u>smashed and destroyed</u>.

revision: The first car in the accident was <u>destroyed</u>.

wordy: I <u>think and believe</u> the way you do.

revision: I <u>think</u> [believe] the way you do.

5. *Avoid opening with "there."*

wordy: <u>There are</u> many things we can do to help.

revision: We can do many things to help.

wordy: <u>There was</u> an interesting mix of people at the party.

revision: An interesting mix of people was at the party.

6. *Reduce the number of prepositional phrases.*

wordy: The increase <u>of</u> violence <u>in</u> this country points to a decline <u>in</u> moral values.

revision: This country's increasing violence points to moral decline.

7. *Reduce the number of "that" clauses.*

wordy: The students asked the instructor to repeat the explanation <u>that she gave earlier</u>.

revision: The students asked the instructor to repeat her
earlier explanation.

wordy: The book <u>that is on the table</u> is yours.

revision: The book on the table is yours.

NOTE: Sometimes words that could be cut out are left in because the sentence works better that way with the sentences before and after it. The trick is to eliminate *annoying* wordiness while using words to achieve a readable style that comes from each sentence flowing well from the previous one. Thus, whether a writer uses "Most people notice right off that Melanie is a sarcastic person" or "Most notice immediately that Melanie is sarcastic" will depend in part on which reads better with the sentences before and after.

Avoid Clichés

A **cliché** is an overworked expression that people are weary of hearing and reading. At one time, a cliché was an interesting way to say something, but as a result of overuse, it has become worn and dull. Below is a list of some clichés you may have heard.

scarce as hen's teeth	vim and vigor	tried but true
sadder but wiser	clear as a bell	bright-eyed and bushy-tailed
cold as ice	black as night	
crawl out from under	over the hill	drank like a sailor
dry as a bone	the quick and the dead	soft as silk
free and easy	free as a bird	hard as nails
cried like a baby		

Avoid clichés and find a more interesting way to express your ideas. Take a look at the following student sentence:

When my father accepted a job in Ohio, my heart sank.

As readers we have no trouble determining what the writer means: He felt bad about his father taking a job in Ohio. Still, the cliché *my heart sank* creates two problems. First, it is vague. Just how bad did the writer feel? Was the writer depressed, scared, or what? Second, the sentence lacks interest because the cliché is dull. Now react to this revision:

When my father accepted a job in Ohio, I lost sleep worrying
about whether I could make new friends.

With this revision, the reader understands both the nature and the extent of the writer's negative feeling. Thus, the revision is the more-effective sentence.

NOTE: Even if you do not view clichés as overworked expressions, keep in mind that a seasoned reader will, which is a good enough reason to avoid them.

Avoid Passive Voice

In the **active voice,** the subject of the sentence *acts.* In the **passive voice,** the subject of the sentence is *acted upon.*

active: The optometrist examined the child's eyes. (The subject, *optometrist,* performs the action of the verb, *examined.*)

passive: The child's eyes were examined by the optometrist. (The subject, *child's eyes,* is acted upon.)

Usually, a writer should use active voice rather than passive voice, because active voice is more vigorous and less wordy, as the following examples reveal.

passive: The ball was thrown into the end zone by the quarterback.

active: The quarterback threw the ball into the end zone.

Another reason to favor active over passive voice is that the passive may not indicate who or what performed the action.

passive: The workers were criticized for their high absentee rate. (Who did the criticizing?)

active: The new corporate vice president criticized the workers for their high absentee rate. (Now we know who did the criticizing.)

Although you should usually choose active over passive voice, sometimes the passive voice is more appropriate, particularly when the performer of the action is either unknown or unimportant.

appropriate passive voice: After germination, the plants are thinned so they are spaced 6 inches apart. (Who thins the plants is not important.)

appropriate passive voice: The chicken was baked until it was tough and tasteless. (The person who baked the chicken is unknown.)

Be wary when a writer or speaker uses the passive voice to hide information.

passive voice used to conceal: I have been told that someone is stealing from the cash register. (The writer or speaker does not want to reveal who did the telling.)

EXERCISE | **Specific Words, Wordiness, Clichés, Active and Passive Voice**

1. Revise the sentences to create more-effective ones by substituting specific words for the general ones. In some cases, you may want to substitute several words for one general word and add additional detail, as in the following example:

   example: The happy boy ran down the street.

   revision: The paper boy sprinted down Ford Avenue, excited that he had finished his route an hour early.

   a. The room was a mess.
   b. By afternoon the child was feeling terrible.
   c. The food tasted awful.
   d. The way that person was driving his car almost caused an accident.
   e. The sound of that baby's cry really bothered me.
   f. The movie was very good.
   g. Carlotta watched the ballplayers practice.

2. Compose a sentence about something you saw, heard, tasted, smelled, or touched today. Revise that sentence until you are satisfied that the diction is specific enough.

3. *Collaborative Activity.* With two classmates, write the following ideas in sentences with specific diction. (You may need to revise a number of times before you are satisfied.)

   example: the pleasant ringing of church bells

   sentence: The melodious ring of St. John's bells announced the start of morning worship.

   a. a squirrel running back and forth across a branch
   b. the smell of brownies baking in the oven
   c. the sound of rain on a roof
   d. a woman wearing too much floral-scented perfume
   e. walking barefoot and stepping on a sharp stone

4. Revise the sentences to eliminate wordiness.

   sample original: The most frightening experience that I think I ever had occurred when I was 15.

   sample revision: The most frightening experience I had occurred when I was 15. [My most frightening experience occurred when I was 15.]

   a. The only audible sound to be heard was the blower of the heater motor as it worked to produce a soft, low hum.
   b. The reason I feel our nation is so great is that both men and women of the species have opportunities to excel.
   c. Until that day I did not realize or consider that people such as Corey are the most dangerous of all because they are so extremely selfish.

    d. In my opinion it seems that a physical education requirement for college students is a complete waste of time.

    e. This particular kind of sport is ideal for the person who desires exercise but is not in the best physical condition in the world.

    f. There are many reasons why beer commercials should be banned from television.

    g. The explanation of my son for why he was home late was the same explanation that he gave me last Saturday night.

    h. The small little package which Jimmy gave Conchetta for her birthday held the ring that was for her engagement.

    i. In the event that I am unable to join you, please start and begin to eat without my presence.

    j. There were six dogs that were roaming the neighborhood which the dog warden found it necessary to take to the city pound.

5. Revise the sentences to eliminate the italicized clichés. You may revise several times before your sentence reads the way you want it to. Also, feel free to add any detail you wish.

    example: My sixth-grade teacher was *mad as a hatter.*

    revision: My sixth-grade teacher was so eccentric that she wore the same faded green dress from September until Christmas break.

    a. Cassandra is never bored because she is always *busy as a beaver.*

    b. *It's a crying shame* that rainy weather spoiled your vacation.

    c. Anyone who can sit through Professor James's lectures deserves a medal, because the man has a *voice that would shatter glass.*

    d. Juan is *happy as a clam* because he got an *A* in calculus.

    e. Poor Godfrey is so clumsy he is *like a bull in a china shop.*

6. Five of the following sentences are in the active voice; five are in the passive voice. Rewrite those in the passive voice so they are in the active voice.

    a. The elaborate sand castle was built by Tina, Jerry, and their father.

    b. By noon, high tide had washed away most of their creation.

    c. While I was shopping in the mall, my purse was snatched by a teenager dressed in torn blue jeans and a green sweatshirt.

    d. The police reported that someone matching that description had stolen three other purses the same day.

    e. The antique necklace I wear so often was given to me by my favorite aunt.

    f. Aunt Sadie collected antique jewelry and gave me a piece every year for my birthday.

    g. A surprise birthday party was thrown for Rhoda by three of her closest friends.

    h. Unfortunately, Rhoda did not arrive when she was expected, so she ruined the surprise.

    i. I asked my academic advisor how to improve my calculus grade.

    j. I was told by my advisor to spend two hours a week in the math lab.

Use Coordination and Subordination

A group of words with both a subject and a verb is a **clause.** If the clause is complete enough to stand as a sentence, it is a **main clause;** if the clause cannot stand as a sentence, it is a **subordinate clause.**

Main clause: this year's citrus crop was damaged by frost

Explanation: This word group has the subject *citrus crop* and the verb *was damaged,* so it is a clause. It is complete enough to be a sentence when a capital letter and period are added, so it is a main clause.

Sentence: This year's citrus crop was damaged by frost.

Subordinate clause: because this year's citrus crop was damaged by the frost

Explanation: This word group has a subject and verb, so it is a clause. However, it is not complete enough to be a sentence, so it is a subordinate clause.

Two main clauses can appear in the same sentence if they are connected by one of the following **coordinating conjunctions.**

and	nor
but	for
or	so
yet	

When writers connect two main clauses in the same sentence, the technique is called **coordination.** Here is an example:

main clause: the storm caused a power failure

main clause: we lit the candles

         main clause   *coordinating conjunction*   *main clause*

coordination: [The storm caused a power failure], <u>so</u> [we lit the candles].

Coordination allows a writer to demonstrate a specific relationship between ideas in the clauses. This relationship is identified by the coordinating conjunction used to connect the clauses, as described below.

1. If the main clauses are connected by *and,* the idea in the second clause functions in addition to the idea in the first:

   The mayor urged a 14 percent budget cut, and he suggested a freeze on municipal hiring.

2. If the main clauses are connected by *but* or *yet*, the idea in the second clause shows contrast to the idea in the first:

   ```
   The temperatures have been unusually warm for December, but
   (yet) it may snow for Christmas.
   ```

3. If the main clauses are connected by *or*, the idea in the second main clause is an alternative to the idea in the first:

   ```
   Your research papers must be handed in on time, or you will
   be penalized.
   ```

4. If the main clauses are connected by *nor*, the idea in the second clause is a negative idea functioning in addition to the negative idea in the first clause:

   ```
   The school board cannot be expected to raise teacher
   salaries, nor can it renovate the high school buildings.
   ```

5. If the main clauses are connected by *for*, the idea in the second clause tells why the idea in the first clause happened or should happen:

   ```
   Television talk shows are popular, for viewers never grow
   weary of watching celebrities talk about themselves.
   ```

6. If the main clauses are connected by *so*, the idea in the second clause functions as a result of the idea in the first clause:

   ```
   Dr. Wesson was ill last week, so our midterm exam is
   postponed until Thursday.
   ```

PUNCTUATION NOTE: As the previous examples show, when two main clauses are joined by a coordinating conjunction, a comma appears before the conjunction.

When writers connect a subordinate clause and a main clause in the same sentence, the technique is called **subordination.** Here is an example:

subordinate clause: `because the storm caused a power failure`

main clause: `we lit the candles`

subordination:
subordinate clause
`[Because the storm caused a power failure],`
main clause
`we lit the candles.`

Subordination allows a writer to demonstrate the specific relationship between the ideas in the two clauses. This relationship is identified by the subordinating conjunction used to introduce the subordinate clause. Below are some common subordinating conjunctions, the relationships they signal, and representative examples. Notice that subordinate clauses can come before or after main clauses.

because
in order that
since
	To show why the idea in the main clause occurs or occurred:
	
	`Because the traffic signal on Dearborn Street`
	`is out, cars are backed up for two blocks.`

after
whenever
as
while
before
when
	To show when the idea in the main clause occurs or occurred:
	
	`Before undergraduates can enroll in upper-`
	`division courses, they must get permission from`
	`their academic dean.`

where
 	
wherever
	To show where the idea in the main clause occurs or occurred:
	
	`Janine always attracts attention wherever she`
	`goes.`

as if
 	
as though
	To show how the idea in the main clause occurs or occurred:
	
	`Jim was out partying last night as if he did not`
	`have any problems.`

if
provided
once
unless
	To show under what condition the idea in the main clause occurs or occurred:
	
	`Once the additional computers are in`
	`place, we can complete the mailing lists.`

although
even though
though
	To admit a point:
	
	`Although enrollment in literature courses has`
	`been down in the last five years, the trend is`
	`beginning to reverse.`

PUNCTUATION NOTE: As the previous examples show, a subordinate clause at the beginning of a sentence is followed by a comma. When the subordinate clause comes at the end of the sentence, a comma is used before the clause only if it shows separation from the rest of the sentence.

Use Parallel Structure

Parallelism means that coordinate sentence elements (elements of equal importance serving the same function) should have the same grammatical form. The following sentence has parallel structure:

`Mrs. Chen found the novel outrageous, offbeat, and shocking.`

The underlined words have the same function (to describe *novel*) and they all have the same degree of importance in the sentence. To achieve parallelism, then, the words all take the same grammatical form—they are adjectives.

If you fail to achieve parallelism, the result is an awkward sentence that weakens style, as in the following example:

```
I have always liked hiking and to swim.
```

Because *hiking* and *to swim* have the same function (they serve as the object of the verb *have liked*), and because they are of equal importance, they should both have the same grammatical form. Yet one is an *-ing* verb form (present participle) and one is a *to* verb form (infinitive). To be parallel, both must be present participles or both must be infinitives.

```
I have always liked hiking and swimming.
I have always liked to hike and to swim.
```

Faulty parallelism occurs most often when writers place items in a series or a pair, when they compare or contrast, and when they use correlative conjunctions. These matters are discussed next.

1. Sentence elements forming a series or pair should have the same grammatical form.

nonparallel: `You can get to Toronto by car, bus, or fly.`

parallel: `You can get to Toronto by car, bus, or plane.`

explanation: The nonparallel series includes two nouns and a verb. Parallelism is achieved by revising to include three nouns.

nonparallel: `Before my first date, Mother told me to be in by midnight and she said I was to be a gentleman.`

parallel: `Before my first date, Mother told me to be in by midnight and to be a gentleman.`

explanation: The nonparallel pair includes a verb (infinitive) phrase and a clause. Parallelism is achieved by revising to include two verb (infinitive) phrases.

2. Items compared or contrasted in a sentence should have the same grammatical form. Consider the following nonparallel sentence.

```
I love a day at the beach more than to spend a day in the
country.
```

This sentence lacks parallelism because the noun phrase *a day at the beach* is contrasted with the verb phrase *to spend a day in the country*. To be parallel, the contrast should be expressed in one of the following ways:

```
I love a day at the beach more than a day in the country. (Two
noun phrases)
```

or

> I love <u>spending a day at the beach</u> more than <u>spending a day in the country</u>. (Two *-ing* verb phrases)

Sometimes parallelism problems crop up because the writer fails to mention the second item being compared or contrasted, as in the following sentence:

> I like small, intimate restaurants better.

This sentence does not indicate what *small, intimate restaurants* is contrasted with. To solve the problem, add the missing contrast.

> I like <u>small, intimate restaurants</u> better than <u>crowded, noisy cafeterias</u>. (Two noun phrases)

3. **Correlative conjunctions** are conjunctions used in pairs. The following are correlative conjunctions.

either . . . or	both . . . and
neither . . . nor	not only . . . but [also]

To achieve parallelism with correlative conjunctions, be sure that the same grammatical structure follows both conjunctions.

nonparallel construction: I want either <u>to spend my vacation in New York City</u> or <u>in Bermuda</u>.

parallel construction: I want to spend my vacation either <u>in New York City</u> or <u>in Bermuda</u>.

explanation: In the nonparallel construction, a verb (infinitive) phrase appears after *either* and a prepositional phrase appears after *or*. In the parallel construction prepositional phrases appear after *either* and *or*.

nonparallel construction: The ballet was both <u>well performed</u> and <u>had lavish sets</u>.

parallel construction: The ballet both <u>was well performed</u> and <u>had lavish sets</u>.

explanation: In the nonparallel construction, *both* is followed by a modifier and *and* is followed by a verb phrase. In the parallel construction, *both* and *and* are followed by verb phrases.

Eliminate Mixed Constructions

A sentence that starts out following a particular sentence pattern and midway switches to another pattern has a problem called **mixed construction.** Consider the following sentences:

> By following my advisor's suggestions, I raised my grade-point average.
>
> Following my advisor's suggestions raised my grade-point average.

If you form one sentence by mixing the patterns of these two sentences, the result is the following problem sentence:

> By following my advisor's suggestions raised my grade-point average.

Here is another sentence with mixed construction:

> Although I need the money will not guarantee I will get the scholarship.

To revise this problem sentence, separate the mixed constructions and use either one of the following improvements:

> Although I need the money, I will not necessarily get the scholarship.
>
> Needing the money does not guarantee that I will get the scholarship.

One way to find mixed constructions is to read your draft aloud or have someone to read it to you so that you can listen for this problem.

NOTE: A mixed construction is often the problem when you sense something is wrong but cannot give the problem a name.

Vary Sentence Structures

To achieve a pleasing rhythm, strive for **sentence variety** by varying sentence structures. With sentence variety you avoid the monotonous rhythm that comes from too many sentences with the same pattern. For example, the following paragraph lacks sentence variety. As you read it, notice how you react.

> My son is in third grade. He told me yesterday that he was one of twelve students selected to take French. Greg is delighted about it. I am annoyed. I feel this way for several reasons. The French classes will be held three days a week. The students will have French instead of their usual reading class. I believe at the third-grade level, reading is more important than French. I do not want my son to miss his reading class. The teacher says Greg reads well enough for his age. I maintain that there is still room for improvement. Some people might say that learning French at an early age is a wonderful opportunity. They say students will be exposed to another language and culture. This will broaden their awareness. This

may be so. I do not think students should be forced into French
for this. They should have a choice of languages to study, the
way they do in high school. Greg might be more interested in
German. He cannot pick German now. He will learn French now.
This means in high school he will probably pick French again.
He will think it will be easier because he already knows some.
He will never be exposed to German or whatever other language
he might like. This is not broadening awareness. This is
narrowing the field. I am concerned about a third grader
learning a new grammar. He does not have English grammar down
pat yet. It would be better to get one thing right before
moving on to another. I suspect Greg will get the two grammars
confused. Teaching French to third graders in place of reading
does not make sense to me.

The paragraph has an unsatisfactory rhythm because all the sentences
begin the same way—with the subject. To achieve sentence variety and improve
your style, include a mix of sentence structures by following the suggestions
below.

1. *Use coordination in some of your sentences.*

examples: Gregory is delighted to be learning French, but I am
annoyed about it.

Third graders are not ready for a foreign language,
and I doubt they will profit much from it.

2. *Begin some sentences with subordinate clauses.*

examples: While I believe the study of French can be
beneficial, I do not feel it should be taught to
third graders at the expense of reading instruction.

If my son is to learn another language, I prefer that
he choose the one he wishes to study.

(For a discussion of coordination and subordination, see page 102–104.)

3. *Begin some sentences with one or two "-ly" words (adverbs).* When you use
two -*ly* words to begin a sentence, these words may be separated in one of four
ways: with a comma, with *and*, with *but*, or with *yet*.

examples: Excitedly, Greg told me of his opportunity to take
French.

Patiently but [yet] firmly, I told Greg I did not want
him to take French.

Loudly and angrily, I told Greg's teacher I did not
want Greg to take French.

> Slowly, thoroughly, Greg's teacher explained why Greg should take French.

PUNCTUATION NOTE: Two -*ly* words are separated by a comma when *and, but,* or *yet* is not used. If one of these words appears, no comma is used. Also, an introductory -*ly* word or a pair of introductory -*ly* words is followed by a comma.

examples: Wearily, I explained to Greg for the fifth time why he would not be taking French.

Loudly and irritably, I argued with the principal about the wisdom of teaching French to third graders.

4. Begin some sentences with the -ing form of a verb. The -*ing* form of a verb is the **present participle,** and it can appear alone, in a pair, or with a phrase.

examples: Sobbing, Greg explained that all his friends were taking French, and he wanted to also.

Whining and crying, Greg left the room convinced that I was a cruel mother.

Understanding his disappointment, I finally agreed to the French instruction.

caution: When you begin a sentence with a present participle—whether it appears alone, in a pair, or with a phrase—be sure the participle and any accompanying words are immediately followed by a word or word group the participle can sensibly refer to. Otherwise you will create an illogical or even silly sentence.

example: Still having trouble with English grammar, it is not the time for Greg to learn French.

correction: Still having trouble with English grammar, Greg is not ready to learn French.

explanation: In the first sentence, the participle and phrase refer to *it,* which causes the sentence to express the idea that *it* was having trouble with English grammar. However, Greg was the one having trouble, so the word *Greg* must appear just after the participle phrase.

5. Begin some sentences with "-ed," "-en," "-n," or "-t" verb forms. These are the **past participle** forms of verbs; they can function alone, in a pair, or with a phrase.

examples: Exasperated, Greg stormed from the room.

Spent from the long discussion with Greg, I took a nap for an hour.

Stricken with grief, Greg cried for an hour because he could not take French.

Frustrated and defeated, I finally allowed Greg to take the French class.

caution: When you begin with a past participle, whether it is alone, part of a pair, or in a phrase, be sure the word or word group immediately following the structure is something the participle can sensibly refer to. Otherwise you will have a silly, illogical sentence.

example: `Delighted by the idea of learning a new language,`
`French class was something Greg looked forward`
`to.`

correction: `Delighted by the idea of learning a new language,`
`Greg looked forward to French class.`

explanation: In the first sentence, *French class* appears just after the past participle phrase. As a result, it seems that the French class was delighted. In the revision, a word to which the participle can sensibly refer appears after the phrase.

PUNCTUATION NOTE: An introductory participle—whether alone, in a pair, or with a phrase—is followed by a comma.

6. *Begin some sentences with "to" and a present-tense verb.* When *to* is used with the present-tense verb form, the structure is called an **infinitive.** Infinitives can appear alone, in pairs, or in phrases, but most often they appear in phrases.

examples: `To understand my reaction, you must realize that I`
`value reading above all other subjects.`

`To be effective, a foreign language curriculum should`
`offer students a choice of languages.`

`To appreciate and to accept my view, you must agree`
`that reading is more important than French.`

PUNCTUATION NOTE: An introductory infinitive—whether alone, in a pair, with a phrase, or with a modifier—is followed by a comma only if the infinitive and any accompanying words are followed by a main clause.

examples: `To study French in third grade, Greg would have`
`to miss his reading class.`

`To study French in third grade seems foolish.`

explanation: In the first sentence, the infinitive phrase *(to study French in third grade)* is followed by a main clause, so a comma is used after the infinitive phrase. In the second sentence, the infinitive phrase *(to study French in third grade)* is not followed by a main clause, so no comma is used after the phrase.

7. *Begin some sentences with a prepositional phrase.* A **preposition** is a word that signals direction, placement, or connection. Common prepositions include the following:

about	among	between	from	of	over	under
above	around	by	in	off	through	with
across	before	during	inside	on	to	within
along	behind	for	into	out	toward	without

A **prepositional phrase** is a preposition plus the words that are functioning with it. Here are some examples:

across the bay   of the United States

before the rush hour   to me

at the new shopping mall   without the slightest doubt

To achieve sentence variety, you can begin some of your sentences with one or more prepositional phrases.

examples: For a number of reasons, I oppose French instruction at the third-grade level.

By my standards, reading is more important than French for third graders.

8. *Vary the placement of transitional words and phrases.* Many transitions can function at the beginning, in the middle, or at the end of a sentence. To achieve sentence variety, vary the placement of these structures.

examples: <u>Indeed</u>, Greg was disappointed that I would not allow him to take French.

He was so disappointed, <u>in fact</u>, that I felt compelled to give in.

This does not mean my belief has changed, <u>however</u>.

9. *Begin some sentences with the subject.* Sentence variety refers to mixing sentence structures to avoid monotony. So by all means, begin some sentences with the subject.

10. *Balance long and short sentences.* Follow a long sentence with a shorter one, or a short sentence with a longer one. While you need not follow this pattern throughout an essay, on occasion it can enhance rhythm and flow.

examples: Although I explained to Greg why I believed he was better off taking reading rather than French, he never understood my view. Instead, he was heartbroken.

I did my best. I reasoned with him, bribed him, and became angry with him, but still I could not convince Greg that he would be better off to wait a few years before studying a foreign language.

| **Coordination and Subordination, Parallelism, Mixed Structures, Sentence Variety**

1. For each general subject, write one sentence with coordination and one with subordination to demonstrate the specific relationships indicated. Try to place some of your subordinate clauses before the main clauses and some of them after. Also remember the punctuation notes on pages 103 and 104. The first one is done for you as an example.

   a. *exams:* (A) coordinate to show contrast; (B) subordinate to admit a point

   > (A.) I have three exams today, but I have time for lunch.
   >
   > (B.) Although Dr. Manolio is known for giving difficult tests,
   >   her exams are always fair.

   b. *spring:* (A) coordinate to show addition; (B) subordinate to show when
   c. *your best friend:* (A) coordinate to show contrast; (B) subordinate to admit a point
   d. *your favorite restaurant:* (A) coordinate to show an alternative; (B) subordinate to show why
   e. *your first day of college:* (A) coordinate to show a result; (B) subordinate to show when
   f. *a miserable cold:* (A) coordinate to continue a negative idea; (B) subordinate to show under what condition
   g. *the first day of summer vacation:* (A) coordinate to show why; (B) subordinate to show when
   h. *a party:* (A) coordinate to show addition; (B) subordinate to show where
   i. *your favorite teacher:* (A) coordinate to show why; (B) subordinate to show how
   j. *a movie you have seen:* (A) coordinate to show result; (B) subordinate to admit a point
   k. *a holiday celebration:* (A) coordinate to show contrast; (B) subordinate to show why

2. Rewrite the following sentences to achieve parallel structure.

   a. The boutique is known for its variety of styles, for its haughty sales clerks, and daring new designs.
   b. The police car sped up the street, its lights flashing, its siren wailing, and roaring its engine.
   c. I find playing tennis to be better exercise than volleyball.
   d. Kim not only has bought a tape deck but also a video recorder.
   e. Susan is beautiful, arrogant, and has been spoiled by her parents.
   f. My neighbor wants either to resurface his driveway or be painting his house.
   g. Carlos plans to attend the university, study biology, and being accepted into medical school.
   h. Neither is the newspaper column timely nor interesting.
   i. Lisa enjoys working for a large corporation for its many chances for advancement, for its excitement, and because of its many fringe benefits.

    j. The research paper was not acceptable because it was late, it was too short, and needed typing.

3. Read each sentence aloud to practice hearing mixed constructions, and then rewrite each sentence to eliminate the mixed patterns.

    a. If we all pitch in and recycle is what will save our environment.

    b. By getting a good night's sleep before an examination will improve a student's performance.

    c. Because rain forests are vital to a stable ecology is the reason they must be protected.

    d. In my residence hall, most of the basketball players live here.

    e. In whole-language learning teaches children all subjects by using speech, reading, writing, and critical thinking.

    f. When students do not pay attention in class causes instructors to lose their patience.

    g. By expanding the mall's hours of operation during the holiday season is one way to increase sales.

    h. Because the building contractor cut corners when he estimated the cost of the job caused a number of things to go wrong with the plumbing and the electrical work.

    i. In assuming the worst will happen creates a self-fulfilling prophecy so the worst does happen.

    j. By exercising regularly can promote psychological well-being as well as physical fitness.

4. Rewrite the paragraph on page 107 to give it sentence variety. Strive for an adequate mix of structures, using as many patterns as you find necessary. You may alter the existing wording, and you may add words (transitions, for example). Of course, there is no single way to revise the paragraph. There may be as many different effective revisions as there are people in your class.

Pitfalls to Avoid

1. **Avoid using an unnatural style.** If you try to impress your reader by sounding overly sophisticated, authoritative, or intellectual, you will end up sounding pretentious. By all means, polish your prose as much as possible, but be yourself and use your own natural style.

2. **Avoid switching levels of diction.** If you are using a formal level of diction for, say, an upper-level research paper, maintain that level. Do not fall into a popular level here and there. Similarly, if you are using the popular level for an essay, do not suddenly become informal or formal. The switches will distract and confuse your reader.

3. **Avoid indiscriminate use of the dictionary and thesaurus.** These are excellent tools when wisely used. However, be sure you fully understand both the denotations and connotations of words you take from these sources. Otherwise, you may lapse into a pretentious style or use words inappropriately.

4. **Avoid potentially offensive usages.** Know your reader well. If your audience is likely to be put off by the use of *chairman*, then use *chair* or *chairperson*; if your reader prefers the term *Asian*, do not lapse into the use of *Oriental*.

Computer Tips

Your word-processing program may have a built-in thesaurus you can use to find more specific alternatives to general words in your draft, or you may be able to buy an add-on program. Be sure, however, that you understand the meanings of words you take from this source.

Use your computer's search-and-replace function to locate general words you are in the habit of using, words like *good, great, nice, awful,* and *bad.* After locating these words, evaluate their appropriateness and make changes as necessary.

Finally, if your computer has a style-check function use it to check your work. Be careful, though, because these tools are not infallible.

Questions for Evaluating Effective Expression

1. Is your level of diction suited to your audience, purpose and topic? Have you maintained that level consistently? Is your diction specific yet simple? Have you avoided clichés?
2. Have you used words with appropriate connotations, being particularly careful of words taken from the dictionary or thesaurus?
3. Have you avoided slang, colloquial usage, and sexist language?
4. Have you avoided potentially offensive usages, wordiness, and passive voice?
5. Have you written in a way that is natural for you? For a mature style, have you used parallel structures and achieved sentence variety? Have you eliminated mixed constructions?

PROCESS GUIDELINES: REVISING FOR EFFECTIVE EXPRESSION

1. If you have trouble finding the "right" words
   a. Read through your draft and underline the words you want to change because they are vague or inaccurate. Study what you have underlined and if you are unable to find the words you want, consult a dictionary or thesaurus for synonyms. Be careful that you understand the meaning of words from these sources.
   b. You may not be able to take out one word and substitute another. Instead, you may have to substitute phrases and sentences for individual words to get the meaning you are after.
   c. If you cannot express your ideas effectively one way, write a different sentence expressing your ideas another way.
   d. When you cannot think of how to word something, imagine yourself explaining what you mean to a friend, and then write the passage the way you would speak it. You may find that you use several words or sentences, but that is fine. You can polish as necessary afterward.
2. If your essay does not flow well
   a. To identify where the flow needs to be improved, read your draft out loud.

b. Look at the structure of your sentences. If too many in a row are the same length, shorten or lengthen where necessary. If too many begin with the same structure, alter the beginning of some sentences.

c. Use coordination and subordination to join ideas.

d. Use transitions to ease flow.

Working Collaboratively: Getting Reader Response

Writers are always looking for advice from others. In fact, professional writers make changes all the time based on the responses of editors, reviewers, and proofreaders. You, too, can benefit from the reactions of others, particularly as you make revision decisions, by asking for reader response.

There is no one correct way to engage in reader response. The best way, of course, is the one that yields the best results for you. You may even find that you favor different procedures for different papers. If you are unsure how to proceed, try one or more of the following procedures:

PROCEDURE 1

Give your reader a copy of your draft, and ask that person to indicate the chief strengths and weaknesses in a summary comment at the end. Ask your reader to be specific, using language like this: "Good intro—it gets my interest; I don't understand the point you are making in paragraph 2—an example would help; paragraph 3 reads well, but I'm not sure how it relates to your thesis; the description at the end is vivid and interesting."

PROCEDURE 2

Give your reader a copy of your draft, and ask that person to write comments directly on the draft and in the margin the way an instructor might. Ask your reader to note strengths and weaknesses.

PROCEDURE 3

Ask your reader to write out the answers to the following questions on a separate sheet of paper.

1. What is the thesis of the essay?
2. Is there anything that does not relate to the thesis?
3. Are any points unclear?
4. Do any points need more explanation?
5. Is there any place where the relationship between ideas is unclear?
6. Does the introduction engage interest?
7. Does the conclusion provide a satisfying finish?
8. What is the best part of the essay?
9. What is the weakest part of the essay?

PROCEDURE 4

Give your reader a list of questions that reflect the concerns you have about the draft, such as "Does the introduction arouse interest?" "Is the example in paragraph 2 detailed enough?" "Is there a better approach to the conclusion?"

PROCESS GUIDELINES: GETTING READER RESPONSE

1. If you are the writer
   a. Use readers who will view your work objectively and who will not be afraid to offer constructive criticism. If your mother likes everything you do no matter what, then do not use her as a reader. If your roommate is uncomfortable giving criticism, that person will not be a helpful reader.
   b. Choose readers who know the qualities of effective writing. A person who has failed English 101 three times may not be the best judge of what is right and wrong with your draft. Students in your writing class, students who have already taken writing and done well, people who write on the job, and writing center tutors all make good choices.
   c. Give your draft to more than one person and look for consensus. When readers agree, their view is likely to be reliable. When readers disagree and you cannot make up your mind about who is right, seek guidance from your instructor or another knowledgeable reader.
   d. Form a group with several classmates and exchange drafts regularly. Meet and discuss with this group several times while your work is in progress.
   e. Evaluate your readers' responses carefully. Weigh the reactions and accept or reject them in a discriminating way. If you are unsure about the reliability of a particular response, ask your instructor to help you decide.
2. If you are the reader
   a. Before commenting, read through the entire draft.
   b. Give reasons for your reactions. For example, rather than say, "Your introduction did not engage my interest," say, "Your introduction did not engage my interest because the opening story is one I have heard many times."
   c. Make suggestions for revision. If you think paragraph 2 needs an example, try to suggest one that the writer might use.
   d. Comment on the strengths as well as the weaknesses.
   e. Avoid commenting on grammar, punctuation, capitalization, and spelling. These are editing concerns. React, instead, to the revision issues: content, organization, and effective expression of ideas.
   f. Avoid overwhelming the writer with too many reactions. Focus on the most important points or the questions the writer has asked you.

Computer Tip

Rather than trading paper copies with your reader, trade disks or send the draft over your computer network. If possible, split the screen and write your reactions next to the draft. Otherwise, use a different font or color to distinguish your comments from the writer's words.

Revising in Stages

As you can tell by now, revising is a time-consuming process that takes in many aspects of the draft. For that reason, the most efficient, effective approach to revision is to work in stages. You might find that one of the following approaches works well for you.

PROCEDURE 1

    a. Read through your draft and make any changes that can be easily handled.
    b. Check that everything is relevant to the thesis and appropriate topic sentence. If something is not relevant, strike it no matter how much it hurts.
    c. Check next to be sure all your points are clear and that all generalizations are supported.
    d. Be sure your points follow logically from one to the next.
    e. Look at your introduction and conclusion. Be sure the former creates interest and the latter brings the essay to a satisfying close.
    f. Go back and attend to anything you were unable to handle earlier.
    g. Finally, review your sentences for effectiveness.

PROCEDURE 2

Start at the top of the revision checklist below, and rework your draft until you can answer yes to every question on the list. As an alternative, answer the questions on pages 82, 90, and 114.

PROCEDURE 3

Revise one paragraph at a time, evaluating and rewriting until one paragraph is polished before going on to the next.

 REVISION CHECKLIST

    1. Did you leave your work before you began to revise and after each complete revision?
    2. Did you view your work from your reader's point of view?
    3. Is your introduction geared to engage your reader's interest?
    4. Does your essay have a clear, narrow thesis that accurately conveys what your essay is about?
    5. Does each body paragraph have a topic sentence (stated or implied) that clearly and accurately conveys what the paragraph is about? Is each topic sentence relevant to the thesis?

6. Are all your points suited to your audience and purpose?
7. Is your supporting detail in each body paragraph adequate? Have you supported every generalization?
8. Is your supporting detail relevant to its topic sentence?
9. Do you have enough support in the body paragraphs to develop your thesis adequately?
10. Are all your ideas clearly expressed?
11. Are the supporting details in a logical order?
12. Did you use transitions to link ideas?
13. Did you write a conclusion geared toward leaving your reader with a positive final impression?
14. Are your sentences and words as effective as you can make them?

Computer Tips

1. Because your screen displays only a small portion of your work at a time, you should study a printed copy of your draft to get a good overall sense of how it is shaping up.
2. Place the revision checklist in a window as a reminder of the revision concerns.
3. If you are unsure whether some parts of your draft need work, place those sections in boldface type to highlight them. Then print your draft and ask a reliable reader to react to the boldface portions.
4. Use your enter key to separate each of your topic sentences from its supporting detail with about five line spaces. With this visual separation, you can better judge how much supporting detail you have for each topic sentence. Add detail as necessary and then reform your paragraphs.

PROCESS GUIDELINES: REVISING STRATEGIES

1. Leave your work after each revision stage or two to restore objectivity. When you return, evaluate your revisions and make further changes before going on.
2. Some writers make their changes directly on the first draft by crossing out, writing above lines and in margins, drawing arrows, and so on. Other writers revise by writing a second draft on fresh paper.
3. Writers often rewrite until they have completed several drafts. It is impossible to know how many drafts a person will write for a particular piece.
4. Some writers cut and tape when they revise. If they decide to alter the sequence of sentences or paragraphs, they can easily move them to a new location.

Student Essay: Revising the Draft

The following is the first revision of the draft that appears on page 77. As you study it, note the attention to content, organization, and effective expression. Also notice that when the author noticed errors, she edited for correctness.

In the '50s or '60s there was a commercial on T.V. that made reference to a big family. It showed the husband and wife looking out their window at a car pulling up to their house with kids in it packed like sardines in a can. The wife screams, "Here come Helen and her hungry brood, what are we gonna do for food?" I really thought at the time that they were referring to my family. Someone in the neighborhood had to have told them about us. My mother's name was Helen. She had seven children. To get us all in the car to go anywhere was a real fiasco. The doctor told her she was built to have ~~kids~~ *babies*.

add family joke about only sleeping together on Saturday

I guess the most devastating fact about being in this large family was not enough money. My dad had a steady job at the bakery as a checker, but the pay was ~~pretty crummy~~ *not very good*. My dad never took a vacation. We needed the money too badly. He had to do some pretty tight budgeting to pay the bills. This lack of money led to many other hardships.

Food was a problem. We never went hungry but the foods we ate were those you could make a large amount of at one time, that stretched a long way and weren't too expensive, like beans, soup, and mush. Since only nine quarts of ~~mild~~ *milk* were delivered to our house, we had to substitute canned milk and water or powdered milk on our cereal quite a few times. We rarely got store bought candy or sweets. We never experienced the privilege of going to a restaurant. ~~Again the culprit is lack of money.~~

never dreaming that one day they would be the in thing and girls would actually want to wear them.

We were never choosy about the clothes we wore. We couldn't afford to be choosy. Since we girls had two older brothers, we ended up wearing old faded jeans,/ₐ I can never remember getting any new clothing. It was always my brothers' or sisters' or someone else's/. The one thing I do remember getting new are shoes. We had one pair each. We wore them a long time ~~till~~ *until* they couldn't be patched and on payday we got a new pair. That was ~~a great~~ *special* feeling.

*tell about
Uncle Charlie*

Professional haircuts were not to be had. We didn't have the money for such frivilous things. My uncle cut everyone's hair. Regular dental work was also out of the question. We only went to the dentist when we had a toothache or when we might loose a tooth through decay.

*3 miles away
in town, &
that was*

We never owned a real nice car. My dad would keep the thing running but you couldn't depend on it to go too far. The grocery store was ∧about the extent of our travel.

As a member of a large family you took a few things for granted: you never took long trips, Christmas was never thought of for its material gain, and birthday parties were unheard of. ⟨These are a few of the disadvantages experienced.⟩?

When I was in eighth grade, I was sitting in English class and the teacher was lecturing. Our principle *pal* appeared in the doorway and calmly said to the teacher that I was supposed to go with him. I wondered what all the mystery was about. I knew I hadn't done anything wrong. What could he want with me? When we reached the corridor I saw my older brother standing there waiting for me. I knew something was wrong. "Dad died," he managed to get out. I couldn't believe it. We hugged and cried.

*tell about
heart attack
from stress.*

Living within a large family structure had meant many hardships, but the hardship of living without a dad was one that would never be overcome. *We seven kids went without a lot, but all we really missed was Dad.*

Collaborative Exercise: Evaluating a Draft

With a group of classmates, study the following draft written by a student. What are the chief strengths and weaknesses of the draft? What revision advice would you give the writer?

The Wrecked Spirit

It was maybe about 4:00 in the morning, the temperature was at a perfect level, and I was feeling good. The sky overhead was clear but down the road a distance, I could see occasional jagged streaks of lightning illuminate the upcoming clouds. I looked over at my friend Rusty, who was sleeping like a baby in the passenger's seat. Unfortunately, the scene did not remain peaceful for much longer. In little less than an hour, we were involved in an accident that was emotionally scarring as well as causing physical scars.

I had been driving about fourteen hours. I was getting a little bleary-eyed. I nudged Rusty out of his slumber, and he took over the wheel. I was startled a while later by a crack of thunder. Rusty seemed to have everything under control, so I went back to sleep. The next time something woke me up, the scene had changed drastically.

Rusty had fallen asleep at the wheel, running off the road into one of the many, very sturdy steel utility poles that line the highway. I tried to move, but my body was pinned down between the seat and the dashboard. After a brief altercation with my surroundings, I was able to get up and over the seat into the back of the car. That's when I found out I was injured. Then I heard the sirens.

The paramedics arrived and did their job. They strapped me to a cot in the ambulance. The last time I had ridden in an ambulance, I was six years old and had been hit by a car. While they worked to get Rusty out of the car, I lay there listening to the buzz saws cutting the wreckage away from his body. After what seemed an eternity, the back door opened and in stepped two men with my best friend between them.

Eventually, we both recovered from the physical injuries. But the emotional side is a different story. Even though it has been six years, I still recall the incident in my memory so vividly. I still have nightmares and feel guilty about talking Rusty into going with me.

I know that accidents are something that you never think about until they happen. Now I know from experience that when they do happen, sometimes you cannot stop thinking about them.

EXERCISE | **Essay in Progress**

Directions: After completing this exercise, save your revision. You will use it later in this chapter as you work toward your completed essay.

1. Review pages 115-119 and make a list of the revising techniques you would like to try—the ones that seem like they might work for you.
2. Use the techniques in your list to revise the draft you wrote in response to the exercise on page 79.
3. Did your revision activities prompt you to return to any earlier stages of the process? If so, which ones?
4. Were you comfortable with the revision procedures you followed? If not, what will you do differently the next time you revise? Why?

EDITING (READER-BASED/REWRITING)

When you edit, you look for mistakes in grammar, usage, capitalization, punctuation, and spelling. Editing is a reader-based activity because even the most tolerant readers are dismayed by misspellings, lack of punctuation, incorrect verbs, and such. If your writing contains frequent or serious lapses in grammar and usage, your reader will doubt your ability and lose confidence in what you have to say. That is, once your reader questions your ability with grammar and usage, that person is a short hop from questioning the validity of your ideas. Furthermore, because many of the rules facilitate communication between writer and reader (the period tells when an idea ends, for example) breaking these rules will undermine your ability to get a message across.

Finding Errors

Before you edit, leave your work to clear your head and restore objectivity. By the time you reach the editing stage, you will be so aware of what you wanted to say that you may see it on the page whether it is there or not. Getting away helps compensate for this tendency.

When you return to your work, look for two kinds of errors: those you have a tendency to make and those that are just slips. Go over your work twice. The first time through, look for the kinds of mistakes you typically make (fragments, lack of parallelism, or whatever), and the second time through identify and edit careless errors. Part 3 of this book is an explanation of the more frequent errors in grammar and usage. Consult this section on points you are unsure of. In addition, the following suggestions can help you find your errors.

PROCESS GUIDELINES: EDITING STRATEGIES

1. Read through your draft *slowly,* studying each word and punctuation mark. To keep your speed down and increase your chances of finding errors, point to each word or punctuation mark with a pen as you go. (Be sure your eyes do not stray past what you are pointing to.)
2. Read your work out loud or speak it into a tape recorder to listen for mistakes. Be very careful to speak *exactly* what appears on the page. It is easy to speak a plural form, for example, when a singular form was actually written; it is easy to speak the word *feel* when *fell* is on the page. To avoid such substitution, speak *very* slowly, focusing for a second on each word. Remember that certain kinds of mistakes cannot be heard. You cannot hear misspellings, nor can you hear certain punctuation, so at least once you should go over your work to check for mistakes visually.
3. Edit typed copy because errors are much easier to spot that way.
4. Professional writers have copy editors who check for errors that the author may have overlooked. You can follow the professionals' lead by asking someone to review your work for mistakes. However, be sure your reader is

knowledgeable enough to spot errors. Also, you cannot relinquish your own responsibility to learn and apply grammar and usage rules by assuming someone else can always correct your errors for you. Ultimately, the responsibility for finding your mistakes rests with you. A reliable reader functions only to catch the occasional errors that get by you.

5. Trust your instincts. If your internal alarm sounds, assume there is a problem. If you cannot identify or solve the problem, get help from your instructor or another knowledgeable reader, perhaps a writing center tutor.

6. Some writers combine revising and editing. As they rework their first draft, they consider grammar and usage at the same time they deal with content, organization, and effective expression. To do this, a writer must have strong grammar and usage skills.

7. Keep track of your mistakes to learn your pattern of error. If your instructor notes your tendency to misuse commas, you can study the comma rules in Part 3 of this text; if your instructor notes frequent misspellings, you can check your dictionary more often.

Computer Tips

1. If your word-processing program has grammar and spelling checkers, use them, but understand their limitations. For example, your program cannot tell if you have used *their* and *there* correctly; it can only tell if your spelling of these words corresponds to what it has in its dictionary.

2. After revising, quadruple space your text. Finding errors may be easier that way because fewer words will enter your field of vision and distract you. After editing, reformat your text.

3. Edit one time looking at the screen and one time looking at printed copy.

4. If you have problems with specific points of grammar, check Part 3 for specific tips on editing with the computer or word processor.

Student Essay: Second Draft with Revisions and Editing

The following draft resulted when the student author revised and edited the draft on page 119.

In the '50s or '60's there was a commercial on T.V. that made reference to a big family. It showed the husband and wife looking out their window at a car pulling up to their house with kids in it packed ~~like sardines in a can~~. The wife

as tightly as olives in a jar.

screams, "Here comes Helen and her hungry brood, what are we gonna do for food?" I really thought at the time that they were referring to my family. Someone in the neighborhood had to have told them about us. My mother's name was Helen. She had seven children. To get us all in the car to go anywhere was a real fiasco. The doctor told her she was built to have babies, and she tried to prove him right by having two in one year. The weird thing about our large family was that my mom and dad only slept together one night a week. My dad was a checker in a bakery and worked all night. He only had Saturday evenings off. The relatives would always kid my parents about this. Nevertheless, seven kids were the end result, and I don't mean lucky number seven.

I guess the most devastating fact about being in this large family was not enough money. My dad had a steady job ~~at the bakery as a checker~~, but the pay was not very good. ~~My dad never took a vacation. We needed the money too badly~~. He had to do some pretty tight budgeting to pay the bills. This lack of money led to many ~~other~~ hardships.

Food was a problem. We never went hungry but the foods we ate were those you could make a large amount of at one time, _and_ that stretched a long way and weren't too expensive. ~~like beans, soup, and mush~~. Since only nine quarts of milk were delivered to our house, we had to substitute canned milk and water or powdered milk on our cereal quite a few times. We rarely got store-bought candy or sweets. We never experienced the privilege of going to a restaurant.

Soups like potato, bean, and vegetable; poor man's stew; hamburgers; oatmeal; and mush were usually on the menu.

We were never choosy about the clothes we wore. We couldn't afford to be choosy. Since we girls had two older brothers, we ended up wearing old faded jeans, never dreaming that one day they would be the in thing and girls would <u>want</u> to wear them. I can never remember getting any new clothing. It was always my brothers' or sisters' or someone else's. The one thing I do remember getting new are shoes. We had one pair each. We wore them a long time until _the holes_ ~~they~~ couldn't be patched _with cardboard_ _then_ and on payday we got a new pair. That was a special feeling.

We would make chocolate oatmeal fudge or ice cream from the snow in the winter.

Professional haircuts were not to be had. We didn't have the money for such fri_v_ilous things. My uncle cut everyone's hair. I can remember my Uncle Charlie coming over with his barber shears and electric razor. He'd start with my dad and go on down the line. "Who's next for a trimming," he'd _ask_ ~~say~~. Only the brave would step forward. His haircuts left something to be desired. Regular dental work was also out of the question. We only went to the dentist when we had a toothache or when we might lose a tooth through decay.

We never owned a real nice car. My dad would keep the thing running, but you couldn't depend on it to go too far. The grocery store *was* three miles away in town, and that was about the extent of our travel.

As a member*s* of a large family ~~you~~ *we* took a few things for granted, ~~you~~ *we* never took long trips, Christmas was never thought of for its material gain, and birthday parties were unheard of.

When I was in eighth grade, I was sitting in English class and the teacher was lecturing. Our principal appeared in the doorway and calmly said to the teacher that I was supposed to go with him. / *Fill this gap* I wondered what all the mystery was about. I knew I hadn't done anything wrong. What could he want with me? When we reached the corridor I saw my older brother standing there waiting for me. I knew something was wrong. "Dad died," he managed to get out. I couldn't believe it. We hugged and cried. Later I found out my dad had a heart attack. The stress of raising a large family with never enough money had taken its *final* toll.

Living ~~within~~ *in* a large family ~~structure~~ had meant many hardships, but the hardship of living without a dad was one that would never be overcome. We seven kids went without ~~a lot~~ *a great deal*, but all we really missed was our dad.

EXERCISE | **Editing**

1. What kinds of grammar and usage errors are you in the habit of making? To answer this question, you can consider the mistakes instructors have pointed out on your past papers.
2. Go to the table of contents. Based on your answer to number 1, what sections of Part 3 should you study? Devise a plan for studying those sections.

PROOFREADING (READER-BASED/REWRITING)

After checking for grammar and usage mistakes and editing accordingly, type your work into its final form, the form for submission. If you are writing for an instructor, he or she may have requirements for the final manuscript. Be sure you understand and fulfill these requirements, which may speak to such things as margins, placement of name and title, the amount of crossing out permitted, and so on.

After typing your essay into its final manuscript form, you should run one last check for errors by proofreading. Proofreading is a necessary final step because writers make mistakes when typing. It is easy to leave a word out, lapse into a misspelling, and so on.

Proofreading can be handled much the same way as editing. The first step is to leave the final version for a while, to clear your head and regain objectivity. Remember, at no other point are writers as close to their work as here at the end, and so the tendency to see what was *intended,* rather than what *is,* is now most pronounced.

Because of this tendency, you must proofread slowly, one word or punctuation mark at a time. A quick reading through of your work is not proofreading. Use your pen to point to each word and punctuation mark as you read to keep yourself from building up speed that can cause you to overlook an error.

If you discover a mistake while proofreading, most instructors will allow you to ink in the correction neatly. However, use your judgment. If you have many corrections on a page, type it over. The overall appearance of your work can affect a reader's reaction. If you do retype a page, remember to proof again for mistakes.

Student Essay: Editing and Proofreading the Draft

After revising, editing, and proofreading the draft that appears on page 123, the student author produced the final version of her essay that appears below.

Helen's Hungry Brood

In the 1950s or 1960s there was a commercial on television that made reference to a big family. It showed the husband and wife looking out their window at a car pulling up to their house with kids in it packed as tightly as olives in a jar. The wife screams, "Here comes Helen and her hungry brood, what are we gonna do for food?" I really thought at the time that they were referring to my family. Someone in the neighborhood had to have told them about us. My mother's name was Helen. She had seven children. To get us all in the car to go anywhere was a real fiasco. The doctor told her she was built to have babies, and she tried to prove him right by having two in one year. The weird thing about our large family was that my mom and dad only slept together one night a week. My dad was a checker in a bakery and worked all night. He only had Saturday evenings off. The relatives would always kid my parents about this. Nevertheless, seven kids were the end result, and I don't mean lucky number seven.

I guess the most devastating fact about being in this large family was not enough money. My dad had a steady job, but the pay was not very good. He had to do some pretty tight budgeting to pay the bills. This lack of money led to other hardships.

Food was a problem. We never went hungry, but the foods we ate were those that you could make a large amount of at one time, that stretched a long way, and that weren't too expensive. Soups like potato, bean, and vegetable; poor man's stew; hamburgers; oatmeal; and mush were usually on the menu. Since only nine quarts of milk were delivered to our house, we had to substitute canned milk and water or powdered milk on our cereal quite a few times. We rarely got store bought candy or sweets. We would make chocolate oatmeal fudge or ice cream from the snow in the winter. We never experienced the privilege of going to a restaurant.

We were never choosy about the clothes we wore. We couldn't afford to be choosy. Since we girls had two older brothers, we ended up wearing old faded jeans, never dreaming that one day they would be the in thing and girls would *want* to wear them. I can never remember getting any new clothing. It was always my brothers' or sisters' or someone else's. The one thing I do remember getting new are shoes. We had one pair each. We wore them until the holes couldn't be patched with cardboard, and then on payday we got a new pair. That was a special feeling.

Professional haircuts were not to be had. We didn't have the money for such frivolous things. My uncle cut everyone's hair. I can remember my Uncle Charlie coming over with his barber shears and electric razor. He'd start with my dad and go on down the line. "Who's next for a trimming?" he'd ask. Only the brave would step forward. His haircuts left something to be desired. Regular dental work was also out of the question. We only went to the dentist when we had a toothache or when we might lose a tooth through decay.

We never owned a real nice car. My dad would keep the thing running, but you couldn't depend on it to go too far. The grocery store was three miles away in town, and that was about the extent of our travel.

As members of a large family we took a few things for granted; we never took long trips, Christmas was never thought of for its material gain, and birthday parties were unheard of.

When I was in eighth grade, I was sitting in English class and the teacher was lecturing. Our principal appeared in the doorway and calmly said to the teacher that I was supposed to go with him. I rose from my seat with my books in hand and followed him into the empty hallway. "Take your books to your locker, Emma," he said. I did as I was told, not saying a word. The slamming of my locker door sounded like a small bomb exploding in the quietness. "Please come with me to the office," he instructed. I wondered what all the mystery was about. I knew I hadn't done anything wrong. What could he want with me? When we reached the corridor I saw my older brother standing there waiting for me. I knew something was wrong. "Dad died," he managed to get out. I couldn't believe it. We hugged and cried. Later I found out my dad had a heart attack. The stress of raising a large family with never enough money had taken its final toll.

Living in a large family had meant many hardships, but the hardship of living without a dad was one that would never be overcome. We seven kids went without a great deal, but all we really missed was our dad.

EXERCISE | **Essay in Progress**

1. Consider how frequently you make errors in grammar, usage, spelling, capitalization, and punctuation. Do you make them often enough to warrant editing in a separate step?
2. Using procedures you already know work for you or ones described in this chapter, edit the draft you revised for the exercise on page 121.
3. Leave your edited draft for at least half a day and then type your essay. Proofread the final version using procedures proven successful for you or ones described in this chapter.
4. If you completed all the "Essay in Progress" exercises, you sampled procedures for each stage of the writing process. Which of these procedures worked well enough for you to use in the future? Which of these procedures will you not use again? Which procedures might you try in place of the ones that did not work well for you?

NOTE: Your instructor may ask you to submit your completed essay.

PART 2

Patterns of Development

CHAPTER 4

Description

Writers of description use words to create pictures in the reader's mind. Sometimes writers use observable, factual details expressed in unemotional language to create an **objective description.** For example, a real estate appraiser who describes a house to determine its fair market value would write an objective description of the house. Other times, writers want to convey their feelings about what they are describing, or they want to create certain feelings in the reader. At such times, writers use more expressive language to describe. This is **subjective description.**

Notice the difference between the factual language of objective description and the expressive language of subjective description in these two examples, taken from selections in this chapter:

objective
description: It was like every other house in Jalco, probably
larger. The adobe walls were thick, a foot or
more, with patches of whitewash where the thatched
overhang protected the adobe from the rain. There
were no windows. The entrance doorway was at one
end of the front wall, and directly opposite the
door that led to the corral. ("A Mexican House")

subjective
description: Night in midtown is the noise of tinseled honky-
tonk and violence. Thin strains of music, usually
the firm beat of rock 'n' roll or the frenzied
outbursts of the discotheque, rise from ground
level. This is the cacophony, the discordance of
youth, and it comes on strongest when nights are
hot and young blood restless. ("The Sounds of the
City")

ESTABLISHING YOUR PURPOSE AND IDENTIFYING YOUR AUDIENCE

People write description for a number of reasons. Sometimes they want to *relate experience* or *express feelings*. For example, you may want to describe your childhood home to a reader, and you may even want that reader to understand *why* you recall that home so fondly. Or perhaps you want your reader to understand the effects your perception has had on you—why, for example, you are so depressed by learning that your childhood home has fallen into disrepair.

Writers can also describe in order to *inform* a reader, perhaps by helping the reader experience something new or come to a fresh appreciation of the familiar. You could, for example, describe a newborn calf for a reader who has never seen one, or you could describe an apple to help your reader rediscover the joys of this simple fruit.

Description can also have a *persuasive* purpose. Say, for example, that you want to convince your reader that music videos often degrade women. You might describe a degrading video to make your point. Of course, good description is always enjoyable to read, so writers can also describe in order to *entertain* their audience.

The purpose for your description will influence detail selection. Say that you wish to describe your car and that you want your reader to understand the car is a reflection of your outgoing personality. In this case, you might describe the flashy colors, custom dash, unusual hood ornament, elaborate sound system, and so forth. Now say you want your reader to come to a fresh appreciation of the familiar. In this case, you might describe the features of your car that show it to be a marvel of engineering. If, however, you want to convince your reader to view your car as you do (as, say, something that does more harm than good), you might describe the features that contribute to air and noise pollution, that contribute to laziness, that can kill, and so on.

Audience, like purpose, affects detail selection. How much your reader knows about your subject, how your reader feels about your subject, how interested your reader is in your subject—these factors influence your choice of details. For example, say you plan to describe the beauty of your campus commons in winter. If your reader is from a warm climate and has never seen snow, you will have to provide more details to create mental images than you would if your reader were familiar with snow. If your reader hates winter, you will have to work harder to help him or her appreciate the beauty than you would if your reader enjoyed winter. Because audience is so important to detail selection, keep clearly in mind who your reader is as you approach your description.

COMBINING DESCRIPTION WITH OTHER PATTERNS

Because description adds interest and helps the reader form mental images, writers often use it with other patterns of development. For example, if you narrate a story, you might describe a person or setting to add vividness. If you compare and contrast two restaurants, you might include a description of their decors; if you explain the effects of not having zoning laws, you might describe what an area without zoning laws looks like; if you classify the kinds of jazz, you might include a description of what the different kinds of jazz rhythms sound like; if you write a definition of *tacky,* you might illustrate with descriptions of tacky items. Thus, description is a good way to provide specific detail; it can often help you show and not just tell. You are likely to use it often, no matter what your dominant pattern of development.

For an example of how to combine description with other patterns, read "The Way to Rainy Mountain" on page 149. In this selection, the author combines description with both narration and cause-and-effect analysis to create a vivid, moving reminiscence.

USING DESCRIPTION BEYOND THE WRITING CLASS

You are likely to find yourself using description in many of your other classes. For example, in a paper for an advertising class, you might describe the persuasive visuals in several print advertisements. In a botany lab report, you might describe a plant cell you view under a microscope; in an exam for an art appreciation course, you might describe the techniques of a particular artist; and in a history paper, you might describe the condition of the economy just after the stock market crash of 1929.

Outside the classroom, there are also many occasions to use description. Travel brochures describe vacation sites to entice people to visit them; your campus admissions office prints brochures with descriptions of your campus to convince prospective freshmen to attend; a magazine cooking column describes what a fresh melon looks, smells, and feels like to help the reader select the best fruit; a newspaper account of a tornado describes the damage done by the storm; a tribute to a retiring executive will describe his traits and accomplishments; a real estate listing describes the property for sale; a recipe describes what the finished dish looks like; and so forth.

SELECTING DETAIL

Assume that the attic of your grandmother's house has intrigued you since you were a small child, so you decide to write a descriptive essay about it. Or assume that your grandmother herself has always interested you, so you decide to describe *her* in an essay. Either way, one thing is clear: you cannot describe *everything* about your subject. If you tried to include every detail about your grandmother or her attic, the result would be an unwieldy essay. Then how do writers decide what to include and what to omit? You already know part of the answer: Writers base their detail selection on their audience and purpose.

Something else you can do to avoid describing everything about your subject is to settle on one *dominant impression* and describe only those features that contribute to that impression. For example, if your grandmother's attic has always intrigued you because it is eerie, full of reminders of the past, and unusual, pick one of these three impressions to form the dominant impression and thereby supply the focus of your description. Then describe only those features of the attic that convey the impression you have settled on. Similarly, if your grandmother is interesting because she is enthusiastic, eccentric, and young at heart, decide which of these three qualities will be your focus and then describe only features that convey that dominant impression.

To see how description can focus on one impression, read the following paragraph written by a student.

> It was late last night as I reluctantly took the steps down to the gloomy fruit cellar. Its dark, dusty shelves are located behind the crumbling basement walls. I fumbled in the dark for the lifeless screw-in light bulb and managed to twist it to a faint glow. With that the musty room was dimly lit, and long dark shadows lurked on the ceiling, picturing enlarged, misshapen jars of fruit. Water condensed and dripped from the ceiling, shattering the eerie silence. Cobwebs suspended in every corner hid their makers in a gray crisscross of lines. Hesitantly I took a step, my sneakers soaking up the black water lying 2 inches deep on the floor. A rat darted through a hole in the wall, and jars of fruit peered at me with their glassy eyes. The rotting shelves looked as if at any moment they would fall to the floor. The cold, gray walls reminded me of an Egyptian tomb forgotten long ago. Yet mummies don't decay, and I distinctly smelled the odor of something rotting.

Concrete Sensory Detail

When you write description, your goal is to create vivid mental images for your reader, and to do that, you will use **concrete sensory detail,** which consists of specific words that appeal to the senses (sight, sound, taste, smell, touch). Look back at the paragraph describing the fruit cellar and notice the strong mental images created with concrete sensory detail. Take, for example, the sentence, "Cobwebs suspended in every corner hid their makers in a gray crisscross of lines." The detail here is *sensory* because it appeals to the sense of sight. It is *concrete* (specific) because of specific words like *suspended* and *crisscross of lines*. This specific detail that appeals to the sense of sight creates a picture in the mind of the reader much more vivid than one that would be formed from something like "cobwebs were in every corner hiding their spiders."

Notice too that the writer appeals to more than just the sense of sight. He also includes sound (water "shattering the eerie silence"), smell ("the odor of something rotting"), and touch ("feeling the dampness at my back"). While description typically relies more on one sense than the others, impressions are most clearly conveyed when the writer brings in as many senses as are pertinent. Be careful, though. Too much concrete sensory detail bombards your reader with mental images; too much of it and your reader will think, "Enough already; give it a rest." To realize that this is true, read and react to the following sentence:

```
The small, fluffy, gray terrier danced and jumped with
excitement and pleasure as her master took the hard, crunchy,
brown dog biscuit from the large red-and-white sack.
```

This overdone sentence illustrates that descriptive writers must exercise some restraint and recognize when enough is enough. This principle of restraint holds true in paragraphs as well. Often when you have a complex, highly descriptive sentence in a paragraph, you should have a more-simple, less-descriptive one next to it. Consider the following two sentences from "The Sounds of the City," on page 142.

```
Trash cans rattle outside restaurants. Metallic jaws on
sanitation trucks gulp and masticate the residue of daily
living, then digest it with a satisfied groan of gears.
```

The second, very descriptive sentence appears next to a shorter and less descriptive one to create balance and prevent the reader from feeling overwhelmed.

NOTE: Concrete sensory detail is best achieved with specific, simple diction, which is explained on page 93.

Similes, Metaphors, and Personification

Similes, metaphors, and personification are forms of figurative language that can help you create vivid descriptions. A *simile* uses the words *like* or *as* to compare two things that are not usually seen as similar. For example, automobile tires are not typically compared to a brook, but they are in this simile from paragraph 2 of "Dawn Watch" on page 144:

```
One car at a time goes by, the tires humming almost like the
sound of a brook a half mile down in the crease of a mountain
I know. . . .
```

A *metaphor* also compares two things not usually seen as similar, but it does so without using the words *like* or *as*. For example, a cat is not usually compared to a "poolroom braggart," but in paragraph 5 of "Dawn Watch," the author writes this metaphor:

```
My neighbor's tomcat comes across the lawn, probably on his way
home from passion, or only acting as if he had had a big night.
I suspect him of being one of those poolroom braggarts who
can't get next to a girl but who likes to let on that he is a
hot stud.
```

Personification grants human qualities, emotions, or sensibilities to nonliving objects, animals, or ideas. Consider this example of personification, which grants a human characteristic to a taxicab, taken from paragraph 7 of "The Sounds of the City":

`Taxicabs blaring, insisting on their checkered priority.`

Although similes, metaphors, and personification can help you create mental images for your reader, you should use them sparingly so that you do not overwhelm your reader with too much figurative language.

ARRANGING DETAIL

The thesis for a descriptive essay can note what you are describing and the dominant impression you have formed about what you are describing, like this:

`As a child, and now as an adult, I have always been drawn to Grandma's attic because it is filled with reminders of the past.`

The thesis indicates that Grandma's attic will be described, and the impression is that it is filled with reminders of the past.

When you form your thesis, express your impression in specific language. Impressions expressed in words like *nice, great, wonderful, awful, terrible,* and *bad* are vague and do not tell the reader much. However, words like *relaxing, scenic, cheerful, depressing, congested,* and *unnerving* are specific and give the reader a clearer understanding of how you feel about what you are describing.

As an alternative, your introduction can state what you are describing *without* specifying your impression. With this technique, the reader gathers the impression from the details in the body.

Of course, your body paragraphs form the heart of your essay. Here you provide the descriptive details that bear out your impression of your subject. You can approach the arrangement of descriptive details several ways. If you are describing a place, **spatial order** is useful. You can move from left to right, top to bottom, near to far, the center to the periphery, or the inside to the outside. Sometimes a **progressive order** is effective. You can arrange your details so that they build to the features that most clearly or strikingly convey your impression. A **chronological order** can even be effective at times, as when you are describing what you see as you move through a place.

Sometimes the best way to organize a description is by sensory impressions. For example, if you are describing a ballpark during a game, you could first describe the sights, then the sounds, next the smells, and so forth.

Annotated Student Essay

Studying the following descriptive essay written by a student, along with the marginal annotations, will help you better understand the points made in this chapter.

🎋 A Child's Room

paragraph 1

The introduction engages interest with background information and amusing exaggeration. The thesis is the last sentence. It notes that the sight [of the son's room] will be described and that the dominant impression is methodical disorder. Some may question whether the detail supports the idea of "methodical."

paragraph 2

The first sentence is the closest thing to a topic sentence. It directs the reader's attention to the floor. Note the personification (the toys are engaged in battle) and concrete sensory detail (words like "flame red cape" and "dilapidated wrecker.") Details appeal to both sight and sound ("wail of a train whistle"). Both subjective and objective description appear.

paragraph 3

The first sentence is the topic sentence. It presents the arsenal as the focus. The transition "another corner" indicates a spatial arrangement. Note the specific nouns ("arsenal"), verbs ("dangles"), modifiers ("spent"), and personification. The description is subjective. The author's purpose seems to be to entertain and relate experience.

paragraph 4

The first sentence is the topic sentence. It presents the focus on the bureau. Spatial and chronological

1   I avoid going into my son's domain as often as I can. I like to keep life and limb intact, but there are times when it is impossible to escape the risk. One such time is in the evening when I have to carry him to his bed after he has fallen asleep in mine. Then, armed with a soporific child and a will to come out unharmed, I reluctantly approach his door and push it open. The sight that greets me is one of methodical disorder.

2   On the floor, a battle is being fought between the Super Heroes and the Ghostbusters. Superman, in his red silk shorts and flame red cape, is mounting the steps of the enemy's headquarters as the Marshmallow Man looms down at him from high atop the chimney. He-Man is fighting a green plastic dragon under a corner of the bed. The wail of a train whistle is heard as the 550 Express bears down on them on its endless journey around the room. Spilling out of one corner is the largest auto salvage yard in the United States. Matchbox cars are everywhere, and they are in every stage of disrepair. A rusted station wagon is missing a wheel, and next to it is a little red Volkswagon minus its hood and a door. A dilapidated wrecker has backed up to a worn-out bus and attempts to haul it away.

3   Another corner boasts an arsenal big enough to appeal to a hostile nation. Water guns, submachine guns, and popguns line the wall expectantly awaiting the next encounter with the enemy. Strewn across the floor are grenades and spent shotgun shells; they lay claim to the proximity of the battleground. A forgotten leather holster dangles from his hobby horse. This is all evidence of a hurried retreat.

4   Still warily treading my way across the room, and with my eyes darting between the floor and the bed, I spot his bureau out of the corner of my eye. The

order are indicated by "still warily treading my way across the room." Concrete sensory detail includes sight and smell ("stinky" socks). The last two sentences are personification. The description is mostly objective.

bureau is a tall, stately antique with a large fuzzy mirror, and it is too short on drawers. It seems to be leaning ever so slightly to the right, as if ready to call it a day, or maybe just to rest its load. The load is made up of various articles of clothing. A grimy baseball shirt hangs from the top of the mirror, and muddy, stinky, rolled-up socks have been tossed about the marble top. Underwear, new and used, hangs from every knob. Clean clothes, half folded, have been tossed out of drawers and left in heaps on the floor. Worn and tired jeans hang from belts caught by the corners of the tall bureau. It pleads to be released from its burden.

paragraph 5
The first sentence is the topic sentence. It presents the focus as the bed. The transition "at last" notes chronological order. Note the personification (stuffed animals are fighting) and the metaphor of the teddy bear as a monarch who "reigns." Specific words include "rumpled," "soulful eyes," and "nestled."

His rumpled bed is within reach at last. As I get ⁵ ready to lighten my load, I see that it is still impossible. His bed has been taken over by the Cleveland Zoo. A woolly bear is curled up at the bottom of the bed. A monkey and an elephant fight for a spot next to him. The soulful eyes of a stuffed beagle look up at me as if to say, "Don't move me." Three pigs are nestled between the pillows, and on top of one pillow is a white furry kitten already in a world of dreams. A large teddy bear reigns over the other pillow and spins his tales of adventure to a crowd of chipmunks. I hold my precious bundle with one hand, and I make a clean sweep of the animals with the other hand only to find sticky candy wrappers, half-eaten candy bars, and more surprises waiting for me under the covers.

paragraph 6
The conclusion completes the chronology (the author leaves the room) and introduces the related idea that tomorrow will bring more play and mess.

At last the moment arrives, and I can gently lay ⁶ him down and tuck him in against the night. I turn around and creep out of this room past all the toys in their various states of play, and I know that tomorrow will bring more imaginative play and a bigger mess for me to wade through.

Pitfalls to Avoid

1. **Avoid creating inadequate mental images.** You cannot describe every feature, so to some extent, your description will necessarily be incomplete. However, you must give your reader enough descriptive details that he or she can form adequate mental images. The best way to do that is to remember that while the object of your description is vivid in *your* mind, your reader probably has not seen what you are describing and, therefore, needs rich detail.

2. **Avoid too much figurative language.** A few similes and metaphors, a little personification—these go a long way. Overdo these techniques and your writing is likely to become too ornate and overwhelming. Also, do not feel you must use all these techniques—or even one of them. If you are not comfortable with one or more of them, do not use them.

3. **Avoid cataloging.** A description—even objective description—must be more than a listing of items. Thus, avoid writing like this: "To the left is my stereo set, and sitting on the speakers are my softball trophies. Immediately to the right of the stereo is my autographed picture of Susan Lucci."

4. **Avoid details that do not convey your dominant impression.** If you are describing your bedroom as a model of order, do not mention the dirty clothes on the closet floor.

5. **Avoid shifting your vantage point.** If you are describing the view from your classroom window, do not describe the ants marching along the sidewalk across the street, as you cannot see them from where you are located.

PROCESS GUIDELINES: WRITING DESCRIPTION

1. To decide on a person or place to describe and on your impression of your subject, fill in the blanks in the following sentence: _____ is the most _____ I know. Fill in the first blank with a person or place (your subject), and fill in the second blank with a characteristic (your impression). You will get something like "The student cafeteria at noon is the most hectic place I know," which will lead to a description of the hectic nature of the cafeteria at 12:00. Be careful to use specific words to fill in your blanks and to pick manageable subjects, so you do not end up with something too broad or vague, something like "Wichita is the most interesting city I know." All of *Wichita* is too much to handle in one essay, and *interesting* is too vague to be useful to the reader.

2. If you are describing a place, select one that you can visit and observe. If this is not possible, select one that is fresh and detailed in your memory.

3. If you have trouble determining a dominant impression, fill in the blanks in these sentences:
   a. My subject makes me feel _____.
   b. My subject is important to me because _____.
   c. My first impression of my subject is _____.

    d. The word that best describes my subject is _____.

    e. When I am near my subject, my mood is _____.

4. To determine your purpose, you can ask yourself these questions:
    a. Can I help my reader understand why I perceive my subject a particular way?
    b. Can I help my reader understand the effect my perception has on me?
    c. Can I help my reader appreciate something he or she has not experienced before?
    d. Can I help my reader achieve a fresh appreciation for something familiar?
    e. Can I convince my reader to view something the same way I do?

5. To establish an audience, you can ask yourself these questions:
    a. Who would enjoy reading my description?
    b. Who would learn something from my description?
    c. Who shares an interest in my subject?
    d. Who could be persuaded to view my subject as I do?
    e. Whom would I like to share my perceptions with?
    f. Who would find my subject important?
    g. Who could come to appreciate my subject by reading my essay?

6. To gear your detail to your reader's needs, you can answer these questions:
    a. How much experience has my reader had with my subject?
    b. How does my reader currently view my subject?
    c. What does my reader need to know about my subject?
    d. What strong feelings does my reader have about my subject?
    e. How much interest does my reader have in my subject?
    f. How receptive will my reader be to my point of view?

7. List writing can be an effective idea-generation technique. When describing a place, make your list at that place. When describing a person, observe the person before describing physical appearance and mannerisms. As you write your list, do not worry about effective sentences, mental images, organization, and such; simply get down as best you can and as quickly as you can the details that convey your impression. A list for an essay about your intimidating grandmother might read, in part, like this:

    gnarled hands

    wrinkled, scary face

    powerful voice

    won't take no for an answer

    pinches my shoulder when angry

    fearsome eyes

8. If you like to secure reader response before revising, see page 115. In addition, ask your reader to circle words and concrete sensory detail that should be reconsidered and place a check mark next to words and concrete sensory detail that are particularly effective.

REVISION CHECKLIST

In addition to the checklist on page 117, you can use this checklist for revising a descriptive essay.

1. Does your thesis include both a subject to be described and a dominant impression?
2. Is your impression expressed in specific language?
3. Given your thesis, audience, and purpose, is your detail appropriately subjective or objective?
4. Are all your supporting details relevant to your subject and impression?
5. Have you used concrete sensory detail to create vivid mental images? Is your concrete sensory detail restrained when necessary?
6. Have you used similes, metaphors, and personification judiciously?

EXERCISE | **Writing Description**

1. Read either "Dawn Watch" (page 144) or "The Sounds of the City" (page 142). Cite three descriptions that you particularly like and underline the concrete sensory detail.
2. Visit the following places and write two different dominant impressions you could use for two different descriptions of each place.
   a. your bedroom
   b. a grocery store
   c. a campus dining hall
   d. an area outside a campus building
3. Select one of the places you visited for number 2 and one of the dominant impressions you had of the place. Then mention three things you could describe to convey that dominant impression.
4. Write one descriptive sentence for each of the items in your list from number 3. Be sure to keep your dominant impression in mind.
5. Write a simile or metaphor for two of the following:
   a. a stubborn child
   b. the sound of a lawn mower
   c. the smell of burning food
   d. the feel of cat fur
6. Write one sentence that includes objective description of an item of clothing you are wearing. Then rewrite that sentence to make the description subjective.
7. *Collaborative Activity.* Form a group with three or four classmates and together write a one-paragraph *objective* description of some part of your writing classroom. Then on a separate sheet, write a one-paragraph *subjective* description of the same thing. Trade paragraphs with at least one other group and note the chief strengths and weaknesses of the paragraphs you receive.

PROFESSIONAL ESSAYS

The Sounds of the City

James Tuite

To create vivid mental images, writers usually rely heavily on the sense of sight. However, author James Tuite does something more unusual: He relies on the sense of sound to describe a city teeming with activity day and night.

New York is a city of sounds: muted sounds and shrill sounds; shattering sounds   *1*
and soothing sounds; urgent sounds and aimless sounds. The cliff dwellers of
Manhattan—who would be racked by the silence of the lonely woods—do not
hear these sounds because they are constant and eternally urban.

The visitor to the city can hear them, though, just as some animals can hear   *2*
a high-pitched whistle inaudible to humans. To the casual caller to Manhattan,
lying restive and sleepless in a hotel 20 or 30 floors above the street, they tell a
story as fascinating as life itself. And back of the sounds broods the silence.

Night in midtown is the noise of tinseled honky-tonk and violence. Thin   *3*
strains of music, usually the firm beat of rock 'n' roll or the frenzied outbursts of
the discotheque, rise from ground level. This is the cacophony, the discordance
of youth, and it comes on strongest when nights are hot and young blood restless.

Somewhere in the canyons below there is shrill laughter or raucous shouting.   *4*
A bottle shatters against concrete. The whine of a police siren slices through the
night, moving ever closer, until an eerie Doppler effect* brings it to a guttural halt.

There are few sounds so exciting in Manhattan as those of fire apparatus   *5*
dashing through the night. At the outset there is the tentative hint of the first-
due company bullying his way through midtown traffic. Now a fire whistle from
the opposite direction affirms that trouble is, indeed, afoot. In seconds, other
sirens converging from other streets help the skytop listener focus on the scene
of excitement.

But he can only hear and not see, and imagination takes flight. Are the   *6*
flames and smoke gushing from windows not far away? Are victims trapped
there, crying out for help? Is it a conflagration, or only a trash-basket fire? Or,
perhaps, it is merely a false alarm.

The questions go unanswered and the urgency of the moment dissolves.   *7*
Now the mind and the ear detect the snarling, arrogant bickering of automobile
horns. People in a hurry. Taxicabs blaring, insisting on their checkered priority.

Even the taxi horns dwindle down to a precocious few in the gray and pink   *8*
moments of dawn. Suddenly there is another sound, a morning sound that taunts
the memory for recognition. The growl of a predatory monster? No, just garbage
trucks that have begun a day of scavenging.

Trash cans rattle outside restaurants. Metallic jaws on sanitation trucks gulp   *9*
and masticate the residue of daily living, then digest it with a satisfied groan of

*The drop in pitch that occurs as a source of sound quickly passes by a listener.

gears. The sounds of the new day are businesslike. The growl of buses, so scattered and distant at night, becomes a demanding part of the traffic bedlam. An occasional jet or helicopter injects an exclamation point from an unexpected quarter. When the wind is right, the vibrant bellow of an ocean liner can be heard.

The sounds of the day are as jarring as the glare of a sun that outlines the 10 canyons of midtown in drab relief. A pneumatic drill frays countless nerves with its rat-a-tat-tat, for dig they must to perpetuate the city's dizzy motion. After each screech of brakes there is a moment of suspension, of waiting for the thud or crash that never seems to follow.

The whistles of traffic policemen and hotel doormen chirp from all sides, 11 like birds calling for their mates across a frenzied aviary. And all of these sounds are adult sounds, for childish laughter has no place in these canyons.

Night falls again, the cycle is complete, but there is no surcease from 12 sound. For the beautiful dreamers, perhaps, the "sounds of the rude world heard in the day, lulled by the moonlight have all passed away," but this is not so in the city.

Too many New Yorkers accept the sounds about them as bland parts of 13 everyday existence. They seldom stop to listen to the sounds, to think about them, to be appalled or enchanted by them. In the big city, sounds are life.

Considering Ideas

1. Who are the "cliff dwellers of Manhattan" (paragraph 1)? Why do they not hear the sounds of the city?
2. Tuite says, "New York is a city of sounds." To prove his point, he describes a wide range of things that can be heard. What do all the diverse sounds have in common?
3. Why do you think Tuite chose to describe New York by focusing on sound rather than sight?
4. Does Tuite's description make you want to visit Manhattan? Why or why not?

Considering Technique

1. What is Tuite's subject? What is his dominant impression of that subject? Where do you find this information?
2. In what order does Tuite arrange his details? Are these details objective or subjective description?
3. Tuite's concrete sensory detail appeals to the sense of hearing, but it still creates visual images. For example, "Taxicabs blaring, insisting on their checkered priority" is auditory detail that evokes a visual image of Manhattan traffic. Cite another example of concrete sensory that plays simultaneously on the auditory and the visual.
4. The effectiveness of Tuite's description comes, in large part, from his simple, specific word choice. Cite three examples of simple, specific verbs; three of specific, simple nouns; three of specific, simple modifiers.

For Group Discussion or Journal Writing

Does Tuite make New York City seem like a city you would like to spend time in? Refer to specific descriptions to support your reaction.

Dawn Watch

John Ciardi

With rich descriptive detail, John Ciardi describes a daily occurrence: sunrise. Note the playful, down-to-earth quality of Ciardi's writing as he works to persuade the reader that sunrise is the best part of the day.

Unless a man is up for the dawn and for the half-hour or so of first light, he has missed the best of the day. 1

The traffic has just started, not yet a roar and a stink. One car at a time goes by, the tires humming almost like the sound of a brook a half mile down in the crease of a mountain I know—a sound that carries not because it is loud but because everybody else is still. 2

It isn't exactly a mist that hangs in the thickets but more nearly the ghost of a mist—a phenomenon like side vision. Look hard and it isn't there, but glance without focusing and something registers, an exhalation that will be gone three minutes after the sun comes over the treetops. 3

The lawns shine with a dew not exactly dew. There is a rabbit bobbing about on the lawn and then freezing. If it were truly a dew, his tracks would shine black on the grass, and he leaves no visible track. Yet, there is something on the grass that makes it glow a depth of green it will not show again all day. Or is that something in the dawn air? 4

Our cardinals know what time it is. They drop pure tones from the hem-lock tops. The black gang of grackles that makes a slum of the pine oak also knows the time but can only grate at it. They sound like a convention of broken universal joints grating uphill. The grackles creak and squeak, and the cardinals form tones that occasionally sound through the noise. I scatter sunflower seeds by the birdbath for the cardinals and hope the grackles won't find them. 5

My neighbor's tomcat comes across the lawn, probably on his way home from passion, or only acting as if he had had a big night. I suspect him of being one of those poolroom braggarts who can't get next to a girl but who likes to let on that he is a hot stud. This one is too can-fed and too lazy to hunt for anything. Here he comes now, ignoring the rabbit. And there he goes. 6

As soon as he has hopped the fence, I let my dog out. The dog charges the rabbit, watches it jump the fence, shakes himself in a self-satisfied way, then trots dutifully into the thicket for his morning service, stopping to sniff everything on the way back. 7

There is an old mountain laurel on the island of the driveway turn-around. From somewhere on the wind a white morning glory rooted next to it and has climbed it. Now the laurel is woven full of white bells tinged pink by the first rays 8 through the not quite mist. Only in earliest morning can they be seen. Come out two hours from now and there will be no morning glories.

Dawn, too, is the hour of a weed I know only as a day flower—a bright blue *9* button that closes in full sunlight. I have weeded bales of it out of my flower beds, its one daytime virtue being the shallowness of its root system that allows it to be pulled out effortlessly in great handfuls. Yet, now it shines. Had it a few more hours of such shining in its cycle, I would cultivate it as a ground cover, but dawn is its one hour, and a garden is for whole days.

There is another blue morning weed whose name I do not know. This one *10* grows from a bulb to pulpy stems and a bedraggled daytime sprawl. Only a shovel will dig it out. Try weeding it by hand and the stems will break off to be replaced by new ones and to sprawl over the chosen plants in the flower bed. Yet, now and for another hour it outshines its betters, its flowers about the size of a quarter and paler than those of the day flower but somehow more brilliant, perhaps because of the contrast of its paler foliage.

And now the sun is slanting in full. It is bright enough to make the leaves *11* of the Japanese red maple seem a transparent red bronze when the tree is between me and the light. There must be others, but this is the only tree I know whose leaves let the sun through in this way—except, that is, when the fall colors start. Aspen leaves, when they first yellow and before they dry, are transparent in this way. I tell myself it must have something to do with the red-yellow range of the spectrum. Green takes sunlight and holds it, but red and yellow let it through.

The damned crabgrass is wrestling with the zinnias, and I stop to weed it *12* out. The stuff weaves too close to the zinnias to make the iron claw usable. And it won't do to pull at the stalks. Crabgrass (at least in a mulched bed) can be weeded only with dirty fingers. Thumb and forefinger have to pincer into the dirt and grab the root-center. Weeding, of course, is an illusion of hope. Pulling out the root only stirs the soil and brings new crabgrass seeds into germinating position. Take a walk around the block and a new clump will have sprouted by the time you get back. But I am not ready to walk around the block. I fill a small basket with the plucked clumps, and for the instant I look at them, the zinnias are weedless.

Don't look back. I dump the weeds in the thicket where they will be smoth- *13* ered by the grass clippings I will pile on at the next cutting. On the way back I see the cardinals come down for the sunflower seeds, and the jays join them, and then the grackles start ganging in, gate-crashing the buffet and clattering all over it. The dog stops chewing his rawhide and makes a dash into the puddle of birds, which splashes away from it.

I hear a brake-squeak I have been waiting for and know the paper has ar- *14* rived. As usual, the news turns out to be another disaster count. The function of the wire services is to bring us tragedies faster than we can pity. In the end we shall all be inured, numb, and ready for emotionless programming. I sit on the patio and read until the sun grows too bright on the page. The cardinals have stopped singing, and the grackles have flown off. It's the end of birdsong again.

Then suddenly—better than song for its instant—a hummingbird the color *15* of green crushed velvet hovers in the throat of my favorite lily, a lovely high-bloomer I got the bulbs for but not the name. The lily is a crest of white horns with red dots and red velvet tongues along the insides of the petals and with an odor that drowns the patio. The hummingbird darts in and out of each horn in turn, then hovers an instant, and disappears.

Even without the sun, I have had enough of the paper. I'll take that hum- *16* mingbird as my news for this dawn. It is over now. I smoke one more cigarette too many and decide that, if I go to bed now, no one in the family need know I have stayed up for it again. Why do they insist on shaking their heads when they find me still up for breakfast, after having scribbled through the dark hours? They always do. They seem compelled to express pity for an old loony who can't find his own way to bed. Why won't they understand that this is the one hour of any day that must not be missed, as it is the one hour I couldn't imagine getting up for, though I can still get to it by staying up? It makes sense to me. There comes a time when the windows lighten and the twittering starts. I look up and know it's time to leave the papers in their mess. I could slip quietly into bed and avoid the family's headshakes, but this stroll-around first hour is too good to miss. Even my dog, still sniffing and circling, knows what hour this is.

Come on, boy. It's time to go in. The rabbit won't come back till tomorrow, *17* and the birds have work to do. The dawn's over. It's time to call it a day.

Considering Ideas

1. Why do you think Ciardi enjoys dawn so much?
2. What can you tell about Ciardi's work habits and lifestyle as a result of reading the essay?
3. What do you think Ciardi means when he says in paragraph 12 that "weeding . . . is an illusion of hope"?
4. Ciardi opens by saying, "Unless a man is up for the dawn and for the half-hour or so of first light, he has missed the best of the day." How do you react to the use of "man" and "he"? Do you think Ciardi is excluding women? Does the fact that the essay was published in 1972 affect your view?
5. *Irony* is the contrast between what is stated or what occurs and what is expected by the reader. What irony occurs at the end of the essay?

Considering Technique

1. Which sentence presents the thesis? What does that thesis say is being described, and what does it note as the author's dominant impression?
2. In what order does Ciardi arrange most of his details? Why does he use this order?
3. Ciardi's description includes similes and metaphors (see page 135). Cite an example of each.

4. Ciardi describes some sounds along with the sights of dawn. Which ones?

5. Is Ciardi's description primarily objective or expressive? Mention a description or two that you particularly enjoy. Why do you like this description? What specific nouns, verbs, and modifiers do these descriptions include?

For Group Discussion or Journal Writing

Ciardi works all night and goes to sleep after sunrise. What are the advantages and disadvantages of such a schedule?

A Mexican House

Ernesto Galarza

Born in Mexico and relocated to California, Ernesto Galarza describes his one-room house in this excerpt from his 1971 autobiography Barrio Boy.

Our adobe cottage was on the side of the street away from the *arroyo*. It was the last house if you were going to Miramar. About 50 yards behind the corral, the forest closed in.

It was like every other house in Jalco, probably larger. The adobe walls were thick, a foot or more, with patches of whitewash where the thatched overhang protected the adobe from the rain. There were no windows. The entrance doorway was at one end of the front wall, and directly opposite the door that led to the corral. The doors were made of planks axed smooth from tree trunks and joined with two cross pieces and a diagonal brace between them hammered together with large nails bent into the wood on the inside. Next to each door and always handy for instant use, there was the cross bar, the *tranca*. On both sides of the door frame there was a notched stub, mortared into the adobe bricks and about six inches long. The door was secured from the inside by dropping the *tranca* into the two notches.

All the living space for the family was in the one large room, about 12 feet wide and three times as long. Against the wall between the two doorways was the *pretil*, a bank of adobe bricks three feet high, three across, and two feet deep. In the center of the *pretil* was the main fire pit. Two smaller hollows, one on either side of the large one, made it a three-burner stove. On a row of pegs above the *pretil* hung the clay pans and other cooking utensils, bottom-side out, the soot baked into the red clay. A low bench next to the *pretil*, also made of adobe, served as a table and shelf for the cups, pots, and plates.

The rest of the ground floor was divided by a curtain hung from one of the hand-hewn log beams, making two bedrooms. Above them, secured to the beams, was the *tapanco*, a platform the size of a double bed made of thin saplings tied together with pieces of rawhide. The top of a notched pole, braced against the foot of the back wall of the cottage, rested against the side of the *tapanco,* serving as a ladder. Along the wall opposite the *pretil,* in the darkest and coolest part of the house, were the big *cantaros,* the red clay jars; the *canastos,* tall baskets made of woven reeds; the rolled straw *petates* to cover the dirt floor where people walked or sat; and the hoes and other work tools.

There was no ceiling other than the underside of the thatch, which was tied 5 to the pole rafters. On top of these, several layers of thatch were laid, making a waterproof cover thicker than the span of a man's hand. The rafters were notched and tied to the ridgepole and mortared on the lower end to the top of the walls. Between the top of the walls and the overhang there was an open space a few inches wide. Through this strip the smoke from the *pretil* went out and the fresh air came in.

It was the roof that gave space and lift to the single room that served as 6 kitchen, bedroom, parlor, pantry, closet, storeroom, and tool shed. The slender rafters pointed upward in sharp triangles tied at the peak with bows of dark brown rawhide that had dried as tight as steel straps. Strings of thatch hung from the ceiling like the fringe of a buggy top, making it appear that the heavy matting of grass did not rest on the rafters but tiptoed on hundreds of threads. It was always half dark up there. My cousins, Jesus and Catarino, and I slept in the *tapanco.* More than a bedroom, to us it was a half-lighted hideaway out of sight of parents, uncles, aunts, and other meddlesome people.

Considering Ideas

1. Write a list of modifiers that could be used to describe Galarza's house.
2. For what reason do you think Galarza describes his boyhood house? For what kind of reader do you think he is writing?
3. How does Galarza feel about his boyhood house? How can you tell that he feels this way?

Considering Technique

1. Is Galarza's description primarily objective or subjective?
2. Cite three examples of concrete sensory details that create clear mental images.
3. Cite one example each of a specific yet simple noun, verb, and modifier.
4. In what kind of order are the details arranged? Cite three transitions that signal this order.

For Group Discussion or Journal Writing

What do you think it is like to live in a house similar to the one Galarza describes? How would the lack of privacy affect family members? How would you be affected?

Combining Patterns of Development

The Way to Rainy Mountain

N. Scott Momaday

A Kiowa who grew up on reservations, N. Scott Momaday is the author of The Way to Rainy Mountain, *from which the the following excerpt is taken. In the piece, Momaday combines* **description** *and* **narration** *in a moving personal memoir and historical account.*

A single knoll rises out of the plain in Oklahoma, north and west of the Wichita 1
Range. For my people, the Kiowas, it is an old landmark, and they gave it the
name Rainy Mountain. The hardest weather in the world is there. Winter brings
blizzards, hot tornadic winds arise in the spring, and in summer the prairie is an
anvil's edge. The grass turns brittle and brown, and it cracks beneath your feet.
There are green belts along the rivers and creeks, linear groves of hickory and
pecan, willow and witch hazel. At a distance in July or August the steaming foliage seems almost to writhe in fire. Great green-and-yellow grasshoppers are
everywhere in the tall grass, popping up like corn to sting the flesh, and tortoises
crawl about on the red earth, going nowhere in the plenty of time. Loneliness is
an aspect of the land. All things in the plain are isolate; there is no confusion of
objects in the eye, but *one* hill or *one* tree or *one* man. To look upon that landscape in the early morning, with the sun at your back, is to lose the sense of proportion. Your imagination comes to life, and this, you think, is where Creation
was begun.

I returned to Rainy Mountain in July. My grandmother had died in the 2
spring, and I wanted to be at her grave. She had lived to be very old and at last
infirm. Her only living daughter was with her when she died, and I was told that
in death her face was that of a child.

I like to think of her as a child. When she was born, the Kiowas were living 3
that last great moment of their history. For more than a hundred years they had
controlled the open range from the Smoky Hill River to the Red, from the head-
waters of the Canadian to the fork of the Arkansas and Cimarron. In alliance
with the Comanches, they had ruled the whole of the southern Plains. War was
their sacred business, and they were among the finest horsemen the world has
ever known. But warfare for the Kiowas was preeminently a matter of disposition
rather than of survival, and they never understood the grim, unrelenting advance
of the U.S. Cavalry. When at last, divided and ill-provisioned, they were driven
onto the Staked Plains in the cold rains of autumn, they fell into panic. In Palo
Duro Canyon they abandoned their crucial stores to pillage and had nothing then
but their lives. In order to save themselves, they surrendered to the soldiers at
Fort Sill and were imprisoned in the old stone corral that now stands as a military
museum. My grandmother was spared the humiliation of those high gray walls

by eight or ten years, but she must have known from birth the affliction of defeat, the dark brooding of old warriors.

Her name was Aho, and she belonged to the last culture to evolve in North *4* America. Her forebears came down from the high country in western Montana nearly three centuries ago. They were a mountain people, a mysterious tribe of hunters whose language has never been positively classified in any major group. In the late seventeenth century they began a long migration to the south and east. It was a long journey toward the dawn, and it led to a golden age. Along the way the Kiowas were befriended by the Crows, who gave them the culture and religion of the Plains. They acquired horses, and their ancient nomadic spirit was suddenly free of the ground. They acquired Tai-me, the sacred Sun Dance doll, from that moment the object and symbol of their worship, and so shared in the divinity of the sun. Not least, they acquired the sense of destiny, therefore courage and pride. When they entered upon the southern Plains, they had been transformed. No longer were they slaves to the simple necessity of survival; they were a lordly and dangerous society of fighters and thieves, hunters and priests of the sun. According to their origin myth, they entered the world through a hollow log. From one point of view, their migration was the fruit of an old prophecy, for indeed they emerged from a sunless world.

Although my grandmother lived out her long life in the shadow of Rainy *5* Mountain, the immense landscape of the continental interior lay like memory in her blood. She could tell of the Crows, whom she had never seen, and of the Black Hills, where she had never been. I wanted to see in reality what she had seen more perfectly in the mind's eye, and traveled 1,500 miles to begin my pilgrimage.

Yellowstone, it seemed to me, was the top of the world, a region of deep *6* lakes and dark timber, canyons and waterfalls. But, beautiful as it is, one might have the sense of confinement there. The skyline in all directions is close at hand, the high wall of the woods and deep cleavages of shade. There is a perfect freedom in the mountains, but it belongs to the eagle and the elk, the badger and the bear. The Kiowas reckoned their stature by the distance they could see, and they were bent and blind in the wilderness.

Descending eastward, the highland meadows are a stairway to the plain. In *7* July the inland slope of the Rockies is luxuriant with flax and buckwheat, stonecrop and larkspur. The earth unfolds and the limit of the land recedes. Clusters of trees and animals grazing far in the distance cause the vision to reach away and wonder to build upon the mind. The sun follows a longer course in the day, and the sky is immense beyond all comparison. The great billowing clouds that sail upon it are shadows that move upon the grain like water, dividing light. Farther down, in the land of the Crows and Blackfeet, the plain is yellow. Sweet clover takes hold of the hills and bends upon itself to cover and seal the soil. There the Kiowas paused on their way; they had come to the place where they must change their lives. The sun is at home on the plains. Precisely there does it have the certain character of a god. When the Kiowas came to the land of the Crows, they could see the dark lees of the hills at dawn across the Bighorn River, the profusion of light on the grain shelves, the oldest deity ranging after the solstices. Not yet would they veer southward to the caldron of the land that lay below; they must wean their blood from the northern winter and hold the mountains a while longer in their view. They bore Tai-me in procession to the east.

A dark mist lay over the Black Hills, and the land was like iron. At the top *8* of a ridge I caught sight of Devil's Tower upthrust against the gray sky as if in the birth of time the core of the earth had broken through its crust and the motion of the world was begun. There are things in nature that engender an awful quiet in the heart of man; Devil's Tower is one of them. Two centuries ago, because they could not do otherwise, the Kiowas made a legend at the base of the rock. My grandmother said:

> "Eight children were there at play, seven sisters and their brother. Suddenly the boy was struck dumb; he trembled and began to run upon his hands and feet. His fingers became claws, and his body was covered with fur. Directly there was a bear where the boy had been. The sisters were terrified; they ran, and the bear after them. They came to the stump of a great tree, and the tree spoke to them. It bade them climb upon it, and as they did so, it began to rise into the air. The bear came to kill them, but they were just beyond its reach. It reared against the tree and scored the bark all around with its claws. The seven sisters were borne into the sky, and they became the stars of the Big Dipper."

From that moment, and so long as the legend lives, the Kiowas have kinsmen in the night sky. Whatever they were in the mountains, they could be no more. However tenuous their well-being, however much they had suffered and would suffer again, they had found a way out of the wilderness.

My grandmother had a reverence for the sun, a holy regard that now is all *9* but gone out of mankind. There was a wariness in her, and an ancient awe. She was a Christian in her later years, but she had come a long way about, and she never forgot her birthright. As a child she had been to the Sun Dances; she had taken part in those annual rites, and by them she had learned the restoration of her people in the presence of Tai-me. She was about seven when the last Kiowa Sun Dance was held in 1887 on the Washita River above Rainy Mountain Creek. The buffalo were gone. In order to consummate the ancient sacrifice—to impale the head of a buffalo bull upon the medicine tree—a delegation of old men journeyed into Texas, there to beg and barter for an animal from the Goodnight herd. She was ten when the Kiowas came together for the last time as a living Sun Dance culture. They could find no buffalo; they had to hang an old hide from the sacred tree. Before the dance could begin, a company of soldiers rode out from Fort Sill under orders to disperse the tribe. Forbidden without cause the essential act of their faith, having seen the wild herds slaughtered and left to rot upon the ground, the Kiowas backed away forever from the medicine tree. That was July 20, 1890, at the great bend of the Washita. My grandmother was there. Without bitterness, and for as long as she lived, she bore a vision of deicide.

Now that I can have her only in memory, I see my grandmother in the sev- *10* eral postures that were peculiar to her: standing at the wood stove on a winter morning and turning meat in a great iron skillet; sitting at the south window, bent above her beadwork, and afterwards, when her vision had failed, looking down for a long time into the fold of her hands; going out upon a cane, very slowly as she did when the weight of age came upon her; praying. I remember her most often at prayer. She made long, rambling prayers out of suffering and hope, having seen many things. I was never sure that I had the right to hear, so exclusive were they of all mere custom and company. The last time I saw her she prayed standing by the side of her bed at night, naked to the waist, the light of a kerosene lamp moving upon her dark skin. Her long, black hair, always drawn and braided in the day, lay upon her shoulders and against her breasts like a shawl. I do not speak Kiowa, and I never understood her prayers, but there was something inherently sad in the sound, some merest hesitation upon the syllables of sorrow. She began in a high and descending pitch, exhausting her breath to silence; then again and again—and always the same intensity of effort, of something that is, and is not, like urgency in the human voice. Transported so in the dancing light among the shadows of her room, she seemed beyond the reach of time. But that was illusion; I think I knew then that I should not see her again.

Considering Ideas

1. What do you think Momaday means when he says that "warfare for the Kiowas was preeminently a matter of disposition rather than of survival" (paragraph 3)?
2. Why does Momaday say that his grandmother "bore a vision of deicide" (paragraph 9)?
3. Explain Momaday's feelings about his grandmother, citing specific passages to support your view.
4. How do you think Momaday feels about his heritage? How can you tell?

Considering Technique

1. Which paragraphs are developed primarily with description? What purpose does the description serve? Is any of that description objective rather than subjective?
2. *Combining Patterns.* What narration (stories) does Momaday provide? What purpose do the narrations serve?
3. Cite three descriptions that you find particularly effective. Underline any specific nouns, verbs, and modifiers.
4. Cite an example of personification in paragraph 1. Cite an example of a simile in that paragraph. Cite an example of a metaphor in paragraph 7.

For Group Discussion or Journal Writing

Momaday is keenly aware of his cultural heritage, and he feels a sense of connection to his past and to his ancestors. How important is a person's cultural heritage? To what extent does it affect who we are and what we do today?

STUDENT ESSAYS TO READ AND EVALUATE

Below are two descriptive essays written by students. Each has definite strengths as well as aspects that could be improved with revision and editing. As you read the selections, consider their strengths and weaknesses. Doing so will give you practice evaluating writing by identifying successful techniques to include in your own pieces and less-successful ones to avoid. It will also sharpen your critical ability so you are better able to make sound revision decisions about your own writing.

Never Intrude

It was early morning, and I was diving just off the shores of Grand   *1*
Cayman Island when I swam through an opening in the coral. At first
I could only hear the intermittent gurgle of exhaust air, but as my
eyes adjusted to the dim light, I was astonished by the assortment
of life in what appeared to be a coral room.

There in the middle of the floor, caught by surprise, a crab   *2*
shuttled from side to side unable to decide which way to go, yet
unbothered nearby, a rust-red starfish worried at a clam it was
trying to pry open. Deadman's fingers, a well-named rubbery sponge
that was dangling from the ceiling, brushed my back. As I hung
suspended just above the floor careful to avoid touching the few
black sea urchins below. Fascinated, I watched as thousands of
shrimp fry floated by like dust on a ray of sunlight, while
hundreds of small fish, called neons, flitted in and out of the
walls, their iridescent bodies giving the room a psychedelic
effect. I looked at the wall on my right. There in a cubbyhole a
porcupine fish had puffed itself up at least twice his normal size
and was wedged tightly into his hole.

Bothered by my intrusion, a spotted jewfish loomed from the   *3*
shadows to assert his territorial rights; when he swam towards me,
lime-green anemones popped shut as if from fear. I could understand
their concern, for he must have weighed over 100 pounds. When I
raised my prod-rod, he seemed to reconsider his approach. With
things at an impasse I had time to think of the position that I was
in. Here in a room with jagged walls of blush pink, their white
tips announcing it was fire coral. If he rammed me that coral would

cut right through my wet suit and at best leave me with a nasty infection. Since I was the intruder, I carefully backed out into the open. Glad to be out of the confines of the coral room.

🎋 *Shopping in Old Jerusalem*

The Holy Land is as ancient as time itself; the beautiful mount of   *1*
Masada, the Sea of Galilee, the Garden of Gethsemane, and many
other sites are etched into my mind forever. One of my fondest
memories, though, is my shopping spree in the Market Place in Old
Jerusalem. The long, winding, snakelike street with its old wooden
huts yawning from both sides contains the precious foods, clothing
and artifacts that I wished to purchase.

As I started down the long runway, a long sinewy brown arm with *2*
mishappen fingers belonging to a merchant, beckoned me to come
inside a gaping hut. Once inside, I was greeted with "Shalom" and
his sweeping arm showed me the menagerie of trinkets on sale. In
front of me on a makeshift counter were all sorts of wooden
artifacts. I picked up a small set of camels made of light-colored
wood, gaudily arrayed with saddles trimmed in red and gold
embroidery. I asked the toothless merchant, "How much?" He replied,
"Three dollars." "No," I told him; so started the bartering.
Deciding that I really did not want the camels, I replaced them on
the counter and started to leave. The merchant, no longer friendly,
shouted obscenities at me, gesturing wildly with his hands as he
followed me onto the street. I kept walking and did not look back.

As I continued to walk down the crowded thoroughfare, a   *3*
familiar aroma caused me to stop and look around; beautiful, fresh
oven-baked breads, pita bread, breads with sesame seeds, and bread
sticks were arranged openly in a neat row on shelves in front of
one of the huts. Walking over to the hut, I observed flies dining
haphazardly on the breads. While standing there, trying not to show
my disappointment, a sickening odor of rotting meat coming from
inside the hut caused me to look up. To my right just inside the
opening, hung several greenish/yellow chickens on a hook, waiting
to be purchased. My stomach did a flip but, as I turned to leave, I
saw those beautiful succulent oranges and grapefruit so I purchased
a couple of oranges and continued down the street.

High noon in Jerusalem. I could hear the cries of priests   *4*
calling for Moslem prayers, bits and pieces of conversations, loud
barterings and shouts of disagreements coming from the huts on
either side of me, as I continued my journey in search of
souvenirs. Finally, I found a hut that was not too crowded and
stepped inside to make several purchases. Smiling smugly, I emerged
with a small olivewood-covered Bible, a skillfully made wooden
carving of Moses with staff, a hideous beige-colored gauze dress
trimmed with bright orange, and a couple of leather key chains with
the Star of David embossed on them.

As I neared the end of the long market place and its carnival   *5*
atmosphere, three Israeli soldiers in camouflage combat fatigues,
green berets atop their heads and carrying Uzi machine guns, walked
towards me. I was abruptly brought back to reality. Though I
enjoyed the giant market with its banters and barkers of life, this
beautiful land and its inhabitants are in a continuous war.

Collaborative Exercise: Evaluating Writing

To help you become a reliable critic—someone who judges writing well—so you can make decisions about your own drafts with confidence, this activity gives you practice evaluating writing and supporting your conclusions.

Form a group with several classmates and read the previous student essays; select one essay to evaluate. As a group, make decisions about the strengths and weaknesses of the essay by answering the evaluation questions that follow. One person should write down the group's responses. If group members disagree on some points, the recorder should make note of that disagreement. When deliberations are complete, one group member should report the group's findings to the rest of the class.

Evaluation Questions

1. *The Thesis*
   What subject and dominant impression are presented? Is the language specific enough?
2. *The Introduction*
   What do you think of the opening? Does it engage your interest?
3. *Supporting Details*
   Note any points you do not understand. Note any points that are not relevant. Is the language specific yet simple? Cite a mental image you like. Comment on the use of concrete sensory details. Note any striking problems with word choice.

4. *Organization*
   Are the details in a logical order? Evaluate the use of transitions.
5. *The Conclusion*
   Does the essay come to a satisfying end? Explain.
6. *Overview*
   What do you like best about the essay? What is the most important revision the author should make?

Essay Topics: Description

When you write your essay, consult Pitfalls to Avoid on page 139, Process Guidelines on page 139, and the Revision Checklist on page 141.

Writing in the Pattern

1. Describe a crowded or hectic spot (a subway station at rush hour, the campus green at noon, your dining hall at the busiest time of day, the freeway at 5:00, and so forth).
2. Describe one of the following:
   a. a favorite campus spot
   b. a favorite night spot
   c. a schoolyard at recess
   d. a gathering storm or the time just after a storm
   e. a room after a big party or celebration
   f. a place you go for solitude
3. Describe an ugly building, room, or painting, being sure to convey why it is so unappealing.
4. Describe a place during a holiday celebration (your grandmother's dining room at Thanksgiving, the outside of your house at Christmas, a park during an Independence Day celebration, and so forth).

Reading Then Writing in the Pattern

1. Like Tuite (page 142), write a description that relies heavily on sensory detail of sound. You might describe the sounds of the student union, your residence hall, a shopping mall, a doctor's office, a park, and so forth. Title your essay "The Sounds of _____." (Fill in the blank with the place you describe.)
2. Pick one of the mental pictures created in Tuite's essay (the discotheque, the fire emergency, the taxis on the street, the garbage collection, etc.) and expand the image to essay proportions using whatever sensory details you wish.
3. If you have spent time in the country, write an essay called "The Sounds of the Country."
4. Like Ciardi (page 144), use description to express your impression of a particular time of day (dawn, dusk, noon, midnight, and so on) at a particular place.

5. Ciardi includes descriptions of both plant and animal life in "Dawn Watch." For example, he describes a tomcat, a hummingbird, weeds, and leaves. Select some form of plant or animal life that you can observe closely, and describe both its features and how you react to those features.

6. Ciardi describes dawn as the "best of the day." Describe what you think is the "worst of the day": rush hour, supper time, the first hour you are awake, and so on. Be sure to convey why this time is unpleasant.

7. Like Galarza (page 147), write an objective description of your house, but focus on only one room. Be sure to convey how you feel about the room.

8. In paragraph 10, Momaday (p. 149) describes his grandmother so that the reader can see her the way he did. Describe a person you know, being sure to include specific details so that the reader forms a clear mental image of that person.

9. In paragraph 1, Momaday describes a plain in Oklahoma, a place "where Creation was begun." Like Momaday, describe a place that has a profound impact on you.

Responding to the Readings

1. Galarza describes his one-room house (page 147). Think about the dwelling (or one of the dwellings) you grew up in and then write how you were affected by the living conditions it created.

2. In paragraph 14, Ciardi (page 144) raises an important issue about newspapers. Explain his opinion and then go on to agree or disagree with him, using examples from newspapers, your own experience, and your own observations to make your point.

3. Momaday (page 149) discusses his family's past and the importance it plays for him. Discuss the role your family's history plays in your life, explaining how your heritage has shaped you.

4. *Connecting the Readings.* Using the information in "A Mexican House" (page 147), "The Sounds of the City" (page 142), and "The Way to Rainy Mountain" (page 149), along with your own experience and observation, explain how we are affected by our physical surroundings.

CHAPTER 5

Narration

"So tell me what happened." You are likely to respond to that request by telling a story—by relating the events that occurred, where they occurred, when they occurred, and who was involved. In writing, such a story is a **narration.**

There are two kinds of narrations. A brief narration, called an **anecdote,** can be written in as little as one paragraph. Anecdotes often serve as body paragraphs to explain, illustrate, or support a thesis. For example, if you wanted to explain the effects of television advertising on young children, you could write a paragraph about the time your three-year-old cousin would not let his babysitter eat Trix because he believed that "Trix are for kids." In this chapter, however, we will be concerned with **extended narrations**—narrations it takes an essay to tell.

ESTABLISHING YOUR PURPOSE AND IDENTIFYING YOUR AUDIENCE

Because nothing amuses more than a good story, you may find yourself writing narration in order to *entertain* your reader. This is particularly true when you tell a funny story. For example, you might narrate an account of your first meeting with your future father-in-law, when you mistook him for an annoying insurance salesman. You can also write narration to *express feelings* or *relate experience,* as when you tell the story of the time you got lost in the woods. Narration can also serve an *informational* purpose, as when you tell the story of the time you were wrongly arrested for shoplifting in order to inform your reader about what happens when a person is arrested. Narration can even serve a *persuasive* purpose. For example, say you want to argue that high schools should require students to perform community service in order to graduate. You could narrate an account of the community service you performed as a senior in order to demonstrate how valuable it was.

The purpose of your narration will influence your detail selection. Say you tell the story about the time your psychology teacher was unfair to you. If your purpose is to express your anger, you might focus on yourself and your feelings. If your purpose is to convince your reader that students need a grievance procedure, you might focus more on what happened. If your purpose is to inform your reader that even the best profs have their bad moments, you might emphasize what happened, why it happened, and the instructor involved. For this purpose, you might also describe the instructor as a typically fair one, which is something you would not do for the first two purposes.

Like your purpose, your audience will influence the detail you include and what you emphasize. Let's return to the story of the unfair psychology professor to illustrate this. If your reader knows little about the workings of a college classroom, you might include more explanatory detail than if your reader is currently attending the university. If your audience is a classmate who witnessed the incident, you might emphasize what happened less than if your audience is someone who did not witness the event.

COMBINING NARRATION WITH OTHER PATTERNS

Description is often part of narration because memorable narrations include specific, descriptive details to make the story vivid. Important details of scene are often described, as are key people and events. To appreciate the importance of description, compare these two versions of a narration.

a. The child drove his tricycle down the driveway into the path of an oncoming car. Fortunately, the driver, who was speeding, was able to swerve in time to avoid a collision.

b. Four-year-old Ishmael hopped on his racing red tricycle and began pedaling furiously down his driveway. By the time he reached the end, he had gathered too much speed to stop. With fear in his eyes, he screamed mightily as his out-of-control trike headed into the path of a speeding Chevy Lumina. The teenage driver, startled into action, swerved just in time to avert disaster.

You probably found version *b* more interesting because of the description.

Because narration can help explain, illustrate, or support a point, it often appears in essays developed primarily with other patterns. For example, assume you are writing a definition of *friendship* and that you note loyalty as one of its characteristics. You could narrate an account of the time your best friend refused to believe rumors about you. The story could explain and illustrate what you mean by loyalty. If you are classifying types of teachers and you establish one type as "the authoritarian," you can tell the story of an encounter you had with an authoritarian teacher to show what that type is like. Similarly, if you are explaining the effects of divorce on children, you can illustrate one of the effects by narrating what happened when your father was not around when you needed him the most. No matter what your dominant pattern of development, there is the possibility that narration can help you achieve your purpose.

For an example of combining narration with cause-and-effect analysis and contrast, see "Looking for Work" on page 175.

USING NARRATION BEYOND THE WRITING CLASS

You might be surprised to discover yourself writing narration in many other college courses: in a political science paper, you might narrate the sequence of events leading up to the failure of the League of Nations; in a history midterm, you might narrate an account of the Teapot Dome scandal. If you take a journalism course, the news articles you write will often be narrative, and if you observe a classroom for an education class, you may write journal entries narrating what occurred in the class. Similarly, if you take an experimental psychology class, your lab assignments may frequently involve narrative accounts of experiments.

Outside the classroom, as well, narration has many uses. Correspondence to friends includes narrations of the events in our lives, and newspapers and magazines narrate accounts of important happenings in the world. Police officers write reports that narrate accounts of crimes; attorneys write briefs that narrate a sequence of events in which the client was involved; doctors chart narrative accounts of their patients' responses to treatment; and recording secretaries take narrative minutes of meetings. If you attend a lecture, you may receive a program book that includes a narration of the highlights of the speaker's life.

SELECTING DETAIL

Let's say two friends run into each other on campus and one says to the other, "What happened? You look terrible." Then the second friend replies, "I just went through the worst registration ever." The conversation that might follow reveals much about storytelling.

John: What happened? You look terrible.

Marsha: I just went through the worst registration ever.

John: Why? What happened?

Marsha: Well, when I tried to call in to the automated registration line, I got a busy signal for 20 minutes, and when I finally got through, my registration was rejected, and I had to go to the records office to find out why. So I went to records and stood in line for another 20 minutes to find out I owed a lousy $1.50 library fine, so I paid the fine. When I tried to register again, I found out I needed the chair's permission to take this biology course I wanted, but I had already asked Dr. Ingles, but he apparently forgot to phone in the permission. So I walked all the way to the science building and the secretary gave me a hard time.

John: Why? What did she say?

Marsha: She told me I needed the biology chairman's permission to take this biology course I wanted. I told her he already said it was OK, but she made a big deal about how she needed his signature. I got ticked and told her off.

John: Why so angry?

Marsha: Well, I'd already wasted almost two hours and didn't have one class scheduled, and I wasn't crazy about trying to run down Dr. Ingles all over again. Anyhow, I went to the library where he was supposed to be and got Ingles's signature. By the way, I saw Lorenzo there and he's leaving for Florida on break.

John: Forget Lorenzo and finish the story.

Marsha: Yeah, well I went back to the science building, and you won't believe what happened this time.

John: I give up, what?

Marsha: The secretary told me to wait a minute—oh I forgot to tell you, this woman told me before that I better straighten out my act or I'd be in trouble.

John: Wait a minute—when? The first or second time? You're losing me.

Marsha: When I told her off. Anyway, when I got to her desk . . .

John: The second time?

Marsha: Yeah. When I got to her desk, she told me to wait—like I hadn't already done enough of that, you know. So I waited, and next thing I know, she's dragging some security guard over to me. And you know what he says?

John: Will you tell the story already?

Marsha: He tells me that unless I can act like an adult, I won't be allowed to register.

John: Why did he say that?

Marsha: I guess because when she made me get Ingles's signature, I called her a dumb broad.

John: Why didn't you tell me that before? Sounds to me like you got what you deserved.

Marsha: Yeah, I suppose.

The conversation between John and Marsha raises several points about effective narration. First, a good narration must include all the significant events. When Marsha neglects to tell John why she was angry, he asks her to supply this information. When she neglects to say that she called the woman a dumb broad, John is annoyed. Second, an effective narration does not bring up unrelated points. When Marsha starts to speak of Lorenzo, John tells her to get back to the matter at hand. Third, good narration follows a logical time sequence. When Marsha mentions the time she was told to straighten out her act, John has to ask a question to get things clear. Fourth, interesting narration does not drag on; its pace is brisk. When Marsha begins to bog down, John tells her to move the story along. Finally, good narration usually has a point that can be drawn from the story. John and Marsha both conclude that she acted badly and deserved to be chastised by the security guard.

The dialogue between John and Marsha illustrates the following points about narration:

1. All the significant details must be supplied.
2. Irrelevant details should be left out.

3. The story should be presented in a logical, understandable time sequence.
4. The story should be paced so it does not drag.
5. The story should make a point or lead to a conclusion.

When deciding what detail to include, you can answer the standard journalist's questions: *who? what? when? where? why? how?* A reader will want to know what happened, when it happened, where it happened, why it happened, how it happened, and who was involved. If you respond to each of these questions, you are likely to include all the significant information.

However, do not get carried away and include ideas not pertinent to the who, what, when, where, why, and how of your narration, or your reader will grow impatient. We have all seen movies that drag because of unnecessary detail, action, explanation, or dialogue. Such movies are boring. To avoid boring your reader, maintain a brisk pace by including only the significant details.

In addition to identifying significant details, you must determine which of these details require major emphasis. For some narrations, the who and where may deserve extended treatment, while the why, when, and how merit less development. Other narrations may dictate detailed discussion of the why. Which details you emphasize will be determined by your purpose and audience.

USING CONVERSATION

You may want to use conversation because what people said can be important to the advancement and meaning of the story, and it can add vitality to an essay. Consider the following two sentences:

    The coach shouted that we should get in there and hustle.

    The coach shouted at us, "Get in there and hustle!"

The second sentence has more power than the first because the coach's exact words appear. As a result, this sentence will have greater impact on the reader and create more interest.

Typically, sentences that contain conversation have two parts: a part that notes what was said, and a part that indicates who did the speaking. How you punctuate depends on where these parts appear.

1. When the spoken words come before the statement of who spoke, the sentence looks like this:

    "Get out of here while you have the chance," the stranger warned.

a. Spoken words are enclosed in quotation marks.
b. Spoken words are followed by a comma, which appears before the final quotation marks. If a question is asked, then a question mark is used.

    "What chance do I have?" Joyce wondered.

c. The first of the words showing who spoke begins with a lower-case letter unless it is a proper noun (like *Ed*) or a word always capitalized (like *I*).

2. When the statement of who spoke comes before the words spoken, the sentence looks like this:

```
Alex responded quietly, "My sister is the one to blame."
```

a. The statement of who spoke is followed by a comma.
b. The spoken words appear in quotation marks.
c. The first of the spoken words is capitalized.
d. The spoken words are followed by a period, which appears before the final quotation marks.

3. When the spoken words come both before and after the statement of who spoke, the sentence will look like one of the following:

```
"I wish I knew," Paulette sighed, "why I always end up doing
most of the work."
```

```
"Please be here by 8:00," Dad cautioned. "We don't want to get
a late start."
```

a. The first and second groups of spoken words appear inside separate sets of quotation marks.
b. The first group of spoken words is followed by a comma.
c. If the first group of spoken words is not a sentence, a comma appears after the statement of who spoke and the second group of spoken words does not begin with a capital letter.
d. If the first group of spoken words forms a sentence, the statement of who spoke is followed by a period, and the second group of spoken words begins with a capital letter.
e. The second group of spoken words is followed by a period, which appears inside the final quotation marks.

4. When the spoken words form a question, a question mark is used instead of the period or comma after the spoken words:

```
Malcolm asked, "Where did you park my van?"
```

```
"When is the last day of the book sale?" Carla questioned.
```

```
"Can we go now," Sis asked, "or do we still have to wait for
Joe?"
```

a. In each case above, the question mark replaces the period or comma because the spoken words form a question.
b. The question mark appears inside the quotation marks.

5. When the entire sentence, rather than just the spoken words, is forming the question, the question mark appears outside of the quotation marks:

```
Can you believe that Professor Golden said, "If you want, we
will postpone the test until Monday"?
```

The question mark is outside the quotation marks because the entire sentence, not the spoken words, forms the question.

6. When you use quotation marks to signal the use of conversation, be careful that you really do have spoken words. Notice the two sentences below:

```
Maria announced that she was quitting her job to attend school
full-time.

Maria announced, "I'm quitting my job to attend school full-
time."
```

   a. Although it is tempting to use quotation marks in the first sentence, no spoken words appear there.
   b. Since the second sentence does have spoken words, quotation marks are necessary.

7. A person's thoughts are often punctuated the same way as spoken words.

```
Joshua thought to himself, "I'm sure I can win this event if I
get a fast start."
```

8. To be more precise and to increase the vitality of your writing, consider these substitutions for *said* and *asked:*

responded	whispered	explained
replied	whimpered	questioned
shouted	announced	inquired
cried	blurted out	wondered
snapped		

ARRANGING DETAIL

Narrative details are arranged in *chronological* (time) order. Usually, you start with what happened first, move to what happened next, and so forth. However, this is not the only chronology available. You can also begin at the end and flash back to the first event and proceed in chronological order from there. Similarly, you can begin somewhere in the middle of a story and then flash back to the beginning.

Let's say I want to narrate an account of preparing for and taking a final exam. If I want to begin with the first event and move chronologically, I might begin this way:

```
I filled the kettle with water—enough to keep me in coffee for
the rest of the night, opened a 16-ounce bag of Fritos,
arranged my statistics notes next to my text, and I was ready
to make sense of T-scores and chi-squares.
```

After this opening sentence, I could describe the night of study, explaining events in the order they occurred. Then I could move on to the next morning and how I felt on the way to the exam. From there I could narrate the events of the exam.

But I could follow a different time sequence: I could begin in the middle.

```
The alarm jarred me from a fitful three hours' sleep, and I
knew the time for preparation was gone. In just two hours I
would be sweating over my statistics exam. "Well, old girl," I
tried to reassure myself, "you certainly studied hard enough."
Yes, I put in some kind of night preparing for the test.
```

From here I could flash back to narrate the night of study, return to the time I woke up, and move through the events up to and including the exam.

Or I could start at the end—in this fashion:

```
As I left the classroom, I knew I would be lucky to get a C-
on my stat exam. Anything higher would call for divine
intervention. Yet, it wasn't like I hadn't prepared for the
test.
```

From this point I could flash back to the night of study and detail the events chronologically up to and including the exam.

To signal your chronological order and help your reader follow along, transitions are important. You will want to use words and phrases like the following:

in the meantime	at first
suddenly	later
soon	that evening
earlier	next
by noon	in the evening

The fact that narration has a logical chronology that is readily recognized by the reader can greatly influence the structure of a narrative piece. For example, topic sentences are not always necessary or desirable because the chronology is often enough to establish a logical presentation. Once the reader grasps the time sequence at work, he or she easily understands why ideas are grouped and presented in the order that they are: They follow the governing chronology.

You can also write a narration without traditional paragraphs of introduction and conclusion. This is particularly true when the events in the narration speak so well for themselves that no formal working up to them (introduction) or tying off of them (conclusion) is necessary. Often, however, writers feel the need for an introductory remark, so they precede their narration with a one- or two-sentence introduction before presenting the first chronological event. Sometimes this preliminary material presents the point the narration makes.

Similarly, instead of a concluding paragraph you may prefer to tie things off with a brief one- or two-sentence closing, which may draw a conclusion from the narration. However, this is not to say that narration cannot have an introduction with thesis and a concluding paragraph.

Finally, at times you will want to comment on the significant aspects of your narration in the introduction, body, or conclusion—whatever seems the most effective. An event, person, location, or time may hold import that is not obvious from the story, and you may want to point out that import. For example, if the site where the story occurred now has special meaning to you as a result of the event you are narrating, you can mention that fact and explain the meaning.

Annotated Student Essay

Studying the following narration, written by a student, along with the marginal notes, will help you better understand the points made in this chapter.

Lots of Locks

paragraph 1
The writer opens with the narration. Notice the description, which adds interest. The questions who, when, and where are answered.

I was 12 years old at the time. It was the summer before I was to enter junior high school. I sat in the beautician's chair, awaiting the first haircut of my life. I stared at my long braided hair stretching down the middle of my back, the tip making a relaxed curl at my waist. As far back as I could remember, my hair had always been that long. Even old photographs of me at the age of three or four showed long locks of hair cascading over my shoulders and covering most of me. What a hassle those locks had been over the years. Most people had nightmares of assailants coming at them with a knife or gun. In my nightmares, I saw my mom coming at me with a wide-tooth comb.

paragraph 2
Sentence 1 is the topic sentence, which sets up the flashback beginning in the next sentence. This paragraph begins the discussion of the significance of an element of the narration (the writer's long hair). Notice the specific word choice.

Combing my hair was always such a huge task. I remember my mom standing me on an old wooden kitchen chair. Then she'd start combing. She'd angle the comb at the top of my head, ever so gently, then pull, tug, and yank until the comb made a jerky exit at the ends of my long strands.

paragraphs 3–10
The details are in chronological order. Notice the use of conversation and the specific words like *yank, taunt,* and *jerky exit.*

"Ow," I'd holler. "That hurts!" "Use the brush," I'd plead.

"Now honey," she'd say calmly, "you know that brush won't get the tangles out."

"I don't care!" I'd start crying, hoping to change her mind.

Of course my whining didn't do a bit of good. My sisters, the brats that they were, hung around just to tease me.

"Whiney Caroliney, Whiney Caroliney," they'd taunt in unison and almost perfect harmony.

I'd cry even harder, and my mom would take a *8*
quick swat at them. She'd try to shut me up by cooing.

"Look honey at this big rat's nest I got out of *9*
your hair. You know that's what these tangles really
are, don't you? If we don't get those buggers out of
your hair today, there'll be twice as many in there
tomorrow."

I would look at the knotted ball of hair wrapped *10*
around the teeth of the comb, with its straggly ends
sticking out all over, and my childlike gullibility
would lead me to believe her fabrication. When she
finished, I imagined what a chicken might feel like
after having all its feathers plucked.

paragraph 11
Sentence 1 is the topic sentence; it establishes that a second flashback is beginning. Note the similes: the comparison of pulling braids to squeezing Charmin and the comparison of the author to an old woman. The body paragraphs are explaining the significance of the author's long hair.

I thought about other times when having long *11*
hair was a real pain (in a different sense of the
word). Some mornings my mom would fix my hair into
two long braids. Not only would family and friends
give them a tug, but even an occasional stranger
could not resist the urge to pull on my braids. It
was as impossible as trying to resist the urge to
"squeeze the Charmin." Another hairdo she liked to
deck me out in was the crisscrossing of the two
braids on the top of my head. I hated my hair like
that. I felt I looked like an old woman. Since I was
a tomboy, most of the time I just wore my hair in a
ponytail. Still my hair would fly around and slap me
in the face while playing kick the can, or homerun
derby, like a horse's tail swatting flies. I would be
glad to get rid of the nuisance. Who wouldn't be? My
long locks were way overdue for a trimming.

paragraph 12
The topic sentence (sentence 1) brings the chronology back to the present of the narration.

Finally, the beautician entered the room. She *12*
picked up a pair of scissors larger than any I had
ever seen. I felt one last, long tug on my hair and
heard the muffled cutting sounds of the scissors. My
long lifeless braid fell limp to the floor.

paragraph 13
Notice the thoughts punctuated as conversation.

"Free at last!" I thought. "No more long tangle *13*
sessions," I sighed to myself. "No one would pull on
my hair now," I mused. "How happy could any one
person be?" I wondered.

paragraph 14

The conclusion gives the last event in the chronology and raises a question for the reader to consider and thereby get at the significance of the narration. The narration emphasizes the journalist's question *why*.

At that moment, I felt a tear forming in the corner of my eye and I wondered why.

14

Pitfalls to Avoid

1. **Avoid telling a story for no reason.** You should tell your story for a specific purposes; for instance, tell it because it is entertaining, points to an important truth, teaches a lesson, or illustrates a fact of life.

2. **Avoid rambling.** You must keep your story on track and moving forward. Side trips into areas that do not advance the story line, do not help you fulfill your purpose, or do not explain the significance of a narrative element will bore a reader.

3. **Avoid made-up stories.** These are better left to creative writing classes. For now, tell stories that come from your own experience or observation.

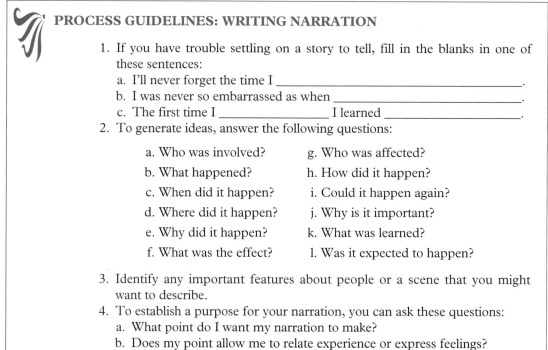

PROCESS GUIDELINES: WRITING NARRATION

1. If you have trouble settling on a story to tell, fill in the blanks in one of these sentences:
   a. I'll never forget the time I _____.
   b. I was never so embarrassed as when _____.
   c. The first time I _____ I learned _____.

2. To generate ideas, answer the following questions:

a. Who was involved?	g. Who was affected?
b. What happened?	h. How did it happen?
c. When did it happen?	i. Could it happen again?
d. Where did it happen?	j. Why is it important?
e. Why did it happen?	k. What was learned?
f. What was the effect?	l. Was it expected to happen?

3. Identify any important features about people or a scene that you might want to describe.

4. To establish a purpose for your narration, you can ask these questions:
   a. What point do I want my narration to make?
   b. Does my point allow me to relate experience or express feelings?
   c. Does my point allow me to inform the reader? If so, of what?
   d. Does my point allow me to persuade the reader? If so, of what?
   e. Does my point allow me to entertain the reader?

5. To settle on an audience, you can ask these questions:
    a. Who would be interested in my story?
    b. Who could learn something from my story?
    c. Who could be influenced by my story?
    d. To whom would I like to relate my experience?
6. To assess the nature of your audience so that you know what kind of detail your reader requires, you can ask these questions:
    a. Are there any of the *who, what, when, where, why, how* questions to which my reader already knows the answers?
    b. Does my reader have any strong feelings that will influence reaction to my narration?
    c. What must my reader know to appreciate my point?
    d. Has my reader had an experience similar to the one I am narrating?
7. If you like to secure reader response as part of your revising process, see page 115. In addition, ask your reader to note any places on the draft where you should comment on or explain the significance of an event. Then ask that person to write out the point your narration makes so you can be sure you are expressing what you want to express.

REVISION CHECKLIST

In addition to the checklist on page 117, you can use this checklist to help you revise your narration:

1. Does your narration make a specific point that is stated or strongly implied? What is that point?
2. Have you answered all the journalist's questions? Have you emphasized the answers to some questions as your audience and purpose warrant?
3. Is the narration well paced and free of irrelevant detail?
4. Are details arranged chronologically, with or without flashbacks?
5. If you have omitted a formal introduction, stated thesis, topic sentences, and/or concluding paragraph, have you done so judiciously?
6. When necessary for clarity, have you interrupted the narration to comment on an event or explain its significance?
7. Have you used conversation, specific diction, and description as necessary for vividness?
8. Have you used transitions to signal your chronology?

EXERCISE | **Writing Narration**

1. Think back over your experiences and identify two narrations you could tell about your family and two that you could tell about college life.
2. For each of the narrations you identified for number 1, establish a purpose and identify a suitable audience.

3. Write sentences according to the directions given, being sure to punctuate correctly.
   a. Write a sentence you recently heard spoken on campus. Place the spoken words before the indication of who spoke.
   b. Write a sentence you have heard spoken in the doctor's office. Place the spoken words after the indication of who spoke.
   c. Write a sentence you have heard spoken in the library. Place spoken words both before and after the indication of who spoke.
   d. Write a question you have heard spoken in class, placing the exact words after the indication of who spoke.
   e. Write something you might think to yourself before a final exam, placing the exact words before the indication of who was thinking.
4. Read paragraph 13 of "Looking for Work" (p. 175) and identify the transitions that signal chronological order.
5. *Collaborative Activity.* Reread the dialogue between John and Marsha on page 160 and then with a classmate, write a narrative paragraph or two telling what happened when Marsha tried to register for classes. Use the details given in the dialogue and any other details that you care to add. Arrange the details in chronological order, and use some description and conversation. Be sure to answer all the journalist's questions.

PROFESSIONAL ESSAYS

The Girl in Gift Wrap

Paul Hemphill

He worked in men's shoes, and she worked in gift wrap. Could he find the courage to speak to her?

He worked in Men's Shoes and she worked in Gift Wrap, and he considered it   *1*
the best part-time job he had ever had during any Christmas holiday. All day long, while he fitted feet to shoes and she wrapped Christmas gifts, they were no more than 30 feet apart. There were only 30 feet separating him and the most beautiful girl he had ever seen, and maybe it would have been better if he had a job on another floor, because the thought of being so close to her but never having spoken to her was driving him out of his mind.

The first thing he had noticed about her was the way she looked at the cus-   *2*
tomers with her eyes. They were the most beautiful eyes in the world. They were dark blue, a very dark blue, with long, black eyelashes protecting them. He would go home every night remembering how she teased people by looking up at them through those long, black eyelashes. Her hair was black, too, a silken, shimmering black streaming down over her shoulders. And her face was soft and white, and her figure was like a ballet dancer's, and every day she wore baby blue or desert tan or mint green to promote all of this to the fullest. Here he was, working 30 feet away, and he did not know how much longer he could stand being so close,

yet so far away. It really was a wonderfully painful kind of job, being in Men's Shoes while she was in Gift Wrap.

And now it was the last week before Christmas. He knew he was going to *3* have to find some way to talk to her before they both went back to school, if she went to school at all, and he did not know how he was going to do it.

Once, he thought he was in love with a girl in high school. That was his se- *4* nior year. All year long he tried to sit near her and her dates during the football and basketball games, and he even prayed he would be in the same classes with her. She had a lot of dates, and this discouraged him, so he never got around to asking her for a date. It wasn't until he had graduated and gone to college that he learned why she had been so popular, and because he had not dreamed she was that kind of girl, that made him feel even more awkward.

But now the Christmas holidays were almost over. The crowds of shoppers *5* were thinning. Those who came now were men buying at the last minute for their wives. There were only three more shopping days until Christmas. Three more days to do something. And he chose to make his move on her coffee break.

The snack bar where she always went for her break was not crowded. That *6* would make it easier for him. He had waited for her to leave, and then he had followed her, and when she took one of the stools at the counter he took another, leaving one stool between them, and after their snacks had come, he cleared his throat and said, "Well, it's almost over now."

"Yes, and I hope I never see another package," she said. "I work in Gift *7* Wrap."

"I know. I work in Men's Shoes. Next to you," he said. She seemed *8* friendly enough. And her eyes really were beautiful.

"Ah, do you go to school?" he asked her. *9*

"No. I'm just trying to make some money for Christmas." *10*

"Yeah. Me, too. I'm in college." *11*

"What are you studying?" *12*

"Engineering. I'm going to be an engineer." *13*

"That's wonderful. That's a good profession, isn't it?" *14*

"It sure is," he said, looking into her beautiful blue eyes. *15*

She said, "What's Santa Claus going to bring you for Christmas?" She *16* laughed, a very nice laugh, when she said it.

"Oh, I don't know. Clothes, I guess. How about you?" *17*

She answered so quickly and easily and pleasantly. That is what made it *18* hurt. "An engagement ring," she said.

"Oh," he said. And he went back to Men's Shoes, and she to Gift Wrap. *19* She was only 30 feet away. There were three miserable days to go.

Considering Ideas

1. How did the young man feel about the girl in gift wrap? Why did he feel that way?
2. Why did the young man wait so long to speak to the girl?

3. What do you judge to be Hemphill's purpose? Who do you judge to be his intended audience?
4. What lesson does the narration teach?

Considering Technique

1. Which of the *who, what, when, where, why, how* questions does Hemphill emphasize the most?
2. *Combining patterns*. What elements of description appear in the essay? What purpose does that description serve? What element of contrast appears?
3. What purpose does the conversation serve?
4. Where in the essay is the statement of the narration's significance?
5. What approach does Hemphill take to his introduction? To the conclusion?

For Group Discussion or Journal Writing

Using the evidence in the essay for clues, develop a list of words that describe the college student who worked in men's shoes.

The Boys

Maya Angelou

In a powerful narrative taken from her autobiography I Know Why the Caged Bird Sings *(1969), Angelou shares a childhood reminiscence of a dark period of American history.*

Weighing the half-pounds of flour, excluding the scoop, and depositing them dust-free into the thin paper sacks held a simple kind of adventure for me. I developed an eye for measuring how full a silver-looking ladle of flour, mash, meal, sugar or corn had to be to push the scale indicator over to eight ounces or one pound. When I was absolutely accurate our appreciative customers use to admire: "Sister Henderson sure got some smart grandchildrens." If I was off in the Store's favor, the eagle-eyed women would say, "Put some more in that sack, child. Don't you try to make your profit offa me." 1

Then I would quietly but persistently punish myself. For every bad judgment, the fine was no silver-wrapped Kisses, the sweet chocolate drops that I loved more than anything in the world, except Bailey. And maybe canned pineapples. My obsession with pineapples nearly drove me mad. I dreamt of the days when I would be grown and able to buy a whole carton for myself alone. 2

Until I was thirteen and left Arkansas for good, the Store was my favorite place to be. Alone and empty in the mornings, it looked like an unopened present from a stranger. Opening the front doors was pulling the ribbon off the unexpected gift. The light would come in softly (we faced north), easing itself over the shelves of mackerel, salmon, tobacco, thread. It fell flat on the big vat of lard 3 and by noontime during the summer the grease had softened to a thick soup. Whenever I walked into the Store in the afternoon, I sensed that it was tired. I alone could hear the slow pulse of its job half done. But just before bedtime, after numerous people had walked in and out, had argued over their bills, or joked about their neighbors, or just dropped in "to give Sister Henderson a 'Hi y'all,' " the promise of magic mornings returned to the Store and spread itself over the family in washed life waves.

Momma opened boxes of crispy crackers and we sat around the meat block *4* at the rear of the Store. I sliced onions, and Bailey opened two or even three cans of sardines and allowed their juice of oil and fishing boats to ooze down and around the sides. That was supper. In the evening, when we were alone like that, Uncle Willie didn't stutter or shake or give any indication that he had an "affliction." It seemed that the peace of a day's ending was an assurance that the covenant God made with children, Negroes and the crippled was still in effect.

Throwing scoops of corn to the chicken and mixing sour dry mash with *5* leftover food and oily dish water for the hogs were among our evening chores. Bailey and I sloshed down twilight trails to the pig pens, and standing on the first fence rungs we poured down the unappealing concoctions to our grateful hogs. They mashed their tender pink snouts down into the slop, and rooted and grunted their satisfaction. We always grunted a reply only half in jest. We were also grateful that we had concluded the dirtiest of chores and had only gotten the evil-smelling swill on our shoes, stockings, feet and hands.

Late one day, as we were attending to the pigs, I heard a horse in the front *6* yard (it really should have been called a driveway, except that there was nothing to drive into it), and ran to find out who had come riding up on a Thursday evening when even Mr. Steward, the quiet, bitter man who owned a riding horse, would be resting by his warm fire until the morning called him out to turn over his field.

The used-to-be sheriff sat rakishly astraddle his horse. His nonchalance was *7* meant to convey his authority and power over even dumb animals. How much more capable he would be with Negroes. It went without saying.

His twang jogged in the brittle air. From the side of the Store, Bailey and I *8* heard him say to Momma, "Annie, tell Willie he better lay low tonight. A crazy nigger messed with a white lady today. Some of the boys'll be coming over here later." Even after the slow drag of years, I remember the sense of fear which filled my mouth with hot, dry air, and made my body light.

The "boys"? Those cement faces and eyes of hate that burned the clothes *9* off you if they happened to see you lounging on the main street downtown on Saturday. Boys? It seemed that youth had never happened to them. Boys? No, rather men who were covered with graves' dust and age without beauty or learning. The ugliness and rottenness of old abominations.

If on Judgment Day I were summoned by St. Peter to give testimony to the *10* used-to-be sheriff's act of kindness, I would be unable to say anything in his behalf. His confidence that my uncle and every other Black man who heard of the

Klan's coming ride would scurry under their houses to hide in chicken droppings was too humiliating to hear. Without waiting for Momma's thanks, he rode out of the yard, sure that things were as they should be and that he was a gentle squire, saving those deserving serfs from the laws of the land, which he condoned.

Immediately, while his horse's hoofs were still loudly thudding the ground, *11* Momma blew out the coal-oil lamps. She had a quiet, hard talk with Uncle Willie and called Bailey and me into the store.

We were told to take the potatoes and onions out of their bins and knock *12* out the dividing walls that kept them apart. Then with a tedious and fearful slowness Uncle Willis gave me his rubber-tipped cane and bent down to get into the now-enlarged empty bin. It took forever before he lay down flat, and then we covered him with potatoes and onions, layer upon layer, like a casserole. Grandmother knelt praying in the darkened Store.

It was fortunate that the "boys" didn't ride into our yard that evening and *13* insist that Momma open the Store. They would have surely found Uncle Willie and just as surely lynched him. He moaned the whole night through as if he had, in fact, been guilty of some heinous crime. The heavy sounds pushed their way up out of the blanket of vegetables and I pictured his mouth pulling down on the right side and his saliva flowing into the eyes of new potatoes and waiting here like dew drops for the warmth of morning.

Considering Ideas

1. Who are "the boys"? How does Angelou feel about them?
2. The "boys" that the sheriff refers to are actually men. What effect is created when these men are called boys?
3. Why is Angelou not grateful for the sheriff's warning?
4. What point does the narration make? That is, what is its significance?

Considering Technique

1. Angelou does not begin her narration until paragraph 6. What purpose do the first five paragraphs serve?
2. Paragraph 3 is largely descriptive. Cite an example of concrete sensory detail (see page 134). Cite an example of personification (see page 135). Cite an example of a simile (see page 135).
3. What purpose does the conversation in paragraph 8 serve?
4. What purpose does paragraph 9 serve? Paragraph 10?
5. "The Boys" closes with an image of Uncle Willie in the vegetable bin. Is this an effective conclusion? Explain.

For Group Discussion or Journal Writing

Imagine that you are Momma, having that "quiet, hard talk with Uncle Willie" (paragraph 11). What do you think Momma might have said in order to convince Uncle Willie to hide? What might Uncle Willie have said in return?

Combining Patterns of Development

Looking for Work

Gary Soto

*In striking clarity and detail, Gary Soto narrates the events of a July day of his youth. From his account, the reader learns something of his dreams and reality. Notice the **cause-and-effect analysis** and **contrast** that appear with the **narration.***

One July, while killing ants on the kitchen sink with a rolled newspaper, I had a   *1*
nine-year-old's vision of wealth that would save us from ourselves. For weeks I
had drunk Kool-Aid and watched morning reruns of *Father Knows Best*, whose
family was so uncomplicated in its routine that I very much wanted to imitate it.
The first step was to get my brother and sister to wear shoes at dinner.

"Come on, Rick—come on, Deb," I whined. But Rick mimicked me and   *2*
the same day that I asked him to wear shoes he came to the dinner table in only
his swim trunks. My mother didn't notice, nor did my sister, as we sat to eat our
beans and tortillas in the stifling heat of our kitchen. We all gleamed like cello-
phane, wiping the sweat from our brows with the backs of our hands as we talked
about the day: Frankie our neighbor was beat up by Faustino; the swimming pool
at the playground would be closed for a day because the pump was broken.

Such was our life. So that morning, while doing-in the train of ants which ar-   *3*
rived each day, I decided to become wealthy, and right away! After downing a bowl
of cereal, I took a rake from the garage and started up the block to look for work.

We lived on an ordinary block of mostly working-class people: warehouse-   *4*
men, egg candlers,[1] welders, mechanics, and a union plumber. And there were
many retired people who kept their lawns green and the gutters uncluttered of
the chewing gum wrappers we dropped as we rode by on our bikes. They bent
down to gather our litter, muttering at our evilness.

At the corner house I rapped the screen door and a very large woman in a   *5*
muu-muu answered. She sized me up and then asked what I could do.

"Rake leaves," I answered smiling.   *6*

"It's summer, and there ain't no leaves," she countered. Her face was   *7*
pinched with lines; fat jiggled under her chin. She pointed to the lawn, then the
flower bed, and said: "You see any leaves there—or there?" I followed her pointing arm, stupidly. But she had a job for me and that was to get her a Coke at the
liquor store. She gave me twenty cents, and after ditching my rake in a bush, off I
ran. I returned with an unbagged Pepsi, for which she thanked me and gave me a
nickel from her apron.

I skipped off her porch, fetched my rake, and crossed the street to the next   *8*
block where Mrs. Moore, mother of Earl the retarded man, let me weed a flower
bed. She handed me a trowel and for a good part of the morning my fingers
dipped into the moist dirt, ripping up runners of Bermuda grass. Worms sur-

---

[1]*egg candler:* one who inspects eggs by holding them up to a light.

faced in my search for deep roots, and I cut them in halves, tossing them to Mrs. Moore's cat who pawed them playfully as they dried in the sun. I made out Earl whose face was pressed to the back window of the house, and although he was calling to me I couldn't understand what he was trying to say. Embarrassed, I worked without looking up, but I imagined his contorted mouth and the ring of keys attached to his belt—keys that jingled with each palsied step. He scared me and I worked quickly to finish the flower bed. When I did finish Mrs. Moore gave me a quarter and two peaches from her tree, which I washed there but ate in the alley behind my house.

I was sucking on the second one, a bit of juice staining the front of my 9 T-shirt, when Little John, my best friend, came walking down the alley with a baseball bat over his shoulder, knocking over trash cans as he made his way toward me.

Little John and I went to St. John's Catholic School, where we sat among 10 the "stupids." Miss Marino, our teacher, alternated the rows of good students with the bad, hoping that by sitting side by side with the bright students the stupids might become more intelligent, as though intelligence were contagious. But we didn't progress as she had hoped. She grew frustrated when one day, while dismissing class for recess, Little John couldn't get up because his arms were stuck in the slats of the chair's backrest. She scolded us with a shaking finger when we knocked over the globe, denting the already troubled Africa. She muttered curses when Leroy White, a real stupid but a great softball player with the gift to hit to all fields, openly chewed his host[2] when he made his First Communion; his hands swung at his sides as he returned to the pew looking around with a big smile.

Little John asked what I was doing, and I told him that I was taking a break 11 from work, as I sat comfortably among high weeds. He wanted to join me, but I reminded him that the last time he'd gone door-to-door asking for work his mother had whipped him. I was with him when his mother, a New Jersey Italian who could rise up in anger one moment and love the next, told me in a polite but matter-of-fact voice that I had to leave because she was going to beat her son. She gave me a homemade popsicle, ushered me to the door, and said that I could see Little John the next day. But it was sooner than that. I went around to his bedroom window to suck my popsicle and watch Little John dodge his mother's blows, a few hitting their mark but many whirring air.

It was midday when Little John and I converged in the alley, the sun blaz- 12 ing in the high nineties, and he suggested that we go to Roosevelt High School to swim. He needed five cents to make fifteen, the cost of admission, and I lent him a nickel. We ran home for my bike and when my sister found out that we were going swimming, she started to cry because she didn't have the fifteen cents but only an empty Coke bottle. I waved for her to come and three of us mounted the bike—Debra on the cross bar, Little John on the handle bars and holding the Coke bottle which we would cash for a nickel and make up the difference that would allow all of us to get in, and me pumping up the crooked streets, dodging

---

[2]*his host:* the wafer that represents, in the Catholic sacrament of Communion, the bread of the Last Supper and the body of Christ.

cars and pot holes. We spent the day swimming under the afternoon sun, so that when we got home our mom asked us what was darker, the floor or us? She feigned a stern posture, her hands on her hips and her mouth puckered. We played along. Looking down, Debbie and I said in unison, "Us."

That evening at dinner we all sat down in our bathing suits to eat our beans, *13* laughing and chewing loudly. Our mom was in a good mood, so I took a risk and asked her if sometime we could have turtle soup. A few days before I had watched a television program in which a Polynesian tribe killed a large turtle, gutted it, and then stewed it over an open fire. The turtle, basted in a sugary sauce, looked delicious as I ate an afternoon bowl of cereal, but my sister, who was watching the program with a glass of Kool-Aid between her knees, said, "Caca."

My mother looked at me in bewilderment. "Boy, are you a crazy Mexican. *14* Where did you get the idea that people eat turtles?"

"On television," I said, explaining the program. Then I took it a step fur- *15* ther. "Mom, do you think we could get dressed up for dinner one of these days? David King does."

"*Ay, Dios,*" my mother laughed. She started collecting the dinner plates, *16* but my brother wouldn't let go of his. He was still drawing a picture in the bean sauce. Giggling, he said it was me, but I didn't want to listen because I wanted an answer from Mom. This was the summer when I spent the mornings in front of the television that showed the comfortable lives of white kids. There were no beatings, no rifts in the family. They wore bright clothes; toys tumbled from their closets. They hopped into bed with kisses and woke to glasses of fresh orange juice, and to a father sitting before his morning coffee while the mother buttered his toast. They hurried through the day making friends and gobs of money, re-turning home to a warmly lit living room, and then dinner. *Leave It to Beaver* was the program I replayed in my mind:

"May I have the mashed potatoes?" asks Beaver with a smile. *17*

"Sure, Beav," replies Wally as he taps the corners of his mouth with a *18* starched napkin.

The father looks on in his suit. The mother, decked out in earrings and a *19* pearl necklace, cuts into her steak and blushes. Their conversation is politely clipped.

"Swell," says Beaver, his cheeks puffed with food. *20*

Our own talk at dinner was loud with belly laughs and marked by our *21* pointing forks at one another. The subjects were commonplace.

"Gary, let's go to the ditch tomorrow," my brother suggests. He explains *22* that he has made a life preserver out of four empty detergent bottles strung to-gether with twine and that he will make me one if I can find more bottles. "No way are we going to drown."

"Yeah, then we could have a dirt clod fight," I reply, so happy to be alive. *23*

Whereas the Beaver's family enjoyed dessert in dishes at the table, our *24* mom sent us outside, and more often than not I went into the alley to peek over the neighbor's fences and spy out fruit, apricot or peaches.

I had asked my mom and again she laughed that I was a crazy *chavalo*[3] as   *25* she stood in front of the sink, her arms rising and falling with suds, face glistening from the heat. She sent me outside where my brother and sister were sitting in the shade that the fence threw out like a blanket. They were talking about me when I plopped down next to them. They looked at one another and then Debbie, my eight-year-old sister, started in.

"What's this crap about getting dressed up?"   *26*

She had entered her *profanity* stage. A year later she would give up such   *27* words and slip into her Catholic uniform, and into squealing on my brother and me when we "cussed this" and "cussed that."

I tried to convince them that if we improved the way we looked we might   *28* get along better in life. White people would like us more. They might invite us to places, like their homes or front yards. They might not hate us so much.

My sister called me a "craphead," and got up to leave with a stalk of grass   *29* dangling from her mouth. "They'll never like us."

My brother's mood lightened as he talked about the ditch—the white water,   *30* the broken pieces of glass, and the rusted car fenders that awaited our knees. There would be toads, and rocks to smash them.

David King, the only person we knew who resembled the middle class,   *31* called from over the fence. David was Catholic, of Armenian and French descent, and his closet was filled with toys. A bear-shaped cookie jar, like the ones on television, sat on the kitchen counter. His mother was remarkably kind while she put up with the racket we made on the street. Evenings, she often watered the front yard and it must have upset her to see us—my brother and I and others— jump from trees laughing, the unkillable kids of the very poor, who got up unshaken, brushed off, and climbed into another one to try again.

David called again. Rick got up and slapped grass from his pants. When I   *32* asked if I could come along he said no. David said no. They were two years older so their affairs were different from mine. They greeted one another with foul names and took off down the alley to look for trouble.

I went inside the house, turned on the television, and was about to sit down   *33* with a glass of Kool-Aid when Mom shooed me outside.

"It's still light," she said. "Later you'll bug me to let you stay out longer. So   *34* go on."

I downed my Kool-Aid and went outside to the front yard. No one was   *35* around. The day had cooled and a breeze rustled the trees. Mr. Jackson, the plumber, was watering his lawn and when he saw me he turned away to wash off his front steps. There was more than an hour of light left, so I took advantage of it and decided to look for work. I felt suddenly alive as I skipped down the block in search of an overgrown flower bed and the dime that would end the day right.

---

[3]*chavalo:* kid.

Considering Ideas

1. Why was the young Soto so taken by the family life he saw depicted on television?
2. Soto looked for work both at the beginning and the end of the narration, but he did so for different reasons each time. What is the difference in his motivation?
3. As a nine-year-old, Soto longed for a different kind of family life than he had. Would you say that he was unhappy? Explain.
4. How would you characterize young Soto's family life?
5. For what reason do you think Soto wrote "Looking for Work"?
6. What point does Soto's narration make? Is that point stated or implied?

Considering Technique

1. "Looking for Work" lacks a separate introduction with thesis. Is that a problem? Explain. What approach does Soto take to his conclusion?
2. In what paragraphs does Soto explain an event or its significance?
3. Soto uses a great deal of description. What does this description contribute? Cite two examples of description that you find effective.
4. What does the conversation contribute to the essay?
5. Which of the journalist's questions are emphasized?
6. *Combining Patterns.* What element of cause-and-effect analysis appears in the essay? (Cause-and-effect analysis explains the causes or the effects of an occurrence.) What element of contrast appears? (Contrast shows differences.)

For Group Discussion or Journal Writing

Soto longed for the kind of home life depicted in the television programs he watched. Discuss the ways television influences what we desire.

STUDENT ESSAYS TO READ AND EVALUATE

The following narrations were written by students. As you read, determine what works well and what could be improved. Doing so will help you become a reliable critic so you can make accurate revision decisions, and it will make you aware of both successful techniques to incorporate into your writing and less-successful techniques to avoid.

The Ball Game

It was midsummer and the Little League baseball playoffs had begun. *1* Many teams from the area participated in them, including the one I coached. My team was made up of 9- and 10-year-olds, all relatively the same size and build, with one exception. Jimmy was much smaller and had much less athletic ability than the others. Still, he was very excited about the playoffs. Jimmy's father was also worked up over the playoffs, maybe too worked up.

When my team went on the field for the pregame warmups, it was easy to pick Jimmy out of the crowd. His uniform was much too big. He was always tripping over his long pants or pulling his sleeves up to throw the ball. His cap was continuously falling over his eyes, blocking his vision. Still, Jimmy was as proud and happy to be a part of that team as the next boy. He never complained about anything; he just went along with what was asked of him.   *2*

It was in the third inning of our first game that I sent Jimmy in to bat. He was so excited when I told him that he ran out on the field without the bat. But when he came back to get it, I reminded him to calm down and take his time. His fast swing at the ball brought a solid single; it was his first hit all year. The big, gleaming smile on Jimmy's face showed how proud he was. But his father, who was watching the game from the side of the dugout, stood still. He neither clapped nor smiled. The look on his face seemed to say, "Is that all?"   *3*

Jimmy's second at-bat was not at all good. He struck out in three straight pitches. As he slowly turned around to make that lonely walk back to the dugout, I could see the disappointment all over his face. I went out to meet Jimmy and started to console him, when suddenly I was pushed from behind and knocked several feet away from him. It was Jimmy's dad who pushed me. It was also Jimmy's dad who was yelling and screaming at Jimmy in front of everyone in the ballpark. Everyone tried to ignore the scene Jimmy's dad was making. The players in the dugout began to talk to each other, coaches looked at the roster sheets, fans stared up at the sky, and Jimmy just looked down at the ground, crying ever so slightly so no one would notice.   *4*

After several minutes, which seemed more like hours, Jimmy's dad finally walked off the field and left the park. Jimmy walked slowly back to the dugout and sat on the end of the bench for the rest of the game. He stared blankly into the ground, not once looking up, as big round tears rolled slowly down his embarrassed cheeks.   *5*

We lost the playoff game that day, but no one seemed to mind that much. We all realized that Jimmy had lost something more important, something it would not be easy to get back. In just a few minutes of cruel and thoughtless yelling, the little bit of pride and confidence that Jimmy had gained was lost.   *6*

I Learned to March

I can still see it clearly even after all these years. A bright   *1*
cheerful fourth-grade room filled with 30 eager children of all
varieties of body and mind. I can also hear it as if it enveloped
me. The music of John Philip Sousa stays with me even today.

She played the records every day, that staunch old woman. Miss   *2*
Thompson was a matriarch. She was close to retirement that year,
and feared by every third-grader walking the halls of Walker
Elementary School. The summer before my fourth school year was one
of great anticipation. Miss Thompson was a legend with a bifurcated
image. She was feared due to her demanding nature, and respected
for her strength. Miss Thompson was crippled. She had survived
polio as a child and as a result walked with the aid of a cane and
was marked with a deformed left foot and leg. The day those fourth-
grade room assignments arrived the phone lines were jammed. Mary
called Cindy, Cindy called Susie, and Susie called me. I alone, of
all my friends, had been placed in Miss Thompson's class.

I wanted to cry, to scream of the injustice of it all. I knew   *3*
what lay ahead. I could feel it in every nerve cell of my body. It
was not the homework; it was not her demand to perform with above-
average capabilities; it was that damned marching!

Every day through the small glass window of Room 11, the   *4*
students of Miss Thompson could be seen marching round the room,
knees up high, heads back, chests out, marching to the music of
"Stars and Stripes Forever." Worse, though, was the fact that the
students of Room 11 could see the jeering faces of the crowds in
the hallway. They laughed and snickered and even pointed! I could
feel the shame even then, reading that small card with her name so
stately printed upon it. I knew how I would look to them!

Yet, deep inside of me, slowly nurturing, was a slight sense of *5*
titillation. I was an extremely shy child. Having no brothers or
sisters and an introverted mother, I too became quiet and reserved.
Still, I was curious about this new twist in my life.

I survived the remainder of the summer by doing deep-breathing   *6*
exercises, and arrived at school on the first day of fourth grade a
total nervous wreck. I seated myself in the back of the room,
unable at any time to remove my gaze from this silver-haired woman
sitting perfectly erect at her desk.

How I learned that first day. I learned of consistent demand   *7*
topped with a dollop of love; I learned to respect the grace of a
woman who had midmorning tea brewed in a cup with a strange heating
coil; I learned that indeed my back did feel better if I sat erect
in my chair; and I learned to march—with my knees high, my head
back, and my chest out, to John Philip Sousa's classic piece,
"Stars and Stripes Forever."

Collaborative Exercise: Evaluating Writing

Form a group with several classmates and select one of the previous student writings. Designate one person to record the group's findings and another to report those findings to the class. Then read the essay closely and answer the evaluation questions below. Answering these questions will help you appreciate how each aspect of an essay contributes to or detracts from its overall quality, and it will point out successful techniques you can bring to your own writing as well as less-successful techniques to avoid.

Evaluation Questions

1. *The Opening*
   Does the opening engage your interest? Why or why not?
2. *Supporting Details*
   Which journalist's questions are answered? Are any treated in too much or too little detail? Note any points that you do not understand. Does the writer interrupt the narration to explain? Evaluate the effectiveness of this technique. Evaluate the use of conversation and description.
3. *Organization*
   Does the writer use or omit an introduction, stated thesis, topic sentences, and conclusion paragraph effectively? Explain. What chronology is followed? Is the time sequence easy to follow? Evaluate the use of transitions.
4. *The Closing*
   Does the narration end in a satisfying way? Explain.
5. *Overview*
   What do you like best about the essay? What is the most important revision the author should make?

Essay Topics: Narration

When you write your essay, consult Pitfalls to Avoid on page 168, Process Guidelines on page 168, and the Revision Checklist on page 169.

Writing in the Pattern

1. Relate an occurrence that caused you to change your view of someone or something, making sure you note your view both before and after

the event. If you like, you can tell why the occurrence caused you to change your view.

2. Tell of an event that had a significant impact on you. Make clear what the impact was/is. You can also tell why the event affected you as it did.

3. Tell a story that describes a single, specific school experience. While it is not necessary, you can use a humorous approach.

4. Tell of a time when things did not go as you, or another, expected them to. Make clear what the expectation was and comment on why things did not go as planned.

5. Write a narration about a specific job experience you have had.

6. Tell the story of a time you were happy or unhappy with your family life.

7. Narrate a moment or event that marked a turning point in your life.

8. Tell of a time when you (or another) were treated unjustly.

9. Write an account of the time you were the angriest you have ever been.

10. Tell of an event that caused you to feel regret. If you like, you can write about a missed opportunity.

11. Relate an incident that caused you to realize something for the first time. Explain what the effect of that realization has been.

12. Tell a story of a time you witnessed (or displayed) courage.

13. Relate a memorable experience you have had in a sports competition.

14. Tell the story of some first-time experience.

Reading Then Writing in the Pattern

1. In paragraph 4 of "The Girl in Gift Wrap" (page 170), Paul Hemphill refers to a specific high school memory. Think back to your own experience and narrate an account of something that happened in high school that continues to affect you today. Try to explain why the event still affects you.

2. In "The Boys" (page 172), Maya Angelou narrates an account of an injustice. Tell of a time when you (or another) were treated unjustly and go on to explain what can be learned from the event.

3. Like Gary Soto in "Looking for Work" (page 175), tell a story that reveals something about the nature of your family life. Also like Soto, use conversation to lend insight into people and events and to advance the narration.

Responding to the Readings

1. In "Looking for Work" (page 175), Gary Soto says he wanted his family to be more like families on television. To what extent do you think television influences our desires? Is this influence largely positive or negative?

2. In "The Boys" (page 172), Uncle Willie is forced to hide even though he is not guilty of a crime. Discuss another example of injustice that you are aware of and try to explain the cause of that injustice.

3. The narrator of "The Girl in Gift Wrap" (page 170) is taken by the girl's beauty. How important is physical attractiveness in our society?

4. *Connecting the Readings.* Hemphill, Soto, and Angelou all narrate accounts of negative experiences. Drawing on their essays and your own experience and observation, explain the role negative experiences play in shaping who we are and what we learn. Consider whether or not negative experiences influence us more profoundly or positively than do good experiences.

CHAPTER 6

Illustration

An illustration is an example—and nothing helps a reader understand a writer's point better than an example. Think about a time when you were reading and feeling unsure about what the writer meant. Just when you were feeling the most uncertain, you may have come across the words, "for example." Remember how hopeful you felt when you read those words, knowing they were introducing an illustration that would clarify things? Remember how much better you understood the writer's point after you read the example? That is because a well-chosen illustration can crystallize meaning.

Even our most routine communications rely heavily on examples to make their point. Say a friend asked you whom to take for geology and you replied, "Take Chung; he's the most reasonable." Well, your friend would probably want you to clarify why Chung is the most reasonable, and you might explain by providing examples. "His tests are graded on the curve, he requires only one research paper, and he's always in his office to help students." Even the question, "What do you want to do tonight?" can prompt the use of examples. If you replied, "Something relaxing," you would not be as clear as if you added examples. "Something relaxing like a movie or a quiet dinner at Alonzo's."

Illustration adds clarity because it makes the general more specific; it allows the writer to nail down a generalization by providing specific instances of ways that generalization is true. Consider, for example, the following four sentences:

> It is not easy today for a young married couple to get off to a good start. House prices are high, making home ownership almost impossible, so the couple may spend many years in a cramped apartment. High-paying jobs are hard to find, so many couples cannot secure their income. Perhaps most significant, young marrieds find that financial worries cause tensions that strain the marriage bond.

The first sentence expresses a generalization, and the three sentences after that provide illustrations that bear out the generalization. In Chapter 2, when supporting detail was discussed, you were cautioned to *show* rather than *tell* (see page 65). Illustrations can help you do that by providing instances to make generalizations concrete.

In addition to providing clarity and concreteness, illustrations add interest. Carefully chosen examples add vitality and create reader interest by bringing things down from the abstract level to a more-specific, easily understood one.

ESTABLISHING YOUR PURPOSE AND IDENTIFYING YOUR AUDIENCE

Using illustration as your primary method of development allows you to achieve a variety of purposes. Assume you have written this thesis: Going to college is more stressful than I thought it would be. To *relate experience* or *express feelings,* you can provide examples of the stress you have experienced while in college. To *entertain* your reader, you could provide amusing examples of the stress. Now assume that you have written this thesis:

    We do not adequately care for the elderly in this country.

To *inform* your reader of the inadequate care or to persuade your reader that improvements in care are needed, you could provide examples of the poor care our elderly get.

Audience is an important consideration because who your reader is will affect your choice of examples. To appreciate this, assume you are writing about why your college is a good one, and you plan to present examples to illustrate some of your school's strengths. If you are writing for an academically oriented audience that does not care much for sports, you would not give the example that your football team is the conference champion. Similarly, a paper aimed at parents of prospective freshmen should not give the example of wild parties on Saturday nights.

Taken together, your purpose and audience will profoundly affect the illustrations you include. For example, assume you are writing about the benefits of running. If you want to express why you enjoy running so your friends—who think you are odd because you run four miles a day, regardless of the weather— will better understand your dedication to the sport, you would provide examples of the benefits you get. However, if your purpose is to inform the average reader that running can control depression and anxiety symptoms, you might provide examples of runners who have enjoyed these benefits from the sport.

COMBINING ILLUSTRATION WITH OTHER PATTERNS

Because examples are so useful for clarifying and proving points, they are frequent components of writing, no matter what the primary method of development. Thus, if you write a narrative essay that tells the story of the time a tornado hit your town, you might include illustrations of the damage done by the storm. If you explain how to grow a beautiful flower garden (process analysis), you might provide examples of the kinds of plants suitable for different kinds of soil and sun exposure. If you classify the kinds of laptop computers, you are likely to give examples of each different kind.

For an example of how to combine illustration with other patterns, see "The Myth of the Latin Woman: I Just Met a Girl Named Maria" on page 199. In this selection, the author combines illustration with definition and cause-and-effect analysis to explain the culture clash that results in the stereotype of Latin women.

USING ILLUSTRATION BEYOND THE WRITING CLASS

Illustration will be a frequent component of your writing in other classes. In essay examinations and required papers, you will often be asked to "explain and illustrate," "define and give examples of," "give examples to show," and so forth. For instance, in a biology class, you might be asked to define and give examples of *natural selection;* in an education class, you might be asked to explain and give examples of various learning strategies; and in a political science class, you might be asked to give examples to illustrate the influence of Tammany Hall.

Outside the classroom, as well, examples are a frequent component of writing. Written tributes to important people give examples of their accomplishments, college recruiting materials include examples of activities students can engage in, campaign literature offers examples of a candidate's virtues, newspaper editorials supporting tax increases give examples of the good the money can accomplish, and so forth.

SELECTING DETAIL

How many examples to use is a key decision. With too few examples you can fail to clarify your generalization and provide the necessary concreteness. With too many examples, you can be guilty of overkill.

In general, you have four options: provide just a few examples—say, two or three, and develop each one in great detail; provide quite a few examples and develop each one in far less detail; provide a moderate number of examples, each developed to a degree somewhere between the other two extremes; or provide several examples, some highly detailed and some less developed. Whatever number of examples you have, it must be enough to explain and support your generalization adequately; and to whatever degree you develop an illustration, you must have enough detail that your reader appreciates the point it makes.

Your examples can come from a variety of sources, including your own experiences and observations, class readings and lectures, personal reading, and television viewing. Notice how each generalization below is followed by an illustration taken from a different source.

> *generalization:* Too often, young children believe that what they see on television is an accurate representation of reality.

example from
personal reading: I recall years ago reading of a young child who died after jumping from a window and trying to fly like the Superman character he had seen on TV.

generalization: Americans are immune to the plight of the homeless.

example from
observation: I watched at least fifty people walk past an obviously sick, homeless man on Federal Street without noticing him.

generalization: Being a salesperson, especially at Christmastime, is difficult.

example from
experience: Last Christmas I worked at the jewelry counter of a local department store. Although it is supposed to be a season of goodwill, Christmas made ordinarily pleasant people pushy and demanding. Once, an elderly woman insisted that I bring out every watch in the stockroom just so she could verify that all the styles were on display.

generalization: Many of the early immigrants to this country found life harder here than it was in their homeland.

example from
class reading
or lecture: My history instructor, for example, explained that many of those who survived the Atlantic crossing spent their lives in sweatshops, working for slave wages.

generalization: People in high-pressure jobs can reduce their risk of heart attack.

example from
television viewing: A recent television documentary explained that executives could strengthen their hearts by parking a mile from their office and walking to work with a heavy briefcase.

Some of your examples may be narrations, because a story can be an excellent way to illustrate. Description, too, can be highly illustrative, so some of your examples may take this form. For example, part of an essay developing the thesis generalization "Being a salesperson, especially at Christmastime, is difficult" could have a paragraph telling the story of the time the elderly woman demanded to see all the watches in the stockroom. Similarly, an essay developing the thesis generalization "Many of the early immigrants to this country found life harder here than it was in their homeland" could have a paragraph describing what it was like to work in the sweatshops.

Hypothetical Examples

When you select examples, you have the option of creating *hypothetical examples*, which are not *actual* instances, but ones you create from what *could* happen or is likely to happen. To be effective, hypothetical examples must be representative of common experience—so much so that their actual occurrence is plausible. Consider, for example, this generalization: "Magazine advertisements create an unrealistic image of the ideal woman." You could give examples from actual ads as support, but you could also create a hypothetical example that is sufficiently similar to actual ads, like this:

> The woman in makeup and fashion advertisements is thin beyond what is desirable—and achievable—for the average woman. She wears designer clothes that most of us cannot afford and sports a hairdo that few can accomplish without a salon of experts showing up to help us every morning. Then there is that makeup: eyeliner, eyeshadow, foundation, powder, blush, lipliner, lipstick, mascara, brow liner. What woman has the time (or the skill) to put all that on? As if that isn't enough, the model is backlit for maximum effect.

While the above example is not a specific one from any particular magazine, it is enough like what typically appears to be representative of actual occurrence.

ARRANGING DETAIL

In an illustration essay, the thesis can express the generalization and the body paragraphs can present and develop the illustrations of that generalization.

When just a few illustrations are used, each one can be presented and developed in its own body paragraph. If an illustration is an extended example, it may require more than one body paragraph for adequate development. When quite a few illustrations are used and each one gets less-extensive development, you can group related examples together in the same body paragraph.

Often, a progressive order is used for the examples. If some of your examples are more telling than others, you can save your most compelling example for last in order to build to a big finish. Or you could begin with your second-best example to impress your reader right off with the validity of your generalization. You can also begin with your *best* example to impress your reader initially, while reserving your second-most-effective example for last to ensure a strong final body paragraph.

Sometimes you can arrange your illustrations in a chronological or spatial order. Say your thesis says the fans at local high school basketball games are rowdy. You could arrange your illustrations chronologically by first giving examples of rowdiness before the game begins, then examples of rowdiness during halftime, and finally examples of rowdiness after the game. You can also sequence your examples in a spatial order. If you are developing the generalization that the playground in the city park was not really designed with children in mind, you could begin at one end of the playground and work your way around, ordering your examples to correspond with this movement through space.

Other logical arrangements are also possible. For example, if some of your examples come from your own, firsthand experience, some from your own observation, and some from the experience of others, you can group together the examples from the same source.

Annotated Student Essay

The following illustration essay was written by a student. If you study it and the marginal notes, you will better understand the points made in this chapter.

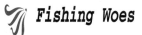 **Fishing Woes**

paragraph 1
The introduction engages interest with background information. The thesis is the second to last sentence. It presents the generalization to be supported with illustrations (agonizing problems occur on charter fishing trips). Some may note the need to edit the dangling modifier.

Every year I go on a chartered fishing trip. It's usually held on a clear and sunny July afternoon, or at least that is the weather prediction we hope for. After consuming two cups of strong coffee, our venture begins at 4 A.M. with a three-hour drive to Port Clinton, Ohio. This is where we board "The Sassy Sal," and head out onto Lake Erie. Seven-thirty finds us on course with the captain's eyes glued on the depth finder in search of a school of walleye. Once they're found, the motor is turned off and we begin to fish. This sounds like a great way to spend a Sunday afternoon, huh? Although charter-boat fishing is very popular, without a doubt, a few agonizing problems always occur to make each trip a memorable one. Let me explain.

1

paragraph 2
The first sentence is the topic sentence, which presents the paragraph's focus as tangled fishing lines. Supporting details include humor. Some may question the relevance of the last two sentences. Note the specific detail, like "spin-cast auto-winder reel," and the process analysis.

One inevitable problem is that the fishing lines get tangled. This usually occurs 10 to 15 seconds after you have dropped your line into the water, and is quickly followed by the cry "I got one!" from the guy on the other side of the boat with whose line you've become entangled, and he almost pulls you overboard trying to reel in his "big one." However, this type of tangle doesn't compare to the 20-line tangle, which occurs when a guy catches a fish and lets it swim across all the lines on his side of the boat while he is patiently trying to figure out how to operate his new ninety-five-dollar spin-cast auto-winder reel. All this can be overcome simply by

2

bringing along a little pair of scissors, and, while everyone is screaming at this guy, proceed to cut all lines wrapped around your own. It is then wise to take your pole and silently move to the opposite side of the boat while the others are trying to figure out where their lines went. I have also found, though, that the best way to avoid other problems is to slip the captain a generous tip before you leave the dock. This will assure you the best spot at the bow of the boat next to the cooler of beer.

paragraph 3

The first sentence is the topic sentence, which gives the paragraph's focus as catching a fish. The example is in the form of narration. The humor establishes the author's purpose as entertaining the reader. Notice the use of conversation and the specific word choice ("17-inch jumping and twisting walleye"). Also note the hypothetical nature of the example.

3

Of course there is always the matter of catching the fish. Yes, this is why we go, but sometimes it's better not to catch any at all. Once you have a fish on your line, you realize you have a coaching staff of nine men, each with his own way of landing the creature. "Reel slower, not so fast," one guy screams in my ear while seven others tell me to "keep the rod tip up." Still another demonstrates for me the correct body motion to use. Once the fish is finally hauled in, you realize no one wants to help you anymore. You're stuck with a 17-inch jumping and twisting walleye who would make Mary Lou Retton look like an amateur, followed by the dilemma of how to get your hook out. After several unsuccessful tries and two bloody fingers (yes, they have teeth) you're ready to smash this fish which you've paid $50 for the opportunity to catch. Eventually the hook is removed; relying on your previous generosity, you appeal to the captain for assistance. You breathe a sigh of relief as the fish is laid to rest in the beer cooler. The deed is done! Alas! here comes our second-time-out expert who feels the need to appraise your catch. He lifts it into the air, sizes it up, and as he minimizes your accomplishment, you watch your fish slip from his grasp and do a two-and-a-half gainer with a one-half twist back into the lake.

paragraph 4

The topic sentence (sentence 1) has a transition ("final"); note that the paragraph focuses on the last problem encountered. Note also that the examples in the entire essay are in chronological order. Some may feel the need for more detail to develop the hypothetical example.

4

The final problem one faces occurs halfway through the day, by which time several beers have been consumed. The pitching and rolling motions of the boat activate regurgitation and before you have time to give homage to the porcelain pot, you find yourself hanging over the rail and wishing you were dead.

paragraph 5
The conclusion gives the last hypothetical event in the chronology and thereby creates an overall reaction.

As the sun sets and you head back to port, you shred   5
up your copy of *Field and Stream* and try to remember where the
nearest fish market is back home.

Pitfalls to Avoid

1. **Avoid unconvincing examples.** All examples are not created equal, so be sure the ones you use do a good job of supporting your thesis or topic sentence generalization. For example, to show that Kevin Kline's performances are under-appreciated, do not cite his performance in *A Fish Called Wanda* as an example because he earned an Academy Award for that role.

2. **Avoid using too few examples.** The cumulative impact of your examples must provide convincing support of your thesis. Thus, to support the thesis idea that parking is a problem on your campus, you must do more than give two examples of times you had difficulty parking—even if those examples are highly detailed.

3. **Avoid unrepresentative examples.** You cannot rely solely on your own experience to prove a generalization is true for more people than you because your experience will not necessarily be representative of a larger population. Thus, to show that parking is a problem on your campus, you must provide examples to show that people other than you have also had difficulty.

4. **Avoid hypothetical examples that are not plausible.** Any hypothetical examples you develop must be sufficiently representative of reality that they *could* happen. Thus, to illustrate that working out with a personal trainer is the best way to get in shape, you cannot make up a story about Chris, who lost 30 pounds in two weeks with a trainer.

PROCESS GUIDELINES: WRITING ILLUSTRATION

1. To settle on a generalization you can support with examples, fill in the blanks in a version of the following sentence:_____ is the most _____ I know. This will give you something like "Taking a three-year-old on a long car trip is the trickiest thing I know." You may alter the words in the sentence to get something like "Registration is the biggest hassle I know."

2. Another way to arrive at a generalization/topic is to take a common saying and show that it is *not* true. For example, provide illustrations to show that a bird in the hand is *not* worth two in the bush, honesty is *not* the best policy, ignorance is *not* bliss, and so on.

3. You can determine your purpose by asking these questions:
   a. Do I want to relate my reaction to or feeling about my subject?
   b. Do I want to help my reader understand why I respond to my subject as I do?

   c. Do I want to clarify the nature of my subject?

   d. Do I want to convince my reader of something?

4. To determine your audience, you can answer the following questions:

   a. To whom do I want to express my feelings or relate experience? Or whom do I want to entertain, inform, or convince?

   b. Who would benefit from reading about my subject?

   c. Who does not know enough about my subject?

   d. Who sees my subject differently than I do?

   e. Who would be influenced by reading about my subject?

5. To determine the nature of your audience, answer these questions:

   a. How much does my reader know about my subject?

   b. Is my reader's knowledge of my subject firsthand?

   c. Does my reader have any strong feelings about my subject?

   d. Does my reader have an interest in my subject?

   e. Is my subject important to my reader?

6. Answering these questions may help you discover examples:

   a. What have I done that illustrates my generalization?

   b. What have I observed that illustrates my generalization?

   c. What have I learned in school that illustrates my generalization?

   d. What have I read that illustrates my generalization?

   e. What have others experienced that illustrates my generalization?

   f. What story can I tell to illustrate my generalization?

   g. What can I describe that illustrates my generalization?

7. List your examples and number them in the order they are to appear in your draft. This will give you an informal outline for your body paragraphs.

8. If you like to secure reader response as part of your revision process, see page 115. In addition, ask your reader to write out the generalization your examples support. Also ask your reader to do the following:

   a. Place a check mark where detail is needed.

   b. Place a question mark where something is unclear.

   c. Place an exclamation point next to anything particularly strong.

REVISION CHECKLIST

In addition to the checklist on page 117, you can use this checklist to help you revise your illustration essay.

1. What generalization do your examples support?

2. Do your examples provide clarity and concreteness?

3. Are your examples appropriate to your audience and purpose?

4. Have you used enough examples to clarify the generalization, but not so many that you belabor the point? Are your examples developed in sufficient detail?

5. Are your examples arranged in a progressive or other suitable order?

EXERCISE | **Writing Illustration**

1. Locate two published essays or articles that include examples. (You might check your textbooks, newsmagazines, and newspapers.) Photocopy the selections and answer these questions:
   a. Is illustration or some other pattern the primary method of development?
   b. What is the source of the examples: personal experience, observation, research, or other?
   c. Are the examples adequately detailed? Do they support their generalization adequately? Explain.
   d. Are any of the examples hypothetical? If so, are they plausible?
2. For each of the following subjects, write one generalization that can be supported with examples.

   education   television   sports

3. Select one of the generalizations you wrote for number 2 and establish a possible audience and purpose for an essay that uses that generalization as a thesis.
4. To support the thesis/generalization, discover one example to fit each of the categories listed below. If you are unable to think of an example for a particular category, then try to come up with two for another category. Also, one example may fill more than one category. For instance, one example may be both a narration and something from personal experience.
   a. Example from personal experience.
   b. Example from observation.
   c. Example from personal reading.
   d. Example from class reading or lecture.
   e. Example from television viewing.
   f. Narrative example.
   g. Descriptive example.
5. *Collaborative Activity.* Write a hypothetical example to support the thesis/generalization. Then give that example to a classmate and have that person evaluate whether or not the example is plausible and effective.

PROFESSIONAL ESSAYS

Darkness at Noon

Harold Krents

Blind from birth, Harold Krents uses examples to educate the reader about the blind in particular and the disabled in general.

Blind from birth, I have never had the opportunity to see myself and have been   *1*
completely dependent on the image I create in the eye of the observer. To date it
has not been narcissistic.

There are those who assume that since I can't see, I obviously also cannot *2* hear. Very often people will converse with me at the top of their lungs, enunciating each word very carefully. Conversely, people will also often whisper, assuming that since my eyes don't work, my ears don't either.

For example, when I go to the airport and ask the ticket agent for assistance *3* to the plane, he or she will invariably pick up the phone, call a ground hostess and whisper: "Hi, Jane, we've got a 76 here." I have concluded that the word "blind" is not used for one of two reasons: Either they fear that if the dread word is spoken, the ticket agent's retina will immediately detach, or they are reluctant to inform me of my condition of which I may not have been previously aware.

On the other hand, others know that of course I can hear, but believe that I *4* can't talk. Often, therefore, when my wife and I go out to dinner, a waiter or waitress will ask Kit if "*he* would like a drink" to which I respond that "indeed *he* would."

This point was graphically driven home to me while we were in England. I *5* had been given a year's leave of absence from my Washington law firm to study for a diploma in law degree at Oxford University. During the year I became ill and was hospitalized. Immediately after admission, I was wheeled down to the X-ray room. Just at the door sat an elderly woman—elderly I would judge from the sound of her voice. "What is his name?" the woman asked the orderly who had been wheeling me.

"What's your name?" the orderly repeated to me. *6*

"Harold Krents," I replied. *7*

"Harold Krents," he repeated. *8*

"When was he born?" *9*

"When were you born?" *10*

"November 5, 1944," I responded. *11*

"November 5, 1944," the orderly intoned. *12*

This procedure continued for approximately five minutes at which point *13* even my saint-like disposition deserted me. "Look," I finally blurted out, "this is absolutely ridiculous. Okay, granted I can't see, but it's got to have become pretty clear to both of you that I don't need an interpreter."

"He says he doesn't need an interpreter," the orderly reported to the *14* woman.

The toughest misconception of all is the view that, because I can't see, I *15* can't work. I was turned down by over 40 law firms because of my blindness, even though my qualifications included a cum laude degree from Harvard College and a good ranking in my Harvard Law School class.

The attempt to find employment, the continuous frustration of being told *16* that it was impossible for a blind person to practice law, the rejection letters, not based on my lack of ability but rather on my disability, will always remain one of the most disillusioning experiences of my life.

I therefore look forward to the day, with the expectation that it is certain to *17* come, when employers will view their handicapped workers as a little child did me years ago when my family still lived in Scarsdale.

I was playing basketball with my father in our backyard according to proce- *18* dures we had developed. My father would stand beneath the hoop, shout, and I would shoot over his head at the basket attached to our garage. Our next-door neighbor, aged five, wandered over into our yard with a playmate. "He's blind," our neighbor whispered to her friend in a voice that could be heard distinctly by Dad and me. Dad shot and missed; I did the same. Dad hit the rim; I missed entirely; Dad shot and missed the garage entirely. "Which one is blind?" whispered back the little friend.

I would hope that in the near future when a plant manager is touring the *19* factory with the foreman and comes upon a handicapped and nonhandicapped person working together, his comment after watching them work will be, "Which one is disabled?"

Considering Ideas

1. Explain the meaning of the title. Is the title a good one? Why or why not?
2. The thesis is implied rather than stated. In your own words, write out the thesis. Where in the essay is this thesis most strongly implied?
3. How does Krents distinguish between a "lack of ability" and a "disability" (paragraph 16)? Why is this distinction important to Krents?
4. What three misconceptions about blind people does Krents illustrate?
5. What do you judge to be the author's purpose? How do the examples help Krents fulfill his purpose?

Considering Technique

1. What is the source of Krent's illustrations?
2. In what order does Krents arrange his detail?
3. Krents uses anecdotes (brief narrations) as examples. What purpose does the basketball narration serve? What other narrative examples appear?
4. "Darkness at Noon" originally appeared in the *New York Times*. Are the illustrations suited to the original audience? Explain.
5. What approach does Krents take to his conclusion? Does that conclusion bring the essay to a satisfying finish? Explain.

For Group Discussion or Journal Writing

In the last paragraph of "Darkness at Noon," Krents expresses a hope for the future. How likely do you think it is that his hope will be realized? Explain.

🎵 Cheap Men

Adair Lara

San Francisco Chronicle *columnist Adair Lara looks at a persistent double standard and asks, "Why* not *dump on cheap men?" The answer may be that they do not deserve it.*

It was our second date, and we had driven one hundred miles up the coast in my car to go abalone-diving. When I stopped to fill the tank at the only gas station in sight, Craig scowled and said, "You shouldn't get gas here. It's a rip-off."   1

But he didn't offer to help pay. And that night, after dinner in a restaurant, he leaned over and whispered intimately, "You get the next one." Though he was sensitive and smart, and looked unnervingly good, Craig was as cheap as a two-dollar watch.   2

This is not an ethical dilemma, you're all shouting. *Lose the guy,* and fast.   3

Lose the guy? Is this fair? My friend Jill is always heading for the john when the check comes, but I don't hear anybody telling me to lose *her.* And she's far from the only cheap woman I know. A lot of us make decent money these days, yet I haven't seen women knocking over tables in fights for the lunch tab. In fact, many women with 20/20 vision seem to have trouble distinguishing the check from the salt, pepper, and other tabletop items. But if a guy forgets to chip in for gas or gloats too long over the deal he got on his Nikes, he's had it.   4

Why is this double standard so enduring? One reason is that, while neither sex has a monopoly on imperfection, there *are* such things as flaws that are much more distasteful in one sex than in the other. Women seem especially unpleasant when they get drunk, swear, or even insist on pursuing an argument they'll never win. And men seem beneath contempt when they're cheap.   5

These judgments are a holdover from the days when women stayed home and men earned the money. Though that old order has passed, we still associate men with paying for things. And besides, there's just something appealing about generosity. Buying something for someone is, in a sense, taking care of her. The gesture says, "I like you, I want to give you something." If it comes from a man to whom we are about to entrust our hearts, this is a comforting message. We miss it when it's not forthcoming.   6

Then why *not* dump on cheap men?   7

Some men are just skinflints and that's it. My friend Skye broke up with her boyfriend because when they went to the movies he doled out M&M's to her one at a time. Craig, my date back at the gas station, liked to talk about how he'd bought his car—which in California, where I live, is like buying shoes—as a special present to himself.   8

This kind of cheapness is ingrained; you'll never change it. That guy who parks two miles away to avoid the parking lot fee was once a little boy who saved his birthday money without being told to. Now he's a man who studies the menu and sputters, "Ten dollars for *pasta?*" His stinginess will always grate on you, since he is likely to dole out his feelings as parsimoniously as his dollars.   9

On the other hand, I know a wonderful man, crippled with debts from a *10* former marriage, who had to break up with a woman because she never paid her share, and he was simply running out of money. Though she earned a lot more than he did, she couldn't expand her definition of masculinity to include "sometimes needs to go Dutch treat."

To men, such women seem grasping. One friend of mine, who spends a lot *11* of money on concerts and theater and sailing but not on restaurants he considers overpriced, has evolved a strategy for women who are annoyed at the bohemian places he favors. If his date complains, he offers to donate to the charity of her choice the cost of an evening at her favorite spot. "Some women have bad values," he says. "And if the idea of spending money on a good cause, but not on her, makes her livid, I know she's one of them."

I had a bracing encounter with my own values when I told my friend *12* Danny the humorous (I thought) story of a recent date who asked if I wanted a drink after a concert, then led me to the nearest water fountain.

Danny gave me one of his wry looks. "Let's get this straight," he said, *13* laughing. "As a woman, you are so genetically precious that you deserve attention just because you grace the planet. So, of course, he should buy you drinks. He should also drive the car, open the door, ask you to dance, coax you to bed. And then when you feel properly pampered, you can let out that little whine about how he doesn't treat you as an equal."

On second thought, I guess I'd rather buy my own drink. *14*

So here's the deal. Before dumping a guy for ordering the sundowner din- *15* ner or the house white, better first make sure that you aren't burdening the relationship with outdated ideas of how the sexes should behave. Speaking for myself, I know that if a man looks up from the check and says, "Your share is eleven dollars," part of me remembers that, according to my mother, *my* share was to look charming in my flowered blouse.

Wanting the man to pay dies hard. What many of us do now is *offer* to split *16* the check, then let our purses continue to dangle from the chair as we give him time to realize that the only proper response is to whip out his own wallet.

Is this a game worth playing? It's up to you, but consider that offering to *17* help pay implies that the check is his responsibility. And this attitude can work both ways. My sister gets angry when her husband offers to help clean the house. "Like it's *my* house?" she snorts. *18*

Like it's *his* check.

Considering Ideas

1. The thesis of "Cheap Men" is implied. State the thesis in your own words.
2. What is your opinion of Craig? Do you agree that Lara's best course of action was to "lose the guy" (paragraph 3)?
3. What double standard is Lara pointing out? Why does she think this double standard endures? Do you agree with her? Explain.

4. How does Lara answer the questions in paragraphs 4 and 7?
5. For what purpose do you think Lara wrote "Cheap Men"? Who would you judge to be her intended audience?

Considering Technique

1. What is the source of Lara's examples?
2. *Combining Patterns.* What element of narration appears in the essay? What element of cause-and-effect analysis (explanation of the causes or effects of an event) appears?
3. Which paragraph includes a hypothetical example? Do you consider that example sufficiently representative of reality to be effective? Explain.
4. Do paragraphs 1–3 make an effective opening? Explain why or why not.
5. Do you think that Lara's examples are convincing? That is, do they support her generalization adequately? Explain your view.

For Group Discussion or Journal Writing

What do you think of present-day dating practices? What are their chief strengths and weaknesses? Evaluate and make suggestions for change, if you like.

Combining Patterns of Development

The Myth of the Latin Woman: I Just Met a Girl Named Maria

Judith Ortiz Cofer

*Combining **illustration** with **cause-and-effect analysis** and **definition,** Judith Ortiz Cofer examines the stereotype of the Latina that emerges from the mixed messages of two cultures.*

On a bus trip to London from Oxford University where I was earning some   *1* graduate credits one summer, a young man, obviously fresh from a pub, spotted me and as if struck by inspiration went down on his knees in the aisle. With both hands over his heart he broke into an Irish tenor's rendition of "Maria" from *West Side Story*. My politely amused fellow passengers gave his lovely voice the round of gentle applause it deserved. Though I was not quite as amused, I managed my version of an English smile: no show of teeth, no extreme contortions of the facial muscles—I was at this time of my life practicing reserve and cool. Oh, that British control, how I coveted it. But "Maria" had followed me to London, reminding me of a prime fact of my life: you can leave the island, master the English language, and travel as far as you can, but if you are a Latina, especially one like me who so obviously belongs to Rita Moreno's gene pool, the island travels with you.

This is sometimes a very good thing—it may win you that extra minute of *2* someone's attention. But with some people, the same things can make *you* an island—not a tropical paradise but an Alcatraz, a place nobody wants to visit. As a Puerto Rican girl living in the United States and wanting like most children to "belong," I resented the stereotype that my Hispanic appearance called forth from many people I met.

Growing up in a large urban center in New Jersey during the 1960s, I suf- *3* fered from what I think of as "cultural schizophrenia." Our life was designed by my parents as a microcosm of their *casas* on the island. We spoke in Spanish, ate Puerto Rican food bought at the *bodega,* and practiced strict Catholicism at a church that allotted us a one-hour slot each week for mass, performed in Spanish by a Chinese priest trained as a missionary for Latin America.

As a girl I was kept under strict surveillance by my parents, since my virtue *4* and modesty were, by their cultural equation, the same as their honor. As a teenager I was lectured constantly on how to behave as a proper *senorita*. But it was a conflicting message I received, since the Puerto Rican mothers also encouraged their daughters to look and act like women and to dress in clothes our Anglo friends and their mothers found too "mature" and flashy. The difference was, and is, cultural; yet I often felt humiliated when I appeared at an American friend's party wearing a dress more suitable to a semi-formal than to a playroom birthday celebration. At Puerto Rican festivities, neither the music nor the colors we wore could be too loud.

I remember Career Day in our high school, when teachers told us to come *5* dressed as if for a job interview. It quickly became obvious that to the Puerto Rican girls "dressing up" meant wearing their mother's ornate jewelry and clothing, more appropriate (by mainstream standards) for the company Christmas party than as daily office attire. That morning I had agonized in front of my closet, trying to figure out what a "career girl" would wear. I knew how to dress for school (at the Catholic school I attended, we all wore uniforms), I knew how to dress for Sunday mass, and I knew what dresses to wear for parties at my relatives' homes. Though I do not recall the precise details of my Career Day outfit, it must have been a composite of these choices. But I remember a comment my friend (an Italian American) made in later years that coalesced my impressions of that day. She said that at the business school she was attending, the Puerto Rican girls always stood out for wearing "everything at once." She meant, of course, too much jewelry, too many accessories. On that day at school we were simply made the negative models by the nuns, who were themselves not credible fashion experts to any of us. But it was painfully obvious to me that to the others, in their tailored skirts and silk blouses, we must have seemed "hopeless" and "vulgar." Though I now know that most adolescents feel out of step much of the time, I also know that for the Puerto Rican girls of my generation that sense was intensified. The way our teachers and classmates looked at us that day in school was just a taste of the cultural clash that awaited us in the real world, where prospective employers and men on the street would often misinterpret our tight skirts and jingling bracelets as a "come-on."

Mixed cultural signals have perpetuated certain stereotypes—for example, 6
that of the Hispanic woman as the "hot tamale" or sexual firebrand. It is a one-
dimensional view that the media have found easy to promote. In their special vocabulary, advertisers have designated "sizzling" and "smoldering" as the adjectives of choice for describing not only the foods but also the women of Latin
America. From conversations in my house I recall hearing about the harassment
that Puerto Rican women endured in factories where the "boss-men" talked to
them as if sexual innuendo was all they understood, and worse, often gave them
the choice of submitting to their advances or being fired.

It is custom, however, not chromosomes, that leads us to choose scarlet over 7
pale pink. As young girls, it was our mothers who influenced our decisions about
clothes and colors—mothers who had grown up on a tropical island where the natural environment was a riot of primary colors, where showing your skin was one
way to keep cool as well as to look sexy. Most important of all, on the island,
women perhaps felt freer to dress and move more provocatively since, in most
cases, they were protected by the traditions, mores, and laws of a Spanish/Catholic
system of morality and machismo whose main rule was: *You may look at my sister,
but if you touch her I will kill you.* The extended family and church structure could
provide a young woman with a circle of safety in her small pueblo on the island; if
a man "wronged" a girl, everyone would close in to save her family honor.

My mother has told me about dressing in her best party clothes on Saturday nights and going to the town's plaza to promenade with her girlfriends in 8
front of the boys they liked. The males were thus given an opportunity to admire
the women and to express their admiration in the form of *piropos:* erotically
charged street poems they composed on the spot. (I have myself been subjected
to a few *piropos* while visiting the island, and they can be outrageous, although
custom dictates that they must never cross into obscenity.) This ritual, as I understand it, also entails a show of studied indifference on the woman's part; if she
is "decent," she must not acknowledge the man's impassioned words. So I do
understand how things can be lost in translation. When a Puerto Rican girl
dressed in her idea of what is attractive meets a man from the mainstream culture
who has been trained to react to certain types of clothing as a sexual signal, a
clash is likely to take place. I remember the boy who took me to my first formal
dance leaning over to plant a sloppy, over-eager kiss painfully on my mouth;
when I didn't respond with sufficient passion, he remarked resentfully: "I
thought you Latin girls were supposed to mature early," as if I were expected to
ripen like a fruit or vegetable, not just grow into womanhood like other girls.

It is surprising to my professional friends that even today some people, including those who should know better, still put others "in their place." It hap- 9
pened to me most recently during a stay at a classy metropolitan hotel favored by
young professional couples for weddings. Late one evening after the theater, as I
walked toward my room with a colleague (a woman with whom I was coordinating an arts program), a middle-aged man in a tuxedo, with a young girl in satin
and lace on his arm, stepped directly into our path. With his champagne glass extended toward me, he exclaimed "Evita!"[1]

[1]A musical about Eva Duarte de Peron, the former first lady of Argentina.

Our way blocked, my companion and I listened as the man half-recited, *10* half-bellowed "Don't Cry for Me, Argentina." When he finished, the young girl said: "How about a round of applause for my daddy?" We complied, hoping this would bring the silly spectacle to a close. I was becoming aware that our little group was attracting the attention of the other guests. "Daddy" must have perceived this too, and he once more barred the way as we tried to walk past him. He began to shout-sing a ditty to the tune of "La Bamba"—except the lyrics were about a girl named Maria whose exploits rhymed with her name and gonorrhea. The girl kept saying "Oh, Daddy" and looking at me with pleading eyes. She wanted me to laugh along with the others. My companion and I stood silently waiting for the man to end his offensive song. When he finished, I looked not at him but at his daughter. I advised her calmly never to ask her father what he had done in the army. Then I walked between them and to my room. My friend complimented me on my cool handling of the situation, but I confessed that I had really wanted to push the jerk into the swimming pool. This same man—probably a corporate executive, well-educated, even worldly by most standards—would not have been likely to regale an Anglo woman with a dirty song in public. He might have checked his impulse by assuming that she could be somebody's wife or mother, or at least *somebody* who might take offense. But, to him, I was just an Evita or a Maria: merely a character in his cartoon-populated universe.   *11*

Another facet of the myth of the Latin woman in the United States is the menial, the domestic—Maria the housemaid or countergirl. It's true that work as domestics, as waitresses, and in factories is all that's available to women with little English and few skills. But the myth of the Hispanic menial—the funny maid, mispronouncing words and cooking up a spicy storm in a shiny California kitchen—has been perpetuated by the media in the same way that "Mammy" from *Gone with the Wind* became America's idea of the black woman for generations. Since I do not wear my diplomas around my neck for all to see, I have on occasion been sent to that "kitchen" where some think I ob- *12* viously belong.

One incident has stayed with me, though I recognize it as a minor offense. My first public poetry reading took place in Miami, at a restaurant where a luncheon was being held before the event. I was nervous and excited as I walked in with notebook in hand. An older woman motioned me to her table, and thinking (foolish me) that she wanted me to autograph a copy of my newly published slender volume of verse, I went over. She ordered a cup of coffee from me, assuming that I was the waitress. (Easy enough to mistake my poems for menus, I suppose.) I know it wasn't an intentional act of cruelty. Yet of all the good things that happened later, I remember that scene most clearly because it reminded me of what I had to overcome before anyone would take me seriously. In retrospect I understand that my anger gave my reading fire. In fact, I have almost always taken any doubt in my abilities as a challenge, the result most often being the satisfaction of winning a convert, of seeing the cold, appraising eyes warm to my words, the body language change, the smile that indicates I have opened some avenue for communication. So that day as I read, I looked directly at that woman. Her lowered eyes told me she was embarrassed at her faux pas, and when I willed her to look up at me, she graciously allowed me to punish her with my full attention. We shook hands at the end of the reading and I never saw her again. She has probably forgotten the entire incident, but maybe not.

Yet I am one of the lucky ones. There are thousands of Latinas without *13* the privilege of an education or the entrees into society that I have. For them life is a constant struggle against the misconceptions perpetuated by the myth of the Latina. My goal is to try to replace the old stereotypes with a much more interesting set of realities. Every time I give a reading, I hope the stories I tell, the dreams and fears I examine in my work, can achieve some universal truth that will get my audience past the particulars of my skin color, my accent, or my clothes.

I once wrote a poem in which I called all Latinas "God's brown daughters." *14* This poem is really a prayer of sorts, offered upward, but also, through the human-to-human channel of art, outward. It is a prayer for communication and for respect. In it, Latin women pray "in Spanish to an Anglo God/ with a Jewish heritage," and they are "fervently hoping/ that if not omnipotent,/ at least He be bilingual."

Considering Ideas

1. In paragraph 2, Cofer mentions the "stereotype that [her] Hispanic appearance called forth." What is that stereotype?
2. Describe the "cultural schizophrenia" (paragraph 3) that Cofer grew up with.
3. Cofer says that the media contribute to the myth of the Latin woman. In what way? Do you agree that the media contributes to the myth? Explain.
4. What do you think Cofer means in paragraph 10 when she says, "But, to him, I was just an Evita or a Maria"?
5. Do you think that the Latin male is also the victim of stereotyping? Explain.

Considering Technique

1. What approach does Cofer take to her introduction? Does that introduction engage your interest? Why or why not?
2. Which paragraphs include examples taken from the author's experience? Are these examples convincing? Why or why not?
3. *Combining patterns.* In what way can paragraphs 3–4, 6–8, 11, and 13 be considered cause-and-effect analysis (the explanation of the causes or effects of an event). What element of definition (the explanation of something's meaning) appears in the essay? What element of narration?

4. Throughout the essay, Cofer mentions women from plays, literature, and movies as examples of the stereotype of minority women in mainstream culture. Do you find these references effective? Explain.

For Group Discussion or Journal Writing

Throughout the essay, Cofer gives examples of how she reacted to being treated as the stereotypical Latina. What do you think of the way she reacted? Should she have done or said anything different? Explain.

STUDENT ESSAYS TO READ AND EVALUATE

The following essays, written by students, are developed with illustrations. Each has strengths and weaknesses for you to notice as you read, so you can practice forming and supporting critical judgments. Reading the essays will also increase your awareness of what does and does not work in writing.

Look Out, Here She Comes

Every morning at 8:30 A.M., there enters a short, overweight, middle-aged woman through the front doors of the Valu King where I am employed, even though we do not officially open for business until 9:00. This lady is always dressed in the same out-of-style, dirty-looking outfit. Her hideous legs are so fat they are fortunate to be supported by a pair of old, black, high-heeled pump shoes. Her gray hair is unsuccessfully dyed with red. From her appearance you would assume that she can't afford new clothes or health and beauty care. The lady is Nora Tompkins.

Nora starts every day off by browsing through the produce section, searching for discolored, old, or bruised fruits and vegetables. Once she has discovered some items, she asks us if she can have them reduced. Sometimes she practically begs us to mark the price down for her. If we do not mark the produce down enough to suit her, Nora throws the items back in the display and wheels her cart away in a huff.

As Nora exits the produce section and enters my dairy department, she slowly grabs a few of my sale items, looking at them to see if they are her idea of real bargains. If she notices some milk products are reduced, she will usually buy all of them, even though the expiration date is near.

The day-old bakery items are her favorites. Upon arriving at   *4*
the day-old rack, she starts glancing over it for bargains. Most of
the time, she fills her cart with these reduced items. But first
she demands they be reduced even more. I have seen her stand there
and argue about the price with the bakery women. She has even taken
a swing at one of them for not reducing the day-old pastries more.

There are only two things she looks at in the grocery   *5*
department: generic products and sale items. These are the only
items she will buy, and she usually does not want just one or two
of each of these products. She usually asks us if she can buy a
full case, regardless of what our ad says is the limited purchase
on these items.

Inexpensive fresh cuts of meat are all she buys out of the meat   *6*
cases. She picks up a piece of meat that she might want and
inspects it better than a health inspector. The meat cutters have
found meat packages with holes in them because of Nora's finger
inspection. She even has enough nerve to ask the meat cutters to
trim off minute pieces of fat for her. Other times she has asked
them to cut one thick piece of beef into two thin pieces of meat
for her.

Over time, everyone in the store, including the cashiers, has   *7*
come to hate Nora. Now most of the employees avoid her by staying
in the back room or slipping into an aisle she has already passed.
She wants to be friends with everyone so that she can save a penny,
but no one even says hello to her anymore. More than once Nora has
asked cashiers not to charge her for some of the food, but they do
anyway. It's not a matter of honesty. They really hate the woman.

We are all relieved when Nora leaves. When she finally does go,   *8*
she takes all of this discount food to her $150,000 home in a
suburban development. Then, after she cleans, cooks, or repacks most
of the food, she drives out to a roadside stand, sells these lower-
priced items to people at a higher price, and pockets the profit.

It's Time to Reform Sex Education

Two years ago, I graduated from a public high school in a large   *1*
metropolitan area. My freshman year, I had to take a health class,
a one-semester course that forced us to learn the bones of the

body, the dangers of drugs, and other equally boring content that I and everyone else paid practically no attention to. One part of that course was labeled "sex education." If that course is representative of the kind of sex education that goes on in this country, then, believe me, we need to revamp the way we teach this subject matter—and fast.

Judging from the number of pregnancies in my school, no one   *2*
paid attention to the portion of the class devoted to birth control. Two girls I was friendly with left high school in December of their senior year to deliver their babies. They never came back. Another high school girl, who already had two children, told me that if she had three children and her own place, she could live nicely on government assistance. I got the distinct impression she was planning on trying for that third kid.

It seems the girls who became pregnant suffered more than the   *3*
boys who helped them get that way. The pregnant girls had to decide whether to have abortions, keep the babies, or put them up for adoption. Even if the decision was easy (how could it be?), these girls either dropped out of school or graduated late. Some of the young mothers got their own places and got help from child care and welfare, but they didn't have much of a life. While their friends (and the babies' fathers) were out having fun and being teenagers, these young mothers were stuck with the responsibility of raising children. Very few, if any, of the girls in my high school received help from the babies' fathers. One boy bragged to me that he was the father to four different children by four different girls. When I asked him who supported his children, he replied, "the system."

I know that many of the girls who were pregnant did not know   *4*
enough to get proper medical care. They were so worried about hiding their pregnancy as long as possible that they did not go to the doctor. A few of the girls went to the free clinic because they could not afford private medical attention. One girl had her child in a restroom during school. The dismissal bell was held up 15 minutes so that the paramedics could remove her and the child to take them to a local hospital.

In addition to the health risks, the pregnant teens were   *5*
starting down a road to nowhere. It seemed that most of the girls came from one-parent families. They, too, were beginning their own one-parent families. Some of the girls would become part of their

mother's or grandmother's extended families. They seemed doomed to a life of struggle and poverty.

Too bad the sex education classes never discussed what happened 6 after the baby was born. That might have led to abstinence. One girl who was on her own with her daughter said that her life was no longer the same. She said her child was not like a doll that she could put away when she got tired of playing. She said that one day she was a carefree adolescent and the next she was a young adult with a baby who needed constant care. When I saw her, the first thing I noticed was how old and tired she looked.

Teenage pregnancy remains a problem, and as long as sex 7 education courses are taught as badly as the one at my high school, I doubt that the problem will be solved.

Collaborative Exercise: Evaluating Writing

For additional practice making critical judgments about writing so you can evaluate your own work reliably, form a group with two classmates and select one of the previous student essays. With your group, prepare a report that notes the chief strengths and weaknesses of the piece. Also decide on the most important revision you would like to see. Be specific. If you say a particular example is not working, explain why and suggest an improvement.

If you like, you can use the following evaluation questions to guide your work.

Evaluation Questions

1. *The Introduction*
   Does the opening engage your interest? Why or why not?
2. *The Thesis*
   Does the thesis make clear what generalization is being presented? What is that generalization?
3. *Supporting Details*
   Are there enough examples to illustrate the generalization? Evaluate the examples. (Are they adequately detailed, relevant, sufficiently specific, and convincing?) Note any points you do not understand.
4. *Organization*
   What do you think of the order of examples? Evaluate the use of transitions. Does the author use topic sentences?
5. *Word Choice and Sentence Effectiveness*
   Cite examples of effective words and sentences. Cite examples of words and sentences to revise.

6. *The Conclusion*
Does the essay come to a satisfying end? Why or why not?

Essay Topics: Illustration

When you write your essay, consult Pitfalls to Avoid on page 192, Process Guidelines on page 192, and the Revision Checklist on page 193.

Writing in the Pattern

1. Write an essay to illustrate that television is (or is not) living up to its potential.
2. Write an essay to illustrate that your campus or local newspaper is (or is not) doing a good job of covering important stories.
3. Write an essay to illustrate the advantages or disadvantages of being your gender.
4. Write an essay illustrating the fact that modern advances are not without some disadvantages.
5. Write an essay to illustrate one of the following:
   a. Things do not always go as planned.
   b. Sports are becoming more violent.
   c. Appearances can be deceiving.
   d. The consumer is often taken advantage of.
   e. Advertising leads people to view luxuries as necessities.
6. Select a modern device (video games, television, washing machines, answering machines, etc.) and write an essay illustrating the problems the device can cause.
7. Illustrate how some group (homemakers, working women, husbands, police officers, etc.) is depicted on television.
8. Illustrate the effect that political correctness has had on television commercials or magazine ads.

Reading Then Writing in the Pattern

1. In "Cheap Men," Adair Lara notes that some behaviors are distasteful in one gender but not the other (paragraph 5). Write an essay that illustrates one or more of these behaviors.
2. In "The Myth of the Latin Woman . . . " Judith Cofer illustrates the stereotype of the Latina. Illustrate another stereotype that you are familiar with (the jock, the divorced woman, the single father, the teenager, and so forth).
3. In "Darkness at Noon" (page 194), Harold Krents illustrates the discrimination he suffers as a result of his disability. Write an essay illustrating how some condition in your life affected you dramatically. You might write about being an only child (oldest child, middle child, etc.), about being the child of divorced parents, about being a member of a minority group, about being tall or short for your age, about being athletic (or musically inclined or artistic), about being the class clown, and so on.

Responding to the Readings

1. Explain how we respond to the disabled and *why* we respond as we do. If you like, you can use some of the information in "Darkness at Noon" (page 194).

2. In "Cheap Men" (page 197), Adair Lara points out that current dating practices are unfair to men. Discuss other practices or customs that are unfair to one gender or the other.

3. In "The Myth of the Latin Woman: I Just Met a Girl Named Maria" (page 199), Judith Cofer notes that the media contribute to the stereotyping of Latinas. Discuss in what ways the media either contribute to or help dispel common stereotypes.

4. *Connecting the Readings.* Using the ideas in "Darkness at Noon" (page 194), "The Myth of the Latin Woman . . . " (page 199), and "It Is Time to Stop Playing Indians" (page 273), along with your own experience and observation, explain how stereotypes influence our behavior.

CHAPTER 7

Process Analysis

A **process analysis** explains how something is made or done. There are two kinds of process analyses: the directional and the explanatory. The **directional process analysis** gives the steps in a process the reader can perform. The directions that explain how to assemble the toy you bought your nephew are a directional process analysis. The instructions in your biology lab manual explaining how to prepare a slide are also a directional process analysis—so are the explanation for making simple repairs given in the owner's manual of your stereo, the magazine article describing how to land the perfect job, and the directions for preparing a gourmet meal found in the cookbook on the kitchen counter.

The **explanatory process analysis** explains how something is made or done, but the reader is not likely to perform the process. For example, "A Delicate Operation" on page 222 explains how brain surgery is performed—that is an explanatory process analysis because the reader is not likely to perform brain surgery. Similarly, explanations of how the body converts carbohydrates to energy, how plants manufacture chlorophyll, and how lightning occurs are all explanatory process analyses.

ESTABLISHING YOUR PURPOSE AND IDENTIFYING YOUR AUDIENCE

The obvious purpose of a process analysis is to *inform* a reader about how something is made or done. Often the process analysis is meant to *help the reader learn how* to make or do something. For example, a process analysis could teach a person how to hang wallpaper and thus avoid paying someone else to do it. Sometimes the reader already knows how to make or do something. In this case, the purpose can be to *make the reader aware* of a better or faster way to perform the process. For example, perhaps your reader already knows how to take an essay examination, but you can describe a process that helps the student budget time better.

A process analysis is often written to *increase the reader's knowledge* about how something works or how it is made. For example, if you wrote a description of how computers work or how alligators hunt their prey, your purpose would be to increase your reader's knowledge.

Another reason to write a process analysis is to *help your reader appreciate the difficulty, complexity, or beauty of a process.* For example, if you think your reader does not appreciate how hard it is to wait on tables, you could describe the process of waiting on tables to heighten your reader's appreciation.

Sometimes the purpose of a process analysis is not to inform but to *persuade.* You could, for example, describe a process in an effort to convince your reader that it is superior to another way of doing things and should be adopted. This would be the case if you wrote to your campus registrar to describe a registration process that is less troublesome than the current process. And sometimes the purpose of a process analysis is to *entertain,* as is the case with the humorous "Some Assembly Required" on page 230.

Your audience is an important consideration because it will affect detail selection. For example, if you are explaining how to use a particular word-processing program for a reader who understands computer operation, you will not have to explain the computer parts (like *disk drive*) or define many terms (like *format a disk*). However, if your audience is someone who just bought a computer and knows little about it, you should identify the parts and define terms. The nature of your audience will also affect to what extent you must explain the importance of the process, provide examples, and explain steps.

COMBINING PROCESS ANALYSIS WITH OTHER PATTERNS

Whenever you need to explain how something is made or done, you will use process analysis, regardless of the dominant pattern of development. For example, if you are writing a definition of *electoral college,* part of your essay is likely to explain how the electoral college works to elect a president. If you are explaining the causes and effects of anorexia nervosa, you may also explain by what process the condition can lead to death. If you are contrasting two exercise programs, you might explain how each one works.

Even when process analysis is your dominant pattern, you are likely to make use of other methods of development. For example, to explain how to choose the best running shoes, you might give examples of the best ones to buy. To explain the process that causes leaves to change color in autumn, you might include a description of the various colors of the leaves.

For an example of an essay that combines process analysis and narration, see "Green Frog Skin" on page 226.

USING PROCESS ANALYSIS BEYOND THE WRITING CLASS

Process analysis is a common component of writing done in a variety of college courses. In science labs of all kinds, you will write lab reports that explain the process you followed to complete an experiment. In an education class, you can be asked to explain the process for developing a good lesson plan; in a marketing class, you may need to write out the process for doing market research; in a political science class, you may need to explain the process for amending the constitution; in a prelaw class, you may be asked to explain the process for bringing a case before the Supreme Court; in a biology class, you may be asked to explain the process of cell division; and so forth.

Outside the classroom, you also encounter process analysis. There are the directions for programming your VCR that you read in the owner's manual, the recipe for preparing poached salmon that you follow in your cookbook, the article about how to train your dog that you read in the pamphlet in the veterinarian's office, the explanation of how paper is made that you find on the Internet, the explanation of how to lose 10 pounds that you see in a magazine, and the explanation of how to eliminate weevils that you look up in a gardening book.

SELECTING DETAIL

Obviously, the primary detail in a process analysis will be the steps in the process. Be careful not to omit any steps, or the reader may not be able to understand or perform the process. However, providing the steps alone may not be enough; you may need to explain just *how* the steps are performed. For example, if you are explaining how to discover ideas to include in an essay, do more than note that a writer can try freewriting; also explain how that freewriting is done.

In addition to explaining *how* steps are performed, you may need to explain *why*, particularly if your reader will not appreciate the importance of a step and perhaps skip it. For example, assume that you are explaining how to land a perfect job and that you mention the reader should send a thank-you note to the personnel director immediately after the interview. If the reader might not appreciate the importance of this step, explain that sending the note impresses the personnel director with your courtesy and follow-through.

Sometimes you may find it necessary to explain what *not* to do, especially when your reader might do something unnecessary or incorrect. Assume again that you are explaining how to land the perfect job. You may want to caution your reader *not* to smile too much, explaining that too much smiling can create a frivolous or insincere image.

If a step in the process can prove troublesome, point out the possible problem and how to avoid it. For example, when you tell a job applicant to write a thank-you note, you can caution the person to use a business-letter format, which can be found in any handbook.

If your reader must assemble materials to perform the process, be sure to mention everything needed, and if your reader needs an understanding of special terms, provide the definitions. For example, if you are explaining how to make the best-ever chocolate cake, tell your reader early on what ingredients to have on hand. If the cake will be baked in a springform pan, explain what this is if your reader is not likely to know.

Examples and descriptions can also be included in a process analysis to help a reader understand the nature and significance of steps in a process. Thus, you might want to describe appropriate dress or give examples of questions to ask during a job interview.

Finally, if your reader does not fully appreciate the importance of performing or understanding the process, include this detail as well. For example, if you are explaining how television advertisements persuade people to buy, you can mention that people should understand this process so that they can recognize attempts to manipulate them.

ARRANGING DETAIL

Chronological order (see page 68) is the likely detail arrangement for process analysis because a reader usually needs the steps presented in the order they are performed. At times, however, chronological order is not necessary. For example, if you are explaining how to dress for success, the order of steps may not be significant.

If you are explaining what is *not* done, you should do this near the step the caution is related to. For example, a cake recipe would explain not to overbake at the point baking time is mentioned. If your process analysis includes several statements of what not to do, you might want to group all the cautions together in their own paragraph.

If you must define a term, do so the first time the term is used. If you explain a troublesome aspect of the process, do so just after presenting the step under consideration. If you explain why a step is performed, do so just before or after your explanation of the step. If necessary materials are listed, group together this information in an early paragraph, perhaps even in the introduction.

The introduction of a process analysis can include a thesis that mentions the process to be explained. In addition, the thesis can note the importance of understanding the process. Here are two examples:

> Car owners can save a great deal of money if they learn to change their own points and plugs. (The process is changing points and plugs; understanding the process is important because it can save the reader money.)

> There is only one efficient way to study for a final examination. (This thesis mentions the process without noting its importance.)

To create interest in your topic, you can explain in the introduction why understanding the process is important (if your thesis does not do this). You can also tell why you are qualified to explain the process, arouse the reader's curiosity about how the process is performed, or combine approaches.

The conclusion can be handled using any of the approaches given for the introduction. However, at times a separate conclusion is unnecessary because the last step in the process provides sufficient closure.

Annotated Student Essay

Studying the following process analysis, written by a student, along with the marginal notes, will help you better understand the points made in this chapter.

🎵 A Disc Jockey's Work

paragraph 1
The introduction establishes that the process to be discussed is the disc jockey's work and that the writer's purpose is to help the reader appreciate what the disc jockey does.

paragraph 2
The topic sentence (the first sentence) presents the first step in the process.

paragraph 3
This paragraph presents the next step (reaching an agreement) and explains how the step is performed. Some may want to know why weddings are more expensive. Notice that throughout the essay details are arranged in chronological order

paragraph 4
Some may find the last sentence confuses the chronology: Was the deposit given earlier?

paragraph 5
This paragraph notes a troublesome aspect of the process.

Most people see the disc jockey as someone who simply plays music. To them, the disc jockey's job is easy. This attitude could be expected from someone who has not actually had the chance to experience the job. A closer examination will reveal that a lot of work goes on before, during, and after the show.   *1*

The process begins when the disc jockey accepts a "booking." That is, someone calls to inquire about his/her services, and the disc jockey accepts the proposal. In order for this to happen, the disc jockey must have a well-established reputation and/or have spent time and money advertising.   *2*

The disc jockey and the interested party reach a mutual agreement. They discuss and settle issues such as a date, time, location, amount of money involved, and the length of the show. Some issues are the responsibility of the interested party, while others such as length of the show and the fee depend more on the disc jockey. An acceptable show length is usually four hours, and the fee can range from $200 to $600. This depends on the disc jockey's reputation and the type of party or special occasion. Weddings, for example, are generally more expensive.   *3*

The date finally arrives and the disc jockey meets with the client at least 30 minutes before the show. This is when final payments and other details are dealt with. Sometimes a deposit is required in advance to hold a date, but usually an oral agreement is sufficient.   *4*

At this point the real work begins. In the next 30 minutes the disc jockey has to unload all of the necessary equipment from the van or truck, and move it inside. This can be a difficult task when you take into account that   *5* some stereo components can weigh in excess of 70 pounds. These components are large, cumbersome, and bulky. It may be necessary to make ten or more trips to unload them all.

paragraphs 6–8
These paragraphs note how steps are performed and troublesome aspects of the process (making the wrong connections and finding music).

When all of the equipment is moved inside, the disc jockey begins to get it ready for playing. In some cases the disc jockey has to connect twenty or more wires and plugs. Each wire has a specific place to go, and can be color and number coded accordingly. Making the wrong connection could send an electrical surge through the system. This could cause a short circuit and destroy the entire system, causing hundreds of dollars worth of damage. With so many different wires and possible connections, to the untrained eye, the system looks like the complicated pieces of a jigsaw puzzle. The disc jockey quickly makes sense of the tangled mess of wires and connects each one to its proper place within minutes.   6

After a careful final check of the entire system, it is time for the show to begin. The first hour is extremely important. The disc jockey has to measure the crowd's tastes and preferences, or their likes and dislikes. This is done by taking requests and by playing a wide variety of different musical selections. After this first hour the disc jockey should know what the audience wants to hear, and choose the right mixture of music accordingly. Upbeat dance songs, slow romantic ballads, country, and top-forty pop rock can all be incorporated into the show.   7

Often, finding the music is difficult. While one song is playing, the disc jockey is rapidly searching for the next selection to be played. Since the average length of a song is four to five minutes, the disc jockey has only this long to find that selection and get ready to introduce it. The disc jockey is constantly busy searching for records, and while this is going on he/she must also take additional requests and dedications. This confusion can last for three or more hours, and can be extremely stressful since you can not please everyone all of the time.   8

paragraph 9
Note the descriptive language: "noisy crowd," "dwindled," "deep, mellow voice."

As the fourth and final hour draws to a close, the disc jockey chooses the final song of the evening. A slow ballad begins to play as the disc jockey announces to the crowd that this will be the last dance of the evening. The   9 once large and noisy crowd has dwindled to only a few remaining couples, who now find their way to the dance floor one final time. As the song slowly fades, the disc jockey says in a deep, mellow voice, "Good night ladies and gentlemen, I've had a wonderful time here this evening and I hope you did too. Thank you for coming—goodnight."

paragraph 10
This paragraph notes the last step in the process.

Some stragglers continue to dance despite the lack of music. Others sit around and talk, and for just a second the disc jockey feels an overwhelming sense of satisfaction. The work, however, is still not done. Now the disc jockey must disassemble and reload all of the equipment that was unloaded just over four and a half hours ago. This does not require as much skill or preparation as setting up does, but it is still time-consuming. After all, this equipment is delicate and expensive, and must be handled carefully.

10

paragraph 11
The conclusion reaffirms the idea in the introduction: that the work of disc jockeys should be appreciated by the reader.

While the party-goers are home in bed the disc jockey is still hard at work putting equipment into storage. This work often takes the disc jockey into the early hours of the morning. The disc jockey's work is not easy, and it's not glamorous. It is a lot of work that can be exhausting, both physically and mentally, but for someone who loves music and entertaining, the sense of personal satisfaction after the show is well worth the aggravation.

11

Pitfalls to Avoid

1. **Avoid explaining a trivial process that does not matter to your reader.** In most cases, this means you do not want to tell how to make a recipe or how to do something everyone already knows how to do, like wash a car, unless you can put a fresh spin on the material.

2. **Avoid stating the obvious.** A recipe might tell you to preheat the oven to 350 degrees, but it will not tell you to turn the oven on first, as that step is too obvious to mention. Similarly, you must keep your audience in mind and avoid insulting or boring your reader with information he or she does not need. For example, if you are explaining how to shop for a car loan, you do not need to explain what the annual percentage rate means for readers likely to have had car loans before. However, this explanation would be useful to a young, first-time buyer and loan applicant.

3. **Avoid giving the steps out of sequence.** Unless the order of steps is unimportant to the successful performance of the process, be sure to give them in the order they are performed.

PROCESS GUIDELINES: WRITING PROCESS ANALYSIS

1. To come up with a topic, consider these:
   a. Your past experiences and activities may suggest processes you can describe. If you were involved in athletics, perhaps you can describe how to coach Little League or how to prepare mentally for a game. If you were a scout, maybe you can explain how to prepare for a hike or how to survive in the wilderness. If you baby-sat, maybe you can explain how to sit for very young children, and so forth.
   b. Think of what you have learned in your classes. Maybe as a result of what you have learned you can explain how to teach reading or how to prepare a slide to view under a microscope.
2. To decide on your purpose, answer these questions:
   a. Do I want to describe a process so that my reader can perform it?
   b. Do I want to describe a process so that my reader is aware of it?
   c. Do I want to describe a process so that my reader will appreciate it more?
   d. Do I want to convince my reader that there is a better way to perform a process?
   e. Do I want to entertain my reader by showing the humor in a process?
3. These questions can help you identify your audience:
   a. Who does not know how to perform the process I am describing?
   b. Who does not fully understand or appreciate the process?
   c. Who should be convinced to perform the process?
   d. Who would be entertained by reading about the process?
4. These questions can help you assess the nature of your audience:
   a. Does my reader appreciate the importance of the process?
   b. Has my reader had any experience with the process?
   c. How interested is my reader in the process?
   d. Does my reader need any terms defined?
   e. Determine whether any steps in the process will prove difficult for your reader to perform or understand.
5. To generate ideas, do the following:
   a. List every step in the process in the order it is performed.
   b. For each step you have listed, answer the following questions:
      • Should I explain how the step is performed?
      • Should I explain why the step is performed?
      • Should I explain something that is *not* done?
      • Should I explain a troublesome aspect of the step?
      • Should I define a term?
      • Should I describe something?
      • Should I illustrate something?
6. If you like to secure reader response as part of your revision process, see page 115. In addition, give your draft to a reader and ask that person if there are any aspects of the process that are hard to follow.

REVISION CHECKLIST

In addition to the checklist on page 117, you can use this checklist to help you revise your process analysis.

1. Does your thesis mention the process and the significance of the process? If not, should it?
2. Will your reader know why it is important to understand the process and/or why you are qualified to describe the process?
3. Have you mentioned all the steps in the process and how they are performed? Have you avoided stating the obvious?
4. Where necessary, have you explained why steps are performed and noted what is not done? If necessary, are steps given in sequence?
5. Have you defined unfamiliar terms and, if necessary, given a list of items needed?
6. Have you explained troublesome aspects of the process?

EXERCISE | **Writing Process Analysis**

1. Explain how you might use process analysis as part of each of the following essays:
   a. a definition of a *good teacher*
   b. the causes and effects of premature birth
   c. a classification of the ways advertisements influence consumers
2. Think of two things that you do well (shop for bargains, make friends, plan a party, buy used cars, study, baby-sit, and so forth). Then list the steps in each process (in the order they are performed, if chronological order is important).
3. Assume you will write a process analysis for each of the processes you identified for number 1, and identify a purpose and audience for each.
4. For each process, answer the following questions keeping your audience and purpose in mind:
   a. Is it necessary to explain *how* any steps are performed?
   b. Is it necessary to explain *why* any steps are performed?
   c. Will the reader understand better if I explain something that is *not* done?
   d. Are there troublesome aspects that should be explained?
   e. Are any materials needed?
   f. Should any terms be defined?
   g. Is it possible to describe anything?
   h. Is it possible to use examples?
5. *Collaborative Activity.* With two or three classmates, write a list of the processes a student should know in order to succeed at your school. Pick one of these processes and write an explanation of how it is performed. Think of your reader as a new freshman.

PROFESSIONAL ESSAYS

How to Take a Job Interview

Kirby W. Stanat

As a former placement officer at the University of Wisconsin-Milwaukee and a former recruiter, Kirby Stanat knows what he is talking about when he explains how the job interview process works. In addition to providing valuable information, Stanat uses specific diction to keep his process analysis lively and engaging.

To succeed in campus job interviews, you have to know where that recruiter is 1
coming from. The simple answer is that he is coming from corporate headquarters.

That may sound obvious, but it is a significant point that too many students
do not consider. The recruiter is not a free spirit as he flies from Berkeley to New
Haven, from Chapel Hill to Boulder. He's on an invisible leash to the office, and
if he is worth his salary, he is mentally in corporate headquarters all the time he's
on the road.

If you can fix that in your mind—that when you walk into that bare-walled 2
cubicle in the placement center you are walking into a branch office of Sears,
Bendix, or General Motors—you can avoid a lot of little mistakes and maybe
some big ones.

If, for example, you assume that because the interview is on campus the re- 3
cruiter expects you to look and act like a student, you're in for a shock. A student
is somebody who drinks beer, wears blue jeans, and throws a Frisbee. No recruiter has jobs for student Frisbee whizzes.

A cool spring day in late March, Sam Davis, a good recruiter who has been 4
on the college circuit for years, is on my campus talking to candidates. He comes
out to the waiting area to meet the student who signed up for an 11 o'clock interview. I'm standing in the doorway of my office taking in the scene.

Sam calls the candidate: "Sidney Student." There sits Sidney. He's at a 45 5
degree angle, his feet are in the aisle, and he's almost lying down. He's wearing
well-polished brown shoes, a tasteful pair of brown pants, a light brown shirt,
and a good-looking tie. Unfortunately, he tops off this well-coordinated outfit
with his Joe's Tavern Class A Softball Championship jacket, which has a big
woven emblem over the heart.

If that isn't bad enough, in his left hand is a cigarette and in his right hand 6
is a half-eaten apple.

When Sam calls his name, the kid is caught off guard. He ditches the ciga- 7
rette in an ashtray, struggles to his feet, and transfers the apple from the right to
the left hand. Apple juice is everywhere, so Sid wipes his hand on the seat of his
pants and shakes hands with Sam.

Sam, who by now is close to having a stroke, gives me that what-do-I-have- 8
here look and has the young man follow him into the interviewing room.

The situation deteriorates even further—into pure Laurel and Hardy. The *9* kid is stuck with the half-eaten apple, doesn't know what to do with it, and obviously is suffering some discomfort. He carries the apple into the interviewing room with him and places it in the ashtray on the desk—right on top of Sam's freshly lit cigarette.

The interview lasts five minutes. . . .   *10*

Let us move in for a closer look at how the campus recruiter operates.   *11*

Let's say you have a 10 o'clock appointment with the recruiter from the *12* XYZ Corporation. The recruiter gets rid of the candidate in front of you at about 5 minutes to 10, jots down a few notes about what he is going to do with him or her, then picks up your résumé or data sheet (which you have submitted in advance). . . .

Although the recruiter is still in the interview room and you are still in the *13* lobby, your interview is under way. You're on. The recruiter will look over your sheet pretty carefully before he goes out to call you. He develops a mental picture of you.

He thinks, "I'm going to enjoy talking with this kid," or "This one's going *14* to be a turkey." The recruiter has already begun to make a screening decision about you.

His first impression of you, from reading the sheet, could come from your *15* grade point. It could come from misspelled words. It could come from poor erasures or from the fact that necessary information is missing. By the time the recruiter has finished reading your sheet, you've already hit the plus or minus column.

Let's assume the recruiter got a fairly good impression from your sheet.   *16*

Now the recruiter goes out to the lobby to meet you. He almost shuffles *17* along, and his mind is somewhere else. Then he calls your name, and at that instant he visibly clicks into gear. He just went to work.   *18*

As he calls your name he looks quickly around the room, waiting for some- *19* body to move. If you are sitting on the middle of your back, with a book open and a cigarette going, and if you have to rebuild yourself to stand up, the interest will run right out of the recruiter's face. You, not the recruiter, made the appointment for 10 o'clock, and the recruiter expects to see a young professional come popping out of that chair like today is a good day and you're anxious to meet him.

At this point, the recruiter does something rude. He doesn't walk across the *20* room to meet you halfway. He waits for you to come to him. Something very important is happening. He wants to see you move. He wants to get an impression about your posture, your stride, and your briskness.

If you slouch over to him, sidewinderlike, he is not going to be impressed. *21* He'll figure you would probably slouch your way through your workdays. He wants you to come at him with lots of good things going for you. If you watch the recruiter's eyes, you can see the inspection. He glances quickly at shoes, pants, coat, shirt; dress, blouse, hose—the whole works.

After introducing himself, the recruiter will probably say, "Okay, please fol- *22* low me," and he'll lead you into his interviewing room.

When you get to the room, you may find that the recruiter will open the ²³ door and gesture you in—with him blocking part of the doorway. There's enough room for you to get past him, but it's a near thing.

As you scrape past, he gives you a closeup inspection. He looks at your ²⁴ hair; if it's greasy, that will bother him. He looks at your collar; if it's dirty, that will bother him. He looks at your shoulders; if they're covered with dandruff, that will bother him. If you're a man, he looks at your chin. If you didn't get a close shave, that will irritate him. If you're a woman, he checks your makeup. If it's too heavy, he won't like it.

Then he smells you. An amazing number of people smell bad. Occasionally ²⁵ a recruiter meets a student who smells like a canal horse. That student can expect an interview of about four or five minutes.

Next the recruiter inspects the back side of you. He checks your hair (is it ²⁶ combed in front but not in back?), he checks your heels (are they run down?), your pants (are they baggy?), your slip (is it showing?), your stockings (do they have runs?).

Then he invites you to sit down. ²⁷

At this point, I submit, the recruiter's decision on you is 75 to 80 percent ²⁸ made.

Think about it. The recruiter has read your résumé. He knows who you are ²⁹ and where you are from. He knows your marital status, your major, and your grade point. And he knows what you have done with your summers. He has inspected you, exchanged greetings with you, and smelled you. There is very little additional hard information that he must gather on you. From now on it's mostly body chemistry.

Many recruiters have argued strenuously with me that they don't make ³⁰ such hasty decisions. So I tried an experiment. I told several recruiters that I would hang around in the hall outside the interview room when they took candidates in.

I told them that as soon as they had definitely decided not to recommend ³¹ (to department managers in their companies) the candidate they were interviewing, they should snap their fingers loud enough for me to hear. It went like this.

First candidate: 38 seconds after the candidate sat down: Snap! ³²
Second candidate: 1 minute, 42 seconds: Snap! ³³
Third candidate: 45 seconds: Snap! ³⁴

One recruiter was particularly adamant, insisting that he didn't rush to ³⁵ judgment on candidates. I asked him to participate in the snapping experiment. He went out in the lobby, picked up his first candidate of the day, and headed for an interview room.

As he passed me in the hall, he glared at me. And his fingers went "Snap!" ³⁶

Considering Ideas

1. For what purpose did Stanat write his process analysis? Who is his intended audience?

2. What does Stanat mean in paragraph 1 when he says that the student needs to know that the interviewer is "coming from corporate headquarters"? Why does the student need to know this fact?
3. Stanat explains how the campus recruiter works. Write out a list of the steps in that process.
4. Explain the reference to Laurel and Hardy in paragraph 10. Do you find that reference appropriate? Why or why not?
5. The recruiter often makes decisions about applicants before meeting them, and he often judges students according to their appearance. Do you think this behavior is fair? Explain.

Considering Technique

1. In which paragraphs does the author do the following:
   a. Explain what *not* to do?
   b. Explain *why* a step is performed?
   c. Explain *how* to perform a step?
2. Stanat explains the behavior of both the interviewer and the student-applicant. Is this dual perspective on the interview process a good idea? Explain.
3. *Combining patterns*. Paragraphs 5–11 form a narration. What purpose does that narration serve? What other paragraphs form a narration? In which paragraphs does Stanat use examples to illustrate aspects of the process?
4. Stanat's simple, specific diction contributes to the essay's engaging, lively quality. Cite three examples of simple, specific diction.

For Group Discussion or Journal Writing

Consider the following questions: What, if anything, did you learn about the interview process as a result of reading "How to Take a Job Interview"? Did you find anything surprising about the interviewer's procedures? As you think back over job interviews you have had in the past, can you recall the interviewer following any of the procedures described in the essay? If so, which ones?

A Delicate Operation

Roy C. Selby, Jr.

Because the following process analysis describes brain surgery, it is obviously not meant to teach the reader how to perform a process. It does, however, help the reader appreciate the complexity—and even the beauty—of a very dramatic undertaking.

In the autumn of 1973 a woman in her early fifties noticed, upon closing one eye   *1*
while reading, that she was unable to see clearly. Her eyesight grew slowly worse. Changing her eyeglasses did not help. She saw an ophthalmologist, who found that her vision was seriously impaired in both eyes. She then saw a neurologist, who confirmed the finding and obtained X rays of the skull and an EMI scan—a

photograph of the patient's head. The latter revealed a tumor growing between the optic nerves at the base of the brain. The woman was admitted to the hospital by a neurosurgeon.

Further diagnosis, based on angiography, a detailed X-ray study of the circulatory system, showed the tumor to be about two inches in diameter and supplied by many small blood vessels. It rested beneath the brain, just above the pituitary gland, stretching the optic nerves to either side and intimately close to the major blood vessels supplying the brain. Removing it would pose many technical problems. Probably benign and slow-growing, it may have been present for several years. If left alone it would continue to grow and produce blindness and might become impossible to remove completely. Removing it, however, might not improve the patient's vision and could make it worse. A major blood vessel could be damaged, causing a stroke. Damage to the undersurface of the brain could cause impairment of memory and changes in mood and personality. The hypothalamus, a most important structure of the brain, could be injured, causing coma, high fever, bleeding from the stomach, and death. *2*

The neurosurgeon met with the patient and her husband and discussed the various possibilities. The common decision was to operate. *3*

The patient's hair was shampooed for two nights before surgery. She was given a cortisonelike drug to reduce the risk of damage to the brain during surgery. Five units of blood were cross-matched, as a contingency against hemorrhage. At 1:00 P.M. the operation began. After the patient was anesthetized her hair was completely clipped and shaved from the scalp. Her head was prepped with an organic iodine solution for 10 minutes. Drapes were placed over her, leaving exposed only the forehead and crown of the skull. All the routine instruments were brought up—the electrocautery used to coagulate areas of bleeding, bipolar coagulation forceps to arrest bleeding from individual blood vessels without damaging adjacent tissues, and small suction tubes to remove blood and cerebrospinal fluid from the head, thus giving the surgeon a better view of the tumor and surrounding areas. *4*

A curved incision was made behind the hairline so it would be concealed when the hair grew back. It extended almost from ear to ear. Plastic clips were applied to the cut edges of the scalp to arrest bleeding. The scalp was folded back to the level of the eyebrows. Incisions were made in the muscle of the right temple, and three sets of holes were drilled near the temple and the top of the head because the tumor had to be approached from directly in front. The drill, powered by nitrogen, was replaced with a fluted steel blade, and the holes were connected. The incised piece of skull was pried loose and held out of the way by a large sponge. *5*

Beneath the bone is a yellowish leatherlike membrane, the dura, that surrounds the brain. Down the middle of the head the dura carries a large vein, but in the area near the nose the vein is small. At that point the vein and dura were cut, and clips made of tantalum, a hard metal, were applied to arrest and prevent bleeding. Sutures were put into the dura and tied to the scalp to keep the dura open and retracted. A malleable silver retractor, resembling the blade of a butter *6* knife, was inserted between the brain and skull. The anesthesiologist began to administer a drug to relax the brain by removing some of its water, making it easier for the surgeon to manipulate the retractor, hold the brain back, and see the tumor. The nerve tracts for smell were cut on both sides to provide additional room. The tumor was seen approximately two-and-one-half inches behind the base of the nose. It was pink in color. On touching it, it proved to be very fibrous and tough. A special retractor was attached to the skull, enabling the other retractor blades to be held automatically and freeing the surgeon's hands. With further displacement of the frontal lobes of the brain, the tumor could be seen better, but no normal structures—the carotid arteries, their branches, and the optic nerves— were visible. The tumor obscured them.

A surgical microscope was placed above the wound. The surgeon had se- 7 lected the lenses and focal length prior to the operation. Looking through the microscope, he could see some of the small vessels supplying the tumor and he coagulated them. He incised the tumor to attempt to remove its core and thus collapse it, but the substance of the tumor was too firm to be removed in this fashion. He then began to slowly dissect the tumor from the adjacent brain tissue and from where he believed the normal structures to be.

Using small squares of cotton, he began to separate the tumor from very 8 loose fibrous bands connecting it to the brain and to the right side of the part of the skull where the pituitary gland lies. The right optic nerve and carotid artery came into view, both displaced considerably to the right. The optic nerve had a normal appearance. He protected these structures with cotton compresses placed between them and the tumor. He began to raise the tumor from the skull and slowly to reach the point of its origin and attachment—just in front of the pituitary gland and medial to the left optic nerve, which still could not be seen. The small blood vessels entering the tumor were cauterized. The upper portion of the tumor was gradually separated from the brain, and the branches of the carotid arteries and the branches to the tumor were coagulated. The tumor was slowly and gently lifted from its bed, and for the first time the left carotid artery and optic nerve could be seen. Part of the tumor adhered to this nerve. The bulk of the tumor was amputated, leaving a small bit attached to the nerve. Very slowly and carefully the tumor fragment was resected.

The tumor now removed, a most impressive sight came into view—the pi- 9 tuitary gland and its stalk of attachment to the hypothalamus, the hypothalamus itself, and the brainstem, which conveys nerve impulses between the body and the brain. As far as could be determined, no damage had been done to these structures or other vital centers, but the left optic nerve, from chronic pressure of the tumor, appeared gray and thin. Probably it would not completely recover its function.

After making certain there was no bleeding, the surgeon closed the wounds 10 and placed wire mesh over the holes in the skull to prevent dimpling of the scalp over the points that had been drilled. A gauze dressing was applied to the patient's head. She was awakened and sent to the recovery room.

Even with the microscope, damage might still have occurred to the cerebral *11* cortex and hypothalamus. It would require at least a day to be reasonably certain there was none, and about 72 hours to monitor for the major postoperative dangers—swelling of the brain and blood clots forming over the surface of the brain. The surgeon explained this to the patient's husband, and both of them waited anxiously. The operation had required seven hours. A glass of orange juice had given the surgeon some additional energy during the closure of the wound. Though exhausted, he could not fall asleep until after two in the morning, momentarily expecting a call from the nurse in the intensive care unit announcing deterioration of the patient's condition.

At 8:00 A.M. the surgeon saw the patient in the intensive care unit. She *12* was alert, oriented, and showed no sign of additional damage to the optic nerves or the brain. She appeared to be in better shape than the surgeon or her husband.

Considering Ideas

1. The thesis of "A Delicate Operation" is implied rather than stated. What is the thesis? Where is it most strongly implied?
2. Whom would you judge to be Selby's intended audience? What is his purpose?
3. Selby uses a considerable amount of technical language ("electrocautery," "angiography," "bipolar coagulation," and so forth). How would the essay be different if the author had not used the technical terms? Do you think you would prefer the essay that way? Why or why not?
4. Given the facts stated in paragraph 4, would you have had the surgery described in the essay? Why or why not?
5. The "delicate operation" occurred in the 1970s. Since then, a number of advancements have occurred in medical science. Does that fact affect your reaction to the essay? Explain.

Considering Technique

1. The introduction is the first three paragraphs. What approach do these paragraphs take?
2. Selby frequently defines medical terms. Cite three terms that he defines. Why does he provide these definitions?
3. In which paragraphs does Selby explain why steps are performed? How do these explanations help Selby fulfill his purpose? In which paragraph does Selby explain how a step is performed? How does this explanation help Selby fulfill his purpose?
4. Paragraph 6 includes description. What purpose does this description serve?
5. In which two paragraphs does Selby note troublesome aspects of the process? What does this contribute?

For Group Discussion or Journal Writing

Selby's process analysis describes brain surgery. However, it also gives us some knowledge of the neurosurgeon. Use the clues in the essay to construct a sketch of the neurosurgeon's personality.

Combining Patterns of Development

Green Frog Skin

John Lame Deer

A tribal priest of the Sioux tribe, John Lame Deer writes seriously about the way whites view money and treat the land. Still, his engaging style lets him do so in an entertaining fashion. Notice, as you read, that the author combines **narration, cause-and-effect analysis,** *and* **process analysis.**

The green frog skin—that's what I call a dollar bill. In our attitude toward it lies the biggest difference between Indians and whites. My grandparents grew up in an Indian world without money. Just before the Custer battle the white soldiers had received their pay. Their pockets were full of green paper and they had no place to spend it. What were their last thoughts as an Indian bullet or arrow hit them? I guess they were thinking of all that money going to waste, of not having had a chance to enjoy it, of a bunch of dumb savages getting their paws on that hard-earned pay. That must have hurt them more than the arrow between their ribs. 1

The close hand-to-hand fighting, with a thousand horses gallyhooting all over the place, had covered the battlefield with an enormous cloud of dust, and in it the green frog skins of the soldiers were whirling around like snowflakes in a blizzard. Now, what did the Indians do with all that money? They gave it to their children to play with, to fold those strange bits of colored paper into all kinds of shapes, making them into toy buffalo and horses. Somebody was enjoying that money after all. The books tell of one soldier who survived. He got away, but he went crazy and some women watched him from a distance as he killed himself. The writers always say he must have been afraid of being captured and tortured, but that's all wrong. 2

Can't you see it? There he is, bellied down in a gully, watching what is going on. He sees the kids playing with the money, tearing it up, the women using it to fire up some dried buffalo chips to cook on, the men lighting their pipes with green frog skins, but mostly all those beautiful dollar bills floating away with the dust and the wind. It's this sight that drove that poor soldier crazy. He's clutching his head, hollering, "Goddam, Jesus Christ Almighty, look at them dumb, stupid, red sons of bitches wasting all that dough!" He watches till he can't stand it any longer, and then he blows his brains out with a six-shooter. It would make a great scene in a movie, but it would take an Indian mind to get the point. 3

The green frog skin—that was what the fight was all about. The gold of the Black Hills, the gold in every clump of grass. Each day you can see ranch hands riding over this land. They have a bagful of grain from their saddle horns, and 4 whenever they see a prairie-dog hole they toss a handful of oats in it, like a kind little old lady feeding the pigeons in one of your city parks. Only the oats for the prairie dogs are poisoned with strychnine. What happens to the prairie dog after he has eaten this grain is not a pleasant thing to watch. The prairie dogs are poisoned, because they eat grass. A thousand of them eat up as much grass in a year as a cow. So if the rancher can kill that many prairie dogs he can run one more head of cattle, make a little more money. When he looks at a prairie dog he sees only a green frog skin getting away from him.

For the white man each blade of grass or spring of water has a price tag on   5
it. And that is the trouble, because look at what happens. The bobcats and coyotes which used to feed on prairie dogs now have to go after a stray lamb or a crippled calf. The rancher calls the pest-control officer to kill these animals. This man shoots some rabbits and puts them out as bait with a piece of wood stuck in them. That stick has an explosive charge which shoots some cyanide into the mouth of the coyote who tugs at it. The officer has been trained to be careful. He puts a printed warning on each stick reading, "Danger, Explosive, Poison!" The trouble is that our dogs can't read, and some of our children can't either.

And the prairie becomes a thing without life—no more prairie dogs, no   6
more badgers, foxes, coyotes. The big birds of prey used to feed on prairie dogs, too. So you hardly see an eagle these days. The bald eagle is your symbol. You see him on your money, but your money is killing him. When a people start killing off their own symbols they are in a bad way.

The Sioux have a name for white men. They call them *wasicun*—fat-takers.   7
It is a good name, because you have taken the fat of the land. But it does not seem to have agreed with you. Right now you don't look so healthy—overweight, yes, but not healthy. Americans are bred like stuffed geese—to be consumers, not human beings. The moment they stop consuming and buying, this frog-skin world has no more use for them. They have become frogs themselves. Some cruel child has stuffed a cigar into their mouths and they have to keep puffing and puffing until they explode. Fat-taking is a bad thing, even for the taker. It is especially bad for Indians who are forced to live in this frog-skin world which they did not make and for which they have no use.

Considering Ideas

1. Lame Deer calls the dollar bill "green frog skin"? Why?
2. How would you describe Lame Deer's attitude toward the soldiers he tells about in paragraph 1?
3. Lame Deer says that the last surviving soldier killed himself when he saw how the Indians were treating the soldiers' money. Do you think Lame Deer is serious here?
4. How do the Indians value the Black Hills? How do whites value them? How do you explain the difference?
5. What does Lame Deer mean when he says that Americans are "consumers, not human beings" (paragraph 7)?

Considering Technique

1. Lame Deer says that the death of a prairie dog after ingesting strychnine is "not a pleasant thing to watch" (paragraph 4), but he does not give specific details of the death? Why?
2. Why does Lame Deer use the present tense in paragraph 3 to describe the soldier killing himself, even though the event took place a long time ago?
3. *Combining Patterns.* In paragraphs 1–3, Lame Deer tells a brief narration. What does this narration contribute to the essay?
4. *Combining Patterns.* What cause-and-effect analysis appears in the essay?

For Group Discussion or Journal Writing

Agree or disagree with Lame Deer's assertion that money is the cause of serious problems.

STUDENT ESSAYS TO READ AND EVALUATE

Each of the following student process analyses has strengths and weaknesses for you to identify. Doing so will help you become a more reliable critic so you can better judge the effective and ineffective features of your own drafts.

Horse Sense

Some people think a horse is just another dumb animal, but they are wrong. Horses are very smart, and their intelligence is clearly shown when you try to break them. If you break horses, you will find that each has an instinctive bag of tricks to try to get you off his back. He'll do this by matching his wits against yours. *1*

The battle of wits will begin the moment you step into the horse's stall. You don't realize it, but he's always watching you. Even if he isn't looking straight at you but pretending to be interested in the wall straight ahead of him, he's watching you out of the corner of his eye. *2*

If you have to walk behind the horse, be careful! If he's in a good mood, you might only get a well-aimed, stinging slap in the face by his tail. If the horse is ornery, you could end up becoming the target of two muscular, hard-kicking hind legs. *3*

The horse knows exactly where your feet are. One well-maneuvered side step from the horse and you could suddenly find your foot anchored to the floor of the stall. As you yell, glad that there is a cushion of straw on the floor, and struggle to push *4*

him off of your foot, he'll glance at you, pretending to wonder
what all the ruckus is about.

When you're ready to put the saddle on him, you'll notice his   5
belly suddenly becomes extended. He does this to keep you from
pulling the cinch as tightly as needed to keep the saddle securely
on his back. He does this hoping that while you're on his back
riding, you'll suddenly find yourself sitting on the ground,
watching him trot away with a loose saddle bouncing under his
belly. From about 15 yards away, the horse will stop, turn his head
toward you, and let out a shrill whinny, which is his way of
laughing at you. To prevent this embarrassing event, you have to be
sure that the cinch is tight.

After the saddle is on properly, you're ready to get on his   6
back to try and stay in the saddle. Since the horse is not broken,
your first ride will be the first of many battles with him to find
out which one of you is going to be the boss. Before you get on
him, he's going to try to intimidate you by snorting loudly, pawing
at the ground, and rolling his eyes. As you get your foot in the
stirrup, he'll turn his head toward your leg and try and leave a
temporary tattoo of the imprint of his teeth on your calf. As soon
as you're seated in the saddle, he'll start rearing up on his hind
legs. Reaching higher and higher towards the sky with his front
hoofs, it'll feel as if you and the horse might topple over
backwards onto the hard ground behind you. Beginning to buck, he'll
leap forward and upward suddenly, trying to dislodge you from the
saddle. After minutes of this bone-jarring ride, he'll spring
straight up into the air, landing stiff legged, making it feel as
if you've just stoved your whole body.

After resting for just seconds, the horse takes off in a dead   7
run with his ears back against his head. You can see that his
destination is a grove of trees with low-hanging branches. You
realize that if you don't duck your head lower than the horse's,
the grabbing fingers of the branches will snatch you off the horse
and leave you lying in a heap on the ground. The horse will also
swerve as close to a tree as possible, trying to batter your leg
against the trunk. By lifting your leg onto the horse's back, you
safely make it past the horse's intended target and through the
tree grove, scratched and bruised but still in one piece. You
wonder, "How did this horse make it through unscathed?"

A horse can also stop and turn on a dime and will use this   *8*
ability to try to dismount you. He'll run straight for a fence and
while you're deciding if this horse can clear the three loosely
stranded, rusted barbed wires, you brace yourself for the jump.
Instead, the horse digs its hoofs into the ground and stops
suddenly, as if he had just slammed into a brick wall. As you're
thrown forward, your arms wrap around the horse's neck
involuntarily, your head is thrown between his ears, and your legs
are tossed up into the air.

As you regain your seat, you glance to the left and right,   *9*
hoping that nobody saw you in that ridiculous-looking acrobatic
position. The horse takes off again. Ahead you see a five-foot-wide
stream. As you approach the swiftly moving water, you wonder if the
horse will run through the current or jump it. Now you're also
prepared for his quick-stop trick. Being only feet from the
obstacle, the horse suddenly makes a lightning-quick 90-degree
right turn in one quick, jolting motion. This move leaves you
dangling from the horse's left side by one leg with a hand grasping
the saddle horn. At this point, you decide it's time for a reprieve
and take the horse back to the weather-beaten barn.

As you leave your spirited, four-legged companion stomping and   *10*
munching grain in his stall, you shuffle across the straw-covered
floor and sink into a pile of loose hay. Before a horse is broken,
it's just a natural instinct for him to use any means to get you
off his back.

🖐 Some Assembly Required

If it hasn't happened to you yet, it will. You will purchase an   *1*
item, it will come in a box, and printed on the box in the tiniest
of letters will be the warning: "Some assembly required." There is
almost always a set of instructions that comes with your purchase.
These are supposed to guide you through the whole torturous
process, but let's face it—fifty pages of tech talk or toy talk
(depending on what you bought) is not your idea of a good read. So
you promptly toss aside these instructions and blithely dive into
the task, thinking, "How hard can this be?" This approach, despite
the beliefs of your friends and family (and the salesperson who
told you the store would assemble the item for $20.00) is the right

one! Forget the suggested order of steps. Forget the diagrams of how things should look. Forget the list of parts with their names. All you need to do is complete the following simple steps, and things will turn out just fine.

The first step in assembling your unassembled item is to lift the box in which it is contained up over your head. With a snap of your wrists, dump its contents haphazardly onto the floor in front of you. This will create a fantastic pile of unidentifiable plastic doodads, metal springy thingies, and other important parts. The purpose of this is to create an air of complexity so that whenever you complete even the simplest step of assembly, it will seem like a *huge* deal. This is good. It builds self-esteem.   *2*

If the item you purchased is electrical, your next step is to take any cords and wires that came with the item and randomly plug them into its main section. Sure you could look at the instruction manual to find out the proper place for these, but then you would only get one-half of the facts. By ignoring the manual, not only can you find out where the wires *should* go, you can also find out where they should *not* go. You may get a shock or two here, a blown circuit there, but hey, you're learning, right? Knowledge is beautiful if not painful.   *3*

If your item is not electrical, you will have to find your challenge elsewhere. One of my favorite methods is to invite my dog in to run through the parts, causing the tiniest screws, nuts, and assorted doohickeys to roll under the furniture and into a black hole. Although the assembly is now rendered more challenging, it often goes much faster, as you have fewer parts to contend with.   *4*

The next step is one of my favorites: swearing at the item. The step may seem vulgar and unnecessary, and perhaps it is. However, swearing at the infernal thing is actually a great motivational tool! It creates for you a sense of power over the item. (This is, of course, a completely false sense of power. You have no control over the situation at all.) However, remember that the assembly process is 50 percent mental. Delusions of grandeur, not to mention competence, are vital to your success. As for the item, it seems less intimidating once you have sworn at it. It has become your small child. You've punished it. It is ready to cooperate now. At this point, the assembly is almost complete. You will quickly put together whatever parts remain within arm's reach and feel supremely confident.   *5*

Now it is time for the final step. You've stepped back and   6
taken a long, hard look at what you have accomplished and realized
that the way you have assembled this thing has rendered it
completely useless! As frustration consumes you, do not forget the
final step: Kick the thing. Kick it hard. There. Now don't you feel
better?

Mission accomplished.   7

Collaborative Exercise: Evaluating Writing

Break into groups of three and select one of the previous student essays. As a group, choose the strongest features of the essay and the features most in need of revision. Then prepare a group report that explains the essay's chief strengths and weaknesses. Be sure the report notes the specific kinds of changes needed. For example, do not just say that more detail is needed in paragraph 3; state that paragraph 3 should explain how the step is performed. When your report is complete, present it to the rest of the class. (The following evaluation questions can be used to guide you through your assessment of the essay.)

Evaluation Questions

1. *The Introduction*
   Does the introduction engage your interest? Why or why not?
2. *The Thesis*
   Does the thesis mention the process and its significance?
3. *Supporting Details*
   Does the essay include all the necessary steps in the process? Where necessary, does the essay explain how steps are performed, why steps are performed, and what is *not* done? Are troublesome aspects of the process explained? Does the essay list needed materials and explain unfamiliar terms? Are any examples or description needed? Is there anything you do not understand?
4. *Organization*
   Do all the body paragraphs have topic sentences? If not, is this a problem? Are there any relevance problems?
5. *Word Choice and Sentence Effectiveness*
   Cite examples of effective word choice. Cite examples of word choice to revise. Are transitions needed? Where? Note any places where sentence variety is needed.

Essay Topics: Process Analysis

When you write your process analysis, consult Pitfalls to Avoid on page 216 and the Revision Checklist on page 218.

Writing in the Pattern

1. Explain a process you perform well so that someone else can perform it—how to change the oil in a car, how to train for an athletic competition, how to build a campfire, how to buy a used car, and so forth. Your responses to the exercise on page 218 may help you here.

2. Explain any of the following processes to help first-year students at your school:

how to register	how to select a major	how to meet people
how to study for an exam	how to select an advisor	how to live with a roommate

3. Think of something you know how to make and describe the process so that someone else can make it.

4. Explain a process that can save a life (CPR, first aid, the Heimlich maneuver, etc.).

5. Explain one of the following processes:

how to survive adolescence	how to buy the perfect gift
how to plan the perfect party	how to choose the right college
how to buy running shoes	how to buy a computer

6. Identify a problem that exists on your campus and then explain a process for solving the problem.

Reading Then Writing in the Pattern

1. In paragraphs 4 through 6 of "Green Frog Skin," John Lame Deer explains a process that hurts the environment, a process set in motion by the killing of the prairie dog. Think of one way people could help the environment and explain that process.

2. As Roy Selby does in "A Delicate Operation," describe a process to increase the reader's appreciation. Possibilities include how to write a poem, how to design clothing, how to raise show dogs, how to design scenery for a play, and how to pass legislation in Congress.

3. Like the author of "Some Assembly Required," write a process analysis for comic effect. Possibilities include how to avoid working, how to make a rotten impression on a first date, how to fail an exam, and how to annoy a professor.

Responding to the Readings

1. Stanat describes the interview process in "How to Take a Job Interview" (page 219). Tell about an experience you had applying or interviewing for a job. Your essay should teach something about how the job applicant should or should not behave.

2. Explain how much of the interview process that Stanat describes in "How to Take an Interview" (page 219) is applicable to Harold Krents in "Darkness at Noon" (page 194). Does Krents deserve special consideration by the interviewer? Explain and support your view.

3. John Lame Deer says in paragraph 7 of "Green Frog Skin" that "Americans are bred like stuffed geese—to be consumers, not human beings." Agree or disagree with this assessment. Be sure to back up your points with specific examples.

4. *Connecting the Readings.* "How to Take a Job Interview" (page 219), "A Delicate Operation" (page 222), and "A Disc Jockey's Work" (page 214) all give insight into kinds of jobs. Consider the kinds of work people do and explain how we ascribe status and value to jobs.

CHAPTER 8

Comparison-Contrast

Comparison-contrast involves setting things side by side to examine their similarities and/or differences. In common classroom usage, to *compare* is to look at both similarities and differences. However, strictly speaking, when you **compare,** you look at similarities, when you **contrast,** you look at differences, and when you **compare and contrast,** you look at both.

Comparison-contrast is so much a part of routine thinking that you may not realize how much you engage in it. To appreciate how fundamental comparison-contrast is to thinking about the world, consider how often you say or think things like, "This television show is not as good as the one I saw last week"; "Your schedule is very similar to mine"; "This soap dries my skin more than my cleansing cream"; "Professor James is every bit as interesting as Professor Aqueros."

When you write comparison-contrast, give careful thought to topic selection. The items compared or contrasted must have enough in common to warrant their side-by-side consideration. Usually this means that the subjects must belong to the same category. For example, you can sensibly compare or contrast a Mercury Villager with a Plymouth Voyager because both of these belong to the same category—minivans. You can compare or contrast two jobs, two teachers, two forms of government, two ways to study, two kinds of dates, two ways to celebrate Christmas, two cities you have lived in, and so on. These comparisons and contrasts are possible and sensible because the items share enough features to make their comparison or contrast logical and meaningful. It would be silly, however, to compare learning to use a personal computer and learning to roller skate. Even if you could manage some corresponding statements about both of these activities, the comparison would be strained, probably more clever than valid, and the contrasts would be so obvious they could go without saying. As a result, the essay would serve no purpose.

ESTABLISHING YOUR PURPOSE AND IDENTIFYING YOUR AUDIENCE

Comparison-contrast can serve a variety of informational purposes. It can *clarify the unknown* by placing it (the unknown) next to something more familiar to determine in what ways the two are alike and in what ways they are different. For example, an essay comparing and contrasting rugby (less understood) with football (well-known) could serve this purpose. Once the lesser-known rugby is explained in light of how it is like and unlike the better-known football, rugby can be better understood. Comparison-contrast can also *lend a fresh insight* into something familiar. This can be achieved when similarities are drawn between things typically viewed as dissimilar or when differences are noted in things usually seen as comparable. Love and hate, for example, are usually seen as opposites, but an essay that explains their similarities by pointing out that both emotions are highly motivating, potentially self-destructive, and sometimes irrational can lead to new awarenesses about these familiar feelings. Comparison-contrast can sometimes *bring things into sharper focus*. For example, while we may understand what Catholicism and Protestantism are, an essay comparing and contrasting their basic tenets may lead to a clearer understanding of each religion.

Finally, a comparison-contrast essay can serve a *persuasive* purpose because when the features of one thing are compared or contrasted with the features of another, you can judge which one is superior. For example, the platforms of two mayoral candidates can be compared and contrasted to determine which candidate would make the better mayor.

Your purpose will influence detail selection. Say that you decide to note the differences between dating practices today and those of 50 years ago. If your purpose is to reveal how women are more assertive now, you can note that they take the initiative today but that 50 years ago they seldom asked men out or paid expenses. If your purpose is to argue that dating was easier 50 years ago, you might mention that relationships were simpler before prescribed codes of conduct relaxed and blurred.

Like purpose, audience will affect detail selection, so identifying and assessing your reader is important. How much your reader knows about your subjects, how your reader feels about your subjects, and how strong these feelings are—these influence the details you choose. For example, consider the essay that contrasts dating practices today with those of 50 years ago. Say your purpose is to convince the reader that dating was more fun 50 years ago. If your reader is a feminist, you will not note that 50 years ago men and women had more prescribed roles and hence were more certain how to act. However, if your reader is a teenager who finds today's sexual freedom frightening, you might note that there was less sexual pressure for teens who dated 50 years ago.

COMBINING COMPARISON-CONTRAST WITH OTHER PATTERNS

Comparison-contrast can be combined with any other pattern of development. If, for example, you are describing blues music, you can compare and contrast its rhythm with jazz rhythm to help your reader understand its qualities. If you are writing an extended definition of old age, you can contrast the activities that the elderly enjoy with those that younger adults enjoy to help explain what old age is like. If you are explaining a better process for determining which patients are chosen to receive organ transplants, you can contrast your procedure with the existing one to show the superiority of your process.

Even when comparison-contrast is the dominant method of development, it may be combined with other patterns. For example, a comparison-contrast of two basketball players can include a process analysis explaining the way each athlete plays defense. A contrast of two colleges that notes differences in the degree of political activism on campus can explain the effects of the activism and give examples of it.

For an example of an essay that combines comparison-contrast with cause-and-effect analysis and definition, see "Sport and the American Dream" on page 252.

USING COMPARISON-CONTRAST BEYOND THE WRITING CLASS

Because comparison-contrast requires you to analyze subjects and draw conclusions about their characteristics, it will be a frequent component of your writing in other college classes. For example, in a political science class, you may be asked to compare and contrast two forms of government, two supreme court justices, or two pieces of civil rights legislation and assess the relative merits of each. In an art appreciation course, you may be asked to explain Monet's use of light by comparing and contrasting two of his paintings. In a business class, you could be asked to compare and contrast two management strategies and determine which would be better in a particular setting.

Beyond the classroom, you will encounter comparison-contrast regularly, particularly as a persuasive strategy. For example, advertisements will contrast forms of pain relievers to persuade you to buy a particular product and campaign literature will compare and contrast candidates to convince you to vote for a particular person. Comparison-contrast will also be integral to your decision-making, as when you compare and contrast courses to decide what to schedule, compare and contrast apartments to decide where to live, compare and contrast movies to decide what to see, and so forth.

SELECTING DETAIL

In most cases, you cannot mention every point of comparison or contrast without writing an overly long, unwieldy essay. Instead, you must select your points judiciously. As noted on page 236, your detail selection will be influenced by your audience and purpose. In addition, you can limit yourself to a single basis of comparison or contrast. For example, if you were comparing two presidents, you could limit yourself to their foreign policies. If that gave you too much to write about, you could limit a step further, perhaps to a comparison of their trade policies.

To achieve adequate detail, you may need to do more than mention similarities and differences—you may also need to explain the points of comparison and contrast. For this, you can draw on the patterns of development you have learned so far. Say you want to compare the ways you have celebrated Christmas before and after you left home for college. This may involve you in two narrations—one of a celebration before you left home and one of a celebration after. If you want to contrast two respected teachers, you may find yourself explaining with illustrations, perhaps of the classroom techniques each uses. If you contrast study techniques, you are likely to rely on some process analysis to explain how each technique works. If you compare and contrast two cars, you may find yourself describing the interiors of the vehicles.

Regardless of your patterns of development, work to maintain balance between the points you discuss for each subject. This means that any point you discuss for one subject should also be mentioned for the other. Say, for example, you are comparing your family life before your parents divorced with your family life after they divorced, for the purpose of arguing that children can be better off if their parents end an unhappy marriage. If you describe mealtime before the divorce as a time of squabbling that made you tense and afraid, then you should say something about what mealtime was like after the divorce.

This need for balance does not require you to treat a point with exactly the same degree of development for each subject. You may describe extensively the mealtime squabbling that occurred before the divorce to give your reader a clear picture of its nature and effect on you. Then you can note the peaceful nature of meals after the divorce in just two or three sentences. Similarly, you may find that either the comparison or the contrast is more detailed, or that one of the subjects gets more development than the other. This is fine. As long as everything treated is developed *adequately*, it need not be developed *equally*.

ARRANGING DETAIL

To develop a thesis for a comparison-contrast essay, you can state the subjects you are considering and indicate whether you are comparing, contrasting, or doing both. Below are three possible thesis statements developed this way.

1. People think that adolescence is more difficult for females than it is for males, but teenage males suffer many of the same anxieties that females do. (This thesis indicates that the anxieties of adolescent males and females will be compared.)
2. Attending high school in Japan for two years gave me a firsthand look at the most important differences in our educational systems. (This thesis notes that the educational systems in Japan and the United States will be contrasted.)
3. The book and movie versions of *The Firm* are alike in many ways, but they differ significantly as well. (The thesis states that the book and movie versions of *The Firm* will be compared and contrasted.)

You can also write a thesis that includes the points of comparison or contrast that you will make, like this:

> People think that adolescence is more difficult for females than it is for males, but teenage males suffer the same anxieties about their appearance, about dating, about their relationship with their parents, and about peer pressure that girls do. (The thesis notes that the points of comparison will be anxiety about appearance, dating, relationships with parents, and peer pressure.)

Comparison-contrast must be carefully organized, or your points will be disconnected and confusing. Two arrangements can help you here. The first is **subject by subject.** With this organization, you make all your points about your first subject, and then you go on to make all your points about your second subject. An outline for an essay with a subject-by-subject organization could look like the following:

> Preliminary thesis: People think that adolesence is more difficult for females than it is for males, but teenage males suffer many of the same anxieties that teenage females do.

    I. Females
        A. Anxiety about appearance
        B. Anxiety about dating
        C. Anxiety about relationship with parents
        D. Anxiety about peer pressure
    II. Males
        A. Anxiety about appearance
        B. Anxiety about dating
        C. Anxiety about relationship with parents
        D. Anxiety about peer pressure

Note the balance in the outline. The points discussed for the first subject (anxiety about appearance, anxiety about dating, anxiety about relationship with parents, anxiety about peer pressure) are also discussed for the second. You need not develop each point equally, but you should treat the same points for each subject and do so in the same order.

The subject-by-subject organization generally works best for an essay that is not long, complex, or developed with a great many points. Otherwise, the reader working through your points on the second subject must keep too many points about the first subject in mind.

Longer, more-complex essays can be organized following the **point-by-point** arrangement. With this pattern you make a point about your first subject and then treat the corresponding point about your second subject. Then you treat the next point about your first subject and follow it with the corresponding point about your second subject. You continue in this alternating fashion until all your points have been presented and developed. An outline for an essay with this pattern could look like the following:

Preliminary thesis: People think that adolesence is more difficult for females than it is for males, but teenage males suffer many of the same anxieties that teenage females do.

```
  I. Anxiety about appearance
     A. Females
     B. Males
 II. Anxiety about dating
     A. Females
     B. Males
III. Anxiety about relationship with parents
     A. Females
     B. Males
 IV. Anxiety about peer pressure
     A. Females
     B. Males
```

You can tell from the outline that balance is important in point-by-point development. You must treat the same points for both subjects, although you need not give the same degree of development to each point for each subject.

For essays that show both similarities and differences, a third method of organization is possible. You can first discuss all the similarities between your subjects and then go on to discuss all the differences, using either point-by-point or subject-by-subject organization.

Preliminary thesis: Although Atlantic City has some things in common with its big sister, Las Vegas, the East Coast gambling town is not the vacation site Las Vegas is.

```
  I. Similarities
     A. Both have gambling.
     B. Both have top-level entertainment.
     C. Both have high-class hotels.
 II. Differences
     A. Gambling is different.
        1. There are more casinos in Vegas.
        2. There is cheaper gambling available in Vegas.
        3. Gambling is available 24 hours a day, 7 days a week
           in Vegas.
     B. Top-level entertainment is different.
        1. There are more big-name entertainers in Vegas.
        2. There is more free entertainment in Vegas.
     C. The high-class hotels are different.
        1. There are more hotels in Vegas.
```

```
2. There is greater variety of accommodations in Vegas.
3. There are lower room rates available in Vegas.
```

In the above outline, first the similarities are noted, using a point-by-point development, and then the differences are cited, again using a point-by-point pattern. However, the similarities can be developed with a point-by-point pattern and the differences with a subject-by-subject pattern. With this organization the outline would look like this:

```
 I. Similarities
    A. Gambling
    B. Top-level entertainment
    C. High-class hotels
II. Differences
    A. Atlantic City
       1. Gambling
       2. Top-level entertainment
       3. High-class hotels
    B. Las Vegas
       1. Gambling
       2. Top-level entertainment
       3. High-class hotels
```

Although in this particular example the same aspects (gambling, entertainment, hotels) are discussed for the similarities and for the differences, this balance is not necessary. You can discuss some features of similarity between both subjects and then go on to discuss different features of contrast. Whether you discuss the similarities first or the differences first depends on which you want to emphasize more. Points treated second get the greater emphasis because the closer to the end, the more emphatic the position.

As you can tell, comparison-contrast has an organization more complex than many other patterns, so transitions are very important for helping your reader find the way. You need to use transitional signposts like *similarly, in like manner, in the same fashion,* and *like* to show comparison and ones like *however, in contrast, on the other hand,* and *unlike* to show contrast. For a review of transitions that signal comparison and contrast, see page 86. Transitions can be particularly important with a subject-by-subject pattern, when the reader needs to be reminded of points made about the first subject before reading about the second subject. Thus, you can achieve transition with sentences such as, "Like females who are self-conscious about their figures, teenage males are worried about their size and physique."

Annotated Student Essay

The following contrast piece was written by a student. Study it and the marginal notes to better understand the points made in this chapter.

Running the Distance

My daughters, Laura and Jennifer, ran with the Columbiana High School Cross-Country Team. Although they both had determination and devotion, their training techniques, running styles, and attitudes toward spectators were quite different.

During training, Laura developed a vigorous stretching routine, which she used before each meet. She made adjustments in her running position to help increase her speed, such as leaning forward when running uphill. Since she wore out easily, she went to bed earlier and watched her diet. She ate balanced meals and believed that a steak dinner was the best meal to have the evening before a meet.

Laura's running style was a pleasure to watch. Her short frame seemed to be made for running. She looked like a thoroughbred horse gracefully running the course. Her legs stretched out as she made strong, even strides. She paced herself so she could, at just the right moment, begin to speed up for her big sprint to the finish. Since she never seemed to sweat, she appeared to still have energy after crossing the finish line.

Laura thrived on the spectators' cheers. The encouragement she received from the crowd motivated her to try harder. She always wanted people positioned along the course to cheer for her and to give her instructions. The coach would run back and forth across the course to give her tips during the race. Her best running time was when the entire boys' team went from point to point along the course and cheered for her from start to finish.

paragraph 5

The first sentence makes a transition to the second subject. Notice that the details covered are the same as the ones for the first subject (see paragraph 2). Also note the use of examples.

paragraph 6

The topic sentence (the first) notes the next point of contrast. This is the most well-developed paragraph. Note the use of description.

paragraph 7

The topic sentence (the first) notes the last point of contrast. Note the use of example. Note the balance in the essay: The same points are discussed for each subject, in the same order.

Jennifer's approach to running was totally   5
different. While she was training, her stretching
routine was kept at the bare minimum, and she
made few adjustments in her running position. She
never went to bed early. When she was hungry, her
stomach came before her runner's diet. For
example, when a county meet was delayed because
of rain, she filled her empty stomach with greasy
french fries. Spaghetti was her ideal meal the
night before a meet.

Since Jennifer had runner's knee, her running   6
style was far from graceful. Her entire body
seemed to be fighting her determination to run.
The agonizing pain of each step could be seen in
her distorted face. She wore a sweatband around
her head to keep the perspiration from streaming
into her eyes. With each stride of her long,
slender legs, her feet appeared to plop heavily to
the ground. Jennifer's speed only varied slightly
during a race. Although she was never able to
sprint, it was evident that she gave all she had
to the race. After she crossed the finish line,
her body would collapse to the ground in gruelling
pain. When describing her running, her younger
brother Kurt jokingly commented, "When Jennifer
runs, she looks like a dog with two legs. And
those two legs have cement blocks on them."

Since the cheering spectators interfered with   7
Jennifer's concentration, she preferred to run
without onlookers. She made me aware of this
preference at her first cross-country meet. As
she ran past me, I cheered, "Come on Jennifer!"
While still running, she turned and looked at me
with glaring eyes. She snapped, "You get out here
and try it!" After the meet, she informed me that
I could continue to come to the meets if I
promised never to cheer for her.

paragraph 8
The conclusion ends on a note of similarity (both girls were acknowledged for their running).

8

Although their training techniques, running styles, and attitudes toward spectators differed, each daughter received awards and trophies for her efforts. Along with acknowledgments for devotion, Laura was recognized for her speed and Jennifer for her determination.

Pitfalls to Avoid

1. **Avoid subjects with no basis for comparison or contrast.** While you may be clever enough to force a comparison of dating and baking a pie, what purpose would the essay serve?

2. **Avoid subjects of no interest to your reader.** Technically you can write an essay with the thesis "While my Uncle Phineas is a generous person, my Cousin Esmeralda is very stingy," but what possible interest could your reader have?

3. **Avoid statements of the obvious.** If you are comparing two cars, it would be silly to mention that they both have engines. Statements of the obvious insult your reader and waste that person's time.

4. **Avoid discussing points out of sequence.** In a subject-by-subject organization, discuss the points for the second subject in the same order you discussed them for the first subject.

PROCESS GUIDELINES: WRITING COMPARISON-CONTRAST

1. If you have trouble thinking of a topic, try discussing the similarities between two things generally thought of as different or the contrasts between two things generally viewed as similar. For example, an essay noting the differences between getting a degree and getting an education could clarify the real essence of education, despite the fact that "getting a degree" is commonly equated with "getting an education." Similarly, an essay discussing the similarities between eccentricity and genius, two very different states in many ways, could foster greater understanding of one or both of these. Be sure your comparisons or contrasts are valid and useful. While you can compare studying for an exam with preparing for war, what purpose would be served?

2. List writing can help generate ideas. Make two lists, one with every similarity you can think of and the second with every difference. Write everything that occurs to you without evaluating the worth of anything.

3. On your lists, circle each comparison and contrast that you find meaningful or interesting.

4. If you are not certain whether to treat similarities, differences, or both, consider the ideas in your lists. However, do not think that if you have circled more similarities than differences that it is obviously similarities you should treat. Consider whether the differences lead to the more significant conclusion.

5. To determine your purpose, you can ask these questions:
   a. Do I want to clarify the nature of one unfamiliar subject by placing it next to another, more-familiar subject?
   b. Do I want to lend a fresh insight into one subject by placing it next to another?
   c. Do I want to bring one or both of my subjects into sharper focus?
   d. Do I want to show that one of my subjects is superior to the other?

6. To determine your audience, you can ask yourself these questions:
   a. Who could learn something by reading my essay?
   b. Who could be influenced to share my point of view?
   c. Who does not currently know much about one of my subjects?
   d. Who would enjoy reading my essay?

7. To determine the nature of your audience, answer these questions:
   a. How much does my reader know about my subjects?
   b. How much interest does my reader have in my subjects?
   c. How does my reader feel about my subjects?
   d. How *strongly* does my reader feel about my subjects?

8. Even if you do not usually outline, you may find that outlining makes organizing comparison-contrast easier. Be sure to check for balance.

9. If you like to secure reader response before revising, see page 115. In addition, ask your reader to place a check mark any place where the movement from subject to subject or point to point seems abrupt. (Consider adding transitions and topic sentences here.) Also ask your reader to place a check mark any place where an idea is unclear.

REVISION CHECKLIST

In addition to the checklist on page 117, you can use this checklist for revising your comparison-contrast.

1. Is there a logical basis for comparing or contrasting your subjects? Is it clear what your subjects are? Are your subjects of interest to the reader?

2. Does your comparison-contrast do one of the following?
   a. Clarify something unknown or not well understood.
   b. Lead to a fresh insight or a new way of viewing something.
   c. Bring one or both of the subjects into sharper focus.
   d. Show that one subject is better than the other.

3. Does your thesis present the subjects and indicate whether you are comparing, contrasting, or both?

4. Have you discussed the same points for both subjects? Have you avoided stating the obvious?
5. Have you used a point-by-point or subject-by-subject pattern to your best advantage?
6. Have you used transitions and topic sentences to help your reader move from point to point and subject to subject?

EXERCISE | **Writing Comparison-Contrast**

1. For each pair of subjects, identify a possible audience and purpose for a comparison-contrast essay.

   what college is like and what you thought it would be like

   two athletes

   two job applicants

2. Select one of the subject pairs in number 1 and write a suitable thesis for a comparison-contrast.
3. What other patterns of development might appear in comparison-contrast essays on the subject pairs in number 1? How would the patterns be used?
4. Assume you will write a comparison-contrast essay about your current writing process and the one you used at some point in the past (perhaps before this term began). Then do the following:
   a. Make one list of the similarities and one list of the differences.
   b. Based on your lists from *a*, decide whether you would rather write an essay treating similarities, differences, or both.
   c. Establish an audience and purpose, and write a preliminary thesis.
   d. Write two outlines, one with a subject-by-subject pattern and one with a point-by-point pattern. Decide which organization is better for your essay.
5. *Collaborative Activity.* Pair up with a classmate. Each of you should keep a log of every comparison-contrast you hear, speak, or read for 24 hours. Be sure to note the nature of each comparison-contrast and its purpose. Compare your lists and write a report that explains and illustrates the functions and importance of comparison-contrast.

PROFESSIONAL ESSAYS

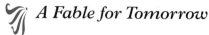 *A Fable for Tomorrow*

Rachel Carson

Rachel Carson is one of the forerunners of environmentalism. Her book Silent Spring *(1962) made the general public aware of the effects of chemical weed and insect killers. "A Fable for Tomorrow," which is an excerpt from* Silent Spring, *uses contrast to warn of the dangers of chemical pesticides.*

There was once a town in the heart of America where all life seemed to live in *1* harmony with its surroundings. The town lay in the midst of a checkerboard of prosperous farms, with fields of grain and hillsides of orchards where, in spring, white clouds of bloom drifted above the green fields. In autumn, oak and maple and birch set up a blaze of color that flamed and flickered across a backdrop of pines. Then foxes barked in the hills and deer silently crossed the fields, half hidden in the mists of the fall mornings.

Along the roads, laurel, viburnum and alder, great ferns and wildflowers *2* delighted the traveler's eye through much of the year. Even in winter the roadsides were places of beauty, where countless birds came to feed on the berries and on the seed heads of the dried weeds rising above the snow. The countryside was, in fact, famous for the abundance and variety of its bird life, and when the flood of migrants was pouring through in spring and fall people traveled from great distances to observe them. Others came to fish the streams, which flowed clear and cold out of the hills and contained shady pools where trout lay. So it had been from the days many years ago when the first settlers raised their houses, sank their wells, and built their barns.

Then a strange blight crept over the area and everything began to change. *3* Some evil spell had settled on the community: mysterious maladies swept the flocks of chickens; the cattle and sheep sickened and died. Everywhere was a shadow of death. The farmers spoke of much illness among their families. In the town the doctors had become more and more puzzled by new kinds of sickness appearing among their patients. There had been several sudden and unexplained deaths, not only among adults but even among children, who would be stricken suddenly while at play and die within a few hours.

There was a strange stillness. The birds, for example—where had they *4* gone? Many people spoke of them, puzzled and disturbed. The feeding stations in the backyards were deserted. The few birds seen anywhere were moribund; they trembled violently and could not fly. It was a spring without voices. On the mornings that had once throbbed with the dawn chorus of robins, catbirds, doves, jays, wrens, and scores of other bird voices there was now no sound; only silence lay over the fields and woods and marsh.

On the farms the hens brooded, but no chicks hatched. The farmers com- *5* plained that they were unable to raise any pigs—the litters were small and the young survived only a few days. The apple trees were coming into bloom but no bees droned among the blossoms, so there was no pollination and there would be no fruit.

The roadsides, once so attractive, were now lined with browned and with- *6* ered vegetation as though swept by fire. These, too, were silent, deserted by all living things. Even the streams were now lifeless. Anglers no longer visited them, for all the fish had died.

In the gutters under the eaves and between the shingles of the roofs, a white *7* granular powder still showed a few patches; some weeks before it had fallen like snow upon the roofs and the lawns, the fields and streams.

No witchcraft, no enemy action had silenced the rebirth of new life in this *8* stricken world. The people had done it themselves.

This town does not actually exist, but it might easily have a thousand coun- *9* terparts in America or elsewhere in the world. I know of no community that has experienced all the misfortunes I describe. Yet every one of these disasters has actually happened somewhere, and many real communities have already suffered a substantial number of them. A grim specter has crept upon us almost unnoticed, and this imagined tragedy may easily become a stark reality we all shall know.

Considering Ideas

1. What point does Carson's contrast make? Where in the essay is that point made known?
2. The town in the fable does not exist. Does that fact undermine the author's point? Why or why not?
3. "A Fable for Tomorrow" was published in 1962. Is the essay still relevant today? What does your answer say about the environmental movement?
4. In paragraph 4, Carson says it was "a spring without voices." Explain the significance of the phrase.
5. What is the "white granular powder" of paragraph 7?
6. Would you (or do you?) pay twice as much money for food grown without chemicals? Why or why not?

Considering Technique

1. What subjects is Carson contrasting? Is the treatment of subjects balanced? Explain.
2. What pattern does Carson use to arrange her details?
3. Carson develops her discussion of the town after the blight in greater detail than she does her discussion of the town before the blight. Is this a problem? Explain.
4. *Combining patterns.* How does Carson use narration? Description?
5. How does Carson make the transition from the first subject to the second?
6. What approach does Carson take to her conclusion? Is it effective? Explain.

For Group Discussion or Journal Writing

Do you think we are doing enough to protect the environment? Explain.

Two Ways to Belong in America

Bharti Mukherjee

The following comparison-contrast, which originally appeared as an Op-Ed piece in the New York Times, *in 1996, is the author's response to efforts to pass legislation that would limit government benefits to resident aliens. It is also a response to her sister's reaction to the initiative.*

This is a tale of two sisters from Calcutta, Mira and Bharati, who have lived in the United States for some 35 years, but who find themselves on different sides in the current debate over the status of immigrants. I am an American citizen and she is not. I am moved that thousands of long-term residents are finally taking the oath of citizenship. She is not.

Mira arrived in Detroit in 1960 to study child psychology and preschool education. I followed her a year later to study creative writing at the University of Iowa. When we left India, we were almost identical in appearance and attitude. We dressed alike, in saris; we expressed identical views on politics, social issues, love, and marriage in the same Calcutta convent-school accent. We would endure our two years in America, secure our degrees, then return to India to marry the grooms of our father's choosing.

Instead, Mira married an Indian student in 1962 who was getting his business administration degree at Wayne State University. They soon acquired the labor certifications necessary for the green card of hassle-free residence and employment.

Mira still lives in Detroit, works in the Southfield, Michigan, school system, and has become nationally recognized for her contributions in the fields of preschool education and parent–teacher relationships. After 36 years as a legal immigrant in this country, she clings passionately to her Indian citizenship and hopes to go home to India when she retires.

In Iowa City in 1963, I married a fellow student, an American of Canadian parentage. Because of the accident of his North Dakota birth, I bypassed labor-certification requirements and the race-related "quota" system that favored the applicant's country of origin over his or her merit. I was prepared for (and even welcomed) the emotional strain that came with marrying outside my ethnic community. In 33 years of marriage, we have lived in every part of North America. By choosing a husband who was not my father's selection, I was opting for fluidity, self-invention, blue jeans and T-shirts, and renouncing 3,000 years (at least) of case-observant, "pure culture" marriage in the Mukherjee family. My books have often been read as unapologetic (and in some quarters overenthusiastic) texts for cultural and psychological "mongrelization." It's a word I celebrate.

Mira and I have stayed sisterly close by phone. In our regular Sunday morning conversations, we are unguardedly affectionate. I am her only blood relative on this continent. We expect to see each other through the looming crises of aging and ill heath without being asked. Long before Vice President Gore's "Citizenship U.S.A." drive, we'd had our polite arguments over the ethics of retaining an overseas citizenship while expecting the permanent protection and economic benefits that come with living and working in America.

Like well-raised sisters, we never said what was really on our minds, but we probably pitied one another. She, for the lack of structure in my life, the erasure of Indianness, the absence of an unvarying daily core. I, for the narrowness of her perspective, her uninvolvement with the mythic depths or the superficial pop culture of this society. But, now, with the scapegoatings of "aliens" (documented or illegal) on the increase, and the targeting of long-term legal immigrants like

Mira for new scrutiny and new self-consciousness, she and I find ourselves unable to maintain the same polite discretion. We were always unacknowledged adversaries, and we are now, more than ever, sisters.

"I feel used," Mira raged on the phone the other night. "I feel manipulated 8 and discarded. This is such an unfair way to treat a person who was invited to stay and work here because of her talent. My employer went to the I.N.S. and petitioned for the labor certification. For over 30 years, I've invested my creativity and professional skills into the improvement of *this* country's preschool system. I've obeyed all the rules, I've paid my taxes, I love my work, I love my students, I love the friends I've made. How dare America now change its rules in midstream? If America wants to make new rules curtailing benefits of legal immigrants, they should apply only to immigrants who arrive after those rules are already in place."

To my ears, it sounded like the description of a long-enduring, comfortable 9 yet loveless marriage, without risk or recklessness. Have we the right to demand, and to expect, that we be loved? (That, to me, is the subtext of the arguments by immigration advocates.) My sister is an expatriate, professionally generous and creative, socially courteous and gracious, and that's as far as her Americanization can go. She is here to maintain an identity, not to transform it.

I asked her if she would follow the example of others who have decided to 10 become citizens because of the anti-immigration bills in Congress. And here, she surprised me. "If America wants to play the manipulative game, I'll play it, too," she snapped. "I'll become a U.S. citizen for now, then change back to India when I'm ready to go home. I feel some kind of irrational attachment to India that I don't to America. Until all this hysteria against legal immigrants, I was totally happy. Having my green card meant I could visit any place in the world I wanted to and then come back to a job that's satisfying and that I do very well."

In one family, from two sisters alike as peas in a pod, there could not be a 11 wider divergence of immigrant experience. America spoke to me—I married it—I embraced the demotion from expatriate aristocrat to immigrant nobody, surrendering those thousands of years of "pure culture," the saris, the delightfully accented English. She retained them all. Which of us is the freak?

Mira's voice, I realize, is the voice not just of the immigrant South Asian 12 community but of an immigrant community of the millions who have stayed rooted in one job, one city, one house, one ancestral culture, one cuisine, for the entirety of their productive years. She speaks for greater numbers than I possibly can. Only the fluency of her English and the anger, rather than fear, born of confidence from her education, differentiate her from the seamstresses, the domestics, the technicians, the shop owners, the millions of hard-working but effectively silenced documented immigrants as well as their less fortunate "illegal" brothers and sisters.

Nearly 20 years ago, when I was living in my husband's ancestral homeland 13 of Canada, I was always well-employed but never allowed to feel part of the local Quebec or larger Canadian society. Then, through a Green Paper that invited a national referendum on the unwanted side effects of "nontraditional" immigration, the government officially turned against its immigrant communities, particularly those from South Asia.

I felt then the same sense of betrayal that Mira feels now. I will never forget *14* the pain of that sudden turning, and the casual racist outbursts the Green Paper elicited. That sense of betrayal had its desired effect and drove me, and thousands like me, from the country.

Mira and I differ, however, in the ways in which we hope to interact with the *15* country that we have chosen to live in. She is happier to live in America as expatriate Indian than as an immigrant American. I need to feel like a part of the community I have adopted (as I tried to feel in Canada as well). I need to put roots down, to vote and make the difference that I can. The price that the immigrant willingly pays, and that the exile avoids, is the trauma of self-transformation.

Considering Ideas

1. Mukherjee notes that the chief contrast between her sister and herself is that one is a United States citizen and one is not. What is the chief cause of that difference?
2. In paragraph 7, the author refers to "the scapegoatings of 'aliens.' " Explain what you think she means.
3. What people do you think might favor legislation denying benefits to resident aliens?
4. In paragraph 8, the author reports that her sister feels that the United States used and manipulated her. Why does she feel this way?
5. "Two Ways to Belong in America" originally appeared in the *New York Times* on the Op-Ed page. How would you characterize the intended audience? For what purpose do you think Mukherjee wrote the piece? How hard do you think it was for the author to fulfill her purpose with that particular audience?

Considering Technique

1. Where does Mukherjee express her thesis? Does that thesis make it clear that the essay is a comparison-contrast? Explain.
2. What elements of comparison appear in the essay?
3. Although "Two Ways to Belong in America" includes comparison, the contrasts are emphasized. What purpose, then, do the comparisons serve?
4. What points of contrast does the author make? Are those points arranged in a subject-by-subject or point-by-point pattern?
5. Mukherjee uses exact words in paragraphs 8 and 10. What do those quotations contribute?

For Group Discussion or Journal Writing

In paragraph 5, Mukherjee says that she celebrates "mongrelization." Explain what she means and whether or not you agree with her and why.

Combining Patterns of Development

Sport and the American Dream

Jeffrey Schrank

In "Sport and the American Dream," Jeffrey Schrank combines **contrast, definition,** *and* **cause-and-effect analysis** *to examine the values at the heart of three popular American sports.*

1

Sport is a ritual, an acting out of a myth or series of myths. A sport that can be considered a national pastime can be expected to reflect national values and wishes. Sports that capture the national fancy are ritualistic enactments of the American Dream. Baseball is still called our national pastime but is rapidly being replaced by American football. That football should become our "national pastime" is understandable to those who can see sports as reflections of national character.

2

American football is passionately concerned with the gain and loss of land, of territory. The football field is measured and marked with all the care of a surveyor and the ball's progress noted to the nearest inch. Football is a precise game and its players are often trained like a military unit on a mission to gain territory for the mother country. The players are the popular heroes but the coaches and owners run the game, using the players to carry out their plans—there is comparatively little room for individual initiative. A score comes as the result of a strategic series of well-executed maneuvers and is bought on the installment plan, yard by yard.

3

The regulation and almost military precision of American football is a reflection of national psychology. Even the words we use to describe the game include throwing the bomb, marching downfield, game plan (which has become nearly a national phrase for any field, from selling toothpaste to covering up political scandals), guards, executions, blitz, zone, platoon, squad, drills, attack, drives, marching bands for entertainment, stars on helmets, lines that can be blasted through, and even war paint. Much of the verbal similarity comes from the fact that war was originally the ultimate game played within the confines of certain rules agreed upon by both "teams."

4

Football, more than any other sport, is a game for spectators to watch superhuman, mythical heroes. Football is a sport that more people watch than play. The game requires too many people, too much space, and is simply too dangerous for the weekend athlete. The size and speed of professional players and their uniforms make them into heroic figures capable of feats that invite admiration but not imitation. The football spectator is in awe of the armored monsters. The viewer of a golf match or even baseball or tennis dreams of going out the next day and doing likewise, but football is played only by the gods who can run the 100-yard dash in 10 seconds, stand six feet three and weigh 260 pounds.

5

The demise of baseball as our national pastime reflects a change in national character. The change does not mean the disappearance of baseball, merely its relocation to a position as just another game rather than *the* game. Professor John Finlay of the University of Manitoba, writing in *Queen's Quarterlay*, compares baseball to an acting out of the robber baron stage of capitalism, whereas football more clearly reflects a more mature capitalism into which we are now moving. Hence, the rise in popularity of football and apparent decline in baseball. He notes that Japan, still in the early stages of capitalism, has taken avidly to baseball but not to football. It is not a question of Japanese physique serving as a determinant since rugby has a large Asian following. He predicts that when their capitalism moves into a higher stage, the Japanese will move on to football as have Americans.

Baseball is a game of a quieter age when less action was needed to hold interest, when going to the park was enjoyable (baseball is still played in ball parks while football is played in stadiums), when aggression was subservient to finesse. Baseball players did not need exposure as college players to succeed as football players do; they play a relatively calm game almost daily instead of a bruising gladiatorial contest weekly. Baseball has room for unique and colorful characters, while football stresses the more anonymous but effective team member. Baseball is a game in which any team can win at any given contest and there are no favorites; only football has real "upsets." Football's careful concern with time adds a tension to the game that is lacking in the more leisurely world of baseball. 6

Football has replaced baseball as the favorite American spectator sport largely because of television. A comparison between a telecast of a football game on one channel and a baseball game on another could reveal baseball as a game with people standing around seemingly with little to do but watch two men play catch. Football would appear as 22 men engaged in almost constant, frenzied action. To watch baseball requires identification with the home team; to watch football requires only a need for action or a week of few thrills and the need for a touch of vicarious excitement. 7

Baseball is a pastoral game, timeless and highly ritualized; its appeal is to nostalgia and so might enjoy periods of revitalization in comparison to football. But for now, the myth of football suits the nation better. 8

According to a 1974 Harris survey, baseball has already been statistically dethroned. In a sports survey a cross section of nearly 1400 fans was asked, "Which of these sports do you follow?" 9

The decision to play or "follow" a certain sport is also the decision to live a certain myth. The team violence of football, the craftiness of basketball, the mechanistic precision of bowling, the auto racer's devotion to machinery are all subworlds within the universe of sport. 10

Golf, for example, is a unique subworld, one of the few left as a sport (unlike hunting, which does not involve scoring or teams) in which the game is played between man and nature. The winner of a match is one who has beaten the opponent, but the game itself is a person versus the environment. To understand the appeal of golf it is again necessary to consider the game as a ritual reenactment of an appealing myth. 11

Golf, perhaps more than any other sport, has to be played to be appreciated. Millions who never played football can enjoy the game on TV, but only a 12 dedicated participant can sit through two hours of televised golf. Golf is growing in participation but still has the stigma of an upper-class game. Eighty percent of the nation's golfers must play on 20 percent of the nation's courses that are open to the public. The ratio of public to private facilities hurts public participation in the game but mirrors the inequities of society and provides a convenient status symbol for those who can afford club membership. Its TV audience is not the largest of any sport but it is the most well heeled.

Golf is a reenactment of the pioneer spirit. It is man versus a hostile environment in search of an oasis. The goal is a series of lush "greens," each protected by natural hazards such as water, sand, and unmanageably long grass. The hazards are no threat to physical life but they are to the achievement of success. Golf is a journey game with a constantly changing field. Golfers start the 18-hole journey, can rest at a halfway point, and then resume until they return to near the point of origination. *13*

The winner of the match is one who has fallen victim to the fewest hazards and overcome the terrain. Many golf courses have Indian names as if to remind the golfer of the frontier ethos. A local course called Indian Lakes invites golfers to use either one of two courses—the Iroquois trail or the Sioux trail. *14*

Golf, like baseball, is a pastoral sport—with a high degree of tensions and drama but relatively little action. It is a game in which players are constantly in awe of the magic flight of the golf ball. To hit any kind of ball 100 or 200 or more yards with accuracy or to hit a small target from 150 yards is an amazing feat to be appreciated only by those who have at least tried the game. Golf is very likely the most difficult game to master, yet one in which the average player occasionally hits a shot as good as the best of any professional. It is this dream of magic results that keeps the golfer on course. *15*

Considering Ideas

1. The thesis of "Sport and the American Dream" is implied rather than explicitly stated. Write a sentence that expresses the thesis idea. Which sentence of the essay comes closest to expressing that thesis idea?
2. According to Schrank, what does the popularity of football say about American values? Do you agree? Explain.
3. Why does Schrank think that baseball is no longer the favorite national sport?
4. Why does Schrank consider baseball and golf to be pastoral sports? What other pastoral sports can you name?
5. What values does Schrank see reflected in golf? Would you add any values to the list? Explain.

Considering Technique

1. Why does Schrank write about the three sports in the order that he does? How would the essay be affected if he first discussed baseball or golf?

2. What points of comparison does Schrank make?
3. What points of contrast does Schrank make?
4. *Combining Patterns*. What elements of cause-and-effect analysis appear? (Cause-and-effect analysis explains the causes and/or effects of an event.) What elements of definition appear? (Definition explains the meaning of something.)
5. The essay lacks a formal conclusion. Do you consider this a problem? Explain.

For Group Discussion or Journal Writing

Americans often draw their heroes and role models from the sports world. Discuss whether or not athletes make suitable heroes and role models and where else our heroes and role models do, or should, come from.

STUDENT ESSAYS TO READ AND EVALUATE

The following comparison-contrast essays written by students have both strengths and aspects that could be improved with revision. Thus, each essay can teach something about techniques to try and strategies to avoid. Evaluating the essays will sharpen your critical abilities and make you a more reliable judge of your own writing.

The Human and the Superhuman: Two Very Different Heroes

In the late 1930s a small company in the fledgling comic book business decided to create something new and different for the public: the superhero. Two of the first characters to be created were opposites of one another. One had the powers of a god while the other was only a man, yet Superman and Batman were the mythic creations that set the stage for all who followed.

Superman was created in 1938 by two imaginative young men named Jerry Siegel and Joe Schuster. They wanted to create a character that was immensely powerful. What emerged was someone "faster than a speeding bullet, more powerful than a locomotive, and able to leap tall buildings in a single bound." The powers that Superman possessed brought about much reader interest. The story of the sole survivor of a doomed planet coming to earth to battle the forces of evil contained the idealism people wanted during those post-Depression days. Although times have changed, the public still enjoys a bit of idealism once in a while, and Superman provides it.

Unlike Superman, Batman was not created for idealistic   *3*
purposes, but rather for vengeance. While Superman was flying far
above society, Batman was stalking the seedy underside of Gotham,
preying on the criminal element. Bob Kane created Batman in 1939
with the human element in mind. The public enjoyed the idea of
having a hero as human as they. Also the concept of revenge
associated with the murder of Batman's parents struck a chord with
the public's conscience. This troubled hero has become more popular
than Superman in recent years because the rise in crime that is
prevalent in society today has been documented within the Batman
books. With urban society becoming increasingly violent, Batman's
methods in combating crime have changed accordingly. Batman is not
an idealistic role model, but rather a warrior fighting a never-
ending battle.

The major differences between Superman and Batman revolve   *4*
around the former's benevolence and the latter's malevolence.
Superman acts with restraint and exudes a noble, benevolent
attitude. Criminals do not fear Superman because of his
personality, but rather they fear his power. Batman, on the other
hand, strikes fear into the criminal element with his methods and
obvious modus operandi: the dark, threatening bat. Criminals are
afraid of Batman simply because they don't know what he will do if
he apprehends them. This psychological factor is employed by Batman
because of his vulnerability. Fear makes the criminal sloppy, and
that sloppiness makes it much easier for Batman to apprehend him.
Because of Superman's obvious invincibility, he does not bother
with such tactics. Also, because of Batman's methods, he is not
much of a team player. He would much rather work alone than with a
group of his fellow costumed heroes. Superman, however, enjoys
working with, and sometimes leading, his fellow superheroes. He is
a group player. The different personalities of these characters can
be compared to day and night.

Superman and Batman have both survived for over 50 years. The   *5*
reason for their longevity can be simply explained. Each was a
pioneer character in the comic book medium. Superman showed readers
that a man could fly. Batman showed them that being human isn't all
that bad. The influence of each character on American culture will
help both heroes survive at least another 50 years.

Like Mother Like Daughter

My mother died of cancer when I was 19 years old. She suffered a   *1*
slow, painful death, and the final five years of her life were
devastating to me. Having been the youngest of her four children,
it was I who remained at home to do the housekeeping chores, plan
and prepare meals, and just give her care and support when
necessary. I felt resentful that my teenage years were marred by
that feeling of being trapped at home. On the other hand, I never
questioned the fact that it was my responsibility to be there when
she needed me. The feelings of sadness, guilt, and denial
completely overshadowed any fond, happy memories I had for my
mother during the years I was growing up and she was healthy. It
was not until seven years following her death that my attitude
toward my mother changed.

By this time I was married and the mother of two sons. I was   *2*
hosting a family reunion—my brother and his family came from
California, and my two sisters and their families arrived from New
York and New Jersey. There were fourteen of us living together at
my house for two whole weeks, and although chaos prevailed, I loved
being together.

To prevent the children from becoming bored, we kept busy   *3*
picnicking, swimming, playing tennis, and visiting relatives. Then
one evening, my brother and I were alone. We were reminiscing about
the fact that I was only six years old when he left home for
college and that he never really knew me. He looked at me and said,
"I want you to know that you are more like Mom than Ruth and Rose
will ever be." He pointed out that I was functioning as a mother
and a homemaker exactly as she did. It was like opening a door to
my past, and the more we talked, the more I realized that my mother
gave me more love and direction than I could ever give back.

I began to remember the lessons I learned. She was the daughter *4*
of Italian immigrants and had a total preoccupation with food. I
was constantly at her side licking cake batter, rolling pie dough,
stirring spaghetti sauce. When family or company visited, we seldom
sat in her immaculate parlor; she ordered everyone to sit at the
old chrome kitchen table while she perked fresh, steaming coffee.
How remarkable that our friends today seem to gather in the kitchen
rather than the family room. Could it be that I lead them there?

To my mother, food was the symbol of life. We were healthy to   *5*
her because we were fat! I too push food in front of my family; if
company arrives, I head for the refrigerator. How I envy my skinny
friends who can fast all day while I have to eat breakfast by 8:30.

My mother taught me respect for food. I can still hear her   *6*
preach, "Eat, eat . . . think of those poor children in India who
don't have food!" How ironic that I have repeated those same words
to my sons as they rush from the table with plates half-full. To
this day, I cannot bear to see food wasted.

Thrift was a profound lesson that I learned. She managed my   *7*
father's paycheck from the mill better than any banker. She took me
to sales and clearances and taught me to bargain-hunt. How
remarkable that I rarely pay full retail price for clothing or
merchandise today.

Finally, the most important trait my mother shared with me was   *8*
a warmth and loyalty to family. Her only job in life was to keep
house and care for her family. And even though I am pursuing an
education and career now, I will never regret staying home with my
family when they were babies and young children. Although my
children never knew their grandmother, I have kept her memory alive
without being consciously aware that I did.

Collaborative Exercise: Evaluating Writing

Form a group and evaluate one of the previous student essays. Designate a
recorder to take down the group's conclusions and a spokesperson to report
those conclusions to the class. If you like, you can use the following evaluation
questions to help you assess the essay's chief strengths and weaknesses.

Evaluation Questions

1. *The Thesis*
   Does the thesis note the subjects and whether comparison, contrast, or
   both will occur? Is there a logical basis for comparing or contrasting the
   subjects? Do the subjects interest you?
2. *The Introduction*
   What do you think of the opening? Does it engage your interest?
3. *Supporting Details*
   Note any points you do not understand, any that are not relevant, or any
   that require additional support. Are the same points discussed for both
   subjects? Are there any statements of the obvious?

4. *Organization*

   How is the detail arranged? Is this the best organization to use? Evaluate the use of transitions and topic sentences to help the reader move from subject to subject and point to point.

5. *The Conclusion*

   Does the essay come to a satisfying end? Explain.

6. *Overview*

   What do you like best about the essay? What is the single most important revision the author should make?

Essay Topics: Comparison-Contrast

When you write your essay, consult Pitfalls to Avoid on page 244, Process Guidelines on page 244, and the Revision Checklist on page 245.

Writing in the Pattern

1. Write an essay that compares and/or contrasts two books, television shows, or movies that have similar themes.

2. Contrast the styles of two athletes who play the same sport.

3. Select two entertainers, movies, television shows, or songs and use comparison and/or contrast to show how they reflect the values of two different groups of people or the climates of two periods of time. For example, contrast *Leave It to Beaver* and *The Simpsons* to show that the former reflects the 1950s and the latter the 1990s.

4. Compare and/or contrast life as it is today with life as it would be without some modern fact of life, such as the car, the telephone, antibiotics, professional or collegiate football, airplanes, computers, alarm clocks, and so on. Be careful not to dwell on the obvious.

5. Compare and/or contrast the way you view something or someone now with the way you did when you were a child.

6. Compare and/or contrast two magazine ads or two television commercials for the same kind of product (wine, cigarettes, cars, jeans, cold remedies, etc.).

7. If you have lived in two cities or countries, write a comparison-contrast of life in those two places.

8. Write a comparison-contrast of one of the following:
   a. the way you thought something would be and the way it really was
   b. two political figures
   c. two people you admire

9. Compare and/or contrast some feature of soap operas with the same feature in real life (the way problems are solved, the way friends interact, the way crimes are solved, and so forth). Make this essay humorous.

Reading Then Writing in the Pattern

1. A fable is a story, written in a simple style, with a moral or lesson. Write a fable in the style of Rachel Carson's "A Fable for Tomorrow" (page 246)

that compares and/or contrasts life today with life as it would be if population growth continued unchecked, if drug usage continued to escalate, or if some other problem continued unresolved. Be sure your moral or lesson is apparent.

2. The author of "Two Ways to Belong in America" (page 248) contrasts being a resident alien and being a citizen of the United States, taking the position that the latter is better than the former. Write a comparison-contrast of the same subjects, but take the opposite position.

3. Like Jeffrey Schrank in "Sport and the American Dream" (page 252), contrast football and baseball, but do not make the same points that appear in his essay.

4. Like Schrank in "Sport and the American Dream" (page 252), write a comparison-contrast of two sports (other than baseball and football) on the basis of what those sports say about American values.

Responding to the Readings

1. In "A Fable for Tomorrow" (page 246), Rachel Carson points out that we are destroying our environment. "Fable" first appeared in Carson's *Silent Spring* in 1962. Do you think our treatment of the environment has improved since the essay was written? Cite specific examples to support your view.

2. In paragraph 8 of "Two Ways to Belong in America" (page 248), the author notes the sentiments of her sister, a resident alien. Agree or disagree with the sentiments expressed in that paragraph.

3. In "Sport and the American Dream" (page 252), Jeffrey Schrank notes that American values are reflected in the sports we enjoy. Select a popular American activity other than sports (fast-food dining, television viewing, mall shopping, and so forth) and explain the national values that it reflects.

4. *Connecting the Readings.* Write an essay that explores the question, "Whom do Americans choose as their heroes and what does that choice say about American values?" You can read "I Learned to March" (page 181), "Sport and the American Dream" (page 252), "About Men" (page 300), "The Way to Rainy Mountain" (page 149), and "The Human and the Superhuman" (page 255) for ideas to use along with your own.

CHAPTER 9

Cause-and-Effect Analysis

A cause-and-effect analysis examines why an event or action occurred (the causes) or what resulted from the event or action (the effects), or both. We engage in cause-and-effect analysis regularly because it helps us make sense of the world. For example, cause-and-effect analysis can help us understand the past if we identify the causes of the stock market crash in 1929 and go on to determine how that event affected our country and its people. Cause-and-effect analysis can also help us look to the future, as when we predict the effects of the current air pollution rate on the quality of life 20 years from now.

ESTABLISHING YOUR PURPOSE AND IDENTIFYING YOUR AUDIENCE

A cause-and-effect analysis can be written to *inform,* to *persuade,* to *express feelings* and *relate experience,* or to *entertain.* For example, to inform your reader, you could explain what causes the consumer price index to rise and fall, or you could explain the effects of divorce on teenagers. To persuade, you could explain the causes of urban blight to convince your reader that city government is not completely responsible, or you could explain the effects of watching too much television to convince parents to limit their children's viewing time. To express feelings and relate experience, you could write about how your father's military career affected you, and to entertain, you could write a humorous account of the effects of technology on the average person.

Of course, everything you have learned about audience applies to writing cause-and-effect analysis. Your purpose, topic, and detail must be geared to your reader. Thus, there is little reason to write about the effects of television viewing on children for an audience of childless married couples if your purpose is to convince your reader to limit viewing time.

Taken together, purpose and audience significantly affect detail selection. Thus, if you are explaining what causes the consumer price index to rise and fall, you need not clarify what the consumer price index is for an audience of students in an economics course, but you would do so for a more general reader. If you want to persuade your reader to address the problem of teenage alcoholism, you might be more inclined to explain both its causes and effects rather than just one or the other.

COMBINING CAUSE-AND-EFFECT ANALYSIS WITH OTHER PATTERNS

Other patterns of development often appear as support in cause-and-effect analysis. One such pattern is illustration. Say you are explaining the effects of moving to a new town when you were in seventh grade, and one of those effects was that you felt like an outsider. You could illustrate this point with the example of the time no one wanted to sit with you at lunch.

You can also use description. For example, if you are discussing the effects of dumping industrial waste into rivers, you can describe the appearance of a river that has had industrial waste dumped into it.

Narration can also appear in a cause-and-effect analysis. Say you are explaining why more women than men suffer from math anxiety, and you note that females are often told that they are not as good at math as males are. To support this point, you can tell the story of the time your guidance counselor advised you not to take calculus because you were a girl.

Process analysis can also be used. Assume you are explaining the long-term effects of using pesticides, and you mention that pesticides work their way into the food chain. To support this point, you could describe the process whereby the pesticide goes from soil to plant to animal to human.

You will also encounter cause-and-effect analysis in essays developed primarily with another pattern. If you are narrating an account of your visit to your childhood home, you might include a discussion of how you were affected by the visit. If you are explaining the process of batiking, you might note what causes the cracking effect of the finished art. If you are comparing and contrasting two cities, you might explain what causes the crime rate to be lower in one of them. Cause-and-effect analysis can be a part of any essay, no matter what the dominant pattern of development.

For an example of an essay that combines cause-and-effect analysis, comparison-contrast, and narration, see "Beauty: When the Other Dancer Is the Self" on page 275.

USING CAUSE-AND-EFFECT ANALYSIS BEYOND THE WRITING CLASS

You are likely to use cause-and-effect analysis often in your other college classes. For example, in a history course, you could be asked to explain the causes and effects of the enclosure movement. In an economics class, you could be asked to explain what causes the federal government to raise and lower the prime interest rate. Your biology instructor could require you to explain what happens when a plant species becomes extinct, your education instructor could ask you to predict the effects of teaching reading to children of a younger age, your sociology instructor could ask you to explain the effects of affirmative action in the workplace, and your health instructor could ask you to note the causes of hyperventilation.

Beyond the classroom, cause-and-effect analysis is common. Whenever you make a decision, you speculate about the effects of that decision. For example, to decide which job offer to accept, you would weigh out the effects of accepting each position. Cause-and-effect analysis is everywhere: in professional journal articles that consider such things as the effects of technology on higher education, the causes of fibromyalgia, and the effects of whole language instruction on reading scores; in a newspaper editorial that offers a theory on the causes of voter apathy; in a doctor's chart that gives the effects of a patient's treatment; in a company vice president's report explaining a sales decline; in a police officer's report to explain the cause of a traffic accident; or in a medical researcher's notes on the effects of a chemical on cancer cell division, in a congressional committee's report predicting the effects of a defense spending cut, and so forth.

SELECTING DETAIL

When you select detail for a cause-and-effect analysis, identify *underlying* causes and effects. For example, if you are examining the causes of the high divorce rate, you might note the increase in two-career marriages. This would be an obvious cause. However, a closer examination of this cause would reveal underlying causes. Two-career marriages mean less clearly defined roles, less clearly defined divisions of labor, added job-related stress, and increased competition between partners. If you are discussing effects, then you should consider underlying effects. For example, say you are examining the effects of being the youngest child in a family. One obvious effect is that the youngest is considered "the baby." Look beyond that obvious effect to the underlying effects: The youngest can come to view himself or herself as the baby and hence less capable, less mature, and less strong; the youngest, viewed as a baby, may not be taken seriously by other family members.

Many cause-and-effect relationships are part of causal chains. A **causal chain** occurs when a cause leads to an effect and that effect becomes a cause, which leads to another effect and that effect becomes a cause leading to another effect, and so on. To understand causal chains, consider the effects of raising the cost of a stamp.

First the government raises the price of a postage stamp. What is the effect? Once the cost of the stamp goes up, it costs more to mail a letter. That is the first effect. This effect becomes a cause: It causes business expenses to rise for companies. What is the effect of this cause? The cost of doing business increases. This effect becomes a cause: It causes companies to raise the prices on their goods and services. What is the effect? Consumers cannot afford the increase, so they buy less. This effect becomes a cause: It causes the economy to slow down. Causal chains like this one are often part of a cause-and-effect analysis.

One way to develop detail for a cause-and-effect analysis is to think of each cause and effect as a generalization to support with adequate detail (see page 65 on supporting generalizations). Often that detail will take the form of other patterns of development, as explained on page 67.

Sometimes explaining why or how something is a cause or effect is necessary. For example, assume that you state that one effect of divorce on young children is to make them feel responsible for the breakup of their parents' marriage.
You should go on to explain why: Young children think that if they had behaved
better, their parents would not have fought and would have stayed married.

Sometimes a cause-and-effect analysis must explain that something is *not* a
cause or effect. Say you are explaining the causes of math anxiety among
women. If your reader believes women are genetically incapable of excelling in
math, then you should note this is untrue. You may also go on to explain *why*
this is not true: No studies have proved that anyone is genetically good or bad at
mathematics.

ARRANGING DETAIL

You can arrange the detail for your cause-and-effect analysis a number of ways.
Often a progressive order is best. In this case, the most significant or obvious
causes or effects are given first, and you work progressively to the least-significant
or obvious causes or effects. You can also move from the least significant or obvious to the most significant or obvious.

A chronological arrangement is possible if the causes or effects occur in a
particular time order. If you are reproducing causal chains, a chronological order
is likely since one cause will lead to effects and other causes that occur in a particular time sequence. When reproducing causal chains, get the sequence of
causes and effects in the correct order.

Sometimes you will group causes and effects in particular categories. For
example, say you are explaining what causes high school students to drop out of
school. You could group together all the causes related to home life, then group
together all the causes related to peer pressure, and then group together all the
causes related to academic environment.

The introduction of a cause-and-effect analysis can be handled in any of
the ways described in Chapter 2. Another approach is to explain why understanding the cause-and-effect relationship is important. For example, if you
want to provide reasons for adolescent drug use, your introduction could note
that understanding the reasons for the problem is a first step toward solving the
problem.

If your essay will treat the causes of a problem, your introduction can
provide a summary of the chief effects. Say you will explain why fewer people
are entering the teaching profession. Your introduction can note some of the
chief effects of this phenomenon: fewer qualified teachers, a decline in the
quality of education, and larger class sizes. Similarly, if your essay will explain
the effects of something, your introduction can note the chief causes. For example, if your essay will discuss the effects of increased tuition fees at your
school, your introduction can briefly explain the causes of the increase: lower
enrollment generating less income, higher operating costs, or perhaps an expensive building program.

A suitable thesis for a cause-and-effect analysis can indicate the relationship to be analyzed. It can also note whether causes or effects, or both, will be treated. Here are some examples:

> To solve the problem of teenage drug abuse, we must first understand what leads teenagers to take drugs. (This thesis notes that the essay will analyze the causes of drug use among teenagers.)

> Not everyone realizes the devastating effects unemployment has on a person's self-image. (This thesis notes that the essay will analyze the effects of unemployment on self-image.)

> The reasons Congress is cutting aid to the homeless are clear, but the effects of this action are less well understood. (This thesis notes that the essay will treat both the causes and effects of cuts in aid to the homeless.)

The conclusion of a cause-and-effect analysis can be handled in any of the ways described in Chapter 2. Often a cause-and-effect analysis ends with a conclusion drawn from the cause-and-effect relationship. For example, if your essay has shown what the causes of teenage drug abuse are, it could end with a conclusion drawn about the best way to combat the problem. A summary can also be an effective way to end. If the cause-and-effect relationship is complex, with several causal chains, your reader may appreciate a final reminder.

Annotated Student Essay

Studying the following cause-and-effect analysis, written by a student, along with the marginal notes, will help you better understand the points made in this chapter.

Gender-Specific Cigarette Advertising

paragraph 1
The introduction engages interest with a question. The thesis is the last sentence. It notes what cause will be dealt with.

paragraph 2
The topic sentence (the first) notes the first cause to be discussed (advertisers preying on women's desire to be desired). Supporting detail is an example. Some may feel the need for a second example.

Everyone knows the dangers of smoking, so why do more people take up the habit each day? The reasons are probably many and complex, but certainly one cause is the seductive power of the gender-specific advertising like that of Virginia Slims and Marlboro.

    One reason women are seduced into smoking Virginia Slims is advertisers' ability to prey on women's desire to be desired. The advertising for Virginia Slims cigarettes epitomizes the approach. One Virginia Slims ad pictures a stunningly beautiful woman at a party. She is surrounded by every man in the room as she tells some sort of amusing little story. In her hand, she holds a cigarette; on her face is a knowing look. The message: Smoke Virginia Slims, and you, too,

1

2

can be the center of male attention, the most desirable woman in the room.

paragraph 3
The topic sentence (the first) gives the second cause (the slogan). Note the transition ("A second reason"). The supporting detail explains how the slogan is a cause.

A second reason women are seduced into smoking Virginia Slims rests in the brilliant slogan, "You've come a long way, baby." The slogan reminds women that they have come a long way in the struggle for equality. Why? Because they are finally allowed to smoke in public without being considered too masculine. The ad campaign focuses on the freedom of women to smoke publicly and with pride, as if that is a real accomplishment. The slogan conveys the message that all successful, liberated women are smoking in celebration because they are finally equal, after all these years, to men, who never had to hide their smoking habit. "Hey, ladies," the picture in the magazine screams, "smoke these cigarettes and everyone will know you are strong, capable, independent, and equal to men." Women who want to project that image are thus seduced into smoking Virginia Slims.

paragraph 4
The first two sentences make the transition from the discussion of women to the discussion of men. The third sentence is the topic sentence, which gives a cause (Marlboro man represents who men want to be). The supporting detail includes objective description. Note the exaggeration for a humorous effect. The last sentence explains why the Marlboro man is a cause.

Women, however, are not the only gender being seduced into smoking. The Marlboro man has done more than his share to seduce men to become addicted to Marlboro cigarettes. One reason men are seduced by the Marlboro man is that he represents the kind of guy all guys want to be. He is tall, well-muscled, handsome. He sits astride his horse with authority, at peace with his surroundings. That Marlboro in his mouth is so much a part of the package that one assumes if you take it away, the man becomes a three-foot, gnarled troll, suitable only for exacting tolls from pedestrians trying to cross a bridge. Because the average male wants to look like the Marlboro man, he lights up. Then (at least in his own mind) he is tall, well-muscled, and handsome.

paragraph 5
The topic sentence (the first) includes a transition ("another reason") and a statement of the next cause. The supporting detail includes objective description and a statement of how something is a cause.

Another reason the Marlboro man seduces men is that he embodies the mystique of rugged individualism. The Marlboro man is never seen at parties. He is always alone, but for his horse. He has no one, he needs no one, he desires no one. All he needs is his cigarette to be complete. Men aspire to that. They want to be loners, dependent upon no one, fully capable of taking care of themselves all by themselves. How do they do that? Why, by smoking Marlboros of course.

paragraph 6
The first two sentences form the topic sentence, which presents the next cause. The supporting detail includes description and how something is a cause. Note the rhetorical question that underscores the irony.

paragraph 7
The conclusion summarizes the main point.

6   The mystique of the rugged individualist calls for man to pit himself against nature. Hence, the Marlboro man is always in the great outdoors. Expansive skies are overhead, snow-capped mountains are in the background, and open land stretches out as far as the eye can see. Now men know that even if they are firmly rooted in Manhattan, if they smoke Marlboros somehow they are at one with nature. The seduction is complete, for the irony goes unnoticed: What could be more unnatural than polluting the lungs with tar and nicotine?

7   Both the Virginia Slims "You've come a long way, baby" and the Marlboro man campaigns have been remarkably long-running, proving that they are incredibly successful. The chief reason for the success of both campaigns is that they appeal to the image people want to project. The Virginia Slims advertisements appeal to women's desire to appear desirable, confident, and equal to men. The Marlboro advertisements appeal to men's desire to appear handsome, independent, and rugged.

Pitfalls to Avoid

1. **Avoid oversimplifying.** Very few things have only one cause or effect, so do not oversimplify by suggesting so. For example, to indicate that drug use is the only cause of the high crime rate is to overlook a number of other significant causes: unemployment, urban decay, the school dropout rate, and so forth. You can certainly say that something is the primary cause or effect, but be careful not to ignore other causes and effects.

2. **Avoid assuming that an earlier event caused a later event.** Enrollment may have declined at your college after a tuition increase was instituted, but you cannot automatically assume that one caused the other. Other factors may have been involved. Perhaps the job outlook became brighter, so more high school grads went to work rather than to college.

3. **Avoid abrupt shifts as you introduce causes and effects.** Use transitions that signal cause-and-effect (such as *consequently, as a result, thus, therefore, hence, for this reason*) and ones that signal addition (such as *furthermore, in addition, also, another*) to smooth the flow. For a review of transitions, see page 84.

4. **Avoid using "the reason is because."** This expression is redundant because "the reason is" *means* "because." Instead, use either "the reason is that" or simply "because."

> *no:* Registration has been a serious problem this term. <u>The reason is because</u> the computer center experienced technical problems.

yes: Registration has been a serious problem this term. <u>The reason is that</u> the computer center experienced technical problems.

yes: Registration has been a serious problem this term <u>because</u> the computer center experienced technical problems.

PROCESS GUIDELINES: WRITING CAUSE-AND-EFFECT ANALYSIS

1. If you need help with topic selection, try the following:
   a. Think of something you do particularly well or particularly badly (run track, do math, make friends, play the piano, paint, etc.). Then consider why you do the thing well or badly and how your ability or lack of it has affected you.
   b. Identify something about your personality, environment, or circumstances and assess how this factor has affected you. You could analyze the effects of poverty, shyness, a large family, moving, and so forth.
2. If you need help generating ideas, try the following:
   a. List every cause and/or effect you can think of. Do not censor yourself; write down everything that occurs to you.
   b. To get at underlying causes and effects, ask *why?* and *then what?* after every cause and effect in your list. For example, if you listed difficulty making friends as an effect of shyness, ask *then what?* and you may get the answer "I was lonely." This answer could be an underlying effect of your shyness. If you listed strong legs as a reason for your success at running track, ask *why?* and you may get the answer "I lifted weights to increase leg strength." This would give you an underlying cause. Asking *then what?* will also help you discover causal chains.
   c. Ask yourself why an understanding of the cause-and-effect relationship is important. The answer can appear in your introduction or conclusion.
3. To identify an audience for your cause-and-effect analysis, answer these questions:
   a. Who would be interested in my cause-and-effect analysis?
   b. Who could learn something from my cause-and-effect analysis?
   c. Whom could the cause-and-effect analysis persuade to think or act a certain way?
   d. With whom would I like to share my feelings or experiences?
4. To establish a purpose for your cause-and-effect analysis, you can answer these questions:
   a. Can I inform my reader of something?
   b. Can I persuade my reader to think or act a certain way?
   c. Can I express my feelings or relate experiences?
   d. Can I entertain my reader?

5. If you like to secure reader response when revising, see page 115. In addition, have your reader ask *why?* and *then what?* after all your causes and effects. If doing so leads your reader to any underlying causes or effects you should discuss, have that person note them on the draft.

REVISION CHECKLIST

In addition to the checklist on page 117, you can use this checklist for revising your cause-and-effect analysis.

1. Is it clear what cause-and-effect relationship will be analyzed and whether causes, effects, or both will be examined?
2. Have you included underlying causes and/or effects and avoided oversimplifying?
3. Have you reproduced causal chains?
4. As necessary, have you explained what is *not* a cause or effect? As necessary, have you shown why or how something is a cause or effect?
5. Have you used transitions to avoid abrupt shifts?
6. Have you avoided assuming that an earlier event caused a later one?

EXERCISE | **Writing Cause-and-Effect Analysis**

1. Check your textbooks in other courses, newsmagazines, and newspapers for a piece of writing that includes cause-and-effect analysis. Read the selection and answer these questions:
   a. Does the cause-and-effect analysis form the primary pattern of development or is it part of a piece developed primarily with another pattern?
   b. Are causes, effects, or both causes and effects discussed?
   c. What purpose does the cause-and-effect analysis serve?
2. Pick an important decision you made sometime in your life (quitting the football team, choosing a college, joining the army, moving away from home, and so forth). Make one list of everything that caused you to make your decision. Then make a second list of all the effects of your decision.
3. Study your list and try to identify one causal chain and list every cause and effect in that chain.
4. Study your list again. If you were to write an essay from the list, would you treat causes, effects, or both? Why? What audience and purpose would you use for the essay?
5. If you were to write an essay, would you note anything that is not a cause or effect? If so, what?
6. *Collaborative Activity.* With two or three classmates, identify a problem on your campus (parking, course availability, lack of computers, overcrowded residence halls, and so forth). Then make a list of all the causes of the problem

and a second list of all the effects. Next, select two of the causes or effects and do the following:

a. Identify a possible audience and purpose for a cause-and-effect analysis of the problem.

b. Explain what supporting detail you would use to develop the selected causes or effects.

PROFESSIONAL ESSAYS

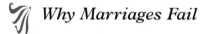

Why Marriages Fail

Anne Roiphe

Novelist Anne Roiphe wrote "Why Marriages Fail" for Family Weekly *magazine. Her examination of what causes marriages to fail also speaks to ways couples can save their marriages.*

These days so many marriages end in divorce that our most sacred vows no *1* longer ring with truth. "Happily ever after" and "Till death do us part" are expressions that seem on the way to becoming obsolete. Why has it become so hard for couples to stay together? What goes wrong? What has happened to us that close to one-half of all marriages are destined for the divorce courts? How could we have created a society in which 42 percent of our children will grow up in single-parent homes? If statistics could only measure loneliness, regret, pain, loss of self-confidence, and fear of the future, the numbers would be beyond quantifying.

Even though each broken marriage is unique, we can still find the common *2* perils, the common causes for marital despair. Each marriage has crisis points and each marriage tests endurance, the capacity for both intimacy and change. Outside pressures such as job loss, illness, infertility, trouble with a child, care of aging parents, and all the other plagues of life hit marriage the way hurricanes blast our shores. Some marriages survive these storms and others don't. Marriages fail, however, not simply because of the outside weather but because the inner climate becomes too hot or too cold, too turbulent or too stupefying.

When we look at how we choose our partners and what expectations exist *3* at the tender beginnings of romance, some of the reasons for disaster become quite clear. We all select with unconscious accuracy a mate who will recreate with us the emotional patterns of our first homes. Dr. Carl A. Whitaker, a marital therapist and emeritus professor of psychiatry at the University of Wisconsin, explains, "From early childhood on, each of us carried models for marriage, femininity, masculinity, motherhood, fatherhood, and all the other family roles." Each of us falls in love with a mate who has qualities of our parents, who will help us rediscover both the psychological happiness and miseries of our past lives. We may think we have found a man unlike Dad, but then he turns to drink or drugs, or loses his job over and over again, or sits silently in front of the T.V. just the way Dad did. A man may choose a woman who doesn't like kids just like his mother or who gambles away the family savings just like his mother. Or he may choose a slender wife who seems unlike his obese mother but then turns out to have other addictions that destroy their mutual happiness.

A man and a woman bring to their marriage bed a blended concoction of conscious and unconscious memories of their parents' lives together. The human way is to compulsively repeat and recreate the patterns of the past. Sigmund Freud so well described the unhappy design that many of us get trapped in: the unmet needs of childhood, the angry feelings left over from frustrations of long ago, the limits of trust, and the recurrence of old fears. Once an individual senses this entrapment, there may follow a yearning to escape, and the result could be a broken, splintered marriage.

Of course people can overcome the habits and attitudes that developed in childhood. We all have hidden strengths and amazing capacities for growth and creative change. Change, however, requires work—observing your part in a rotten pattern, bringing difficulties out into the open—and work runs counter to the basic myth of marriage: "When I wed this person all my problems will be over. I will have achieved success and I will become the center of life for this other person and this person will be my center, and we will mean everything to each other forever." This myth, which every marriage relies on, is soon exposed. The coming of children, the pulls and tugs of their demands on affection and time, place a considerable strain on that basic myth of meaning everything to each other, of merging together and solving all of life's problems.

Concern and tension about money take each partner away from the other. Obligations to demanding parents or still-depended-upon parents create further strain. Couples today must also deal with all the cultural changes brought on in recent years by the women's movement and the sexual revolution. The altering of roles and the shifting of responsibilities have been extremely trying for many marriages.

These and other realities of life erode the visions of marital bliss the way sandstorms eat at rock and the ocean nibbles away at the dunes. Those euphoric, grand feelings that accompany romantic love are really self-delusions, self-hypnotic dreams that enable us to forge a relationship. Real life, failure at work, disappointments, exhaustion, bad smells, bad colds, and hard times all puncture the dream and leave us stranded with our mate, with our childhood patterns pushing us this way and that, with our unfulfilled expectations.

The struggle to survive in marriage requires adaptability, flexibility, genuine love and kindness, and an imagination strong enough to feel what the other is feeling. Many marriages fall apart because either partner cannot imagine what the other wants or cannot communicate what he or she needs or feels. Anger builds until it erupts into a volcanic burst that buries the marriage in ash.

It is not hard to see, therefore, how essential communication is for a good marriage. A man and a woman must be able to tell each other how they feel and why they feel the way they do; otherwise they will impose on each other roles and actions that lead to further unhappiness. In some cases, the communication patterns of childhood—of not talking, of talking too much, of not listening, of distrust and anger, of withdrawal—spill into the marriage and prevent a healthy exchange of thoughts and feelings. The answer is to set up new patterns of communication and intimacy.

At the same time, however, we must see each other as individuals. "To *10* achieve a balance between separateness and closeness is one of the major psychological tasks of all human beings at every stage of life," says Dr. Stuart Bartle, a psychiatrist at the New York University Medical Center.

If we sense from our mate a need for too much intimacy, we tend to push *11* him or her away, fearing that we may lose our identities in the merging of marriage. One partner may suffocate the other partner in a childlike dependency.

A good marriage means growing as a couple but also growing as individuals. *12* This isn't easy. Richard gives up his interest in carpentry because his wife, Helen, is jealous of the time he spends away from her. Karen quits her choir group because her husband dislikes the friends she makes there. Each pair clings to each other and are angry with each other as life closes in on them. This kind of marital balance is easily thrown as one or the other pulls away, and divorce follows.

Sometimes people pretend that a new partner will solve the old problems. *13* Most often extramarital sex destroys a marriage because it allows an artificial split between the good and the bad—the good is projected on the new partner and the bad is dumped on the head of the old. Dishonesty, hiding, and cheating create walls between men and women. Infidelity is just a symptom of trouble. It is a symbolic complaint, a weapon of revenge, as well as an unraveler of closeness. Infidelity is often that proverbial last straw that sinks the camel to the ground.

All right—marriage has always been difficult. Why then are we seeing so *14* many divorces at this time? Yes, our modern social fabric is thin, and yes the permissiveness of society has created unrealistic expectations and thrown the family into chaos. But divorce is so common because people today are unwilling to exercise the self-discipline that marriage requires. They expect easy joy, like the entertainment on TV, the thrill of a good party.

Marriage takes some kind of sacrifice, not dreadful self-sacrifice of the soul, *15* but some level of compromise. Some of one's fantasies, some of one's legitimate desires have to be given up for the value of the marriage itself. "While all marital partners feel shackled at times it is they who really choose to make the marital ties into confining chains or supporting bonds," says Dr. Whitaker. Marriage requires sexual, financial, and emotional discipline. A man and a woman cannot follow every impulse, cannot allow themselves to stop growing or changing.

Divorce is not an evil act. Sometimes it provides salvation for people who *16* have grown hopelessly apart or were frozen in patterns of pain or mutual unhappiness. Divorce can be, despite its initial devastation, like the first cut of the surgeon's knife, a step toward new health and a good life. On the other hand, if the partners can stay past the breaking up of the romantic myths into the development of real love and intimacy, they have achieved a work as amazing as the greatest cathedrals of the world. Marriages that do not fail but improve, that persist despite imperfections, are not only rare these days but offer a wondrous shelter in which the face of our mutual humanity can safely show itself.

Considering Ideas

1. According to Dr. Carl A. Whitaker, what kind of marriage partners do we choose? What implications does this choice have for the quality of our marriages?
2. What are the earliest clues that Roiphe will examine causes?
3. Roiphe says that the women's movement and the sexual revolution have strained modern marriages. Explain why this is so.
4. Roiphe's essay concludes on a positive note. She says that divorce can be healthy and that marriages that survive are a "wondrous shelter." Why do you think she ends in such an upbeat way?
5. Roiphe's original audience was the readers of *Family Weekly* magazine. For what purpose do you think she wrote her essay for this audience?
6. Did you learn anything as a result of reading "Why Marriages Fail"? Explain.

Considering Technique

1. Which sentence is Roiphe's thesis? Which words indicate that the author will discuss causes?
2. Which paragraphs begin with a topic sentence that presents a cause to be examined?
3. *Combining Patterns.* Which two paragraphs support a cause-and-effect generalization with examples? How does Roiphe use process analysis to examine a cause of marital failure?
4. In which paragraphs does Roiphe explain *why* something is a cause? Is this detail important to developing the thesis? Explain.
5. In paragraph 13, Roiphe offers infidelity as an *obvious* cause of marital failure. Does she also offer an *underlying* cause? Explain.

For Group Discussion or Journal Writing

Study paragraph 14 and consider to what extent you agree or disagree with Roiphe's explanation for the current increase in the divorce rate.

It Is Time to Stop Playing Indians

Arlene B. Hirschfelder

Arlene Hirschfelder, a staff member of the Association on American Indian Affairs and a longtime advocate of Native American rights, examines the detrimental effects of using Native American symbols for merchandising, holiday images, and sports mascots.

It is predictable. At Halloween, thousands of children trick-or-treat in Indian costumes. At Thanksgiving, thousands of children parade in school pageants wearing plastic headdresses and pseudobuckskin clothing. Thousands of card shops stock Thanksgiving greeting cards with images of cartoon animals wearing feathered headbands. Thousands of teachers and librarians trim bulletin boards with Anglo-   1 featured, feathered Indian boys and girls. Thousands of gift shops load their shelves with Indian figurines and jewelry.

Fall and winter are also the seasons when hundreds of thousands of sports 2 fans root for professional, college, and public school teams with names that summon up Indians—"Braves," "Redskins," "Chiefs." (In New York State, one out of eight junior and senior high school teams call themselves "Indians," "Tomahawks," and the like.) War-whooping team mascots are imprinted on school uniforms, postcards, notebooks, tote bags, and car floor mats.

All of this seems innocuous: Why make a fuss about it? Because these trap- 3 pings and holiday symbols offend tens of thousands of other Americans—the Native American people. Because these invented images prevent millions of us from understanding the authentic Indian America, both long ago and today. Because this image-making prevents Indians from being a relevant part of the nation's social fabric.

Halloween costumes mask the reality of high mortality rates, high diabetes 4 rates, high unemployment rates. They hide low average life spans, low per capita incomes, and low educational levels. Plastic war bonnets and ersatz buckskin deprive people from knowing the complexity of Native American heritage—that Indians belong to hundreds of nations that have intricate social organizations, governments, languages, religions and sacred rituals, ancient stories, unique arts and music forms.

Thanksgiving school units and plays mask history. They do not tell how 5 Europeans mistreated Wampanoags and other East Coast Indian peoples during the seventeenth century. Social studies units don't mention that, to many Indians, Thanksgiving is a day of mourning, the beginning of broken promises, land theft, near extinction of their religions and languages at the hands of invading Europeans.

Athletic team nicknames and mascots disguise real people. Warpainted, 6 buckskin-clad, feathered characters keep the fictitious Indian circulating on decals, pennants, and team clothing. Toy companies mask Indian identity and trivialize sacred beliefs by manufacturing Indian costumes and headdresses, peace pipes, and trick-arrow-through-the-head gags that equate Indianness with playtime. Indian figures equipped with arrows, guns, and tomahawks give youngsters the harmful message that Indians favor mayhem. Many Indian people can tell about children screaming in fear after being introduced to them.

It is time to consider how these images impede the efforts of Indian parents 7 and communities to raise their children with positive information about their heritage. It is time to get rid of stereotypes that, whether deliberately or inadvertently, denigrate Indian cultures and people.

It is time to bury the Halloween costumes, trick arrows, bulletin-board pin- 8 ups, headdresses, and mascots. It has been done before. In the 1970s, after student protests, Marquette University dropped its "Willie Wampum," Stanford University retired its mascot, "Prince Lightfoot," and Eastern Michigan University and Florida State modified their savage-looking mascots to reduce criticism.

It is time to stop playing Indians. It is time to abolish Indian images that sell 9 merchandise. It is time to stop offending Indian people whose lives are all too often filled with economic deprivation, powerlessness, discrimination, and gross injustice. This time next year, let's find more appropriate symbols for the holiday and sports seasons.

Considering Ideas

1. What problems does Hirschfelder see with Halloween costumes?
2. Explain what Hirschfelder means when she says, "Thanksgiving school units and plays mask history" (paragraph 5). What is interesting about her use of the word *mask*?
3. According to Hirschfelder, how do toy companies contribute to the problem by making fake Native American weapons and clothes?
4. Why do you think some schools like Marquette University and Stanford University agreed to change their mascots? Do you think they did the right thing? Explain.

Considering Technique

1. For what purpose do you think Hirschfelder wrote "It Is Time to Stop Playing Indians"?
2. Hirschfelder examines the effects of "playing Indian." Why didn't she look at the causes of this behavior?
3. Which paragraph embodies the thesis of the essay?
4. Which paragraphs include examples? What purpose do these examples serve?
5. Paragraphs 4–6 cite the effects of using Indian images for athletic teams and holiday celebrations. Many effects are given, but none is developed in much detail. Why? Is the original audience a factor? Explain. (The essay first appeared in the Los Angeles *Times*.)
6. What is the effect of opening each of the last three paragraphs with "It is time"?

For Group Discussion or Journal Writing

Hirschfelder hopes that we can find "more appropriate symbols for the holiday and sports seasons" (paragraph 9). Make a list of possible symbols for each of the following: Halloween, Thanksgiving, a baseball or football team. Explain why the symbols are appropriate.

Combining Patterns of Development

Beauty: When the Other Dancer Is the Self

Alice Walker

Poet, essayist, and novelist Alice Walker won the Pulitzer Prize for her novel The Color Purple. *In the following autobiographical account, the author explains the effects of her disfiguring accident. Be sure to notice the combination of **cause-and-effect analysis**, **narration**, and **comparison-contrast**.*

It is a bright summer day in 1947. My father, a fat, funny man with beautiful *1* eyes and a subversive wit, is trying to decide which of his eight children he will take with him to the county fair. My mother, of course, will not go. She is knocked out from getting most of us ready: I hold my neck stiff against the pressure of her knuckles as she hastily completes the braiding and then beribboning of my hair.

My father is the driver for the rich old white lady up the road. Her name is *2* Miss Mey. She owns all the land for miles around, as well as the house in which we live. All I remember about her is that she once offered to pay my mother thirty-five cents for cleaning her house, raking up piles of her magnolia leaves, and washing her family's clothes, and that my mother—she of no money, eight children, and a chronic earache—refused it. But I do not think of this in 1947. I am two and a half years old. I want to go everywhere my daddy goes. I am excited at the prospect of riding in a car. Someone has told me fairs are fun. That there is room in the car for only three of us doesn't faze me at all. Whirling happily in my starchy frock, showing off my biscuit-polished patent-leather shoes and lavender socks, tossing my head in a way that makes my ribbons bounce, I stand hands on hips, before my father. "Take me, Daddy," I say with assurance; "I'm the prettiest!"

Later, it does not surprise me to find myself in Miss Mey's shiny black car, *3* sharing the back seat with the other lucky ones. Does not surprise me that I thoroughly enjoy the fair. At home that night I tell the unlucky ones all I can remember about the merry-go-round, the man who eats live chickens, and the teddy bears, until they say: that's enough, baby Alice. Shut up now, and go to sleep.

It is Easter Sunday, 1950. I am dressed in a green, flocked, scalloped-hem *4* dress (handmade by my adoring sister, Ruth) that has its own smooth satin petticoat and tiny hot-pink roses tucked into each scallop. My shoes, new T-strap patent leather, again highly biscuit-polished. I am six years old and have learned one of the longest Easter speeches to be heard that day, totally unlike the speech I said when I was two: "Easter lilies / pure and white / blossom in / the morning light." When I rise to give my speech I do so on a great wave of love and pride and expectation. People in the church stop rustling their new crinolines. They seem to hold their breath. I can tell they admire my dress, but it is my spirit, bordering on sassiness (womanishness), they secretly applaud.

"That girl's a little *mess*," they whisper to each other, pleased. *5*

Naturally I say my speech without stammer or pause, unlike those who *6* stutter, stammer, or, worst of all, forget. This is before the word "beautiful" exists in people's vocabulary, but "Oh, isn't she the *cutest* thing!" frequently floats my way. "And got so much sense!" they gratefully add . . . for which thoughtful addition I thank them to this day.

It was great fun being cute. But then, one day, it ended. *7*

I am eight years old and a tomboy. I have a cowboy hat, cowboy boots, *8* checkered shirt and pants, all red. My playmates are my brothers, two and four years older than I. Their colors are black and green, the only difference in the way we are dressed. On Saturday nights we all go to the picture show, even my mother; Westerns are her favorite kind of movie. Back home, "on the ranch," we pretend we are Tom Mix, Hopalong Cassidy, Lash LaRue (we've even named one of our dogs Lash LaRue); we chase each other for hours rustling cattle, being outlaws, delivering damsels from distress. Then my parents decide to buy my brothers guns. These are not "real" guns. They shoot "BBs," copper pellets my brothers say will kill birds. Because I am a girl, I do not get a gun. Instantly I am relegated to the position of Indian. Now there appears a great distance between us. They shoot and shoot at everything with their new guns. I try to keep up with my bow and arrows.

One day while I am standing on top of our makeshift "garage"—pieces of   *9* tin nailed across some poles—holding my bow and arrow and looking out toward the fields, I feel an incredible blow in my right eye. I look down just in time to see my brother lower his gun.

Both brothers rush to my side. My eye stings, and I cover it with my   *10* hand. "If you tell," they say, "we will get a whipping. You don't want that to happen, do you?" I do not. "Here is a piece of wire," says the older brother, picking it up from the roof; "say you stepped on one end of it and the other flew up and hit you." The pain is beginning to start. "Yes," I say, "Yes, I will say that is what happened." If I do not say this is what happened, I know my brothers will find ways to make me wish I had. But now I will say anything that gets me to my mother.

Confronted by our parents we stick to the lie agreed upon. They place me   *11* on a bench on the porch and I close my left eye while they examine the right. There is a tree growing from underneath the porch that climbs past the railing to the roof. It is the last thing my right eye sees. I watch as its trunk, its branches, and then its leaves are blotted out by the rising blood.

I am in shock. First there is intense fever, which my father tries to break   *12* using lily leaves bound around my head. Then there are chills: my mother tries to get me to eat soup. Eventually, I do not know how, my parents learn what has happened. A week after the "accident" they take me to see a doctor. "Why did you wait so long to come?" he asks, looking into my eye and shaking his head. "Eyes are sympathetic," he says. "If one is blind, the other will likely become blind too."

This comment of the doctor's terrifies me. But it is really how I look that   *13* bothers me most. Where the BB pellet struck there is a glob of whitish scar tissue, a hideous cataract, on my eye. Now when I stare at people—a favorite pastime, up to now—they will stare back. Not at the "cute" little girl, but at her scar. For six years I do not stare at anyone, because I do not raise my head.

Years later, in the throes of a mid-life crisis, I ask my mother and sister   *14* whether I changed after the "accident." "No," they say, puzzled. "What do you mean?"

What do I mean?   *15*

I am eight, and, for the first time, doing poorly in school, where I have been   *16* something of a whiz since I was four. We have just moved to the place where the "accident" occurred. We do not know any of the people around us because this is a different county. The only time I see the friends I knew is when we go back to our old church. The new school is the former state penitentiary. It is a large stone building, cold and drafty, crammed to overflowing with boisterous, ill-disciplined children. On the third floor there is a huge circular imprint of some partition that has been torn out.

"What used to be here?" I ask a sullen girl next to me on our way past it to   *17*
lunch.

"The electric chair," says she.   *18*

At night I have nightmares about the electric chair, and about all the people   *19*
reputedly "fried" in it. I am afraid of the school, where all the students seem to
be budding criminals.

"What's the matter with your eye?" they ask, critically.   *20*

When I don't answer (I cannot decide whether it was an "accident" or not),   *21*
they shove me, insist on a fight.

My brother, the one who created the story about the wire, comes to my res-   *22*
cue. But then brags so much about "protecting" me, I become sick.

After months of torture at the school, my parents decide to send me back to   *23*
our old community, to my old school. I live with my grandparents and the
teacher they board. But there is no room for Phoebe, my cat. By the time my
grandparents decide there *is* room, and I ask for my cat, she cannot be found.
Miss Yarborough, the boarding teacher, takes me under her wing, and begins to
teach me to play the piano. But soon she marries an African—a "prince," she
says—and is whisked away to his continent.

At my old school there is at least one teacher who loves me. She is the   *24*
teacher who "knew me before I was born" and bought my first baby clothes. It is
she who makes life bearable. It is her presence that finally helps me turn on the
one child at the school who continually calls me "one-eyed bitch." One day I
simply grab him by his coat and beat him until I am satisfied. It is my teacher
who tells me my mother is ill.

My mother is lying in bed in the middle of the day, something I have never   *25*
seen. She is in too much pain to speak. She has an abscess in her ear. I stand
looking down on her, knowing that if she dies, I cannot live. She is being treated
with warm oils and hot bricks held against her cheek. Finally a doctor comes. But
I must go back to my grandparents' house. The weeks pass but I am hardly
aware of it. All I know is that my mother might die, my father is not so jolly, my
brothers still have their guns, and I am the one sent away from home.

"You did not change," they say.   *26*

Did I imagine the anguish of never looking up?   *27*

I am 12. When relatives come to visit I hide in my room. My cousin   *28*
Brenda, just my age, whose father works in the post office and whose mother is a
nurse, comes to find me. "Hello," she says. And then she asks, looking at my recent school picture, which I did not want taken, and on which the "glob," as I
think of it, is clearly visible, "You still can't see out of that eye?"

"No," I say, and flop back on the bed over my book.   *29*

That night, as I do almost every night, I abuse my eye. I rant and rave at it,   *30*
in front of the mirror. I plead with it to clear up before morning. I tell it I hate
and despise it. I do not pray for sight, I pray for beauty.

"You did not change," they say.   *31*

I am 14 and baby-sitting for my brother Bill, who lives in Boston. He is my   *32* favorite brother and there is a strong bond between us. Understanding my feelings of shame and ugliness he and his wife take me to a local hospital, where the "glob" is removed by a doctor named O. Henry. There is still a small bluish crater where the scar tissue was, but the ugly white stuff is gone. Almost immediately I become a different person from the girl who does not raise her head. Or so I think. Now that I've raised my head I win the boyfriend of my dreams. Now that I've raised my head I have plenty of friends. Now that I've raised my head classwork comes from my lips as faultlessly as Easter speeches did, and I leave high school as valedictorian, most popular student, and *queen,* hardly believing my luck. Ironically, the girl who was voted most beautiful in our class (and was) was later shot twice through the chest by a male companion, using a "real" gun, while she was pregnant. But that's another story in itself. Or is it?

"You did not change," they say.   *33*

It is now 30 years since the "accident." A beautiful journalist comes to visit   *34* and to interview me. She is going to write a cover story for her magazine that focuses on my latest book. "Decide how you want to look on the cover," she says. "Glamorous, or whatever."

Never mind "glamorous," it is the "whatever" that I hear. Suddenly all I   *35* can think of is whether I will get enough sleep the night before the photography session: If I don't, my eye will be tired and wander, as blind eyes will.

At night in bed with my lover I think up reasons why I should not appear   *36* on the cover of a magazine. "My meanest critics will say I've sold out," I say. "My family will now realize I write scandalous books."

"But what's the real reason you don't want to do this?" he asks.   *37*

"Because in all probability," I say in a rush, "my eye won't be straight,"   *38*

"It will be straight enough," he says. Then, "Besides, I thought you'd made   *39* your peace with that."

And I suddenly remember that I have.   *40*

I remember: *41*

I am talking to my brother Jimmy, asking if he remembers anything unusual   *42* about the day I was shot. He does not know I consider that day the last time my father, with his sweet home remedy of cool lily leaves, chose me, and that I suffered and raged inside because of this. "Well," he says, "all I remember is standing by the side of the highway with Daddy, trying to flag down a car. A white man stopped, but when Daddy said he needed somebody to take his little girl to the doctor, he drove off."

I remember: *43*

I am in the desert for the first time. I fall totally in love with it. I am so over-   *44* whelmed by its beauty, I confront for the first time, consciously, the meaning of the doctor's words years ago: "Eyes are sympathetic. If one is blind, the other will likely become blind too." I realize I have dashed about the world madly, looking at this, looking at that, storing up images against the fading of the light. *But I might have missed seeing the desert!* The shock of that possibility—and gratitude for

over 25 years of sight—sends me literally to my knees. Poem after poem comes—
which is perhaps how poets pray.

ON SIGHT   *45*

I am so thankful I have seen   *46*
The Desert
And the creatures in the desert
And the desert Itself.

The desert has its own moon   *47*
Which I have seen
With my own eye.
There is no flag on it.

Trees of the desert have arms   *48*
All of which are always up
That is because the moon is up
The sun is up
Also the sky
The stars
Clouds
None with flags.

If there *were* flags, I doubt   *49*
the trees would point.
Would you?

But mostly, I remember this: *50*

I am 27, and my baby daughter is almost three. Since her birth I have wor-   *51*
ried about her discovery that her mother's eyes are different from other people's.
Will she be embarrassed? I think. What will she say? Every day she watches a
television program called "Big Blue Marble." It begins with a picture of the earth
as it appears from the moon. It is bluish, a little battered-looking, but full of light,
with whitish clouds swirling around it. Every time I see it I weep with love, as if it
is a picture of Grandma's house. One day when I am putting Rebecca down for
her nap, she suddenly focuses on my eye. Something inside me cringes, gets
ready to try to protect myself. All children are cruel about physical differences. I
know from experience, and that they don't always mean to be is another matter. I
assume Rebecca will be the same.

But no-o-o-o. She studies my face intently as we stand, her inside and me   *52*
outside her crib. She even holds my face maternally between her dimpled little
hands. Then, looking every bit as serious and lawyerlike as her father, she says, as
if it may just possibly have slipped my attention: "Mommy, there's a *world* in
your eye." (As in, "Don't be alarmed, or do anything crazy.") And then, gently,
but with great interest: "Mommy, where did you *get* that world in your eye?"

For the most part, the pain left then. (So what, if my brothers grew up to   *53*
buy even more powerful pellet guns for their sons and to carry real guns themselves. So what, if a young "Morehouse man" once nearly fell off the steps of
Trevor Arnett Library because he thought my eyes were blue.) Crying and

laughing I ran to the bathroom, while Rebecca mumbled and sang herself off to sleep. Yes indeed, I realized, looking into the mirror. There *was* a world in my eye. And I saw that it was possible to love it: that in fact, for all it had taught me of shame and anger and inner vision, I *did* love it. Even to see it drifting out of orbit in boredom, or rolling up out of fatigue, not to mention floating back at attention in excitement (bearing witness, a friend has called it), deeply suitable to my personality, and even characteristic of me.

That night I dream I am dancing to Stevie Wonder's song "Always" (the 54 name of the song is really "As," but I hear it as "Always"). As I dance, whirling and joyous, happier than I've ever been in my life, another bright-faced dancer joins me. We dance and kiss each other and hold each other through the night. The other dancer has obviously come through all right, as I have done. She is beautiful, whole and free. And she is also me.

Considering Ideas

1. How did Walker see herself before she lost her eye? How was Walker affected by the loss of her eye? Why does Walker come to love her eye?
2. How was Walker affected by her daughter's reaction to her eye? Why did the child react the way she did?
3. What incident of racism is highlighted in the essay?
4. Why do you think Walker did poorly in school after the accident? Why did she perform well in school again when the scar tissue was removed?
5. What point about beauty is Walker making in the essay?

Considering Technique

1. In what order does Walker arrange her details?
2. *Combining patterns.* Explain how Walker uses cause-and-effect analysis, narration, and comparison-contrast in the essay.
3. Why do you think Walker includes the poem and her reaction to the desert?
4. Walker repeats the words, "You did not change" a number of times. Why does she do this?

For Group Discussion or Journal Writing

Using the evidence in the essay, tell what you think Walker's parents and siblings were like. Also, explain how you think her immediate family affected Walker's reaction to her injury.

STUDENT ESSAYS TO READ AND EVALUATE

The following cause-and-effect analyses, written by students, have strengths and weaknesses. As you read them, identify the chief strong and weak points. This will help you become a reliable judge of writing so you can better decide how to revise your own work.

Athletes on Drugs: It's Not So Hard to Understand

On June 17, 1986, Len Bias, a basketball star from the University   1
of Maryland, was the second pick in the National Basketball
Association amateur draft. Bias had everything going for him; he
was a 22-year-old kid about to become a millionaire and superstar.
He was on top of the world (or so it seemed). Forty hours later Len
Bias was dead—from an overdose of drugs. The Len Bias story is
tragic, but it is just one of many cases. Just eight days following
the Bias tragedy, Cleveland Browns all-pro safety Don Rogers, then
23, died of a drug overdose. Steve Howe, once a dazzling pitcher,
now finds himself out of baseball because of his drug problems. And
the list goes on. Why? Why are professional athletes, people who
have money, success, fame, and power, destroying their lives with
drugs?

To most people the life of professional athletes is filled with   2
glamour. All they see are the sports cars, the million-dollar
contracts, and the adoring fans. People do not realize the mental
anguish that is involved with being a professional athlete. The
loneliness, the fear of failure, and the insecurities of their jobs
are just a few of the pressures that athletes have to deal with
every day. In some sports, such as baseball, basketball, and
hockey, the teams play five to seven games a week, so the athletes
must travel to two or three different cities. This constant travel
has an adverse effect on athletes' ability to cope with daily
pressures. They begin to miss family and friends, often becoming
lonely and depressed. As an alternative to this depression, they
turn to drugs.

In most cases, professional athletes of today have been the   3
best in their sports since childhood. They have won honors and
awards for their talents all through their lives. They have seldom
been failures, and fear of becoming one is their worst nightmare.
The athletes are surrounded by family, friends, and coaches who
tell them they are the best. These people attempt to make the
athletes feel flawless, incapable of making a mistake. Therefore,
when players do have a bad day, they not only let themselves down
but those people too. Again, in order to deal with the pressure,
drugs become a solution.

For most of today's professional athletes, sports is all they   *4*
know. Many do not have a college education, and, more than likely,
without sports they would not have a career. Athletes must remain
above the competition to keep their jobs. In some cases, when the
God-given ability is not enough, the player uses drugs for
improvement. Athletes have found that some drugs, such as
amphetamines, can increase their physical abilities. These drugs
help the athlete to perform better, therefore giving her or him a
greater chance of success. For example, steroids have almost become
a norm in some sports. Bodybuilders and football players have
discovered that these drugs speed up the development of strength
and muscles. In professional football, large numbers of offensive
and defensive linemen claim to have used steroids at least once in
their careers. Those professional athletes who refuse to use
amphetamines and steroids are no doubt at a disadvantage.

In today's sports athletes are bigger, stronger, and faster;   *5*
therefore, more injuries are occurring. Injuries are part of the
game, and all players have suffered at least one in their careers.
The most discomforting fact about injuries for professional
athletes of today is not the pain but the drugs that are used to
ease their discomfort. In many cases, coaches and trainers strongly
encourage the use of such drugs. In the high-priced world of
sports, time is money. Athletes cannot afford to sit out and allow
their injuries to heal properly. They often turn to drugs to help
speed up the healing process. Often these drugs are illegal;
sometimes they are more dangerous than the injury itself, but for
the athlete the use of the drug appears to be the only choice.
Without the drugs, the players face the loss of thousands of
dollars as well as their livelihoods.

The professional athlete has to deal with a great deal of   *6*
pressure. As the mental struggles begin to mount and the aches and
pains begin to multiply, the athlete becomes more susceptible to
drug use. Drug use should never be accepted, but in the case of the
professional athlete, condemning the problem will not solve it. The
fans, owners, and especially the players themselves must reexamine
the pressures and stop the drug problem before it destroys more
people's lives.

Small but Mighty

"Adam Ant! Adam Ant!" I can still hear it echo through my head, a   *1*
name that has plagued me my entire life. Ever since my youth, I was
the smallest kid in class, and I couldn't do anything about it. I
was born a midget. Well, maybe I wasn't a midget, but sometimes I
felt like I was.

My height problem began even before I can remember. When I was   *2*
four years old, I was able to enter kindergarten. My parents, being
unsure of enrolling me because of my age, had taken me to a
psychologist to get her opinion. I was scholastically ready for
school. I could tie my shoes, I could recite the alphabet, I could
distinguish the colors; I knew all the things I would learn in
kindergarten. I also would have been a year and a half younger than
all the others. Because of my height and age, the psychologist did
not advise that I go. She was afraid my abilities would deteriorate
if I was teased about my size. I didn't start until the next year.

In grade school, everyone was small, but I, of course, was the   *3*
smallest. Back then I didn't worry much about it. If someone did
tease me, I was told not to let it bother me because I would grow
as I got older. I grew, but not as much as I expected to. Anyway, I
was a normal kid. I played games, made fun of girls, and did all
the usual stuff kids do. I was pretty popular in school, and I had
a lot of friends, too. No one really made a big deal about my
height because none of them were towering giants either. It wasn't
until the fourth or fifth grade that my height really began to
bother me.

I started to feel insecure about myself the first year I played   *4*
football. I was on the pee-wees. Go figure! It was my coach who
labeled me with the infamous name "Adam Ant." At first I laughed
and paid no attention; it wasn't until the other kids started
calling me it that I became bothered. I tried not to show that it
bothered me. I just played a little harder. I decided that I would
be the best no matter how small I was. I became a starter. That
made me feel good. I also played baseball. Along with me came the
name. I worked hard and made the All-Stars. I wanted to show
everyone that I was not handicapped.

My height kept me from doing things that I liked. For instance,   5
I didn't try out for the basketball team. I was only a freshman, a
small freshman. I felt very insecure about myself, so I skipped it.

I was in the seventh grade when I tried to do something about   6
my size. I knew that I couldn't make myself taller, so I decided to
make myself bigger. Bulkier, that is. A couple of friends and I
began weight training. I was surprised at the amount of weight I
could lift. At first, I wasn't very serious, but I was excited. It
was something new to me.

After a couple of months, I could feel myself getting stronger   7
and growing bigger. Other people also noticed. I'd hear things
like, "Wow! You look huge" and "What's your mom feeding you?" This
really helped build my confidence. No one talked about my height
anymore. In fact, my height is kind of a blessing. Because I have a
small frame, the muscle builds up more and I look like a monster.

I now realize that I was dubbed "Adam Ant" not only because of   8
my height, but because I performed activities that were considered
out of reach.

Collaborative Exercise: Evaluating Writing

Form a group and select one of the previous student essays. Designate a recorder
to take down the group's findings and a spokesperson to report those findings to
the class. Then study the essay to identify its chief strengths and weaknesses. If
you like, you can use the following evaluation questions as a guide.

Evaluation Questions

1. *The Thesis*
   What is the thesis? If it does not indicate whether causes and/or effects
   will be discussed, should it?
2. *The Introduction*
   Does the introduction engage your interest? Why or why not?
3. *Supporting Details*
   Note any points you do not understand, any points that are not relevant,
   and any points that need more development. Is there a faithful repro-
   duction of causal chains? If necessary, does the author explain something that is *not* a cause or effect? If necessary, does the author explain
   why or how something is a cause or effect? Has the author avoided oversimplifying and assuming an earlier event caused a later one?
4. *Organization*
   Are all the details in an easy-to-follow, logical order? Evaluate the use of
   transitions and topic sentences.

5. *The Conclusion*
   Does the essay come to a satisfying end? Explain.
6. *Overview*
   What do you like best about the essay? What is the single most important revision the author should make?

Essay Topics: Cause-and-Effect Analysis

When you write your essay, consult Pitfalls to Avoid on page 267, Process Guidelines on page 268, and the Revision Checklist on page 269.

Writing in the Pattern

1. Explain either the causes or effects of racial or religious prejudice.
2. Analyze the effects of some technological innovation, such as the VCR, the answering machine, video games, caller ID, and so forth.
3. Explain the causes of increased violence among spectators at sporting events.
4. Select a popular trend and analyze its causes and/or its effects.
5. Explain why some college students drop out of school.
6. Analyze the causes and/or effects of one of your bad habits.
7. Explain the effects college has had on your life.
8. Where we grow up has an enormous effect on who and what we become. How did the place you grew up (big city, small town, farm, poor neighborhood, affluent suburb, etc.) affect you?
9. Explain how the way we dress affects how people perceive us.
10. Explain how television influences our view of the world.
11. Explain the long-term effects of a childhood experience.
12. If you or a family member has been unemployed, explain the effects of this unemployment.
13. Identify a problem on your campus (inadequate housing, crowded classes, outdated requirements, high tuition, etc.) and analyze its causes and/or effects.

Reading Then Writing in the Pattern

1. Anne Roiphe (page 270) explains why marriages fail. Write an essay that explains why students fail.
2. In paragraph 7 of "Why Marriages Fail," Roiphe comments on the concept of romantic love. Describe the popular concept of romantic love and what is responsible for that concept and/or what the effects of that concept are.
3. In "Beauty: When the Other Dancer Is the Self" (page 275), Alice Walker explores the notion of what is beautiful. Explain what you think the prevailing concept of beauty is. Then explore either the causes or the effects of that concept.

4. In "Athletes on Drugs: It's Not So Hard to Understand" (page 282), the author discusses the causes of drug abuse among athletes. Explain the causes of some other problem behavior: cheating on exams, smoking, overeating, shoplifting, road rage, and so on.

Responding to the Readings

1. Pick a holiday that you think we celebrate inappropriately and, like Arlene Hirschfelder in "It Is Time to Stop Playing Indians" (page 273), explain what is wrong with the way we celebrate the holiday.

2. Agree or disagree with the description of romantic love that Anne Roiphe presents in paragraph 7 of "Why Marriages Fail" (page 270).

3. The student author of "Athletes on Drugs: It's Not So Hard to Understand" (page 282) explains why athletes turn to drugs. What do you think can be done to solve the problem? Describe a specific plan to address the issues in the student's essay and any other you find pertinent.

4. *Connecting the Readings.* Using the ideas in "Small but Mighty" (page 284), "Beauty: When the Other Dancer Is the Self" (page 275), and "It Is Time to Stop Playing Indians" (page 273), along with your own experience and observation, write an essay about self-image, considering how it is formed and how it affects us.

CHAPTER 10

Definition

To discover what a word means, you go to the dictionary, but sometimes the dictionary is not enough. Sure, you can check a dictionary to learn the meaning of a word like *fun,* but what is fun to you may not be fun to someone else, and so the full meaning of that word will vary among individuals to an extent. Some words symbolize abstractions, with subtleties that cannot all be taken in by an inch or so of space in a dictionary. What, for example, does *justice* mean? Certainly, it is a concept with complexities far beyond its neat dictionary definition. In addition, some words have meanings so complex that a dictionary definition can only hit the high points, leaving quite a bit unexplained. *Democracy* is such a word. Not only is its meaning complex, but it varies greatly depending on which country's democracy is referred to.

Thus, dictionary definitions can tell us much, but when it comes to the controversial, abstract, or complex, something more may be needed. This something can be an extended definition. An **extended definition** goes beyond the concise, formal definition in a dictionary to explore the *nature* of something, including the aspects, significances, nuances, or complexities that are not part of what a dictionary takes in.

ESTABLISHING YOUR PURPOSE AND IDENTIFYING YOUR AUDIENCE

Many concepts—like *wisdom, courage, freedom, hate,* and so on—are multifaceted and difficult to grapple with. In fact, people do not always agree on what these concepts mean. An extended definition of such a term can *offer clarification.*

A second purpose of an extended definition can be to bring to the reader's attention something that is taken for granted. For example, an extended definition of a *free press* can *lead the reader to a fresh appreciation* of something so much a part of daily life that it is undervalued.

An extended definition can also *bring the reader to a sharper awareness* of something familiar but only vaguely understood. An essay defining the *microchip* might serve this purpose. An extended definition can also *explain the meaning and nature of something not at all understood by the reader,* say, a *token economy.* You can even *inform* the reader of something new by defining the commonplace. An extended definition of *senior citizen* might lead to a new knowledge of what it means to grow old in this country. Sometimes definition *makes a statement about some issue* that goes beyond the subject defined. For example, an essay that defines *rock music* can also comment on the orientation, values, and thinking of young people. That is, because musical preferences among youth are often an index to the prevailing needs and attitudes of young people, a definition of one makes significant statements about the other.

In addition to informing, an extended definition can allow a writer to *express feelings and relate experience,* as when you tell about your childhood experiences with your best friend in order to explain the meaning of *friendship.* Finally, definition can serve to *entertain,* as is the case with the amusing "Tacky Hits Home" on page 303, and to *persuade,* as when you define the horrors of *poverty* to convince your reader to do something about it.

Your purpose will influence your detail. Say you decide to define *fear* to give your reader a fresh outlook on this feeling by showing that fear is really a positive emotion. You might note that fear is adaptive because it ensures our survival. You might also note instances when we would endanger ourselves needlessly were it not for fear. However, a different purpose would mean different detail. If you want your definition to show that fear keeps us from realizing our potential, you might include detail that relates lack of achievement to fear of failure and fear of taking risks.

Detail selection is also affected by audience. Assume that you are writing an essay defining *teenager* and your purpose is to make your reader aware of how difficult the teen years are. If your reader is 25 and likely to remember adolescence, you can explain less than if your audience is much further removed from those years and needs to be reminded of a few things. Similarly, if your audience is a neighbor who has been expressing concern over "what the youth in this country have come to," you may want to explain why teenagers behave as they do in order to address and discharge your reader's negative feelings. However, if your audience is a teenager, there will be no ill will to overcome, so you might instead include detail to reassure the teen that he or she is not alone in the struggle.

COMBINING DEFINITION WITH OTHER PATTERNS

Definition combines readily with other patterns of development to help you achieve your purpose. For example, to inform your reader, you might first define *pornography* and then use cause-and-effect analysis to explain its effects. To convince your reader that even upper-middle-class people can become homeless, you can define *homelessness* and then go on to use process analysis to explain how one can become homeless. An essay on heroism can first define *heroism* and then classify the types of heroism. An essay on stress can combine three patterns by first defining *stress,* then explaining its causes, and finally noting what can be done to cope with it. For an example of an essay that combines definition and cause-and-effect analysis, see "About Men" on page 300.

USING DEFINITION BEYOND THE WRITING CLASS

Definition will be a frequent part of your essay examination answers and papers in courses outside your writing class. An environmental science class may call for a definition of *ecosystem;* a political science class may require a definition of *gerrymander,* and a philosophy class may require a definition of *epistemology.* You will often be given assignments with instructions like "define and illustrate" or "define and explain the significance of." For example, in a finance class, you may need to define and explain the effects of *bear and bull markets;* in a literature class, you may be asked to define and illustrate *metaphysical conceit;* and in an anthropology class, you may be required to define and note the various kinds of *family.*

Outside the classroom, you will also encounter definition. A pamphlet put out by the National Rifle Association might define *gun control* to show its problems; *Seventeen* magazine might define *anorexia nervosa* to help teenagers recognize the causes and symptoms of the disorder; a church bulletin might offer a definition of *charity* to encourage parishioners be more charitable; a brochure at a natural history museum might define the various geologic ages to inform museum visitors; and a newspaper editorial might define *the good citizen* to move readers to behave more like one.

SELECTING DETAIL

An extended definition can include any of the patterns of development or combination of patterns discussed in this book. If you are defining *Christmas spirit,* you could *tell a story* that reveals what Christmas spirit is, or you could *compare and contrast* Christmas spirit with the feelings people get on other holidays in order to clarify the nature of the spirit. You could *provide a number of examples* to illustrate the nature of Christmas spirit, or you could *describe* how it makes people feel and what it makes people do. If you were defining *loyalty,* you might use *cause-and-effect analysis* to explain what causes loyalty and its effects. You could use *classification* to note the various kinds of loyalty, and you could use *process analysis* to explain the process whereby loyalty is created and built upon.

In addition to the patterns of development, you may at times want to include a *stipulative definition,* which restricts the parameters of your explanation. If a word has more than one meaning or if its meaning includes many aspects, a stipulative definition can narrow your scope by establishing the boundaries of your definition. For example, the term *pornography* means different things to different people.

To set the scope of your discussion of meaning, you can include a stipulative definition like this: "Pornography is any material in any medium that sexually arouses some people but creates a threat to the well-being of others."

Sometimes, you will want to explain what your subject is *not.* For example, if you are defining *freedom,* you may want to say that freedom is *not* doing anything you want, it is *not* a privilege, and it is *not* necessarily guaranteed to everyone. From here you could go on to explain what freedom *is.* This technique can be useful for making important distinctions or dispelling common misunderstandings.

ARRANGING DETAIL

Your thesis can indicate what you are defining and what point can be drawn from the definition. Such a thesis might be "Christmas spirit is not what it used to be" or "Christmas spirit is a natural high."

Each of your body paragraphs can present a characteristic of what you are describing, which can be noted in the topic sentence. For example, if you are defining *jealousy,* you could use topic sentences like these:

```
Jealousy is an all-consuming emotion.

Jealousy causes people to behave in hurtful ways.

Jealousy destroys friendships.
```

Your supporting detail for the paragraph can explain and clarify the characteristic noted in the topic sentence.

If your body paragraphs are developed with particular patterns of development, follow the organization principles that govern these techniques. Otherwise, a progressive arrangement is frequently effective, perhaps beginning and ending with your strongest points.

Interesting introductions can be crafted a variety of ways. You can explain what many people believe your subject means if you plan to show it means something else, or you can explain why it is important to arrive at a definition of your subject. Often an anecdote about your subject can pave the way for a definition of that subject. It can also be interesting to explain what your subject used to mean if your essay will go on to show how that meaning has changed. Usually, however, you should avoid including a dictionary definition in your introduction. Your reader will know, at least approximately, how your subject is defined in *Webster's,* so a formal definition will probably bore your audience.

If you are stuck for an approach to your conclusion, try elaborating on the significance of the definiton—the points to be drawn from it.

Annotated Student Essay

Reading the following extended definition and the accompanying marginal notes will help you better understand many of the points made in this chapter.

Parenthood: Don't Count on Sleeping until They Move Out

paragraph 1
The introduction—the author engages reader interest by explaining what she used to think the term *parents* meant. The thesis (the last

Before I had children, I thought I had a crystal clear understanding of the word "parents." Parents were those people who fed me, clothed me, put a roof over my head, and took me to the doctor when I was ill. They were not, however, people who should be inquiring into my personal life, worrying about the

1

sentence) notes the term means something different. The thesis includes what will be defined and the point to be drawn (the parent has the "world's most difficult job").

paragraph 2
The topic sentence (the first) notes the first characteristic of the thing being defined (the parent is a guesser). The rest of the paragraph is the supporting detail to develop the topic sentence. Note the use of questions to convey the sense of uncertainty and the hypothetical situations to illustrate situations requiring guessing.

paragraph 3
The topic sentence (the first) gives the next characteristic (vulnerability). The

choices I made as I grew into my teens and demanded more freedom. Most of all, they were insensitive people whose feelings could not be hurt by anything I said or did. Yes, I thought I knew all about parents—right up until the time my first child was born. That's when I discovered that my assumptions about parents were dead wrong. A parent, I've learned, is a person both blessed and cursed with the world's most difficult job.

First and foremost, a parent is a guesser. At best, the *2* guess is an educated one; at worst, it's a blind shot in the dark. An educated guess, for example, would be Mom's choice of the right toy for an eight-year-old boy's birthday gift, based on what every other eight-year-old boy in the neighborhood owns. Simple, right? The educated guess, however, can get scarier: Should a child be taken to the emergency room at midnight with an earache and a fever, or can treatment safely be delayed until morning? The sleepless parent, rocking the sleepless child through the night, makes and unmakes the decision. Yes, little Jen has had earaches before, and she's usually better by morning. But what if this time is different? What if she's worse? What if she loses her hearing? But it's rainy and miserable outside. What if taking her out makes her worse? What if she has to wait hours in the emergency room? What if . . . well, you get the picture. As if the educated guess isn't bad enough, though, a parent often must also be a guesser in the dark, blindly hoping that some of the guesses are the right ones. Was it right or wrong to ground the thirteen-year-old for lying? How about for screaming in her mother's face? And what's the appropriate curfew for a seventeen-year-old, anyway? How much freedom is too much? How much is too little? Is the parent encouraging rebellion and possibly dangerous behavior by being too strict or too permissive? The awful truth, of course, is seldom voiced: Parents are people who NEVER, EVER learn whether all those blind guesses were right or wrong, foolish or wise, helpful or damaging.

All of this guessing helps parents become sensitive souls, *3* exquisitely vulnerable to their offspring. The flinching probably starts with the first child's departure for kindergarten (or maybe even preschool) without a backward

supporting detail is examples. The last sentence gives another characteristic (silent sufferers) that is an effect.

glance at Mom and Dad, standing tearfully at the door. Then there's that terrible moment of truth when a child first realizes that parents aren't really gods, that they don't have all the answers, even on fourth-grade homework. What can hurt worse than the astonished look on a child's face that says, "You let me down, Mom" or "I always thought you knew everything, Dad"? I'll tell you what hurts worse: the teen-aged boy who finds his mother's mere presence a total embarrassment, the teen-aged girl who tells her father that he doesn't understand ANYTHING, or the five-year-old who screams "I hate you! I hate you!" Eventually, to avoid those painful scenes, many parents become silent sufferers, developing high blood pressure as well as a high tolerance for mental anguish.

paragraph 4
The last paragraph gives another characteristic in the first sentence ("anxious bargainers with God"), and the second-to-last sentence gives another characteristic ("grateful believers"). The last provides the closure.

Finally, as they lay exhausted in the dark at midnight, or *4* pace the floor at 3:00 A.M., many parents become anxious bargainers with God. If You just let her come home safely, God, I'll never swear at her again. If You'll just help him stop drinking, God, I promise I'll spend more time with him. Then, when the door cracks open and footsteps creak up the stairs, every parent—whatever the religious background—becomes a grateful believer. Thankfully, we whisper, "Someday, if there's a God, you'll have a kid *just like you*."

Pitfalls to Avoid

1. **Avoid stating the obvious.** For example, if you are defining *Christmas spirit* and you state that it is a mood that occurs at Christmastime, you run the risk of insulting your reader, who does not need to be reminded of such an obvious point.
2. **Avoid using the writing style found in dictionaries.** It lacks the vitality essential to a good essay. If you write that "Christmas spirit is that seasonal mood of ebullience and feeling of goodwill and generosity characteristic of and emanating from the yearly celebration of the birth of Jesus," you will not hold your reader's interest.
3. **Avoid using "according to *Webster's*."** Unless citing the dictionary definition serves an important purpose—perhaps as a contrast to the definition you plan to offer—there is no reason to cite *Webster's* or any other dictionary.
4. **Avoid circular definitions.** Circular definitions merely restate what is being defined without adding helpful information, so they contribute nothing.

circular: Freedom of speech is speech that is spoken freely.

better: Freedom of speech is the one constitutional guarantee without which no democracy can survive.

PROCESS GUIDELINES: WRITING DEFINITION

1. If you have trouble discovering a topic, try the following:
   a. Leaf through a dictionary and consider the entries. List words you might like to define and then choose one subject from this list.
   b. Consider your own experience. What moods or emotions have you known lately? Depression, anger, surprise, love—these can all be defined using narrations and illustrations from your own life. Also, think of people you have observed recently. Coaches, teachers, salespeople, doctors—these can be defined on the basis of your own observation.
2. If you have trouble generating ideas, try the following:
   a. Write a letter to someone with whom you are comfortable (see page 34), and begin this way: "I would like to explain what _____ means to me."
   b. Answer as many of these questions as are pertinent:
      • What does my subject look, smell, feel, and sound like?
      • How does my subject work?
      • What are some examples of my subject?
      • What is my subject like and different from?
      • What different types of my subject are there?
3. To determine your purpose, you can answer these questions:
   a. Do I want to clarify the nature of a familiar subject?
   b. Do I want my reader to become more aware of something taken for granted?
   c. Do I want my reader to better understand an unfamiliar subject?
   d. Do I want to give my reader a fresh outlook on my subject?
   e. Do I want to make a statement about an issue that goes beyond (but is related to) the subject defined?
   f. Do I want my reader to appreciate my subject more?
   g. Do I want to entertain my reader?
   h. Do I want to inform my reader?
   i. Do I want to persuade my reader?
4. To target a specific audience, you can answer the following questions:
   a. With whom would I like to share my view?
   b. Who would be influenced by my essay?
   c. Who sees my subject differently than I do?
   d. Who does not fully understand my subject?
   e. Who takes my subject for granted?
   f. Who would enjoy reading my definition?
5. If you like to secure reader response during revision, consult page 115. In addition, ask your reader to note any distinguishing characteristics of your subject that you neglected to mention. Also, ask your reader to write out the significance of your definition so that you can check to be sure this point is clear.

REVISION CHECKLIST

In addition to the checklist on page 117, you can use this checklist for revising your extended definition.

1. Does your definition do one of the following?
   a. Clarify a complex subject.
   b. Create appreciation for or a fresh awareness of something taken for granted.
   c. Inform about something not understood.
   d. Provide a new understanding of a familiar subject.
   e. Make a statement about an issue related to the subject defined.
2. If your definition includes other patterns of development, have you conformed to the conventions for handling those patterns?
3. Have you explained the distinguishing characteristics of your subject?
4. When appropriate, have you explained what your subject is *not?*
5. Have you avoided a dictionary-style definition, a circular definition, and statements of the obvious?
6. Is the significance of your definition clearly stated or strongly implied?

EXERCISE | **Writing Definition**

1. Select a concept (freedom, justice, good taste, sportsmanship, etc.), object (compact disc, microchip, etc.), person (a good teacher, a friend, etc.), or movement (environmentalism, feminism, etc.) to define.
2. What is the most distinguishing characteristic of the subject you selected for number 1? The second-most distinguishing characteristic? What patterns of development could you use to explain each of those characteristics in an essay?
3. Come up with three additional points you could make to help define your subject by answering any of the following questions that are pertinent:
   a. What story can I tell to help define my subject?
   b. What features of my subject can I describe?
   c. What examples would help define my subject?
   d. To what can I compare my subject? With what can I contrast it?
   e. What is my subject *not?*
4. Write out a thesis that includes your subject and a point that could be drawn from you definition.
5. *Collaborative Activity.* With two or three classmates read the following paragraph and evaluate how effective it would be as an introduction for an extended definition. Be prepared to cite reasons for your view.

   ```
   Although I feel that it is not extremely difficult for two
   people to begin establishing a relationship, maintaining that
   relationship may not be quite as easy. Undoubtedly, we all have
   ```

our faults and flaws, our marks of imperfection, and as two
people come to know more about one another, these flaws become
more and more evident. It is the degree of emphasis placed on
these flaws that determines whether or not a relationship
blossoms into a true friendship. If a person is truly your
friend, then even after he has come to know a lot about you, he
will still care very much for you. A true friend is fun to be
with, trustworthy, and reliable.

PROFESSIONAL ESSAYS

Spanglish Spoken Here

Janice Castro, with Dan Cook and Cristina Garcia

"Spanglish Spoken Here" first appeared in Time *magazine. The essay helps the reader
understand the growing effect Spanish is having on English by defining the hybrid dialect,
Spanglish.*

In Manhattan a first grader greets her visiting grandparents, happily exclaiming,   *1*
"Come here, *siéntate!*" Her bemused grandfather, who does not speak Spanish,
nevertheless knows she is asking him to sit down. A Miami personnel officer understands what a job applicant means when he says, "*Quiero un* part time." Nor
do drivers miss a beat reading a billboard alongside a Los Angeles street advertising CERVEZA—SIX-PACK!

This free-form blend of Spanish and English, known as Spanglish, is com-   *2*
mon linguistic currency wherever concentrations of Hispanic Americans are
found in the United States. In Los Angeles, where 55 percent of the city's three
million inhabitants speak Spanish, Spanglish is as much a part of daily life as
sunglasses. Unlike the broken-English efforts of earlier immigrants from Europe,
Asia, and other regions, Spanglish has become a widely accepted conversational
mode used casually—even playfully—by Spanish-speaking immigrants and na-
tive-born Americans alike.

Consisting of one part Hispanicized English, one part Americanized Span-   *3*
ish and more than a little fractured syntax, Spanglish is a bit like a Robin
Williams comedy routine: a crackling line of cross-cultural patter straight from
the melting pot. Often it enters Anglo homes and families through the children,
who pick it up at school or at play with their young Hispanic contemporaries. In
other cases, it comes from watching TV; many an Anglo child watching *Sesame
Street* has learned *uno dos tres* almost as quickly as one two three.

Spanglish takes a variety of forms, from the Southern California Anglos   *4*
who bid farewell with the utterly silly "*hasta la* bye-bye" to the Cuban-American
drivers in Miami who *parquean* their *carros*. Some Spanglish sentences are mostly
Spanish, with a quick detour for an English word or two. A Latino friend may
cut short a conversation by glancing at his watch and excusing himself with the
explanation that he must "*ir al* supermarket."

Many of the English words transplanted in this way are simply handier than   *5*
their Spanish counterparts. No matter how distasteful the subject, for example, it
is still easier to say "income tax" than *impuesto sobre la renta.* At the same time,
many Spanish-speaking immigrants have adopted such terms as VCR, mi-
crowave, and dishwasher for what they view as largely American phenomena.
Still other English words convey a cultural context that is not implicit in the
Spanish. A friend who invites you to *lonche* most likely has in mind the brisk
American custom of "doing lunch" rather than the languorous afternoon break
traditionally implied by *almuerzo.*

Mainstream Americans exposed to similar hybrids of German, Chinese, or   *6*
Hindi might be mystified. But even Anglos who speak little or no Spanish are
somewhat familiar with Spanglish. Living among them, for one thing, are 19 million Hispanics. In addition, more American high school and university students
sign up for Spanish than for any other foreign language.

Only in the past 10 years, though, has Spanglish begun to turn into a na-   *7*
tional slang. Its popularity has grown with the explosive increases in U.S. immigration from Latin American countries. English has increasingly collided with
Spanish in retail stores, offices, and classrooms, in pop music, and on street corners. Anglos whose ancestors picked up such Spanish words as *rancho, bronco,*
tornado, and *incommunicado,* for instance, now freely use such Spanish words as
gracias, bueno, amigo, and *por favor.*

Among Latinos, Spanglish conversations often flow easily from Spanish   *8*
into several sentences of English and back.

Spanglish is a sort of code for Latinos: The speakers know Spanish, but   *9*
their hybrid language reflects the American culture in which they live. Many lean
to shorter, clipped phrases in place of the longer, more graceful expressions their
parents used. Says Leonel de la Cuesta, an assistant professor of modern languages at Florida International University in Miami: "In the U.S., time is money,
and that is showing up in Spanglish as an economy of language." Conversational
examples: *taipiar* (type) and *winshi-wiper* (windshield wiper) replace *escribir a*
máquina and *limpiaparabrisas.*

Major advertisers, eager to tap the estimated $134 billion in spending   *10*
power wielded by Spanish-speaking Americans, have ventured into Spanglish to
promote their products. In some cases, attempts to sprinkle Spanish through
commercials have produced embarrassing gaffes. A Braniff airlines ad that
sought to tell Spanish-speaking audiences they could settle back *en* (in) luxuriant
cuero (leather) seats, for example, inadvertently said they could fly without
clothes *(encuero).* A fractured translation of the Miller Lite slogan told readers the
beer was "Filling, and less delicious." Similar blunders are often made by Anglos
trying to impress Spanish-speaking pals. But if Latinos are amused by mangled
Spanglish, they also recognize these goofs as a sort of friendly acceptance. As
they might put it, *no problema.*

Considering Ideas

1. Where do the authors indicate why an understanding of the definition is important? What is that importance?
2. "Spanglish Spoken Here" first appeared in *Time* magazine. How do the authors meet the needs of their readers? For what purpose do you think the authors wrote the essay?
3. In paragraph 3, the authors refer to the "melting pot" that the United States is often said to be. Explain the reference to the United States as a melting pot. Do you think the United States today is a melting pot? Why or why not?
4. Ten years from now, do you think Spanglish will still exist? Why or why not?

Considering Technique

1. Which sentence forms the thesis because it indicates what will be defined?
2. *Combining Patterns*. The authors use several patterns of development to create their definition. Cite an example of a paragraph that includes each of these patterns: illustration, comparison-contrast, and cause-and-effect analysis.
3. "Spanglish Spoken Here" is a lively essay, partly because of the specific yet simple diction. For example, the authors refer to Spanglish as "a crackling line of cross-cultural patter" (paragraph 3). Cite three other examples of specific, simple word choice.
4. What approach do the authors take to their conclusion?

For Group Discussion or Journal Writing

Discuss whether or not you enjoyed "Spanglish Spoken Here." Develop a list of reasons for why you did or did not like the essay.

Appetite

Laurie Lee

British author Laurie Lee has done it all. He has written poems, plays, children's books, scripts, travel books, and his autobiography. The following selection from one of his longer works says as much about anticipation as it does about appetite.

One of the major pleasures in life is appetite and one of our major duties should   *1*
be to preserve it. Appetite is the keenness of living; it is one of the senses that tells you that you are still curious to exist, that you still have an edge on your longings and want to bite into the world and taste its multitudinous flavours and juices.

By appetite, of course, I don't mean just the lust for food, but any condition   *2*
of unsatisfied desire, any burning in the blood that proves you want more than you've got, and that you haven't yet used up your life. Wilde said he felt sorry for

those who never got their heart's desire, but sorrier still for those who did. I got mine once only, and it nearly killed me, and I've always preferred wanting to having since.

For appetite, to me, is that state of wanting, which keeps one's expectations 3 alive. I remember learning this lesson long ago as a child, when treats and orgies were few, and when I discovered that the greatest pitch of happiness was not in actually eating a toffee but in gazing at it beforehand. True, the first bite was delicious, but once the toffee was gone one was left with nothing, neither toffee nor lust. Besides, the whole toffeeness of toffees was imperceptibly diminished by the gross act of having eaten it. No, the best was in wanting it, in sitting and looking at it, when one tasted an inexhaustible treasure-house of flavours.

So, for me, one of the keenest pleasures of appetite remains in the wanting, 4 not the satisfaction. In wanting a peach, or a whisky, or a particular texture or sound, or to be with a particular friend. For in this condition, of course, I know that the object of desire is always at its most flawlessly perfect. Which is why I would carry the preservation of appetite to the extent of deliberate fasting, simply because I think that appetite is too good to lose, too precious to be bludgeoned into insensibility by satiation and overdoing it.

For that matter, I don't really want three square meals a day—I want one 5 huge, delicious, orgiastic, table-groaning blow-out, say every four days, and then not be sure where the next one is coming from. A day of fasting is not for me just a puritanical device for denying oneself a pleasure, but rather a way of anticipating a rarer moment of supreme indulgence.

Fasting is an act of homage to the majesty of appetite. So I think we should 6 arrange to give up our pleasures regularly—our food, our friends, our lovers—in order to preserve their intensity, and the moment of coming back to them. For this is the moment that renews and refreshes both oneself and the thing one loves. Sailors and travellers enjoyed this once, and so did hunters, I suppose. Part of the weariness of modern life may be that we live too much on top of each other, and are entertained and fed too regularly. Once we were separated by hunger both from our food and families, and then we learned to value both. The men went off hunting, and the dogs went with them; the women and children waved goodbye. The cave was empty of men for days on end: nobody ate, or knew what to do. The women crouched by the fire, the wet smoke in their eyes; the children wailed; everybody was hungry. Then one night there were shouts and the barking of dogs from the hills, and the men came back loaded with meat. This was the great reunion, and everybody gorged themselves silly, and appetite came into its own; the long-awaited meal became a feast to remember and an almost sacred celebration of life. Now we go off to the office and come home in the evenings to cheap chicken and frozen peas. Very nice, but too much of it, too easy and regular, served up without effort or wanting. We eat, we are lucky, our faces are shining with fat, but we don't know the pleasure of being hungry any more.

Too much of anything—too much music, entertainment, happy snacks, or 7 time spent with one's friends, creates a kind of impotence of living by which one can no longer hear, or taste, or see, or love, or remember. Life is short and precious, and appetite is one of its guardians, and loss of appetite is a sort of death. So if we are to enjoy this short life we should respect the divinity of appetite, and keep it eager and not too much blunted.

It is a long time now since I knew that acute moment of bliss that comes   8
from putting parched lips to a cup of cold water. The springs are still there to be enjoyed—all one needs is the original thirst.

Considering Ideas

1. Why did [Oscar] Wilde feel sorry for people who "got their heart's desire" (paragraph 2)?
2. In a sentence or two, explain Lee's view of appetite and fasting. Do you agree with this view? Why or why not?
3. What do you judge to be the purpose of Lee's definition?
4. What is the significance of Lee's definition? Where is this significance presented?

Considering Techniques

1. *Combining Patterns.* In which paragraphs does the author use examples to illustrate the subject's distinguishing characteristics? Which elements of cause-and-effect analysis appear in the essay?
2. Where does Lee explain the importance of the topic?
3. Where does Lee explain what the subject is *not?*
4. What approach does Lee take to the conclusion?
5. You probably noticed and enjoyed Lee's diction and style. Cite two sentences that you particularly like and explain why you like them.

Combining Patterns of Development

About Men

Gretel Ehrlich

Gretel Ehrlich defines the cowboy to dispel the mistaken, stereotypical notion many of us have about what the cowboy is like. To increase our understanding, Ehrlich includes **cause-and-effect analysis** *with* **definition** *to explain why the cowboy acts as he does.*

When I'm in New York but feeling lonely for Wyoming I look for the Marlboro   1
ads in the subway. What I'm aching to see is horseflesh, the glint of a spur, a line of distant mountains, brimming creeks, and a reminder of the ranchers and cowboys I've ridden with for the last eight years. But the men I see in those posters with their stern, humorless looks remind me of no one I know here. In our hellbent earnestness to romanticize the cowboy we've ironically disesteemed his true character. If he's "strong and silent," it's because there's probably no one to talk

to. If he "rides away into the sunset," it's because he's been on horseback since four in the morning moving cattle and he's trying, 15 hours later, to get home to his family. If he's a "rugged individualist" he's also part of a team: Ranch work is teamwork and even the glorified open-range cowboys of the 1880s rode up and down the Chisholm Trail in the company of 20 or 30 other riders. Instead of the macho, trigger-happy man our culture has perversely wanted him to be, the cowboy is more apt to be convivial, quirky, and softhearted. To be "tough" on a ranch has nothing to do with conquests and displays of power. More often than not, circumstances—like the colt he's riding or an unexpected blizzard—are overpowering him. It's not toughness but "toughing it out" that counts. In other words, this macho, cultural artifact the cowboy has become is simply a man who possesses resilience, patience, and an instinct for survival. "Cowboys are just like a pile of rocks—everything happens to them. They get climbed on, kicked, rained and snowed on, scuffed up by wind. Their job is 'just to take it,' " one old-timer told me.

A cowboy is someone who loves his work. Since the hours are long—10 to 15 hours a day—and the pay is $30, he has to. What's required of him is an odd mixture of physical vigor and maternalism. His part of the beef-raising industry is to birth and nurture calves and take care of their mothers. For the most part his work is done on horseback and in a lifetime he sees and comes to know more animals than people. The iconic myth surrounding him is built on American notions of heroism: the index of a man's value as measured in physical courage. Such ideas have perverted manliness into a self-absorbed race for cheap thrills. In a rancher's world, courage has less to do with facing danger than with acting spontaneously—usually on behalf of an animal or another rider. If a cow is stuck in a boghole he throws a loop around her neck, takes his dally (a half hitch around the saddle horn), and pulls her out with horsepower. If a calf is born sick, he may take her home, warm her in front of the kitchen fire, and massage her legs until dawn. One friend, whose favorite horse was trying to swim a lake with hobbles on, dove under water and cut her legs loose with a knife, then swam her to shore, his arm around her neck lifeguard-style, and saved her from drowning. Because these incidents are usually linked to someone or something outside himself, the westerner's courage is selfless, a form of compassion. 2

The physical punishment that goes with cowboying is greatly underplayed. Once fear is dispensed with, the threshold of pain rises to meet the demands of the job. When Jane Fonda asked Robert Redford (in the film *Electric Horseman*) if he was sick as he struggled to his feet one morning, he replied, "No, just bent." For once the movies had it right. The cowboys I was sitting with laughed in agreement. Cowboys are rarely complainers; they show their stoicism by laughing at themselves. 3

If a rancher or cowboy has been thought of as a "man's man"—laconic, hard-drinking, inscrutable—there's almost no place in which the balancing act between male and female, manliness and femininity, can be more natural. If he's gruff, handsome, and physically fit on the outside, he's androgynous at the core. Ranchers are midwives, hunters, nurturers, providers, and conservationists all at once. What we've interpreted as toughness—weathered skin, calloused hands, a 4 squint in the eye and a growl in the voice—only masks the tenderness inside. "Now don't go telling me these lambs are cute," one rancher warned me the first day I walked into the football-field-sized lambing sheds. The next thing I knew he was holding a black lamb. "Ain't this little rat good-lookin'?"

So many of the men who came to the West were southerners—men looking for work and a new life after the Civil War—that chivalrousness and strict codes of honor were soon thought of as western traits. There were very few women in Wyoming during territorial days, so when they did arrive (some as mail-order brides from places like Philadelphia) there was a stand-offishness between sexes and a formality that persists now. Ranchers still tip their hats and say, "Howdy, ma'am" instead of shaking hands with me.

Even young cowboys are often evasive with women. It's not that they're Jekyll and Hyde creatures—gentle with animals and rough on women—but rather, that they don't know how to bring their tenderness into the house and lack the vocabulary to express the complexity of what they feel. Dancing wildly all night becomes a metaphor for the explosive emotions pent up inside, and when these are, on occasion, released, they're so battery-charged and potent that one caress of the face or one "I love you" will peal for a long while.

The geographical vastness and the social isolation here make emotional evolution seem impossible. Those contradictions of the heart between respectability, logic, and convention on the one hand, and impulse, passion, and intuition on the other, played out wordlessly against the paradisical beauty of the West, give cowboys a wide-eyed but drawn look. Their lips pucker up, not with kisses but with immutability. They may want to break out, staying up all night with a lover just to talk, but they don't know how and can't imagine what the consequences will be. Those rare occasions when they do bare themselves result in confusion, "I feel as if I'd sprained my heart," one friend told me a month after such a meeting.

My friend Ted Hoagland wrote, "No one is as fragile as a woman, but no one is as fragile as a man." For all the women here who use "fragileness" to avoid work or as a sexual ploy, there are men who try to hide theirs, all the while clinging to an adolescent dependency on women to cook their meals, wash their clothes, and keep the ranch house warm in winter. But there is true vulnerability in evidence here. Because these men work with animals, not machines or numbers, because they live outside in landscapes of torrential beauty, because they are confined to a place and a routine embellished with awesome variables, because calves die in the arms that pulled others into life, because they go to the mountains as if on a pilgrimage to find out what makes a herd of elk tick, their strength is also a softness, their toughness, a rare delicacy.

Considering Ideas

1. Why do you think Ehrlich considers it important to define the cowboy?
2. According to Ehrlich, what characteristics does the stereotypical cowboy possess?

3. Ehrlich mentions many characteristics of the real cowboy in her definition. Name five of them.
4. What do you think Ehrlich means in paragraph 1 when she refers to the stereotypical cowboy as a "cultural artifact"? What do you think she means in paragraph 4 when she calls the real cowboy "androgynous"?
5. Explain the significance of the title.

Considering Technique

1. In your own words, write out Ehrlich's thesis. Which sentence in the essay comes close to expressing the idea in your sentence?
2. Where does Ehrlich indicate what a cowboy is *not?* What does this element contribute to the essay?
3. *Combining Patterns.* Which paragraphs include illustrations? What do these illustrations contribute to the essay?
4. *Combining Patterns.* Much of the essay (paragraphs 5, 6, 7, and 8) is developed with cause-and-effect analysis. What information does the cause-and-effect analysis provide? Why do you think Ehrlich wants the reader to have that information?
5. Cite two examples of phrases or sentences that you find particularly appealing because of specific word choice.

For Group Discussion or Journal Writing

Ehrlich admires the cowboy, in part, because he is androgynous. That is, he possesses both male and female characteristics. Does our society encourage the development of androgynous males? Explain why or why not. Should we do more to encourage the development of androgynous males? Explain.

STUDENT ESSAYS TO READ AND EVALUATE

The extended definitions that follow were written by students. Each has strengths and weaknesses. As you study the essays, you will improve your ability to assess strengths and weaknesses so that you can better judge your own writing. You will also learn successful techniques to incorporate into your own work and unsuccessful techniques to avoid.

Tacky Hits Home

Because my own family is overrun with tackiness, I have become an   *1*
authority on the subject. There is no tackiness, regardless of how
subtle, that I cannot recognize and become instantly repulsed by.
First, tacky is Aunt Sonya in polyester pants. I find myself
cringing at the sight of her fat dimples poking through the tight,
scratchy material. Even worse, most of her pants are purchased in

an array of carnival colors that include blinding aqua, iridescent lime, and resonant red. Because these shades are so difficult to match, most of her shirts (which may look nice with other pants) also appear tacky because of the clashing colors.

Tacky is also Aunt Sonya's daughter Betsy wearing bulky sweat socks with dress shoes. The very thought of her cramming those thick socks into those delicate shoes irritates me. 2

Tackiness is not limited to the women in my family. Uncle Harold, Aunt Sonya's husband, tucks his pants into his cowboy boots. Those who have never heard of *GQ* may find this appealing, but I find it appalling. Then there is Uncle Sammy, who is stuck in a clothing time warp wearing his favorite sky-blue leisure suit. To compound the offense, he combines this relic with a flashy disco shirt and white fake leather shoes. 3

The most tacky male award goes to my Uncle Earl, who belongs to that intriguing breed of men who find it impossible to purchase clothing that fits properly. I lose my appetite when I see Uncle Earl hunched over the counter with his derriere protruding out over his jeans for all to see. As if that weren't bad enough, he insists on wearing his favorite tee shirts that have stupid sayings such as "six-pack attack" on the front of them. 4

In the field of home decorating, it is my Aunt Sue and Uncle Mort who win the tackiness-of-the-year award. In their front yard, they have these stupid Dutch kids kissing. They must have been at it a long time because the paint on their lips has peeled off. In the center of the back yard is a rusted swing set, with no swings attached. The inside of the house is even worse. Tacky is definitely Aunt Sue and Uncle Mort's kitchen: plastic mustard and ketchup bottles sit on the dinette, dried yellow and red goop clinging to the sides; the cat's litter box is in the corner, and that mangy feline roams the kitchen counters at will. 5

Although I grew up with tackiness, I am sure anyone can recognize it. Pink flamingos in the front yard, bowling trophies on the mantle, plastic daisies on the kitchen table, parents diapering babies in public, people smoking on elevators, teenagers singing out loud the songs they hear on their headphones—tackiness is everywhere. There really ought to be a law against bad taste. 6

What Is Writer's Block?

I have writer's block. For the last two days I have sat at this   *1*
table, staring at a blank piece of paper. My mother calls to ask
what I'm doing, and I say I'm writing. She asks me what, and I say
nothing, for I have writer's block. "Well, write something," she
replies. Something? Obviously, she does not understand writer's
block.

Writer's block is pacing. Up and down in front of the table   *2*
with pen in hand. Wearing a ragged trail in an otherwise OK carpet.
Pacing. Palms sweating. Knowing you have a deadline that is
creeping up on you like a fairy tale troll, following behind, and
steadily getting closer and closer with each tick of the clock.

Writer's block is trying. Sitting down ready and willing to   *3*
work. Picking up a freshly sharpened pencil and advancing on a
clean crisp piece of paper only to have a sense of emptiness come
over you. The pencil falters above the paper, and the words
stubbornly refuse to leave their hiding places in the recesses of
my mind. Now the sweaty hand forces the pencil down onto the paper.
Write something. Doodles. Lots and lots of doodles. Squiggly little
lines. Bold black circles. Delicate little spider webs. Angry dots!
Names . . . Julie . . . Mike . . . John . . . Jimmy. Why won't the
words come? What are they afraid of? Try, make those sweaty palms
produce. Deadlines.

Writer's block is doubting myself, being convinced I can't   *4*
write. It is waiting, waiting for the block to recede. It is
starting, stopping, starting over, stopping again.

Writer's block is anticipation. I know they will come, if I can *5*
just be patient a few more minutes. I can feel them; the words are
there. As soon as they're ready, they will come spilling out,
tumbling all over each other, mixing letters and vowels in their
rush to be heard. Then the pencil will have to restrain them and
take them one by one and put them in their proper order.

Until that time, I can only see a dam. I can feel the force of *6*
the words straining behind it. I can see them bouncing off the
tall, unyielding walls. Occasionally, one or two escape through the
overflow. Open those floodgates, and let them flow.

Collaborative Exercise: Evaluating Writing

Form a group and select one of the previous student essays. Take three sheets of paper; label one sheet *Introduction,* label one sheet *Body,* and label one sheet *Conclusion.* On the appropriate sheets record what you agree are the strengths and weaknesses of the essay. Also record an explanation for why each noted feature is strong or weak. You need not record *every* strength and weakness—just the major ones. If group members disagree, note this disagreement. You can refer to some or all of the evaluation questions that follow.

Evaluation Questions

1. *The Thesis*
   What is the thesis? Is it a clear indication of what is being defined?
2. *The Introduction*
   Does the introduction engage your interest? Why or why not?
3. *Supporting Details*
   Note any points you do not understand, any points that are not relevant, and any points that need more development. Has the author avoided a dictionary style, circular definition, and statements of the obvious? Is the reason for the definition clear?
4. *Organization*
   Are all the details in a logical order? Evaluate the use of transitions and topic sentences.
5. *The Conclusion*
   Does the essay come to a satisfying end? Explain.
6. *Overview*
   What do you like best about the essay? What is the single most important revision the author should make?

Essay Topics: Definition

When you write your essay, consult Pitfalls to Avoid on page 293, Process Guidelines on page 294, and the Revision Checklist on page 295.

Writing in the Pattern

1. Write a definition of a stereotype (of lawyers, doctors, teachers, fathers, teenagers, etc.) depicted on television or in a magazine advertisement.
2. Define one of the following:

male chauvinism	frustration	excitement
feminism	anticipation	dread
maturity	adolescence	success
patriotism	satisfaction	greed
bureaucrat	hero	inner strength
Christmas spirit	hospitality	cynicism
sportsmanship	jealousy	runner's high

3. Define *superhero* (Wonder Woman, Superman, Batman, John Wayne, Spiderman, etc.).
4. Define the nature of a successful (popular, not necessarily good) television show.
5. Define an ethnic term (*chutzpah, gringo,* etc.).

Reading Then Writing in the Pattern

1. In "About Men" (page 300), Louise Ehrlich defines the cowboy. Write a definition that reflects the cowboy stereotype depicted on television and in the movies.
2. Like Ehrlich, write a definition to correct the stereotype of some group: athletes, blondes, police officers, "brains," housewives, teenagers, single parents, and so forth. Also like Ehrlich, present both the stereotype and the correct version.
3. In paragraph 4 of "Appetite" (page 298), Laurie Lee says that "one of the keenest pleasures of appetite remains in the wanting, not the satisfaction." Write a definition of *satisfaction.*
4. Using "What Is Writer's Block?" (page 305) for a guide, write an essay with the title "What Is Inspiration?"

Responding to the Readings

1. The authors of "Spanglish Spoken Here" (page 296) consider the influence of Spanish on English. Explain other influences of Spanish culture on American culture.
2. In "Appetite" (page 298), Laurie Lee argues that anticipation is better than satisfaction. Write an essay arguing that the opposite is true.
3. Summarize what "About Men" (page 300) says about the relationship between men and women and go on to explain whether this commentary reflects positively or negatively on the ways the genders interact.
4. *Connecting the Readings.* Using the ideas in "About Men" and "The Myth of the Latin Woman: I Just Met a Girl Named Maria" (page 199) along with your own experience and observation, write an essay that considers the effects of stereotyping people.

Classification

Life is so filled with facts and figures, people, places, and things, aspects, devices, stimuli, and information that, without some way to order the myriad elements, chaos would ensue. **Classification** provides that ordering mechanism. It is a way of ordering items and information by grouping things according to their characteristics.

Without classification, life would be enormously difficult. Imagine a library without a classification system. If you wanted to read a mystery, you would have to scan the shelves until you got lucky and ran across an appropriate book. Fortunately, libraries have classification systems that allow you to go quickly to the area where all the mysteries are shelved. Shopping, too, would be daunting. Imagine taking your list to a grocery store that shelved items randomly, instead of grouping canned goods together, produce together, dairy products together, and so forth. Or imagine trying to find a business phone number in the yellow pages of a phone book that did not group numbers by type of business.

ESTABLISHING YOUR PURPOSE AND IDENTIFYING YOUR AUDIENCE

People often classify because ordering information *makes for easier study*. In biology, for example, grouping animals into classifications such as mammals, birds, reptiles, and amphibians allows scientists to study animal life more efficiently. You, too, may classify in order to facilitate the examination of information or items. For example, if you wanted to determine the best bicycle to buy, you could classify the available models (racing, touring, dirt bikes, etc.) according to their chief characteristics (price, frame design, tire size, etc.) to make a careful study of their chief features.

Classification is also a way to *clarify similarities and differences*. For example, if you classified diet programs, you would discover how these programs are similar and different. Such information could help you decide which program is the best for you. In addition, such a classification could point out which features are shared by successful programs. Knowing this information can help you predict the chances of success for any program you encounter.

Classification can also *bring the reader to a fresh way of viewing something.* For example, television programs are usually classified as dramas, situation comedies, game shows, soap operas, variety shows, and so forth. However, an essay that classifies programs according to how they portray women can lead to a greater awareness of how television influences our perception of women.

Classification can also help readers understand something with which they may not be familiar. For example, you could classify Eastern religions to *inform* a reader who knows little about Eastern beliefs.

Classification can also *persuade.* For example, to persuade the reader that telephone solicitors should be treated with more respect, you could classify them according to why they take the job. One group could include those who are unprepared for other work (high school dropouts, the unskilled, those with low intelligence, etc.); one group could include those who are housebound (mothers who have no one to care for their children, those with no transportation, etc.); another group could include those who are physically unable to perform other work (the disabled, the elderly, etc.).

Additionally, you can use classification to *express feelings and relate experiences,* as when you classify your childhood birthday celebrations to tell about your youth. Or you can use classification to *entertain,* as Russell Baker does in the funny essay "The Plot against People" on page 318.

You will want to consider your audience as carefully as your purpose because your reader will affect detail selection. Say you are classifying home computers. If your reader knows little about computers, you may have to define terms like *byte.* Similarly, how extensively you use examples may depend on your reader. For instance, if you are classifying video games for a parent who has never played them, you may need to give many examples of each type; however, if your reader is a teenager who plays the games often and is knowledgeable about them, fewer examples will be called for.

COMBINING CLASSIFICATION WITH OTHER PATTERNS

When you classify, you set up categories and note the items in those categories. Often you explain the characteristics of the elements in the categories, and to do so you may rely heavily on various patterns of development. Assume, for example, that you are writing a humorous classification of baby sitters. You could *describe* the appearance of the slovenly teenage sitter, *narrate* an account of the time the cleanliness nut washed the children *and* the walls, and *illustrate* the inattentive sitter with the example of the sitter who talked on the phone while the child wandered through the neighborhood. You could also explain nervous sitters with a *process analysis* of the elaborate procedure they go through to feed the child to guard against choking, *compare* the elderly sitter to a doting grandparent, and *define* the perfect sitter.

Classification can also be included in essays with other dominant patterns of development. An essay explaining the effects of social stratification might first classify socioeconomic categories people fall into; an essay noting the causes of cheating among college students could begin with a classification of kinds of cheating; and an essay that explains how employers can effectively communicate with employees might include a classification of the ways these two groups talk to each other. For an example of an essay that combines classification with definition and cause-and-effect analysis, see "The Ways of Meeting Oppression" on page 325.

USING CLASSIFICATION BEYOND THE WRITING CLASS

To demonstrate your comprehension of material, you are likely to use classification in your writing for a variety of classes. A film course might require you to classify kinds of horror movies, a speech course might require you to classify persuasive strategies, a communications course might require you to classify types of political rhetoric, and an education class might require you to classify methods of classroom management. All of these classifications would allow you to show that you have grasped important material.

Sometimes you will be asked to classify and then evaluate which category is the best. For example, a labor relations class may require you to classify methods of collective bargaining and evaluate which is the least confrontational; a sports physiology class might ask you to classify kinds of aerobic exercise and evaluate which are the most efficient and least harmful to joints.

Outside of the classroom, you will encounter classification all the time. On the job, you may list all the tasks you must perform in the near future and then classify them according to importance or level of difficulty. When you arrange your books on your shelves, you might do so according to category, placing books in your major together, books you plan to sell together, novels together, and so forth. The yellow pages section of your phone book groups businesses by type; libraries shelve books according to subject; your college catalog explains degree requirements according to school and major; *TV Guide* lists programs according to the day of the week and time of day; classified ads list job vacancies under headings such as *secretarial, sales,* and *medical;* and textbooks arrange information according to topics.

SELECTING DETAIL

To be meaningful, a classification must group elements according to some principle. This principle provides the logic for the classification. Consider, for example, a classification of teachers. One group could be those who lecture, one group could be those who use a question-and-answer format, and one group could be those who guide student discussion. The *principle of classification* in this case is instructional methods.

Of course, most elements can be classified according to more than one principle. Teachers, for example, could also be classified according to degree of interest in students, levels of formality, testing techniques, amount of skill, and so forth. The principle of classification used, in large measure, depends on your audience and your purpose. For example, if your audience is teachers, it would be silly to classify according to testing techniques because teachers are already aware of these techniques. However, if you believe teachers are not sufficiently aware of how levels of formality affect students, you might classify this way. Your purpose could be informational (to let teachers know how students are affected by varying degrees of formality; or your purpose could be persuasive (to persuade teachers to be more informal because informality engages student interest).

When you classify, place elements in groups according to your principle of classification. Your supporting detail can indicate what the groups are, what elements are in each group, and what the characteristics of the elements are. Assume, for example, that you are classifying aerobics classes according to the amount of impact they have on the joints. Your supporting detail would note your categories (perhaps high impact, moderate impact, and low impact). Your detail would also note which classes (perhaps dance aerobics, step aerobics, and walk aerobics) fall into each category. Finally, your detail would describe the relevant aspects of the classes in each category (perhaps kind of movements, speed of movements, number of repetitions). In other words, your detail will arrange items in groups and explain what the elements in the group are like.

Do not feel you must develop each grouping in equal detail, for some groupings may need more explanation than others. As long as all groupings are explained *adequately,* they need not be explained *equally.*

ARRANGING DETAIL

The introduction of a classification can be handled a number of ways. You can, for example, explain the value of the classification. If you are classifying movies recently released on videocassettes and your audience consists of parents, you can explain that the classification is important because it helps parents choose suitable movies for their youngsters. Your introduction can also explain why you are capable of making the classification. Thus, if you are classifying cookbooks, you can explain that you have been a cookbook collector and gourmet cook for many years. This approach gives your classification credibility because you establish yourself as knowledgeable. Another approach is to explain how you discovered the classification. If you are classifying baseball coaches, you can note that you arrived at your classification after years of observing your children's coaches.

A suitable thesis can be shaped by stating what you are grouping and your principle of classification. Here are two examples:

Commercial weight-loss programs can be distinguished by the kind of positive and negative reinforcement they provide. (This thesis states that commercial weight-loss programs will be grouped; the principle of classification is the positive and negative reinforcement provided.)

Some students classify teachers according to whether they are hard or easy, but a better way to classify them is according to their teaching techniques. (This thesis notes that teachers will be classified; the principle of classification is teaching techniques.)

Another way to shape a thesis is to state your topic and provide words that indicate you will classify (without mentioning the principle of classification). Here is an example:

> After working as a waitress for five years, I have concluded that four kinds of people eat out regularly. (Here, the topic is people who eat out regularly; the words *four kinds* indicate that classification will occur.)

Another approach is to state your groupings in your thesis:

> White lies can be harmless, embarrassing, or hurtful.

In your body paragraphs, topic sentences can introduce each grouping as it is presented. For example, the following topic sentences could appear in a classification of white lies:

> Most white lies are harmless.
> At times, white lies prove embarrassing to the teller.
> Unfortunately, a small percentage of white lies are hurtful.

After the topic sentence that presents the grouping, you can provide the supporting details that give the characteristics of the elements in the group.

At times, you can arrange your groups in a progressive order. For example, in the classification of white lies, the groupings can be arranged according to how serious the consequences of the lies are. You can discuss the harmless lies first, then the embarrassing lies, then the hurtful ones.

Sometimes you can arrange groups in chronological order. For example, if you are classifying ways to discipline children, you can do so according to the age of the child.

Many times you can present your groupings in a random order because no organizational pattern is apparent or called for. However, if you discuss the same characteristics for each grouping, use the same order each time. For example, if you classify salespeople and discuss personality, technique, and willingness to help for each group, present these aspects in the same order each time.

Annotated Student Essay

Reading the following classification, written by a student, along with the marginal notes, will help you better understand the points made in this chapter.

Grocery Shoppers

paragraph 1
The introduction engages interest with background information and gives the author's qualifications (she has shopped for over 30 years).
The thesis (last sentence) gives

While entering Giant Eagle to do my usual Saturday grocery *1*
shopping, I found myself behind a trim young woman with
three children in tow, their ages approximately one,
three, and five. Although I have been shopping for

the topic (grocery shoppers) and words indicating classification will occur ("fall into several basic categories").

paragraph 2
Topic sentence (the first) notes the first category (The Mother). Supporting detail (the characteristics of the category) is a narrative example. Note the specific detail and word choice.

groceries for well over 30 years, it was only then that I realized that grocery shoppers fall into several basic categories.

The woman I entered behind fit perfectly into the category I call "The Mother." Technically, a mother can be any woman shopping with a child. However, shopping with only one kid presents no substantial challenge, so "The Mother" must be accompanied by at least two children. "The Mother" I entered behind illustrated that women in this category have two organizational problems. The first is where to find space in the cart to pile the groceries. In the case of "The Mother" I entered behind, child #1, the eldest, was instructed to sit on the bottom shelf of the grocery cart, while #2 child sat in the carriage, and #3 child, the youngest, in the child seat. This arrangement temporarily controlled the number-two problem: how to restrain the six extra hands she had brought along. It was not long, however, before #2 child became buried in Pampers, tissues, and cereal boxes. Child #2 was then transferred to the bottom shelf, freeing #1 to walk and help Mommy. "See, Mommy, I can count the eggs," piped a little voice. "Cleanup in aisle seven," sounded the P.A. system. Such announcements are a sure indicator that "The Mother" is in the store. The bottom shelf of a shopping cart is not without hazard for the child riding thereupon. That day, "The Mother," mumbling to herself something about not forgetting the laundry detergent, abruptly turned left at the end of an aisle, while child #2, anticipating another pass through the cereal section, inclined right. Cries of pain and surprise rang out (another sure indicator that "The Mother" is in the store), as child #2's head unceremoniously clunked to the floor. "The Mother" administered loving kisses and murmured assurances that "Yes, we will go find the Crispy Mermaid Cereal right now." During this disturbance, the youngest child remained calm and occupied by carefully peeling the little red price stickers from the grocery items within her reach.

2

paragraph 3
Discussion of first category
continues. The topic sentence
(the first) notes the focus on
solving the problem of hungry
kids. The supporting detail is
narration.

Seeing all the food in the store typically makes the children hungry, so "The Mother" I was observing solved the problem as many of her kind do. A stop at the delicatessen for packages of bologna and cheese, and another at the produce department for apples and grapes, and lunch was served. A box of vanilla wafers, its top unceremoniously ripped open, became dessert. With six little hands busy feeding three little mouths, "The Mother" now hurried to finish the rest of her shopping.

3

paragraph 4
The topic sentence (the first)
notes the second category
(Mother's Helper). Notice the
transition ("another
category"). Supporting detail
explains the chief
characteristics of the items in
the category. Notice the
specific word choice.

Another category of shopper is the "Mother's Helper." "Mothers' Helpers" are pre-teens sent to the store by their mothers for some urgently needed item. An unusual phenomenon happens when "Mothers' Helpers" enter a grocery store—they suddenly become avid readers! Cereal boxes are removed from the shelves and are read front and back. After scrutinizing the candy-bar labels (as well as smelling and palpitating the contents), the "Mothers' Helpers" usually find time to read the comic books and muscle magazines. Of course, the final stop before making their purchase is the video department, where they avidly review any new titles and some of their old favorites as well. You probably have seen "Mothers' Helpers" on their way home—pedaling slowly with hands, not on the handlebars, but carefully clutching the urgently needed item for Mom.

4

paragraph 5
The topic sentence (the first)
notes the third category (Ms.
Organization). Notice that the
sentence begins with a
transition. Supporting detail to
give characteristics is
description. Notice that the
classification's principle of
organization is the behavior of
shoppers. The writer's purpose
is to entertain.

Another frequently seen shopper is "Ms. Organization." "Ms. Organization" is identifiable by the coupon box (usually the size of a small fishing tackle box) in the childseat of the grocery cart, her 32-function solar calculator, her pencil chiseled to a lethal point, and her detailed grocery list with items arranged in the order of aisles in the store. The list, I am sure, was compiled while consulting the recipe cards for next week's menus. Methodically, "Ms. Organization" moves up and down each aisle, scanning prices, matching items to coupons, recording each purchase on her calculator, then canceling the item from her list with a neat, impeccably straight line. Never get behind "Ms. Organization" at the checkout because she never lets the clerk ring anything up until

5

everything is out of the cart. Then she monitors the ringing up of each item and finds a reason to demand a price check. Even worse, she is known to demand a recheck of an entire register tape, so out comes every item from the bags, and out comes the "Use Next Lane" sign. On the way out of the store, "Ms. Organization" can be seen clutching her purse while giving instructions in economics to the boy helping her take her groceries to the car.

paragraph 6
The topic sentence (the first) presents the next category (Hapless Husbands). Supporting detail notes the chief characteristics (by contrasting Hapless Husbands with Ms. Organization) and includes description.

At the other end of the spectrum from "Ms. Organization" is the "Hapless Husband," a male who has been coerced into grocery shopping. Far from organized, he walks erratically up and down the aisles, head and eyes inclined upward to read each aisle's contents. His disorganized list, often scrawled on the back of an envelope, is so illegible that he must often guess whether he is to buy Frosted Flakes or french fries. Unlike "Ms. Organization," he has no clue how the store is set up, so he is frequently seen doubling back, repeatedly pushing the cart up and down the same aisle, and stopping other shoppers to ask where the toilet paper or some other item is. When he does manage to find what he needs, "Hapless Husband" grabs it with no regard for price and, with great relief, tosses it into the cart. Once he makes it to the checkout, he pays no attention to the prices being punched into the register, pays whatever the clerk tells him to, and leaves the store dazed and confused. While you do *not* want to get behind "Ms. Organization," you *do* want to be behind "Hapless Husband" because he never challenges anything at the checkout.

paragraph 7
The conclusion provides closure by giving the significance of the classification—the types are part of us all.

In truth, there is a little bit of each kind of shopper in all of us. At times, each of us can be as frazzled as "The Mother," as easily distracted as the "Mother's Helper," as efficient as "Ms. Organization," or as confused as the "Hapless Husband," which makes all shoppers fall into the largest category of all—"The Human Being."

Pitfalls to Avoid

1. **Avoid classifications that are not useful to your audience.** Say, for example, that you are classifying movies recently released on videocassette. Obviously, this can be done several ways: according to genre (comedy, drama, science fiction, etc.), according to critical response, according to rating (G, PG, PG-13, R, NC-17), according to theme, and so forth. However, if your audience consists of parents trying to decide which movies are suitable for five- to eight-year-olds, some of these classifications are not useful. One useful way to classify would be according to the amount of violence in the movies and the nature of that violence.

2. **Avoid having only two groupings in your classification.** If you have only two groupings, you are probably writing a comparison-contrast essay.

3. **Avoid omitting groupings or your classification will be incomplete.** If you are classifying ways freshmen can make friends, you do not want to omit "join an interesting club," or you will leave out an important category. If necessary, narrow the scope of your classification so you can include all the groupings. For example, rather than classify kinds of employment available to liberal arts majors, classify kinds of employment in the nonprofit sector for liberal arts majors.

4. **Avoid groupings incompatible with your principle of classification.** If you are classifying teachers according to their teaching style, you would not include categories for male and female teachers because gender is not necessarily related to teaching style.

PROCESS GUIDELINES: WRITING CLASSIFICATION

1. If you need help with idea generation, try the following:
   a. Write each element that can be grouped on a separate index card. On the back of each card list all the characteristics of the element.
   b. To discover a principle of classification, study the characteristics on the back of the index cards, and then make a list of every possible principle classification.
   c. Once you have your principle, select the index cards with the elements that will appear in your classification. You are not likely to use every card, every element, and every characteristic.

2. If you need help with organization, try the following:
   a. Place the index cards in piles to correspond to the groupings in your classification.
   b. As an alternative, make columns on a sheet of paper, one column for each grouping. Label each grouping at the top of its column and list the elements of each group in the appropriate column. Also list the characteristics of the elements in the group.
   c. As another alternative, construct a formal outline. Because outlines are themselves forms of classification, they can be particularly helpful in planning a classification essay.

3. To determine your purpose, you can ask yourself these questions:
   a. Do I want to clarify by showing how elements are alike and different?
   b. Do I want to bring the reader to a fresh way of viewing something?
   c. Do I want to persuade the reader to think or act a particular way?
   d. Do I want to entertain the reader?
   e. Do I want to relate my experience or express my feelings?
4. To determine your audience, you can ask these questions:
   a. Who could learn something from my classification?
   b. Who could be brought to a fresh appreciation of what I am classifying?
   c. Who could be persuaded to think or act a particular way?
   d. Who would enjoy reading my classification?
5. You can establish the nature of your audience with these questions:
   a. How much does my reader know about the elements I am classifying?
   b. What strong feelings does my reader have?
   c. How much interest does my reader have in what I am classifying?
   d. What information does my reader need in order to appreciate and accept my classification?
6. If you like to secure reader response during revision, consult page 115. In addition, ask your reader to write out your principle of classification and the significance of the classification to be sure these points are clear.

REVISION CHECKLIST

In addition to the checklist on page 117, you can use this checklist when you revise your classification.

1. Does your classification group elements according to some principle?
2. Does your classification serve one of these purposes?
   a. Order information to make for easier study.
   b. Clarify by identifying how elements are alike and different.
   c. Bring the reader to a fresh way of viewing something.
   d. Persuade the reader to think or act a particular way.
   e. Entertain the reader, relate experience, or express feelings.
3. Does your thesis do one of the following?
   a. State what is being grouped and the principle of classification.
   b. State the topic and include words that indicate that classification will occur.
   c. State what the groupings are.
4. Have you presented the groupings in topic sentences?
5. If the same characteristics are discussed for each grouping, are they arranged in parallel order?
6. Is the value of the classification clear? Do you have at least two groupings?
7. Have you included all categories, and are all categories compatible with your principle of classification?

EXERCISE | **Writing Classification**

1. For one 24-hour period, list every classification that you encounter.
2. *Collaborative Activity.* List as many principles of classification as you can for an essay that classifies restaurants.
3. Identify a principle of classification for each of these subjects: friends, teachers, students.
4. Write a thesis for each subject and principle of classification from number 3. Each thesis should include words that indicate you will classify or words that present the principle of classification.
5. Note the categories that could appear in an essay using one of the thesis statements from number 4.
6. Pick one of the categories identified in number 5 and list the elements in that category.
7. What patterns of development could you use to help explain the elements noted in number 6?

PROFESSIONAL ESSAYS

The Plot against People

Russell Baker

Newspaper columnist Russell Baker won the Pulitzer Prize in 1979 for distinguished commentary. "The Plot against People" is an entertaining classification that achieves its humor through a mock scientific tone.

Inanimate objects are classified scientifically into three major categories—those 1 that break down, those that get lost, and those that don't work.

The goal of all inanimate objects is to resist man and ultimately to defeat 2 him, and the three major classifications are based on the method each object uses to achieve its purpose. As a general rule, any object capable of breaking down at the moment when it is most needed will do so. The automobile is typical of the category.

With the cunning peculiar to its breed, the automobile never breaks down 3 while entering a filling station which has a large staff of idle mechanics. It waits until it reaches a downtown intersection in the middle of the rush hour, or until it is fully loaded with family and luggage on the Ohio Turnpike. Thus it creates maximum inconvenience, frustration, and irritability, thereby reducing its owner's lifespan.

Washing machines, garbage disposals, lawn mowers, furnaces, TV sets, tape 4 recorders, slide projectors—all are in league with the automobile to take their turn at breaking down whenever life threatens to flow smoothly for their enemies.

Many inanimate objects, of course, find it extremely difficult to break 5 down. Pliers, for example, and gloves and keys are almost totally incapable of breaking down. Therefore, they have had to evolve a different technique for resisting man.

They get lost. Science has still not solved the mystery of how they do it, and *6* no man has ever caught one of them in the act. The most plausible theory is that they have developed a secret method of locomotion which they are able to conceal from human eyes.

It is not uncommon for a pair of pliers to climb all the way from the cellar *7* to the attic in its single-minded determination to raise its owner's blood pressure. Keys have been known to burrow three feet under mattresses. Women's purses, despite their great weight, frequently travel through six or seven rooms to find hiding space under a couch.

Scientists have been struck by the fact that things that break down virtually *8* never get lost, while things that get lost hardly ever break down. A furnace, for example, will invariably break down at the depth of the first winter cold wave, but it will never get lost. A woman's purse hardly ever breaks down; it almost invariably chooses to get lost.

Some persons believe this constitutes evidence that inanimate objects are *9* not entirely hostile to man. After all, they point out, a furnace could infuriate a man even more thoroughly by getting lost than by breaking down, just as a glove could upset him far more by breaking down than by getting lost.

Not everyone agrees, however, that this indicates a conciliatory attitude. *10* Many say it merely proves that furnaces, gloves, and pliers are incredibly stupid.

The third class of objects—those that don't work—is the most curious of *11* all. These include such objects as barometers, car clocks, cigarette lighters, flashlights, and toy-train locomotives. It is inaccurate, of course, to say that they *never* work. They work once, usually for the first few hours after being brought home, and then quit. Thereafter, they never work again.

In fact, it is widely assumed that they are built for the purpose of not working. Some people have reached advanced ages without ever seeing some of these objects—barometers, for example—in working order.

Science is utterly baffled by the entire category. There are many theories *13* about it. The most interesting holds that the things that don't work have attained the highest state possible for an inanimate object, the state to which things that break down and things that get lost can still only aspire.

They have truly defeated man by conditioning him never to expect anything of them. When his cigarette lighter won't light or his flashlight fails to illuminate, it does not raise his blood pressure. Objects that don't work have given man the only peace he receives from inanimate society.

Considering Ideas

1. Why does Baker say that inanimate objects are classified scientifically (paragraph 1) when the reader knows this is not really the case?
2. When does Baker say that an inanimate object is most likely to break? What do you think his view is of inanimate objects?

3. For what purpose does Baker make his classification? Who is his intended audience?
4. Although much of Baker's essay cannot be taken seriously, it does point to a basic truth. What is that truth?

Considering Technique

1. Write out Baker's thesis, underline the words that indicate what will be classified, and bracket the words that indicate the groupings.
2. The first topic sentence is in an unusual place. Where is that topic sentence? Would you recommend a different placement for the topic sentence? Explain. What topic sentence introduces the second grouping? The third grouping?
3. What is Baker's principle of classification? In what order does he arrange his groupings?
4. For what purpose does Baker use illustration?
5. What techniques contribute to the humor of the classification?

For Group Discussion or Journal Writing

Explain the significance of the title of Baker's essay and why you think he used that title. Then compose an alternate title and explain whether or not you like it as well as Baker's and why.

The Truth about Lying

Judith Viorst

Judith Viorst is a poet and essayist. "The Truth about Lying" originally appeared in Redbook. *In the essay, which classifies lies, Viorst examines her position on lying and asks the reader to do the same.*

I've been wanting to write on a subject that intrigues and challenges me: the subject of lying. I've found it very difficult to do. Everyone I've talked to has a quite intense and personal but often rather intolerant point of view about what we can—and can never, *never*—tell lies about. I've finally reached the conclusion that I can't present any ultimate conclusions, for too many people would promptly disagree. Instead, I'd like to present a series of moral puzzles, all concerned with lying. I'll tell you what I think about them. Do you agree?   1

Social Lies

Most of the people I've talked with say that they find social lying acceptable and necessary. They think it's the civilized way for folks to behave. Without these little white lies, they say, our relationships would be short and brutish and nasty. It's arrogant, they say, to insist on being so incorruptible and so brave that you cause other people unnecessary embarrassment or pain by compulsively assailing them with your honesty. I basically agree. What about you?   2

Will you say to people, when it simply isn't true, "I like your new hairdo," *3*
"You're looking much better," " It's so nice to see you," "I had a wonderful time"?

Will you praise hideous presents and homely kids? *4*

Will you decline invitations with "We're busy that night—so sorry we can't *5* come," when the truth is you'd rather stay home than dine with the So-and-sos?

And even though, as I do, you may prefer the polite evasion of "You really *6* cooked up a storm" instead of "The soup"—which tastes like warmed-over coffee—"is wonderful," will you, if you must, proclaim it wonderful?

There's one man I know who absolutely refuses to tell social lies. "I can't *7* play that game," he says; "I'm simply not made that way." And his answer to the argument that saying nice things to someone doesn't cost anything is, "Yes, it does—it destroys your credibility." Now, he won't, unsolicited, offer his views on the painting you just bought, but you don't ask his frank opinion unless you want *frank,* and his silence at those moments when the rest of us liars are muttering, "Isn't it lovely?" is, for the most part, eloquent enough. My friend does not indulge in what calls "flattery, false praise, and mellifluous comments." When others tell fibs he will not go along. He says that social lying is lying, that little white lies are still lies. And he feels that telling lies is morally wrong. What about you?

Peace-Keeping Lies

Many people tell peace-keeping lies; lies designed to avoid irritation or argument; *8* lies designed to shelter the liar from possible blame or pain; lies (or so it is rationalized) designed to keep trouble at bay without hurting anyone.

I tell these lies at times, and yet I always feel they're wrong. I understand *9* why we tell them, but still they feel wrong. And whenever I lie so that someone won't disapprove of me or think less of me or holler at me, I feel I'm a bit of a coward, I feel I'm dodging responsibility, I feel . . . guilty. What about you?

Do you, when you're late for a date because you overslept, say that you're *10* late because you got caught in a traffic jam?

Do you, when you forget to call a friend, say that you called several times *11* but the line was busy?

Do you, when you didn't remember that it was your father's birthday, say *12* that his present must be delayed in the mail?

And when you're planning a weekend in New York City and you're not in *13* the mood to visit your mother, who lives there, do you conceal—with a lie, if you must—the fact that you'll be in New York? Or do you have the courage—or is it the cruelty?—to say, "I'll be in New York, but sorry—I don't plan on seeing you"?

(Dave and his wife Elaine have two quite different points of view on this *14* very subject. He calls her a coward. She says she's being wise. He says she must assert her right to visit New York sometimes and not see her mother. To which she always patiently replies: "Why should we have useless fights? My mother's too old to change. We get along much better when I lie to her.")

Finally, do you keep the peace by telling your husband lies on the subject of *15* money? Do you reduce what you really paid for your shoes? And in general do you find yourself ready, willing, and able to lie to him when you make absurd mistakes or lose or break things?

"I used to have a romantic idea that part of intimacy was confessing every *16* dumb thing that you did to your husband. But after a couple of years of that," says Laura, "have I changed my mind!"

And having changed her mind, she finds herself telling peace-keeping lies. *17* And yes, I tell them too. What about you?

Protective Lies

Protective lies are lies folks tell—often quite serious lies—because they're con- *18* vinced that the truth would be too damaging. They lie because they feel there are certain human values that supersede the wrong of having lied. They lie, not for personal gain, but because they believe it's for the good of the person they're lying to. They lie to those they love, to those who trust them most of all, on the grounds that breaking this trust is justified.

They may lie to their children on money or marital matters.   *19*

They may lie to the dying about the state of their health.   *20*

They may lie about adultery, and not—or so they insist—to save their own *21* hide, but to save the heart and the pride of the men they are married to.

They may lie to their closest friend because the truth about her talents or *22* son or psyche would be—or so they insist—utterly devastating.

I sometimes tell such lies, but I'm aware that it's quite presumptuous to *23* claim I know what's best for others to know. That's called playing God. That's called manipulation and control. And we never can be sure, once we start to jug- gle lies, just where they'll land, exactly where they'll roll.

And furthermore, we may find ourselves lying in order to back up the lies *24* that are backing up the lie we initially told.

And furthermore—let's be honest—if conditions were reversed, we cer- *25* tainly wouldn't want anyone lying to us.

Yet, having said all that, I still believe that there are times when protective *26* lies must nonetheless be told. What about you?

If your Dad had a very bad heart and you had to tell him some bad family *27* news, which would you choose: to tell him the truth or lie?

If your former husband failed to send his monthly child-support check and *28* in other ways behaved like a total rat, would you allow your children—who be- lieved he was simply wonderful—to continue to believe that he was wonderful?

If your dearly beloved brother selected a wife whom you deeply disliked, *29* would you reveal your feelings or would you fake it?

And if you were asked, after making love, "And how was that for you?" *30* would you reply, if it wasn't too good, "Not too good"?

Now, some would call a sex lie unimportant, little more than social lying, a *31* simple act of courtesy that makes all human intercourse run smoothly. And some would say all sex lies are bad news and unacceptably protective. Because, says

Ruth, "a man with an ego that fragile doesn't need your lies—he needs a psychiatrist." Still others feel that sex lies are indeed protective lies, more serious than simple social lying, and yet at times they tell them on the grounds that when it comes to matters sexual, everybody's ego is somewhat fragile.

"If most of the time things go well in sex," says Sue, "I think you're allowed 32 to dissemble when they don't. I can't believe it's good to say, 'Last night was four stars, darling, but tonight's performance rates only a half.' "

I'm inclined to agree with Sue. What about you? 33

Trust-Keeping Lies

Another group of lies are trust-keeping lies, lies that involve triangulation, with *A* 34 (that's you) telling lies to *B* on behalf of *C* (whose trust you'd promised to keep). Most people concede that once you've agreed not to betray a friend's confidence, you can't betray it, even if you must lie. But I've talked with people who don't want you telling them anything that they might be called on to lie about.

"I don't tell lies for myself," says Fran, "and I don't want to have to tell 35 them for other people." Which means, she agrees, that if her best friend is having an affair, she absolutely doesn't want to know about it.

"Are you saying," her best friend asks, "that if I went off with a lover and I 36 asked you to tell my husband I'd been with you, that you wouldn't lie for me, that you'd betray me?"

Fran is very pained but very adamant. "I wouldn't want to betray you, 37 so . . . don't ask me."

Fran's best friend is shocked. What about you? 38

Do you believe you can have close friends if you're not prepared to receive 39 their deepest secrets?

Do you believe you must always lie for your friends? 40

Do you believe, if your friend tells a secret that turns out to be quite im- 41 moral or illegal, that once you've promised to keep it, you must keep it?

And what if your friend were your boss—if you were perhaps one of the 42 President's men—would you betray or lie for him over, say, Watergate?

As you can see, these issues get terribly sticky. 43

It's my belief that once we've promised to keep a trust, we must tell lies to 44 keep it. I also believe that we can't tell Watergate lies. And if these two statements strike you as quite contradictory, you're right—they're quite contradictory. But for now they're the best I can do. What about you?

Some say that truth will out and thus you might as well tell the truth. Some 45 say you can't regain the trust that lies lose. Some say that even though the truth may never be revealed, our lies pervert and damage our relationships. Some say . . . well, here's what some of them have to say.

"I'm a coward," says Grace, "about telling close people important, difficult 46 truths. I find that I'm unable to carry it off. And so if something is bothering me, it keeps building up inside till I end up just not seeing them any more."

"I lie to my husband on sexual things, but I'm furious," says Joyce, "that 47 he's too insensitive to know I'm lying."

"I suffer most from the misconception that children can't take the truth," says Emily. "But I'm starting to see that what's harder and more damaging for them is being told lies, is *not* being told the truth." 48

"I'm afraid," says Joan, "that we often wind up feeling a bit of contempt for the people we lie to." 49

And then there are those who have no talent for lying. 50

"Over the years, I tried to lie," a friend of mine explained, "but I always got found out and I always got punished. I guess I gave myself away because I feel guilty about any kind of lying. It looks as if I'm stuck with telling the truth." 51

For those of us, however, who are good at telling lies, for those of us who lie and don't get caught, the question of whether or not to lie can be a hard and serious moral problem. I liked the remark of a friend of mine who said, "I'm willing to lie. But just as a last resort—the truth's always better." 52

"Because," he explained, "though others may completely accept the lie I'm telling, I don't." 53

I tend to feel that way too. 54

What about you? 55

Considering Ideas

1. Of the four types of lies, which does Viorst find the most serious? Why? Do you agree?
2. Viorst presents lying in terms of "a series of moral puzzles" (paragraph 1). Explain how deciding whether or not to lie is like a "moral puzzle."
3. Even though it makes Viorst feel guilty, she will tell lies. Why?
4. If your best friend were having an affair, would you lie for him or her? Why or why not?

Considering Technique

1. Evaluate Viorst's approach to her introduction. There is no thesis that indicates that classification will occur. Is that a problem? Explain.
2. What is the principle of classification? In what order does Viorst arrange her categories?
3. *Combining Patterns.* How does Viorst use each of the following to develop her classification: definition, illustration, narration, cause-and-effect analysis?
4. Viorst repeatedly asks, "What about you?" Explain the purpose of this refrain.

For Group Discussion or Journal Writing

People disagree about when it is okay to lie and when it is not. They even disagree about whether it is *ever* okay to lie. What factors do you think determine the position an individual takes on lying?

Combining Patterns of Development

The Ways of Meeting Oppression

Martin Luther King, Jr.

Martin Luther King, Jr., who won the Nobel Peace Prize in 1964, was the most prominent civil rights leader of the 1950s and 1960s. In the following essay, taken from his book Stride toward Freedom, *King **classifies** responses to oppression and evaluates the effectiveness of those responses, relying, in part, on **definition, illustration,** and **cause-and-effect analysis.***

Oppressed people deal with their oppression in three characteristic ways. One *1* way is acquiescence: The oppressed resign themselves to their doom. They tacitly adjust themselves to oppression, and thereby become conditioned to it. In every movement toward freedom some of the oppressed prefer to remain oppressed. Almost 2,800 years ago Moses set out to lead the children of Israel from the slavery of Egypt to the freedom of the promised land. He soon discovered that slaves do not always welcome their deliverers. They become accustomed to being slaves. They would rather bear those ills they have, as Shakespeare pointed out, than flee to others that they know not of. They prefer the "fleshpots of Egypt" to the ordeals of emancipation.

There is such a thing as the freedom of exhaustion. Some people are so *2* worn down by the yoke of oppression that they give up. A few years ago in the slum areas of Atlanta, a Negro guitarist used to sing almost daily: "Been down so long that down don't bother me." This is the type of negative freedom and resignation that often engulfs the life of the oppressed.

But this is not the way out. To accept passively an unjust system is to coop- *3* erate with that system; thereby the oppressed become as evil as the oppressor. Noncooperation with evil is as much a moral obligation as is cooperation with good. The oppressed must never allow the conscience of the oppressor to slumber. Religion reminds every man that he is his brother's keeper. To accept injustice or segregation passively is to say to the oppressor that his actions are morally right. It is a way of allowing his conscience to fall asleep. At this moment the oppressed fails to be his brother's keeper. So acquiescence—while often the easier way—is not the moral way. It is the way of the coward. The Negro cannot win the respect of his oppressor by acquiescing; he merely increases the oppressor's arrogance and contempt. Acquiescence is interpreted as proof of the Negro's inferiority. The Negro cannot win the respect of the white people of the South or the peoples of the world if he is willing to sell the future of his children for his personal and immediate comfort and safety.

A second way that oppressed people sometimes deal with oppression is to *4* resort to physical violence and corroding hatred. Violence often brings about momentary results. Nations have frequently won their independence in battle. But in spite of temporary victories, violence never brings permanent peace. It solves no social problem; it merely creates new and more complicated ones.

Violence as a way of achieving racial justice is both impractical and im- 5
moral. It is impractical because it is a descending spiral ending in destruction for
all. The old law of an eye for an eye leaves everybody blind. It is immoral because it seeks to humiliate the opponent rather than win his understanding; it
seeks to annihilate rather than to convert. Violence is immoral because it thrives
on hatred rather than love. It destroys community and makes brotherhood impossible. It leaves society in monologue rather than dialogue. Violence ends by
defeating itself. It creates bitterness in the survivors and brutality in the destroy-
ers. A voice echoes through time saying to every potential Peter, "Put up your
sword."* History is cluttered with the wreckage of nations that failed to follow
this command.

If the American Negro and other victims of oppression succumb to the 6
temptation of using violence in the struggle for freedom, future generations will
be the recipients of a desolate night of bitterness, and our chief legacy to them
will be an endless reign of meaningless chaos. Violence is not the way.

The third way open to oppressed people in their quest for freedom is the 7
way of nonviolent resistance. Like the synthesis in Hegelian philosophy, the principle of nonviolent resistance seeks to reconcile the truths of two opposites—the
acquiescence and violence—while avoiding the extremes and immoralities of
both. The nonviolent resister agrees with the person who acquiesces that one
should not be physically aggressive toward his opponent; but he balances the
equation by agreeing with the person of violence that evil must be resisted. He
avoids the nonresistance of the former and the violent resistance of the latter.
With nonviolent resistance, no individual or group need submit to any wrong,
nor need anyone resort to violence in order to right a wrong.

It seems to me that this is the method that must guide the actions of the 8
Negro in the present crisis in race relations. Through nonviolent resistance the
Negro will be able to rise to the noble height of opposing the unjust system while
loving the perpetrators of the system. The Negro must work passionately and un-
relentingly for full stature as a citizen, but he must not use inferior methods to
gain it. He must never come to terms with falsehood, malice, hate, or destruction. 9

Nonviolent resistance makes it possible for the Negro to remain in the
South and struggle for his rights. The Negro's problem will not be solved by running away. He cannot listen to the glib suggestion of those who would urge him
to migrate en masse to other sections of the country. By grasping his great opportunity in the South he can make a lasting contribution to the moral strength of
the nation and set a sublime example of courage for generations yet unborn. 10

By nonviolent resistance, the Negro can also enlist all men of good will in
his struggle for equality. The problem is not a purely racial one, with Negroes set
against whites. In the end, it is not a struggle between people at all, but a tension
between justice and injustice. Nonviolent resistance is not aimed against oppres-
sors but against oppression. Under its banner consciences, not racial groups, are
enlisted.

* The apostle Peter had drawn his sword to defend Christ from arrest. The voice was Christ's, who
surrendered himself for trial and crucifixion (John 18:11).

Considering Ideas

1. Explain the advantages and disadvantages of each way of meeting oppression.
2. King says that some oppressed people accept their oppression because they "would rather bear those ills they have . . . than flee to others that they know not of" (paragraph 1). Why is this the case?
3. What does King mean when he says, "Under [nonviolent resistance's] banner consciences, not racial groups, are enlisted" (paragraph 10)?
4. King says, "To accept passively an unjust system is to cooperate with that system; thereby the oppressed become as evil as the oppressor" (paragraph 3). What does King mean? Do you agree with him? Why or why not?

Considering Technique

1. Which sentence is the thesis of the essay?
2. What is King's principle of classification? In what order does King present his groupings?
3. What is the purpose of King's classification? How do you know?
4. *Combining Patterns.* What purpose does the cause-and-effect analysis in paragraphs 5 and 6 serve? What purpose does the cause-and-effect analysis in paragraphs 8–10 serve?
5. *Combining Patterns.* What definition occurs in paragraph 7? What purpose does that definition serve? Which paragraphs include examples? What purpose do the examples serve?

For Group Discussion or Journal Writing

Martin Luther King, Jr., believed that nonviolent resistance was superior to violence because "violence never brings permanent peace" (paragraph 4). Are there ever times when violence is the best solution? Explain, using examples if possible.

STUDENT ESSAYS TO READ AND EVALUATE

The classification essays that follow were written by students. Each has strengths and aspects that could be improved with revision. As you study these essays, you will improve your ability to assess strengths and weaknesses so that you can better judge and revise your own work.

They're Off and Running

Waterford Park is a rather remote horse-racing track wedged between   *1*
the mountains of West Virginia. I go there often, not so much to
test my luck as to observe the fascinating people.

Upon entering Waterford Park, a person first encounters a sign   *2*
that reads, "Lucky Louie's Daily Selections." Beneath the sign sits

the founder, selling his "winners" for one dollar. A portly man, Louie is usually dressed in an outlandish plaid sports jacket accessorized with a shirt and tie bearing the remains of his meals for the past week. A smoking cigar clenched between decayed teeth juts from his mouth, emitting a stench that keeps his clientele on the move. Every so often in his sandpaper voice Louie emits a garbled announcement: "Get your winners here!"

Another character frequently seen at Waterford Park is the inebriated bum. He looks like he stumbled down from his moonshine still in the mountains to gamble his last two bucks. Clothed in a pair of grimy overalls and a stained jacket of indeterminate color, the sot can usually be found sleeping it off in a sheltered area of the grandstand, his nip bottle in one hand and his tattered ticket in the other. More often than not the bum loses, and when he does, he begins staggering around cursing the ponies for his rotten luck. *3*

Of course there are those who have worries other than money: the flamboyant and well-heeled. They have their own club on the premises, known as the Cap and Whip. As the grandstand crowd eat their sausage sandwiches and guzzle their beer, this elite group dines on filet mignon and Asti Spumante served at their reserved tables. Protected from the elements, they sit back for a night of racing. There is no need for them to challenge the betting lines, since they have their own courtesy betting service. They lavishly toss two or three hundred dollars into the hands of the club steward who places the bets for them. Beautifully tailored three-piece suits and designer evening gowns are the standard attire of these affluent people. The air around them is heavy with the scent of Giorgio perfume and the aroma of Cuban cigars. *4*

The hustlers, the sots, and the privileged can be viewed on any given evening at Waterford Park. By 7 P.M., they are all in their places as the familiar cry echoes over the track: "They're off and running!" *5*

Horror Movies

Horror movies started out harmless enough, but they have developed over the years into stomach-turning trash. *1*

The first popular horror movies were the mass destruction movies. These include *The Blob, Invasion of the Body Snatchers,* and the classic *War of the Worlds.* In these movies the human race is threatened with destruction by odd creatures, usually from another planet. The early mass destruction movies are the least gory of the horror flicks. There is no graphic violence, murder, or mutilation. The camera cuts away at the moment someone is done in, and eerie music hints at the mayhem that occurs. The early mass destruction movies give an audience plenty of frightening moments without turning anyone's stomach. They are harmless fun for those who like a good scare.

2

The supernatural thrillers came next. These movies tend to be very scary and even more nauseating. They deal with the satanic and the occult, and vampires and evil spirits are often wreaking havoc on unsuspecting, average human beings. In *The Exorcist,* a young girl was possessed by the devil who caused her to vomit green goop, spin her head in a full circle, and otherwise disgust the audience. *The Omen and Rosemary's Baby* fit into this class of movies that causes knee-clanking fear while souring the stomach.

3

The worst group of horror movies is undoubtedly the psychopath chop 'em up group. These movies, unlike many of the supernatural thrillers, have weak plots. They rely solely on gore to keep the audience interested. Take, for example, the movie series *Friday the Thirteenth.* In these, indestructible Jason uses an ice pick and an axe to attack his victims. The violence is graphic; blood flies everywhere. *The Texas Chainsaw Massacre, Halloween,* and *Nightmare on Elm Street*—all of these depict mutilation, murder, and mayhem vividly and in detail. Strangely, these movies should be the most disturbing, but audiences love them, returning for sequel after sequel. What does this say about us? Why do the simple, scary mass destruction movies no longer provide sufficient thrills? Perhaps the answers to these questions are even scarier than the movies.

4

Collaborative Exercise: Evaluating Writing

Form a group with two classmates and select one of the previous student essays. Prepare a report noting the chief strengths of the essay and the revisions you would like to see. If you like, you can use the following evaluation questions as a guide.

Evaluation Questions

1. *The Thesis*
   What is the thesis? Is it clear what is being classified and what the principle of classification is?
2. *The Introduction*
   Does the introduction engage your interest? Why or why not?
3. *Supporting Details*
   Note any elements omitted from a grouping and any place where the characteristics of a grouping are unclear. Also note anything that is not relevant or that is inadequately developed.
4. *Organization*
   Are there at least three groupings? Are the groupings placed in a logical order? Evaluate how effectively the author moves from grouping to grouping.
5. *The Conclusion*
   Does the essay come to a satisfying end?
6. *Overview*
   What do you like best about the essay? What is the single most important revision the author should make?

Essay Topics: Classification

When you write your classification, consult Pitfalls to Avoid on page 316, Process Guidelines on page 316, and the Revision Checklist on page 317.

Writing in the Pattern

1. Classify any of the following people according to type:

college students	automobile drivers
professors	salespeople
bosses	table servers
roommates	disc jockeys
talk-show hosts	game-show hosts

2. Classify one of the following:

your friends	study techniques
fads or trends of the last 10 years	radio stations
advertisements for a particular kind of product	coaches
sports fans	movie comedies
situation comedies	

Reading Then Writing in the Pattern

1. Like Russell Baker, in "The Plot against People" (page 318), write a humorous classification of inanimate objects. Perhaps you can classify Christmas gifts, wedding presents, or kitchen gadgets.

2. In "The Truth about Lying" (page 320), Judith Viorst classifies kinds of lies. Using her categories or ones of your own, classify the kinds of lies told in school.

3. In "The Ways of Meeting Oppression" (page 325), Martin Luther King, Jr., classifies the ways to deal with oppression and notes which of the ways is best. In similar fashion, write an essay that classifies the ways to deal with one of the following: sexual harassment, sex discrimination, stress, depression, or peer pressure. Be sure to note which way is the best.

Responding to the Readings

1. Russell Baker uses humor to express the frustration that can be caused by inanimate objects. On a more serious note, discuss whether or not the "things" that we own unnecessarily complicate our lives. Do we pay a price for using modern conveniences?

2. Do you agree with those who Viorst says find social lying "the civilized way for folks to behave" (paragraph 2)? Or do you take the position that it is morally wrong (paragraph 7)? Explain and defend your view.

3. Cite one or more examples of oppression that you have experienced or observed and explain how that oppression could be addressed using the nonviolent resistance that Martin Luther King, Jr., advocates in "The Ways of Meeting Oppression" (page 325).

4. *Connecting the Readings.* Harold Krents (see "Darkness at Noon," page 194) suffers humiliation and oppression, as do Native Americans (see "It Is Time to Stop Playing Indians," page 273). Explain which of the ways of meeting oppression (see "The Ways of Meeting Oppression") the essays note have been used to deal with the oppression. Evaluate the success of these methods and comment on whether other methods would be more successful.

CHAPTER 12

Argumentation-Persuasion

In writing, argumentation is *not* a form of fighting, and persuasion is *not* a form of unfair manipulation. Instead, argumentation-persuasion involves stating and defending your view so well that you convince your reader to think a certain way (perhaps to believe that affirmative action is a good policy), to act a certain way (perhaps to vote for a tax cut), or to support a solution to a problem (perhaps to agree to drug testing in schools as a way to reduce drug use among teens).

Sometimes writers use cool logic and sound reasoning to convince—that is **argumentation.** Sometimes they appeal to our emotions—that is **persuasion.** Most often, however, argumentation and persuasion are combined to sway us to specific lines of thought or courses of action. For example, to convince you to help the homeless, I could appeal to your intellect by explaining that helping the homeless reduces crime, and I could appeal to your emotions by describing the abominable living conditions of the homeless.

ESTABLISHING YOUR PURPOSE AND IDENTIFYING YOUR AUDIENCE

You might think that establishing audience and determining purpose are simple: Your purpose is to *convince the reader,* and the reader is someone who disagrees. However, that is only part of the picture.

Certainly your audience will be someone who disagrees with you to some extent, for why bother trying to convince someone who already agrees with you? However, you must establish how great the disagreement is. Say you are writing in opposition to dispensing birth control in schools. If your audience is a member of Planned Parenthood, you will need to be far more persuasive than if your reader is the parent of a sexually active teen.

You must also determine how much your reader knows about your issue. Say you are writing in support of the legislative veto. If your audience is knowledgeable about the workings of the federal government, you can supply less background information than if your reader has only limited knowledge in this area.

Your purpose also deserves careful consideration. Sure, you want to convince your reader to see things just as you do, but that may be an unreasonable expectation. If you favor gun control and are writing to a member of the National Rifle Association, it would be realistic to set your purpose as convincing the reader we need stricter enforcement of existing laws. It might be unrealistic to expect you can convince your reader that handguns should be banned.

Sometimes a particular audience is so opposed to your view that the best you can hope for is *that the reader will consider your points and agree that they have some merit.* For example, if you are writing to the president of the local teachers' union about the hardships of teachers' strikes, you cannot expect your reader to come out against such strikes. However, if you present a good enough case, your reader can *come to understand something he or she never realized before,* and become more sympathetic to your view. Perhaps this new understanding will influence the reader's thinking and actions in the future.

COMBINING ARGUMENTATION-PERSUASION WITH OTHER PATTERNS

If you are to convince your reader to think or act a particular way, then it is crucial that you support your points adequately. To that end, you will draw heavily on the patterns of development you have learned so far. Narration, description, illustration, comparison-contrast, process analysis, cause-and-effect analysis, definition, classification—one or more of these may appear in your essay. Say, for example, that you wish to convince your reader to vote for Chris Politician. You might *narrate* an episode that reveals Politician's integrity. You might also *describe* the various personality traits that identify Politician as the best candidate, or you might *illustrate* Politician's strengths with several examples. You could *compare and contrast* Politician with one or more of the other candidates. You could explain the *effects* of electing Politician. You could even *define* what a good public official is and then show how Politician fits this definition.

Of course, since persuasion is very much a purpose for writing and not just a pattern of development, any essay in any pattern may have argumentation-persuasion as an important component. For example, a comparison-contrast of exercise videos may be done to persuade the reader that one is better than the other; a description of the Florida Keys may be written to convince the reader to vacation there; an explanation of the effects of teenage pregnancy may be written to persuade the reader to support sex education.

USING ARGUMENTATION-PERSUASION BEYOND THE WRITING CLASS

Argumentation and persuasion are everywhere. A friend tries to talk you into skipping a class and catching an afternoon movie; a politician delivers a speech to win your vote; a newspaper editor writes an editorial to convince you of the dangers of tax reform; an advertising executive creates an ad to make you believe that the surest path to popularity is using the right deodorant soap—all of these are examples of argumentation-persuasion.

In addition, you will write argumentation-persuasion in almost every class you take in college. A criminal justice class may require you to suggest a solution to the repeat-offender rate and argue for its adoption; a history class may require you to explain how the westward expansion affected a particular Native American tribe and argue for or against the payment of reparations; an education class may require you to explain how whole language instruction works and argue for or against its adoption in elementary classrooms; a management class may require you to support or attack the use of flex-time; an ethics class may require you to devise and defend an equitable procedure for allocating transplant organs. The possibilities are endless because argumentation-persuasion is so important to the education process.

SELECTING DETAIL

Because argumentation-persuasion is written on a controversial subject (on a debatable issue with at least two sides), there is no clear right and wrong side; both sides will have some merit, and you must respect that fact. You cannot present your view as the only correct one, but you *can* present it as the *more* correct one. To do so, your argumentative detail must be firmly rooted in reason. If a thoughtful reader is to adopt your view, that person must see the wisdom of your stand as a result of your well-reasoned evidence.

That evidence can come from a variety of sources, including your own experience and observation, your reading and television viewing, class lectures, the experience of others, information researched in reliable sources, and testimony of authorities. Assume you are arguing that high school students should have to submit to regular drug testing. The following shows how you could argue a case with evidence from a variety of sources.

> *evidence from personal experience and observation:* "A classmate of mine was a regular marijuana user from his sophomore year until his death the morning of high school graduation. Perhaps if she had been discovered as a user as a result of routine drug testing, she would not have died high behind the wheel of her car."

> *evidence from reading and television viewing:* "A recent local news report indicated that over half of the teenagers surveyed admitted to regular recreational use of drugs and alcohol. With drug use that common, drug testing is needed."

> *evidence from class lectures:* If you learned in a health class that drug testing has been shown to be a deterrent among Olympic athletes, you could note this and say that it could also be a deterrent for high school students as well.

> *evidence from the experience of others:* "In my senior year, a classmate transferred to our public school from a private school in another state. He reported that he was afraid to use drugs there because of drug testing, but he felt free to use them in our school, where no such drug testing existed."

evidence from information researched in reliable sources: You could find in your campus library statistics on teenage drug use or statements by educators and health officials in support of routine drug testing of high school students.

evidence from testimony of authorities: You could interview high school principals and drug counselors in favor of your view and include their testimony.

NOTE: When you use evidence from library research or the testimony of authorities, be sure to document according to the conventions explained in Chapter 14.

Another effective technique is to consider what would happen if your view were adopted (or what would happen if it were *not* adopted). To convince your reader to vote for Chris Politician, you could say that if Politician were elected, a bigger budget would be allotted to the safety forces so that police and fire protection would improve. Or you could explain something negative that would happen if Politician were *not* elected: Police and fire protection would continue at substandard levels.

As any attorney knows, sound logic and compelling facts are not all that influence a person. Emotion, too, plays a role. After all, when we make up our minds about something, how we *feel* about the issue can determine our decision along with what we *think* about it. For this reason, a writer may include persuasive detail to move the reader's emotions. This is why the writer of a toothpaste ad may emphasize fewer cavities *and* a brighter smile. Our intellect makes us understand the virtue of fewer cavities, but our emotional desire to be attractive makes us want a bright smile.

Still, you must be careful with emotional appeals. They should be used sparingly and with restraint. You can call upon the reader's patriotism to earn support for defense spending, but it is unfair, inflammatory, and illogical to whip up emotions by saying that anyone who does not support the spending is un-American. Use emotional appeals only to enhance your logical argument, not to replace it.

Creating Goodwill

No matter how misguided you think the opposing view is, no matter how little regard you have for your opposition, you are unlikely to convince a reader if you assume a confrontational stance. You are more likely to convince your reader if you create some goodwill. One way to do that is to *find some common ground with your reader* to lessen the amount of disagreement between you and your audience. Say, for example, you are writing to convince your reader to support mandatory drug testing of high school students. You can establish common ground by noting that you both want to ensure the safety and well-being of young people. Once your reader realizes you share some ideas or beliefs, you are positioned closer together and you have less opposition to overcome.

A second way to create goodwill is to *demonstrate that you understand your reader's viewpoint and take it seriously.* Doing so validates your reader's view and makes that person less defensive and less inclined to dig in and hold fast to a position at all costs. For example, when arguing for mandatory drug testing of teenagers, you could say something like this to show that you understand and respect your reader's view: "Mandatory drug testing does raise important privacy issues and presents a challenge to the Bill of Rights, facts which make the issue a particularly thorny one."

Another way to create goodwill is to *concede a point or two in the spirit of compromise,* like this: "Opponents of drug testing have a valid concern about what the cost will do to already-stressed education budgets. There is simply no way to deny that the cost will be significant. What we must ask ourselves is whether the cost is worthwhile."

The key to creating goodwill is recognizing that no matter what stand you take on an issue, some intelligent, reasonable people will disagree with you. Ignoring their opposing views will weaken your position because you will not come across as someone who has weighed all sides before drawing conclusions. However, if you acknowledge and come to terms with the most significant arguments on the other side, you help incline your reader to your position because it appears more carefully thought out. Furthermore, even if you ignore the opposition's points, your reader will have them in mind. To be convincing, then, you must deal with the chief objections head-on to dispel some of your reader's disagreement. The process of acknowledging and coming to terms with opposing views is called *raising and countering objections.*

Raising and countering objections is a two-part operation. First, you state the opposition's point; this is **raising the objection.** Then, you make the point less compelling by introducing a point of your own; this is **countering the objection.**

Let's return to the paper written to convince a reader to vote for Chris Politician to see how raising and countering objections works. Your first step is to identify your reader's most compelling objections. Let's say they are these:

1. Politician lacks experience in city government.
2. Politician's proposed safety forces budget is inflationary.
3. Politician's health problems will undermine her effectiveness.

After identifying the chief objections, you must find a way to soften their force. You can do this in one of two ways: by offering an equally compelling point of your own to balance out the opposition or by showing that the opposition's point is untrue. Here are some examples:

Offering an Equally Compelling Point

Some people claim that Politician's lack of experience in
municipal government will make him a poor city manager.
(objection raised) However, while she has not had actual experience
in city government, 10 years as president of City Bank have

provided Politician with all the managerial skills any mayor could need. Furthermore, our current mayor, who came to the job with five years of experience on City Council, has mismanaged everything from Street Department funds to the city's public relations efforts. Thus, experience in city government does not guarantee success. *(objection countered)*

Although some contend that the increased safety forces budget that Politician supports is inflationary, *(objection raised)* the fact remains that without adequate police and fire protection, we will not attract new industry to our area. *(objection countered)*

Showing That the Opposition's Point Is Untrue

Some of Politician's detractors say that he is not well enough to do the job. *(objection raised)* However, Politician's physical examination last month shows he to be in perfect health and any discussion to the contrary is based on rumor and falsehood. *(objection countered)*

As the examples show, an objection is sometimes countered in a single sentence and sometimes countered in several sentences. If an objection is particularly compelling, you may need to devote one or more paragraphs to the counter. Usually, you need not raise and counter every objection to your view. You can identify your reader's most important objections and deal with those.

Using Induction and Deduction

To convince a reader, the reasoning in your argumentation-persuasive essay must be flawless. For this reason, you should understand the two most common patterns of reasoning: induction and deduction.

Induction is a movement from specific evidence to a general conclusion, like this:

specific evidence: The number of adolescent suicide attempts is increasing.

specific evidence: In the last year, the local high school has reported four attempted suicides.

specific evidence: Guidance counselors in the middle school and high school are counseling more students for depression than ever before.

specific evidence: Today's high school students are under a great deal of stress.

conclusion: Our high school should institute a suicide prevention program.

Inductive reasoning allows you to argue your case by showing how specific evidence (facts, statistics, cases, examples, etc.) lead to the point you want to convince your reader of. Thus, if you wanted to convince your reader that the local high school should institute a suicide prevention program, you could do so by stating and explaining each piece of evidence that—by way of induction—leads to your conclusion that the program is a good idea.

In inductive reasoning, your conclusion is sound only if it is based on sufficient evidence and only if that evidence is accurate. Thus, you cannot reasonably conclude that today's teens are suicidal solely on the basis that there are four attempted suicides in one high school. Nor can you make that conclusion if you are wrong about the amount of depression counselors are seeing in teenagers.

Here is an example of a paragraph developed with inductive reasoning:

evidence
[Maxine Phillips reports that approximately 9.5 million

preschoolers have mothers with jobs outside the house.] [Many
evidence
of these mothers are the sole support of their children, so
evidence
they cannot stay home, although they may want to.] [An alarming

number, says Philips, also cannot afford quality day care, so

their children are in substandard situations or worse—
evidence
unsupervised.] [Given the compelling evidence that the child's

early years are key to good development, we must ensure that

those years are spent in sound, enriching environments like the
evidence
ones quality day care can provide] [Yet, if that day care is

not affordable, large numbers of children will suffer.] [That
conclusion
is something we have it in our power to prevent:] [The federal

government should subsidize day-care programs for single

parents.]

A second reasoning pattern is **deduction,** which involves moving from a generalization (known as a **major premise**) to a specific case (known as a **minor premise**) and on to a conclusion. Deduction works like this:

generalization
(major premise): Our city has a serious unemployment problem.

specific case
(minor premise): A proposed federal prison would create 500 new
jobs.

conclusion: If the new federal prison is built in our city,
we could put 500 people to work.

Deductive reasoning can help you organize the argument for your stand on an issue. Say you want to convince your reader that your city should compete for the new federal prison. You can support your view by reproducing your deductive reasoning: the city needs jobs, and the prison will provide them.

To argue well, however, you must avoid the illogical conclusions that result from inaccurate or sweeping generalizations. Notice the problems with the following deductive reasoning:

> *generalization*
> *(major premise):* All students cheat at one time or another.
>
> *specific case*
> *(minor premise):* Lee is a student.
>
> *conclusion:* Lee cheats.

This conclusion is illogical because the first generalization is inaccurate—all students do not cheat.

> *generalization*
> *(major premise):* Foreign cars are better made than American cars.
>
> *generalization*
> *(minor premise):* My car was made in Germany.
>
> *conclusion:* My car is better made than American cars.

This conclusion is illogical because the first generalization is sweeping—many foreign cars are not better made than American cars. Remember, your conclusion is valid only when your premises are valid.

Here is an example of a paragraph developed with deductive reasoning:

> *major premise*
> [No one argues with the fact that preschool children
> *minor premise*
> require a nurturing environment.] [No one disagrees either that
>
> the best nurturing environment is a stable home combined, if
> *minor premise*
> necessary, with a quality day care center.] [Lately, however,
>
> there is evidence that many preschoolers are not getting the
>
> nurturing they need because their mothers find it necessary to
>
> work to make ends meet and there is too little money for
> *support for minor premise*
> adequate day care.] [Maxine Phillips reports that over half the
>
> mothers of preschoolers are in the workforce. She also explains
>
> that many of these mothers, who are the sole support of their
>
> children, cannot afford to stop working, nor can they afford
>
> adequate day care, so children end up in substandard
> *conclusion*
> environments or unsupervised.] [In light of this, the need for
>
> federally subsidized day care becomes apparent.]

Avoiding Logical Fallacies

Errors in reasoning, called **logical fallacies,** will weaken your case. If they are serious or frequent enough, your reader will reject your position outright. When you read about induction and deduction, you learned about three types of faulty logic: basing a conclusion on insufficient evidence, using sweeping generalizations, and using inaccurate generalizations. In addition, you should guard against the following logical fallacies:

1. Do not attack an idea on the basis of the people associated with that idea.

> *example:* Only liberals oppose balancing the federal budget, and we all know the mess they've gotten this country into.
>
> *explanation:* The people who do or do not champion an idea or action have nothing to do with the validity of that idea or action.

2. Avoid name calling.

> *example:* The president of this college is an idiot if he thinks students will sit still for another tuition increase.
>
> *explanation:* It is legitimate to criticize what people do or think, but it is unfair to attack the personalities of the people themselves.

3. Do not defend or attack an idea or action on the grounds that people have always believed that idea or performed that action.

> *example:* Children have always learned to read in first grade, so why should we begin teaching them any earlier now?
>
> *explanation:* Everything believed and done in the past and present is not always for the best. Perhaps new research in education indicates children are capable of reading before the first grade.

4. Avoid illogical comparisons.

> *example:* The voters in this city have not passed a school levy for seven years. They will never vote for a teacher to become our next senator.
>
> *explanation:* How voters feel about school levies has nothing to do with how they feel about a political candidate who happens to be a teacher. The comparison is not logical.

5. Do not assume that what is true for one person will be true for everybody.

example: When I was a child, my parents spanked me
regularly, and I turned out just fine. Clearly,
there is no harm in spanking as a form of
punishment.

explanation: It does not hold that because one person suffered
no ill effects from spanking, no one will suffer
ill effects from spanking.

6. Do not assume that a debatable point is the truth, or you will be guilty of
begging the question.

example: Unnecessary programs like shop and home economics
should be eliminated to balance the new school
budget.

explanation: The importance of shop and home economics is
debatable, so you cannot assume they are
unnecessary and argue from there. You must first
prove they are unnecessary.

7. Avoid drawing a conclusion that does not follow from the evidence. This
is called a **non sequitur.**

example: Feminism is a potent social force in the United
States. No wonder our divorce rate is so high.

explanation: Many factors contribute to the divorce rate; no
logical reason establishes feminism as the sole
cause or even one cause.

8. Do not present only two options when more than two exist. This is the
either/or fallacy.

example: Either you support the strike, or you are opposed
to organized labor.

explanation: The sentence ignores other possibilities, such as
opposing the strike but believing the union's
demands should be met, and opposing the strike
but calling for further negotiations.

9. Avoid bandwagon appeals that argue that everyone believes something
so the reader should too.

example: All the professors I spoke to in the political
science department favor the trade agreement with
Japan, so it must be a good idea.

explanation: The issue should be argued on the merits of the
trade agreement, not on the basis of who favors
it.

10. Do not assume that an event that precedes another event is the cause of that event. This is called a **post hoc fallacy.**

> *example:* After the freshman class read <u>Catcher in the Rye</u>, the number of teen pregnancies increased. The book causes promiscuity.

> *explanation:* Although the pregnancies followed reading the book, other factors may have caused the increase in pregnancy rate.

11. Do not digress from the matter at hand by introducing a distraction (called a **red herring**).

> *example:* We should not spend more money on AIDS research because so many AIDS victims chose to put themselves at risk.

> *explanation:* The behavior of some people who contract AIDS is not the issue but a distraction (a red herring) meant to direct the reader's attention away from the issue—whether or not more money should be spent on AIDS research.

ARRANGING DETAIL

A progressive order from the least to the most compelling points is effective for argumentation-persuasion because the potency of your argument gradually builds. An effective alternative is to begin with your second-strongest point and then build from your least to most compelling reasons. This arrangement allows you to begin and end powerfully, creating strong initial and final impressions.

At times, the reasons in support of a view have a particular relationship to each other that dictates a particular arrangement. Often that relationship is one of cause and effect. For example, assume you are arguing against raising the driving age to 18 and you give as a reason the fact that teenagers who work would have trouble getting to and from the job. You might then note the effect of that fact as your next reason: Teens who cannot get to work may have to quit their jobs, in many cases depriving their families of needed income.

You must also determine where to raise and counter objections. Usually, the most effective way is to raise and counter objections at the points where the objections logically emerge. Say you are arguing that children should not be allowed to play with toy guns, and you explain that violent play leads to violent behavior. In that paragraph (or immediately after), you can raise and counter the objection that gun play can vent violent tendencies harmlessly and thus reduce violent behavior.

Another way to handle objections is to raise them all in your introduction or in your first body paragraphs. The rest of the essay can counter the objections. This arrangement is useful when your stand is unpopular, with many objections to it. Then you can make your point by showing how the prevailing beliefs are mistaken. Such an approach would work if you were taking the unpopular stand that military service should be mandatory for all 18-year-olds. For this argument, you could cite all the reasons people are opposed to this and then go on to show why these reasons are not good ones.

Typically, the thesis for argumentation-persuasion notes both the issue and your stand on the issue, like one of the following:

> All college students should be required to become proficient in a foreign language. *(The issue is learning a foreign language and the stand is that college students should do so.)*

> Because of the number of mothers in the workforce, we need federally funded day care. *(The issue is federally funded day care and the stand is that we need it.)*

Annotated Student Essay

Studying the following essay written by a student, along with the marginal notes, will help you better understand the points made in this chapter.

It's Just Too Easy

paragraph 1
The introduction creates interest with images of parents, and it demonstrates the importance of the issue with statistics on teen accidents from the testimony of an authority.

As their adolescent children approach driving age, parents 1 lie awake at night staring at the ceiling. Why? Terror keeps them awake and wide-eyed. Sure, the convenience of having an extra driver around to run to the drugstore, pick up little Sally at her dance lesson, and swing by the dry cleaners sounds heavenly, yet the appeal of the extra driver is offset by the sobering reality that driving poses a threat to the safety of teenagers and those around them. It was explained to me by one of my driver's education instructors that teenagers cause a disproportionate number of accidents. Although they represent only 7 percent of the drivers on the road, they are responsible for 16 percent of all accidents and 14 percent of all fatal crashes. I would not have admitted this when I got my own license and began to drive a few years ago, but in the interest of everybody's safety, we need tough guidelines for licensing teenage drivers.

paragraph 2
This paragraph raises an objection in the first sentence (the topic sentence) and

Immediately, teenagers and others are probably 2 thinking that this is a classic case of discrimination, that young people are not inherently worse drivers than

counters it in rest of paragraph with an equally compelling point.

people in any other age group and should not be singled out. Of course, teenagers have all the natural ability to be as safe as anyone else on the road (and maybe even safer than the octogenarians out there driving), but they do lack experience behind the wheel, and that is what causes their accidents. The standards I am proposing will do nothing more than give teens the experience they need to be among the safest motorists out there.

paragraph 3
The first sentence is the topic sentence. This paragraph includes personal experience to demonstrate that getting a license is currently too easy. Supporting detail is narrative. Note the inductive reasoning.

When I got my driver's license, it was a joke. The day of my sixteenth birthday, I took a written test so easy that an impaired chimpanzee would have passed. I did not even study, and I got a 90 percent. That entitled me to get a learner's permit for a modest fee. Now I could drive anywhere, anytime, as long as I was with a licensed driver. My parents were strict, so I could only drive with them or my driver's ed instructor, but many of my friends were out driving with older brothers and sisters (not older by much) and with other friends. It was the blind leading the blind because the licensed drivers were only barely more experienced than the ones with the learner's permits. To get my real license, I took six hours of driver's education. I had three teachers who rotated taking me out on the road. One of them was a loser who was just one rung above a derelict. We went out three times, two hours at a time, and bingo I was allowed to take my driver's test. I passed—barely. Next thing I knew, I was licensed and on the road anytime I could wheedle the car out of my parents. Although I did not know it then, I was no more ready to drive than to be an astronaut.

3

paragraph 4
This paragraph uses the author's experience and that of others to show that teens have accidents and do not drive safely. Supporting detail is illustration.

Soon my friends and I were having accidents, nothing serious, but they could have been. I rear-ended a van on an exit ramp. My best friend got a speeding ticket. His girlfriend changed lanes, cut off a pickup, and narrowly escaped injury. Others I know had freeway collisions, parking lot fender-benders, and various moving violations. We were all accidents waiting to happen because we had no experience and no appreciation for the damage we could inflict. What I am proposing would give teenagers more driving experience before they strike out on their own,

4

and it would help them better appreciate what it means to drive.

paragraph 5
The last two sentences raise and counter an objection. The counter is an equally compelling point. Paragraphs 1–4 present a problem; paragraphs 5–8 present a solution. Note that the solution is specific and detailed. Information is also given on why the solution would work. Presenting a solution is a good persuasive strategy because the author is doing more than complaining. He is suggesting a way to deal with the complaint.

paragraphs 6–8
Note the use of cause-and-effect analysis to show what would happen if the writer's view were adopted.

First, the test for securing a learner's permit   5
should be rigorous. In addition to covering all rules of the road and all traffic signs, it should present various driving scenarios and ask what the proper response should be. Passing this test should not be easy. People should have to study, and they should have to score in the 90s. Then, we could be sure that people who get their learner's permit at least have a certain basic knowledge. Some people might think this test would be unfair to people who are not very bright and have trouble taking tests. Is it any more fair to put unknowledgeable people behind the wheels of cars, where their lack of information could cause injury and death?

Once a teenager has a learner's permit, he or she   6
should have to have a great deal of experience behind the wheel before being permitted to take the test for a permanent license. At least 20 hours would not be unreasonable, with at least five hours at night and five hours on a busy highway or interstate. This requirement would help ensure that teens were experienced in a variety of driving situations so they knew what to do and how to respond in tricky driving situations. Even better would be to increase the requirement to 22 hours and require two hours of driving in inclement weather—rain, snow, fog, and so forth. This way young drivers could learn about handling skids, driving on wet pavement, increasing stopping time, and all the other precautions necessary in less-than-ideal conditions.

Until they have their permanent licenses, teenagers   7
should not be able to drive with anyone other than a parent, guardian, driver's education instructor, or person over 21. This requirement would serve two purposes. First, it would help ensure that teens were getting their driving hours in with responsible, experienced drivers. Second, it would create more parental involvement in the driver's education process.

Finally, passing the actual driving test should be   *8*
difficult. Teenagers should have to demonstrate ability on
the highway, in heavily trafficked areas, and at night.
They should also demonstrate the ability to maneuver a car
in tight areas, operate safely in reverse, and park. If
they can do that, then we will be putting more
experienced, capable drivers on the road.

paragraph 9
The conclusion includes
emotional appeal and a
restatement of the thesis.

Young people are at risk today from so many sources,   *9*
including drugs, alcohol, stress, street violence, and
broken homes. Anything we can do to protect them should be
a top priority. Of course, on the road, teens are not the
only ones at risk. With tougher requirements for getting a
driver's license, we can protect young drivers and
everybody else in a vehicle.

Pitfalls to Avoid

1. **Avoid issues that are not debatable.** Your issue must have at least two
sides to it. It would serve no purpose, for example, to argue that everyone needs
some relaxation, for no one would disagree with you. It *would* be purposeful,
though, to argue that places of business should have recreation areas to allow employees to relax during lunch and break periods.
2. **Avoid issues of personal taste.** To argue that it is more pleasant to listen to
Mozart than Bach makes little sense because the issue is strictly a matter of individual preference.
3. **Avoid arguing both sides of an issue.** While it is important to raise and
counter compelling objections, do not treat all the arguments on one side and
then give all the arguments on the other side. Your mission is to present a case
for just one side.

PROCESS GUIDELINES: WRITING ARGUMENTATION-PERSUASION

1. To decide on a topic, try the following:
   a. Review the editorial pages and letters to the editor in your campus and
      community newspapers for controversial issues that can serve as topics.
   b. Fill in the blank in the following sentence: I think it is unfair that
      _____. If, for example, you complete the sentence
      to get "I think it is unfair that students cannot go on strike," you can
      write an essay arguing that students should be permitted to strike.
      Other fill-in-the-blank sentences that can lead to a topic include

- I have always been angry that _____. (Argue for a change in what angers you.)
- The worst feature of this university is _____. (Argue for a change that would improve the feature.)
- If I had the power, I would _____. (Argue for the advisability of what you would do.)
- I disagree with people who believe _____. (Show why these people are wrong and support your view.)

2. To generate ideas to support your view, answer the following questions:
   a. Why is my issue important?
   b. What would happen if my view were adopted?
   c. What would happen if my view were not adopted?
   d. What are the two strongest objections to my view?
   e. How can these objections be countered?

3. To help generate ideas *and* determine methods of development, answer these questions:
   a. What story can I tell to support my view?
   b. Is there anything I can describe to support my view?
   c. What examples can I provide to support my view?
   d. Are there any comparisons I can make to support my view?
   e. Are there any contrasts I can draw to support my view?
   f. Do any aspects of my topic require definition? classification?
   g. Do any cause-and-effect relationships support my view?

4. List every reason you can think of to support your stand. Do not evaluate the strength of these reasons; just get down everything that occurs to you. When you can think of no more reasons, take a second sheet and list every reason you can think of to oppose your view. This second list will be a source of ideas for raising and countering objections. Next to each opposition point, jot down a few words about how the objection can be countered.

5. The following can help you settle on a purpose compatible with your audience.

If your audience . . .	*a possible purpose is . . .*
a. is well informed and strongly opposed to your view,	a. to lessen the opposition by convincing the audience that some of your points are valid and worth consideration.
b. is poorly informed and opposed to your view,	b. to inform the audience and to change the audience's view.
c. would find it difficult to perform the desired action,	c. to convince the audience that it is worth the sacrifice or to convince the audience to do some part of what is desired.

d. would not find it difficult to perform the desired action,

e. has no interest one way or the other in the issue,

d. to convince the audience to perform the action.

e. to arouse interest and persuade the audience to your view.

6. If you like to secure reader response during revision, consult page 115. In addition, ask your reader to note any important objections you failed to raise and counter. Also ask your reader to note any convincing points you failed to include.

REVISION CHECKLIST

In addition to the checklist on page 117, you can use this checklist when you revise your argumentation-persuasion.

1. Is your issue debatable and not a matter of taste?
2. Does your thesis note the issue and your stand?
3. Have you avoided logical fallacies?
4. Are your emotional appeals properly restrained?
5. Have you raised and countered compelling objections and otherwise maintained goodwill with your reader?
6. Where appropriate, have you speculated about what would happen if your view were (or were not) adopted?
7. Have you provided and explained all the reasons for your view?

EXERCISE | **Writing Argumentation-Persuasion**

1. Pick two of the following subjects and write a thesis statement for each that would be suitable for an argumentation-persuasion essay. Be sure each thesis mentions the issue and your stand on the issue.

television	rock music	college life
sports	graduation requirements	politics

2. For each thesis below, note a particular concern the indicated audience is likely to have and how hard it will be to convince the reader with that concern.

   a. In order to graduate from college, students should be required to perform 40 hours of community service. *(audience = college students)*

   b. In order to graduate from college, students should be required to perform 40 hours of community service. *(audience = college administrators)*

   c. Building a water tower on Cadillac Drive will allow water to reach the north quarter of the township, allowing new businesses to locate there and revitalize the area. *(audience = homeowners on Cadillac Drive)*

d. Building a water tower on Cadillac Drive will allow water to reach the north quarter of the township, allowing new businesses to locate there and revitalize the area. *(audience = township administrators)*

e. Establishing a curfew for people under 18 will help keep our youth out of trouble. *(audience = parents)*

f. Establishing a curfew for people under 18 will help keep our youth out of trouble. *(audience = teenagers)*

3. Select one of the following thesis statements:

a. High school seniors should be required to pass a proficiency test in order to graduate.

b. High school seniors should not be required to pass a proficiency test in order to graduate.

Assume that your audience will be the members of your local school board. With that audience in mind, write out two possible objections to your stand and explain how you can counter those objections.

4. Each of the following includes one or more logical fallacies. Identify what they are.

a. The proposed assisted-living facility is an unnecessary expenditure of public funds. The elderly in this city have always been cared for by family members or in nursing homes.

b. Those who favor school prayer are the same reactionaries who bomb abortion clinics.

c. The last generation has seen a marked increase in the number of working mothers, which explains the similar increase in the rate of violent crime.

d. Because football players care less about their schoolwork than their sport, the university should eliminate athletic scholarships.

e. How can any union member not vote for Chris Politician? After all, every major labor group in the country has endorsed him.

5. *Collaborative Activity.* With two or three classmates, analyze the chief strengths and weaknesses of a persuasive editorial in your local or campus newspaper.

PROFESSIONAL ESSAYS

Parents Also Have Rights

Ronnie Gunnerson

Ronnie Gunnerson argues that parents, not the pregnant teenager, should be legally empowered to decide the fate of the teen's unborn child. Her essay first appeared in Newsweek's *"My Turn" column.*

"What's a parent to do?" is the punch line to many a joke on the perils of raising *1* children. But what a parent does when a teenager gets pregnant is far from a joke: It's a soul-searching, heart-wrenching condition with responses as diverse as the families affected.

In an era besotted with concern for both the emotional and social welfare of   *2*
teenage mothers and their babies, anger seems to be forbidden. Yet how many
parents can deny anger when circumstances over which they have no control
force them into untenable situations?

And untenable they are. What I discovered after my 16-year-old step-   *3*
daughter became pregnant shocked me. Parents have no rights. We could neither
demand she give the baby up for adoption, nor insist on an abortion. The choice
belongs to the teenage mother, who is still a child herself and far from capable of
understanding the lifelong ramifications of whatever choice she makes.

At the same time, homes for unwed mothers, at least the two we checked in   *4*
Los Angeles, where we live, will house the teenager at no cost to the family, but
they will not admit her unless her parents sign a statement agreeing to pick up
both her and her baby from a designated maternity hospital. Parents may sit out
the pregnancy if they so desire, but when all is said and done, they're stuck with
both mother and baby whether they like it or not.

In essence, then, the pregnant teenager can choose whether or not to have   *5*
her baby and whether or not to keep it. The parents, who have the legal responsibility for both the teenage mother and her child, have no say in the matter. The
costs of a teenage pregnancy are high; yes, the teenager's life is forever changed by
her untimely pregnancy and childbirth. But life is forever changed for the rest of
her family as well, and I am tired of the do-gooders who haven't walked a yard, let
alone a mile, in my shoes shouting their sympathy for the "victimized" teen.

What about the victimized parents? Are we supposed to accept the popular   *6*
notion that we failed this child and that therefore we are to blame for her lack of
either scruples or responsibility? Not when we spend endless hours and thousands of dollars in therapy trying to help a girl whose behavior has been rebellious since the age of 13. Not when we have heart-to-heart talks until the wee
hours of the morning which we learn are the butt of jokes between her and her
friends. And not when we continually trust her only to think afterward that she's
repeatedly lied to us about everything there is to lie about.

Yes, the teenager is a victim—a victim of illusions fostered by a society that   *7*
gives her the right to decide whether or not to have an illegitimate baby, no matter what her parents say. Many believe it is feelings of rejection that motivate girls
to have babies; they want human beings of their own to love and be loved by. I
wouldn't disagree, but another motive may be at work as well: the ultimate rebellion. Parents are forced to cope with feelings more devastating than adolescent
confusion. And I'm not talking about the superficial, what-will-the-Joneses-think
attitudes. I mean gut-gripping questions that undermine brutally the self-confidence it can take adults years to develop.

We can all write off to immaturity mistakes made in adolescence. To what   *8*
do we attribute our perceived parental failures at 40 or 50? Even as I proclaim
our innocence in my stepdaughter's folly, I will carry to my grave, as I know my
husband will, the nagging fear that we could have prevented it *if only* we'd been
better parents.

And I will carry forevermore the sad realization that I'm not the compas- *9*
sionate person I'd tried so hard to be and actually thought I was. My reaction to
my stepdaughter's pregnancy horrified me. I was consumed with hatred and
anger. Any concern I felt for her was overridden by the feeling that I'd been had.
I'd befriended this child, housed her and counseled her for years, and what did I
get in return? Not knowing her whereabouts that culminated in her getting pregnant with a boy we didn't even know. At first I felt like a fool. When I discovered
how blatantly society's rules favor the rule breaker, I felt like a raving maniac.

Resentment and rage: It took more hours of counseling for me to accept my *10*
anger than it did for my stepdaughter to deal with her pregnancy. But then, she
had the support of a teenage subculture that reveres motherhood among its own
and a news-media culture that fusses and frets over adolescent mothers. Few ears
were willing to hear what my husband and I were feeling. While I can't speak for
my husband, I can say that today, a year after the baby's birth, he still turns to ice
when his daughter is around. Smitten as he is with his first grandchild, he hasn't
forgotten that the joy of the boy's birth was overshadowed by resentment and rage.

Fortunately, my stepdaughter recently married a young man who loves her *11*
son as his own, although he is not the father. Together, the three of them are a
family who, like many a young family, are struggling to make ends meet. Neither
my stepdaughter nor her husband has yet finished high school, but they are not a
drain on society as many teenage parents are. She and her husband seem to be
honest, hard workers, and I really think they will make it. Their story will have a
happy ending.

My stepdaughter says she can't even understand the person she used to be, *12*
and I believe her. Unfortunately, the minds of adults are not quite as malleable as
those of constantly changing adolescents. My husband and I haven't forgotten—
and I'm not sure we've forgiven—either our daughter or ourselves. We're still
writing the ending to our own story, and I believe it's time for society to write an
ending of its own. If a pregnant teenager's parents are ultimately responsible for
the teenager and her baby, then give those parents the right to decide whether or
not the teenager keeps her baby. Taking the decision away from the teen mother
would eliminate her power over her parents and could give pause to her reckless
pursuit of the "in" thing.

Considering Ideas

1. Why does Gunnerson consider the parents of a pregnant teenager to be
   in an "untenable" position?
2. Do you agree or disagree that the choice about her pregnancy "belongs
   to the teenage mother, who is still a child herself and far from capable of
   understanding the lifelong ramifications of whatever choice she makes"
   (paragraph 3)? Explain your view.
3. For what reasons does Gunnerson believe that parents should decide the
   fate of their teenager's baby?

4. "Parents Also Have Rights" first appeared in *Newsweek*. Is the strong emotional appeal in the essay likely to move the author's intended audience? Explain.

5. Does the fact that Gunnerson's stepdaughter ultimately married and made a life for herself (although a difficult one) detract from the author's argument? Explain.

Considering Technique

1. The most direct statement of Gunnerson's issue and stand does not appear in the introduction but in the conclusion. Which sentence provides this statement?

2. What approach does Gunnerson take to her introduction?

3. What purpose do paragraphs 2 and 3 serve?

4. In which paragraphs does Gunnerson raise and counter objections? How does she counter each objection?

5. Where does Gunnerson speculate about what would happen if her view were adopted?

For Group Discussion or Journal Writing

Ronnie Gunnerson admits to feeling angry about her stepdaughter's pregnancy and its effect on the family. Consider to what extent Gunnerson's anger adds to or detracts from the convincingness of her essay.

Why I Dread Black History Month

Wayne M. Joseph

In this essay, which first appeared in Newsweek, *middle school principal Wayne M. Joseph, argues that Black History Month misses the point that black history cannot be separated from American history.*

Every year when the month of February approaches, I'm overcome with a feeling *1* of dread. February is hailed as Black History Month, a national observance that is celebrated neither at the school in which I am the principal nor in my own home. This may come as a surprise to the even casual observer, since I am black. In my humble estimation Black History Month is a thriving monument to tokenism which, ironically, has been wholeheartedly embraced and endorsed by the black community.

For at least 28 days we are bombarded by the media with reminders of *2* great black Americans. Teachers across America dust off last year's lesson plans and speak of African kings and queens. Dr. Martin Luther King's "I Have A Dream" speech is played repeatedly and there are festivities where people wear traditional African garb and may even speak a few words of Swahili.

So, you might ask, what is wrong with this? *3*

Black contribution to American history is so rich and varied that attempting 4
to confine the discussion and investigation to four weeks a year tends to trivialize
the momentous impact that blacks have had on American society.

There is also a tendency to somehow feel that "black" history is separate 5
from "*American*" history. "Black" history *is* American history—they are not mu-
tually exclusive. The struggles of black people in America strike at the core of our
country's past and its development. One cannot, for instance, hope to thoroughly
study the factors leading to the Civil War or Reconstruction without investigating
the issue of slavery and the emancipation of those slaves. American music and
dance has little significance without the recognition of black influences. Spiritu-
als, jazz and the blues are a vital and important part of American culture. To
speak of the experience of black people in America (as some are inclined to do
during the month of February) as independent of the American social, political,
and economic forces at work in our country is a misreading of history at best and
a flagrant attempt to rewrite it at worst.

Of course very few people will be courageous enough during February to 6
say that it's irrelevant whether or not Cleopatra and Jesus were black, since their
experiences have not the slightest kinship with those of black Americans.

It is not very difficult to understand why the distant (usually African) past 7
is used as a way to give blacks a sense of cultural identity. In the final analysis,
however, it's a hollow attempt to fill a vacuum that was created by the institution
of slavery. It is widely acknowledged that one of the more insidious aspects of
American slavery was that Africans of different cultures and languages were
stripped of their cultural base and were forced to learn the enslaver's tongue to
survive. Unlike the German, Italian, and Jewish immigrants who came to this
country with their own languages, religions, and customs, Africans of different
backgrounds were compelled to eschew their own roots in order to survive on
American soil.

Slavery and Segregation

Instead of African kings and queens who never set foot in America, it is the black 8
people who survived the infamous "middle passage" and endured slavery who
should be heralded as "kings" and "queens" for their courage and perseverance.
After slavery, there were scores of blacks who endured beatings, lynchings, and
daily degradations indigenous to the system of discrimination in both the North
and the South; yet these paragons of endurance are seldom lauded. It's as if the
words "slavery" and "segregation" are to be mentioned only fleetingly during
February. We should look to our own grandfathers and grandmothers to find examples of real heroism. Unfortunately, the significance of these black men and
women as well as the traditional black icons—Dr. King, Malcolm X, Jackie
Robinson, et al.—are lost in a month in which people are studied in isolation instead of within the historical context that produced them.

Black parents must try to instill in children a sense of their own history. 9
This should include a sense of family—the accomplishments of parents, grandparents, and ancestors has more relevance than some historical figure whose only

connection to the child is skin color. We in the schools are often expected to fill the gaps that parents have neglected in their child's development; but for every child a knowledge of identity and self-worth must come from home to be meaningful and long-lasting. For the black child, a month-long emphasis on black culture will never fill that void.

There will be those, I'm sure, who will say that I should feel pleased that 10 black people are recognized one month out of the year, knowing the difficulty black Americans have historically encountered validating their accomplishments. But being black does not entitle one to more or less recognition based solely on heritage. In a multicultural society, there is a need to celebrate our cultural differences as well as our commonalities as human beings. No one group has a monopoly on this need.

One month out of every year, Americans are "given permission" to com- 11 memorate the achievements of black people. This rather condescending view fails to acknowledge that a people and a country's past should be nurtured and revered; instead, at this time, the past of black Americans is handled in an expedient and cavalier fashion denigrating the very people it seeks to honor.

February is here again, and I'll be approached by a black student or parent 12 inquiring as to what the school is doing to celebrate Black History Month. My answer, as always, will be that my teachers and I celebrate the contributions of *all* Americans *every* month of the school year.

Considering Ideas

1. What reasons does Joseph give for his opposition to Black History Month?
2. Do you find Joseph's reasons convincing? Why or why not? Are there any reasons he should have included but did not?
3. Do you think Joseph's position on Black History Month is popular among African-Americans? Why or why not?
4. Joseph dwells on the negative aspects of Black History Month. What positive aspects are associated with it? Do the positive aspects outweigh the negative? Explain.

Considering Technique

1. In paragraph 1, Joseph identifies himself as a black school principal. Why does he do so?
2. What element of emotional appeal appears in paragraphs 1 and 2? In paragraph 4? What does the emotional appeal contribute to the persuasive quality of the essay?
3. What objection does Joseph raise, and how does he counter it? Is the counter effective? Are there any other objections that he should have raised and countered?
4. How does Joseph use examples in paragraph 5? What do the examples contribute to the persuasive quality of the essay?
5. What technique does Joseph use to create goodwill in paragraph 7?

For Group Discussion or Journal Writing

Joseph says that an alternative to Black History Month is for children to learn about their own family histories. What can be gained when people study their family histories? Is this endeavor a suitable alternative to Black History Month?

Combining Patterns of Development

Four-Letter Words Can Hurt You

Barbara Lawrence

College professor and writer Barbara Lawrence argues that obscene words are hurtful because of their negative, sexist connotations. As you read, notice the author's use of **cause-and-effect analysis, exemplification,** *and* **definition.**

Why should any words be called obscene? Don't they all describe natural human *1*
functions? Am I trying to tell them, my students demand, that the "strong, earthy, gut-honest"—or, if they are fans of Norman Mailer, the "rich, liberating, existential"—language they use to describe sexual activity isn't preferable to "phony-sounding, middle-class words like 'intercourse' and 'copulate'?" "Cop You Late!" they say with fancy inflections and gagging grimaces. "Now, what is *that* supposed to mean?"

Well, what is it supposed to mean? And why indeed should one group of *2*
words describing human functions and human organs be acceptable in ordinary conversation and another, describing presumably the same organs and functions, be tabooed—so much so, in fact, that some of these words still cannot appear in print in many parts of the English-speaking world?

The argument that these taboos exist only because of "sexual hangups" *3*
(middle-class, middle-age, feminist), or even that they are a result of class oppression (the contempt of the Norman conquerors for the language of their Anglo-Saxon serfs), ignores a much more likely explanation, it seems to me, and that is the sources and functions of the words themselves.

The best known of the tabooed sexual words, for example, comes from the *4*
German *ficken,* meaning "to strike"; combined according to Partridge's etymological dictionary *Origins,* with the Latin sexual verb *futuere:* associated in turn with the Latin *fustis,* "a staff or cudgel"; the Celtic *buc,* "a point, hence to pierce"; the Irish *bot,* "the male member"; the Latin *battuere,* "to beat"; the Gaelic *batair,* "a cudgeller"; the Early Irish *bualaim,* "I strike"; and so forth. It is one of what etymologists sometimes called "the sadistic group of words for the man's part in copulation."

The brutality of this word, then, and its equivalents ("screw," "bang," *5*
etc.), is not an illusion of the middle class or a crotchet of Women's Liberation. In their origins and imagery these words carry undeniably painful, if not sadistic, implications, the object of which is almost always female. Consider, for example, what a "screw" actually does to the wood it penetrates; what a painful, even mutilating, activity this kind of analogy suggests. "Screw" is particularly interesting

in this context, since the noun, according to Partridge, comes from words meaning "groove," "nut," "ditch," "breeding sow," "scrofula," and "swelling," while the verb, besides its explicit imagery, has antecedent associations to "write on," "scratch," "scarify," and so forth—a revealing fusion of a mechanical or painful action with an obviously denigrated object.

Not all obscene words, of course, are as implicitly sadistic or denigrating to 6 women as these, but all that I know seem to serve a similar purpose: to reduce the human organism (especially the female organism) and human functions (especially sexual and procreative) to their least organic, most mechanical dimension; to substitute a trivializing or deforming resemblance for the complex human reality of what is being described.

Tabooed male descriptives, when they are not openly denigrating to 7 women, often serve to divorce a male organ or function from any significant interaction with the female. Take the word "testes," for example, suggesting "witnesses" (from the Latin *testis*) to the sexual and procreative strengths of the male organ; and the obscene counterpart of this word, which suggests little more than a mechanical shape. Or compare almost any of the "rich," "liberating" sexual verbs, so fashionable today among male writers, with that much-derived Latin word "copulate" ("to bind or join together") or even that Anglo-Saxon phrase (which seems to have had no trouble surviving the Norman Conquest) "make love."

How arrogantly self-involved the tabooed words seem in comparison to ei- 8 ther of the other terms, and how contemptuous of the female partner. Understandably so, of course, if she is only a "skirt," a "broad," a "chick," a "pussycat" or a "piece." If she is, in other words no more than her skirt, or what her skirt conceals; no more than a breeder, or the broadest part of her; no more than a piece of a human being or a "piece of tail."

The most severely tabooed of all the female descriptives, incidentally, are 9 those like a "piece of tail," which suggests (either explicitly or through antecedents) that there is no significant difference between the female channel through which we are all conceived and born and the anal outlet common to both sexes—a distinction that pornographers have always enjoyed obscuring.

This effort to deny women their biological identity, their individuality, their 10 humanness, is such an important aspect of obscene language that one can only marvel at how seldom, in an era preoccupied with definitions of obscenity, this fact is brought to our attention. One problem, of course, is that many of the people in the best position to do this (critics, teachers, writers) are so reluctant today to admit that they are angered or shocked by obscenity. Bored, maybe, unimpressed, aesthetically displeased, but—no matter how brutal or denigrating the material—never angered, never shocked.

And yet how eloquently angered, how piously shocked many of these same 11 people become if denigrating language is used about any minority group other than women; if the obscenities are racial or ethnic, that is, rather than sexual. Words like "coon," "kike," "spic," "wop," after all, deform identity, deny individuality and humanness in almost exactly the same way that sexual vulgarisms and obscenities do.

No one that I know, least of all my students, would fail to question the val- *12* ues of a society whose literature and entertainment rested heavily on racial or ethnic pejoratives. Are the values of a society whose literature and entertainment rest as heavily as ours on sexual pejoratives any less questionable?

Considering Ideas

1. In your own words, write out the thesis of "Four-Letter Words Can Hurt You." Which paragraph best expresses that thesis idea?
2. Why does Lawrence avoid using obscene words in paragraphs 4 and 7? If she had chosen to include obscene words, would you consider her essay obscene? Why or why not?
3. In paragraph 10, Lawrence says that many people are "reluctant . . . to admit that they are angered or shocked by obscenity." If you agree, why do you think this is the case? If you disagree, tell why.
4. Considering that most people are unaware of the history of specific obscene words like the ones discussed in paragraphs 4 and 5, do you agree that these words demean women? Explain. Has your attitude about or will your use of these words change as a result of reading the essay? Explain.
5. Using the evidence in the essay for clues, what do you think Lawrence's attitude toward pornography is?

Considering Technique

1. Lawrence begins and ends her essay with questions. What purpose do these questions serve?
2. Why does Lawrence include a description of her students' reactions to obscene words (paragraph 1)?
3. What objections does Lawrence raise, and how does she counter them? Are the counters effective? Explain.
4. *Combining Patterns.* What aspect of definition appears in the essay? What does the definition contribute to the persuasive quality of the essay? What aspect of illustration appears, and what does it contribute to the persuasive quality? What element of cause-and-effect analysis appears, and what does it contribute to the persuasive quality?
5. How does Lawrence use emotional appeal to persuade the reader? Is her pattern of reasoning inductive or deductive?

For Group Discussion or Journal Writing

Since Lawrence wrote her essay, obscenities have become more prevalent both in society and in the media. Explain why you think this is the case and evaluate whether or not the trend is a harmful one.

STUDENT ESSAYS TO READ AND EVALUATE

Each of the argumentation-persuasion essays that follow was written by a student. Each has strengths and weaknesses. Reading and evaluating these essays will make you a more knowing judge of your own writing. Also, by studying what others have done, you can discover successful techniques to incorporate into your own writing and less successful techniques to avoid.

The Old Ball Game

"For it's one, two, three strikes you're out at the old ball game."   *1*
A catchy tune if you happen to be singing it, agonizing reality if you happen to be six or seven years old and playing in an organized baseball league. Six- and seven-year-old children are simply not emotionally ready, and therefore should simply not be permitted, to play on an organized baseball team.

Consider this not-so-uncommon scene: The pitch is made. The bat   *2*
and ball connect, and the grounder heads toward the 3 1/2-foot-tall first baseman. He opens his glove. He just has to pick up the ball, tag first base, and the runner will be out. He misses the ball. Hurriedly trying to retrieve it, the first baseman's attempt is futile, and the runner is safe. The manager, the father of one of the boys, stops the game, walks out halfway toward the first baseman, and yells, "What are you doing, Michael? You should have had that ball. Now settle down." There's nothing like public humiliation to damage a tender psyche.

Some people argue that just as much, if not more, yelling goes   *3*
on during backyard neighborhood games. This is true, but the yelling there goes back and forth among the kids. In the organized leagues, the manager yells at, and sometimes even humiliates, his players. The player, of course, is not permitted to respond, and thus frustration and feelings of inadequacy can build. He can only try to cope with these feelings that have been heaped on him, which can be quite an emotional struggle for a child so young.

Even major league baseball players make mistakes on the field;   *4*
can a six- or seven-year-old player be expected to be any better? If a player misses the ball, no one feels worse than he does. Instead, why not praise the good plays made by the kids and ignore

the mistakes? Unfortunately, this doesn't seem to be what happens in many cases.

I believe the goal of organized sports is for the children   5
involved to have fun. Unfortunately, this frequently does not happen. Too much emphasis is placed on winning by both the managers and the parents. This inevitably leads to feelings of disappointment and failure in the children. Imagine being six years old and up to bat. One hit is all you need to win the ball game. This would create a lot of pressure for many adults. It is simply too much pressure for six- and seven-year-olds. The pitch is made and you're out. Some might say that children must learn to deal with disappointment and failure. I also believe this is true, but certainly not at such a young age.

It has been said that organized sports are a good source of   6
discipline. However, children should be learning discipline in the home, as well as in school. Further sources of discipline are unnecessary.

To me, there is nothing more heartbreaking than watching a six-   7
or seven-year-old baseball player crying because he just struck out, he missed the ball, or he just got yelled at by his manager. I guess I'm old-fashioned—I prefer games that make children laugh and leave them smiling.

🎐 It Is Just That Simple

The United States has, by far, the highest number of shooting   1
deaths in the world. We have a hundred times more shooting deaths than Great Britain, Germany, and Israel combined. Banning hand guns would decrease the number of murders in the United States. It is just that simple.

All gun owners should be required to turn their guns back in   2
for the amount of money they were bought for. What's that you say? That will leave guns in the hands of the criminals, while ordinary, law-abiding citizens will be left unarmed and at the mercy of the criminal element? No, criminals will not voluntarily turn in their weapons, but we can create some effective deterrents to committing

crimes with guns. Mandatory sentences of at least twenty years would be effective, especially if we eliminated all plea bargaining in such cases. Furthermore, when criminals know that their victims are unarmed, they will be less likely to arm themselves with guns when they commit their crimes.

We have to remember that shooting deaths at the hands of criminals are only part of the issue. The number of accidental deaths, often involving children, is frightening. Lately, students have been opening fire in schools. We now have children angry over grades, distraught over being dumped, and depressed over a teacher's comment taking guns from legal owners and wreaking havoc. None of this could happen if guns were not available. Lives would definitely be saved. We have to ask ourselves how we got to this point that children think that a gun is a legitimate way to solve a problem or settle a score.

3

Gun control opponents are fond of trotting out the Constitutional right to bear arms as a defense for owning handguns. However, no longer do people need to keep a gun handy for fear of invasion by British soldiers. The Constitution can and should be amended. In fact, one of the strengths of the document is that it has provisions for change. If it did not recognize the need to change with the times, then women would not be voting today.

4

I have also heard it said that if a person is angry enough, he or she will kill, whether a gun is available or not. That argument does not work because guns allow people to kill more easily in the heat of passion. Knives, rocks, bows and arrows, and any other weapon you can think of is less likely to be lethal. Thus, while the number of attacks might not decrease when it comes to crimes of passion, the number of deaths certainly will.

5

Another argument for handguns that I often hear is the now clichéd comment, "Guns don't kill people. People kill people." That's absurd. People *do* kill people, but they are doing it with guns. Take away the guns and you take away the ability to kill easily.

6

Perhaps the most convincing argument for banning guns is the fact that, in countries where guns are outlawed, the murder rate is significantly less than it is in the United States. What greater proof than that is there?

7

Like discussions of religion and abortion, debates about   *8*
handguns are sure to get people screaming at each other. However,
if we can forget the emotion and look at the statistics, we would
see that like other countries, the United States can reduce the
number of shooting deaths by banning handguns.

Collaborative Exercise: Evaluating Writing

Form a group, select one of the previous essays, and identify its chief strengths
and weaknesses. Have a recorder note these and a spokesperson report them to
the rest of the class. If you like, you can use the following evaluation questions to
guide your study.

Evaluation Questions

1. *The Thesis*
   What is the thesis? What does it present as the issue and the writer's
   stand on the issue? Is the issue debatable and not a matter of taste?
2. *The Introduction*
   Does the introduction engage your interest? Why or why not?
3. *Supporting Details*
   Note any details that are unclear or irrelevant. Note any logical fallacies
   or unrestrained appeals to emotion. Evaluate the raising and countering
   of objections. How convincing is the essay? Why?
4. *Organization*
   Are the details placed in a progressive or other logical order? Evaluate
   the use of transitions and topic sentences.
5. *The Conclusion*
   Does the essay come to a safisfying end? Why or why not?
6. *Overview*
   What do you like best about the essay? What is the single most important revision the author should make?

Essay Topics: Argumentation-Persuasion

When you write your essay, consult Pitfalls to Avoid on page 346, Process
Guidelines on page 346, and the Revision Checklist on page 348.

Writing in the Pattern.

1. Write an argumentation-persuasion essay on one of the following:

bilingual education	advertising in children's programming
school prayer	a longer school year
athletic scholarships	mandatory retirement
open admissions policies	violence in the media
the salaries of professional athletes	

2. Write an essay arguing for a specific change at your college or place of employment.

3. Write an essay arguing that high school students should (or should not) have to pass a proficiency test in order to graduate.

4. If you had the power to draft one piece of legislation, what would it be? Write an essay that explains the legislation and argues for its passage.

5. If you believe that the current movie rating system is inadequate, explain why, describe a better system, and argue for its adoption.

Reading Then Writing in the Pattern

1. Argue for or against the point of view reflected in "Parents Also Have Rights" (page 349). That is, argue that pregnant, unwed teens, not their parents, should decide the fate of their babies.

2. Taking the view opposite that of the student who wrote "The Old Ball Game" (page 358), defend organized baseball leagues for six- and seven-year-olds.

3. Taking the view opposite that advanced in "Why I Dread Black History Month" (page 352), argue that Black History Month is a positive celebration of black culture and accomplishment.

4. Write an essay entitled "Four-Letter Words Cannot Hurt You" and argue a position opposite that expressed by Barbara Lawrence (page 354).

Responding to the Readings

1. "Parents Also Have Rights" (page 349) deals with the problem of teen pregnancy. Although a number of solutions to the problem of teenage pregnancy have been tried, the problem persists. Explain why you think the problem endures. As an alternative, explain what you think can be done to solve the problem.

2. In paragraph 7 of "Why I Dread Black History Month" (page 352), Wayne M. Joseph notes that African-Americans have been stripped of their cultural base. Explain why that is the case and go on to explore what happens when people lose their cultural base.

3. Barbara Lawrence (page 354) maintains that obscenities are harmful. Yet over the years the use of obscenities has increased both among individuals and in the media. Explain what has caused this increase, and explore what it says about our culture.

4. *Connecting the Readings.* What points can you draw about the way we celebrate diversity, as a result of reading "It Is Time to Stop Playing Indians" (page 273) and "Why I Dread Balck History Month" (page 352)? Describe a celebration of which you think Hirschfelder and Joseph would approve.

Persuasion in Advertising

On television, on radio, on billboards, on ballpark fences, on subways, on busses, on milk cartons, on cereal boxes, in newspapers, in magazines, in movie theatres, at bus stops, on telephone poles, on Web pages, on match books, on the backs of grocery receipts, on flyers in our mailboxes, in airports, in train stations, in shopping malls, even in schools on Channel 1, advertising is—almost literally—everywhere. And this advertising has one goal only: To persuade you and me to buy products.

Clearly, the advertising is overwhelmingly effective because companies spend tremendous amounts of money on their advertising campaigns, and we are buying in greater volume than every before. It would be wise of us, therefore, to take a look at just how advertising persuades us so successfully.

To appreciate how print advertising utilizes the persuasive techniques discussed in this chapter, examine the advertisements for similar products that appear on the next two pages. Then write an essay that identifies and discusses the persuasive strategies apparent in the ads. To guide your thinking, you can consider all or some of the following questions:

1. What are the ads trying to persuade the reader to think or do?
2. What audience(s) does each ad target?
3. How does each ad address its audience(s)?
4. What are the visual elements in each ad? How do those visual elements contribute to each ad's persuasive quality? How important are the visual elements?
5. How is language used in each ad? What does the language contribute to each ad's persuasive quality? How important is the language?
6. What element of emotional appeal appears in each ad? How important is that emotional appeal to the persuasive quality of each ad?
7. What element of logical reasoning appears in each ad? How important are those elements to each ad's persuasive quality?
8. How effective is each ad likely to be in persuading its audience?

Some artwork you value above all others. That's because it was created by your child. To help protect your budding artist, LeSabre comes with standard anti-lock brakes. Visit www.lesabre.buick.com or call 1-800-4A-BUICK.

LeSabre *by* Buick

PEACE OF MIND

CHAPTER 13

Writing in Response to Reading

The reading you do in college must be thoughtful reading; it requires you to pay close attention to ideas, evaluate their merit, and consider how they relate to other ideas you have encountered both in and out of the classroom. It requires you to question assumptions, draw conclusions, form opinions, test ideas, weigh things out, judge the significance of points, reconsider, and perhaps change your mind. When you do all this, you are **reading analytically.**

After reading analytically, you will often be called upon to write in response to what you have read. In fact, writing in response to reading is the most important way scholars, including student scholars, communicate with one another. One person writes something he or she thinks is significant, and someone else reacts by writing a response, which may prompt yet another person to write a reaction. All these written responses make up scholarly journals, newsletters, books, student newspapers, theses, and dissertations—the means by which teachers and other scholars communicate with one another.

As a college student, you are a part of this community of writers—this group of people who read and react in writing to share ideas, inform others of developments, and argue points of view. In addition, writing in response to reading is an important part of your college life because it helps you grapple with the ideas of others and shape your reactions to those ideas. In short, writing in response to reading is one way you learn.

This chapter will help you become more comfortable reading analytically and writing in response to that reading so you can take your place in the ongoing written exchange and so you can use writing as a means of learning.

READING ANALYTICALLY

To read analytically, you must focus your attention to make certain discoveries about the material and draw important conclusions. To do this, you may need to read the material more than once—even several times if the material is challenging enough—to learn the answers to questions like those in the following box.

QUESTIONS TO ANSWER WHEN READING ANALYTICALLY

1. **What is the thesis?**
2. **Is the thesis adequately supported?** Is there enough detail? Is all the detail relevant? Are there any logical flaws? Is the support convincing? Is the author offering facts, opinions, or both?
3. **What is the source of the author's detail?** Is the author writing from personal experience and observation? The testimony of authorities? Research? Is the source of the detail reliable?
4. **Does the author reveal any particular bias or point of view?**
5. **What is the significance of the material?** Do I agree or disagree with the author? Do any points relate to other material I have studied, read, or otherwise learned about? How does the material compare and contrast with other things I have read? How important are the author's ideas? How can the author's thesis and ideas be applied?
6. **What is the author's purpose and who is his intended audience?**
7. **What have I learned from the material?** How can I relate the material to my life?
8. **Is the material well written?**

Marking a Text

You can facilitate analytical reading by reading with a pencil or pen in hand and marking the text in the following way as you go:

1. Underline the thesis if it is stated.
2. Underline the main points (often given in topic sentences). Avoid underlining subpoints, or the page will be cluttered with underlining.
3. In the margins, write your responses, including areas of agreement and disagreement, personal associations the text evokes, questions that arise, and so forth. Your marginal notations can include jottings like these: "yes," "I disagree," "reminds me of Dale," and "I don't get this."
4. Also in the margins, evaluate what you are reading. Note whether you find something untrue, biased, fair, unproven, unclear, interesting, unsupported, angry, surprising, sarcastic, or dated. You can write things like "unclear"; "not true where I live"; "where's the proof?"; "good example"; "seems strange"; "sounds great"; and "not true anymore."
5. Place a star (★) next to words, phrases, or sentences that you find particularly appealing.
6. Place a question mark next to anything you do not understand, including words to look up in the dictionary.

Remember, you may need to read a text more than once to give it proper attention. Each time you read, do so with a pencil or pen and mark the text. Here is an example of how an analytic reader might mark an essay.

School Is Bad for Children

John Holt

John Holt (1923–1985) was a teacher and writer who gained notoriety in the 60s and 70s for advocating that children control their own learning. His most famous book is How Children Fail *(1964).*

<u>Almost every child, on the first day he sets foot in a school building, is smarter, more curious, less afraid of what he doesn't know, better at finding and figuring things out, more confident, resourceful, persistent and independent than he will ever be again in his schooling</u>—or, unless he is very unusual and very lucky, for the rest of his life. Already, by paying close attention to and interacting with the world and people around him, and without any school-type formal instruction, he has done a task far more difficult, complicated, and abstract than anything he will be asked to do in school, or than any of his teachers has done for years. He has solved the mystery of language. He has discovered it—babies don't even know that language exists—and he has found out how it works and learned to use it. He has done it by exploring, by experimenting, by developing his own model of the grammar of language, by trying it out and seeing whether it works, by gradually changing it and refining it until it does work. And while he has been doing this, he has been learning other things as well, including many of the "concepts" that the schools think only they can teach him, and many that are more complicated than the ones they do try to teach him.

In he comes, this curious, patient, determined, energetic, skillful learner. We sit him down at a desk, and <u>what do we teach him</u>? Many things. First, that <u>learning is separate from living</u>. "You come to school to learn," we tell him, as if the child hadn't been learning before, as if living were out there and learning were in here, and there were no connection between the two. Secondly, that <u>he cannot be trusted to learn and is no good at it</u>. Everything we teach about reading, a task far simpler than many that the child has already mastered, says to him, "If we don't make you read, you won't, and if you don't do it exactly the way we tell you, you can't." In short, (he) <u>comes to feel that learning is a passive process, something that someone else does *to* you, instead of something you do for yourself.</u>

Sexist: What about females?

<u>In a great many other ways, he learns that he is worthless, untrustworthy, fit only to take other people's orders, a blank sheet for other people to write on</u>. Oh, we make a lot of nice noises in school about respect for the child and individual differences, and the like. <u>But our acts, as opposed to our talk, say to the child, "Your experience, your concerns, your curiosities,</u> your needs, what you know, what you want, what you wonder about, what you hope for, what you fear, what you like and dislike, what you are good at or not so good at—all this <u>is of not the slightest importance, it counts for nothing</u>. What counts here, and the only thing that counts, is what we know, what we think is important, what we want you to do, think, and be." <u>The</u>

Yes! I've seen this happen many times.

1

2

3

child soon learns not to ask questions—the teacher isn't there to satisfy his curiosity. Having learned to hide his curiosity, he later learns to be ashamed of it. Given no chance to find out who he is—and to develop that person, whoever it is—he soon comes to accept the adults' evaluation of him.

School becomes a game.

Yes, just do the minimum to get by.

He learns many other things. He learns that to be wrong, uncertain, *4* confused, is a crime. Right Answers are what the school wants, and he learns countless strategies for prying these answers out of the teacher, for conning her into thinking he knows what he doesn't know. He learns to dodge, bluff, fake, cheat. He learns to be lazy. Before he came to school, he would work for hours on end, on his own, with no thought of reward, at the business of making sense of the world and gaining competence in it. In school he learns, like every buck private, how to goldbrick, how not to work when the sergeant isn't looking, how to know when he is looking, how to make him think you are working even when he is looking. He learns that in real life you don't do anything unless you are bribed, bullied, or conned into doing it, that nothing is worth doing for its own sake, or that if it is, you can't do it in school. He learns to be bored, to work with a small part of his mind, to escape from the reality around him into daydreams and fantasies—but not like the fantasies of his preschool years, in which he played a very active part.

This guy really hates teachers.

The child comes to school curious about other people, particularly *5* other children, and the school teaches him to be indifferent. The most interesting thing in the classroom—often the only interesting thing in it—is the other children, but he has to act as if these other children, all about him, only a few feet away, are not really there. He cannot interact with them, talk with them, smile at them. In many schools he can't talk to other children in the halls between classes; in more than a few, and some of these in stylish suburbs, he can't even talk to them at lunch. Splendid training for a world in which, when you're not studying the other person to figure out how to do him in, you pay no attention to him.

Nice sarcasm.

In fact, he learns how to live without paying attention to anything *6* going on around him. You might say that school is a long lesson in how to turn yourself off, which may be one reason why so many young people, seeking the awareness of the world and responsiveness to it they had when they were little, think they can only find it in drugs. Aside from being boring, the school is almost always ugly, cold, inhuman—even the most stylish, glass-windowed, $20-a-square-foot schools.

I disagree here.

And so, in this dull and ugly place, where nobody ever says anything *7* very truthful, where everybody is playing a kind of role, as in a charade, where the teachers are no more free to respond honestly to the students than the students are free to respond to the teachers or each other, where the air practically vibrates with suspicion and anxiety, the child learns to live in a daze, saving his energies for those small parts of his life that are too trivial for the adults to bother with, and thus remain his. It is a rare child who can come through his schooling with much left of his curiosity, his independence, or his sense of his own dignity, competence, and worth.

No! Lots of kids thrive in this environment.

So much for criticism. What do we need to do? Many things. Some 8 are easy—we can do them right away. Some are hard, and may take some time. Take a hard one first. <u>We should abolish compulsory school attendance</u>. <u>At the very least we should modify it</u>, <u>perhaps by giving children every year a large number of authorized absences</u>. Our compulsory school-attendance laws once served a humane and useful purpose. They protected children's right to some schooling, against those adults who would otherwise have denied it to them in order to exploit their labor, in farm, store, mine, or factory. Today the laws help nobody, not the schools, not the teachers, not the children. To keep kids in school who would rather not be there costs the schools an enormous amount of time and trouble—to say nothing of what it costs to repair the damage that these angry and resentful prisoners do every time they get a chance. Every teacher knows that any kid in class who, for whatever reason, would rather not be there not only doesn't learn anything himself but makes it a great deal tougher for anyone else. As for protecting the children from exploitation, the chief and indeed only exploiters of children these days *are* the schools. Kids caught in the college rush more often than not work 70 hours or more a week, most of it on paper busywork. For kids who aren't going to college, school is just a useless time waster, preventing them from earning some money or doing some useful work, or even doing some true learning.

Objections. "If kids didn't have to go to school, they'd all be out in the 9 streets." No, they wouldn't. In the first place, even if schools stayed just the way they are, <u>children would spend at least some time there because that's where they'd be likely to find friends</u>; it's a natural meeting place for children. In the second place, <u>schools wouldn't stay the way they are</u>, <u>they'd get better</u>, <u>because we would have to start making them what they ought to be right now</u>—places where children would *want* to be. In the third place, <u>those children who did not want to go to school could find</u>, <u>particularly if we stirred up our brains and gave them a little help</u>, <u>other things to do—the things many children now do during their summers and holidays</u>.

There's something easier we could do. <u>We need to get kids out of the</u> 10 <u>school buildings</u>, <u>give them a chance to learn about the world at first hand</u>. It is a very recent idea, and a crazy one, that the way to teach our young people about the world they live in is to take them out of it and shut them up in brick boxes. Fortunately, educators are beginning to realize this. In Philadelphia and Portland, Oregon, to pick only two places I happen to have heard about, plans are being drawn up for public schools that won't have any school buildings at all, that will take the students out into the city and help them to use it and its people as a learning resource. In other words, students, perhaps in groups, perhaps independently, will go to libraries, museums, exhibits, courtrooms, legislatures, radio and TV stations, meetings, businesses, and laboratories to learn about their world and society at first hand. A small private school in Washington is already doing this. It makes sense. We need more of it.

No way!

Kids still need protection.

Jobs aren't that plentiful.

Get real!

I agree.

We did something like this in 8th grade & it was great.

As we help children get out into the world, to do their learning there, *11* we can get more of the world into the schools. Aside from their parents, most children never have any close contact with any adults except people whose sole business is children. No wonder they have no idea what adult life or work is like. <u>We need to bring a lot more people who are *not* full-time teachers into the schools, and into contact with the children.</u> In New York City, under the Teachers and Writers Collaborative, real writers, working writers—novelists, poets, playwrights—come into the schools, read their work, and talk to the children about the problems of their craft. The children eat it up. In another school I know of, a practicing attorney from a nearby city comes in every month or so and talks to several classes about the law. Not the law as it is in books but as he sees it and encounters it in his cases, his problems, his work. And the children love it. [It is real, grown-up, true, not *My Weekly Reader,*] not "social studies," not lies and baloney.

Something easier yet. <u>Let children work together, help each other, *12* learn from each other and each other's mistakes.</u> We now know, from the experience of many schools, both rich-suburban and poor-city, that children are often the best teachers of other children. What is more important, we know that when a fifth- or sixth-grader who has been having trouble with reading starts helping a first-grader, his own reading sharply improves. A number of schools are beginning to use what some call Paired Learning. This means that you let children form partnerships with other children, do their work, even including their tests, together, and share whatever marks or results this work gets—just like grownups in the real world. It seems to work.

<u>Let the children learn to judge their own work.</u> A child learning to talk *13* does not learn by being corrected all the time—if corrected too much, he will stop talking. *He* compares, a thousand times a day, the difference between language as he uses it and as those around him use it. Bit by bit, he makes the necessary changes to make his language like other people's. In the same way, kids learning to do all the other things they learn without adult teachers—to walk, run, climb, whistle, ride a bike, skate, play games, jump rope—compare their own performance with what more skilled people do, and slowly make the needed changes. <u>But in school we never give a child a chance to detect his mistakes, let alone correct them. We do it all for him.</u> We act as if we thought he would never notice a mistake unless it was pointed out to him, or correct it unless he was made to. Soon he becomes dependent on the expert. We should let him do it himself. Let him figure out, with the help of other children if he wants it, what this word says, what is the answer to that problem, whether this is a good way of saying or doing this or that. If right answers are involved, as in some math or science, give him the answer book, let him correct his own papers. Why should we teachers waste time on such donkey work? Our job should be to help the kid when he tells us that he can't find a way to get the right answer. Let's get rid of all this nonsense of grades, exams, marks. We don't know now,

A good way for high school kids to learn about careers.

Nice!
I hate group work. Someone always takes over.

Take tests together? Is this fair?

and we never will know, how to measure what another person knows or understands. We certainly can't find out by asking him questions. All we find out is what he doesn't know—which is what most tests are for, anyway. Throw it all out, and let the child learn what every educated person must someday learn, how to measure his own understanding, how to know what he knows or does not know.

Yes! Yes! Yes! In college too.

We could also abolish the fixed, required curriculum. People remem-   *14* ber only what is interesting and useful to them, what helps them make sense of the world, or helps them get along in it. All else they quickly forget, if they ever learn it at all. The idea of a "body of knowledge," to be picked up in school and used for the rest of one's life, is nonsense in a world as complicated and rapidly changing as ours. Anyway, the most important questions and problems of our time are not *in* the curriculum, not even in the hotshot universities, let alone the schools.

Children want, more than they want anything else, and even after   *15* years of miseducation, to make sense of the world, themselves, and other human beings. Let them get at this job, with our help if they ask for it, in the way that makes most sense to them.

WRITING IN RESPONSE TO READING

The writing you do in response to your analytical reading can take a variety of forms. Sometimes your instructors will ask you to summarize an author's main points to be sure you have read and comprehended important material. Other times, they will ask you to analyze an author's view and assess its worth. On still other occasions, you will be asked to express your personal reactions and share the associations and feelings the writing strikes within you. Although you most often will be writing as a student for a teacher, make no mistake—you are part of the exchange of views and information that is at the heart of the academic community.

When you write in response to reading, you will often combine patterns of development. For example, say you are responding to "School Is Bad for Children," on page 366, by explaining the advantages of collaborative learning. You might define collaborative learning, describe collaborative learning procedures, include examples of successful collaborative learning activities, and then explain the effects of collaborative learning—all this would combine definition, process analysis, illustration, and cause-and-effect analysis.

In addition to combining patterns of development, you may find yourself paraphrasing and quoting from the reading you are responding to. (Paraphrasing and quoting are discussed on page 404 and page 406.) For example, consider again a response to "School Is Bad for Children." This time, assume that you wish to disagree with the author and argue that we should not abolish compulsory school attendance laws. To do this, you can bring up the author's points by paraphrasing and quoting them and then go on to counter those points with your own ideas. For an example of how this is done, see the student essay "Compulsory School Attendance Laws Make Sense," on page 374.

Detail for your essay can come from your own experience and observation, as well as from material you have learned in your classes and from books and articles in the library. If you borrow material from books and articles, however, remember to document these borrowings according to the conventions described in Chapter 14.

Sharing Personal Reactions and Associations

The following student essay is an example of a piece that shares personal reactions and associations. After reading "School Is Bad for Children," the student was moved to draw on her own school experiences to bear out Holt's point that in school a child "learns that he is worthless, untrustworthy, fit only to take other people's orders." To make her point, the student combines illustration, narration, and cause-and-effect analysis.

School Was Bad for Me

I share John Holt's view that school harms children. My own   *1*
negative experiences in elementary school have haunted me over the
years and affected the way I present myself to my college
professors. In fact, it has taken two years of college life for me
to really feel comfortable talking to my instructors, largely
because of my early school experiences with teachers.

Holt says that a child in school "learns that he is worthless,   *2*
untrustworthy, fit only to take other people's orders," and I
couldn't agree more. I can remember walking into Crestview
Elementary School on the first day of first grade, anxious,
nervous, and very shy. The first thing the teacher did was go over
all the rules and procedures for the class: we were not allowed to
speak without raising our hands; we could only get a drink when we
went to the lav and we could only go to the lav once in the morning
and once in the afternoon; both of our feet had to be on the floor
at all times; and we had to respect the rights of others (that was
a big one, but I was never sure what it meant). Of course, the
teacher was careful to point out that any infraction of the class
rules would be swiftly and severely punished. From that moment, I
was terrified that I would break a rule. To be sure that I didn't,
I didn't do anything. I didn't speak, I didn't ask questions, and I

didn't participate in any way. From the start, I knew that she was the general and I was the soldier trying to get through basic training without getting into any trouble. I was so intimidated that when any child broke a rule, I shook in sympathy. When Tommy's spelling words weren't written neatly enough and he had to do them over, my stomach ached. When Erica's math paper had messy erasure smudges and she was accused of having a messy mind, I smarted with humiliation. I was always sure I would be the next to break a rule.

I made it through first grade by keeping my mouth shut, but *3* second grade proved more troublesome. My coping strategy failed me almost at once. Soon into the year, the teacher asked a question, but rather than call on someone whose hand was waving wildly in the air, she called on me. I instantly panicked. The words stuck in my throat and my lips froze. I couldn't utter a sound. "What's the matter; has the cat got your tongue?" the teacher cleverly asked. I've never forgotten the humiliation of that moment.

Although I have had positive experiences with teachers over the *4* years, that initial put-down made me hesitant to speak out in class by voicing an opinion or asking a question. Even in college, I could not at first participate in class or ask a question when I did not understand. Yes, as Holt points out, I felt worthless and fit only to take orders. That's what I learned in school.

Writing a Summary

To summarize, you restate an author's main ideas in your own words and writing style. You are not to add your own thinking in any way, so you may not comment on the ideas, interpret them, evaluate them, or add anything that does not appear in the original selection. Teachers often ask students to summarize material to check their comprehension. Sometimes teachers ask students to first summarize reading material and then go on afterwards to respond to it in some way. However, unless specifically directed to do so, do not add your own ideas.

The following suggestions can help you write summaries:

1. **Underline or list the main points in the selection.** Do not note supporting details, as they will not appear in the summary.
2. **Write an opening sentence that includes the author's name, the title of the reading selection, and the thesis of the selection.**
3. **Use a present-tense verb with the author's name.**
4. **Draft the body of the paper by writing in your own words and style the main points you underlined or listed.**

5. **If some of the main points are difficult to express in your own words, quote them, but use quotation sparingly.**
6. **Revise to be sure you have not included ideas that did not appear in the original and that you have not altered the meaning of the original.**
7. **Check, too, that you have used transitions to ease the flow from point to point, including repeating the author's name with a present-tense verb.**

The following example summarizes the first six paragraphs of "School Is Bad for Children."

What John Holt Finds Wrong with Schools

In "School Is Bad for Children," John Holt notes the failure of modern education. He claims that most children are brighter and more intellectually inclined on the first day of school than at any other time during the educational process. Holt identifies the reason for this phenomenon as the fact that we teach children some unfortunate things, including the notions that "learning is separate from living" and that children do not know how to learn on their own. He says that American education casts children in the role of passive learners, whose questions, experiences, and concerns are of no interest. Once children learn these unfortunate things, Holt explains that they cease asking questions and recognize that "to be wrong, uncertain, confused, is a crime." Then students become lazy, maneuvering to get the right answers out of the teacher rather than discovering them on their own. They work to create the illusion that they are knowledgeable when they are not. Holt further explains that once their curiosity is extinguished, students become indifferent to other children and turned off in general, a fact Holt believes explains drug use among young people.

Evaluating an Author's Ideas

The following student essay responds to reading by evaluating an author's ideas. The student argues that Holt is wrong—abolishing compulsory education would be a mistake. To make his point, he cites ideas in Holt's essay and refutes them, and he also draws on examples from his personal experience.

Compulsory School Attendance Laws Make Sense

In "School Is Bad for Children," John Holt says, "We should abolish   *1*
compulsory school attendance." He believes that only those who want
to go to school should attend and that children should be allowed
unauthorized absences. I disagree with Holt completely. School is
not bad for children. On the contrary, children need to be
educated, and for that to happen, children need to be in school.
Compulsory attendance laws, therefore, should not be abolished.

Holt claims that at one time mandatory attendance laws made   *2*
sense because children needed to be protected from adults who would
keep them out of school and send them to work. Sad to say, children
still need the protection the laws afford, for exploitive and
abusive adults still exist and children still need protection from
them. Without the law, plenty of parents would force their children
into the workforce and worse. For children born into poverty and
abusive homes, education may be the only way to a better life. If
compulsory attendance laws did not exist, then these children would
lose their tickets out of difficult situations.

Even if children do not need protection from adults, they must   *3*
be required to attend school to improve their situations. Holt says
that "for kids who aren't going to college, school is just a
useless time waster, preventing them from earning some money."
Sure, they can earn money doing minimum wage jobs that do not
require a diploma. But how can people support themselves as well as
a family earning a little more than four dollars an hour? An
education is more important than a low-paying job at an early age
because a person must have a chance at a better job in the future.
I know of one person who dropped out of school, and today he is on
welfare trying to support three children. He is twenty-six and has
little to look forward to. Furthermore, his children are already at
a disadvantage because their needs cannot be met, and they cannot
enjoy the benefits that many of us had when we were young.
Fortunately, these children will be required to go to school, so
they may find a way out of their poverty.

Holt also blames compulsory attendance for the problems that   *4*
exist in schools today. Those who don't want to be in school, says
Holt, make things difficult for those who do. Perhaps, but the

solution is not to let young people leave school. Instead, the solution is to find ways to make these people *want* to be in school. We need to do whatever it takes to attract the most talented people into teaching so all students can be motivated to stay in school and learn.

Some might think that Holt's suggestion that students be given   5 unauthorized absences makes sense. But here too I see problems. How is a teacher supposed to maintain continuity with a steady stream of students coming and going? The teacher would spend more time repeating lessons to bring students up to date than teaching necessary material.

Mandatory attendance should not be abolished. Students need to   6 be in school to receive the education they need to make a satisfactory life for themselves. Doing away with compulsory attendance laws would do more harm than any Holt sees with the existing laws.

Essay Topics: Writing in Response to "School Is Bad for Children"

1. Summarize Holt's suggestions for change; then explain what change or changes should be instituted to improve the public school system in your area. Your audience will be the local school board, and your purpose will be to convince the board to implement the change you suggest.

2. Holt says, "We should abolish compulsory school attendance." Do you agree? Write an essay arguing for or against Holt's view. Be sure to speak to the points Holt offers to support his view as well as to the objections he counters. Your audience is your classmates, and your purpose is to convince them of the wisdom of your stance.

3. Holt says that in school, children learn that "to be wrong, uncertain, confused, is a crime." Did you learn this in school? If so, write an essay narrating specific events that taught you this. Your audience is your classroom teacher, and your purpose is to relate a portion of your past.

4. Do you share Holt's view that students are dishonest, that they learn "to dodge, bluff, fake, cheat"? If so, explain how this happens and what can be done about it. Your audience is the local PTA, and your purpose is to describe a serious problem and suggest a solution.

5. What event in your previous schooling had the greatest impact on you? Describe the event and tell how it affected you and why you believe it affected you the way it did. Your purpose is to express feelings and relate experience, and your audience is your teacher and classmates.

6. Holt believes in paired learning, which is today called **collaborative learning.** In the library, find some books and articles that discuss

collaborative learning. Read about this technique, and then write an essay advocating or denouncing its use as a classroom practice. Your audience consists of members of the National Education Association, and your purpose is to convince your readers to use (or not to use) collaborative learning in their classrooms. (Review the conventions for handling library research in Chapter 14.)

ESSAYS TO READ AND RESPOND TO

The rest of this chapter contains previously published essays, each of which is followed by a selection of topics that will give you experience writing in response to reading.

Values and Violence in Sports Today

Brenda Jo Bredemeier and David L. Shields

Brenda Jo Bredemeier is a professor of sport psychology and David L. Shields is a physical education researcher. In the following essay, the authors examine the ethics of violence and aggression in athletics.

To be good in sports, you have to be bad. Or so many athletes, coaches, and *1* sports fans believe. Heavyweight champion Larry Holmes, for example, revealed a key to his success during a "60 Minutes" interview with Morley Safer: Before he enters the ring, he said, "I have to change, I have to leave the goodness out and bring all the bad in, like Dr. Jekyll and Mr. Hyde."

Even sports fan Ronald Reagan suggested that normally inappropriate ways *2* of thinking and acting are acceptable in sports. When he was governor of California, he reportedly told a college team during a pep talk that in football, "you can feel a clean hatred for your opponent. It is a clean hatred since it's only symbolic in a jersey."

Does success today really depend on how well an athlete or team has mas- *3* tered the art of aggression? The question is usually answered more by ideology than by evidence. But there is a more fundamental question that needs to be asked: Is it really OK to be bad in sports? In particular, is aggression an acceptable tactic on the playing field? If it is morally unacceptable, the debate about its utility misses the mark.

It seems odd to ask whether being bad is all right. But in contact sports par- *4* ticularly, acts of aggression are seldom condemned, usually condoned, and often praised. Sport is a "world within a world" with its own unique conventions and moral understandings.

Lyle and Glenn Blackwood of the Miami Dolphins are nicknamed "the *5* bruise brothers." Their motto—"We don't want to hurt you, just make you hurt"—aptly expresses the ambiguity many people feel about sport aggression. To reduce such ambiguity, many athletes appeal to game rules, informal agreements or personal convictions to decide the legitimacy of aggressive acts. As one collegiate basketball player told us in an interview: "It's OK to try to hurt somebody if it is legal and during the game. If the guy doesn't expect it, it's a cheap shot. That's no good. You can be aggressive and do minor damage without really hurting him and still accomplish your goal."

As social scientists, we are interested in the moral meaning athletes and fans   *6* attach to aggression. Do sport participants think about aggression in moral terms? Does the maturity of athletes' moral reasoning influence their aggressive behavior? What are the unique characteristics of sport morality and how does this "game reasoning" influence the perceived legitimacy of aggression?

Most recommendations for reducing sport aggression have focused on   *7* rules and penalties against fighting, beanballs, slugging, and other forms of violence. We believe, however, that reducing athletic aggression requires the transformation of both external sports structures such as rules and penalties and internal reasoning structures. To reduce aggression, we must first understand the meaning athletes attach to it.

By aggression, we mean acts that are intended to inflict pain or injury. Robust, physically forceful play not meant to harm another player is better termed assertion. Unfortunately, this distinction is often blurred on the mat, the ice, and the Astroturf.   *8*

We believe that aggression is more than a convention; it is a moral issue   *9* and can be investigated as such. If this is true, there should be an inverse relationship between the maturity of athletes' moral reasoning and their acceptance of aggression. Our research suggests that this relationship exists. The higher their level of moral reasoning, the less aggression athletes practice and condone.

Establishing a link between moral reasoning and sport aggression is only the   *10* first step in understanding it. It is still not clear why many people find everyday aggression objectionable but have few moral qualms when they or others hurl a beanball at a batter. We can develop a more complete portrait of athletic aggression by exploring the unique patterns of moral reasoning that sport encourages.

Some social scientists have noted a curious fact that athletes and fans take   *11* for granted. Sport is set apart both cognitively and emotionally from the everyday world. Anthropologist Don Handelman, for example, has observed that play "requires a radical transformation in cognition and perception." Sociologist Erving Goffman has described play activities as enclosed within a unique "social membrane" or conceptual "frame."

In a 1983 interview, Ron Rivera, then a linebacker with the University of California at Berkeley and now with the Chicago Bears, described the personality transformation he undergoes on the field. The off-field Ron, he said, is soft-spoken, considerate, and friendly. When asked to describe the on-field Ron, he replied, "He's totally opposite from me. . . . He's a madman. . . . No matter what happens, he hits people. He's a guy with no regard for the human body." Elaborating further, Rivera revealed, "I'm mean and nasty then. . . . I'm so rotten. I have a total disrespect for the guy I'm going to hit."   *12*

Does this personality transformation include a fundamental change in   *13* moral reasoning? To explore this possibility, we designed a study to see whether the same people would use similar levels of moral reasoning in response to hypothetical dilemmas set in sport-specific and daily life contexts. One "sport dilemma," for example, centered on Tom, a football player who is told by his coach to injure an opponent to help Tom's team win. One of the "daily life" dilemmas hinged on whether a person should keep his promise to deliver some money to a rich man or use it to help his hungry kin.

We presented four dilemmas to 120 high school and college athletes and   *14* nonathletes and asked them to reason about the best way to resolve each dilemma. Most of the students clearly perceived a difference between morality in sport and in everyday life. One comment by a high school female basketball player exemplified this perspective: "In sports, it's hard to tell right from wrong sometimes; you have to use game sense." Both athletes and nonathletes used lower-level egocentric moral reasoning when thinking about dilemmas in sport than when addressing moral issues in other contexts.

These and other findings suggest that moral norms which prescribe equal   *15* consideration of all people are often suspended during competition in favor of a more egocentric moral perspective. One male college basketball player explained the difference this way: "In sports you can do what you want. In life it's more restricted. It's harder to make decisions in life because there are so many people to think about, different people to worry about. In sports you're free to think about yourself."

This theme was echoed by many others who referred to sport as a field   *16* where each person or team seeks personal triumph and where opponents need not be given equal consideration.

There are several reasons sports may elicit an egocentric style of game rea-   *17* soning. The very nature of competition requires that self-interest be temporarily adopted while the athlete strives to win. In everyday life, such preoccupation with self almost inevitably leads to moral failings. But in sport, participants are freed to concentrate on self-interest by a carefully balanced rule structure that equalizes opportunity. Players are guarded against the moral defaults of others by protective rules and by officials who impose sanctions for violations. Moral responsibility is thus transferred from the shoulders of players to those of officials, the enforcers of the rules, and to coaches, whom the players learn to see as responsible for all decisions.

If the nature of competition encourages egocentricity, the "set aside" char-   *18* acter of sport helps to justify it. Sport consists of artificial goals that are achieved through arbitrarily defined skills and procedures. Although running across a line or shooting a ball through a hoop is all-important in the immediate game context, neither has significant consequences outside sports. This lack of any "real world" meaning to sport actions helps make egocentric reasoning seem legitimate.

Not all sport goals, of course, lack real-world implications. In boxing, for   *19* example, where the goal involves damage to another person, serious injury or even death is possible. Another exception is professional sports, and even some collegiate and high school sports, where winners may receive prizes, bigger paychecks, more perks, or expanded educational and professional opportunities. The moral implications of harm as a sport goal (boxing) and extrinsic rewards contingent on sport performance (in professional and quasiprofessional sports) still need to be investigated.

The dynamic of competition, the structural protection provided by officials 20 and rules and the relatively inconsequential implications of sport intentions combine to release sport participants from the usual demands of morality. But game-specific moral understandings do not completely replace everyday morality. Just as sport exists in a unique space and time within the everyday world, so game reasoning is a form of "bracketed morality." The transformed morality that occurs in sport does not take the place of everyday morality; rather, it is embedded in the broader, more encompassing morality of daily life.

Because of this, most athletes limit the degree of sport aggression they ac- 21 cept as legitimate in line with their general understanding of the rights of others. Coordinating these two sets of standards is not easy. Consider, for example, how one athlete reasoned about the football dilemma in which Tom is told to injure his opponent:

"If Tom looks at it as a game, it's OK to hurt the guy—to try to take him 22 out of the game. But if he looks at the halfback as a person, and tries to hurt him, it's not OK." Asked, "How do you decide which to go by?" the athlete explained, "When you're on the field, then the game is football. Before and after, you deal with people morally."

This man recognized that aggression can be viewed from two contrasting 23 viewpoints but eliminated his ambivalence by subordinating everyday morality to game reasoning. For him, an opponent is a player, not a person. This objectification of opponents reduces an athlete's sense of personal responsibility for competitors.

Among some of the other athletes we interviewed, accountability was allevi- 24 ated by simply "not thinking about it." As one athlete stated succinctly, "In sports you don't think about those things [hurting others]; mostly you don't think about other people, you just think about winning."

Most athletes, however, tried to coordinate game and everyday morality by 25 distinguishing between legitimate and illegitimate aggression. As one man explained: "Some [aggressive acts] are not acceptable. The game is a game. You go out to win, but there's a line—limitations—there are rules. . . . You try to dominate the other player, but you don't want to make him leave the game."

Another athlete put it this way: "Tom shouldn't try to hurt him. He should 26 just hit him real hard, stun him, make him lose his wind, make sure he's too scared to run the ball again."

Players use a complex moral logic in attempts to coordinate the goal of win- 27 ning with the need to respect limits to egocentricity. Some athletes identify the rules as the final arbiter of legitimacy, but most appeal to less formal criteria. Themes such as intimidation, domination, fairness, and retribution are continuously woven into participants' fabric of thought, providing a changing picture of what constitutes legitimate action.

Shifting expectations, created by the fast-paced and emotionally charged *28* action, can readily lead to perceived violations or "cheap shots." Cheap shots, of course, are in the eye, or ribs, of the beholder. As a college basketball player explained, physical contact may be interpreted by athletes as either assertive or aggressive, depending on their perception of intent: "I've played with guys who try to hurt you. They use all kinds of cheap shots, especially elbows in the face and neck. But that's different than trying to maintain position or letting a guy know you're there. An elbow can be for intimidation or it can be for hurting. I just use elbows in the regular course of the game."

Given the complex and variable conditions of sport, it is not surprising that *29* among the athletes we interviewed there was not a clear consensus about the line between legitimate and illegitimate aggression. Generally, we found that the more mature the athletes' moral reasoning, the less aggression they accepted as legitimate—both for the fictitious character Tom in the hypothetical football dilemma and for themselves as they reasoned about personal aggression.

Yet even the more morally mature athletes often accepted minor forms of *30* aggression as legitimate game strategy. In fact, such minor aggression was sometimes viewed as a positive, enhancing aspect of the game. As a high school player explained: "Football is a rough game and if it weren't for rules people would get hurt real bad—even killed. Some people just want to hurt other people real bad." Asked, "Should the present rules be changed to reduce football injuries?" he replied, "No. Nobody will want to play if the rules get so upright that you can't hit hard."

Moral research inevitably leads beyond descriptions about what people do *31* to questions about what people ought to do. Perhaps most athletes accept some aggression as "part of the game," but should they? Should any degree of aggression be considered legitimate?

Based on what we have learned about game reasoning, we believe two criteria *32* can be employed to distinguish morally mature athletes' judgments of aggression which they may perceive as legitimate from aggression which certainly is not. First, any act intended to inflict an injury that is likely to have negative consequences for the recipient once the game has ended is illegitimate. The legitimacy of game reasoning depends partly on the irrelevance of sport action to everyday life. Consequently, inflicting such "game-transcending" injuries as a broken leg or a concussion cannot be morally justified.

Second, game reasoning is also legitimated because it occurs within a situation *33* that is defined by a set of rules that limit the relevant procedures and skills which can be used during the game. Therefore, any act is illegitimate if it occurs apart from the strategic employment of game-relevant skills, even if such an act is intended to cause only minor injury or mild discomfort. Such behavior impinges upon the protective structure that releases participants from their normal moral obligations.

The implications of our research on athletes' game reasoning may extend to *34* other spheres of life. If game reasoning is distinct from the morality of general life, are there other context-specific moralities, such as business reasoning or political reasoning? Perhaps the list could be extended indefinitely. While every context raises unique moral issues, however, we agree with most moral-development theorists that the fundamental structure of moral reasoning remains relatively stable in nearly all situations.

Sport is employed frequently as a metaphor for other endeavors, and game   *35* language is often utilized in discussions of such diverse topics as business, politics, and war. A recent book by Thomas Whisler of the University of Chicago, *Rules of the Game,* has little to do with sport and everything to do with corporate boardrooms.

The borrowing of sport images and language may reflect a tendency to   *36* transplant game morality from its native soil to foreign gardens. If this is the case, game reasoning has social implications that extend far beyond the limited world of sport. Game morality is legitimated by protections within the sport structure, but most other contexts lack such safeguards. If game reasoning leads to manipulation to gain job advancement, for example, are adequate laws available and enforced to guarantee equal opportunity? Can the dirty tricks of politics be legitimated as if they were just a game? Does game reasoning encourage a view that nuclear war is winnable, propelling us toward the "game to end all games"? And if it does, who consents to play these games?

Essay Topics: Writing in Response to "Values and Violence in Sports Today"

1. Bredemeier and Shields say that many people believe that "to be good in sports, you have to be bad." Explain the meaning of this quotation, and go on to agree or disagree with it. Draw your supporting details from the essay and your own experience with sports, either as a player or spectator. Your audience is the parents of student athletes, and your purpose is to inform them of the nature of athletic competition.

2. Do you agree that "sport is a 'world within a world' with its own unique conventions and moral understandings"? Argue your point of view. Draw your supporting details from the essay and your own experience with sports, either as a player or spectator. Your audience is your classroom teacher.

3. Assume that you are one of the starting five on a scholastic basketball team playing in the finals of an important championship. At the start of the fourth quarter, your team is behind by twelve points, and your point guard has twisted an ankle and is on the bench. Your coach sends you in as a replacement with orders to "take out" the other team's star shooter. You do not have to injure the player seriously, just hurt the person enough to return him or her to the bench for a few minutes so that your team can take the lead. Explain whether you will follow the coach's orders and why or why not. Also explain the effects of your decision on you and your teammates. Your audience is student athletes, and your purpose is to convince them that your course of action is the correct one.

4. Consider your own experiences with athletics (either as a player or a spectator) and write an essay that cites specific examples of violence in sports. Explain whether this violence was justifiable. Your audience is your classmates, and your purpose is to relate your experiences and convince your reader that violence in sports is (or is not) justifiable.

5. When does aggression in sports go too far? Write guidelines explaining how much aggression is acceptable in high school football or basketball. Your audience is high school coaches, athletic directors, and players. Your purpose is to convince your audience to adopt your guidelines.

6. The violence among spectators at athletic events is becoming a greater concern. In the library, research violence among spectators and write an essay that describes the nature and extent of this violence and recommends a solution to the problem. Consider limiting yourself to discussion of violence among fans of a particular sport such as soccer, baseball, or football. Your audience will be the readers of *Sports Illustrated,* and your purpose will be to inform them of the extent of the violence and convince them of the wisdom of your proposal for curtailing it.

Born Beautiful: Confessions of a Naturally Gorgeous Girl

Ellen Paige

Is life easier for the beautiful people of the world? Ellen Paige, a staff writer for a national women's magazine, seems to think so.

My blind date is trudging up the four flights to my New York apartment. I'm   *1*
waiting, in suspense. Will he be a little like William Hurt? Have a touch of Tom Hanks' winsomeness? When there's one flight to go, I can't wait any longer. I poke my head out the door and over the bannister to check him out. Not bad—except that he looks like his best friend just died.

Until he glances up and sees me. In a second his brow relaxes, his eyes   *2*
brighten, a wave of visible relief sweeps across his face. He grins and bounds up the last few steps. Why is this man suddenly so cheerful? I already know the reason: It's because I'm pretty. And does this little scene make me feel great? Well, yes. But I'm used to it.

I've been pretty most of my life, except for a few awkward phases. I know   *3*
this because people tell me—both directly and in more subtle ways (like the way my blind date's face did). Sometimes when I look in the mirror, I can see what they mean; other times—as with every woman who has her good and bad days—I can't. But even when I can't, there's no denying the effect of my good looks; it wraps around me like a cocoon, my magic charm. Being beautiful can keep pain at bay.

It's like this: I've made a stupid mistake at work and am feeling embar-   *4*
rassed and worthless—or my ego has been bruised by a particularly bad fight

with my boyfriend. So I put on something I think I look great in and head for the door. Outside, what happens usually cheers me up: Men turn and react appreciatively as I walk by. I don't mean they catcall or harass me (although no woman on earth can successfully escape that kind of attention). And I'm not talking about the chorus of whistles you get from construction workers or truck drivers. I mean that nice-looking men, well-dressed, carrying briefcases—men I might want to go out with—check me out in a way I think is flattering. Women also look at me, but in a different, more investigative way. They eye me, taking in everything as if they're gathering details, maybe shopping for a new look for themselves.

Sure, I'd probably feel even better if my boss told me how smart I was or if 5
my boyfriend showed up on my doorstep apologetic and holding roses. But who can count on that happening? What I can count on are the turned heads, the appreciative glances, the "hey, beautiful." And that goes a long way toward making me feel good.

Shallow, you say? Dating success shouldn't depend on how pretty someone 6
is; a setback at work shouldn't be soothed by skin-deep compliments. Maybe not, but it's also undeniable: Looks count. If you were hoping to hear that being beautiful isn't all it's cracked up to be, I'm going to disappoint. It *is* what it's cracked up to be—and more.

By now you're probably wondering what I look like. Most of what I know 7
about my looks comes from other people, who tell me I'm the earthy, natural type. But I do know my features are small and even, my brown eyes and hair are a good match, I'm tall and fit, and I can look sexy and sophisticated when I want. I wasn't the type of child adults cooed over; my parents let me know they were proud of my looks, partly because all parents do, but mainly to instill confidence. For the most part, though, beauty was not a big deal in my family. There was some sibling rivalry between my younger sister and me that we now know stemmed from the disparity in our looks—she kept her baby fat well into her teens and I didn't.

I suppose she was right to be jealous of my looks, because in school, beauty 8
was definitely a big deal. Being cute had a lot to do with the number of friends I had. My popularity certainly wasn't due to my outgoing personality (I was and am very shy) or my academic record (unremarkable). Girls, I could tell, admired my looks, but it was the boys who first let me know they thought I was good-looking, usually by threatening to pummel my little brother after school if he didn't dish the latest dirt on me. (Unfortunately he always complied, which accounts for how the entire fifth grade knew when I got my first bra.) As I got older, the boys got braver and started to say things—not compliments exactly, but as close to them as adolescents ever get. Sometimes it was flattering, and I liked it. But other times it was unsettling.

I'm at the beach. I'm 13 and an "older" man (actually a boy of about 18) is 9
talking to me while I wait in line for ice cream. He asks me how old I am. When I tell him, he stops cold, steps back and stares at my skimpy bikini, and says one word: "Wow." The way he utters that word—slowly, solemnly—is a revelation, both frightening and enlightening. I realize then that beauty bestows power.

I was just starting to get wise to what my looks could mean to me when I *10* headed to high school. That's where I got an advanced degree in "pretty politics." Once, in the restroom, I overheard someone say about me, "She's pretty and she knows it." Translated, that meant I was vain, conceited, stuck-up. Nice girls, you see, weren't supposed to know they were pretty. I got the message. I learned to deny what was as obvious as the nose, and every other feature, on my face. The way to be liked—and being liked is paramount to a teenager—was to be pretty and *not* know it. So I tried hard to get voted Best Personality; I always won Best-Looking instead.

In high school there were no secrets. Our reputations as freshmen followed *11* us to senior year. When I went to college, though, to a university the size of a small city, I faded into the crowd. I no longer stood out because of the way I looked. In fact, there were many girls in my dorm, not to mention on the whole campus, who were more than my equals in the looks department. Instead of feeling inferior, I was less self-conscious about my appearance. The pressure was off, and that let me relax enough to start enjoying my looks. When someone told me I was attractive, I felt as though I'd earned the compliment. "Pretty" was no longer just a label that showed my high-school status.

Once during the summer between my sophomore and junior years, I ran *12* into a guy I knew from high school. He was surprised to hear I was studying biology at a prestigious university. "You never seemed like the type," he said. Maybe I should have been offended, but instead I just laughed; I *was* the type, and always had been. But college had freed me from my looks.

Now that I'm on my own, out of school and working in New York, it's be- *13* come clearer exactly what being attractive can do for me. It doesn't guarantee glamour, excitement, or adventure, or that I'll marry Mr. Right. But it does make some good things come my way—and make life more comfortable.

For one thing, people notice me: a waiter at a nearby café gives me deli- *14* cious whole-wheat rolls for free; a grocery clerk offers me (but not my date) change for the bus; the guy working out next to me breaks training to flirt. After they've noticed me, people usually want to get to know me, and that's helped to open some doors. My looks hold people's attention long enough for me to strut my stuff—to show them I can produce. If my looks intrigue someone, I don't mind using them. That doesn't mean I'd wear a bustier and miniskirt to a job interview, but I don't try to hide my looks either. It's highly unlikely that someone will hire me on appearance alone, but at least I'll get the interview.

I haven't quite figured out why my looks intrigue. It seems to boil down to *15* simple curiosity; maybe people wonder if I have as much luck in other areas as I've had with my looks. But people do seem attracted to attractiveness, pleased by it, happy to be in the company of it.

I know I am. Sometimes just being with someone I think is good-looking *16* makes me feel special by association. I don't choose my friends because they're beautiful, but still, looks *are* alluring. People tend to assign positive traits to those they find attractive. That's why new acquaintances often seem to have decided that they like me almost as soon as we've met. My appearance can speed up the process that makes people choose to be my friends.

It's my first day on the job at a publishing house. I'm making the rounds, *17* introducing myself to co-workers. One woman is so absorbed in her work, and so uninterested in meeting the new kid on the block, that she doesn't even look up when she says hello. A few days later, she suddenly becomes cordial, even palsy. I realize that I've passed her test; she's sized me up and I look right. She's intrigued, I can tell, not by who I am—she's barely spoken to me before this burst of chumminess—but rather by how I look.

The effect of my looks is even more apparent in my romantic involvements. *18* I'm not the first to have noticed that people pair up with their equals—10s with 10s, 7s with 7s, and so on. Studies have proven it. It's certainly true for my boyfriend, Josh, and me. I think he's at least as good-looking as my friends tell me I am. But there's one big difference: My looks matter more to him than his do to me. I'm not sure why, but it doesn't bother me. In fact, I'm happy Josh is proud of the way I look. If I thought he loved me only for my looks, that would be different.

But then there are those middle-of-the-night doubts. What if he wakes up *19* one day and sees me looking lousy? I don't mean being caught without makeup, since I rarely use cosmetics anyway. What I'm talking about is getting older. I worry about it. So I work out—a lot, sometimes two hours a day. Makeup can disguise the effects of aging, but exercise can actually delay them. I won't hand over my looks to age without a fight. I worry that if time robs me of my beauty, I'll also lose my magic, the power my looks give me. I've felt a twinge of this already. At my 10-year high-school reunion last year, I panicked that my former classmates would think I'd gone downhill, and I'm not sure that some of them didn't. But before I started yearning for my old Best-Looking banner, I told myself that nobody looks as good as they did when they were 17.

I guess admitting that losing my looks worries me is a giveaway that I care *20* about them a great deal. But while I have them, I might as well capitalize on them. If they can make me feel better when I'm blue, why not?

It's a Sunday, a couple of years ago. I'm out running errands when I bump *21* into Craig—a man I've just started dating. He's friendly but not exactly passionate in his hello—not like last Friday night, anyway. I ask him if he'd like to catch a movie tonight, but he hedges. He then tells me that he's started seeing his old girlfriend again. The next moment, he hops in a cab and is gone. I feel like I've been socked in the stomach, but I catch a glimpse of myself in a store window and automatically think, "Well, at least I look good." It doesn't bring Craig back, but I do feel better.

When I feel good about my looks, others pick up on it. The day I met my *22* current boyfriend, I was feeling fabulous about my work, my friends, and the way I looked. I was waiting in the tiny backseat of a Triumph for a ride home from a party when there he was—a gorgeous man scrunching his six-foot-one frame in beside me. He was first attracted to me, he says, mostly by my looks, but also my attitude—enough to fold himself in two to sit next to me.

This doesn't happen every day, though. Let me dispel the myth that pretty *23* women have men knocking down doors or squeezing into sports cars just to be near them. I've gone through several long and lonely stretches without a single eligible man in sight, stretches made worse by the loaded question, "How come a pretty girl like you doesn't have a boyfriend?"

True, being pretty may help me catch a man's eye across a room or spark 24 his interest during a brief encounter in an elevator, but more often I end up getting propositioned by overly aggressive guys who aren't my type at all. During my dating dry spells, I used to rationalize that men must have assumed that I had a boyfriend, and were afraid to ask me out. Although there's no way to prove it, I don't really think this was often the case. Instead, the reasons I found it hard to meet the right men were the same reasons all women have trouble meeting men—but that's another story.

There can be a kind of beauty backlash in other social situations, too. I've 25 noticed some women giving me nasty looks for no apparent reason; I've also felt them act strangely aloof. Rather than instantly *liking* me because of how I look, they seemed to take an instant *dislike* to me. That they may have been jealous doesn't make me feel any better about their reactions.

My exercise class is small: only two other women and our instructor. It's 26 hard to ignore the fact that my classmates won't talk to me. I am shy, but at least I try to be friendly. I try small talk in the locker room, but I get no response. I ask our instructor, Todd, why he thinks they're so aloof. "Two reasons—you're tall and lean. Period," he says. That's ridiculous. Judy has a great job and Beth's got a husband worth bragging about. Two things I envy them for. How can they be jealous of me? I'm hurt, but I'm also angry. How can they judge me on such trivial grounds? But then I think: How can I be annoyed if they judge me negatively on looks alone, when I love it if people assume I'm great just because I'm attractive?

Still, all things considered, if you ask me how I'd like to be known, I'd say 27 I'd rather be considered intelligent. Why then, I wonder, was I so disappointed after I met my boyfriend's brother for the first time? He told Josh later he thought I was really bright. Didn't he think I was sort of, well . . . beautiful?

Essay Topics: Writing in Response to "Born Beautiful"

1. Paige's thesis is that "looks count." Drawing on the points made in the essay and your own experience, agree or disagree with that thesis. Your audience consists of your classmates, and your purpose is to convince your readers of the truth of your view.
2. Paige says, "In high school there were no secrets. Our reputation as freshmen followed us to senior year." Write an essay that tells whether your own experience and that of your classmates is reflected in Paige's statement. Your audience is your instructor, and your purpose is to relate your experience and inform your reader.
3. Explain how some aspect of your physical makeup (such as your height, your athletic ability, your overall appearance, your gender, or your skin color) has affected your life, and provide examples to illustrate your

points. Your audience is your classmates, and your purpose is to express feelings, relate experience, and inform.

4. Paige worries about getting older, afraid she will "lose [her] magic, the power [her] looks give [her]." Predict what Paige's life will be like when she is sixty and her beauty has faded. Also, recommend what Paige should do when "time robs [her] of [her] beauty." Your audience is Paige herself, and your purpose is to inform.

5. Are Paige's essay and the point of view it reflects sexist? What impact does the author's point of view have on women's drive for equality? Argue your point of view for a local chapter of the National Organization of Women, a politically active feminist group.

6. Is what Paige says about physical beauty also true for males? Answer this question in an essay meant to inform readers of *Esquire*.

7. Degree of physical attractiveness is only one of several accidents of birth that affect who we are. Birth order, gender, number of siblings, age of parents, location in an urban or rural area, living in a large or small town—all these influence our personality. In the library, research the effects of one of these accidents of birth on scholastic achievement, and write a report to inform members of the National Education Association.

Democracy

Amy Tan

Best-selling author of The Joy Luck Club, *Amy Tan ponders the meaning of democracy for her family in China.*

How much we Americans take our freedoms for granted. We already have the rights: freedom of expression, contracts and legal departments to protect them, the right to put differences of opinion to a vote. We put those rights in writing, carry them in our back pockets all over the world, pull them out as proof. We may be aliens in another country, but we still maintain that our rights are inalienable.

I try to imagine what democracy means to people in China who dream of it. I don't think they are envisioning electoral colleges, First Amendment rights or civil lawsuits. I imagine that their dreams of democracy begin with a feeling in the chest, one that has been restrained for so long it grows larger and more insistent, until it bursts forth with a shout. Democracy is the right to shout, "Listen to us."

That is what I imagine because I was in China in 1987. I saw glimpses of another way of life, a life that could have been mine. And along with many wonderful things I experienced in my heart, I also felt something uncomfortable in my chest.

In Shanghai in 1987, I attended the wedding of my niece. After the ceremony, she and her husband went home to the three-room apartment shared with her mother, father and brother. "Now that you're married," I said with good humor, "you can't live at home anymore."

"The waiting list for government-assigned housing is 16 years," replied my   *5*
niece's husband. "We will both be 48 years old when we are assigned our own
place."

My mouth dropped. He shrugged.   *6*

While on a boat trip down the Huangpu River, I asked a tour guide how   *7*
she had chosen her career. She told me matter-of-factly that people in China did
not choose careers. They had jobs assigned to them.

She saw my surprised expression. "Oh, but I'm lucky. So many people   *8*
can't get any kind of good job. If your family came from a bad background—the
bourgeoisie—then, no college. Maybe only a job sweeping the streets." At a family dinner in Beijing, I learned that my sister's husband could not attend our get-
together. He was away at his job, said my sister.

"When will he return?" I asked. My mother explained that his job was in a   *9*
city thousands of miles away. He had been living apart from my sister for the
past 10 years. "That's terrible," I said to my sister. "Tell him to ask for a trans-
fer. Tell him you miss him."

"Miss, not miss!" my mother sniffed. "They can't even ask."   *10*

One of my sisters did ask. Several years ago, she asked for a visa to leave   *11*
China. Now she lives in Wisconsin. A former nurse, she now works six days a
week, managing a take-out Chinese restaurant. Her husband, trained as a surgeon, works in the kitchen. And recently I've met others who also asked, a waiter
who was once a doctor in China, a taxi driver who was formerly a professor of
entomology, a housekeeper who was an engineer. Why did they ask to leave? I
found it hard to understand how people could leave behind family, friends, their
motherland, and jobs of growing prestige.

My sister in Wisconsin helped me understand. After my novel was pub-   *12*
lished, she wrote me a letter. "I was once like you," she said. "I wanted to write
stories as a young girl. But when I was growing up, they told me I could not do
so many things. And now my imagination is rusted and no stories can move out
of my brain."

My sister and I had the same dream. But my brain did not become rusted. I   *13*
became a writer. And later, we shared another dream, that China and our family
were on the verge of a better, more open life. We did not imagine that the blood
that is thicker than water would be running through the streets of Beijing. We did
not believe that one Chinese would kill another. We did not foresee that an invisible great wall would rise up, that we would be cut off from our family, that letters
would stop, that the silence would become unbearable.

These days I can only imagine what has happened to my family in China.   *14*
And I think about the word democracy. It rolls so easily off my English-speaking
tongue. But in Beijing it is a foreign-sounding word, so many syllables, so many
clashing sounds. In China, democracy is still not an easy word to say. Many cannot say it.   *15*

Hope then.

Essay Topics: Writing in Response to "Democracy"

1. In paragraph 1, Tan states that "Americans take our freedoms for granted." Look up the Bill of Rights in an encyclopedia. Select one of the rights it guarantees and explain what life would be like without it. Your audience is your classmates, and your purpose is to help them come to a greater appreciation of one of their freedoms.

2. In paragraph 11, Tan tells of the Chinese who left everything behind to come to the United States. If you had to leave everything behind and emigrate to a new country, what do you think you would miss the most? Why? Write your essay for your classroom instructor to help that person learn more about what is important to you.

3. Tan's niece and new husband were forced to live with her mother, father, and brother in a three-room apartment. Explain what effects this kind of living arrangement is likely to have on the family members. Your audience is your sociology professor, and your purpose is to show that you understand how people are affected by their living conditions.

4. Write your own definition of *democracy* and explain how that definition might compare and contrast with the meaning of the word for people who live in dictatorships. Your audience will be non-U.S. citizens, and your purpose is to inform them of what democracy means to one citizen of the United States.

5. In your campus library, research the Chinese democratic movement over the last 10 years or so, and then write an account of that movement. Your audience is the students in a history class, and your purpose is to inform.

Animal Rights versus Human Health

Albert Rosenfeld

Albert Rosenfeld presents his side of the controversy surrounding animal experimentation. As you read, consider how fairly he presents both his view and the opposing perspective.

Stray dogs and cats by the hundreds of thousands roam the streets of our cities. *1* Usually they wind up in animal shelters, where hard-pressed staffs must find ways to dispose of them. One legitimate disposal route has been the research laboratory. But in southern California—with its impressive collection of research centers—antivivisectionists and animal rights groups recently have been leaning hard on animal shelters, effectively cutting off much of the supply.

About 30 years ago Los Angeles voters soundly defeated a proposal to *2* prohibit the release of animals for laboratory use. But today, with new proposals being submitted to city councils and county boards, the results could well be different. And the new proposals are much more sweeping. They would, for instance, create review boards for all animal experimentation, requiring researchers to justify in advance any experiment they were planning and to submit a detailed research protocol before even applying for a grant. Alarmed, a group of southern California investigators have organized a committee for animal research in medicine.

"Most scientists don't realize the danger," says Caltech neurobiologist John 3 M. Allman, who uses monkeys to study the organization of the brain. "Such movements in the past—in this country, at least—have largely been the efforts of small, fragmented, and relatively ineffective groups. But this new movement is carefully orchestrated, well organized, and well financed. Moreover, this is not just a local issue. It is going on intensively at the national and even at the international level. We'd be foolish to underestimate these people. They have clout. And if they attain their goals, it will effectively kill a lot of important research."

To doubly ensure the protection of human experimental subjects, a num- 4 ber of restrictions and regulations that admittedly are burdensome have been adopted over recent years. They take a great deal of time and energy. They generate a considerable amount of extra paper work. They often slow research (indeed, make some projects impossible) and render it much more difficult and costly at a time when budgets are shrinking and inflation is making further inroads. While these procedures are accepted as the price of seeing that human subjects volunteer freely and with fully informed consent, are we willing to pay a similar price on behalf of animal subjects who can in no way either give or withhold consent?

It is easy to look at the history of animal experimentation and compile a cat- 5 alog of horrors. Or, for that matter, to look around today and find research projects that might be hard to justify. But the day is long past when a researcher can take any animal and do anything he pleases to it with a total disregard for its welfare and comfort. "People don't realize," says Allman, "that we are already extensively reviewed. In my work I must follow the ethical codes laid down by the National Institutes of Health and the American Physiological Society, among others. And we might have a surprise visit at any time from the U.S. Department of Agriculture's inspectors. It's the USDA field veterinarians who do the enforcing. Believe me, these inspections are anything but routine, and these fellows have a great deal of power. Because their reports can adversely affect federal funding, their recommendations are, in reality, orders.

"More than that, we are all required to keep detailed reports on all our ani- 6 mal experiments. And if pain or surgery is involved, we must tell them what anesthetics we used and in what dosages, what postoperative pain relievers and care were given, and so on. These reports are filed annually with the USDA, and they keep tabs on what goes on all over the country."

For all these precautions, however, it is fair to say that millions of animals— 7 probably more rats and mice than any other species—are subjected to experiments that cause them pain, discomfort, and distress, sometimes lots of it over long periods of time. If you want to study the course of a disease with a view to figuring out its causes and possible therapies, there is no way that the animal to whom you give the disease is going to be happy about it. All new forms of medication or surgery are tried out on animals first. Every new substance that is released into the environment, or put on the market, is tested on animals.

In fact, some of the tests most objected to by animal advocates are those re- *8* quired by the government. For instance, there is a figure called the LD-50 (short for "lethal dose for 50 percent") that manufacturers are required to determine for any new substance. In each such case, a great many animals are given a lot of the stuff to find out how much it takes to kill half of them—and the survivors aren't exactly in the pink.

The animal rights advocates, except for the more extreme and uncompro- *9* mising types, are not kooks or crackpots. They tend to be intelligent, compassionate individuals raising valid ethical questions, and they probably serve well as consciousness raisers. It is certainly their prerogative—or anyone's—to ask of a specific project: Is this research really necessary? (What's "really necessary" is of course not always obvious.)

But it's important that they not impose their solutions on society. It would *10* be tragic indeed—when medical science is on the verge of learning so much more that is essential to our health and welfare—if already regulation-burdened and budget-crunched researchers were further hampered.

In 1975, Australian philosopher Peter Singer wrote his influential book *11* called *Animal Liberation,* in which he accuses us all of "speciesism"—as reprehensible, to him, as racism or sexism. He freely describes the "pain and suffering" inflicted in the "tyranny of human over nonhuman animals" and sharply challenges our biblical license to exercise "dominion over the fish of the sea, and over the fowl of the air, and over every living thing that moveth upon the Earth."

Well, certainly we are guilty of speciesism. We do act as if we had dominion *12* over other living creatures. But domination also entails some custodial responsibility. And the questions continue to be raised: Do we have the right to abuse animals? To eat them? To hunt them for sport? To keep them imprisoned in zoos—or, for that matter, in our households? Especially to do experiments on these creatures who can't fight back? To send them into orbit, spin them on centrifuges, run them through mazes, give them cancer, perform experimental surgery?

Hardly any advance in either human or veterinary medicine—cure, vaccine, *13* operation, drug, therapy—has come about without experiments on animals. And it may be impossible to get the data we need to determine the hazards of, say, radiation exposure or environmental pollutants without animal testing. I certainly sympathize with the demand that we look for ways to get the information we want without using animals. Most investigators are delighted when they can get their data by means of tissue cultures or computer simulations. But as we look for alternative ways to get information, do we meanwhile just do without?

I wonder about those purists who seek to halt all animal experimentation on *14* moral grounds: Do they also refuse, for themselves and others, to accept any remedy—or information—what was gained through animal experimentation? And do they ask themselves if they have the right to make such moral decisions on behalf of all the patients in cancer wards and intensive care units and on behalf of all the victims of the maladies that afflict our species? And what of the future generations that will be so afflicted—but who might not have been—had the animal rightists not intervened?

Essay Topics: Writing in Response to "Animal Rights versus Human Health"

1. If an AIDS cure could be found at the expense of thousands of monkeys who would suffer and die during laboratory experiments, could the use of the animals be justified? Argue your view for an audience of animal rights activists.

2. Draft a law explaining under what circumstances and in what ways research labs may use animals in experiments. Then argue for the passage of this law.

3. Do we, as Rosenfeld asks, have the right to keep animals in zoos? Write an essay to convince your classmates of the correctness of your view.

4. We do not need to eat animal products, including meat, to survive. If you believe in the rights of animals, write an essay to persuade your classmates to become vegetarians.

5. Define *speciesism* and go on to explain whether you are guilty of speciesism. Consider what you eat, whether you hunt or fish, what you wear, and whether you have a pet. Your audience is your instructor, and your purpose is to relate experience and inform.

6. Research the use of animals in cosmetics manufacturing, and then argue for or against a law that would outlaw this use of animals.

CHAPTER 14

Writing the Research Paper

The research paper is a common component of college courses—for good reason. When you research, you learn things you never knew before and make important discoveries you often never anticipated. For example, researching depression could lead you to learn that college students are at high risk for depression; it could also uncover the surprising discovery that most suicides occur in the spring, not in December, as you thought. The research process also helps you gather information so you can make informed decisions and form sound judgments. Researching automobile safety, for instance, could help you determine the safest car to buy, and researching statistics on handgun deaths could help you form an opinion about handgun control. The research process can also help you test the validity of your opinions and come to new understandings. For example, researching the extent of teenage pregnancy could help you determine the wisdom of your current view on distributing birth control in high schools.

Actually, you probably already do a considerable amount of research without realizing it. Research is just fact-finding, so when you question your friends to learn which courses they recommend taking, you are engaged in research—as you are when you check the classified ads for the best prices on used cars, call local electronics stores to find the best place to purchase a reliable portable telephone, and surf the Internet to learn how to fix your leaking faucet. This chapter will expand on your current research abilities by explaining how to research in your campus library to discover information, evaluate that information, and give the results in a paper written according to the conventions for handling research material.

SURVEYING THE LIBRARY

If you have little experience with your campus library, you should familiarize yourself with it before beginning your research project. Most libraries offer guided or self-paced tours to acquaint you with the most frequently used areas and services. In particular, you should locate the following in your library:

the card or

computer catalog

the reference room

frequently used bibliographies and indexes

general knowledge and specialty encyclopedias

the computer terminals for conducting CD-ROM and online searches

current and past magazines

current and past journals

current and past newspapers

the circulation desk

the microforms room

the reading rooms

the photocopiers

If your library does not offer a tour, ask about the location of the above features.

THE RESEARCH PROCESS

Without an understanding of the research process, you can waste a great deal of time and become frustrated and confused. However, with the right procedures, you can work efficiently and achieve results to be proud of. A sound research process requires you to do the following:

Choose a subject

Narrow to a topic

Survey materials to test your topic and develop a preliminary thesis

Compile a working bibliography

Evaluate your sources

Take notes

Reconsider your preliminary thesis

Outline

Draft

Revise and edit

The rest of this chapter will explain these stages of the research process.

Choose a Subject

Because you will work on your research project for an extended period, be sure to select a subject that interests you, so you do not become bored. Perhaps you have long been curious about the civil rights movement in the 1970s, or maybe you wish you knew more about the space program. A research project presents the perfect opportunity to indulge your curiosity.

If an interesting subject does not strike you right off, try some of these strategies:

1. Browse through newspapers and newsmagazines for ideas.
2. Think about subjects covered in your classwork.
3. Consider what you have read lately.
4. Leaf through a general knowledge encyclopedia like *World Book Encyclopedia.*
5. Surf the Internet, especially the reference sites.

Even if they interest you, some subjects are not suitable and should be avoided.

1. Avoid subjects that do not require research because one good book will say it all. These are subjects like "the circulatory system" and "the life of Abraham Lincoln."
2. Avoid subjects that are so current or so regional in scope that finding sources will be difficult.
3. Avoid subjects that have been researched so extensively that nothing new can be said, subjects like legalizing marijuana and abolishing capital punishment.
4. Avoid subjects that lack scientific foundation, subjects like UFOs, the Bermuda Triangle, reincarnation, and ESP.

Narrow to a Topic

After choosing a subject, you must narrow that subject to a topic that meets the terms of the assignment and that can be completed in the appropriate length. The following guidelines can help:

1. Be sure you understand the terms of the assignment. Has your instructor asked you to write a problem-solution paper, a persuasive paper, or a report? Are there requirements for length, kinds of sources, or number of sources? When is the paper due? The answers to questions like these will help you make decisions about suitable topics.
2. Avoid topics that have little academic significance. Instead of researching the many moods of Madonna, you would do better to research how MTV has shaped popular culture.
3. Avoid topics that are too broad. Broad topics (like "media violence") cover so much territory that you cannot treat them adequately in a standard research paper. Narrower topics (like "the effects of cartoon violence on preschoolers") allow for a more in-depth discussion in a manageable length.
4. Be sure your campus library has enough material on your topic. Relying heavily on interlibrary loan can be risky because the material may not arrive in time.

One way to move from subject to topic is to frame questions about your subject. For example, for the general subject *televised violence,* you could ask these questions to discover topics:

Questions	*Narrow Topic*
1. How does televised violence affect preschoolers?	1. The Effects of Televised Violence on Preschoolers
2. Why do teenagers enjoy televised violence?	2. Why Teenagers Enjoy Televised Violence
3. Should the government regulate the amount of violence on television?	3. The Benefits [or: The Drawbacks] of Government Regulation of Violence on Television

If asking questions does not yield a suitable topic, try some of the other idea-generation techniques discussed in Chapter 1, as well as the survey procedures explained in the next section.

Survey Materials to Test Your Topic and Develop a Preliminary Thesis

Early in your research process, you should survey the library materials available to you. Doing so serves a number of purposes. First, if you do not have a topic, surveying the materials on your subject is a good way to get that topic. If you *do* have a topic, an overview of library materials will tell you whether your topic is workable. Your topic will be workable if it meets the criteria explained on pages 20 and 395 and if your survey shows that there is enough material in the library and that the material is not too technical to understand. Be aware that if there is too much information on your topic, you may not have narrowed sufficiently. Take time to narrow further, or you will be overwhelmed by the scope of the research.

Surveying materials does more than help you form and test a topic; it also helps you develop a preliminary thesis to guide your research. As the name implies, a **preliminary thesis** is a tentative, early statement of what you expect your research paper to be about. Because it is preliminary, this version of your thesis is subject to change—in fact, the odds are that it *will* change. For now, though, it focuses your research and helps you decide what material to take notes on and what material to pass by. Always remember, though, that the preliminary thesis is subject to change in light of information your research brings forth. Here are some examples of suitable preliminary thesis statements:

1. Charter schools offer a positive alternative to traditional public schools.
2. Television violence contributes to the violence in our society.
3. Paying women to be stay-at-home mothers would reduce the number of people on welfare.

NOTE: For a review of the qualities of an effective thesis, see page 40.

How to Survey Materials

Remember, when you survey materials, your purpose is to test or discover your topic and to form your preliminary thesis. You will not be reading closely, and you will not be taking notes. Instead, you will be looking at titles, tables of contents, and headings to identify subcategories, major headings, recurring arguments, and dominant themes that point to workable topics and productive thesis statements, following this procedure:

1. **Survey book titles in the computer or card catalogs.** Most libraries have replaced the card catalog with a computerized catalog of their book holdings. If you have never used a computerized catalog, you need not worry, as the screen presents you with all the prompts you need to look up books on your topic. Take the plunge; it's easier than you think. Just follow the directions to type in your subject or topic. You will then get one or more screens listing the titles of books your library has on the heading you typed in. (Academic libraries use the Library of Congress system of headings, so if the term you type in does not yield what you need, consult the *Library of Congress Subject Headings* book in the reference room. It will tell you what heading to type in for your subject or topic.)

Survey the book titles on the screen to get ideas for a topic or preliminary thesis. If a title looks particularly intriguing or useful, and you want to get information on the publisher, date of publication, call number, and so forth, follow the instructions on the screen to get bibliographic information. Jot down the author, title, and call number, retrieve the book, and scan its table of contents and skim some chapters for additional ideas. (Some systems allow you to print out the information you are interested in.)

In addition to searching the computer catalog by subject, you can search for books by author and title by following the simple directions on the screen.

If your library is not computerized, you will use the traditional card catalog. Like the computer version, the card catalog files every book in the library three ways: by author, by title, and by one or more subjects. Some catalogs file all the cards together, and some catalogs have two parts. First is the catalog file of books alphabetized according to author and title. In this section, every book will have a card filed under its title and another card filed under its author's last name (books with two or more authors will have two or more author cards). Second, the card catalog has a subject file that arranges books alphabetically according to the subjects they treat. To survey material, look up your subject, review the titles, record bibliographic information and call numbers for intriguing titles, and take a look at the tables of contents and skim some chapters of these books. Remember, if you do not find what you are looking for, check the *Library of Congress Subject Headings* for the official headings used in the catalog.

An example of a subject card that can be found in many card catalogs appears on the next page. The numbered features are explained below it.

```
                        ② TELEVISION AUDIENCES
  ① PN          ③ Seldes, Gilbert Vivian, 1893-
    1991.6            ④ The great audience. New York, Viking Press, 1950.
    .54               ⑤ viii, 299 p. 22 cm




                  ⑥    1. Moving-picture audiences. 2. Radio audiences. 3. Television
                      audiences. I. Title
                      PN1991.6.54  (   )        791.4              50-10499
                      Library of Congress         ₍30₎
```

① call number
② subject heading that card is filed under
③ author and date of birth (date of death often given as well)

④ title of book and publication data
⑤ pages before the first Arabic-numbered page, number of pages, height of book

⑥ tracings noting other headings this book is filed under

2. **Read encyclopedia entries.** They will give you an overview of your subject or topic and a good sense of the subcategories it is broken down into, information that will help you shape or test a topic and form a preliminary thesis. Be sure to look at both the general-knowledge encyclopedias, such as *Encyclopedia Britannica,* and the relevant specialty encyclopedias, like *Encyclopedia of Economics.* You can find the names of specialty encyclopedias under the appropriate subject headings of the card and computer catalog. Here is a partial list:

Encyclopedia of American Ethnic Groups

Encyclopedia of American Political History

Encyclopedia of Economics

Encyclopedia of Education

Encyclopedia of Feminism

Encyclopedia of Film and Television

Encyclopedia of Judaica

Encyclopedia of Psychology

Encyclopedia of World Art

International Encyclopedia of Social Sciences

World Encyclopedia of Film

Encyclopedias are designated in the card or computerized catalog with "Ref." above the call number. They are shelved in the reference room, but they cannot be checked out, so you must use them in the library.

3. **Survey general periodicals. Periodicals** are magazines, newspapers, and journals that come out at regular intervals (daily, weekly, monthly, quarterly—that is, "periodically"). They are important to the researcher because they contain the most current material available on a subject since, unlike books, they are updated frequently. Because periodicals contain the most up-to-date information, responsible researchers always investigate them.

General periodicals are magazines and newspapers meant for the average general reader. They include daily newspapers like the *Washington Post* and *The Wall Street Journal* and magazines like *Time, Newsweek,* and *Sports Illustrated.* Think of general periodicals as the publications you can buy at a newsstand.

To find titles of magazine articles on your subject or topic, you can use the *Reader's Guide to Periodical Literature,* which is published twice a month, and monthly in July and August. The *Reader's Guide* indexes articles by subject from over 100 popular, general interest magazines, including *Time, Sports Illustrated,* and *U.S. News and World Report.* The *Reader's Guide* is available in print form and in many libraries on a CD-ROM (compact disc—read only memory). Other indexes to magazine articles that may be available in your library on CD-ROM include *General Periodicals Index, ProQuest,* and *Magazine Index/Plus.* To find newspaper articles, The *New York Times Index* and *The Wall Street Journal Index* may be available in paper form, while *National Newspaper Index* may be available on CD-ROM.

In addition to paper and CD-ROM indexes, your library may have online databases of periodical articles that you access through a computer terminal. The instructions for conducting a search by subject will be available on screen or in a nearby manual.

To shape or test your topic and form your preliminary thesis, use the indexes to general periodicals to review the titles of relevant articles. If you encounter titles that look particularly intriguing or useful, write down the author, title, date, page, and call number. Then retrieve the article and skim it for ideas.

4. **Survey scholarly material.** General periodicals, because they are meant for the average reader, rarely provide the in-depth treatment that you should be looking for as a college student. For that, you must turn to **journals,** which are periodicals published by scholarly, professional organizations like the American Psychological Association and the Modern Language Association. Journals are publications like *American Economic Review* and *Modern Fiction Studies.* They are not available at your local newsstand. The treatment of subjects in journals is more detailed because it is meant for readers knowledgeable in the given field. However, this fact should not discourage you from using journal articles because they can be understood by the college student. In fact, their more-detailed discussions usually make them more satisfying than magazine articles.

To discover useful journal articles, check the indexes appropriate to your subject. In addition, check the abstracts and bibliographies. An **abstract** lists articles by subject matter and provides a brief summary of each article's content in addition to information about where the article can be found; a **bibliography** includes both books and journal articles. Following is a list of some of the most common indexes, bibliographies, and abstracts that may be available in print, on CD-ROM, or on an online database.

Agricultural Index

Applied Science and Technology Index

Art Index

Basic Books and Periodicals of Home Economics

Bibliography of Modern History

Bibliography on Women

Biological Abstracts

Business Periodicals Index

Chemical Abstracts

Drama Bibliography

Education Abstracts

Education Index

Energy Index

Engineering Index

Film Index

Health and Development: An Annotated Indexed Bibliography

Historical Abstracts

Humanities Index

Index to Economic Journals

Index to Religious Periodical Literature

International Bibliography of Geography

International Bibliography of Political Science

International Computer Bibliography

International Nursing Index

MLA International Bibliography of Books & Articles on the Modern Languages & Literature

The Music Index

Nursing Literature Index

Philosopher's Index

Psychology Abstracts

Social Sciences Index

Sociological Abstracts

Women: A Bibliography

To show you what a periodicals index can look like, here is a page from the paper form of the *Humanities Index*.

1. subject
2. pertinent titles listed under headings below

3. title of article
4. author of article
5. abbreviated title of journal that article appears in
6. volume number of journal
7. pages article spans
8. date of journal
9. article is *about* William Marshall, rather than written *by* him
10. article contains a bibliography

① MARRIAGE
  ② *See also*
Endogamy and exogamy
Married people
Early feminist themes in French utopian socialism: the St-Simonians and Fourier. L. F. Goldstein. J. Hist Ideas 43:91–103 Ja/Mr '82
                  Protestant churches
③ To preserve the marital state: the Basler Ehegericht, 1550–1592.
    T. M. Safley. bibl. J Fam Hist 7:162–79 Summ '82
    ④   ⑩   ⑤ Ghana ⑥ ⑦   ⑧
State and society, marriage and adultery: some considerations towards a social history of pre-colonial Asante. T. C. McCaskie. J Afric Hist 22 no 4:477–94 '81
MARRIAGE (canon law)
    See also
Clandestinity (canon law)
MARRIAGE, Clandestine (canon law) See Clandestinity (canon law)
MARRIAGE and employment. See Married people-Employment
MARRIAGE in literature
    See also
Courtship in literature

Of sex and the shrew, M. D. Perret. Ariel 13:3–20 Ja '82
Thel. Thelyphthora, and the daughters of Albion. E. B. Murray. Stud Romant 20:275–97 Fall '81
Third text of Sav me viit in be brom. O. S. Pickering. Eng Stud 63:20–2 F '82
MARRIAGE law
              Great Britain
Thel. Thelyphthora, and the daughters of Albion. E. B. Murray. Stud Romant 20:275–97 Fall '81
              Switzerland
To preserve the marital state: the Basler Ehegericht. 1550–1592. T. M. Safley, bibl J Fam Hist 7:162–79 Summ '82
MARRIED people
              Employment
'Til newsrooms do us part. B. Buresh. Colum Journalism R 21:43–6 My/Je '82
MARRS, Suzanne
  Eudora Welty's snowy heron. Am Lit 53:723–5 Ja '82
MARSHALL, John
  Hypothetical imperatives. Am Philos Q 19:105–14 Ja '82
MARSHALL, Peter
  Nicole Oresme on the nature, reflection, and speed of light. Isis 72:357–74 S '81
MARSHALL, William, fl 1630–1650
              about
⑨ Milton's Greek epigram. J. K. Hale. II Milton Q 16:8–9 Mr '82
MARSHALS
    See also
Montgomery of Alamein, Bernard Law Montgomery, 1st viscount
Ypres, John Denton Pinkstone French, 1st earl of

As part of your efforts to test or form your topic and shape your preliminary thesis, you should survey the titles of scholarly materials. Do this by identifying the indexes, bibliographies, and abstracts for your subject or topic and then look at the titles listed for your subject or topic. The titles will suggest ideas to you; particularly intriguing titles should be noted for examination.

5. **If you have access to the Internet, survey titles of available materials.** Keep in mind, though, that the Internet is still in its infancy. It is unregulated and a bit like the Wild West, so anything goes. That means you must carefully evaluate the quality of the sources you encounter there, using the guidelines on page 403. As you survey the titles, consider ways to shape or test your topic and form a preliminary thesis. Also, write down the address of any promising sources.

Compile a Working Bibliography

A **working bibliography** is a list of potentially useful sources—sources you should look at closely later, when you take notes. To compile a working bibliography, follow these steps:

1. Look up your subject in the card or computer catalog and make a bibliography card for any book that looks promising. Although some people place their working bibliography on notebook paper, index cards are a better choice. The wise researcher writes up the cards to follow the appropriate works-cited forms, which are given beginning on page 412. The following is an example of a bibliography card.

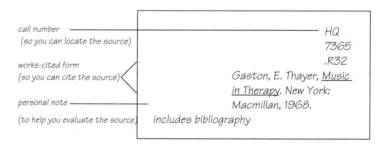

2. Look up your topic in the appropriate indexes, bibliographies, and abstracts and make bibliography cards for promising sources, following the forms beginning on page 414.
3. Check the Internet if you have access to it and make bibliography cards for promising sources, following the forms beginning on page 415.

NOTE: Admittedly, you will decide what to include in your working bibliography on flimsy evidence: whether the title of the source sounds promising. For this reason, you should err on the side of caution, making a card for any source that holds even a slight hope of usefulness. You can always discard the source later if it proves disappointing.

Whether you are dealing with a book or periodical, any source you encounter will be one of two kinds: primary or secondary. A **primary source** is one that forms the subject of your essay. For example, if you were writing about the symbolism in *Moby Dick*, then *Moby Dick* would be a primary source. Similarly, if you were writing about the lives of pioneer women, a diary written by a pioneer woman would be a primary source. A **secondary source** is an author's commentary on your subject. A journal article about the symbolism in *Moby Dick* is a secondary source, as is a book written in 1999 that describes the lives of pioneer women. Both primary and secondary sources are important to a researcher, and whenever possible you should check both.

Evaluate Your Sources

When you wrote your working bibliography, you made preliminary decisions about the usefulness of sources on the basis of their titles. Before taking notes, you must take a closer look at the sources to determine which of them are good enough to take notes on. Answering the following questions can help:

1. Is the material recent enough? For some topics, older material may be fine, but other topics, particularly scientific ones, require the most up-to-date materials available.
2. Does the author have suitable credentials? On the back cover, in the preface, or on the last page of a book, you can learn such things as where an author went to school, the degrees earned, the relevant work or research history, the publications authored, and the awards received. Similar material is often available in headnotes or footnotes of articles.
3. Is the author expressing fact, opinion, or both? Remember, a fact is verifiable information and an opinion is the author's interpretation of the facts. Thus, it is a fact that the stock market is at a three-year high but an opinion that it will decline before the end of the year.
4. Is the material free of manipulative emotion and bias? Be sure the author is as objective as possible. For example, while you can find many balanced articles on abortion, you can also find (and should avoid) materials that whip up emotions and border on propaganda.
5. Is the material sufficiently scholarly, complete, and accessible? Skim to see if it includes references to relevant research. Look at the table of contents, index, and headings to check coverage. Read a few paragraphs to be sure the writing is not too technical or difficult for you to understand. At the same time, be sure the material is not too general and superficial to be useful.

Evaluating Internet Sources

Internet sources present a special challenge because the quality of the materials varies so greatly. When evaluating Internet sources, ask the following questions:

1. Who is sponsoring the page? Generally, you should work with informational pages (ones whose purpose is to present information). The

addresses of such sites often end in .edu or .gov because the pages are sponsored by universities or government agencies.

2. Can you verify the sponsor of the page? Look for a phone number or postal address for this purpose.
3. Are the sources of information listed, and are these reliable?
4. Do you notice grammar, usage, or spelling errors? If you do, they may indicate a shoddy site.
5. Is the site free of advertising? If there is advertising, is it unrelated to the content? Sites with advertising, particularly advertising related to the content, may have a bias.
6. Is the coverage complete and is the material updated regularly?

Take Notes

Once you have judged a source acceptable, you are ready to take notes on index cards, but avoid the temptation to fill each card. Instead, write one piece of information on each card. This way, you can shuffle your note cards into a suitable order later when you organize your paper. Indicate on each card the source and page number the note is taken from so that you can document the material in your paper. If you forget to do this, you will run around at the last minute to locate sources of information. You can also label your card to categorize its content. Here is an example of an acceptable note card.

Why some children like   *Atkin, p. 6*
to watch violence.

    Children will choose to
    watch television shows that
    correspond to their own
    tendencies toward aggression.

There are four main kinds of note cards: paraphrase, quotation, summary, and personal. These will be discussed next.

Paraphrasing

To **paraphrase,** you restate an author's ideas in your own words and style. Most of your notes should be paraphrases so that your paper has your own distinctive style. When you paraphrase, remember the following points:

1. You must alter the style and wording of the original material.
2. You may not add any ideas.
3. You may not alter the meaning of the original material in any way.

A good procedure for paraphrasing is to read the original material several times until you understand its meaning. Then pretend to explain to a friend what you just read and write the paraphrase the way you would form the explanation. Check the note to be sure you have altered style and wording without altering or adding meaning. To paraphrase a long passage, break it down into parts and write the paraphrase part by part.

To appreciate the difference between an acceptable and unacceptable paraphrase, study the following examples:

source: When advertising executives are called upon to defend the advertisements they create for television, they do so by noting that such ads make consumers aware of the best products in a given field. However, this is far from the truth, for rather than informing us about the *best* products, TV ads are more likely to create in us the desire for products we don't really need.

unacceptable paraphrase: When people in advertising have to defend television ads, they do so by saying that the ads tell consumers what the best products in a particular area are. Yet this is not the truth because these ads really make us desire products we do not really need and that is really immoral.

explanation: The paraphrase is unacceptable for two reasons: The style is too close to that of the original, and the last sentence of the paraphrase includes an idea that does not appear in the original.

acceptable paraphrase: Television commercials have been defended on the grounds that these ads let people know which of the available products are the best ones. Actually, this is not really the case. Instead, these ads cause people to want unnecessary products.

explanation: This paraphrase has a style different from that of the original, but the meaning of the original has not been changed, nor has any meaning been added.

When you paraphrase, you may find it necessary or desirable to retain a key word or phrase from the original. If the word or phrase is part of the author's distinctive style, place it in quotation marks, as this example illustrates:

Television commercials have been defended on the grounds that these ads let people know about "the best products in a given field." Actually, this is not really the case. Instead, these ads cause people to want unnecessary products.

Quoting

So that your paper retains your distinctive style, most of your notes should be paraphrases. However, when you encounter material expressed in a particularly effective way, or when you encounter material very difficult to paraphrase, you can use quotation. When you quote, remember these guidelines:

1. With very few exceptions (noted below) you may not alter the spelling, capitalization, punctuation, or wording of anything you quote.

2. Short quotations (those fewer than five lines in your paper) are worked into your sentence or paragraph, but long quotations (those five or more lines in your paper) are set off by starting a new line and by indenting the quote one inch or 10 spaces on the left. Indent the first word 1 1/4 inches or 13 spaces if the quotation marks the beginning of a paragraph in the source. No quotation marks are used unless they appeared in the source, in which case double quotation marks are used. The introduction to a long quote is followed by a colon.

3. To omit some portion from the middle of a quotation use ellipses (three spaced dots). Place brackets around the ellipses to distinguish them from other spaced periods you occasionally see in a source. Be sure when you omit words that you do not distort the original meaning.

> *source:* Professional sport is in fact no more violent than it used to be.

> *quotation with*
> *ellipses:* "Professional sport is [. . .] no more violent than it used to be."

NOTE: The word *no* cannot be omitted, for the meaning would be altered. If the omission comes at the end of a sentence, use a period and then the ellipses.

> *source:* It's a poorly kept NFL secret that hooliganism increases during Monday-night games, which, when played in the east, start at the relatively late hour of 9 p.m. to accommodate west coast TV viewers.

> *quotation with*
> *ellipses:* "It's a poorly kept NFL secret that hooliganism increases during Monday-night games, which, when played in the east, start at the relatively late hour of 9 p.m. [. . .] ."

4. When you must add a word or phrase to a quotation to clarify something or work the quotation into your sentence, note the addition by placing it inside brackets.

> *source:* The OTA awarded a contract to the UCLA School of Public Health for a study of adverse effects of Agent Orange on American ground troops in Vietnam.

quotation with
addition: "The OTA [Office of Technology Assessment] awarded a contract to the UCLA School of Public Health for a study of adverse effects of Agent Orange on American ground troops in Vietnam."

5. When part of the material you are quoting appears in italics, underline the part in italics, if your computer or word processor has no italics capability.

source: Acupuncture relieves pain *even after the needles are withdrawn.*

quotation with
underlining: "Acupuncture relieves pain <u>even after the needles are withdrawn</u>."

6. Sometimes all or part of what you are quoting is itself a quotation. In this case, use single quotation marks wherever double quotation marks appear in the original. Continue to use double quotation marks to mark the place where the quoted material begins and ends.

source: "Crowd behavior is the most sensitive issue in sports today," says a Pinkerton's, Inc., official, who coordinates security at several racetracks and arenas.

quotation with
single quotation
marks: "'Crowd behavior is the most sensitive issue in sports today,' says a Pinkerton's, Inc., official, who coordinates security at several racetracks and arenas."

7. When you work the quotation into your paper with an introduction containing the word *that,* the first word of the quotation is not capitalized (unless it is a proper noun) and no comma is used after the introduction. If the introduction in your text does not have the word *that,* then a comma is used and the first word of the quotation is capitalized.

example
with "that": Smith says that "few adolescents feel secure."

example
without "that": Smith says, "Few adolescents feel secure."

Combining Paraphrase and Quotation

Many passages lend themselves to a combination of paraphrase and quotation, as the following example shows:

source: The commission of crimes by using a computer is a growing phenomenon. One only has to pick up a newspaper or watch TV news to get frequent updates on one of the newest forms of white-collar crime. The most frequently reported stories involve sophisticated computer technology; these can readily be sensationalized. Most Americans, for example, know the term "hackers" and have heard of their high-tech intrusions into some of the nation's largest, most-sensitive computer systems.

paraphrase and
quotation: The number of computer-assisted crimes is increasing, as anyone who watches TV or reads the newspaper knows. Most well known are the cases involving "sophisticated computer technology," including "high-tech intrusions into some of the nation's largest, most-sensitive computer systems."

Summarizing

Like paraphrasing, summarizing involves restating an author's ideas in your own words and style. The difference between summarizing and paraphrasing is that summarizing involves bigger chunks of material. You usually paraphrase one or more sentences or a paragraph at a time. You can summarize several paragraphs or more at once by noting the key ideas without supporting details. For more on how to write a summary, see page 372.

Writing Personal Note Cards

As you take notes, ideas of your own will occur to you. You may think of a way to handle your introduction, or you may have an idea in response to what you have read, or you may think of a piece of information you should look up. When comments, insights, and other brainstorms strike you, write them on note cards too, so you do not forget them—just be sure to label these ideas as your own, so you do not confuse them with borrowed information.

Reconsider Your Preliminary Thesis

After notetaking, you will know much more about your topic than you did when you wrote your preliminary thesis. As a result, you may want to rewrite your thesis to refine it or to take it in a new direction. First, review your note cards to refresh your memory about the information you collected. Then shape your thesis to reflect what you discovered in the library. Even this version of your thesis is still not final, however. You may continue to rework it during drafting and revising.

Outline

Because writing up research findings is a complex process, you should write a formal outline, even if you do not customarily favor outlining. You may even need to outline more than once before you are satisfied with the organization. The following guidelines can help:

1. List your own ideas on your topic. If necessary, do some idea generation.
2. Review your list of ideas and cross out the ones you do not want to include. Place the remaining ideas on index cards, one idea per card.

3. Sort your note cards and the cards with your ideas into piles so all the related cards are stacked together.
4. Label each card "main idea" or "supporting detail." (You may not use all your cards because you cannot know during notetaking exactly what will prove to be useful and what will not.)
5. Using your cards as a guide, write a formal outline with the format explained on page 47.
6. While outlining, you may discover that you need additional information to support a point or explain an issue. If so, do additional research.

WRITING THE FIRST DRAFT

Using your outline as a guide, write out your first draft the best way you can without worrying over anything, particularly grammar, spelling, punctuation, capitalization, or usage. (See page 54 for more on handling the first draft.) Although your outline is a guide, feel free to depart from it if a better idea occurs to you.

When you get to the point where you will write out a paraphrase, quotation, or summary, you can tape the appropriate note card to the draft, if you like.

As you draft, avoid stringing borrowings together one after another. Instead, comment on borrowings by analyzing them, showing their significance, indicating their relationships to something else, and so forth. Here is an example of commenting on a borrowing. Notice that the student author comments on the borrowing by showing its application.

paraphrase

> Professor Charles Atkin explains another reason children should not be completely restricted from viewing violence. He suggests that children will choose to watch television shows that correspond to their own tendencies toward aggression (6).

student comment on paraphrase

> Thus by observing the types of programs their children prefer, parents can gain a better understanding of their personalities. A child who continually elects to watch violence may have aggressive tendencies. Parents need to know whether their children are too aggressive so they can intervene, and one way they can discover this is to observe their children's viewing preferences.

Finally, when you draft, you must document borrowed material by introducing paraphrases and quotations, writing parenthetical text citations, and including a works cited page. These issues will be taken up next.

DOCUMENTING BORROWED MATERIAL

Documentation refers to the system for acknowledging that you are using the words or ideas of another person. It is also the system of conventions for noting the source of your borrowed material so that your readers can locate this material if they want to. (These conventions will be discussed in the next sections.) In order to document and thereby avoid plagiarism, you must be diligent about doing the following for every paraphrase, summary, and quotation in your paper:

1. Introduce the borrowing with the author or source.
2. Provide a parenthetical text citation for the borrowing.
3. Enclose all quotations in quotation marks.
4. Provide a "works cited" entry.

If you neglect to do any of these things, you will be guilty of plagiarism. You will also be guilty of plagiarism if you use another person's paper as your own, quote or paraphrase inaccurately, or fail to use your own style when paraphrasing.

What to Document

Every time you use the words, ideas, or opinions of others, you must document that material. You must document facts that are not common knowledge, including statistics, references to studies, descriptions of experiments, an author's original ideas, an author's opinion, or an author's conclusion—regardless of whether this material appears in your paper as quotation, paraphrase, or summary.

Facts that are common knowledge need not be documented. Thus, you need not document that Lincoln was assassinated by John Wilkes Booth, that gravity holds the planets in orbit, or that plants bend toward the sun. You need not document dates that are not debatable, like the date Lincoln was shot, or common sayings, like "Fools rush in where wise men fear to tread."

If you are in doubt about whether to document a point, err on the side of caution. It is better to document too much than to document too little and plagiarize as a result. Of course, your instructor can advise you when you are unsure.

How to Document

The next sections explain the Modern Language Association's conventions for documenting borrowed material. These conventions include introducing borrowings, providing parenthetical text citations, and writing a "works cited" page. Keep in mind that all the rules are designed to make it clear to your reader what material you have borrowed and where that material can be found, and the rules will seem logical and easier to remember.

Introducing Borrowings

Because your paper will include your own ideas along with those you have discovered in the library or on the Internet, you must distinguish what is yours from what is borrowed. This is done by introducing each borrowing with a phrase that indicates its source. Consider, for example, the following passage taken from a student paper. The introductions are underlined as a study aid.

Businesses in the United States and the world over lose great sums of money because of the alcoholic employee. Estimates of the Department of Health, Education, and Welfare

<u>and a study done by Roman and Trice show that</u> the number of alcoholics ranges from as high as ten out of every one hundred workers to a low of three to four out of one hundred (Williams and Moffat 7). Alcoholism, <u>as Joseph Follman states</u>, is "a problem so far reaching and so costly [it] must have an effect upon the business community of the nation." <u>Follman goes on to say</u>, "The result is impaired production, labor turnover, and increased costs of operation" (78). In terms of impaired productivity, the cost in the United States alone is said to be $12.5 billion a year, <u>as the National Council on Alcoholism estimates</u> (Follman 81–82). Obviously, someone must pay these costs, and no doubt it is the consumer who pays higher prices for goods and services. Yet reduced productivity because of alcoholic employees and the resulting higher prices could be held in check by the sound implementation of company programs to rehabilitate the alcoholic employee.

The paragraph includes both borrowed material and the writer's own ideas. Each borrowing is introduced to identify it as someone else's words or ideas. A close look reveals these points about introducing borrowed material.

1. Regardless of when the source material was written, the introduction is in the present tense. This **present-tense convention** is followed because printed words live on, even if their author died long ago.
2. Introductions usually appear before the borrowing, but they can also be placed in the middle or at the end.
3. The verbs used in your introductions should be varied to avoid monotony. For example, instead of repeatedly writing "Smith says," use "Smith explains" (notes, reveals, demonstrates, believes, contends, and so on).
4. An introduction can refer to the author of the borrowing ("Smith finds"), or to the credentials of the author ("one researcher believes" or "a prominent sociologist contends"), or to the title of the source ("according to *Advertising Age*").

Writing Parenthetical Text Citations

In addition to introducing your borrowings, you must cite your source of information within parentheses immediately after the borrowing. This is true whether your borrowing is a paraphrase, a summary, or a quotation. You must document this way so your reader knows exactly where the borrowing comes from.

1. When your borrowing has been introduced with the author's name, your parenthetical note includes the page number or numbers the borrowing appeared on in the source; the period appears after the citation:

```
Ruth Caldersen agrees that corporal punishment is not a
legitimate form of discipline in schools (104).
```

2. When the introduction does not include the author's name, your parenthetical citation should note this name along with the appropriate page number or numbers:

```
One high school principal remarks, "I've never known
corporal punishment to improve the behavior of unruly
students" (Hayes 16).
```

3. When more than one source by the same author is cited in your paper, include the author's name in the introduction and use a short form of the title in the parenthetical citation:

```
Rodriguez feels that a teacher who resorts to corporal
punishment is acting out of frustration (Discipline 86).
```

The above title is a short form of *Discipline in the Public Schools*. It distinguishes the source from another of Rodriguez's works cited, *Education in an Enlightened Age*.

NOTE: A citation for a long quote that is set off appears after the period. (See p. 406 on long quotes.)

Writing the "Works Cited" Page

In addition to introducing borrowings and providing parenthetical text citations, proper documentation requires you to provide a "works cited" page (or pages) at the end of your paper. This is an alphabetical listing of all the sources from which you paraphrased, summarized, and quoted—it is *not* a listing of all the sources you consulted during your research. For an example of a "works cited" page, see page 426. Notice that you list the entries alphabetically by the author's last name. If the source has no known author, alphabetize the work according to the first important word in the title (excluding *a, an,* or *the*). Double-space each entry and double-space between each entry.

Below are the forms you should model for papers written according to the Modern Language Association (MLA) style sheet. Most humanities papers are written in accordance with MLA guidelines. Instructors in the social sciences may want you to use the American Psychological Association (APA) style sheet (see page 416), while science instructors may favor the American Chemical Society (ACS) format. When in doubt, check with your instructor.

FORMS TO USE FOR BOOKS

Book with One Author

```
Johnson, Paul. Birth of the Modern: World Society 1815-1830.

New York: Harper, 1991.
```

Book with Two Authors or Three Authors

> Fisher, Seymour, and Rhoda L. Fisher. <u>What We Really Know about</u>
>
> <u>Child Rearing</u>. New York: Basic, 1976.

Book with More Than Three Authors

> Shafer, Raymond P., et al. <u>Marijuana: A Signal of</u>
>
> <u>Misunderstanding</u>. New York: NAL, 1972.

Book with an Editor

> Arnold, Matthew. <u>Culture and Anarchy</u>. Ed. J. Dover Wilson.
>
> Cambridge: Cambridge UP, 1961.
>
> Marshall, Sam A., ed. <u>1990 Photographer's Market</u>. Cincinnati:
>
> Writer's Digest, 1989.

Edition Other Than the First

> Langacker, Ronald W. <u>Language and Its Structure: Some</u>
>
> <u>Fundamental Linguistic Concepts</u>. 2nd ed. New York:
>
> Harcourt, 1973.

Selection in an Anthology

> Kafka, Franz. "The Metamorphosis." Trans. Edwin and Willa Muir.
>
> <u>Literature: Reading Fiction, Poetry, Drama and the Essay,</u>
>
> Ed. Robert DiYanni. 4th ed. New York: McGraw, 1998.
>
> 215-45.

Encyclopedia Article

> "Lombard." <u>The World Book Encyclopedia</u>. 1973 ed.

Book with a Translator

> Medvedev, Zhores A. <u>Nuclear Disaster in the Urals</u>. Trans.
>
> George Sanders. New York: Norton, 1979.

More Than One Work by the Same Author

> Tannen, Deborah. <u>That's Not What I Meant</u>! New York: Ballantine,
>
> 1986.

> ---. <u>You Just Don't Understand: Women and Men in Conversation</u>.
>
> New York: Ballantine, 1990.

FORMS TO USE FOR PERIODICALS

Author Unknown

> "Night of Horror." <u>Sports Illustrated</u> 13 Oct. 1980: 29.

Article from a Scholarly Journal (Continuous Pagination)

> Crumley, E. Frank. "The Adolescent Suicide Attempt: A Cardinal
>
> Symptom of a Serious Psychiatric Disorder." <u>American</u>
>
> <u>Journal of Psychotherapy</u> 26 (1982): 158-65.

Article from a Scholarly Journal (Separate Pagination)

> Tong, T.K. "Temporary Absolutisms versus Hereditary
>
> Autocracy." <u>Chinese Studies in History</u> 21.3 (1988): 3-22.

Magazine Published Monthly

> "TV and Movies May Contribute to Crime." <u>Ebony</u> Aug. 1979: 88.

Magazine Published Weekly

> Kanfer, Stefan. "Doing Violence to Sport." <u>Time</u> 31 May 1976:
>
> 64-65.

Newspaper Article

> Farrell, William E. "Ex-Soviet Scientist, Now in Israel, Tells of
>
> Nuclear Disaster." <u>New York Times</u> 9 Dec. 1976, late ed.: A8.

Editorial

> "Patience on Panama." Editorial. <u>Philadelphia Inquirer</u> 12 May
>
> 1989, late ed.: A22.

OTHER FORMS

Radio or Television Show

>   Bly, Robert. <u>A Gathering of Men</u>. Interview with Bill Moyers
>
>   PBS. WNET, New York. 8 Jan. 1990.

Personal Interview

>   Humphrey, Neil. Personal interview. 1 March 1998.

ELECTRONIC SOURCES

NOTE: The second date is the date of access.

An Online Scholarly Project or information Database

>   <u>The Labyrinth: Resources for Medieval Studies</u>. 1977. Georgetown
>
>   University. 30 April 1999 <http://www.georgetown.edu/
>
>   labyrinth/labyrinth-home.html>.

NOTE: The second date is the date the material was accessed.

Material from an Online Scholarly Project or Information

>   "Abbott, Bernice." <u>Women in American History</u>. Encyclopedia
>
>   Britannica. 9 April 1999 <http://women.eb.com/women/
>
>   articles/abbott_bernice. html>.

Personal or Professional Site

>   Hinto, Kip Austen <u>Zora Neale Hurston</u> 25 Apr. 1999
>
>   <http://pages.prodigy.com/zora/>.

Material from a Professional Site

>   National Stroke Association.
>
>   "Hemorrhagic Stroke." 10 Oct. 1997 <http://www.stroke.org/
>
>   HEM_ol.html>.

Note: The second date is the date of access.

>   *Journal Article in an Online Periodical: Scholarly*
>
>   Krueger, Ellen. "Media Literacy Does Work." <u>English Journal</u>
>
>   Jan. 1998. 5 Feb. 1998 <http://digit.soe.ycu.edu/
>
>   ej/krueger.htm>.

NOTE: The date is the date the material was accessed.

Article in an Online Periodical: Newspaper

> "Off Welfare, Yes. But No Job." <u>The Christian Science Monitor</u> 9
>
>   April 1998. 24 April 1998 <http://www.csmonitor.com/plweb-
>
>   turbo/cgi-bin/fastweb?getdoc+plain1+archives+1>.

NOTE: The date is the date the material was accessed.

Article in an Online Periodical: Magazine

> Fromatz, Samuel. "Groovin' with Scofield, Medeski, Martin, and
>
>   Wood." All about Jazz. April 1998. 10 April 1998
>
>   <http://www.allaboutjazz.com/Bios/jxsbio.htm>.

Material from a Portable Database (CD-ROM, Diskette, Magnetic Tape)

> "Nuclear Energy: How Protons and Neutrons Change." <u>Compton's</u>
>
>   <u>Interactive Encyclopedia</u>. 1995 ed.
>
>   CD-ROM. New York: Softkey Multimedia, 1996.

Using APA Documentation

The methods for documenting borrowed material explained so far have been those of the Modern Language Association (MLA). They are appropriate for papers written in the humanities (including writing courses). For papers written in the social sciences, your instructor may want you to follow the American Psychological Association (APA) format. The APA format for handling parenthetical citations and the final list of sources is different from the MLA format.

PARENTHETICAL CITATIONS

In the APA format, parenthetical citations include the publication date, but page numbers are *required* for quotations and only *recommended* for paraphrases. Also, *p.* or *pp.* is used before the page number(s). There is another difference as well: A comma appears between the name of the author and year, and between the year and the page number. Here are some examples:

> *quotation:* For mutual gains bargaining to work, "all
>   parties must undergo rigorous training in
>   nonconfrontational dispute resolution" (Haines,
>   1991, p. 40).

paraphrase: For mutual gains bargaining to work, everyone involved must have extensive training in how to resolve conflict without confrontation (Haines, 1991).

when borrowing is introduced: For mutual gains bargaining to work, Haines (1991) says that "all parties must undergo rigorous training in nonconfrontational dispute resolution" (p. 40).
For mutual gains bargaining to work, Haines (1991) says that everyone involved must have extensive training in how to resolve conflict without confrontation.

LIST OF REFERENCES

Rather than a "Works Cited" page, APA format calls for a list of sources with the heading "References." The "References" page includes the same information as the "Works Cited" page, but it is presented in a different format, as the following representative examples illustrate.

Book with One Author

Dretske, F. (1988). <u>Explaining behavior: Reasons in a world of</u>

<u>causes</u>. Cambridge: MIT.

Book with Two or More Authors

Bosworth, J., & Toller, T. N. (1898). <u>An Anglo-Saxon</u>

<u>dictionary</u>. New York: Oxford University Press.

Magazine Article

McIntyre, R. S. (1988, April 2). The populist tax act of 1989.

<u>The Nation</u>, pp. 445, 462–464.

Journal Article with Continuous Pagination

Sudrann, J. (1970). <u>Daniel Deronda</u> and the landscape of exile.

<u>ELH</u>, <u>37</u>. 433–455.

NOTE: If you write a paper with the APA format, be sure to get a copy of the complete style sheet, so you have models of all the possible forms.

REVISING AND EDITING

Revising and editing research writing is complex because, in addition to all the usual revising and editing concerns, you must consider the special conventions of research. Thus, you should increase the time you spend revising and editing, and you should revise and edit in stages so you stay alert. In addition to the checklist on page 117, the following checklist can help you revise and edit.

1. Have you commented on your paraphrases, summaries, and quotations so you do not string borrowings together?
2. Have you introduced each borrowing?
3. Have you provided a parenthetical citation for each borrowing?
4. Are your quotations accurate?
5. For quotations, have you
   a. Used ellipses with brackets for omissions?
   b. Used brackets for additions?
   c. Underlined or used italics where italics appeared in the source?
   d. Used single quotation marks for quotations within quotations?
   e. Set off quotations of more than four lines?
6. For paraphrases, have you
   a. Used your own style and wording?
   b. Avoided adding meaning?
   c. Avoided altering meaning?
7. Are your "Works Cited" entries in alphabetical order and in the correct form?

EXERCISE | **Writing Research**

1. Below is a sample catalog card for a book. Examine it and answer questions that follow it.

LONELINESS.

HM
132
G66

Gordon, Suzanne, 1945-
    Lonely in America / Suzanne Gordon.
New York : Simon and Schuster, c1975.
318 p. ; 22 cm.
    Bibliography: p. 311–318

    1. Loneliness.   2. Social isolation.
3. United States—Social conditions—
1960-   I. Title

○

PSrS   SRSSdc   75-28318

---

    a. Is the card an author, title, or subject card?

    b. What is the title of the book? Who is the author?

    c. When was the book published? Who is the publisher?

    d. How do you know where to find the book?

2. Write a bibliography card in the correct format for the book. What personal note about the book's usefulness should you make on the card?

3. Assume that you are writing a paper on how magazine advertisements influence people to buy, and you are seeking explanations of specific persuasive techniques used. With this in mind, do the following:

    a. Check the subject file of the card or computerized catalog and write two bibliography cards for two different, promising books.

    b. Refer to the list on page 400 and name the abstracts, bibliographies, and indexes you should check.

    c. Check the titles you named for *b* and write two bibliography cards for promising articles.

4. Examine the following excerpt from *Reader's Guide to Periodical Literature* and respond to the questions that follow it.

Economic conditions

Displaced homemaker. A. McCarthy. Common-
weal 103:38+   Ja 16 '76

Employment

Job strategies '76. N. A. Comer. Mademoiselle
82:112-15   F '76

Women on the job. McCalls   103:68+   F '76

See also

Women—Occupations

    a. What is the title of the article about economic conditions? Who is the author?

    b. In what periodical does the article appear? In what issue? On what page does the article begin?

    c. Write a bibliography card for the article.

5. Assume you are interested in the general subject, *The President of the United States*. Look up the subject in a general-interest encyclopedia and list five aspects of the general topic that you could explore further if you were working to narrow to a topic.

6. Write correct works-cited citations for the following:

    a. A book titled *Into the Flames* by Irene Gut Opdyke, published by San Bernardino, California, publisher Borgo Press in 1992.

b. A book edited by Ronald Catanare titled *Alcoholism: The Total Treatment Approach*, published by Springfield, Illinois, publisher Charles C. Thomas in 1977.

c. An article from the *Washington Post*, titled "NFL Tests Replays for Officials," that appeared March 9, 1977, on page 7.

d. An article by Leslie Kaufman and John McCormick, titled "Year of the Employee," that appeared in the July 2, 1998, issue of *Newsweek* on pages 38–41.

e. An article titled "The Free Verse Spectrum," by Eleanor Berry, which appeared in the continuously paginated journal *College English*, volume 59, in December 1997 on pages 873–897.

7. Paraphrase paragraph 5 of "Animal Rights versus Human Health" on page 389. If you like, you may include some quotation. Be sure to introduce the paraphrase and alter style but not meaning.

8. Quote directly the first sentence of paragraph 4 of "Animal Rights versus Human Health" on page 389. Introduce the quotation with the author's name and *that*. Then rewrite the quotation without *that* in the introduction.

9. Quote the first sentence of paragraph 7 in "Animal Rights versus Human Health" on page 389, omitting the word *however*. Remember to use ellipses and introduce the quotation.

10. Quote the second sentence of paragraph 11, adding *Peter Singer* after *He*. Remember to introduce the quotation and use brackets, underlining (or italics), and single quotation marks as needed.

SAMPLE RESEARCH PAPER

The following research paper, written by a student, illustrates many of the points discussed so far. The marginal notes call your attention to some of the key features.

Wasser 1

William Wasser
Professor Gabriel
English 103
May 17, 1992

Human Impact on the Freshwater Mussel Fauna
of the Eastern United States

Intro provides background

1   In recent years, scientists and naturalists have expressed great concern about the alarming rate at which biological diversity is being lost. Many of our species have suffered significant population reductions, while others are extinct or in danger of becoming extinct. As a result, much of the genetic variability characteristic of earlier periods is being lost. The diversity problem has not gone unrecognized by the U.S. government; in a 1987 report by the Office of Technology Assessment, the authors note that "the rate of diversity loss is now far greater than the rate at which diversity is created" (U.S. Congress, Office of Technology Assessment 82). Kyu Chin Kim attributes the loss to "human activity" which fragments and pollutes many natural habitats (128).

Quotations and paraphrases help establish the problem and lead into thesis.

Thesis ——→ Evidence for such destruction caused by humans has been clearly documented for the rivers of the eastern United States, where there has been a dramatic depletion of the freshwater mussel fauna.

2   Dr. David H. Stansbery, a leading authority on freshwater mussels, estimates that seventy-eight species of mussels inhabited Ohio's rivers approximately two hundred years ago; he adds that only fifty-nine of these species exist there today (qtd. in Laycock 26). This is a 24 percent reduction in mussel species for the state. Similar results have been reported for single-river

Author's name in parenthetical citation because Stansbery is referred to in Laycock article.

Wasser 2

Transitions link
borrowings.

studies. For example, Reginald W. Taylor reports that six
of the twenty-one species of mussels recorded in earlier
investigations were not found during his survey of Elk
River in West Virginia (25). Likewise, Charles R. Bursey
reports an apparent 28 percent reduction in freshwater
mussel species for the Shenango River, in Mercer County,
Pennsylvania (43). Several factors have contributed to the
decline in mussel populations, most of which are related
to human activity. Kenneth W. Cummins notes that a

Borrowing
introduced with
author's name.

significant reduction in the dissolved oxygen content, a
dramatic increase in fine sediments, heavy metal ions, and
pesticides directly eliminate the majority of
macroinvertebrate species from our rivers by producing
conditions that underlie or exceed their limits of
tolerance (187). Interestingly, various human activities
have been responsible for creating such conditions in our
rivers. With respect to these detrimental factors, the

Introduction to
paraphrase is in
present tense.

freshwater mussel is not exempt. As Samuel Fuller points
out, there can be no doubt that man-made substances and
activities have seriously harmed our mussel fauna (246).

3 The construction of dams has caused serious, adverse
effects on mussel populations. The damming of a river
changes its character dramatically. Stansbery reports that

Paraphrase has key
word in quotation
marks.

dams convert the shallow "riffles" of the river into slow-
flowing pools that are prone to collect silt and
precipitated organics on their substrates; he adds that
the accumulation of organics reduces the dissolved oxygen
content, elevates the carbon-dioxide level, and as a

No capital letter or
comma preceding
quotation because
of "that."

consequence lowers the pH (<u>Rare and Endangered</u> 6). Fuller
stresses that "these conditions are inimical to the great
majority of mussels" (252). Obviously, such changes in the

Student author
comments on
borrowing.

oxygen/carbon dioxide content would pose a serious threat
to these animals since they depend upon the gradient for

Wasser 3

respiration. Silt presents yet another problem for
bivalves. Stansbery reports that forest clearing and
agricultural tilling allow large amounts of topsoil (<u>Rare
and Endangered</u> 9), silt, and clay to be carried into the
streams (<u>Eastern</u> 10). He adds that the silt and clay
could, in effect, suffocate some species by "clogging the
gills or stimulating excess mucous secretion" (<u>Eastern</u>
10). In either case, gas exchange would be dramatically
hindered.

4   Organic waste discharged from sewage plants creates
a similarly intolerable situation for mussels. With the
release of organic materials into a stream, bacteria
already present in the water begin to breakdown these
organics through oxidative processes. As the bacterial
count increases, more and more oxygen is utilized and the
result is an environment with an extremely low, dissolved
oxygen content. A study of mussels in the Big Vermilion
River, Illinois, found the river to be completely devoid
of mussels for 22 km downstream of a domestic sewage input
(Wilhm 383). In reference to domestic pollution, Robert
Pennak states that "the zone of recovery may begin
anywhere between one-quarter mile and 100 miles downstream
from the source of pollution" (11). Thus it is evident
that the construction of dams which restrict the flow of
water, forest clearing, agricultural tilling, and organic
wastes all have the effect of depriving the mussel of
essential oxygen, and if the condition persists, metabolic
processes cease.

5   Pesticide runoff has also been considered a factor in
the decline of mussels. While Stansbery points out that
there is no scientific data concerning the specific
effects of pesticides on freshwater mollusks (<u>Eastern</u> 10),
it is probable that they at least indirectly contribute to

No need to
document
scientific fact.

Author's name is
in introduction
to quotation, so
only page
number is given
in parenthetical
citation.

Abbreviated title
of work in
citation because
two sources by
Stansbery are
used.

mussel mortality. A study has shown that mussels exposed to toxic substances will close their shells and cease the filtration process for extended periods of time (Bedford, Roelofs, and Zabik 123). With regard to this effect, J.W. Bedford, E.W. Roelofs, and M.J. Zabik consider the presence of pesticides in the water or starvation to be the probable cause of mussel mortality in their experiment (123). This again reminds us of the importance of the filtration process in obtaining food and oxygen.

Student author draws a conclusion.

6   The industrial discharge of heavy metals has also been responsible for eliminating mussels from our streams. While most aquatic organisms are affected by exposure to high levels of heavy metal toxins, Tackett holds that "mollusks [the phylum to which mussels belong] are the least resistant [. . .] (qtd. in Wilhm 383). Wurtz proposes a hierarchy of the most toxic heavy metals; he holds that zinc is the most toxic, and copper, mercury, and silver decrease in toxicity respectively (Fuller 246). Wurtz further stesses that "mollusks would be the first animals eradicated when the heavy metal content of a stream started to rise" (qtd. in Whitton and Say 293).

Brackets mark addition to quotation. Ellipses with brackets mark deletion from quotation.

Parenthetical citation for work by two authors.

7   Human activity continues day after day with little or no regard for the fragile river ecosystem and its community. The decimation of freshwater mussel populations throughout the eastern United States attests to that fact. Vast segments of our rivers have been rendered completely uninhabitable for many species. Efforts to preserve these natural resources have been hindered by a lack of funds. Stansbery points out that neither industry, the U.S. Army Corps of Engineers, nor the U.S. Environmental Protection Agency has been willing to fund his inexpensive mussel research (Laycock 27). Additionally, the authors of a U.S. document concerning biological diversity urge that

Wasser 5

The conclusion restates the thesis and draws a conclusion from the research. Note the blend of borrowed material and student's analysis.

additional public and private funds are needed to support conservation efforts (U.S. Congress, Office of Technology Assessment 83). Undoubtedly, little can be done to preserve our freshwater mussels without a cooperative effort on the part of industry, government, and the private sector. Until such an effort is made, the river will continue to be a graveyard of countless empty shells.

Works Cited

Bedford, J.W., E.W. Roelofs, and M.J. Zabik. "The Freshwater Mussel as a Biological Monitor of Pesticide Concentrations in a Lotic Environment." <u>Limnology and Oceanography</u> 13 (1968): 118-26.

Bursey, Charles R. "The Unionid (Mollusca: Bivalvia) Fauna of the Shenango River in Mercer County, Pennsylvania." <u>Proceedings of the Pennsylvania Academy of Science</u> 61 (1987): 41-43.

Cummins, Kenneth W. "Macroinvertebrates." <u>River Ecology</u>. Ed. Brian A. Whitton. Los Angeles: U California, 1975. 170-98.

Fuller, Samuel L.H. "Clams and Mussels (Mollusca: Bivalvia)." <u>Pollution Ecology of Freshwater Invertebrates</u>. Ed. Samuel L.H. Fuller and C.W. Hart, Jr. New York: Academic, 1974. 215-73.

Kim, Kyu Chin. "Assessing and Monitoring Our Biological Diversity: A National Biological Survey." <u>Proceedings of the Pennsylvania Academy of Science</u> 61 (1987): 127-32.

Laycock, George. "Vanishing Naiads." <u>Audubon</u> Jan. 1983: 26-28.

Pennak, Robert W. <u>Fresh-water Invertebrates of the United States</u>. 2nd ed. New York: Wiley, 1978.

Stansbery, David H. "Eastern Freshwater Mollusks: The Mississippi and St. Lawrence River Systems." <u>Malacologia</u> 10.1 (1970): 9-22.

---. "Rare and Endangered Freshwater Mollusks in the Eastern United States." <u>Proceedings of a Symposium of Rare and Endangered Mollusks (Naiads) of the U.S.</u> Ed. Sven Jorgensen. United States Department Interior, Fish and Wildlife Service, Sport Fisheries and Wildlife, Region 3, 1971. 5-18.

Journal article with continuous pagination

Selection in an anthology

Monthly magazine

Edition other than first

Two sources by same author

Wasser 7

Journal article
with separate
pagination

Government
document

Taylor, Reginald. "The Freshwater Naiads of Elk River,
    West Virginia with a Comparison of Earlier
    Collections." <u>The Nautilus</u> 95.1 (1981): 21-25.
United States. Cong. Office of Technology Assessment.
    <u>Technologies to Maintain Biological Diversity</u>. OTA-F-
    330. Washington: GPO, 1987.
Whitton, Brian A., and P. J. Say. "Heavy Metals." <u>River</u>
    <u>Ecology</u>. Ed. Brian A. Whitton. Los Angeles:
    U California, 1975. 286-91.
Wilhm, J. L. "Biological Indicators of Pollution." <u>River</u>
    <u>Ecology</u>. Ed. Brian A. Whitton. Los Angeles:
    U California, 1975. 375-402.

PART 3

An Editing Guide to Frequently Occurring Errors

CHAPTER 15

Editing for Word Choice

TROUBLESOME WORDS AND PHRASES

Below are some tips for eliminating words and phrases likely to annoy an experienced reader.

1. Eliminate phrases like *"as this paragraph will explain," "my paper will prove," "as I have shown,"* and *"the following paragraphs will tell."* These formal announcements of intent are common conventions in certain business, scientific, and technical writing, but in informal essays they are considered poor style.

2. Eliminate the phrase, "In conclusion." Over the years, it has been so overworked that it seems trite.

3. Do not refer to people with the relative pronoun, *which.* Instead, use *who, whom,* or *that.*

avoid: Donna is the woman <u>which</u> won the essay contest.

  use: Donna is the woman <u>who</u> won the essay contest.

  use: Donna is the woman <u>that</u> won the essay contest.

4. Do not use *plus* as a synonym for *and.*

avoid: My car needs new tie rods <u>plus</u> shock absorbers.

  use: My car needs new tie rods <u>and</u> shock absorbers.

5. Avoid using *etc., and more, and so forth,* and *and such.* They suggest that you could say more but do not want to. At times, these expressions are appropriate, but usually you *should* say whatever you *could* say.

avoid: For his camping trip, Kevin bought a tent, a sleeping bag, a lantern, <u>etc.</u>

> *use:* For his camping trip, Kevin bought a tent, a sleeping
> bag, a lantern, <u>a stove</u>, <u>and a first-aid kit</u>.

6. Do not use *etc.* with *such as. Such as* notes you are listing items representative of a group, so there is no need to use *etc.* to indicate other things are included.

> *avoid:* For his camping trip, Kevin bought several items, <u>such</u>
> <u>as</u> a tent, a sleeping bag, a lantern, <u>etc.</u>
>
> *use:* For his camping trip, Kevin bought several items, <u>such</u>
> <u>as</u> a tent, a sleeping bag, and a lantern.

7. Do not use *and etc. Etc.* means *and so forth;* therefore, *and etc.* means *and and so forth.*

8. Avoid phrases such as *I believe, in my opinion, it seems to me,* and *I think* when the ideas expressed are clearly your beliefs, opinions, and thoughts. Reserve these expressions for distinguishing your ideas from another person's.

> *avoid:* <u>In my opinion</u>, the mayor's refusal to endorse the
> safety forces' pay raise is shortsighted.
>
> *use:* The mayor's refusal to endorse the safety forces' pay
> raise is shortsighted.
>
> *use:* The city council president believes that the mayor is
> right to criticize the pay raise for the safety
> forces, but <u>I believe</u> the mayor's refusal to endorse
> the raise is shortsighted.

9. Do not use *irregardless.* Use *regardless* or *irrespective of.*

10. Replace *a lot* and *a lot of* with *many, much,* or *a great deal of*

> *avoid:* Juan earned <u>a lot of</u> respect when he told Peter he
> would not cheat for him.
>
> *use:* Juan earned <u>a great deal of</u> respect when he told Peter
> he would not cheat for him.

NOTE: If you do find it appropriate to use *a lot* (in quoting conversation, for example), remember that it is two words.

11. Eliminate *at this point in time* and *in today's world.* These phrases annoy the experienced reader; use *now* or *currently* instead.

> *avoid:* <u>At this point in time</u>, our public schools need more
> financial support.
>
> *avoid:* <u>In today's world</u>, our public schools need more
> financial support.
>
> *use:* Our public schools <u>currently</u> need more financial
> support.

12. Eliminate *the reason is because.* Use *the reason is that* or *because* instead.

avoid: <u>The reason</u> fewer people are becoming teachers <u>is</u> <u>because</u> teachers' salaries are not competitive.

use: <u>The reason</u> fewer people are becoming teachers <u>is that</u> teachers' salaries are not competitive.

use: Fewer people are becoming teachers <u>because</u> teachers' salaries are not competitive.

13. Do not use *very* to intensify things that cannot be intensified. The temperature can be *hot* or it can be *very hot*, but words like *dead, gorgeous, incredible, outstanding, unique,* and *perfect* cannot be made stronger by adding *very*.

14. Avoid using *so* as an intensifier unless it is followed by a clause beginning with *that*.

avoid: After studying for midterm exams, I was <u>so</u> tired.

use: After studying for midterm exams, I was <u>very</u> tired.

use: After studying for midterm exams, I was <u>so</u> tired <u>that</u> <u>I slept for twelve hours.</u>

15. Eliminate *vice versa*. If you want to indicate that the opposite is also true, write out exactly what that opposite is.

avoid: My mother is always criticizing me and vice versa.

use: My mother is always criticizing me, and I am always criticizing her.

16. Avoid *being as* or *being that* as synonyms for *since* or *because*.

avoid: <u>Being that</u> final exams begin next week, I must take a leave of absence from my job to study.

use: <u>Because</u> final exams begin next week, I must take a leave of absence from my job to study.

use: <u>Since</u> final exams begin next week, I must take a leave of absence from my job to study.

17. Avoid using *expect* as a synonym for *suppose*.

avoid: I <u>expect</u> dinner will be ready in an hour.

use: I <u>suppose</u> dinner will be ready in an hour.

18. Do not use *of* to mean *have*.

avoid: He could <u>of</u> (should <u>of</u>, would <u>of</u>) gone if he had had the time.

use: He could <u>have</u> (should <u>have</u>, would <u>have</u>) gone if he had had the time.

19. Avoid using *real* to mean *very*.

avoid: The weather was <u>real</u> hot in Arizona.

use: The weather was <u>very</u> hot in Arizona.

20. Use *try to* rather than *try and*.

avoid: Try and understand my position.

  use: Try to understand my position.

21. Avoid modifying nouns and adjectives with the suffix *-type*. Find the accurate word for what you mean.

avoid: She likes a desert-type climate.

  use: She likes a dry climate.

22. Avoid unnecessary qualifications using words such as *really, different,* and *particular.* They add no meaning to your sentences, but make them wordy.

avoid: In this particular case, I agree.

  use: In this case, I agree.

avoid: She served three different kinds of sandwiches.

  use: She served three kinds of sandwiches.

E X E R C I S E | **Troublesome Words and Phrases**

Directions: Edit the following paragraph to eliminate the troublesome words and phrases:

Irregardless of how busy you are, you can become more organized and efficient if you get in the habit of making a to-do list. To keep the list from doing more harm than good, however, decide what you need to do plus establish a reasonable amount of time to allocate to each task. A lot of people become frustrated because they make up lists with goals very impossible to achieve in a reasonable amount of time, such as cleaning the entire house, grocery shopping, studying, etc. in one day. Being that a list that is too ambitious can add to your stress, your goals must be attainable. In my opinion, you should identify reasonable goals, set priorities, allow flexibility, and cross items out as they are completed. Most important, you should try and avoid annoyance if all your goals are not met, for another list can be made tomorrow. The most productive people which I know are list-type people, but they content themselves with what they *do* accomplish and do not not worry about what they do *not* accomplish.

DOUBLE NEGATIVES

The following words are **negatives** because they communicate the sense of *no.*

no	none	nothing	hardly
not	nowhere	no one	scarcely
never	nobody		

Be sure to use only *one* negative to express a single negative idea.

no (two negatives): <u>No one</u> can do <u>nothing</u> to help.

yes (one negative): <u>No one</u> can do anything to help.

no (two negatives): I <u>cannot</u> go <u>nowhere</u> with you.

yes (one negative): I <u>cannot</u> go anywhere with you.

yes (one negative): I can go <u>nowhere</u> with you.

Contractions often include a form of *not*, which is a negative.

no (two negatives): She <u>can't hardly</u> wait for Leonard to arrive.

yes (one negative): She <u>can't</u> wait for Leonard to arrive.

yes (one negative): She can <u>hardly</u> wait for Leonard to arrive.

no (two negatives): Henry <u>wouldn't</u> be <u>nothing</u> without you.

yes (one negative): Henry would be <u>nothing</u> without you.

yes (one negative): Henry <u>wouldn't</u> be anything without you.

E X E R C I S E | **Double Negatives**

Rewrite the following sentences to eliminate the double negatives.

1. The school board will not never agree to abolish the dress code.
2. In the back row, we can't hardly hear what the actors are saying.
3. I don't know nothing about cars, but I will try to help you change your oil.
4. We baked so many cookies that the dozen we ate won't hardly be missed.
5. That stupid dog won't never learn to fetch my slippers.

FREQUENTLY CONFUSED WORDS

accept, except

Accept is a verb that means "to receive" or "to agree to."

Mary was pleased to <u>accept</u> the scholarship.
I <u>accept</u> the conditions of employment you explained.

Except is a preposition that means "excluding."

Except for the color, Joe liked the car.

advice, advise
Advice is a noun that means "a recommendation."

> Harriet always values Jan's <u>advice</u>.

Advise is a verb that means "to recommend."

> I <u>advise</u> you to quit while you are ahead.

affect, effect
Affect is a verb meaning "to influence."

> The trade deficit <u>affects</u> the strength of our economy.

Effect is a noun meaning "result."

> The <u>effects</u> of the drug are not fully known.

Effect is a verb meaning "to bring about."

> The new company president plans to <u>effect</u> several changes in corporate policy.

all right, alright
A knowledgeable reader is likely to prefer *all right*.

allusion, illusion
Allusion is a noun meaning "indirect reference."

> I resent your <u>allusion</u> to my past.

Illusion is a noun meaning "something false or misleading."

> Having money can create the <u>illusion</u> of happiness.

already, all ready
Already means "by this time."

> I would stay for dinner, but I have <u>already</u> eaten.

All ready means "prepared."

> Now that I have packed, I am <u>all ready</u> to leave.

among, between
Between is usually used to show the relationship of two things.

> The animosity <u>between</u> Lee and Ann has existed for years.

Between can be used for more than two things when it means "within."

> The floor <u>between</u> the stove, refrigerator, and table is hopelessly stained from years of wear.

Among is used to show the relationship of more than two things.

> The friendship <u>among</u> Kelly, Joe, and Stavros began in third grade and has continued for 15 years.

amount, number

Amount is used for a unit without parts that can be counted individually.

> The <u>amount</u> of suffering in the war-torn nation cannot be measured.

Number is used for items that can be counted.

> The <u>number</u> of entries in the contest will determine the odds of winning the grand prize.

beside, besides

Beside means "next to."

> Dad put his book down <u>beside</u> his glasses.

Besides means "in addition to" or "except for."

> <u>Besides</u> a crib, the expectant parents bought a dresser.
> I have nothing to tell you <u>besides</u> watch your step.

breath, breathe

Breath is a noun.

> The skaters held their <u>breath</u> as the judges announced the scores.

Breathe is a verb.

> At high altitudes it is more difficult to <u>breathe</u>.

coarse, course

Coarse means "rough."

> Because wool is <u>coarse</u>, I do not like to wear it.

Course means "path," "route," or procedure."

> To speed your progress, summer school is your best <u>course</u>.

complement, compliment

Complement means something that completes.

> Red shoes will <u>complement</u> the outfit nicely.

Compliment is "praise" or "flattery."

> Your <u>compliment</u> comes at the right time because I was beginning to doubt myself.

conscience, conscious

Conscience is an awareness of right and wrong.

    When in doubt, follow your conscience.

Conscious means "aware."

    Eleni is always conscious of the feelings of others.

dessert, desert

Dessert is the sweet at the end of a meal.

    Ice cream is everyone's favorite dessert.

Desert means "abandon."

    Kim is a good friend because he never deserts me in my time of
    need.

Desert is dry, sandy land.

    When driving across the desert, a person should have a survival
    kit in the car.

different than, different from

Experienced readers are likely to prefer *different from*.

disinterested, uninterested

Disinterested means "impartial."

    In labor disputes, a federal mediator acts as a disinterested
    third party.

Uninterested means "lacking interest" or "bored."

    Giselle is uninterested in my problem because she has troubles
    of her own.

farther, further

Farther refers to distance.

    It is not much farther to the restaurant I told you about.

Further means "in addition" or "additional."

    The senator believed further that the tax favored the rich.
    Any further discussion is a waste of time.

fewer, less

Fewer is used for things that can be counted individually.

    There were fewer A's on the test than I expected.

Less is used for one unit without individual members that can be counted.

    The less you know about what happened, the happier you will be.

human, humane

Human refers to men and women and the qualities men and women possess.

    If we did not make mistakes, we would not be <u>human</u>.

Humane means "compassionate."

    Our society is not known for <u>humane</u> treatment of the elderly.

imply, infer

Imply means "to suggest something without stating it."

    Your attitude <u>implies</u> that you do not care.

Infer means "to draw a conclusion from evidence."

    I can <u>infer</u> from your sarcasm that you do not agree with me.

it's, its

It's is the contraction form of *it is* or *it has.*

    <u>It's</u> unfair to accuse Lee of lying without proof.
    <u>It's</u> been three years since I saw George.

Its is a possessive pronoun.

    The dog buried <u>its</u> bone at the base of the oak tree.

loose, lose

Loose means "unfastened" or "not tight."

    Joey's <u>loose</u> tooth made it hard for him to eat corn on the cob.

Lose means "misplace."

    Every time I buy an expensive pen, I <u>lose</u> it.

passed, past

Passed means "went by."

    Summer <u>passed</u> far too quickly.

Past refers to previous time.

    The <u>past</u> week was hectic because I had to work overtime at the
    store and study for final exams.

precede, proceed

Precede means "to come before."

    A preface <u>precedes</u> the main part of a book.

Proceed means "continue."

    I am sorry I interrupted you; <u>proceed</u> with your plan.

principal, principle
Principal is a school administrator (as a noun); as an adjective *principal* means "first in importance."

```
The principal suspended the students for fighting.
The principal issue here is whether we can afford the trip.
```

Principle is a truth or a moral conviction.

```
My principles will not allow me to lie for you.
```

set, sit
Set is a verb that takes a direct object.

```
For daylight saving time, set your clock ahead one hour.
```

Sit is a verb that does not take a direct object.

```
Sit near the door, and I will find you when I arrive.
```

stationary, stationery
Stationary means "unmoving" or "unchanging."

```
This fan is stationary; it does not rotate.
```

Stationery is writing paper.

```
More men are using pink stationery for personal correspondence.
```

than, then
Than is used for comparisons.

```
The car I bought is more fuel efficient than yours.
```

Then is a time reference; it also means "next."

```
I went to college in the 1970s; students were politically
active then.
Spade the ground thoroughly; then you can plant the seeds.
```

there, their, they're
There indicates place. It is also a sentence opener when *their* or *they're* does not apply.

```
I thought my car was parked there.
There are twelve people going on the ski trip.
```

Their is a possessive pronoun.

```
Children rarely appreciate what their parents do for them.
```

They're is the contraction form of *they are*.

```
Lyla and Jim said they're coming, but I will believe it when I
see them.
```

threw, through, thorough

Threw is the past tense of *throw*.

> The pitcher <u>threw</u> the ball to third base.

Through means "finished" or "into and out of."

> We should be <u>through</u> by noon.
> When I drove <u>through</u> the Lincoln Tunnel, I forgot to put my headlights on.

Thorough means "complete."

> In the spring, many people give their houses a <u>thorough</u> cleaning.

to, too, two

To means "toward." It is also used with a verb to form the infinitive.

> After five years, Kathleen saved enough money <u>to</u> go <u>to</u> Italy.

Too means "also" or "excessively."

> The child whined because he did not get to go skating <u>too</u>.
> When the curtain went up, I was <u>too</u> frightened to say my lines.

Two is the number.

> Lenny gets along well with his <u>two</u> roommates.

whose, who's

Whose is the possessive form of *who*.

> <u>Whose</u> books are on the kitchen table?

Who's is the contraction form of *who is* and *who has*.

> <u>Who's</u> going with you?
> <u>Who's</u> been in the cookie jar?

your, you're

Your is the possessive form of *you*.

> <u>Your</u> car is parked in a tow-away zone.

You're is the contraction form of *you are*.

> Let me know when <u>you're</u> coming with us.

EXERCISE | **Frequently Confused Words**

Select five sets of frequently confused words that you are not completely comfortable using. Use each word in a sentence that you compose.

CHAPTER 16

Editing for Sentence Fragments

A **sentence fragment** results when you punctuate and capitalize a phrase or subordinate clause as if it were a sentence.

> *phrase*
> *fragment:* The bus driver and his wife spent over $500 on toys for their children. <u>Most of it on the two girls</u>.

Although the period and capital letter give the underlined phrase the appearance of a sentence, the words do not have enough completeness for sentence status. Hence, they are a fragment. Here is another example.

> *subordinate*
> *clause fragment:* <u>Since she was graceful as well as daring</u>. She was an excellent dancer.

The underlined subordinate clause forms a fragment. Despite the period and capital letter, the word group lacks enough completeness to function as a sentence.

NOTE: For a more complete discussion of subordinate clauses, see page 102.

A fragment also results when an incomplete or incorrect form of a verb is used, as the following examples illustrate.

> *incomplete*
> *verb fragment:* The game been delayed because of rain.
> *incorrect*
> *verb fragment:* The band being too loud.

CORRECTING SENTENCE FRAGMENTS

1. To correct a fragment that results when a phrase is punctuated and capitalized like a sentence, you can connect the fragment to the appropriate sentence before or after it, or you can rewrite the fragment so that it forms a sentence. These correction methods are illustrated on the opposite page.

442

fragment: The bus driver and his wife spent over $500 on toys for their children. <u>Most of it on the two girls</u>.

correction: The bus driver and his wife spent $500 on toys for their children, most of it on the two girls.

correction: The bus driver and his wife spent over $500 on toys for their children. Most of the money was spent on the two girls.

2. To correct a fragment that results when a subordinate clause is punctuated and capitalized like a sentence, connect the fragment to the appropriate sentence before or after it, as the following example illustrates:

fragment: <u>Since she was graceful as well as daring</u>. She was an excellent dancer.

correction: Since she was graceful as well as daring, she was an excellent dancer.

3. To correct a fragment that results from an incomplete verb, add the missing verb part, like this:

fragment: The game been delayed because of rain.

correction: The game has been delayed because of rain.

4. To correct a fragment that results from an incorrect verb, correct the verb form, like this:

fragment: The band being too loud.

correction: The band is too loud.

PROCESS GUIDELINES: FINDING SENTENCE FRAGMENTS

If you have a tendency to write sentence fragments, you should edit a separate time, looking just for fragments. Study each group of words you are calling a "sentence." Read each group aloud and ask yourself if it sounds complete enough to be a sentence. Do not move on to the next group until you are sure the one you are leaving behind is a sentence. For this method to be effective, you must move slowly, listening to each word group independent of what comes before and after it. Otherwise, you may fail to hear a fragment because you complete its meaning with a sentence coming before or after.

Computer Tips

1. These words often begin sentence fragments:

after	as if	because	for example	such as	when
although	as long as	especially	if	unless	whenever
as	as though	even though	since	until	while

Use your computer's search function to locate these words in your draft. Each time you locate a word group beginning with one of them, check to be sure you have a sentence rather than a fragment.

2. Isolate every word group you are calling a sentence by inserting eight spaces before each capital letter that marks a sentence opening. Then read each word group separately to check for completeness. With word groups visually isolated this way, you are less likely to overlook a fragment by mentally connecting it to a sentence before or after it. After checking everything, reformat the text.

EXERCISE | **Sentence Fragments**

Where necessary, edit the following to eliminate the fragments. Some are correct as they are.

1. After returning from the beach. The children were exhausted.
2. The rain showed no signs of letting up, so flash flood warnings were issued.
3. After Howie had attended drama class several times and bought a subscription to *Variety*. He was sure he would become a big star.
4. Although Marie missed several training sessions. She learned to use the new computer.
5. By midnight the party was over.
6. John neglecting his assigned duties and spending time on independent research.
7. The reigning dictator, being an excellent administrator and former army officer.
8. Being the most indispensable of the Channel 27 news team. Antonio got a raise.
9. Karen dropped calculus. Which she had dropped several times before.
10. Sean went to his karate class and when he came home. He had been burglarized.
11. After awhile, the fog cleared.
12. How can you expect that of me?
13. Carlotta skipped breakfast. Although she needed the nourishment.
14. Working together to save our environment. We can leave the world a better place than we found it.
15. Dad cleaning the hull of the boat, helping to set the lobster traps and still finding time to teach his younger daughter how to bait her own hook.

Edit the paragraphs below to eliminate the fragments:

16. Virgil Trucks won a World Series game for the Detroit Tigers without ever winning a regular season game. Because he was in the navy at the time. Trucks missed most of the season in 1945. Discharged after the war. He returned in time to pitch five innings against the St. Louis Browns and help the Tigers win the pennant. On the last day of the season. He was not credited with the win, though, and finished the season with a record of 0–0. The Tigers faced the Chicago Cubs in the World Series that year. The Tigers triumphed in seven games. Trucks, who had not won a game that year, went

the distance in the second game. Beating the Cubs 4–1. As a result, Trucks being the only pitcher to win in the World Series without winning during the regular season.

17. Much literature written for adolescents is of the highest quality. For example, *IOU'S,* by Ouida Sebestyen, being a well-written story of adolescent conflict that both teens and adults would enjoy. The main character is 13-year-old Stowe. A boy who lives with his divorced mother. The novel chronicles Stowe's efforts as he wrestles with an important decision, struggles with friendships, and makes peace with his family. Like most adolescents, Stowe longs for the independence of adulthood at the same time he fears it. Briskly paced, tightly narrated, and thought-provoking, *IOU'S* is a novel teens will see themselves in. And a novel that will remind adults of the struggles inherent in adolescence. It is poignant, funny, and subtle. And above all realistic.

CHAPTER 17

Editing for Run-On Sentences and Comma Splices

A **run-on sentence** occurs when two or more main clauses are written without any separation. (Main clauses, discussed on page 102, are word groups that can stand as sentences.)

> *main clause:* the power was out for two days
>
> *main clause:* most of the food in my refrigerator spoiled
>
> *run-on sentence:* The power was out for two days most of the food in my refrigerator spoiled.

A **comma splice** occurs when two or more main clauses are separated by nothing more than a comma.

> *main clause:* Rocco studied hard for his final exams
>
> *main clause:* he passed them all with high marks
>
> *comma splice:* Rocco studied hard for his final exams, he passed them all with high marks.

CORRECTING RUN-ON SENTENCES AND COMMA SPLICES

Run-ons and comma splices can be corrected in four ways.

1. You can separate the main clauses with a period and capital letter to form two sentences.

> *run-on:* The power was out for two days most of the food in my refrigerator spoiled.
>
> *correction:* The power was out for two days. Most of the food in my refrigerator spoiled.
>
> *comma splice:* Rocco studied hard for his final exams, he passed them all with high marks.
>
> *correction:* Rocco studied hard for his final exams. He passed them all with high marks.

2. You can separate the main clauses with a semicolon.

> *run-on:* The personnel department was praised for its efficiency all the workers received a bonus.

> *correction:* The personnel department was praised for its efficiency; all the workers received a bonus.

> *comma splice:* I never like to wear wool, its coarseness irritates my skin.

> *correction:* I never like to wear wool; its coarseness irritates my skin.

3. You can separate the main clauses with a comma and coordinating conjunction *(and, but, or, nor, for, so, yet)*.

> *run-on:* The new computer's manual is very clear Enrico learned to use the machine in an hour.

> *correction:* The new computer's manual is very clear, so Enrico learned to use the machine in an hour.

> *comma splice:* The hospital layed off 100 workers, most of them will be called back in three months.

> *correction:* The hospital layed off 100 workers, but most of them will be called back in three months.

NOTE: A frequent cause of run-ons and comma splices is confusing the following conjunctive adverbs for coordinating conjunctions:

therefore	moreover	thus
however	hence	for example
also	consequently	furthermore
indeed	nevertheless	nonetheless

Conjunctive adverbs cannot be used to join main clauses with a comma; only the coordinating conjunctions *(and, but, or, nor, for, so, yet)* can do this.

> *run-on:* I was certain my interview went well therefore I was surprised when I was not among the finalists for the job.

> *correction:* I was certain my interview went well; therefore, I was surprised when I was not among the finalists for the job.

> *comma splice:* The Christmas party was dull, consequently I left early.

> *correction:* The Christmas party was dull; consequently, I left early.

4. You can change one of the main clauses to a subordinate clause.

> *run-on:* My car stalls when I accelerate quickly the carburetor needs to be adjusted.

correction: Because the carburetor needs to be adjusted, my car stalls when I accelerate quickly.

comma splice: Spring is supposed to be a happy time, many people get depressed.

correction: Although spring is supposed to be a happy time, many people get depressed.

PROCESS GUIDELINES: FINDING RUN-ON SENTENCES AND COMMA SPLICES

If you have a tendency to write run-ons and comma splices, edit a separate time, checking just for these errors. Study each group of words you are calling a "sentence," and ask yourself how many main clauses there are. If there is more than one, be sure the proper separation exists. When you find a run-on or a comma splice, make the correction according to the following guidelines:

run-on: The door slammed shut the dog awoke with a start.

comma splice: The door slammed shut, the dog awoke with a start.

correction with semicolon: The door slammed shut; the dog awoke with a start.

correction with comma and coordinating conjunction: The door slammed shut, and the dog awoke with a start.

correction with period and capital letter: The door slammed shut. The dog awoke with a start.

correction with subordinate clause: When the door slammed shut, the dog awoke with a start.

Computer Tips

1. Use your computer's search function to locate these conjunctive adverbs in your draft.

therefore	moreover	thus
however	hence	for example
also	consequently	furthermore
indeed	nevertheless	nonetheless

Each time you locate one of these conjunctive adverbs, check for main clauses on both sides. Wherever you have main clauses on both sides, be sure you have used a semicolon before the word.

2. Isolate every word group you are calling a sentence by inserting eight spaces before each capital letter marking the beginning of a sentence. The visual separation will allow you to check the number of main clauses more easily. After finding and eliminating run-ons and comma splices, reformat your text.

EXERCISE | **Run-on Sentences and Comma Splices**

Correct the following run-ons and comma splices using any of the methods discussed.

1. My first bike will always be special to me it was a yellow dirt bike named Thunderball.
2. Brad loves to gossip about others he becomes angry if he even thinks someone is gossiping about him.
3. Yesterday the fire trucks raced up our street three times it must be the summer brushfire season.
4. The large black ants marched upside down across the kitchen ceiling, I wonder where they came from.
5. The package of chicken fryer parts was obviously spoiled he returned it to the manager of the market demanding a refund.
6. My daughter's baseball pants are impossible to get clean, why does the league insist on purchasing white pants?
7. Randy is a terrible soccer coach, he cares more about winning than he does about the children he manages.
8. Stevie is so warm and open that it is hard to resist his charm, he seems to smile all the time.
9. Cotton material is all that they claim it is—lightweight, soft, and comfortable be careful when laundering it often shrinks.
10. My mother has often been my best friend, she is caring, supportive, and nonjudgmental.

Rewrite the paragraphs below to eliminate the run-on sentences and comma splices.

11. My day off made me wish I was back at my job everything went wrong. First I overslept and neglected to get my son to day camp on time. Then there was no milk for breakfast my son ate pizza. The dog had raided the wastebasket during the night half-chewed paper and bits of garbage littered the living room carpeting. I plugged in the sweeper, one of the prongs broke off in the outlet. I drove to the local hardware store to purchase new plugs. I returned home to discover the plug was the wrong size for the sweeper cord I drove back to the store to exchange the plug for the proper size. Then I cut my finger when the screwdriver slipped while I was trying to attach the new plug. In the middle of all this chaos, the phone rang, the neighbor was calling to tell me that my German shepherd had chased the letter carrier away from

her house. By the time I was finished listening to her, I started to itch I looked down to see the unmistakable red blotches of poison ivy rising on my arms and calves.

12. Every object in the universe pulls on every other object, this is called gravitation. Interestingly, the strength of the gravitational pull depends on two things, how much matter a body contains and the distance between the objects. Objects with very little matter have very little gravitation, for example, the earth has more matter than the moon, so the earth's gravitational pull is stronger than the moon's. Also, the closer together objects are, the greater their gravitational pull. The earth has more matter than a human being, so its gravitation pulls the human to the earth. However, the earth acts as if all matter were at its center thus the strength of gravity at a location depends on its distance from the earth's center. This means that gravity is stronger at sea level than on a mountain top.

CHAPTER 18

Editing for Subject–Verb Agreement and Tense Shifts

SUBJECT–VERB AGREEMENT

The rule for **subject–verb agreement** is straightforward: a verb should always agree with its subject *in number*. That is, a singular subject requires a singular verb, and a plural subject requires a plural verb.

> *singular subject,*
> *singular verb:* Green <u>ink is</u> often difficult to read.

> *plural subject,*
> *plural verb:* The <u>desks are</u> highly polished.

Most of the time subject–verb agreement is easily achieved. However, some instances present special agreement problems, and these are discussed below.

Compound Subjects

A **compound subject** occurs when two or more words, phrases, or clauses are joined by *and, or, nor, either . . . or,* or *neither . . . nor.*

1. If the parts of a compound subject are linked by *and,* the verb is plural.

The <u>lioness and her cub share</u> a close bond.

2. If subjects are preceded by *each* or *every,* then a singular verb is used.

<u>Each lioness</u> and <u>each cub faces</u> starvation on the drought-stricken plain.

3. Singular subjects linked by *or* or *nor* (or by *either . . . or* or *neither . . . nor*) take a singular verb.

<u>Drought or famine threatens</u> all wildlife.

4. Plural subjects linked by *or* or *nor* (or *either . . . or* or *neither . . . nor*) take a plural verb.

> <u>Neither the children nor their parents are</u> enjoying the play.

5. When a plural subject and a singular subject are joined, the verb agrees with the nearer subject.

> <u>Disease or predators are</u> also a danger to newborn cubs.
>
> <u>Neither the scouts nor their leader is</u> willing to camp out on such a cold night.

NOTE: For a more pleasant-sounding sentence, place the plural form last: <u>Neither the leader nor the scouts are</u> willing to camp out on such a cold night.

Subject and Verb Separated

Words, phrases, or clauses that come between the subject and verb do not affect the subject–verb agreement rule.

> The <u>chipmunks</u>, burrowing under my flower bed, also <u>raid</u> my garden.

The subject *chipmunks* is plural, so the plural verb *raid* must be used. The phrase *burrowing under my flower bed* does not affect that. Here is another example:

> <u>One</u> of the demonstrators <u>was</u> fined $100.

Although the phrase between the subject and verb contains the plural word *demonstrators,* the singular subject *one* still requires the singular verb *was.*

Inverted Order

1. When the verb appears before the subject, the word order is *inverted.* Be sure the verb agrees with the subject and not some other word close to the verb.

> Floating on the water <u>were three lilies</u>.

2. Sentences that begin with *there* or *here* often have inverted order, as do sentences that ask a question.

> There <u>are</u> many <u>causes</u> of cancer.
>
> Here <u>is</u> the <u>box</u> of records.
>
> Why <u>are</u> your <u>questions</u> so hard to answer?

Indefinite Pronouns

1. *Indefinite pronouns* refer to some part of a group of people, things, or ideas without specifying the particular members of the group referred to. The following indefinite pronouns are singular and require singular verbs.

anyone	everybody	something
anybody	everything	none
anything	someone	no one
each	either	nobody
one	neither	nothing
everyone	somebody	

```
Nobody ignores an insult all the time.
Everybody retaliates once in a while.
No one likes to be the butt of a joke.
```

NOTE: Although *everyone* and *everybody* clearly refer to more than one, they are still singular in a grammatical sense and take a singular verb.

```
Everyone is invited to the party after the show.
```

2. It is tempting to use a plural verb with a singular indefinite pronoun followed by a phrase with a plural word. However, in this case too the singular verb is used in formal usage.

```
Each of the boys is willing to help rake the leaves.
Neither of us plans to contribute a week's salary to the
Christmas fund.
```

3. The following indefinite pronouns may be singular or plural, depending on the meaning of the sentence.

all	some	most
any	more	

```
Most of the players are injured.
Most of the pie is gone already.
All of the bills are paid.
All of the hem is torn.
```

Collective Nouns

Collective nouns have a singular form and refer to a group of people or things. The following are examples of collective nouns.

audience	class	majority
committee	family	faculty
crew	team	jury

1. Collective nouns take a singular verb when the noun refers to the group as a single unit.

The <u>number</u> of people attending the concert <u>was</u> staggering.

The women's basketball <u>team is</u> still in contention for the state championship.

2. Collective nouns take a plural verb when the members of the group are functioning individually.

A <u>number</u> of those in attendance <u>were</u> over 30 years old.

The <u>faculty have</u> agreed among themselves to promote tougher admissions standards.

EXERCISE | **Subject–Verb Agreement**

Choose the correct verb form in the following sentences.

1. Three wolves and a grizzly bear (stalk/stalks) the grazing caribou herd.
2. The hunter, not natural enemies, (is/are) responsible for the decline in the bald eagle population.
3. Only recently (has/have) we seen the rebirth of violent protest.
4. There (is/are) few American holidays more popular than Thanksgiving.
5. None of us really (know/knows) anyone else.
6. All of us often (disguise/disguises) our real feelings.
7. Neither of the cubs born to the huge female grizzly (appear/appears) undernourished.
8. The chief reasons for the country's high unemployment rate (has/have) been the attempts to bring inflation under control.
9. Each of the campers (is/are) responsible for bringing cooking utensils.
10. A majority of people (feel/feels) insecure about something.
11. There (is/are) few presidents more admired than Lincoln.
12. Neither time nor progress (has/have) diminished the affection most Americans feel for our sixteenth president.
13. One of my favorite poems (is/are) "The Rime of the Ancient Mariner."
14. Most of the beetles (is/are) trapped.
15. Either Whitney Houston or Elton John (deserve/deserves) the Grammy for record of the year.
16. Your family often (demand/demands) to know your innermost secrets.
17. Each of us (decide/decides) whom we will trust.
18. Everyone (need/needs) someone to talk to.
19. Fifteen adult white-tailed deer and a single fawn (was/were) observed by the backpackers.
20. All the elements of nature (act/acts) to maintain the balance of the animal population.

Rewrite the following paragraph to eliminate problems with subject–verb agreement.

One of the islands in the Caribbean Sea is called Bonaire. A number of tourists are attracted to Bonaire because it is a nesting site for pink flamingos. However, the clear waters of the sea makes the area a perfect spot for diving. There is numerous underwater attractions for either the experienced diver or the amateur who requires a guide. On the coral reef is groupies and moray eels. Also, there are small "cleaner fish," called hogfish, who eat the harmful parasites off the larger fish. The colorful reef itself is a spectacular sight where one can observe a variety of coral. Throughout the reef is sea anemones, shrimp, and crabs for the diver to observe. Although the underwater attractions of Bonaire is not commonly known, time and word of mouth will bring more vacationers to this island off the coast of northern South America.

TENSE SHIFTS

Verbs have **tense** to indicate past, present, and future time. Once you begin with a particular verb tense, maintain that tense as long as you are referring to the same period of time. Switching tense without a valid reason creates a problem called **tense shift.** The following paragraph contains unwarranted tense shifts (the verbs are underlined to help you recognize the shifts).

> Hockey player Bill Mosienko <u>dreamed</u> of making his way into the record books, and on March 23, 1952, his dream <u>comes</u> true. His team, the Black Hawks, <u>was playing</u> the New York Rangers. Black Hawk Gus Bodnar <u>gets</u> the puck and <u>passes</u> it to Mosienko, who <u>scores</u>. At the following face-off, Bodnar <u>gains</u> possession, <u>passes</u> to Mosienko, who <u>scored</u> again. Bodnar <u>won</u> the face-off again and <u>passed</u> to Gee. Gee <u>passed</u> to Mosienko, who <u>scores</u> again—for three goals in twenty-one seconds.

The verbs in this paragraph shift back and forth from present to past, interfering with an accurate representation of the action of the game. To prevent confusion about time sequence, once you use a verb tense, maintain that tense consistently and shift time only when the shift is justified.

A corrected version of the example paragraph reads like this:

> Hockey player Bill Mosienko dreamed of making his way into the record books, and on March 23, 1952, his dream came true. His team, the Black Hawks, was playing the New York Rangers. Black Hawk Gus Bodnar got the puck and passed it to Mosienko, who scored. At the following face-off, Bodnar gained possession and passed to Mosienko, who scored again. Bodnar won the face-off again and passed to Gee. Gee passed to Mosienko, who scored again—for three goals in twenty-one seconds.

A shift from one tense to another is appropriate when the time frame at issue has changed.

```
When I first began working as a waiter, I hated my work. Now I
am enjoying my job more than I thought possible.
```

In the above example, each shift (from past to present to past) is justified because each verb accurately reflects the time period referred to.

<table>
<tr><td>E X E R C I S E</td><td>

Tense Shifts

Revise the following sentences to eliminate inappropriate tense shifts. One sentence is correct.

1. While you were turned around, a miracle happened. The line drive hits the base runner, so no runs were scored.
2. Just when Katya thought her homework was finished, she remembers she has history questions to answer.
3. Grandma Rodriguez seemed totally bored with the baseball game when suddenly she jumps up and screams, "Park it, Jimmy!"
4. Many educators in the United States believe in the principle of grouping students according to ability because as long as bright students were competing against other bright students, they performed better.
5. By the end of her essay exam, Jeanine had her facts all confused; she is positive, though, that she passes the multiple-choice section of the test.
6. The governor announced a new tax proposal and explained that he is confident it will solve the state's budget problems.
7. Young people in the 60s demanded a religion that calls for a simple, clean, and serene life.
8. Marty asked Lynn if she wants to go out with him, but she brushed him off and left with Jerome.
9. As Sue collected her clubs and new golf balls, she thinks how difficult this tournament will be.
10. Consequently, we can see that the human race has progressed or at least seemed to have progressed.

Rewrite the following paragraph to eliminate unwarranted tense shifts:

</td></tr>
</table>

Theatre has a long history. The Chinese first performed dramalike dances in temples; later a playhouse is used that is a platform without curtains and a roof like that of a temple. The ancient Japanese developed a form of theatre called Kabuki that was also performed on a platform with a temple roof. In ancient India, dramatic performances were given on raised platforms with drapes for background. The ancient Greeks developed a form of drama performed to audiences seated on a hillside. The play took place in a grassy circle, and a building called a skene is used for the entrances of actors, dressing, and scenic background. In the Middle Ages, the Christian church condemns drama, but later religious drama becomes an important part of church life. During the reign of Elizabeth I, the English theatre takes a leap forward and the first playhouse is built, known simply as "The Theatre." Soon other theatres were built, including the Globe, where many of Shakespeare's plays were performed. The audience stood in a pit, in front of and around the sides of the stage, or were seated in boxes around and above the stage. Our modern theatre had its beginnings with these early English theatres.

CHAPTER 19

Editing for Problems with Pronouns

A **pronoun** substitutes for a noun to help writers and speakers avoid unpleasant repetition, as the following example shows:

> *unpleasant repetition:* The kitten licked the kitten's paw.
>
> *pronoun used:* The kitten licked <u>her</u> paw.

PRONOUN CASE

Pronouns that can function as the subject of a sentence are in the **nominative case.** Pronouns that can function as the direct object, indirect object, or object of a preposition are in the **objective case.** Here is a chart of nominative and objective pronouns.

Nominative Case	Objective Case
I	me
we	us
you	you
he	him
she	her
it	it
they	them
who	whom
whoever	whomever

Choose pronouns on the basis of their function in the sentence, not on the basis of how the pronoun sounds.

subject pronoun
in nominative case: <u>She</u> gave a pint of blood at Red Cross
                     headquarters.

object pronoun
in objective case: Mark cooked dinner for <u>her</u>.

Most of the time, choosing the correct pronoun is not a problem. However, in a few special circumstances, pronoun choice can be tricky. These circumstances are described below.

Choosing Pronouns in Compounds

1. Use nominative case for subjects and objective case for objects:

subject: <u>He and I</u> prefer to drive to Nashville.

object: Police authorities gave <u>them and us</u> citations for
          bravery. (indirect object)

object: Professor Whan asked <u>her and me</u> to help out after
          class. (direct object)

object: Joyce sat down near <u>him and her</u>. (object of preposition)

2. When a pronoun is paired with a noun, you can often tell which pronoun is correct if you mentally cross out everything except the pronoun.
For example, which is it?

Ricardo asked Dale and <u>me</u> to leave.

or

Ricardo asked Dale and <u>I</u> to leave.

Cross out everything except the pronoun to find out.

Ricardo asked ~~Dale and~~ <u>me</u> to leave.
Ricardo asked ~~Dale and~~ <u>I</u> to leave.

Now you can tell that the correct form is

Ricardo asked Dale and <u>me</u> to leave.

Choosing Pronouns after Forms of *To Be*

In strict formal usage, the nominative case is used after forms of *to be (am, is, are, was, were).*

It is <u>I</u>.

The stars of the play are Carlotta and <u>she</u>.

Choosing Pronouns in Comparisons

1. When *than* or *as* is used to compare, some words may go unstated. You can choose the correct pronoun by mentally adding the unstated words.

For example, which is it?

```
Jackson works longer hours than I.
Jackson works longer hours than me.
```

Add the unstated words to decide.

```
Jackson works longer hours than I do.
Jackson works longer hours than me do.
```

With the unstated words added, the correct choice is clear.

```
Jackson works longer hours than I.
```

2. Sometimes the pronoun chosen affects the meaning of the sentence.

```
I enjoy Ivan as much as she.
```
(This sentence means that I enjoy Ivan as much as she does.)

```
I enjoy Ivan as much as her.
```
(This sentence means that I enjoy Ivan as much as I enjoy her.)

Choosing Pronouns in Appositives

Appositives are words that rename. When a pronoun is followed by an appositive, you can choose the correct form by mentally crossing out the appositive.
For example, which is it?

```
We students resent the tuition increase.
```

or

```
Us students resent the tuition increase.
```

Cross out the appositive.

```
We students resent the tuition increase.
Us students resent the tuition increase.
```

Now the choice is clear:

```
We students resent the tuition increase.
```

Choosing *Who, Whoever, Whom, and Whomever*

1. *Who* and *whoever* are the nominative forms and are used as subjects.

```
Henry is the one who understands Phyllis.
```
(*Who* is the subject of the verb *understands*.)

2. *Whom* and *whomever* are the objective forms and are used for direct objects, indirect objects, and objects of prepositions.

direct object: <u>Whom</u> did you take with you? (You did take <u>whom</u> with you.)

indirect object: Give the job to <u>whomever</u> you want.

object of preposition: Seat yourself near <u>whomever</u> you wish.

3. Choosing between *who* and *whom, whoever* and *whomever* can be tricky when you are dealing with questions. The choice is easier if you recast the questions into statements and then decide whether the nominative or objective pronoun is needed. For example, which is it?

<u>Who</u> did you see at the concert?

<u>Whom</u> did you see at the concert?

Recast the question as a statement and you see that the object pronoun is needed to function as a direct object.

You did see <u>whom</u> at the concert.

Now it is clear that the correct sentence is

<u>Whom</u> did you see at the concert?

When you recast questions into statements, use the nominative *who* and *whoever* after forms of *to be (am, is, are, was, were)*. For example, which is it?

<u>Who</u> was the top point scorer in the game?

<u>Whom</u> was the top point scorer in the game?

Recast the question as a statement.

The top point scorer in the game was <u>who</u>.

Now it is clear that the correct form is

<u>Who</u> was the top point scorer in the game?

EXERCISE | **Pronoun Case**

Fill in the blank with the correct form given in parentheses.

1. (She and I/Her and me/She and me) _____ expect to graduate a year early because we attended summer school.
2. (I/me) Gloria is a much better math student than _____.
3. (we/us) The union plans to strike to win a 10 percent pay raise for _____ dock workers.
4. (who/whom) Ask Lionel _____ he plans to train as his replacement.
5. (We/Us) _____ adult learners add an important dimension to the classroom.

6. (he/him) It is _____ who can tell you what you need to know.

7. (who/whom) Mario is the young man _____ I was telling you about.

8. (they/them) Give that box of records to Alice and _____ to store in the basement.

9. (he/him) If I were as good at science as _____, I would major in chemistry or physics.

10. (I/me) Because of our vision problems, all colors look similar to Lisa and _____.

PRONOUN–ANTECEDENT AGREEMENT

Pronouns must agree with the nouns to which they refer (**antecedents**) in **gender** (masculine, feminine, or neuter) and **number** (singular or plural). Many times this agreement is easily achieved, as is the case in the following example:

```
Kurt lost his tennis racket, but he eventually found it.
```

The pronouns *he* and *his* are singular and masculine to agree with the number and gender of the antecedent *Kurt*, and the pronoun *it* is singular and neuter to agree with *racket*.

At times, pronoun–antecedent agreement is not as obvious as in the above sentence, and these instances are discussed in the rest of this chapter.

Compound Subjects

A **compound subject** is formed by two or more words, phrases, or clauses joined by *and, or, nor, either . . . or,* or *neither . . . nor.*

1. If the parts of the antecedent are joined by *and,* a plural pronoun is used.

The shoes and baseball cap were left in their usual places.

Linda, Michelle, and Audrey finished their group project early.

2. If the antecedent is preceded by *each* or *every,* the pronoun is singular.

Every citizen and each group must do its part to elect responsible officials.

Each school and athletic department must submit its budget to the superintendent.

3. Singular antecedents joined by *either . . . or* or *neither . . . nor* require singular pronouns.

Has either Sean or Frank taken his batting practice today?

Neither Melissa nor Jennifer has finished packing her bag.

4. Plural antecedents joined by *either . . . or* or *neither . . . nor* require plural pronouns.

> <u>Neither the teachers nor the students</u> have <u>their</u> coats.

5. If one singular and one plural antecedent are joined by *or, either . . . or,* or *neither . . . nor,* the pronoun should agree with the antecedent closer to it.

> <u>Either Clint Black or the Oak Ridge Boys</u> will release *their* new album soon.

NOTE: Placing the plural antecedent second makes a smoother sentence.

Collective Nouns

Collective nouns have a singular form and refer to a *group* of people or things. Words like these are collective nouns:

group	committee	jury
class	society	audience
team	panel	band

1. If the collective noun is functioning as a single unit, the pronoun that refers to it is singular.

> A civilized <u>society</u> must protect <u>its</u> citizens from violence.

2. If the members of the group are functioning individually, a plural pronoun is used.

> Yesterday the <u>team</u> signed <u>their</u> contracts for next season.

Indefinite Pronouns

Indefinite pronouns refer to some part of a group of people, things, or ideas without specifying the particular members of the group referred to. Indefinite pronouns can be antecedents.

1. The following indefinite pronouns are singular, and in formal usage the pronouns referring to them should also be singular.

each	somebody	one
everybody	someone	either
everyone	anybody	neither
nobody	anyone	none
no one		

> <u>Anyone</u> who has finished <u>his</u> or <u>her</u> essay may leave.
>
> <u>Nobody</u> on the football team should assume that <u>his</u> position is safe.
>
> <u>Neither</u> of the young mothers forgot <u>her</u> exercise class.

NOTE: See the discussion on nonsexist pronouns that follows.

2. In formal usage, a pronoun referring to a singular indefinite pronoun is singular, even when a phrase with a plural word follows the indefinite pronoun.

<u>Each</u> of the boys selected <u>his</u> favorite bat.

3. *Few* and *many* are plural, so pronouns referring to them are also plural.

<u>Many</u> of my friends have already bought <u>their</u> tickets.

4. The following indefinite pronouns may be singular or plural, depending on the meaning of the sentence.

all   some   most

any   more

<u>Some</u> of the book is still attached to <u>its</u> binding.

<u>Some</u> of the band forgot <u>their</u> sheet music.

Nonsexist Pronouns

In the past, when a singular noun or indefinite pronoun designated a person who could be either male or female (*lawyer, student, director, pianist, anybody,* and so on), agreement was achieved by using the masculine pronoun.

<u>Each</u> contestant must bring <u>his</u> birth certificate.

Today, while this method is grammatically correct, it is considered sexist because it does not acknowledge the presence of females. For this reason, many people prefer the following methods for achieving agreement.

1. Use a masculine and feminine pronoun.

<u>Each</u> contestant must bring <u>his or her</u> birth certificate.

2. Recast the sentence into the plural.

<u>All</u> contestants must bring <u>their</u> birth certificate.

EXERCISE | **Pronoun–Antecedent Agreement**

Choose the correct pronoun.

1. Neither Angelo nor Doug volunteered (his, their) services for the Downtown Cleanup Crusade.
2. Each teacher and principal agreed that (he or she, they) would contribute to the United Way.
3. The secretary of the Scuba Club urged everybody to pay (his or her, their) dues by the end of the month.
4. Anyone wanting a successful college experience must spend much of (his or her, their) time studying.
5. A dog and two cats could take care of (itself, themselves) very nicely with just our family's table scraps.
6. The hostess asked that either Cara Smith or the Kanes move (her, their) car.

7. Both Matt and Joey lost (his, their) lunch money.
8. Few of these candlesticks are in (its, their) original boxes.
9. That tribe holds (its, their) sacred initiation rites each autumn.
10. When asked to make statements, the sheriff and his deputy insisted on (his, their) right to remain silent.
11. The company fired (its, their) inefficient workers.
12. The herd moves ever westward as (it, they) grazes.
13. The Ski Club held (its, their) first meeting after the holiday season.
14. The squad of police antiterrorists took (its, their) positions around the abandoned warehouse.
15. The city council debated whether (it, they) should pass the new antismoking ordinance.
16. No one should force (his or her, their) vacation choice on other members of the family.
17. Questioned by the precinct worker, neither Annette nor DeShawn would reveal (her, their) party affiliation.
18. To prepare for hurricanes, each coastal town has (its, their) own special warning system.
19. Most of the Pep Club had (its, their) pictures taken for the yearbook.
20. Both Jeff and Greg took (his, their) lunch to work.

Rewrite the following paragraph to eliminate problems with pronoun–antecedent agreement.

The kind of voice a person has depends on their vocal cords, which are composed of elastic fibers. The bundle of cords is very flexible; in fact, they can become tense or slack to assume 170 different positions. If slack, the cords vibrate at about 80 times per second, creating a deep tone. If tense, they vibrate rapidly, perhaps a thousand times a second, producing a high-pitched tone. As a child grows, his vocal cords elongate, causing the voice to deepen. The length of a man's and woman's vocal cords differ. He will have longer cords than her, which explains his deeper voice. A boy grows so quickly that they cannot control the pitch well, which is why young boys experience a "break" in their voices. The quality of men's and women's voices, however, depends on other factors, especially the resonating spaces such as his or her windpipe, lungs, and nasal cavities. Someone whom has a beautiful voice has well-shaped resonating spaces, which they know how to control.

PRONOUN REFERENCE

If you fail to provide a clear, stated antecedent for a pronoun, you create a problem with **pronoun reference.** The most common kinds of pronoun reference problems are described below.

Ambiguous Reference

Ambiguous reference occurs when your reader cannot tell which of two possible antecedents a pronoun refers to.

ambiguous
reference: When I placed the heavy vase on the shelf, <u>it</u> broke. (What broke, the vase or the shelf? Because of the ambiguous reference, the reader cannot tell.)

To eliminate the ambiguous reference, replace the pronoun with a noun.

correction: When I placed the heavy vase on the shelf, <u>the shelf</u> broke.

Unstated Reference

Unstated reference occurs when you fail to supply an antecedent for a pronoun to refer to. Unstated reference occurs in the following situations:

1. Unstated reference occurs when a pronoun refers to an unstated form of a stated word.

unstated reference: Carla is very ambitious. <u>It</u> causes her to work sixty hours a week. (*It* is meant to refer to *ambition,* but that word does not appear; *ambitious* does.)

To correct a problem with unstated reference, substitute a noun for the pronoun.

correction: Carla is very ambitious. <u>Her ambition</u> causes her to work sixty hours a week.

2. Unstated reference occurs when *this, that, which, it,* or *they* has no stated antecedent. To eliminate the problem, supply the missing word or words.

unstated reference: When I arrived at the office, <u>they</u> said my appointment was cancelled. (*They* has no antecedent to refer to.)

correction: When I arrived at the office, <u>the receptionist</u> said my appointment was cancelled.

unstated reference: At my last appointment with my advisor, I decided to major in marketing. <u>This</u> has made me feel better about school. (*This* has no word to refer to.)

correction: At my last appointment with my advisor, I decided to major in marketing. This decision has made me feel better about school.

3. Unstated reference occurs when *you* appears with no antecedent. To solve the problem, replace the pronoun with a noun.

unstated reference: A teacher becomes frustrated when <u>you</u> do not ask questions. (*You* has no antecedent to refer to.)

correction: A teacher becomes frustrated when <u>students</u> do not ask questions.

4. Unstated reference occurs when a subject pronoun refers to a possessive noun. To solve the problem, replace the noun with a pronoun and the pronoun with a noun.

> *unstated reference:* In Barbara Kingsolver's novels, <u>she</u> writes about strong women.

> *correction:* In her novels, Barbara Kingsolver writes about strong women.

EXERCISE | **Pronoun Reference**

Rewrite the sentences to eliminate problems with pronoun reference.

1. The song lyrics were particularly offensive to women. This caused many radio stations to refuse to play it.
2. Doris explained to Philomena that she had to help clean the apartment.
3. I left the spaghetti sauce and the milk on the counter, and when I answered the phone, my cat knocked it over.
4. I was nervous about today's midterm examination. It made sleep impossible last night.
5. Rodney's car is double-parked. He is certain to get a ticket.
6. Dale is a very insecure person. It is his most unattractive trait.
7. The personnel director explained that I am entitled to twelve vacation days a year, which is guaranteed by the union contract.
8. By the time I arrived at the Dean's office, they had left for lunch.
9. Julius was on the phone with Roberto when he realized that he forgot to go to the bank and cash a check.
10. Dr. Wang is known to be a patient math instructor. It is the reason so many students sign up for his course.

PERSON SHIFTS

When you refer to yourself, you use **first-person pronouns.** When you speak to other people directly, you use **second-person pronouns.** When you refer to other people and things, you use **third-person pronouns.**

> *first-person*
> *pronouns:* I, we, me, us, my, mine, our, ours

> *second-person*
> *pronouns:* you, your, yours

> *third-person*
> *pronouns:* he, she, it, they, his, her, hers, its, their, theirs, him, them

When using the above pronouns, be consistent in person because shifts can be confusing and annoying.

> *shift from third*
> *to second person:* If a football player works hard, <u>he</u> has many chances for financial aid, and <u>you</u> might even be eligible for a full scholarship.

shift eliminated: If a football player works hard, <u>he</u> has many chances for financial aid, and <u>he</u> might even be eligible for a full scholarship.

shift from second to first person: An empathetic friend is one <u>you</u> can tell your most private thoughts to. This kind of friend also knows when <u>I</u> want to be alone and respects <u>my</u> wish.

shift eliminated: An empathetic friend is one <u>you</u> can tell your most private thoughts to. This kind of friend also knows when <u>you</u> want to be alone and respects <u>your</u> wish.

EXERCISE | **Person Shifts**

Revise the following sentences to eliminate person shifts.

1. In high school, I liked geometry because it came easily to me, and you could progress at your own rate.
2. I enjoy riding to the top of the city's tallest building where you can see for miles in all directions.
3. After we received our boots and uniforms, you were shown how to polish and fold them according to army regulations.
4. We are all painfully aware that you can't depend on the boss for help.
5. While taking part in a marathon, a runner should never think about what you're doing.
6. When I ask Sybil to help with some typing, she never turns you down.
7. When a person drinks to excess, you should never attempt to drive a car.
8. In July, people welcome a cool evening, but you know that it is probably only a temporary relief from the heat.
9. By the end of a person's first term as committee secretary, you feel that you are finally beginning to understand the job.
10. I liked my research course better than any other this year. You were on your own searching the library for references.

Eliminate the unwarranted person shifts from the following paragraph:

As soon as we entered the room, you could sense the tension in the atmosphere. This was the day for the first exam to take place. Students were quietly taking his and her places. Pencils were being sharpened; papers were being prepared. Once the class was under way, the quiet tension spread. The only sounds were of paper shuffling and pens scratching. We all hoped that your first efforts would be successful. Finally, the instructor announced, "Anybody who is finished can turn in your papers and leave." Exhausted and relieved, the tired students filed from the room leaving their papers on the teacher's desk.

Editing for Problems with Modifiers

A **modifier** is a word or word group that describes. Modifiers make sentences more vivid and interesting. However, you must be careful to avoid two problems: dangling modifiers and misplaced modifiers.

DANGLING MODIFIERS

A modifier with no stated word to describe is a **dangling modifier.** Dangling modifiers impair meaning and often create silly sentences. Consider the following sentence with a dangling modifier:

> While basting the turkey, the sweet potatoes burned.

While basting the turkey is a modifier, but there is no word for the modifier to refer to or describe. As a result, it seems that the sweet potatoes basted the turkey.

There are two ways to correct a dangling modifier. One method is to leave the modifier as it is and supply a word for the modifier to refer to. *This word should appear immediately after the modifier.*

dangling modifier: <u>Listening for the telephone</u>, the doorbell rang.

explanation: Because there is no word for *listening for the telephone* to refer to, the phrase is a dangling modifier. The sentence indicates that the doorbell listened for the telephone.

correction: Listening for the telephone, I heard the doorbell ring.

explanation: The word *I* is placed immediately after the modifier as a word to which the modifier can logically refer.

A second way to eliminate a dangling modifier is to rewrite the modifier as a subordinate clause (see page 102).

dangling modifier: <u>Jogging along the side of the road</u>, a car splashed me with mud.

explanation: Because there is no word for *jogging along the side of the road* to refer to, the phrase is a dangling modifier. The sense of the sentence is that the car did the jogging.

correction: While I was jogging along the side of the road, a car splashed me with mud.

explanation: The modifier is rewritten as a subordinate clause to eliminate the dangling modifier.

As the above examples illustrate, dangling modifiers often occur when sentences begin with an *-ing* verb form (present participle). However, a dangling modifier can also occur when a sentence begins with an *-ed, -en, -n,* or *-t* verb form (past participle) or when it begins with the present-tense verb form used with *to* (infinitive).

dangling modifier (present participle): <u>While rocking the baby</u>, the cat purred contentedly.

correction: While rocking the baby, I heard the cat purr contentedly.

correction: While I was rocking the baby, the cat purred contentedly.

dangling modifier (past participle): <u>Tired from the day's work</u>, weariness overcame me.

correction: Tired from the day's work, I was overcome with weariness.

correction: Because I was tired from the day's work, weariness overcame me.

dangling modifier (infinitive): <u>To excel in sports</u>, much practice is needed.

correction: To excel in sports, a person needs much practice.

correction: If a person wants to excel in sports, he or she needs much practice.

EXERCISE | **Dangling Modifiers**

Rewrite the following sentences to eliminate the dangling modifiers.

1. Feeling it was too late to apologize, the disagreement was never resolved.
2. While sitting at the drive-in movie, shooting stars could be seen in the clear night sky.

3. Climbing across the pasture fence, Peter's pants were torn in two places.
4. To understand the latest computer technology, these courses should be taken.
5. Faced with the possibility of suspension, studying became attractive to me.
6. When listening to the stereo, cleaning the apartment does not seem so hard.
7. To get to class on time, my alarm is set for 6:00 A.M.
8. Struggling to earn enough money to pay next term's tuition, the job came along just in time.
9. To study in quiet surroundings, the library is the best place to go.
10. After ending the relationship with Joe, loneliness was Ann's biggest problem.

MISPLACED MODIFIERS

A **misplaced modifier** is positioned too far away from the word it describes. The result is an unclear, silly, or illogical sentence.

misplaced modifier: The strolling musicians played while we were eating dinner <u>softly</u>.

explanation: The modifier *softly* is intended to describe *played*. However, the modifier is too far removed from that word, so *softly* seems to describe *were eating*.

To correct a sentence with a misplaced modifier, move the modifier as close as possible to the word it describes.

The strolling musicians played <u>softly</u> while we were eating dinner.

A misplaced modifier can be a word, a phrase, or a clause:

misplaced modifier (word): There must be something wrong with this cookie recipe, for it <u>only</u> requires a half-cup of sugar. (Placement of *only* indicates no other ingredients are needed.)

correction: There must be something wrong with this cookie recipe, for it requires <u>only</u> a half-cup of sugar.

misplaced modifier (phrase): Across the street, <u>playing far too wildly</u>, we saw the young children. (The phrase seems to describe *we*.)

correction: Across the street we saw the young children <u>playing far too wildly</u>.

misplaced modifier (clause): We brought the rubber tree into the house <u>which was at least eight feet tall</u>. (The clause seems to describe the house.)

correction: We brought the rubber tree, which was at least eight feet tall, into the house.

EXERCISE | **Misplaced Modifiers**

Rewrite the following sentences to eliminate the misplaced modifiers:

1. The mattress was built for people with bad backs with extra firmness.
2. Most viewers have misinterpreted the significance of the president's State of the Union address completely.
3. The Chevrolet's muffler fell off after we turned the corner with a loud bang.
4. Kathleen sold her bike to a neighbor with stripped gears for $25.
5. The little girl wore a flower in her hair that had pink petals.
6. We were fortunate to get a cabin by the lake with three bedrooms.
7. The child ran after the ball pulling the rusty wagon down the street.
8. The old car raced down the street with its muffler dragging.
9. The missing wallet was finally found by my aunt Norma under the couch.
10. Turning to go, Lee waved to the gang in the van listening to the stereo.

EXERCISE | **Dangling and Misplaced Modifiers**

Eliminate the dangling and misplaced modifiers in the following paragraph.

The Egyptian Pharaoh Ramses II had temples built at Abu Simbel about 3,200 years ago. Carving stone out of the face of a cliff, the temples were built by workers beside the River Nile. Carved 197 feet into the cliff, The Great Temple had 14 rooms. Four huge stone figures of Ramses flanked the entrance seated on his throne. In the 1960s, the new Aswan Dam blocked the Nile, causing its waters to rise. To save the structures, huge blocks of the temples were cut by workmen weighing 20–30 tons each. They raised these to the nearby hilltop and fitted them together again. To help pay for this project, 50 nations gave money.

CHAPTER 21

Editing for Punctuation

Punctuation marks aid communication because they signal where ideas end, how ideas relate to one another, which ideas are emphasized, which ideas are downplayed, and which ideas are expressed in someone's spoken words. Most of the time, specific rules govern the placement of punctuation, and experienced readers will expect you to follow those rules.

THE COMMA (,)

Writers who do not know the comma rules often place commas wherever they pause in speech. However, listening for pauses is an unreliable way to place commas, so if you have not yet learned the rules, study the next pages carefully.

Commas with Items in a Series

A **series** is formed by three or more words, phrases, or clauses. Use commas to separate each item in the series.

words in a series: The gardener sprayed the <u>grass, trees, and shrubs</u> with pesticide.

phrases in a series: George Washington was <u>first in war, first in peace, and first in the hearts of his countrymen</u>.

clauses in a series: Before his first day of school, <u>Shonda took her kindergartner on a tour of the school, she introduced him to the principal, and she bought him school supplies</u>.

If the items in the series are separated by *and* or *or,* do not use a comma.

The only vegetables Tom will eat are carrots or peas or corn.

Some writers omit the comma after the last item in the series, but you should get in the habit of using the comma to avoid misreading.

473

EXERCISE | **Commas with Items in a Series**

Place commas where they are needed in the following sentences. One sentence is already correct.

1. The vacation brochure promised us fun relaxation and excitement.
2. The trouble with the mayor is that she does not delegate responsibility she does not manage city finances well and she does not work well with city council.
3. Before you go, clean your room and sweep the porch and take out the trash.
4. The instructor explained that the class could write a paper on a childhood memory on a decision recently made or on a favorite teacher.
5. When you edit, be sure to check spelling punctuation and capitalization.

Commas with Introductory Elements

Elements placed before the subject are usually followed by a comma.

    1. Follow an introductory subordinate clause with a comma (see p. 102).

<u>Although she promised to meet me for lunch</u>, Caroline never arrived at the restaurant.

    2. Follow an introductory phrase with a comma.

<u>By the end of the first half of the tournament</u>, our team had won nine games.

    3. Follow introductory adverbs with a comma. (See also page 108.)

<u>Reluctantly</u>, Mr. Simpson told his oldest employee that he was selling his business.

<u>Quickly yet cautiously</u>, the store detective moved in on the suspected shoplifter.

    4. You may omit the comma after a very brief opener.

<u>Unfortunately</u>, the exam grades were lower than expected.

or

<u>Unfortunately</u> the exam grades were lower than expected.

EXERCISE | **Commas with Introductory Elements**

Insert commas in the following sentences where they are needed.

1. When Sherry arrived at the resort she was disappointed to find that there were no rooms available.
2. When he was twenty he believed that everything would work out for the best.
3. Very slowly and silently the deer moved toward the water hole.

4. As a result of the devastating heat wave the death toll rose to 108.
5. Frequently we accuse others of the behavior we dislike most in ourselves.
6. After we checked to be sure all the doors were locked we left the beach house until next summer.
7. During the bleak evenings of winter a cozy fire in the fireplace is welcome.
8. At the time of the space shuttle's arrival the crosswinds had finally died down.
9. Lovingly the young mother stroked her new daughter's chubby cheek.
10. Hastily the six-year-old wiped the telltale signs of strawberry jam from the corners of his mouth.

Commas to Set Off Nouns of Direct Address

The names of those directly addressed are set off with commas.

```
"Dorrie, you must get ready for school now."

"Get away from that hamburger, you mangy dog."

"If you ask me, Juan, we should turn left."
```

EXERCISE | **Commas to Set Off Nouns of Direct Address**

Supply commas to set off the nouns of address.
1. "Ben help me carry the groceries into the house."
2. "You know Son it's too cold to be outside without a jacket."
3. "Friends may I have your attention please?"
4. "Heidi make sure you give fresh seed and water to the bird."
5. "Can you help me with my math tonight Alice?"

Commas with Nonessential Elements

Nonessential elements are words, phrases, and clauses that are not necessary for the clear identification of what they refer to.

nonessential element: Uncle Ralph, who has been on the police force 20 years, believes handgun legislation is the key to reducing violent crime.

explanation: *Who has been on the police force 20 years* is nonessential because the person it refers to (Uncle Ralph) is already clearly identified.

essential element: The student who wins the state finals in speech will get $1,000.

explanation: *Who wins the state finals in speech* is necessary for identifying which student will win $1,000; therefore, it is an essential element.

1. Use commas to set off nonessential clauses.

Sara Summers, <u>who is a senior</u>, was voted president of senior council.

My roommate collects beer cans, <u>which she stacks against the wall</u>.

but

Dr. Kingsley is a person <u>whose opinion I respect</u>. (Clause is essential.)

2. Use commas to set off nonessential phrases.

The sparrows, <u>hunting for food in the snow</u>, sensed the cat's approach and took off suddenly.

but

The child <u>playing in the sandbox</u> is my nephew. (Phrase is essential.)

3. Use commas to set off nonessential appositives. An **appositive** is a word or word group that renames the noun it follows.

nonessential
appositive: My brother, an investment banker, makes $200,000 a year. (*An investment banker* renames *my brother,* so it is an appositive. However, since it is not necessary for identification, commas are used.)

essential
appositive: My son the doctor is not as happy as my son the actor. (*The doctor* is an appositive renaming *my son,* and *the actor* is an appositive renaming the second *my son.* In both cases the appositives are essential for identifying which son is referred to, so no commas are used.)

EXERCISE | **Commas with Nonessential Elements**

Place commas where they are needed in the following sentences:

1. My father who worked for the Bell System for over 30 years has made many sacrifices for me.
2. A Democratic city councilperson who supports his party will try to support the policies of a Democratic mayor.
3. The Luray Caverns which I visited this year are a breathtaking sight.
4. A blue wool suit sporting brass buttons and a traditional cut is always in style.
5. The Empire State Building once the tallest building in the world still dominates the New York City skyline.
6. Dale Norris a brilliant teacher will retire next month.

Commas with Interrupters

Interrupters are words and phrases that "interrupt" the flow of a sentence; they function more as side remarks than as integral parts of sentences. Sometimes transitions interrupt flow and are considered interrupters, which is why the following partial list of interrupters includes some transitions.

```
in a manner of speaking      after all

as a matter of fact          in fact

to tell the truth            in the first place

it seems to me               to say the least

for example                  consequently

by all means                 of course
```

Interrupters are usually set off with commas. However, commas may be omitted after short interrupters coming at the beginning of sentences.

commas used: The students' behavior at the concert, <u>it seems to me</u>, was exemplary.

comma omitted for short introductory interrupter: <u>Of course</u> not everyone shares my concern about this issue.

comma for short interrupter: <u>Of course</u>, not everyone shares my concern for this issue.

EXERCISE | **Commas with Interrupters**

Set off the interrupters with commas in the following sentences:

1. The children it seems will always find something to complain about.
2. As a matter of fact the lamp needs a larger-watt bulb.
3. This report I feel is inadequately prepared.
4. The customer insists in fact that the bike was never properly assembled.
5. However this is the right time to begin our fundraising project.

Commas with Main Clauses

1. When two main clauses are connected with a coordinating conjunction *(and, but, or, nor, for, so, yet),* place a comma before the conjunction (see page 102).

The match was over, <u>but</u> the spectators refused to leave.

The garden was heavily fertilized, <u>so</u> the yield of vegetables was even higher than expected.

2. Do not use a comma before a coordinating conjunction linking two elements that are not main clauses.

> *no:* Lee asked for forgiveness, and promised to try harder.
>
> *yes:* Lee asked for forgiveness and promised to try harder.

EXERCISE | **Commas with Main Clauses**

Place commas where needed in the following sentences.

1. Janice had been rejected many times yet she retained her sense of humor and her cheerful disposition.
2. The pipe to the house was broken and we would have to assume the cost of fixing it.
3. Jake wanted to fly to Maine but Jo had always wanted to drive across country.
4. The students were confused so the instructor assigned extra pages to study.
5. Karen fastened red bows to the lampposts for the holiday season was fast approaching.

Commas between Coordinate Modifiers, Commas for Clarity, and Commas to Separate Contrasting Elements

1. **Coordinate modifiers** are two or more modifiers referring equally to the same word. Commas separate such modifiers when they are not already separated by *and* or *but*. (If the order of the modifiers can be reversed or if *and* can be used to join the modifiers, they are coordinate and should be separated with a comma.)

> An <u>expensive, well-tailored</u> suit is a necessary investment for a young executive. (Order of modifiers can be reversed: a well-tailored, expensive suit.)
>
> They ate their picnic lunch under the <u>blossoming apple</u> tree. (*And* cannot be used between the modifiers, nor can the order be reversed.)
>
> She is certainly a <u>happy and carefree</u> person. (No comma because *and* is used.)

2. Sometimes a comma is necessary for clarity, to prevent the misreading of a sentence.

> For Easter, lilies are the most popular flower. (Without the comma, a reader might read the first three words as a single phrase.)

3. Commas set off an element that contrasts with what comes before it.

> Dale is only lazy, not stupid.

EXERCISE | **Commas between Coordinate Modifiers, Commas for Clarity, and Commas to Separate Contrasting Elements**

Place commas where needed in the following sentences:

1. The muddy rough course was made even worse by the two-day downpour.
2. Ohio State's noisy enthusiastic Pep Club congregated in the middle section of the bleachers.

3. The twins were young not inexperienced.
4. Many new songwriters use concrete visual images to set a mood.
5. The rough manuscript is promising although rambling.
6. Of all spectator sports fans seem to enjoy football most.

When Not to Use the Comma

Below are some cautions about when *not* to use commas.

1. Do not use a comma to separate a subject and verb.

no: The governor-elect, promised to work to change the way public education is funded in our state.

yes: The governor-elect promised to work to change the way public education is funded in our state.

2. Do not use a comma between a preposition and its object.

no: The United States has a government of, the people.

yes: The United States has a government of the people.

3. Do not use a comma between a verb and its object.

no: Carl smacked, the ball out of the park.

yes: Carl smacked the ball out of the park.

4. Do not use a comma between a verb and its complement.

no: Louise will become, a concert pianist if she continues to practice.

yes: Louise will become a concert pianist if she continues to practice.

5. Do not use a comma after a coordinating conjunction linking main clauses.

no: I have tried to understand Juan but, his behavior continues to puzzle me.

yes: I have tried to understand Juan, but his behavior continues to puzzle me.

6. Do not use a comma before the first item or after the last item in a series.

no: The math test covered, improper fractions, common denominators, and, mixed fractions.

yes: The math test covered improper fractions, common denominators, and mixed fractions.

7. Do not use a comma between a modifier and the word it modifies.

no: The frayed, curtains must be replaced.

yes: The frayed curtains must be replaced.

8. Do not use a comma after *such as* or *like*.

no: Kurt believes in some unusual ideas such as,
    reincarnation, transmigration, and mental telepathy.

yes: Kurt believes in some unusual ideas, such as
    reincarnation, transmigration, and mental telepathy.

no: Medical technology students must take difficult courses
    like, physiology, biochemistry, and pharmacology.

yes: Medical technology students must take difficult courses
    like physiology, biochemistry, and pharmacology.

9. Do not use a comma between *that* and a direct quotation.

no: The school board president said that, "we are
    considering a ten-month school year."

yes: The school board president said that "we are
    considering a ten-month school year."

EXERCISE | **Using Commas**

In the following paragraph, add any commas that are needed and omit any that
are inappropriately placed.

Carry Nation achieved prominence at the end of the nineteenth century in
the temperance movement the movement to ban liquor. Born Carry Moore in
Kentucky she experienced poverty her mother's mental instability and, frequent
bouts of ill health. Although, she held a teaching certificate her education was intermittent. In 1867, she married a young physician Charles Gloyd whom she left after
a few months ironically because of his alcoholism. Later she married David Nation
a lawyer journalist and, minister who divorced her on the grounds of desertion. She
entered the temperance movement in 1890. She believed saloons were illegal so she
felt they could be destroyed by anyone. Alone or accompanied by hymn-singing
women Nation would march into a saloon and proceed to sing pray, and smash the
bar fixtures and stock with a hatchet. A formidable severely dressed woman, Nation became a figure of notoriety. Her fervor, at one point, led her to invade the
governor's chambers at Topeka. Jailed many times she paid the fines from her own
money not from donations. She made $300 a week lecturing and selling souvenir
hatchets. Temperance was not Nation's only cause for she also supported women's
suffrage and fought against fraternal orders tobacco foreign foods corsets and
provocative art. Nation died in Kansas after a period of hospitalization.

THE SEMICOLON (;)

1. A **semicolon** separates two main clauses not linked by a coordinating
conjunction.

The canvas raft floated near the edge of the pool; it was
pushed by a gentle summer breeze.

The A team wore the old uniforms; the B team wore new ones.

2. Use a semicolon before a conjunctive adverb that joins two main clauses. Here is a list of conjunctive adverbs:

also	however	thus
besides	instead	meanwhile
nonetheless	therefore	certainly
likewise	then	nevertheless
next	furthermore	similarly
subsequently	still	consequently
moreover	indeed	finally

When you join two main clauses with a semicolon and conjunctive adverb, place a comma after the conjunctive adverb.

```
The car I want to buy is a real bargain; furthermore, the bank
is offering me an excellent financing rate.

The test grades were low; consequently, Dr. Barnes allowed us
to retake the exam.
```

3. For clarity, a semicolon separates items in a series that already contains commas.

```
The following sun-belt cities have experienced phenomenal
growth in the past five years: Las Vegas, Nevada; Phoenix,
Arizona; and Orlando, Florida.
```

EXERCISE | **The Semicolon**

Place semicolons where they are appropriate in the following sentences:

1. The ideal football player is dedicated, for he must work long, hard hours intelligent, for the game is very much one of strategy and physically tough, for he must endure a great deal of punishment.
2. The hand-tied rope hammock was made to hold the weight of two people it was the hook that broke sending Christie and Jim crashing to the ground.
3. The quarterback hesitated for an instant then he passed the ball to the wide receiver, who waited in the end zone.
4. College can create anxiety because of the pressure for grades, which is constant the concern for future job opportunities, which is always present and the uncertainties of life away from home, which are the most unnerving of all.
5. We tried for two hours to start the car finally we gave up and started the long trek back to town.
6. The trip was canceled because of the snow storm however, it has been rescheduled for next weekend.

THE COLON (:)

Use a colon after a main clause to introduce a word, phrase, or clause that explains or particularizes.

Colon to introduce a
phrase that particularizes: Five occupations were represented in the union membership: secretaries, data processors, maintenance workers, cafeteria workers, and bookkeepers.

Colon to introduce a
word that explains: Rick writes soap opera scripts for one reason: money.

Colon to introduce a
clause that explains: All of Terry's efforts were directed toward one goal: She wanted to be a dancer.

Do not use a colon between a verb and its object or complement, or between a preposition and its object.

colon: The following students will compete in the debate: David Haynes, Lorenzo Ruiz, and Clara Jakes.

no colon: The students who will compete in the debate are David Haynes, Lorenzo Ruiz, and Clara Jakes.

colon: I am afraid of these: heights, small rooms, and water.

no colon: I am afraid of heights, small rooms, and water.

EXERCISE | **The Colon**

Place colons where appropriate in the following sentences. (Two sentences do not require a colon.)

1. My courses for next semester are these political science, algebra, biology, and Advanced Composition I.
2. The basket overflowed with fresh fruit peaches, grapes, apples, and bananas.
3. Mr. Grantley seems to have one mission in life making everyone around him miserable.
4. There are complicated reasons for our company's poor safety record we do not supply incentives for employees to exercise more care on the job, our safety equipment is obsolete and ineffective, and we do not require enough proper training for new employees.
5. I knew that success in my journalism class would require curiosity, energy, and writing skill.
6. Of all the distance runners, only one seems to run effortlessly Mark.

THE DASH (—)

A **dash** (formed on the typewriter or word processor without a dash key with two hyphens) indicates a pause for emphasis or dramatic effect. It should be used sparingly and thoughtfully so that its emphatic or dramatic quality is not weakened by overuse. Often dashes can be used in place of commas, semicolons, colons, or parentheses; the mark used depends on the effect you want to create.

```
Jake told me--I can't believe it--that he would rather stay at
home than go to Las Vegas. (Parentheses may also be used.)

I know why Tony's bike disappeared--it was stolen from the
backyard. (Semicolon or colon may also be used.)

Vinnie is 35--although he won't admit it. (A comma may also be
used.)
```

EXERCISE | **The Dash**

Place dashes where appropriate in the following sentences:

1. The new Corvette red, shiny, and powerful was just the thing to make her friends drool.
2. Certain members of this family I won't mention any names are going to lose their allowances if they don't start doing their chores.
3. My history professor at least he calls himself a professor is the most boring teacher on campus.
4. I have only one comment to make about your room yuk!
5. There is a very obvious solution to your school problems study.

PARENTHESES ( )

1. Parentheses enclose elements you want to downplay. Often parentheses signal a side comment or incidental remark.

```
Louise Rodriguez (you remember her) has been elected president
of the Women's Action Council.

When I was in college (over 20 years ago), writing was taught
very differently.
```

Commas or dashes often set off material that could also be enclosed in parentheses. However, commas and dashes will emphasize the material, whereas parentheses will deemphasize it.

parentheses
deemphasize: This week's lottery prize (an incredible
$12 million) will be split between two winners.

dashes emphasize: This week's lottery prize--an incredible
$12 million--will be split between two
winners.

commas give more
emphasis than
parentheses but
less than dashes: This week's lottery prize, an incredible
$12 million, will be split between two winners.

2. Do not place a comma before the element enclosed in parentheses.

no: Most of the class, (easily 30 of us) felt the test was
too long to complete in an hour.

yes: Most of the class (easily 30 of us) felt the test was
too long to complete in an hour.

3. A comma or end mark of punctuation is placed *outside* the closing parenthesis.

The new parking deck is an imposing structure (it has
15 levels), but it has a serious drawback (people have trouble
finding their cars in it).

4. Use a period and capital letter with a complete sentence enclosed in parentheses when the sentence is not interrupting another sentence.

no: After three days (Most of us wondered what took so
long.) the winners were announced.

yes: After three days the winners were announced. (Most of
us wondered what took so long.)

yes: After three days (most of us wondered what took so
long) the winners were announced.

5. Parentheses can enclose numbers and letters in a list of items.

The Citizens' Coalition has three reservations about endorsing
Smith for mayor: (1) she is inexperienced, (2) she opposes
increasing city taxes, and (3) she has no clear position on
minority hiring practices.

Because numbers in a list can distract a reader, writers generally try to avoid them.

The Citizens' Coalition has three reservations about endorsing
Smith for mayor: she is inexperienced, she opposes increasing
city taxes, and she has no clear position on minority hiring
practices.

EXERCISE | **Parentheses**

Place parentheses where they are appropriate in the following sentences:

1. The police officer gave David a ticket he was traveling 50 miles per hour in a
   school zone.
2. Recent reports indicate that fewer workers are smoking probably because of
   increased awareness of the health hazards.

3. Sales of trucks particularly those with luxury features are at an all-time high.
4. At Debby and Antonio's wedding what a fiasco Antonio forgot the ring, Debby tripped on the hem of her dress, the best man was late, and the caterer served undercooked chicken.
5. Lee's favorite meal scrambled eggs, spaghetti, and corn disgusts most people.

THE APOSTROPHE (')

The apostrophe is used most frequently to show possession. It is also used to form contractions and certain kinds of plurals.

The Apostrophe to Show Possession

The apostrophe is used with nouns and certain indefinite pronouns (see page 463 for an explanation of indefinite pronouns) to signal possession.

1. To form the possessive of a noun or indefinite pronoun that does not end in *s,* add an apostrophe and an *s.*

apartment + 's

The <u>apartment's</u> bedroom is much too small.

anybody + 's

<u>Anybody's</u> help would be appreciated.

women + 's

The university has agreed to fund a library for <u>women's</u> studies.

2. To form the possessive of a *singular* noun that ends in *s,* add an apostrophe and an *s.*

Charles + 's

<u>Charles's</u> stolen car was found across town.

business + 's

The <u>business's</u> stock climbed three points.

3. To form the possessive of a *plural* noun that ends in *s,* add just the apostrophe.

governors + '

The five <u>governors'</u> council on aging will examine the issue of adequate health care.

4. To show joint possession of one thing, use an apostrophe only with the last noun. To show individual ownership, use an apostrophe with every noun.

<u>Manuel and Louise's</u> committee report was thorough and clear. (One report belonging to both Manuel and Louise.)

<u>Jason's and Helen's</u> financial problems can be solved with better money management. (Jason and Helen have separate financial problems.)

5. To show possession with a hyphenated word, use the apostrophe only with the last element of the word.

The <u>editor-in-chief's</u> salary was cut in half after the magazine's circulation decreased dramatically.

I have planned a surprise party to celebrate my <u>mother-in-law's</u> 60th birthday.

6. Do not use apostrophes with possessive pronouns *(its, whose, hers, his, ours, yours, theirs)*.

incorrect: The expensive vase fell from <u>it's</u> shelf and shattered.

  correct: The expensive vase fell from <u>its</u> shelf and shattered.

incorrect: The book that is missing is <u>her's</u>.

  correct: The book that is missing is <u>hers</u>.

The Apostrophe to Indicate Missing Letters or Numbers and for Some Plurals

1. A **contraction** is formed when two words are joined and one or more letters are omitted. In a contraction the apostrophe stands for the missing letter or letters. Here are some common contractions; notice that the apostrophe appears where the letter or letters are omitted.

isn't (is not)	we'll (we will)
hasn't (has not)	who's (who is, or who has)
they're (they are)	that's (that is, or that has)
we're (we are)	she'll (she will)
haven't (have not)	it's (it is or it has)
I'll (I will)	shouldn't (should not)

2. When you reproduce dialect or casual speech, use the apostrophe for missing letters in words that are not contractions.

add 'em up (add them up)

sugar 'n' spice (sugar and spice)

ma'am (madam)

3. The apostrophe stands for missing numbers.

```
The class of '67 will hold its annual reunion the day after
Thanksgiving.
```
(The apostrophe stands for the missing *19*.)

4. The apostrophe and an *s* form the plural of letters, numbers, and words meant to be taken as terms.

```
If I get any more D's, I will lose my scholarship.

How many t's are in omit?

Mark makes his 3's backwards.

Janice is too polite; I am tired of all her yes sir's and no
ma'am's.
```

NOTE: Underline letters, numbers, and words used as terms. In printed copy, these words may be set in italics.

EXERCISE | **Apostrophes**

Use apostrophes where they are needed in the following sentences. In some sentences, you will need to add an apostrophe and an *s*.

1. The panel awarding the scholarships spoke to several instructors about the three finalists grades and motivation.
2. In 85, my sister-in-laws German shepherd saved the life of a five-year-old by dragging the sleeping child from her burning bedroom.
3. I can never read Harrys writing because his *os* look like *as*.
4. No one thought that Al and Janets business would do so well in its first three months of operation.
5. Todays women still dont earn equal pay for equal work, but in some ways womens lot has improved.
6. Charles older sister is encouraging him to major in computer science, but he isn't sure he wants to.
7. The hot dog vendor bellowed, "Get em while theyre hot."
8. Recent studies confirm that televisions effects on childrens attention spans should be a source of concern.
9. When I graduated in 70, students social awareness was at an all-time high.
10. Lois new car must be a lemon, because its engine is not running well, and its been in the shop three times in a month.

QUOTATION MARKS (" ")

1. Quotation marks enclose the exact words somebody spoke or wrote. For information on this use of quotation marks, see page 162 and page 406.

2. Use quotation marks to enclose the titles of short published works (poems, short stories, essays, and articles from periodicals). Titles of longer, full-length works (books, magazines, and newspapers) are underlined in type and italicized in print.

```
"To His Coy Mistress" is my favorite poem, and The Sun Also
Rises is my favorite novel.
```

Do not use quotation marks or underlining for unpublished titles, including the titles of your own writings.

3. Use quotation marks around words used in a special sense.

```
Your "humor" is not funny.
```

EXERCISE | **Quotation Marks**

Add quotation marks where needed in the following sentences:

1. Be sure to read The Rime of the Ancient Mariner on page 99 of your poetry anthology.
2. Tell me the whole story, I said to Linda.
3. I always worry when someone tries to fix me an interesting meal.
4. Chapter 1, Idea Generation, is the most important chapter in the writing book.
5. Your frugal ways are costing me money.

THE HYPHEN (-)

1. If a word is too long to fit at the end of a line, use a hyphen to divide the word between syllables. If you are unsure of the correct syllable break, check your dictionary. (Never divide a one-syllable word.)

```
Duane hired a clown, a magician, and an acro-
bat to perform at his daughter's birthday party.
```

2. Use a hyphen between two or more words used to form an adjective or noun.

```
high-interest loan        state-of-the-art computer
low-cost mortgage         sister-in-law
```

The exception to this rule: Do not use a hyphen with an *ly* adverb.

```
eagerly devoured meal     badly reviewed play
```

3. Use a hyphen with the prefixes *all-*, *ex-*, and *self-*.

```
all-inclusive     ex-husband     self-starter
```

CHAPTER 22

Editing for Mechanics

CAPITALIZATION

Below are rules governing the most frequent uses of capital letters. In addition, if you are unsure whether to capitalize a word, you can consult a dictionary.

1. Capitalize proper names of people and animals.

```
Harry          Rover
Joe Popovich   Einstein
```

2. Capitalize names of nationalities, languages, and races.

```
American    Asian                   Chinese art
Spanish     Italian architecture    French cooking
```

3. Capitalize names of specific countries, states, regions, places, bodies of water, and so on.

```
Minnesota    Crandall Park     North Pole
Zimbabwe     Trumbull County   Fourth Avenue
Lake Huron   Europe            Brooklyn
```

Do not capitalize: the park, the beach, a large city, the town hall

4. Capitalize proper names and titles that precede them, but not general terms.

```
Judge Walters          Chairman Mao
Prime Minister Gandhi   Mayor Johnson
Professor Kline         President Clinton
```

Do not capitalize: the judge, a president, the chairman

5. Capitalize words designating family relationships only when these are not preceded by a possessive pronoun or article.

Grandma Moses	Mom (as in I asked <u>Mom</u> to come along.)
Aunt Donna	Cousin Ralph

Do not capitalize: my uncle, his aunt, her mom

6. Capitalize specific brand names but not the type of product.

Coca-Cola	Colgate
Crisco	Nike

Do not capitalize: soda pop, toothpaste, oil, tennis shoes

7. Capitalize directions when they refer to specific geographic regions.

the Midwest	the Middle East	the South
the East Coast	the Pacific Northwest	the North

Do not capitalize: east on I-680, three miles south, the northern part of the state

8. Capitalize specific courses titles and all language courses.

History 101	Intermediate Calculus II
French	English

Do not capitalize studies which do not name specific courses: math class, chemistry, drama

9. Capitalize the names of ships, planes, and spacecraft.

the *Enterprise*	the *Challenger*
the *Queen Elizabeth*	the *Titanic*

10. Capitalize the names of specific buildings, institutions, and businesses.

the Empire State Building	South Bend Water Department
Chrysler Corporation	Harvard University

11. Capitalize names of religions, sacred books, and words that refer to God.

the Almighty	Jewish	the Koran
Moslem	the Holy Bible	Buddha
Jesus Christ	Catholic	Jehovah
the Old Testament	the Scriptures	Mohammed
Christianity	Protestantism	the Trinity

12. Capitalize modifiers derived from proper nouns.

French accent	Renaissance art
Georgian hospitality	Shakespearean comedy

13. Capitalize the first and last word of a title; in between capitalize everything except articles, short prepositions, and short conjunctions.

Star Wars	Of Mice and Men
The Grapes of Wrath	The Last of the Mohicans
The Sun Also Rises	The Sound and the Fury

NOTE: For discussions of capitalization rules for direct quotation, see page 162 and page 406.

EXERCISE | **Capitalization**

Capitalize where necessary in the following sentences:

1. Jessica lived in the south all her life.
2. When Mrs. Torres read *Gone with the wind,* she became fascinated with the old south.
3. One of our most unpopular presidents was president Nixon.
4. After my mother died, my aunt raised my sister and me.
5. As professor Wu entered the room, his history 505 class became quiet.
6. The Monongahela and Allegheny rivers flow into the Ohio river.
7. The Republican party's presidential nominee is the incumbent president.
8. Most people believe that the first day of spring is march 21st.
9. Davy Crockett, a confirmed westerner, spent several years as a congressman living in washington.
10. Learning french was very difficult for harry.
11. Of all the fast-food restaurants, burger king is aunt Mandy's favorite.
12. The national centers for disease control, at its Atlanta headquarters, announced its findings on Legionnaire's disease.
13. Lovers of jazz think miles davis was the world's finest jazz trumpeter.
14. Designed by frank lloyd wright, falling water has been acclaimed for its unique structure and its harmonious coexistence with the natural beauty that surrounds it.
15. The Golden Gate bridge is a modern architectural wonder.

UNDERLINING AND ITALICS

Material that is machine-printed in **italics** (slanted type) is underlined in handwriting and typewriter type.

1. Underline or italicize the titles of full-length works (books, magazines, newspapers, plays, and movies). However, do not underline or italicize unpublished titles, including the titles of your own works.

Animal Dreams is the last novel I read, and

Phantom of the Opera is the last play I saw.

Shorter works, such as poems, and parts of longer works, such as magazine articles, appear in quotation marks. (See page 487)

2. Underline or italicize foreign words and phrases.

```
Enrico graduated magna cum laude.
```

3. Underline or italicize words, letters, and numbers used as words.

```
Your 3's look like B's to me.
```

4. Underline or italicize words or phrases that you want to emphasize.

```
What do you mean, we have a problem?
```

EXERCISE | **Underlining and Italics**

Add underlining where necessary in the following sentences:

1. The company president wants to build an esprit de corps among white-collar and blue-collar workers.
2. As both a book and movie, Schindler's List is powerful.
3. You forgot to cross the t's in tattoo.
4. What does politically correct mean to you?
5. I Love Lucy and The Dick Van Dyke Show are classic television comedies.

ABBREVIATIONS AND NUMBERS

1. Use A.M. (a.m.) and P.M. (p.m.) for exact times of day. Either uppercase or lowercase is acceptable; just be consistent.

```
We left home at 6:30 A.M. and arrived at 7:00 P.M.
```

2. Use A.D. before the year and B.C. after the year.

```
The artifact is dated 50 B.C., but it is similar to items dated
A.D. 500.
```

3. Do not use periods with abbreviations of common terms.

```
FBI     CIA     NATO
AT&T    UFO     MTV
```

4. Some titles come before a person's name, and some come after.

```
Ms. Jenkins          Mr. Hank DuBos
Dr. Louise Garcia     Louise Garcia, MD
Tony Minelli, CPA     Mrs. Atwood
```

Ordinarily, do not use titles both before and after a person's name.

no: Professor Lee Morrison, Ph.D.
yes: Professor Lee Morrison
yes: Lee Morrison, Ph.D.

5. Use U.S. as a modifier and *United States* all other times.

```
The U.S. ski team did well in the olympics.

The United States no longer has a huge national debt.
```

6. Do not abbreviate place names, except in addresses.

no: The Metropolitan Museum of Art in N.Y. has over a
million exhibits.

yes: The Metropolitan Museum of Art in New York has over a
million exhibits.

7. Avoid *etc.* in humanities writing. Use *and so on, and so forth,* and *and the like* instead. Never use *and etc.*

8. Although publishers often fail to do so, you should use words rather than numbers for anything that can be written in one or two words. Two-word numbers between 21 and 99 are hyphenated. Numbers that require three or more words are written with numerals (a hyphenated number is one word). Finally, any number that opens a sentence should be spelled out.

```
eighteen    fourth    twenty-five    1,503    one-third
```

9. Use numerals for measurements, time, addresses, page numbers, decimals, and percentages.

```
5 A.M.           2' 3"         page 3
100 Oak Street   15 percent    1.5 ounces
```

EXERCISE | **Abbreviations and Numbers**

Correct any problems with abbreviations and numbers.

1. 3 of my best friends have job interviews with I.B.M.
2. At 8:00 pm, we left for Cooks Forest with Dr. Joshua Schwartz, MD.
3. The Centers for Disease Control in Atlanta, GA, is aggressively researching the origin of a new strain of virus.
4. Here in the U.S., 1/4 of all women are victims of abuse.
5. People between 30 and 45 make up one-third of our student body.

Acknowledgments

Angelou, Maya. From *I Know Why the Caged Bird Sings* by Maya Angelou. Copyright © 1969 and renewed 1997 by Maya Angelou. Reprinted by permission of Random House, Inc.

Baker, Russell. "The Plot Against People" by Russell Baker, *The New York Times*. Copyright © 1968 by The New York Times Company Reprinted by permission.

Bredemeier, Brenda J. and David L. Shields. "Values and Violence in Sports Today" by Brenda Jo Bredemeier and David L. Shields from *Psychology Today*, October 1985. Reprinted with permission from *Psychology Today* Magazine. Copyright © 1985 (Sussex Publishers, Inc.).

Buick. Photography © 1998 Jamey Stillings.

Carson, Rachel. "A Fable for Tomorrow," *Silent Spring* by Rachel Carson. Copyright © 1962 by Rachel L. Carson, renewed 1990 by Roger Christie. Reprinted by permission of Houghton Mifflin Co. All rights reserved.

Castro, Janice. "Spanglish Spoken Here" by Janice Castro with Dan Cook and Cristina Garcia from *Time*, July 11, 1988. © 1988 Time, Inc. Reprinted by permission.

Chevrolet. Provided courtesy of Chevrolet.

Ciardi, John. From *Manner of Speaking* by John Ciardi, © 1972. Reprinted by permission of the Ciardi Family Publishing Trust.

Cofer, Judith Ortiz. From *The Latin Deli* by Judith Ortiz Cofer. Copyright © 1993. Reprinted by permission of The University of Georgia Press.

Ehrlich, Gretel. "About Men" from *The Solace of Open Spaces* by Gretel Ehrlich. Copyright © 1985 by Gretel Ehrlich. Used by permission of Viking Penguin, a division of Penguin Putnam Inc.

Engle, Paul. Reprinted from *A Lucky American Childhood* by Paul Engle, © 1996. Used by permission of the University of Iowa Press.

Galarza, Ernesto. From *Barrio Boy* by Ernesto Galarza. © 1971 by University of Notre Dame Press. Used by permission of the publisher.

Rosenfeld, Albert. "Animal Rights versus Human Health" by Albert Rosenfeld from *Science* 1981. Reprinted by permission of the author.

Schrank, Jeffrey. From *Snap, Crackle, and Popular Taste: The Illusion of Free Choice in America* by Jeffrey Schrank. Copyright © 1977 by Jeffrey Schrank. Used by permission of Delacorte Press, a division of Random House, Inc.

Selby, Roy. "A Delicate Operation" by Roy Selby. Copyright © 1975 by *Harper's Magazine*. All rights reserved. Reproduced from the December issue by special permission.

Soto, Gary. "Looking for Work" by Gary Soto © 1985. Used by permission of the author.

Stanat, Kirby. "How to Take a Job Interview" from *Job Hunting and Secrets and Tactics* by Kirby Stanat and Patrick Reardon. Reprinted by permission.

Tan, Amy. "Democracy" by Amy Tan. Copyright by Amy Tan. Used by permission of Amy Tan and the Sandra Dijkstra Literary Agency.

Tuite, James. "The Sounds of the City" by James Tuite, *The New York Times*, 1966. Copyright © 1966 by the New York Times Co. Reprinted by permission.

Viorst, Judith. "The Truth About Lying" by Judith Viorst. Copyright © 1981 by Judith Viorst. Originally appeared in *Redbook*. Reprinted by permission.

Walker, Alice. "Beauty: When the Other Dancer is the Self" from *In Search of our Mothers' Gardens: Womanist Prose,* copyright © 1983 by Alice Walker, reprinted by permission of Harcourt Brace & Company.

From *Humanities Index,* Vol. 9, page 1110. Copyright © 1943 by The H. W. Wilson Company. Material reproduced with permission of the publisher.

Wright Barbara. "How I Wrote Fat Chance" by Barbara Wright from *College English,* March 1982. Copyright © 1982 by the National Council of Teachers of English. Reprinted with permission.

Index

Y